PUBLICATIONS OF

THE NAVY

RECORDS SOCIETY

VOL. 168

ANGLO-AMERICAN-CANADIAN

NAVAL RELATIONS

1943–1945

THE NAVY RECORDS SOCIETY was established in 1893 for the purpose of printing unpublished manuscripts and rare works of naval interest. The Society is open to all who are interested in naval history, and any person wishing to become a member should either complete the online application form on the Society's website, www.navyrecords.org.uk, or apply to the Hon. Secretary, email address honsec@navyrecords. org.uk. The annual subscription is £40, which entitles the member to receive one free copy of each work issued by the Society in that year, and to buy earlier issues at much reduced prices.

SUBSCRIPTIONS should be sent to the Membership Secretary, 19 Montrose Close, Whitehill, Bordon, Hants, GU35 9RG.

Members are advised that the Annual General Meeting of THE NAVY RECORDS SOCIETY takes place in London on a Wednesday in July. Members should consult the Society's website, www.navyrecords.org.uk, for more details.

THE COUNCIL OF THE NAVY RECORDS SOCIETY wish it to be clearly understood that they are not answerable for any opinions and observations which may appear in the Society's publications. For these the editors of the several works are entirely responsible.

Admiral Sir Bruce Fraser, C-in-C, British Pacific Fleet, has just invested Admiral Chester W. Nimitz with a knighthood, 1945. By permission of the Imperial War Museum – Image 30133.

ANGLO-AMERICAN-CANADIAN NAVAL RELATIONS, 1943–1945

Edited by

MICHAEL SIMPSON, M.A., M.Litt., F.R.Hist.S.,
Reader in History (ret.),
Swansea University

PUBLISHED BY ROUTLEDGE
FOR THE NAVY RECORDS SOCIETY
2021

LONDON AND NEW YORK

First published 2021
by Routledge
2 Park Square, Milton Park, Abingdon, Oxon OX14 4RN

and by Routledge
605 Third Avenue, New York, NY 10158

Routledge is an imprint of the Taylor & Francis Group, an informa business

British Library Cataloguing-in-Publication Data
A catalogue record for this book is available from the British Library

Library of Congress Cataloging-in-Publication Data
Names: Simpson, Michael (Michael A.), editor. ǀ Navy Records Society
  (Great Britain)
Title: Anglo-American-Canadian naval relations, 1943–1945 / edited by
  Michael Simpson.
Description: Abingdon, Oxon ; New York, NY : Routledge, [2021] ǀ
  "Published by Routledge for the Navy Records Society."
Identifiers: LCCN 2020054940 (print) ǀ LCCN 2020054941 (ebook)
Subjects: LCSH: World War, 1939–1945—Naval operations. ǀ United
  States—Military relations—Great Britain—Sources. ǀ Great
  Britain—Military relations—United States—Sources. ǀ United States.
  Navy—History—World War, 1939–1945—Sources. ǀ Great Britain.
  Royal Navy—History—World War, 1939–1945—Sources. ǀ Canada.
  Royal Canadian Navy—History—World War, 1939–1945—Sources. ǀ
  United States—Military relations—Canada—Sources. ǀ Canada—Military
  relations—United States—Sources.
Classification: LCC D770 .A55 2021 (print) ǀ LCC D770 (ebook) ǀ DDC
  940.54/5—dc23
LC record available at https://lccn.loc.gov/2020054940
LC ebook record available at https://lccn.loc.gov/2020054941

ISBN: 978-1-032-00929-2 (hbk)
ISBN: 978-1-032-00934-6 (pbk)
ISBN: 978-1-003-17643-5 (ebk)

Typeset in Times LT Std
by Apex CoVantage, LLC

THE COUNCIL
OF THE NAVY RECORDS SOCIETY
2020–21

CONTENTS

This volume is dedicated to the memory
of His Royal Highness The Prince Philip,
Duke of Edinburgh, KG KT OM GCVO GBE,
Lord High Admiral of the United Kingdom.
Patron of the Navy Records Society, 1952–2021.

In memory of Wren Phyllis M. Thomas, B.E.M.
(1919–2015)
Secretary to Lieutenant General Sir Frederick Morgan
and Admiral Sir Bertram Ramsay
for the planning of Operations OVERLORD and
NEPTUNE.

PREFACE

This is the final volume of a set of five. The first volume, *Anglo-American Naval Relations, 1917–1919*, was published in 1991, and the second, *Anglo-American Naval Relations, 1919–1939*, in 2010. Other publications (including three volumes for the Navy Records Society) have precluded the completion of the series. Mr Robin Brodhurst, author of a biography of Admiral of the Fleet Sir Dudley Pound, is editing two volumes corresponding to Pound's time as First Sea Lord (June 1939–October 1943), one covering the years 1939–1941 and the second dealing with the period 1941–1943. The account in this volume begins with Admiral of the Fleet Sir Andrew Cunningham's assumption of the First Sea Lordship on 5 October 1943 and concludes with the formal surrender of Japan on 2 September 1945. This volume is entitled *Anglo-American-Canadian Naval Relations, 1943–1945*, for the very good reason that, by the end of the war, the Royal Canadian Navy was the third largest in the world, after its two great partners, and Canadian naval and air forces played a major role in anti-submarine warfare in the Atlantic, and rendered important service also in other theatres.

The period covered by this volume was the time in which victory was forged and the three major Allies enjoyed an almost unbroken series of maritime triumphs. In Part I, the relationships of the senior commanders, their services and their countries is discussed. Part II deals with the last stage of the fight against the U-boats, a war which by 1943 had spread to most of the world's seas. Part III deals with the Western Allies' eventual return to north-west Europe. In Part IV, the final operations in the Mediterranean, including the landings in Southern France and at Anzio in Italy, are covered. Part V recounts the participation of the British Pacific Fleet in the concluding operations against Japan.

I have drawn on the Admiralty, Premiership and Chiefs of Staff Sub-Committee papers at the National Archives, Kew, London. The National Maritime Museum at Greenwich, London, has permitted access to the papers of Admiral of the Fleet Lord Fraser, C-in-C of the British Pacific Fleet. The Churchill Archives Centre at Churchill College, Cambridge, has allowed access to the papers of Admiral Sir Bertram Ramsay, the Allied Naval C-in-C for the invasion of north-west Europe. In the

United States, I have consulted papers at the Madison Library, Library of Congress, Washington, D.C. I have studied other papers at the Operational Archives at the Washington Navy Yard. Further material came from the National Archives in Washington and College Park, Maryland. I used the extensive collections at the Franklin D. Roosevelt Presidential Library at Hyde Park, New York. Other material came from the archives of the Naval War College, Newport, Rhode Island. For the Canadian documents, I have been fortunate to have had the invaluable assistance of Mr Michael Whitby, Senior Naval Historian at the Department of Defence in Ottawa.

Punctuation marks have been inserted on occasion to clarify passages or to mark omissions. At times, numbered paragraphs in official communications have been omitted, resulting in breaks in their sequence; this is indicated by ... Missing words are indicated thus: [–]. If there is some doubt about a word it is expressed thus: [? word]. Place names are contemporaneous. Places and dates of origin, where known, are placed at the heads of documents. All Admiralty communications emanated from London and those from the Navy Department from Washington. Details of warships can be obtained from a variety of sources, such as *Conway's All the World's Fighting Ships, 1922–1946*, and *Jane's Fighting Ships*; they are not included in the footnotes – there are simply too many of them. Information about merchant vessels is not so easily obtainable and full details are given. Dates are given for the first flight of an aircraft, followed by other details. Career notes have been compiled from the *Navy List* for officers of the Royal Navy and Commonwealth navies; for the United States Navy, recourse has been had to the American equivalent, with the co-operation of the library of the Navy Department. Details of the lives of some service and civilian personnel have been obtained from the *New Dictionary of National Biography*, the *Dictionary of American Biography*, and *Who Was Who*.

ACKNOWLEDGMENTS

I wish to record my gratitude to the Navy Records Society, its Publications Committee, and especially to its successive General Editors, Dr Roger Morriss and Dr Ben Jones, for their encouragement and guidance. My thanks are due also to the former Membership Secretary, Mrs Annette Gould, and her successor, Mrs Janet Gould. I owe thanks, too, to my former colleagues in the History and other departments of Swansea University and to former doctoral students Professor James Levy and Dr Simon Rofe, and M.Phil students Martin Jones and Stan May. I have to thank Mr Aleister Smith of Ealing and my former college in Cambridge, Fitzwilliam, for their hospitality. The Scouloudi Foundation has assisted with the costs of the research.

I have received the most helpful and courteous service from The National Archives in Kew; Crown Copyright material has been reproduced by kind permission of The Stationery Office. I would like to thank the people at the Churchill Archives Centre for their kind assistance. As usual, I have received efficient and cheerful assistance from the National Maritime Museum. In the United States, I have depended on the cordial and ready help of the archivists and librarians of the Manuscript Collection at the Madison Library; the Operational Archives and the Navy Department Library at the Washington Navy Yard, especially Sandra L. Fox; and the National Archives in Washington and College Park, notably Susan Elter. At the Roosevelt Library in Hyde Park, New York, I have profited from the help of several people, notably Robert Parks. Evelyn Cherpak, Archivist at the Naval War College, Newport, Rhode Island, earns my special thanks. I am indebted particularly to my colleagues in the Navy Records Society, and to Professors Chris Bell, Paul Halpern and Paul Kennedy. Many other friends have assisted me with perceptive comments and additional information and with hospitality.

Most important of all, I have to thank my long-suffering late wife Susan, who put up not only with my frequent absences on research but also accompanied me on research trips to Canada and the United States, sitting quietly in corners of the archives and libraries, reading (non-naval) books. I regret that she did not live to see it published.

GLOSSARY OF ABBREVIATIONS

All abbreviations are British except where stated.

A/Actg	Acting
(A)	(Air)
AA	Anti-Aircraft
AB	Able Seaman
AC	Collier [US]
ACAS	Assistant Chief of the Air Staff
ACM	Air Chief Marshal
ACNS	Assistant Chief of Naval Staff
	(H): Home
	(UT):U-boat Warfare and Trade
ACOS (P)	Assistant Chief of Staff (Plans) [US]
ACRD	Airfields and Carrier Requirements Department
ACV	Auxiliary Aircraft Carrier
Adm	Admiral
Ady/Admy	Admiralty
AE	Ammunition Ship [US]
AEF	American Expeditionary Force [WWI]
AEF	Allied Expeditionary Force [WWII]
AF	Air Force
AF	Stores Ship [US]
AGC	General Communications Vessel [US]
AH	Hospital Ship [US]
AKA	Attack Cargo Ship [US]
AKS	Store Issuing Ship [US]
AM	Air Marshal
AM	Minesweeper [US]
Amb	Ambassador
AMC	Armed Merchant Cruiser
amph	amphibious
AN	Net Laying Ship [US]
ANCXF	Allied Naval Commander Expeditionary Force

AO	Oiler [US]
AOC-in-C	Air Officer Commanding-in-Chief
AoF	Admiral of the Fleet
AP	Armour Piercing
APA	Attack Transport [US]
APD	High Speed Transport [US]
ARH	Heavy Hull Repair Ship [US]
ARL	Landing Craft Repair Ship [US]
ARS	Salvage Ship [US]
A/S	Anti-Submarine
Asst	Assistant
ASW	Anti-Submarine Warfare
AT	Ocean Tug [US]
ATA	Auxiliary Ocean Tug [US]
Atl F	Atlantic Fleet [US]
ATR	Rescue Tug [US]
Aus	Australian
Aux	Auxiliary
AVM	Air Vice Marshal
AW	Distilling Ship [US]
AWI	America and West Indies Station
BAD	British Admiralty Delegation [Washington]
BASR	British Admiralty Supply Representative
BatDiv	Battleship Division [US]
BB	battleship [US]
BCS	Battle Cruiser Squadron
BEF	British Expeditionary Force
Bde	Brigade
BPF	British Pacific Fleet
Brig	Brigadier
Brig	Gen Brigadier General
b/s	battleships
BS	Battle Squadron
BU	Broken Up
Bu	Bureau [US]
C	Central
CA	Cruiser Attack [US] [Heavy Cruiser]
Cab	Cabinet
Capt	Captain
	(D): Destroyers
CAS	Chief of the Air Staff
CC	Constructor Corps [US]

CCS	Combined Chiefs of Staff
Cdo	Commando
Cdr	Commander
Cdre	Commodore
Cdt	Commandant [of a US Navy Yard]
Chf	Chief
Chmn	Chairman
CID	Committee of Imperial Defence
CIGS	Chief of the Imperial General Staff
C-in-C	Commander-in-Chief
CL	Cruiser Light [US]
Cmd	Command
Cmdg	Commanding
CNO	Chief of Naval Operations [US]
CNS	Chief of the Naval Staff
Cntrlr	Controller
CO/c/o	Commanding Officer
Col	Colonel
Coll	College
COMINCH	Commander-in-Chief, United States Fleet
COMNAVEU	Commander US Naval Forces, Europe
COMNAVNAW	Commander US Naval Forces, North African Waters
Con	Conservative MP
Conf	Conference
CPO	Chief Petty Officer
CortDiv	Escort Division [US]
COS	Chiefs of Staff Sub-Committee
CoS	Chief of Staff
COSSAC	Chief of Staff to the Supreme Allied Commander
CruDiv	Cruiser Division [US]
CS	Cruiser Squadron
CSO	Chief Staff Officer
CTF	Carrier Task Force [US]
Cttee	Committee
CV	Aircraft Carrier
CVA	Aircraft Carrier Attack [US]
CVE	Aircraft Carrier Escort
DACR	Director of Airfields and Carrier Requirements
DASW	Director of Anti-Submarine Warfare
DC	Depth Charge
DC	District of Columbia

DCAS	Deputy Chief of the Air Staff
DCNO	Deputy Chief of Naval Operations [US]
DCNS	Deputy Chief of Naval Staff
DCoS	Deputy Chief of Staff
DD	Destroyer [US]
DD	Duplex Drive [tank]
DDNI	Deputy Director of Naval Intelligence
DDP	Deputy Director of Plans
DE	Destroyer Escort [US]
Dem	Democrat [US]
Dep	Deputy
Dept	Department
DesRon	Destroyer Squadron [US]
DF	Destroyer Flotilla
DF	Direction Finding
DFSL	Deputy First Sea Lord
Dir	Director
Div	Division
DNE	Director of Naval Engineering
DNI	Director of Naval Intelligence
DNO	Director of Naval Ordnance
DOD	Director of Operations Division
	(H): Home
	(F): Foreign
DP/DoP	Director of Plans
DPD	Director of Plans Division
DPS	Director of Personal Services
DSD	Director of Signal Division
DSIR	Department of Scientific and Industrial Research
DTM	Director of Torpedo and Mining
DTSD	Director of Training and Staff Duties
DY	Dockyard
E	East
ed	editor
EF	Eastern Fleet
EIF	East Indies Fleet
elec	electrical
eng	engineering
Engr	Engineer
ent	entered
EO	Executive Officer
esp	especially

Eur	Europe
F	Fleet
FAA	Fleet Air Arm
FAdm	Fleet Admiral [US]
FBA	Fellow of the British Academy
FCapt	Flag Captain
Fcs	Forces
FDR	President Franklin Delano Roosevelt
FDS	Fighter Direction Ship
FE	Far East
FFN	Free French Navy
FGO	Fleet Gunnery Officer
FL	First Lord of the Admiralty
FM	Field Marshal
F/O	Flying Officer
FO	Flag Officer
	(S): Submarines
FOIC	Flag Officer-in-Charge
Fr	French
FS	French Ship
FSL	First Sea Lord
FY	Fiscal Year [US]
Gen	General
Gen Bd	General Board [US]
Ger	German
GOC	General Officer Commanding
Govr	Governor
Govt	Government
Grand F	Grand Fleet
Grp	Group
Grt	gross registered tonnage [merchantmen]
gun	gunnery
HC	Heavy Cruiser
H Cmnr	High Commissioner
HDML	Harbour Defence Motor Launch
HE	High Explosive
HF/DF	High Frequency/Direction Finding
HM	His Majesty['s]
HMAS	His Majesty's Australian Ship
HMCS	His Majesty's Canadian Ship
HMG	HM Government
HMNS	Her Majesty's Netherlands Ship

HMNZS	His Majesty's New Zealand Ship
HMS	His Majesty's Ship
Home F	Home Fleet
HR	House of Representatives [US]
HS	Home Secretary
HVAR	High Velocity Aircraft Rocket [US]
i/c	in charge; in command
IDC	Imperial Defence College
IE	Immediate Effectives
Imp	Imperial
in	inch
Inspr	Inspector
instr	instructor
IR	Immediate Reserve
JCS	Joint Chiefs of Staff [US; Australian]
JPS	Joint Planning Staff
JSM	Joint Staff Mission
k	knots
Lab	Labour MP
LC	Light Cruiser
LCA	Landing Craft Assault
LCF	Landing Craft Flak
LCG	Landing Craft Gun
LCI	Landing Craft Infantry
LCM	Landing Craft Mechanised
LCP	Landing Craft Personnel
LCS	Landing Craft Support
LCT	Landing Craft Tank
Ld	Lord
Ld-Lt	Lord-Lieutenant
Ldr	Leader
Lib	Liberal MP
Lt	Lieutenant
Lt Col	Lieutenant Colonel
Lt Cdr	Lieutenant-Commander
L/S	Leading Seaman
LSD	Landing Ship Dock
LST	Landing Ship Tank
m	miles
M, Min	Ministry
MAB	Munitions Assessment Board [US]
MACAF	Mediterranean Coastal Air Force

Maj Gen	Major General
MAP	Ministry of Aircraft Production
MAS	Motor Boat [German]
Mass	Massachusetts
Md	Maryland
ME	Middle East
Med F	Mediterranean Fleet
mg	machine gun
mgr	manager
MGB	Motor Gun Boat
ML	Motor Launch
mm	millimetre
MNBDO	Mobile Naval Base Defence Organisation
Mo	Missouri
MONAB	Mobile Naval Air Base
MP	Member of Parliament
mph	miles per hour
MRAF	Marshal of the Royal Air Force
MTB	Motor Torpedo Boat
m/s	Minesweeper
MV	Merchant Vessel
MWT	Minister of War Transport
N	North
N Af	North Africa
NAS	Naval Air Station
Natnl	National
NATO	North Atlantic Treaty Organisation
Nav	Navigator
navig	navigation
NAWI	North America and West Indies Station
NC	North Carolina
ND	Navy Department [US]
N Dist	Naval District [US]
NOIC	Naval Officer-in-Charge
NJ	New Jersey
NLO	Naval Liaison Officer
NRS	Navy Records Society
NS	Naval Secretary
NSC	Naval Staff College
NWC	Naval War College [US]
NY	Navy Yard
NY	New York

NW	North West
NZ	New Zealand
OC	Officer Commanding
OD (F)	Operations Division (Foreign)
OIC	Officer-in-Charge
OIC	Operational Intelligence Centre
ONI	Office of Naval Intelligence [US]
ONO	Office of Naval Operations [US]
Ont	Ontario
Ops	Operations
ordnc	ordnance
ORP	Polish Ship
Pa	Pennsylvania
Pac F	Pacific Fleet [US]
Parl	Sec Parliamentary Secretary
PC	Submarine Chaser [US]
PD	Plans Division
PCZ	Panama Canal Zone [US]
PLUTO	Pipe Line Under The Ocean
PM	Prime Minister
Pmnt	Sec Permanent Secretary
PO	Petty Officer
POA	Pacific Ocean Areas [US]
PoW	Prisoner of War
Pres	President
Prof	Professor
PT	Motor Torpedo Boat [US]
Q	Quartermaster
RA	Rear Admiral
	(A): Air
	(D): Destroyers
RAF	Royal Air Force
RAFT	Rear Admiral Fleet Train
RAN	Royal Australian Navy
RCAF	Royal Canadian Air Force
RCN	Royal Canadian Navy
RCNVR	Royal Canadian Navy Volunteer Reserve
Reprv	Representative [US]
Rep	Republican [US]
Res F	Reserve Fleet
ret	retired
RFC	Royal Flying Corps

RM	Royal Marines
RML	Rescue Motor Launch
RN	Royal Navy
RNC	[Britannia] Royal Navy College
RNethN	Royal Netherlands Navy
RNVR	Royal Naval Volunteer Reserve
RNZN	Royal New Zealand Navy
RP	Rocket Projectile
RoP	Report of Proceedings
S	South
SAC	Supreme Allied Commander
S Af	South Africa
S Atl	South Atlantic
SBNO	Senior British Naval Officer
SC	South Carolina
SC	Submarine Chaser [US]
SCAEF	Supreme Commander Allied Expeditionary Force
SD	State Department [US]
SEAC	South East Asia Command
Sec	Secretary
Sec N	Secretary of the Navy [US]
Sen	Senate, Senator [US]
S Fr	South of France
SGB	Steam Gun Boat
SHAEF	Supreme Headquarters Allied Expeditionary Force
sig	signal
SL	Sea Lord
SNLO	Senior Naval Liaison Officer
SNO	Senior Naval Officer
S of N	Secretary of the Navy [US]
SO	Senior Officer
spist	specialist
Sqdn	Squadron
S/M	Submarine
SSt	Secretary of State
Supt	Superintendent
SW	South West
SWPA	South West Pacific Area
t	tonnage [displacement]
TAF	Tactical Air Force

TB	Torpedo Boat
TBR	Torpedo Bomber Reconnaissance
TF	Task Force [US]
trng	training
TSD	Trade and Staff Duties
tt	torpedo tubes
U	University
UK	United Kingdom
UN	United Nations
unpub	unpublished
US,USA	United States of America
USAAC	United States Army Air Corps
USec	Under Secretary
USNA	United States Naval Academy [Annapolis]
USNR	United States Naval Reserve
USSR	Union of Soviet Socialist Republics
VA	Vice Admiral
VCIGS	Vice Chief of the Imperial General Staff
VCNO	Vice Chief of Naval Operations [US]
VCNS	Vice Chief of the Naval Staff
Visct	Viscount
VP	Vice President [US]
W	West
W Af	West Africa
W Apps	Western Approaches
War Cab	War Cabinet
W/Cdr	Wing Commander
W Front	Western Front
WI	West Indies
WNTF	Western Naval Task Force
WO	War Office
WPD	War Plans Division [US]
W Point	West Point [US Military Academy]
WSA	War Shipping Administration [US]
W/T	Wireless Telegraphy
WW I	World War I
WW II	World War II
YF	Covered Lighter [US]
YMS	Motor Minesweeper [US]
YOG	Gasoline Barge [US]
YW	Water Barge [US]

A BRIEF BIBLIOGRAPHY

C. Barnett, *Engage the Enemy More Closely: The Royal Navy in the Second World War* (London, 1991).

C. Bell, *Churchill and Sea Power* (Oxford, 2012).

W. A. B. Douglas, R. Sarty, M. Whitby et al., *A Blue Water Navy: The Official Operational History of the Royal Canadian Navy in the Second World War, 1943–1945*, volume II, part 2 (St Catherine's, Ontario, 2007).

D. Hobbs, *The British Pacific Fleet* (Barnsley, Yorks., 2011)

W. Jackson & D. Bramall, *The Chiefs: The Story of the United Kingdom Chiefs of Staff* (London, 1992).

W. F. Kimball, ed., *Churchill and Roosevelt: The Complete Correspondence*, 3 volumes (Princeton, NJ, & London, 1984).

R. W. Love, jr, *History of the United State Navy*, volume 2 (1942–91), (Stackpole, PA, 1992).

S. E. Morison, *United States Naval Operations in World War II*, volumes IX, X, XI, XIV (Boston, MA, 1957–90).

S. W. Roskill, *Churchill and the Admirals* (London, 1977).

S. W. Roskill, *The War at Sea*, 3 volumes (London, 1954–61).

M. A. Simpson, ed., *The Cunningham Papers*, volume II, *The Triumph of Allied Sea Power, 1942–1946* (Navy Records Society, volume 150; Aldershot, 2006).

M. A. Simpson, ed., *The Somerville Papers* (Navy Records Society, volume 134; Aldershot, 1995).

D. Syrett, ed., *The Battle of the Atlantic and Signals Intelligence: U-boat Trends and Situations, 1941–1945* (Navy Records Society volume 139; Aldershot, 1998).

D. Syrett, ed., *The Battle of the Atlantic and Signals Intelligence: U-boat Tracking Papers, 1941–1947* (Navy Records Society volume 144; Aldershot, 2002).

D. W. Waters, ed. E. J. Grove, *The Defeat of the Enemy Attack on Shipping, 1939–1945* (Navy Records Society volume 137; Aldershot, 1997).

PART I

THE HIGH COMMAND

The grand strategy for the winning of the Second World War was the responsibility of the elected heads of state of the three Atlantic powers – Franklin D. Roosevelt, the President of the United States of America, Winston Churchill, the Prime Minister of Great Britain, and Mackenzie King, the Prime Minister of Canada. In practice major decisions were made by the two senior figures, though King made adroit use of his association with the two great leaders, notably at the summit conferences held at the Château Frontenac in Quebec in 1943 and 1944.[1]

Roosevelt had begun the war-long, fruitful and ultimately triumphant partnership with Churchill by writing to him on 11 September 1939, shortly after Churchill had returned to office as First Lord of the Admiralty. FDR, ever the shrewd politician, foresaw that if the war continued for more than a year, or went badly for the Allies, Churchill might well become Prime Minister. Roosevelt told his Ambassador in London, Joseph Kennedy, that he 'wanted to get his hand in now'. During the years from the autumn of 1939 to the autumn of 1943, they corresponded almost daily, met several times, and sent emissaries when they could not travel themselves; Harry Hopkins, the President's most trusted aide, was a frequent 'go-between'.[2]

Roosevelt and Churchill had developed a firm working relationship by the latter part of 1943. It was based on a genuine but not truly intimate friendship and, like most relationships, it had its differences, though these were largely political rather than strategic. On grand strategy, they were agreed that their immediate effort must be devoted to overcoming the most serious threat to themselves and their Soviet ally – Hitler's

---

[1]Franklin Delano Roosevelt (1882–1945): Dem politician; NY State Sen 1911–13; Asst S of N 1913–29; VP candidate 1920; severe polio 1921; Govr NY 1929–32; Pres 1933–45.

Winston L. S. Churchill (1874–1965): subaltern, India & Sudan 1890s; war correspondent, Cuba & Boer War 1898–1900; MP, Con, Lib, Con, most of 1900–64; Pres Board of Trade, Home Sec, FL 1906–15; Col, W Front 1915–16; Min of Munitions 1917–19; SSt War & Air 1919–21; Chancellor of the Exchequer 1924–9; political wilderness 1929–39; FL 1939–40; PM 1940–45 & 1951–4.

W. L. Mackenzie King (1874–1950): Canadian Lib PM for most of period 1927–50.

M. A. Stoler, *Allies and Adversaries: The JCS, the Grand Alliance and US Strategy in World War II* (Chapel Hill, NC, & London, 2000); K. Sainsbury, *Churchill and Roosevelt at War* (Basingstoke, 1996).

Quebec conferences: QUADRANT, 14–25 Aug 1943; OCTAGON, 12–16 Sept 1944.

[2]W.F. Kimball, ed., *Churchill and Roosevelt: The Complete Correspondence*, 3 vols (Princeton, NJ, & London, 1984), esp I, p. 7, II, pp. 429–31.

Joseph P. Kennedy (1888–1969): Wall Street financier; Dem politician; US Amb to UK 1937–41.

Harry L. Hopkins (1890–1946): social work; head, New Deal relief programmes 1933–8; Sec of Commerce 1938–40; personal asst & roving Amb 1940–45; head, Lend-Lease 1941.

Germany. The 'Europe-first' strategy was encapsulated in Admiral Harold R. Stark's 'Plan Dog' of October 1940.[1]

Their principal military advisors were the Combined Chiefs of Staff (CCS), which was composed of the British Chiefs of Staff (COS) and the American Joint Chiefs of Staff (JCS). Whereas the British Chiefs had a pedigree going back to 1924, the JCS was newly formed. The CCS, the apex of the military co-operation hierarchy, began during the December 1941–January 1942 meeting of Churchill and Roosevelt in Washington (ARCADIA). Japan had recently struck powerful blows against the Western powers in the Pacific and Indian Oceans and many Americans, including senior officers, wished to strike back at Japan first but FDR held firm and would permit only a holding operation against the Japanese, followed by a limited offensive, going over to a full offensive only when Germany and Italy had been defeated. There was also an awkward but effective alliance with the Soviet Union, though in large part the wars in the west and that on the German-Soviet front were entirely separate.[2]

Whereas Churchill, a self-styled Minister of Defence as well as Premier, was an energetic and ever-present participant in the COS's discussions (much to their chagrin, as they had to fight the Prime Minister's wilder ideas as well as their three overseas' enemies), Roosevelt, while retaining the final decisions on strategy firmly in his own hands, left the JCS to operate without interference. He was enabled to do this in part because the Chairman of the JCS was his own Chief of Staff, Admiral William D. Leahy, a longstanding personal friend, who acted as an effective liaison between the President and his JCS. Leahy, a man of great service and diplomatic experience, was a wise and calm figure. Once the CCS had been formed, it was natural that Leahy should become its Chairman, too.[3]

The British COS was chaired by the Chief of the Imperial General Staff, General Sir Alan Brooke, who also represented the Army. The

---

[1]Adm Harold R. Stark, US Navy (1890–1972): destroyer & staff service; Med & UK 1917–19; NWC; Navy Dept; battleship cmd; Chf, Bu Ordnance; cruiser cmd; CNO 1939–42; Cdr, US Naval Fcs in Eur 1942–5; ret 1946; B. M. Simpson III, *Admiral Harold R. Stark: Architect of Victory* (Colombia, SC, 1989).

Plan Dog: Stark's plan for defeat of Germany first, Oct 1940.

[2]ARCADIA was held largely at Churchill's instigation. He feared US would now desert 'Germany first' for knee-jerk concentration against Japan. D. Rigby, 'The CCS and Anglo-American Strategic Coordination in World War II' (unpub. PhD thesis, Brandeis U, 1996), pp. ii, v, ix; this was brought to my attention by Prof J. B. Hattendorf; W. Jackson & D. Bramall, *The Chiefs: The Story of the UK Chiefs of Staff* (London, 1992).

[3]FAdm William D. Leahy, US Navy (1875–1959): RA 1927; CNO 1937–9; Govr Puerto Rico; Amb to Vichy France 1941–2; Pres's CoS & Chmn, JCS & CCS, July 1942; FAdm 1944; ret 1949; W. D. Leahy, *I Was There* (New York, 1950).

Chief of the Air Staff, Air Chief Marshal Sir Charles Portal, was the longest-serving member but at the outset of our period (5 October 1943), the First Sea Lordship was assumed by Admiral of the Fleet Sir Andrew Cunningham, in place of the dying Admiral of the Fleet Sir Dudley Pound, who had held the office since June 1939; Pound died on Trafalgar Day (21 October 1943).[1]

Cunningham was the Royal Navy's pre-eminent figure. He had achieved great renown by his aggressive command of the Mediterranean Fleet throughout the period between June 1939 and February 1942, a time of tragedy as well as triumph. When the ailing Pound tendered his resignation, Cunningham would have been not only the Royal Navy's but also the people's choice as his successor. He was not the Prime Minister's preferred choice, however, and several days of wrangling were necessary before his appointment. Churchill regarded him, rightly, as a 'no' man, who would not tolerate the Prime Minister's interference and schoolboyish ideas. What counted at least as much as anything else in Churchill's eventual and reluctant decision to offer him the post was that senior American figures wanted him on the CCS. He had an impeccable fighting reputation but, more to the point, he had served for several months in the spring and summer of 1942 as head of the British Admiralty Delegation in Washington, where he had become well known to the

[1]FM Visct Alanbrooke (Sir Alan Brooke) (1883–1963): Royal Artillery; Lt Col 1918; Maj Gen 1935; Mobile Div 1937; Lt Gen 1938; AA Cmd; C-in-C, Southern Cmd Aug 1939; cdr, II Corps, BEF Sept 1939; C-in-C, Home Forces July 1940; CIGS Dec 1941–Jan 1946; FM 1944; A. Danchev & D. Todman, eds, *War Diaries, 1939–45: FM Lord Alanbrooke* (London, 2001); D. Fraser, *Alanbrooke* (London, 1982).

MRAF Visct Portal of Hungerford (Sir Charles Portal) (1893–1971): RFC 1914–18; RAF 1918; AVM, Air Member for Personnel 1939; Actg AM Sept 1939; AOC-in-C, Bomber Cmd April 1940; ACM & CAS Oct 1940; MRAF Jan 1944; ret 1945; D. Richards, *Portal of Hungerford* (London, 1977).

AoF Sir A. Dudley P. R. Pound (1877–1943): ent RN 1891; CO of a torpedo boat 1897; Cdr 1909; Capt 1914; *Colossus* Jutland 1916; DOD (H) 1917; *Repulse* 1920–2; DPD 1922; CoS, Med F 1925; RA 1926; ACNS 1927; BCS 1929; VA 1930; 2SL 1932; Adm 1935; C-in-C, Med 1936–9; FSL 1939–43. R. Brodhurst, *Churchill's Anchor: Admiral of the Fleet Sir Dudley Pound* (Barnsley, 2000).

AoF Visct Cunningham of Hyndhope (Sir Andrew Browne Cunningham) (1883–1963): ent RN 1897; Boer War 1900; destroyer cmds 1908–19; Capt 1920; Capt (D) 6 & 1 DFs 1922; FCapt *Calcutta & Despatch*, N America & WI 1926–8; IDC 1929; CO *Rodney* 1929; RA 1932; RA (D), Med F 1934–6; VA 1936; VA, BCS & 2 i/c, Med F 1937–8; DCNS 1938–9; Actg Adm & C-in-C Med June 1939-Apr 1942; Adm Jan 1941; Head, BAD 1942; Naval C-in-C, TORCH Nov 1942; C-in-C Med Jan–Oct 1943; AoF Jan 1943; FSL Oct 1943–June 1946; autobiography, *A Sailor's Odyssey* (London, 1951); M. A. Simpson, ed., *The Cunningham Papers,* 2 vols (Aldershot, 1998 & 2006; NRS vols 140 & 150); M. A. Simpson, *A Life of Admiral of the Fleet Andrew Cunningham: A 20th Century Naval Leader* (London, 2004).

JCS and had earned their profound respect. When the Allies planned to invade North Africa in November 1942, Cunningham was the Americans' choice as Allied Naval Commander in the Mediterranean, and he continued in that role through the invasions of Sicily and Italy, during which he had built up a strong relationship with the Supreme Allied Commander in the Mediterranean, the American General Dwight D. Eisenhower.[1]

All three of the British services were represented on the COS but at that time the Americans did not have an independent air force; most aviation was in the hands of the US Army and consequently the head of the Army Air Corps, General H. H. ('Hap') Arnold, was given a place on both the JCS and the CCS, to balance Portal. Arnold was in the awkward position of sitting with his chief, the head of the US Army, General George C. Marshall. The naval leader was Admiral Ernest J. King, the Chief of Naval Operations, who also doubled as C-in-C of the US Fleet.[2]

King was an able but tough character; Roosevelt said that he shaved with a blow torch. He was notorious for not getting on with most people. Everyone recognised his firm and astute grasp of naval and related military affairs and he earned great respect for his strategic acumen as well as for his high administrative ability. Cunningham, who exchanged many broadsides with him, was, like most people, grudgingly complimentary.

---

[1]Simpson, *Life of Cunningham*, pp. 173–87; Simpson, ed., *Cunningham Papers*, II, pp. 141–54, 317–18.

Gen of Army Dwight D. Eisenhower, US Army (1890–1969): able staff officer; Col March 1941; Brig Gen Sept 1941; Chf, War Plans, then Ops, Dec 1941; Cmdg Gen, US Forces in Eur June 1942; Cmdg Gen, N Africa, Sicily, Italy, 1942–3; Gen Feb 1943; Supreme Cdr, AEF 1944–5; Gen of Army Dec 1944; CoS 1945–8; Pres, Columbia University 1948–50; Supreme Cdr, NATO 1950–52; Pres (Rep) 1953–61; S. E. Ambrose, *Eisenhower the Commander* (London, 1984).

[2]Gen of the Army George C. Marshall, US Army (1880–1959): AEF 1917–18; Brig Gen 1936; Chf, War Plans 1938; DCoS & CoS 1939-Nov 1945; Gen of Army Dec 1944; China mission 1946; Sec State 1947–9; Sec Defense 1950–1. F. C. Pogue, *George C. Marshall*, vol III (New York, 1973).

Gen H. H. ('Hap') Arnold, US Army (1886–1950): Asst Chief, USAAC 1918; Maj Gen & Chief of USAAC 1938; DCoS Oct 1940; Chief, USAAF June 1941; Lt Gen Dec 1941; Cmdg Gen March 1942; Gen of USAAF 1945.

FAdm Ernest J. King, US Navy (1877–1956): USNA 1897–1901; Lt 1906; instructor, staff & eng appointments; staff of Adm Mayo, C-in-C, Atl F 1915–19; S/M Division 11 1922–6; Capt *Wright* 1926; qualified pilot 1927; Bu Aeronautics & other air cmds; *Lexington* 1930–2; NWC 1932; RA & Chf, Bu Aeronautics 1933–6; further air cmds; Cdr Patrol Force Atl 1940; Adm & C-in-C Atl F Feb 1941; COMINCH Dec 1941; CNO March 1942-Dec 1945; T. B. Buell, *Master of Sea Power* (Boston, 1980); E. J. King & W. M. Whitehill, *Fleet Admiral King* (London, 1953).

Cunningham, diary, 9 June 1944, *Cunningham Papers*, II, p. 158.

'Not content with fighting the enemy,' wrote Cunningham, 'he was usually fighting someone else on his own side as well.'[1]

The CCS accompanied the President and the Prime Minister to their several summits and some of them met each other on other occasions, too, but their permanent base was in Washington. This was sensible, as it was far from the war zones and the US was likely to become the Western Allies' senior partner. As the COS were required to be based in London, a British Joint Services Mission was formed in Washington, consisting of the heads of the British service delegations in America, presided over by Field Marshal Sir John Dill, who became a great friend of many Americans, notably General Marshall. After Dill's death on 4 November 1944, he was succeeded by the then-Supreme Allied Commander in the Mediterranean, Field Marshal Sir Henry Maitland Wilson.[2]

The heads of the British Admiralty Delegation, established in 1941 before the US had become a belligerent, changed periodically. In October 1943, the incumbent was Admiral Sir Percy Noble, who was succeeded in October 1944 by Admiral Sir James Somerville, lately C-in-C, Eastern Fleet, and responsible for the Indian Ocean. Noble, a diligent officer, had felt worn down by having to deal with King. Somerville, a man of wide talents, much experience and great humour, had just concluded a difficult but ultimately triumphant spell as head of the Eastern Fleet, As Japan was about to become the Anglo-Americans' principal enemy, the appointment made sound sense.[3]

---

[1] Cunningham, *Odyssey*, p. 466.

[2] FM Sir John Dill (1881–1944): Brig Gen 1918; I Corps, BEF 1939–40; VCIGS Apr 1940; CIGS May 1940–Dec 1941; Head, JSM, Washington Dec 1941–Nov 1944.

FM Sir Henry M. Wilson (1881–1964): Lt Gen, British Troops in Egypt Sept 1939; Military Govr, Cyrenaica 1940–41; GOC, Greece 1941; GOC Palestine & Transjordan May 1941; Syria June–Aug 1941; Gen Dec 1941; 9 Army, Levant; Persia-Iraq Command Aug 1942; C-in-C ME Jan 1943; SAC Med Jan 1944; Head JSM Dec 1944–7; FM Jan 1945.

[3] Adm Sir Charles J. C. Little (1882–1973): ent RN 1897; Capt 1917; RA 1929; VA 1933; Adm 1937; 2SL 1938–41; Head, BAD, Washington 1941–2; C-in-C Portsmouth 1942.

Adm Sir Percy Noble (1880–1955): ent RN 1894; *Ribble* i/c 1907–8; sig spist; Cdr 1913; Grand F 1914–18; Capt 1918; *Calliope, Calcutta* 1919; *Barham* 1922; *Ganges* (trng); *St Vincent* 1925–7; DOD 1928–9; RA 1929; Dir Naval Eqpt 1931; 2CS, Home F 1932; VA & 4SL 1935; C-in-C China 1937–40; Adm 1939; C-in-C W Apps 1941; BAD Oct 1942-June 1944; ret 1945.

AoF Sir James F. Somerville (1882–1949): ent RN 1897; Lt March 1904; sig spist; W/T Officer, E Med 1915; F W/T O, Grand Fleet 1917; Capt Dec 1921; *Benbow* Aug 1922; DSD Feb 1925; Tactical School March 1927; *Barham, Warspite* May 1927; IDC staff June 1929; Tactical School Sept 1931; *Norfolk* Dec 1931; Cdre Portsmouth Barracks Oct 1932; RA Oct 1933; DPS May 1934; Tactical School Feb 1936; RA (D) Med F April 1936; VA Sept 1937; C-in-C E Indies Oct 1938; invalided home, suspected tuberculosis April 1939; ret July 1939; pioneered naval radar 1939–40; assisted Ramsay in Dunkirk evacuation May–June 1940; Force H June 1940; C-in-C, EF Feb 1942; Active List Aug 1944;

By late 1943, the tide of war was running the Allies' way on all fronts. The Russians were poised to enter Poland. Italy had surrendered and changed sides, though the Allies had invaded Italian territory. In the Pacific, the American offensive was by now well-honed and well-resourced; the Japanese were being outflanked and forced back towards their home islands. The U-boats had been effectively defeated by the spring of 1943. The American war effort was now reaching heights unmatched by any of the belligerents, Allied and enemy alike. It provided military and economic support for Britain, its Commonwealth, the Soviet Union and China, besides smaller allies, as well as furnishing its own burgeoning forces. By July 1943 the US Navy exceeded the Royal Navy in size and, despite British naval wartime expansion on a heroic scale, the US Navy pulled rapidly away, dwarfing British and Commonwealth efforts. Many of the ships and aircraft and naval equipment in general came from America. The BAD and many of the CCS's subordinate committees were concerned with allocating the outpouring of this cornucopia as between America and her allies.

Apart from routine activities, such as arbitrating on the allocation of resources, and on-going topics, such as the strategic bombing of Germany, the struggle against the U-boats, and the ferrying of supplies to Russia and China, the CCS had to decide three major issues. The first one was the date, place and scale of the return to North West Europe, the launching pad for a land assault on Germany. The second was what to do about the Mediterranean – should the Allies continue all the way up the Italian peninsula, or should they switch a major part of their forces to a landing in Southern France, or combine both advances? As the European war was entering its final stages, the third question was how Japan was to be defeated after the Western Allies and their Soviet partner had overcome Hitler.

Prior to the invasion of the Italian mainland in September 1943, it is generally acknowledged that the British held the upper hand in the high command's strategic decisions – reflected in a series of large-scale Mediterranean operations. Their forces in the European theatre were still larger than the Americans' and, more importantly, the COS was a polished, experienced, united and, for the most part, clear-sighted body, whereas the US JCS was still on its shake-down voyage. The American services were traditionally mutually antagonistic, little used to co-operating, had a new structure and machinery to get used to in the midst

---

Head BAD Oct 1944–Dec 1945; AoF May 1945; ret April 1946; Ld-Lt, Somerset 1946–9; D. Macintyre, *Fighting Admiral* (London, 1961); M. A. Simpson, ed., *Somerville Papers* (Aldershot, 1996; NRS vol. 134).

of a genuinely world war, and had but a vague idea of the Allies' future strategy. As summer shaded into autumn in 1943, the Americans had 'hit their stride' in respect of their war effort, their forces were now as strong as (and daily growing stronger than) those of their Western Allies, the JCS was running relatively smoothly, and the Americans were beginning to assert their increasingly overwhelming might by forcing the British to adopt their preferred strategy. The traditional American grand strategy had always been one of going straight for the jugular – a frontal assault with maximum forces against the chief enemy's heartland.

A clear indication of the shape the post-war world would take had been given at the conferences in Cairo (SEXTANT, 22–28 November and 3–7 December 1943) and, more significantly, the meeting in Tehran (EUREKA, 28 November–1 December), at which Roosevelt and Churchill together met Stalin and his entourage for the first time. Roosevelt, looking ahead to the probable post-war order, courted Stalin assiduously, reasoning, correctly, that America and Russia, now dubbed 'superpowers', would mastermind the post-war settlement. Roosevelt assumed, rightly, that Churchill and Britain would have to follow in their wake; an exhausted small nation now had little choice. Churchill was disgruntled throughout the Tehran meeting; he felt jealous and jilted. Roosevelt also won Stalin to his nation's strategy of an early descent on the North West European shore, though Stalin, who had been calling for an effective Western 'second front' since 1942, needed little persuasion.[1]

The British had agreed in early 1942 to an invasion of Northern France but had managed to stave off American attempts to fix a date, fearing that a premature landing would lead to a stalemate like the First World War's Western Front. By the spring of 1943, however, the Japanese advance in the Pacific had been held and reversed, the Soviet Union was tying down the bulk of German land and air forces in Eastern Europe, the war against the U-boats was on the verge of being won, and America was increasingly becoming the dominant Western partner in the war. At the SEXTANT conference in Cairo (22–28 November 1943), the Americans, making good use of these favourable trends, secured a British commitment to launch NEPTUNE/OVERLORD, the invasion of Normandy, on 1 May 1944 [16].[2]

---

[1] Josef V. Stalin (1879–1953): Communist political commissar 1918–20; unquestioned dictator of USSR by 1927–8; effectively C-in-C.

P. M. Kennedy, *Strategy and Diplomacy* (London, 1983), pp. 45, 66, 81; Jackson & Bramall, *COS*, pp. 221, 229, 252.

[2] NEPTUNE was the naval component and OVERLORD the land campaign of the invasion of NW Eur, June 1944.

Outline planning for NEPTUNE/OVERLORD began in the summer of 1943 but it was to take a full nine months to complete. The chief problems surrounding the naval operations on D-day were the provision of enough landing craft and other specialised vessels. 'The basic problem is obviously one of landing craft availability', the CCS concluded in October 1943 [4] and there were frequent further references to this bottleneck in the lead-up to the invasion [8, 11, 16–19]. As the scope of the invasion was enlarged and became clear, all members of the CCS were convinced that other operations, extant or planned, must be subordinated to NEPTUNE/OVERLORD. The Mediterranean and the Indian Ocean were combed for precious landing craft, production was given high priority, and crew training was expanded. In the event, it was decided to postpone the invasion until 1 June 1944 to take advantage of an extra month's production of landing craft.

The complexities of this massive and unprecedented operation are often forgotten in popular historical accounts. These generally ignore the vast amount of planning and the great mass of supporting forces necessary for the invasion. Tugs, possibly the most humble and ungainly of sea-going vessels, for instance, were a vital element in operational support, as important as ships of the line; a paper issued by the US JCS in November 1943 forecast a need for at least 275 [9]. There were occasional disputes between the British and Americans on the assignment of specialised vessels and quarrels had to be referred upwards to the CCS for final decisions [1–3]. Of equal importance was the provision of adequate escort, bombardment and anti-submarine and anti-destroyer patrols. As landing forces were increased, so the need for additional naval cover expanded and Admiral King was vexed by a British acknowledgment that they could not find all the extra forces called for, leaving the Americans to plug gaps in the covering forces [28].

A second major strategic decision facing the CCS in late 1943 was what to do about the Mediterranean, the centrepiece of Allied efforts for some 18 months. The Americans were keen to dispose of this albatross, feeling that it was a strategic dead end which would not assist materially in the central objective – the defeat of Hitler's Germany. They suspected, moreover, that the British were using American might to re-establish the pre-war Imperial position in the Middle Sea. Between the spring of 1942 and the autumn of 1943, the US had been inveigled into one Mediterranean adventure after another, with the result that OVERLORD had been postponed until at least the spring of 1944. A combination of mounting American frustration and swelling military strength, overshadowing Britain's increasingly limited growth, led first to the commitment to launch OVERLORD on 1 May 1944. The Americans then moved swiftly to seal off further major Mediterranean operations. They refused assistance to Churchill's vain Aegean campaign of late 1943, which they regarded as strategically unsound and inchoate [7, 16]. They also curtailed offensive operations in Italy, which had turned quickly into a costly, slow and dispiriting slog up the peninsula; reinforcements of men, weapons and supplies were limited, notably the region's amphibious lift. They overrode British protestations that the near-stalemate in Italy was 'extremely dangerous' [11]. The Americans proposed that Italy should become a military backwater and their preferred Mediterranean option was really designed as a support to OVERLORD. ANVIL, a joint US-Free French landing in the south of France, was designed to open a second front in France, in the rear of the main German forces, and to provide additional logistic support through the ports of Toulon and Marseille and their communications with the north via the Rhône valley. The COS felt that it should be of at least two-divisional strength, to avoid the risk of failure [16, 20].[1]

The decision for ANVIL was fraught with as many sharp differences between the COS and the JCS as OVERLORD, for the British political, diplomatic and military leadership saw the Mediterranean as a key theatre. Operations there would stretch and weaken German forces, enabling a successful OVERLORD. Italy would be eliminated from the war and, with her defeat, the way would be open to strike at Germany from the south. The route to the Far East via the Mediterranean and Suez Canal would be able to be re-opened, saving vast quantities of shipping and much valuable time. As Soviet advances in Eastern Europe threatened to replace German domination of the Balkans with Communist suzerainty, Churchill in particular became concerned to reassert traditional British power in the region. The contrast in strategic traditions between the two nations was brought into sharper relief over the Mediterranean question than about any other theatre. The American tradition of committing the Allies' main effort directly against Germany clashed with Britain's encircling, attritional, maritime-based strategy [7, 11, 16]. American pressure won the day, for not only were they now the preponderant power, their strategic arguments were more soundly based, whereas the British case was less relevant by late 1943 and their ideas confused and vague. Leahy summed up the differences succinctly:

This controversy [over ANVIL] is of long standing. It is caused by all-out American concentration on an early defeat of Nazi Germany, and a

---

[1]M. Jones, *Britain, the United States and the Mediterranean, 1942–44* (Basingstoke & New York, 1996); S. Weiss, *Allies in Conflict: Anglo-American Strategy, 1938–44* (Basingstoke & New York, 1996).

British intention to combine with a defeat of the Nazis the acquisition of post-war advantages in the Balkan States for Great Britain.

[39]

By the SEXTANT meeting, the British had capitulated, agreeing not only to a definite date for OVERLORD but also to ANVIL [16, 17]. They did so with great misgivings and up until a month before its launch on 15 August 1944 (that is, over two months after the landings in Normandy), they were expressing these, telling their American counterparts that 'neither HMG nor the British COS consider that ANVIL is our correct strategy' [41]. It was, however, no more than a formal registration of difference, for they added that 'having accepted the decision we will of course do our very utmost to make ANVIL a success' [41].

As the German war wound down, the thoughts of the high command turned to how Japan should be defeated. The Americans had first halted the Japanese advance and then, from the summer of 1942, pushed back the frontiers established in the first six months of that year. By the autumn of 1943 they had seized the initiative and had developed a well-honed war machine featuring all the services and all arms. They had divided the Pacific into two Supreme Commands. General Douglas MacArthur commanded the South West Pacific Area (SWPA), using Australian bases, while Admiral Chester Nimitz controlled the Central Pacific from his headquarters in Hawaii.[1] Most of the effort was American in men and weapons, though Australia, New Zealand, the Dutch and the Chinese made contributions; the Royal Navy's share had shrunk dramatically since the spring of 1942. The bulk of US naval forces were under Nimitz's control. By spring 1944, he was sure that he had the resources and battle experience 'to continue the further westward movement in the Pacific with confidence' [31, 13, 38]. It was likely that American efforts would be enough to bring Japan to the peace table without significant input from anyone else, though the Americans courted an eventual Soviet intervention to ensure Japan's defeat. Otherwise, most American naval men wished to bask in the US Navy's unfettered victory.

---

[1]Gen of the Army Douglas MacArthur, US Army (1880–1964): W Point 1899–1903; engr; Philippines; Gen Staff 1913–17; Col 1917; Brig Gen AEF 1917–18; Supt W Point 1919; Philippines 1922–30; Maj Gen 1925; CoS Nov 1930–Oct 1934; Military Advisor Philippine Govt 1935; Cdr US Army in FE July 1941; SAC, SWPA March 1942–April 1945; Gen of Army Dec 1944; Supreme Cdr, Allied Powers in Japan 1945–51; UN C-in-C Korea 1950–51; relieved of all cmds by Pres Truman April 1951 following disputes over policy & strategy.

FAdm Chester W. Nimitz, US Navy (1885–1966): s/m; RA 1938; Chf, Bu Navigation 1939; Adm & C-in-C Pac F Dec 1941; FAdm Dec 1944; CNO Nov 1945.

'The Americans ... have always shown a desire to carry the full burden of Pacific operations', said an Admiralty paper [49].

It was into this almost-exclusively American campaign that the British now wished to intrude, though it was questionable that they could provide substantial forces before the issue was decided. The envisaged large-scale participation was the subject of several months of wrangling between the Minister of Defence and the COS. Churchill, the embodiment of the Edwardian Empire, wished to recover Britain's lost Imperial territories – without the US doing it for him or even lending their aid [49]. If Churchill's strategic ideas were followed, Britain's final and augmented effort against Japan would be centred chiefly on the Indian Ocean, with the possibility of some assistance to MacArthur's SWPA [38]. The COS, however, argued that the quickest way to defeat Japan was to join the Americans in a direct drive from the Central Pacific aimed straight at Japan's home islands. This would ensure the collapse of all Japanese power and thus the captured colonies would fall into our hands at no great cost. It would, moreover, establish Britain as a major influence in the post-war settlement in Japan and also in the wider Far Eastern area.[1]

After much exasperating debate, Churchill acceded to the Chiefs' wisdom. In the case of Japan, they refrained from the indirect approach which so annoyed the Americans in the European theatre [38]. At the OCTAGON conference in Quebec in September 1944, Churchill offered a 'balanced and self-supporting' fleet to take part in the 'main operations against Japan' [49]. Roosevelt answered promptly that it was no sooner offered than accepted.[2]

The Royal Navy had a hard task, however, to make the Prime Minister's offer good. Their first formidable handicap was King. While forced to accept a British task force of considerable size and substantial offensive power, he threw many obstacles in the way of its despatch. Some of his objections were quite genuine. He insisted that the British Pacific Fleet (BPF) be entirely self-supporting. The Americans had a splendid fleet train but, with the swelling tide of US naval forces, King knew that it would be unable to support another major task force. He had to think how to employ the BPF and required specific British proposals; in any case, in the early autumn of 1944, he was in no position to allot it a particular role [44].

Most of King's objections, however, were smokescreens designed to hide his real ambition of a solely American and preferably naval victory against Japan. He mounted a furious and sustained opposition against the

---

[1]Simpson, *Life of Cunningham*, pp. 199–200.
[2]Simpson, ed., *Cunningham Papers*, II, pp. 155–74.

BPF, doubting even the President's enthusiastic acceptance of Churchill's offer. He then argued that the offer and its acceptance contained no reference to the Central Pacific theatre. If the BPF did enter the Pacific, he would not withdraw any American units to make way for it. No British forces would be welcomed into the Pacific until all the naval needs of NEPTUNE/OVERLORD and ANVIL had been met in full [28, 44].

Brooke and Portal gave Cunningham valuable support in repulsing King's onslaught. They stuck rigidly to their baseline and were supported by Leahy; after a difficult session, the CCS 'agreed that the British fleet should participate in the main operations against Japan in the Pacific' [44].

The Royal Navy's problems now moved across the Atlantic. They needed vital information on the strength, nature and fighting ability of their Japanese opponents, information which the US Navy was slow to supply, through either disorganisation or, taking their cue from the man at the top, a downright refusal to co-operate [30, 40, 56, 57]. The Royal Navy had to gather together the most powerful fleet that it had ever assembled, though this was somewhat easier than putting together a suitable and adequate fleet train, a subject which had never entered Royal Navy thought. The Admiralty confessed that it had 'great difficulty in providing the necessary logistical support to enable it [the BPF] to operate with the same prolonged activity as the American Fleet, backed as this is by abundant resources' [38, 49]. The question remained whether 'it would be possible, in view of the acceleration of US operations in the Pacific, for British forces to arrive in time to be of real value to the US operations envisaged' [38]. The US Navy had been focused on fighting a major maritime war with Japan in the Pacific since at least 1907 and in the Second World War, despite the official emphasis on 'Germany first', 'there was a constant tendency to divert larger forces, particularly air forces, to the Pacific theatres'. The BAD also noted 'a very marked Naval jealousy regarding the Pacific war' and observed that even the JCS failed to scotch service and press rumours that Britain lacked the will to play a significant part in the final defeat of Japan [56].

The American preference was for the Royal Navy to concentrate its forces in the Indian Ocean area (SEAC), with occasional forays in support of MacArthur (SWPA). King suggested diversionary activities in the Indian Ocean and even Leahy observed that Singapore was a good target [44]. In reply to Cunningham's assertion that major offensives in the Indian Ocean were 'not worth the candle'[19], King responded that if the British forces were used 'aggressively' against Japanese ports, oil installations, shipping and (especially) airfields, this would keep Japan from concentrating her strength, particularly air forces, in the Pacific. He felt, too, that it would give the BPF valuable experience against Japanese opposition. Though King had reservations about the apparent inaction of the Eastern Fleet, he moved quickly to condemn US Navy officers' criticism of its role [5, 19, 28, 29, 38, 44].

The great strategic decisions were not the sole concern of the CCS. An issue which had assumed critical importance up to the spring of 1943 had been U-boat warfare. The U-boat threat had been countered effectively by May 1943 and thereafter represented a nuisance rather than a possible strangulation of the Allies' entire effort but the Allies felt compelled to divert considerable forces to keeping it in check [8, 14]. The Germans recognised this and their object was now to frustrate the Allied build-up to the final victory by instituting a cat-and-mouse game in inshore waters with conventional submarines, which proved hard to detect [14, 50]. The Allies were forced also to address a new undersea threat in 1944–45 – the prospect of a new generation of submarines which appeared to have greater speed, more torpedoes, better defences, longer range and could profit from the 'schnorkel'. The new boats may not have proved so great a threat as the high command imagined in 1943–45, though they could have caused increased sinkings and proved less vulnerable to detection and destruction.

The Allies now possessed such a preponderance of escort vessels and air support, together with sophisticated weapons and detection devices (which were being continuously improved and new ones devised), that a full-scale recrudescence of the dramatic battles of 1940–43 was virtually impossible. Nevertheless, Cunningham and his colleagues felt that they represented a serious enough concern that every effort had to be made to counter it. They relied on a steady Red Army advance westwards to deny the new U-boats training and base areas in the Baltic. Cunningham endeavoured to persuade Portal and Arnold to increase the bombing of U-boat bases and assembly yards. All available escort craft were employed in an attempt to saturate the seas and aircraft patrols were strengthened. Mines were laid in inshore areas to force the U-boats back to deep water. In the event, the Germans experienced innumerable teething troubles with the new boats and only a handful got to sea before the war ended; they accomplished little. It is easy with hindsight to decry the Germans' efforts with these newer yet still conventional submarines, but Cunningham bore the ultimate responsibility for Allied safety at sea, much magnified by the immense traffic in troops and supplies to feed the several land campaigns, and wisely decided not to take risks until the threat could be managed [14, 35, 50, 51].

Much of the traffic between Washington and London was handled by the British Admiralty Delegation, part of the Joint Services Mission. The head of BAD presided over a vast and complex organisation whose activities were much more mundane – in short, administering the Lend-Lease scheme. This meant visiting American military and private production facilities all over that vast country, and liaising with Navy Department officials at all levels and in all Bureaus. From time to time, special missions arrived from the Admiralty and officers posted to BAD went back home to discuss matters with the Admiralty

For the most part co-operation was very productive and the British Empire, the Free French and the Dutch received a cornucopia of ships, planes, guns, ammunition, equipment and training facilities [58, 63]. There were wrangles, generally the result of personal mis-matches, crossed wires or disputes over the allocation of resources. As the war drew to a close, American demands on productive capacity increased and BAD officials had to fight to hold the US to its prior agreements on material; the British got most of what they asked for but towards the war's close they were disappointed more frequently [48, 60, 62, 63, 64].

Many of the Royal Navy's ships came from American yards. These were chiefly CVEs, DEs, landing craft, minesweepers, MTBs and auxiliaries and amounted to hundreds of vessels. In 1943, over 800,000 tons of shipping for the Empire's navies came from America, compared with 700,000 tons from the Empire's own resources [8, 57]. Destroyer escorts were commissioned no more than two months after keels were laid. In addition, numerous Allied ships were repaired and modernised in US yards, ranging from battleships and fleet carriers, cruisers, destroyers and submarines to escort vessels, minesweepers, auxiliaries and other naval craft. The repair programme dwindled rapidly in 1944 owing to increased US Navy demands, and a growing sense that the war was coming to an end and that many ships could not be repaired or modernised in time to play their parts in the war [8, 64].

Many of the FAA's aircraft, especially in the second half of the war, came from the USA; there were several thousand of them, generally superior to equivalent British types, though again the supply dwindled greatly in the last few months of the war [47, 48, 60]. A large number of FAA pilots and other aircrew and mechanics were trained in the USA [62, 63]. In particular, FAA personnel took part in the early trials of helicopters [61, 62].

In the early stages of the war, Britain produced equipment either unknown to the Americans or superior to theirs but by the later stages of the war, the Americans had caught up and even surpassed British standards – especially in radar [57]. While the supply of torpedoes was satisfactory, there were quarrels over the allocation of Oerlikon guns; VT fuses, however, represented 'A good example of rapid co-operation' [57,

26, 27, 64]. Captain Stephen Roskill, who in the latter stages of the war headed the BAD's Ordnance Section, observed that British imprecision in formulating requests was at least as much a cause of bad relations as American desire to harbour almost all production [64].[1] The Americans, who had a far larger and more modern industrial base, achieved astonishing results in getting into mass production innovations which just a month or two earlier were still on the drawing boards. British officers were also appreciative of the vast array of American scientific and technical research; there was closer co-operation between the universities and the military in America than was generally the case in Britain, and the American research effort was much better resourced and had been sustained in peacetime; 'it pays to divert money to research in peacetime', wrote one officer wistfully [59]. He also noted, ruefully, that 'US Navy Yards are far better equipped than our Navy Yards' [59].

It was natural for the Americans to maintain a degree of surveillance over their Lend-Lease products when the British took them over. The US Navy was especially critical of the tardiness with which the Royal Navy put its CVEs into service and of the inefficient way in which they were used [7, 10]. The Admiralty countered by claiming that the escort carriers needed modifications, particularly to improve inflammability [12]. British CVEs were less efficient than their American counterparts – in part because they were crewed less lavishly, in part, perhaps, because of a latent British conservatism [10, 12]. The Americans were also critical of British failure to man new destroyer escorts in 1943, leaving valuable new units swinging to their anchors when they should have been usefully employed. The First Lord explained that the reason was that the Americans had produced the ships ahead of schedule [22].[2] He outlined, too, a more fundamental manpower problem. It was partly a matter of numbers, for from March 1944 'the Fleet will be unable to expand much further', as the pool of recruits was shrinking. It was also, more

---

[1]Capt Stephen W. Roskill (1903–82): ent RN 1917; gun spist; *Warspite* 1936–39; Naval Staff 1939–41; *Leander* (NZ) 1941–44; A/Capt, CSO Admin & Weapons, BAD, March 1944; Capt 1945; Bikini 1946; DDNI 1946–8; ret (deafness) official naval historian, 1946–61; *War at Sea*, 3 vols (London, 1954–61); FBA; Fellow, Churchill Coll & founder and 1st keeper, Churchill Archives Cambridge.
VT fuses: a proximity AA fuse.
Oerlikon gun: Swiss 20mm AA gun.
[2]Albert V. Alexander (later Earl of Hillsborough) (1885–1965): local govt officer; Capt Artists' Rifles, WWI; lay preacher; leader in co-op & union movements; Lab MP, Hillsborough, Sheffield, 1922–31, 1935–50; Parl Sec, Board of Trade 1924; FL 1929–31 & May 1940–Dec 1946; Minister of Defence 1946; Chllr Duchy of Lancaster & Visct 1950; Lab Ldr, House of Lords 1955; Earl 1963.

importantly, a result of the Royal Navy's long fight in adversity, in which it suffered high casualties. Alexander explained that 'we have been under the necessity of putting the highest proportion of our strength and our men into the battle line'. As a consequence, experienced officers and senior rates had been required to serve on the front line and those that survived had not been able to be spared for training duties [12, 22, 23, 35]. The Americans made unfavourable comparisons with the British in other areas, too, such as anti-submarine training [7]. An American report on British Dockyards found them 'old-fashioned, the equipment is out-of-date' [34]. Much of the criticism stemmed from King himself; he was not only sharply critical of Royal Navy practices but believed the wily British (led by Churchill) had designs on American ships [6, 10]. King had more serious operational reasons by 1944 for questioning the repair and modernisation of British vessels in American yards, refusing to dock those that could not be dealt with by the war's end and those of questionable naval value [42]. Relations were good, however, at the operational level. Stark, who came to London to head the American Naval forces in Europe, was distinctly friendly and got on well with Vice Admiral Sir Geoffrey Blake, his link with the Admiralty, while Cunningham was equally well-disposed [32, 33, 34].[1]

The BAD reporting officers were also generally agreed that, overall, co-operation had been effective [57, 58, 59]. 'It can be fairly stated,' wrote one, 'that the vast majority of the US Navy did everything in their power to help and a more co-operative crowd would be difficult to find anywhere' [61]. Almost all of them offered pointers to good co-operation. It was necessary to establish good personal relations with one's contacts. British officers should appreciate that their American counterparts were officers of a foreign navy. They should make watertight cases for their requirements, employ tact and understanding, show a willingness to co-operate and display a mastery of their subjects. 'Frankness and openness' were much valued by the Americans [57, 58, 59, 61, 64].

General harmony in co-operation notwithstanding, most British officers were aware of a marked American coolness in the latter part of the war. This was in part a reflection of the US Navy's growing size and commitments, which compelled American officers to prioritise American needs [57, 58, 64]. It sprang also from an increased self-confidence on the part of the US Navy; gone was that reverence for the

---

[1]Adm Sir Geoffrey Blake (1882–1968): ent RN 1897; Lt 1904; gun spist; Grand F 1914–18; Capt 1918; NA, Washington 1919–20; *Queen Elizabeth* 1921–23; N War Coll 1923–5; Dep Dir & Dir N Staff Coll 1925–29; Cdre, NZ Station 1929–32; RA 1931; 4SL 1932; VA 1935; BCS 1935–7; ret 1938 after heart attack; ACNS (F) 1940; FO Liaison, US Naval Forces in Eur 1942–5; Black Rod 1945.

Royal Navy which existed before the war.[1] The fortunes of the war had exposed the Royal Navy's shortcomings and America's recent successes in the Pacific fuelled this subtle change of attitude. As America looked towards the war's end, its interpretation of Lend-Lease tightened, not least because President Truman succeeded the more generous Roosevelt; 'After VE-Day,' observed one officer, 'the attitude of the Navy Department changed considerably' [58, 56].[2]

Indeed, Rear Admiral Dorling had noticed a definite deterioration in American attitudes from late 1943 onwards.[3] This he ascribed to the political situation, for the Presidential election was due in November 1944 and there is always a long lead up to an American election; 'as time went on', he said, 'these effects became more and more marked in those quarters antagonistic to us'. Many difficulties were placed in the way of warm and effective co-operation 'and could only be overcome by cultivating friendly relations with those disposed to be friendly and being tough with those who were not so disposed'. He pointed the finger firmly at King: 'It is reasonably certain that this attitude was inspired by the Cominch', who took advantage of his relative immunity from Presidential interference during the prolonged election campaign; as so often, the US Navy as a whole took its cue from the policy of the man at the top [57]. American government and military leaders were anxious to curtail their post-war commitments and costs within a couple of years; this was noticeable in their 'attitude ... towards Lend-Lease supplies' [52]. The British were concerned to keep the close wartime relationship going, notably in the fields of scientific research and standardisation [36, 57].

When the war in Europe drew to a close, the Americans and the British were agreed on three matters. They wished to keep a reformed Italy in the Western camp by leaving the Italians with a modest navy, though they recognised that Italy's neighbours would not wish it to remain too powerful. They were mindful, too, of the Soviet Union's somewhat exaggerated claims on Italian ships; during the war, the Russians had been fobbed off with old British and American warships but after the war were allowed a dozen Italian vessels of the main classes [53]. The military chiefs were embarrassed by Roosevelt's airy offer to Stalin of one-third of the Italian navy and the COS pointed out, in some depth, the very real difficulties that would ensue [25]. They were agreed that the German

---

[1]M. A. Simpson, ed., *Anglo-American Naval Relations, 1919–1939* (Aldershot, 2010; NRS vol. 156).

[2]Pres Harry S. Truman (1884–1972): Dem; artillery capt, 1917–18; Sen, Missouri, 1935–44; VP 1945; Pres April 1945–1953.

[3]RA J. W. S. Dorling (1889–1966): Dir Naval Eqpt Aug 1939; RA Sept 1939; *Sultan* June 1941; A/VA *Saker* (BAD) April 1942; VA ret & FOIC *Eaglet* (Liverpool) Aug 1944.

Navy's surviving warships should be parcelled out between themselves and the Soviet Union, with a share for France, too. The British and the Americans were keen to learn from German shipbuilding technology and use the ships for experimental purposes. There were few surviving and intact surface warships but they were reluctant to increase the number of U-boats allotted to each power beyond 10 each. 'The Admiralty's aim', it was stated, 'is to keep U-boats out of undesirable hands, particularly Russian hands'. The British noted smugly that 137 of them were in British ports, 'a potent argument' [54]. Finally, all three major powers agreed to a Tripartite Naval Mission, centred in Berlin, to oversee German naval disarmament [43, 45, 46, 54, 55].

1.   *Memorandum from the Chairman, Munitions Assessment*
Board. Port Repair Ships

[CAB 88/19]   Washington,
                                                  7 October 1943

1. At its 81st. meeting on 1 September 1943, the MAB, with the UK representatives dissenting, assigned to the US four vessels N3-M-A1 for conversion into port repair ships. This action revoked an earlier assignment of the four vessels to the UK. In view of the British dissent, and of the importance attached to the matter from an operational point of view by both sides, the decision of the Board is submitted to the CCS for review.

CCS 367/1: Memorandum by the US Chiefs of Staff.

12 October 1943.

The US COS have considered CCS 367 … and recommend:

1) that the CCS reaffirms the reassignment of three N3-M-A1 vessels to the British for use in OVERLORD;
2) that one N3-M-A1 vessel be assigned to the US to be converted into a port repair ship for use in OVERLORD.

2.   *Combined Chiefs of Staff: 122nd Meeting.*
Supplementary Minutes

[CAB 88/3]   Washington,
                                                  8 October 1943

9. Assignment of four N3-M-A1 Vessels for conversion into Port Repair Ships (CCS 367) [not reproduced].
    Admiral Leahy said … he believed their [the JCS's] attitude would be that the four vessels in question should be allocated to the US.
    …
    Captain Tollemache[1] explained that there was no difference of opinion as to the need for port repair ships. The special vessels under consideration, however, were specifically designed to provide the heavy lift required before cranes were available in a captured port. The vessels had been built to a British order specifically for operation OVERLORD, and would be used to unload barges and then to take the place of cranes in captured harbours until the harbours had been rehabilitated.

---

[1]Capt Tollemache, US Navy: unidentified.

The British regarded these ships as a vital link in the build-up imme-diately after the assault phase. If they were not supplied, OVERLORD would be deprived of an essential adjunct to its success. With regard to port repair ships the British considered that smaller and less specialised vessels could be used and were converting smaller coastal vessels them-selves for this purpose.

...

The CCS: Agreed to defer action on CCS 367.

3. *Combined Chiefs of Staff: 123rd. Meeting*

[CAB 88/3]   Washington,
                                                      15 October 1943

3. *Assignment of four N3-m-A1 vessels for conversion into port repair ship (CCS367–367/1)* [not reproduced].

Sir John Dill [said] ... The British, however, had laid great store on this type of ship which had been laid down at their request. British experts were convinced it would be a great pity to convert any of these ships from the role for which they were designed. With a lift of 70 tons they were immensely valuable for clearing cargo ships at anchor during the build-up after an assault and also for use as cranes in a captured harbour until the full port facilities could be restored. ... He asked that the first three heavy-lift ships should be assigned to the British for OVERLORD.

Admiral King said that the ships must be ready in time for OVER-LORD whatever their use. He pointed out that if one were converted to a port repair ship this work would take longer than the preparation of the ship as a heavy-lift ship.

The CCS: ...

(b) Agreed that it was very necessary to get all four N3-M-A1 ships ready in time for OVERLORD and took note that the US Navy Department would explore the possibility of this.

(c) Took note that the US Navy Department would examine the prac-ticability of the first three of these ships being allotted to Britain.

4. *Combined Chiefs of Staff Memoranda*

[CAB 88/14]   Washington,
                                                      19 October 1943

CCS 286/5: Memorandum from the US Chiefs of Staff: OVERLORD Assault.

The US Chiefs of Staff are of the opinion that the assault forces for OVERLORD should be strengthened by every practicable means. In view of our recent discussions with General Morgan,[1] however, we are not now prepared to express a firm opinion whether the increased strength should go into the initial assault, the immediate follow-up or to provide a floating reserve. The basic problem is obviously one of landing craft availability; exactly how they are to be utilised should await the decision of the Supreme Commander. As to the provision of additional craft, we consider the Mediterranean, the Middle East, increased production and miscellaneous activities here and in the UK are the only acceptable sources. We understand that you have initiated a comb-out in the UK and we are doing the same in the US. Increased production in the US cannot be felt in the UK in time to help OVERLORD. We do not consider that Eisenhower's minimum lift should be further reduced at this time but recognise that after his northward advance in Italy has ended next spring it may prove desirable to take additional craft from the Mediterranean at that time for OVERLORD. We do not know exactly what landing craft there are in the Mediterranean but feel that some assistance may be possible from that source. We are in agreement with General Marshall's desire to strengthen the OVERLORD assault by exploiting the tremendous air lift that will be available in the UK by the OVERLORD target date.

The US Chiefs of Staff propose:

(a) The British and US Chiefs of Staff continue the comb-out of landing craft in the UK and the US, respectively, and report the results to the Combined Chiefs of Staff.

(b) C-in-C, NATO [?], be directed to consult with C-in-C, Middle East, with a view (1) to determining the assistance which might be rendered OVERLORD by transfers of landing craft to the Western Mediterranean, thus releasing some from this area to OVERLORD, and (2) to make appropriate recommendation to the Combined Chiefs of Staff.

...

Although we agree as a broad principle, British forces should be carried in British-manned landing craft and US forces should be carried in US-manned landing craft, circumstances may arise where we will both find

---

[1]Lt Gen Sir Frederick Morgan (1894–1967): Royal Artillery 1913; W Front; Capt 1918; BEF 1939–40; A/Maj Gen, cmdg 55 Div 1941–2; I Corps 1942–3; COSSAC, March 1943; later on SHAEF staff. Real architect of Normandy D-day; DCOS 1944–5; ret 1946; atomic development 1951–6.

that it will be expedient to depart from this principle. Consequently, we are reluctant to adopt any fixed rule in this regard.

5. *Captain L. E. Porter, RN,*[1]*to Captain A. D. Douglas,*
US Navy[2]

[SPD 243]   Washington,
                                                    20 October 1943

I suggest that the time has now come for the British to request the assignment of the next two LSD building at Newport and completing in February and March [1944] respectively. Not only do we have considerable warning of the manning of these ships, but in addition I understand that they have got to the stage where certain British characteristics must be incorporated.

It may interest you to know our latest thoughts on the employment of this class of warships. In CCS 329/2 [not reproduced] three British LSD were shown as available for OVERLORD because it was thought that:

(a) they would be too light for operations in South East Asia Command, and
(b) we should be short of docking facilities in the UK.

Now that the South East Asia operations have been postponed, and NL pontoon gear has been allocated for OVERLORD, neither of these considerations now apply. In any case COSSAC has never been told that he can have them and there is no part such valuable ships can play which would be worth the risks.

On the other hand, the more we look into South East Asia operations, with their lack of bases and long lines of communications, the more we realise the enormous value of these ships. We are therefore intending to send both *Eastway* and *Highway,*[3] our first two LSD to India now, and we urgently require the two completing in February and March as soon as we can get them out to this theatre. Quite apart from their most valuable docking and repair facilities, they will be essential for the transport

---

[1]Capt L.E. Porter: Cdr June 1937; *Kent* Aug 1939; SO (I), *Tana* Jan 1941; *Suffolk* May 1941; A/Capt, BAD May 1942; Capt June 1945; *Condor* Sep 1945.
[2]Capt A.D. Douglas, US Navy: unidentified.
[3]*Eastway, Highway*: LSD; built under Lend-Lease, 1943; 4500t, 15.4k, 1×5in.

of support craft, for which we have no other means of getting to the right place at the right time.

I have therefore asked BASR to request the assignment now of these next two ships, and I would be very grateful if you would consider the matter at your end.

6.   *King to Secretary of the Navy Knox*

[Op Arch, King 4]   Washington,
                                                      23 October 1943

With reference to the attached despatch from Admiral Stark [not reproduced], I would prefer that the name of this vessel not be made public. The pressure from London to emphasise in the public mind the association of this vessel with the Home Fleet is, I think, part and parcel of an Admiralty scheme to force us to make permanent the assignment of this carrier group to the British Fleet. This unit actually was loaned to the British for the purpose of meeting a temporary emergency in UK waters. The Admiralty is resisting my efforts to have it return to its normal station. It would be unfortunate if this temporary loan were to be manoeuvred into the status of a permanent commitment.[1]

7.   *Stark to King*

[Op Arch, Stark A2]   London,
                                                      23 October 1943

... After Syfret[2] had depicted their generally tight situation, and particularly in the Mediterranean, I said in substance:

'Well, Admiral Syfret, I do not know your general plan in the Mediterranean, ... it does strike me that in your playing around in the Aegean you just keep on losing ships, and then turn to us to help you out of a hole. If the sacrifices you are making down there are getting you anywhere, or are worth the price, that would be one thing, but personally

---

[1]USS *Ranger*.

[2]Adm Sir E. Neville Syfret (1884–1971): ent RN 1904; gun spist; Harwich 1914–18; Capt 1929; Naval Sec to FL Nov 1939; RA, 18 CS 1940; Malta convoys 1941–2; cdr, Force H April 1942; Madagascar 1942; N Africa Nov 1942; VA & VCNS; Adm 1946; C-in-C, HF 1946–8; ret 1948.

I can't see where you are going, or what you are leading up to in that corner – also you apparently are getting the worst of it – and possibly detracting from the Italian area. Also it seems to me, with Crete in German hands – the situation in the little islands off South West Turkey will continue to be precarious.

We also have our nooks and corners in the Pacific – but they are part of a well laid plan of advance – they lead somewhere, and when you lose in the Mediterranean, and if to no real purpose, and then ask us to make up your losses, it is bound to hurt effort elsewhere. There just isn't enough to go around.'

Syfret replied –

'We have been considering that situation very carefully and two nights ago we had a session on it with the Prime Minister. I shall bring your thoughts to others concerned.'

… Also Fraser[1] told me that he'd like to get another 12 destroyers from us – that he needed them, etc., etc. I stalled that off, but I know the Admiralty is considering it – and I thought it time to tell them.

P. S.: … Pryce states that Mansfield certainly laid it strongly on the line as regards our CVE operations; in fact telling the British that they were way, way behind us and that they ought to realize it. He supported this statement with data as to flying hours work which Pryce says amazed the British.[2]

Mansfield also compared our A/S training at Bermuda with British training, and very favourably from our standpoint.

I have pointed out personally to the British how much more we have been operating our CVEs than the British have those which have been allocated to them.

I do think the British need waking up on some of these things, and I'm hoping some of these efforts will bear fruit.

---

[1] AoF Lord (Sir Bruce) Fraser (1888–1981): ent RN 1902; Indian Ocean & E Med 1915–16; Gun Div 1926–9; *Effingham*, E Indies 1929–32; DNO 1933–5; *Glorious* 1935–7; RA & CoS to C-in-C Med, Nov 1938; 3SL & Cntrlr March 1939–June 1942; VA 1940; 2inC, HF June 1942–May 1943; C-in-C, HF May 1943–June 1944; Adm 1943; C-in-C, EF & BPF June 1944–June 1946; C-in-C Portsmouth May 1947; AoF & FSL Sept 1948-April 1952. R. Humble, *Fraser of North Cape* (London, 1983).

[2] VA J. M. Mansfield (1893–1949): ent RN 1906; s/m 1915–21; battleships & cruisers 1920s; RN Coll, Greenwich 1931; Capt 1934; RN War Coll 1934–7; F Capt, *Norfolk*, E Indies 1937–9; CoS, NA & WI 1941–3; RA 1943; 15 CS 1944–5; ACNS (UT) May 1945; FO Ceylon 1945–6; VA & FO (S) 1946.

Pryce, US Navy: unidentified.

8. *BAD Report for the period 1–31 October 1943*

[ADM 199/1469]   Washington,
                                                     [c. November 1943]

1. *New Construction.*
During the month of October, one CVE, one frigate, 14 destroyers, two POEs, four BAMs, 11 BYMS, 146 YMSs, two ATRs, and two APCs were accepted and/or commissioned, bringing the total number of ships accepted to:

25 CVEs, AVCs, and BAYGs (including four BAYGs handed over as
   conversions by BAMR)
37 BDEs and Destroyers
12 BAMs and AMs
8 PCEs
134 BYMS and YMS
3 BARs
21 APCs
18 BATs and ATRs
2 BYTs
54 MTBs
32 72-ft MLs
40 Aircraft Rescue Boats
78 LSTs
2 LSTs converted to LSE
1 18,000 ton drydock
1 1800 ton drydock.

CVEs:
CVEs 32 (*Slinger*), 37 (*Trumpeter*), and 39 (*Khedive*) have sailed from the East Coast for the UK. Trials of 35 (*Ameer*), the first ship to complete modification at Vancouver, have been held up owing to engine room defects, but should probably take place during the first week of November.

Destroyers and PFs:
…
During the month, DE 88 (*Fitzroy*) commissioned, having been laid down a little less than two months ago. …
    Unless weather conditions later in the year become too arctic, it is intended that all Destroyers and PFs shall proceed to Casco Bay for a two weeks' shakedown, prior to sailing for Bermuda.

Another record-breaking attempt is now in course, and it is probable that DE 91 (*Halsted*) will be completed within a month from date of keel laying to commissioning.[1]

...

II. *Landing Craft:*

Landing Craft have resumed their position of highest priority, replacing DEs.

Except for an additional 2000 LCM(3), there have been no new contracts issued during the month, but the heat is on again and efforts are being made to expedite production.

... Arrangements have been made for training British LCI(L) crews on arrival in the US at this base [Solomon's Island, Chesapeake Bay] and for familiarising them with the craft. They also return to this base in their own craft to shake-down after commissioning.

The Base is well organised and the standard of discipline of the British crews showed a marked improvement on those who manned the earlier programme.

The possibility of building some small wooden Landing Craft in Canada, engined from US production, is again being investigated.

In addition to the LCT and small craft, the 62 LST now sailed have carried some 7000 passengers, over 50,000 tons of cargo, oil and about the same weight of tanks and solid cargo.

...

MTBs:

MTBs of the 25th and 26th Flotillas are virtually completed, with some awaiting shipment. Those of the 25th are a little behind time as special generators for SO Radar had to be obtained. These are now becoming available, and the boats should be loaded in short order. Some further delay has been occasioned by a bout of cases of overheating of thrust bearings. This matter is now being thoroughly investigated, and it is hoped that a solution will be forthcoming.

...

18-in Torpedoes:

The 15 torpedoes made by the Precision Company have been sent to range. The first three have passed range with British made propellers and the balance are awaiting Bullard Propellers.

---

[1]*Halsted*: DE. Irreparably damaged by E-boat 1944.

...

The prospects of the Bureau [of Ordnance] developing a welded air vessel for the British Mk XV torpedoes varies with the wind, which has been highly changeable in recent weeks. The Bureau of Ordnance scheduling officers' mind[s] veers towards releasing forging capacity to us for the present and not bothering with a new type of welded air vessel. The situation is, however, far from crystallised and by the time this reaches London the wind may be in the other quarter. In any event, we are reasonably assured of a supply of air vessels.

...

VI. *A/S Warfare:*
Instruction –

(a) Key West Sound School

During the month of October the following numbers of Officers and Ratings underwent courses at the British Section of the Fleet Sound School, Key West:

11 Officers, 33 Ratings.

(b) Echo Sounding Courses in New York

During the month of October the following number of Ratings underwent courses in US Echo Sounding equipment at New York:

32 Ratings.

(c) Convoy Escort Courses

The 10th and 11th series of lectures and demonstrations for Officers in New York [were] held in the HQ of the 3rd Naval District, 90 Church Street, New York City, from 4 to 8 October, and 25 to 29 October respectively.

Appendix I

RN Ships in Hand for Repairs, etc., in USA on 1 November 1943:

		Arrived	Completion
Indomitable	Aircraft Carrier	31 Aug	end Feb 1944
Argonaut	Cruiser	30 April	1 Nov 1943
Arethusa	Cruiser	30 March	1 Dec 1943

Bittersweet	Corvette	27 Sept	9 Nov 1943
L26	Submarine	5 Sept	16 Feb 1944
Newfoundland	Cruiser	21Aug	2 Jan 1944
Collingwood	Corvette	12 Oct	21 Dec 1943 RCN
Dunvegan	Corvette	20 Oct	27 Dec 1943 RCN
St Albans	Destroyer	28 Oct	10 Dec 1943 RNethN
Chevreuil	Corvette	26 Aug	15 Dec 1943 Free French

Number of HM Ships repaired in USA up to 1 Nov 1943

Battleships	7	Corvettes	30
Cruisers	16	Submarines	15
AMCs	15	Auxiliary Craft	4
Aircraft Carriers	6	Seaplane Tender	1
Minelayers	3	Transport	1
Depot Ships	2	BYMS	1
ACV	8	Escort Vessel	1
Destroyers	40	Frigate	1
BEC	1	Minesweepers	3
Submarine Chasers	1	Fleet Tender	1

HM Ships due to come in hand after 1 November 1943

Uganda	Cruiser	23 Nov 1943	
Mayflower	Corvette	1 Dec 1943	
Igonish	Minesweeper	15 Nov 1943	RCN
Lockeport	Minesweeper	12 Jan 1944	RCN
Remoncule	Corvette	17Nov 1943	Free French
Lobelia	Corvette	under consideration	Free French
Cleopatra	Cruiser	23 Nov 1943	
P553	Submarine	–Feb 1944	
Leander	Cruiser	–Jan 1944	RNZN
Drumheller	Corvette	11 Nov 1943	RCN
Kamsack	Corvette	26 Dec 1943	RCN
Oakville	Corvette	15 Dec 1943	RCN
Wetaskiwin	Corvette	15 Dec 1943	RCN
Warspite	Battleship	mid Dec 1943	
Agassiz	Corvette	15 Dec 1943	RCN
Pictou	Corvette	7 Jan 1944	RCN
Arvida	Corvette	15 Jan 1944	RCN

Ships completed (i.e., repaired) during October

Ajax	Cruiser	
Roxburgh	Destroyer	
Guysborough	Corvette	RCN
P554	Submarine	
Seawolf	Submarine[1]	

9. *Joint Chiefs of Staff: 121st Meeting*

[RG 218/196]   Washington,
                                              2 November 1943

...

6. *Provision of Tugs for OVERLORD and for artificial harbour purposes.*

Admiral Leahy said that in CCS 307/3 [not reproduced] the representatives of the British COS had examined the availability of tugs for OVERLORD and had concluded there would be a deficit of 40 tugs in the immediate requirements which could not be provided from UK resources. The British COS had expressed the belief that unless this shortage of 40 tugs were provided, OVERLORD would be prejudiced and suggested an immediate examination of US resources to provide the 40 tugs still required.

In JCS 552 [not reproduced] the Joint Logistics Committee had thoroughly examined the availability of tugs and found that a large number had already been sent to the UK, which apparently had not been considered by the British COS in their examination of the position.

The Committee concluded that the US commitment of 25 sea-going tugs or towing vessels for OVERLORD were now being met and that, moreover, an additional 235 tugs, many of which could be temporarily diverted for OVERLORD, had been allocated to the European theater of operations. Further that 25 sea-going tugs or towing vessels are now scheduled for delivery to the British prior to 1 April 1944 under Lend-Lease.

10. *King to Stark*

[Op Arch, King 4]   5 November 1943

I refer to your letters to me of 23 [see Document 7], 25 and 28 October [not reproduced]. The seeming 'helping' of our cousins strikes me as

---

[1]*Guysborough*, torpedoed 17 Mar 1945, appears in Part II.

amusing when it is not annoying. I am sure that what they wish in their hearts is that we would haul down the Stars and Stripes and hoist the White Ensign in all our ships. What particularly 'irks' me is their strong liking for 'mixed forces' which, as you know, approaches 'anathema' to me. I am willing to take over additional tasks – and we have done so – but I cannot be expected to agree to help them cling to tasks that they themselves say they are unable to do unless we lend them our ships and other forces. I think we have done enough for them in the Home Fleet!

It is good to know that Mansfield 'laid it on the line' to his people about their CVE operations. Captain Green should be able to help them, if they want to be helped.[1] Informal information from the *Ranger* indicates that the high command of the Home Fleet does not understand – as yet – that if he wants to get full value out of carriers, the carrier group (cruisers, destroyers, etc.) must conform to the requirements of carrier operations.

Another thing that is giving the JCS some concern is the increasing trend of the British COS to take unilateral action, chiefly regarding Mediterranean matters. We know perfectly well who inspires this unilateral action![2]

The matter of squadrons operating in the Bay has been settled – for the time being – as best we could manage. It is important to Arnold to free the two Army squadrons in Morocco – and we have arranged to do just that but not as soon as would have been the case if the *two* squadrons had been transferred from the so-called Bay Offensive.

I am happy to confirm that we propose to have you home for a conference, arriving here about 20 December. In the meantime, many things will have happened – as you no doubt know.

The award of a Naval DSM to Admiral Pound was gotten under way as soon as his retirement from the Admiralty was announced.

11. *Combined Chiefs of Staff: 126th Meeting*

[CAB 88/3]   Washington,
                                                              5 November 1943

. . .

5. *Operations in the Mediterranean (CCS 379/3, 4 & 5)* [not reproduced]
In general, the Naval C-in-C felt that the holding of LSTs in the Mediterranean until 15 December would reflect seriously on OVERLORD preparations and in particular training.

. . .

---

[1]Capt Green, US Navy: unidentified.
[2]Churchill.

Sir John Dill said that the Prime Minister, the British Cabinet, and the British Chiefs of Staff all regarded the Italian situation as being extremely dangerous. They were anxious not only that General Eisenhower should have a one-divisional amphibious lift, but that he should have at least sufficient landing craft and ships to lift two divisions amphibiously, in order that they could operate on both the east and west coasts of Italy and thus afford a greater threat to both German flanks. They regarded the present situation where our forces were held up as dangerous and they believed that the holding of 60 LSTs in the Mediterranean would not materially affect OVERLORD.

12. *CCS 392: Memorandum by US Chiefs of Staff:*

Assignment of Combat and Merchant Ships to Great Britain

[CAB 88/19]   9 November 1943

1. The C-in-C, US Fleet and CNO has been advised that after about 15 November the British will be unable to man on schedule the DEs now under construction in the Boston area. He is also advised that approximately 10 of these vessels would have to be laid up in the Boston area with British skeleton crews for a period of about two months, after which time the British expect to catch up on the manning schedule.

2. Because of the intensive campaign which has been carried on to stimulate construction of vessels of this class, laying up of a number of vessels for a period of two months in that locality would affect the morale and efficiency of the production forces. Steps have been initiated by the C-in-C, US Fleet and the BAD to move these ships with temporary crews to some British port.

3. Notification of the completion of these vessels was made to British authorities on 15 June 1943. The inability to furnish crews to meet the manning schedule is a matter of grave concern to the US COS not only because of repercussions on our production forces, but more particularly because of the failure to promptly and effectively employ these ships in prosecution of the war. The US COS have also felt much concern over the delays that have ensued before the CVEs assigned to the British have been put to use against the submarine.

4. The US COS appreciate the difficult manpower situation with which the British are faced. They consider that if the delays are an indication that lack of manpower will prevent immediate manning of US construction now allocated to the British, the interests of both Nations will be best served if immediate steps are taken to adjust the US building and allocation programs accordingly.

5. Advice from the British COS in the premises is requested.

CCS 392/1: Memorandum by representatives of the British COS.

16 November 1943.

1. The subject matter of CCS 392 has been discussed fully between the BAD and the Navy Department. It is, therefore, not understood why this memorandum is brought before the CCS.

2. The reason why approximately 10 DEs from Boston may not be manned properly on completion is because the dates of delivery of these vessels have been advanced beyond those originally given, progressively of some two weeks in September 1943, to some six weeks by March 1944.

3. The reference to CVEs appears to be irrelevant, as none of those vessels have been through manning difficulties. The delay in making them active in the submarine war has been due to structural alterations that the Admiralty consider necessary, largely on account of the fact that we have not the manpower to man them on the same scale as the US Navy, and, also, that in recent operations covering the landing of the [US] Fifth Army all four CVEs taking part in giving fighter cover were those of the British programme.

4. It is noted that this paper is headed 'Assignment of Combat and Merchant Ships to Great Britain'. It is not understood why merchant ships have been included as they do not form the subject of any [part] of the paper.

5. The First Sea Lord has recently informed the C-in-C, US Fleet and the CNO at Ottawa of our manning difficulties, and full details of these difficulties and the hopes of clearing them have been given to the Navy Department.

6. It is now becoming clear that the events of the past four years are restricting further expansion of our Navy. After the fall of France it was realised that landing craft in large numbers would be required and their crews would have to be highly trained. We could not, at that time, when so much was needed in other ways, expand our training establishments and our intake of men to meet the additional demand. The enormous demands for landing craft crews in the various theatres of war, when our own and USA warship programmes are coming to fruition, means that our manning capabilities are stretched to the limit. It does not yet mean that we have not sufficient over-all numbers, but our shortage is in the higher trained ratings and officers. This cannot be solved by numbers of men alone. If we could have expanded sufficiently in 1940, these highly trained men would probably be available, but that was not possible.

7. It will be remembered that in 1941 we were faced with intensive warfare in the Mediterranean,[1] and during that period incurred tremendous

---

[1] See *Cunningham Papers*, I.

naval casualties. In passing it may be of interest to note that that through-out the war we have lost over 500 warships sunk, as well as the much greater number that have been damaged in action; and although losses of ships somewhat eased the over-all situation, the casualties deprived us of many of the higher-trained ratings which has consistently affected our ability to train newly enlisted men.

8. At the moment we are examining our position, and hope to be able to produce a solution that will see us through OVERLORD. We are deter-mined, however, to see that escort vessels for the Battle of the Atlantic have a high place in our priorities and, whatever the improvisations that we have to resort to, all the vessels assigned to us by the USA will be manned and placed in service as speedily as possible.

9. Delays have not yet occurred, but arrangements must be made to meet them if they do. We are therefore seeking ways and means of having a reserve to call on if unexpected new commitments place us in difficulties that might otherwise lead to delay. We are looking into the possibility of ferrying ships over and manning them in the UK to save the delay in shipping a crew for each particular ship. The RCN are coming to our assistance, and we are drawing up a list of old ships in which so many defects have occurred and which we feel sure will have to spend so much time in dockyard that we must soon pay them off as worn out. These will be kept ready in commission but earmarked to pay off to supply us with crews if we run short.

10. By these means we hope to get through the period of the next few months without crises, and we expect that the period of about two months, as stated in paragraph 1 of CCS 392 will prove to be very much reduced.

13. *Memorandum by US Chiefs of Staff:*

CCS 300/2: Estimate of Enemy Situation, 1944 – Pacific and Far East

[CAB 88/14]   17 November 1943

(For SEXTANT)
Enclosure

...

3. (f) *South West and Central Pacific:*

We believe that Japan will remain on the strategic defensive, continuing her efforts to build up her local defensive forces and facilities and her naval striking force.

...

Appendix A

...

5. Basic factors in the Japanese situation:

(a) *Objectives*

Japan's basic objective is to establish undisputed control of an area in East Asia and the Western Pacific which shall be militarily secure and as nearly self-sufficient economically as possible. The area now occupied by her approximates the territorial requirements of this objective. ...

(b) *Relationship to the Axis*

Japan's connection with the Axis is a matter of expediency only. Her action will be to coordinate with Germany only in so far as she estimates that such coordination will contribute to the realization of her basic objective.

...

6. The existing overall situation:

(a) *Military Strength*

We estimate the present strength of her armed forces as follows:

(1) *Navy*

11 battleships, 7 carriers, 5 auxiliary carriers, 14 heavy cruisers, 18 light cruisers, 78 destroyers
89 submarines.

...

(c) *Limitations on Japanese Power*

(1) *Shipping*
Japan's defensive position requires secure and adequate ocean transport over long lines of communication. The Japanese shipping situation has become acute, with her total tonnage being further eroded by sinkings in excess of total construction. We estimate that 50–60% of her tonnage is committed to maintaining her military forces outside the homeland and that the remainder is used primarily to maintain the essential part of her war economy. From this latter bracket some tonnage might still be found for new operations by diverting it from trade, and, provided such diversions were temporary, this would not necessarily have serious effects on Japan's capacity to wage war. Since, however, Japan's rate of building, though on the increase, cannot keep pace even with the present rate of sinkings, she would be reluctant to risk adding further to her shipping commitments. Although attempts are being made to improve the position

by building a large number of small and medium-sized wooden ships, the general shipbuilding position is becoming increasingly difficult and may well become precarious in 1944. The situation in regard to tankers is also acute. Japan is attempting to meet a deficiency in this respect by continuing to fit out dry-cargo ships for use as oil carriers.

...

3. *Naval requirements*

Japan cannot afford to risk large commitments of naval strength except for the defense of vital areas. Her extended lines of communication already entail a large commitment of naval strength for the protection of essential shipping. The further extension, or indecisive action entailing heavy attrition, might well be unacceptable.

...

7. The existing local situation:

...

(g) *Central Pacific*

At present Japan bases 50–60% of her naval strength at Truk. The total air strength of this area has been increasing, particularly in the Marshalls and Gilberts.

8. Strategic reserves:

...

(c) *Navy*

Normally Japan maintains her battleship and carrier strength in home waters and at Truk, shifting the center of gravity according to circumstances. A formidable striking force, which can reach any threatened part of the perimeter in from six to nine days, can be quickly assembled in either of these central areas. However, destroyer shortage is becoming critical.

...

9. Prospective developments through 1944:

...

(b) *Naval strength*

Disregarding attrition, we estimate that Japanese naval strength should increase as a result of new construction to the following totals:

	BB	CV	Aux CV	HC	LC	DD	SM
1 Nov 1943	11	7	5	14	18	78	89
1 Jan 1944	12	8	5	14	18	85	97
1 Jun 1944	12	10	6	15	19	95	113
1 Jan 1945	13	14	7	16	20	105	130

(d) *Shipping*

Despite Japan's strenuous shipbuilding efforts, estimates of the rate of loss and rate of construction of steel ships indicate that the Japanese may suffer a net loss of 1,500,000 grt of steel operating tonnage from 1 November 1943 to the end of 1944. However, construction of wooden vessels and further substitution of land transport may offset a part of the estimated net loss of steel ships.

14.   *Memorandum by US Chiefs of Staff:*

CCS 300/3: Estimate of the Enemy Situation, 1944 – Europe

[CAB 88/14]   18 November 1943

(For SEXTANT)
Enclosure

...

Appendix

...

6. The existing overall situation:

...

(c) Naval Forces

(1) Submarines

Germany now (1 November 1943) possesses about 400 German-built submarines of which about 200 are attached to the operating forces. Of the ex-Italian submarines a few in use as supply vessels or blockade runners may be operational but no others. None of the ex-French submarines are believed to be operational.

The rate of completion of new submarines (all German-built) may be expected to continue at approximately 20 a month.

Germany is encountering great difficulty in manning submarines. The quality and morale of the personnel have on the average declined, and in some instances are very low, but there are no reliable indications that any general breakdown of morale is imminent.

(2) Surface vessels (effective combat types, 1 November 1943)

The major units are two battleships, two heavy cruisers, and four light cruisers. Of these, the battleship *Tirpitz* (damaged to an unknown extent) and *Scharnhorst* are in North Norway waters; the rest are in the Baltic with their effectiveness much reduced with the transfer of experienced personnel to submarines. (The carrier *Graf Zeppelin* is not operational). Some 30 destroyers and 40 torpedo boats are in waters from the Bay of Biscay northward (including the Baltic). In service in Mediterranean waters are perhaps two destroyers and three torpedo boats in the Western Basin and perhaps five destroyers and torpedo boats in the Aegean (all ex-French or ex-Italian); as many as 40 or more of such Italian units might be placed in service but no major units.[1]

New construction in progress consists of about 18 destroyers and possibly two ex-Netherlands light cruisers.

We believe that morale is low in the major units but reasonably high in the light forces.

...

7. The situation by fronts – 1 November 1943:

(a) The war against shipping

Germany's war against ocean shipping has fallen far short of achieving its objective of preventing effective support from overseas of UN operations. It has, however, succeeded in delaying such support and limiting its scale, and its effects are still felt in such ways.

Moreover, the Germans realize that as long as they continue their submarine attacks, or threaten them, on a serious scale, they will force the UN to divert to A/S escorts large amounts of manpower, energy and materials which could advantageously be used for other war purposes and will prevent them from making the most efficient use of available shipping. We believe that the effectiveness of the war against shipping will not increase.

---

[1] *Graf Zeppelin*: Ger: carrier: 1936; uncompleted.

15.   *Operational Functions and the Design and Armament of Aircraft Carriers and Naval Aircraft*

[ADM 205/33]   18 November 1943

…

35. *Standardisation*

In order that British and American aircraft should be able to use Carriers of both Navies, some measure of standardisation must be aimed at. These essentials are height of hangar, size and weight capacity of lifts, and mechanical and dynamic features of arrester and take-off gear. Discussion is to be opened with the Americans on these points. So far as hangar heights and lift sizes are concerned existing British Carriers could not under present circumstances be altered to become standardised with American Aircraft Carriers. A further difficulty is likely to be the stressing of British aircraft to withstand the arrester gear on American ships. American aircraft and arrester gear are designed for a maximum deceleration of 3.5g, and it is under consideration to adopt the figure for future British aircraft as well.

36. As far as possible in Carriers under design or construction we are making arrangements which will standardise our practice with that of the US Navy. This will not be possible before the 'Ark Royals' and the 1943 LFCs.[1]

…

Following the loss of *Avenger* and *Dasher* American and British designs of CVEs has been compared from the point of view of vulnerability. On the whole the British design would appear to be the less vulnerable. It has better sub-divisions both longitudinal and transverse and the petrol tanks are cylindrical, more stoutly built and surrounded by water, whereas *Avenger* had less sub-divisions and flat tanks grouped together in a space which is normally air-filled (but can be filled with CO2). So far as experience goes we have had a number of carriers torpedoed but only *Avenger* has blown up as a result, and this was not due to petrol but to the explosion of the bomb room. *Dasher* blew up as a result of a petrol explosion. It is felt that American-built carriers of the *Avenger* [class] should be improved by installing cylindrical petrol tanks and that this has been approved as a long term policy.[2]

---

[1] 'Ark Royal' Fleet Carriers & most of Light Fleet Carriers completed post-war.
[2] *Avenger*: torpedoed *U-155*, 15 Nov 1942; *Dasher*: internal explosion, Clyde, 27 Mar 1943.

16. *Leahy: Diary*

[LC, Leahy]   Cairo,
                                                    24 November 1943

[The Prime Minister] gave a long and unconvincing talk about the advantages of operations in the Aegean Sea and against the island of Rhodes.

Cairo,
                                                    25 November 1943

[We] discussed at length and without agreement a British proposal to delay cross-Channel operations in order to put forth more effort in the Aegean Sea and in Turkey.

Tehran,
                                                    30 November 1943

... we finally succeeded in getting the British to launch the cross-Channel attack on Germany in France during the month of May 1944, and to make at the same time a supporting attack on Southern France in such force as can be handled by the landing craft available in the Mediterranean at that time ...

17. *Combined Chiefs of Staff: 132nd Meeting*

[CAB 88/3]   Tehran,
                                                    30 November 1943

...

   Sir Andrew Cunningham said that unless BUCCANEER landing craft were to be used, it would not be possible, except at the expense of OVERLORD, to have more than a one-division lift for the South of France, a lift which in his opinion, was not sufficient.[1]

   Admiral King said that the Prime Minister had laid great stress on the importance of keeping employed all the forces now in the Mediterranean. He agreed with this in principle but drew attention to the two-and-a-half months' inactivity that would ensue for the 35 divisions in the UK if the OVERLORD date was postponed from 1 May [1944]. He had always felt that the OVERLORD operation was the way to break the back of Germany.

---

[1]BUCCANEER: proposed operation against Andaman Islands.

Sir Andrew Cunningham questioned the two-and-a-half months referred to by Admiral King, saying that the earliest possible date for OVER-LORD would be 1 June. Both Admiral King and Admiral Leahy then said that this came to them as a complete surprise as 1 May was the date agreed upon.

The CCS agreed that:

(a)   That we should continue to advance in Italy to the Pisa-Rimini line. This means that the 68 LST which are due to be sent from the Mediterranean to the UK for OVERLORD must be kept in the Mediterranean until 15 January.

(b)   That an operation should be mounted against the South of France on as big a scale as landing craft permitted. For planning purposes D-day [was] to be the same as OVERLORD D-day.

(c)   To recommend to the President and the Prime Minister respectively that we should inform Marshal Stalin that we shall launch OVER-LORD during May, in conjunction with a supporting operation against the South of France on the largest scale that is permitted by the landing craft available at that time.[1]

18.   *Combined Chiefs of Staff: 133rd Meeting*

[CAB 88/3]   Cairo,
3 December 1943

...

3. *OVERLORD and operations against the South of France*

Sir Alan Brooke ... suggested that the Combined Staff Planners should examine this [the invasion of Southern France] at once on the basis that the OVERLORD operation took place during May [1944] and that a two-divisional assault should take place against the South of France.

Admiral King pointed out that the decision at EUREKA was only that the operation against the South of France should be undertaken in as great a strength as the availability of landing craft permitted and that there was no decision on the strength of the assaulting force.

Sir Alan Brooke said that he regarded a two-division assault as the minimum which could be accepted. The attack must be planned with such strength as to make it successful.

---

[1] This became ANVIL; see Part IV.

Sir Charles Portal suggested ... that an assault with less than two divisions was asking for failure. ... It appeared that in order to carry out a successful operation in the South of France, other operations would have to suffer.

Admiral Leahy felt that the planners should be told that this operation should be carried out without interference with operation OVERLORD.

...

Sir Andrew Cunningham said that in considering the availability of resources, all operations must be taken into consideration except OVER-LORD. He considered that if no strength was set, the planners could not examine the availability of resources properly. He said that they should be told [firstly] to report on the required strength for the assault, and secondly, to put forward proposals from which the landing craft resources could be made available.

...

It was agreed that the CSP should be directed in collaboration, as necessary, with the Combined Administrative Committee, to examine the agreed operation against the South of France on the following premises:

(a) That the operation should be carried out with a minimum of two assault divisions, and
(b) The necessary resources should not be found at the expense of OVERLORD.

This report should include a statement showing where the necessary resources particularly in assault shipping and landing craft might be found.

19.   *Combined Chiefs of Staff: 135th Meeting*

[CAB 88/3]   Cairo,
                                         December 1943

1. *Draft Agreement by the CCS (CCS 423 & 423/1)* [not reproduced]

...

Sir Andrew Cunningham said that there were admittedly advantages in the taking of the Andaman Isles. They would form a base not only for reconnaissance, but for some extent bombing Bangkok and Japanese lines of communication. They would also form a good stopping off place for a further advance on Sumatra. Their seizure would, however, produce for ourselves a very heavy commitment in maintenance. They were 1000 miles from our nearest base. They were surrounded by Japanese air and it would be difficult to supply them to an extent which would make their use possible. In his opinion, the capture of the Andamans was not worth the candle, except as a stepping stone to a southward advance. In this connection, however, it had been agreed that the main effort should be made in the Pacific, and therefore neither amphibious operations against the Andamans nor against Ramree were worthwhile.

Admiral King said that all were agreed that the capture of Ramree would not give us much. He realised that the abandonment of BUCCA-NEER might fit in with the British view that it would be best to withdraw the Eastern Fleet to the Mediterranean.

Sir Andrew Cunningham denied this suggestion.

Admiral King, continuing, said that he felt that the Commander of the Eastern Fleet would feel more secure if he had an air base in the Andamans. He (Admiral King) was much concerned over the success of TAR-ZAN.[1] He had always felt that the Andaman operation was the most useful one with the means available, far better, for instance, than CULVERIN.[2] On purely military grounds he considered that operation BUCCANEER was as much a part of TARZAN as ANVIL was of OVERLORD.

...

Sir Charles Portal asked if it was agreed that if BUCCANEER was abandoned and the amphibious lift of 35,000 men was transferred to Europe, it would be of the greatest assistance to OVERLORD and ANVIL.

Admiral King said that on this basis it might be suggested that resources should be given up from the Pacific to OVERLORD and ANVIL.

Sir Charles Portal said that this consideration, too, ought not to be ruled out. The British Chiefs of Staff felt no doubt that the abandonment of BUCCANEER must increase the chances of success of OVERLORD and ANVIL and must therefore be accepted. We could not afford to take chances with either of these two operations. The abandonment of BUC-CANEER would give far greater military advantages to the war as a whole than the disadvantages entailed in its postponement.

After further discussion,

The CCS:

Agreed to put forward a memorandum to the President and Prime Minister setting out the various points of agreement and disagreement (subsequently circulated as CCS 423/2) [not reproduced].

---

[1]TARZAN: proposed land offensive in Burma.
[2]CULVERIN: proposed operation against N Sumatra; a PM favourite.

20.   *Combined Chiefs of Staff: 136th Meeting*

[CAB 88/3]   Cairo,
                                                5 December 1943

1. *Operations in South East Asia.*

...

[After SEAC representatives had explained operations in South East Asia] The CCS then discussed the relationship of Operation BUCCA-NEER to Operation ANVIL.

Sir Alan Brooke said that as regards ANVIL, the critical part of the operation would be the seizure of a bridgehead, including a port through which the build-up could take place. The assault must be in sufficient strength to tide us over this dangerous period, otherwise we were in danger of being thrown back into the sea.

General Marshall, in discussing the timing of Operation ANVIL, said that he felt that it should take place after rather than before OVERLORD and suggested that a period of approximately one week should elapse between the launching of the two operations.

Sir Alan Brooke said that he agreed with this view. COSSAC had been of the same opinion. He did not wish France to rise before the launching of Operation OVERLORD, nor could the timing of Operation OVERLORD itself be exact in view in view of weather conditions in the Channel.

...

2. *Operation ANVIL.*

The CCS considered a report by the CSSP (CCS 424) [not reproduced] on Operation ANVIL.

Admiral Leahy said that he considered that forces should be taken from BUCCANEER only if they were essential to the success of ANVIL. They should not be taken for diversionary operations, such as Rhodes.

Sir Andrew Cunningham pointed out that an early decision would have to be taken with regard to Operation BUCCANEER, since otherwise we were in danger of 'falling between two stools' and the necessary time for the training of any craft which might be withdrawn would not be available.

...

The CCS:

(a) Approved CCS 424 [ANVIL] ... [and said it should be] forwarded to General Eisenhower.

(b) Agreed that the detailed planning for this operation should be left entirely to General Eisenhower's planning staff.

21. *Combined Chiefs of Staff: 137th Meeting*

[CAB 88/3]   Cairo,
                                                                6 December 1943

4. *Overall Plan for the Defeat of Japan.*

...

Sir Andrew Cunningham asked if the CCS were prepared to approve the general concept that the main effort against Japan should be made in the Pacific.

Admiral King said that he agreed with this plan in principle.

22. *Alexander to Stark*

Aide Memoire on British Manpower Problem.

[Op Arch, King 4]   10 December 1943

Our recent inability to man all the escort vessels and CVEs completing for the Royal Navy in the USA is partly due to manpower difficulties dealt with below. They are *chiefly* due, however, [to the fact] that the delivery date of these ships has been accelerated. We greatly appreciate the strenuous efforts which American yards have made and admire the success they have achieved. Nevertheless the fact remains that it is not possible, particularly in the conditions described below, suddenly to speed up a planned programme for the provision of crews for these ships. The DEs have been completed before their scheduled completion dates, and the recent change in the choice of CVEs to be assigned to us meant a sudden acceleration of the delivery dates, and was coupled with a decision that the Royal Navy should take over the ships at the builder's yard instead of at Vancouver.

2. The general manpower difficulties referred to above are two-fold, qualitative and quantitative. The former is a current difficulty which is remediable. The latter sets a limit to what we can do from about March 1944 onwards.

3. Until that date we probably have enough men to meet our commitments in theory, but we cannot use them all to the best effect for the time being, owing to temporary shortage of other higher ratings.

4. Owing to the over-riding needs of the general war situation at various times, we have been unable to divert as much effort to higher training as we should have wished from a purely Naval point of view. In the earlier stages of the war it was vital to manufacture as much war equipment as possible and this restricted the number of skilled men who could be withdrawn from industry. After the fall of France, we were left virtually alone at sea until the entry of America into the war. For a long time, even after the entry of America, the situation was not sensibly altered, owing to the severe losses sustained by the American Navy and ours in the early months of the Japanese war. For most of the war up-to-date, we have therefore been under the necessity of putting the highest proportion of our strength and our men into the battle line, and training facilities and opportunities have in consequence been a good deal less than they might otherwise have been. For instance, at no time have we been able to use any major warships exclusively, or indeed primarily, for training purposes.

5. The effect of these circumstances would have been overcome by the various measures we took to meet them, but the demands of the large-scale amphibious operations which became an essential part of our strategy as a result of the fall of France have called for large numbers of men to man landing craft and to provide beach parties, port parties and the other ancillary services of such operations. These demands include a much higher proportion of higher ratings than is needed for other manning commitments. Experience alone can provide a reliable basis for the advance estimation of requirements for Combined Operations, and experience takes time to acquire.

6. Everything possible is being done to rectify the position by a continual process of dilution, by training to capacity and by the introduction of new measures to speed up the training of higher ratings.

7. It is hoped that this position will have been restored by the end of next year, but by then the overall shortage of manpower owing to the completion of the process of mobilisation in this country will be an irremediable limiting factor. From the end of next March, the Fleet will be unable to expand much further, save at the expense of the other Services – either fighting services or supply services. Only big strategic changes would enable any such redistribution of the Nation's manpower to be effective, or any large redistribution of manpower made within the Navy itself.

23. *Alexander to Stark*

[Op Arch, King 4]   12 December 1943

I understand from Admiral Brind[1] that what you wanted in connection with our manpower situation was a factual statement which you could use when discussing this problem in Washington.

[Enclosure]

The expansion of the Royal Navy in the last few years is as follows:
No. of officers and men borne on:

	31 Dec 1940	31 Dec 1941	31 Dec 1942	31 Dec 1943
	325,000	450,000	570,000	765,000
Increase:	----	125,000	120,000	195,000

To man all the ships expected to complete for the Royal Navy in 1944 both in this country and in America and to meet other prospective commitments without paying off useful vessels it is expected that 247,000 men and 41,500 women would be required. Owing, however, to the fact that this country is now fully mobilized and owing to the need to replace some of the accumulated wastage in certain special industries, such as coal-mining, the total numbers available for the Forces in 1944 (in the present strategical situation) are estimated to be only 250,000 and a few tens of thousands of women. As a result of this stringency the Navy can be allotted only 50,000 men for certain with some prospect of an additional 17,000 for the FAA. Estimated wastage based on actual experience is 49,000 for 12 months on the total bearing likely to be achieved at the end of this year. The intake of 50,000 in 1944 will barely cover wastage. The additional 17,000, if they are allotted, and this is not yet decided upon, will be trained as flying or maintenance personnel for the FAA so that they will be ready to pursue the war against Japan as soon as possible if Germany is defeated next year.

---

[1]Adm Sir E. J. Patrick Brind (1892–1963): Capt 1933; cruisers; *Excellent*; CoS, Home F 1940–42; RA & ACNS (H) 1942–44; VA & 4 CS, BPF 1945; Pres, RNC, Greenwich 1946–8; Adm & C-in-C, FE, 1949–51; C-in-C, Allied Forces, N Europe 1951–3; ret 1953.

24. *Admiralty Memorandum.*

Relations with US Navy

[Op Arch, Stark A2] 12 December 1943

The US Naval Commander is in charge of US warships, landing craft and bases assigned to OVERLORD and US-operated ports in captured territory.[1]

For operations he acts under the orders or directions of Allied Naval C-in-C.

For administrative matters and logistical support including increases in complement and facilities he deals directly with Commander 12th Fleet (Commander US Naval Forces in Europe). On other matters directly affecting his Forces he deals with C-in-C, US Fleet and Chief of Naval Operations.

25. *Chiefs of Staff to Joint Chiefs of Staff, via the Joint Staff Mission*

[ADM 199/452] 23 December 1943

Transfer of Italian Warships to Russia.

Following is our appreciation of the situation created by the President's instructions to the CCS:

2. As we understand it the situation before the Tehran Conference was that the Russians had laid claim to the following Italian Fleet units and merchant shipping:

One battleship, one cruiser, eight destroyers, four submarines [and] 40,000 tons of merchant shipping.

3. During his visit to Moscow the Foreign Secretary[2] informed the Soviet Government that we agreed in principle that they should have a share of the captured Italian ships and that the proportion for which they asked was reasonable. Details and dates of delivery were to be

---

[1]Adm Alan G. Kirk, US Navy: Capt & Naval Attaché, UK 1939–40; ND 1941; RA & cdr, WNTF, Normandy June 1944; Cdr, US Naval Forces, France, Sept 1944.

[2]Anthony Eden (later Earl of Avon) (1897–1977): Oxford 1st Oriental Languages; Con MP Warwick & Leamington 1923–57; Minister for League Affairs, then Foreign Sec 1935–8; SSt Dominions 1939; SSt War 1940; Foreign Sec 1940–5, 1951–5; PM 1955–7.

set with regard to operations and not losing Italian aid by precipitate publicity.

4. It now appears the President, on the basis of a discussion at Tehran, has informed Harriman[1] that 'it is his intention that Italian ships to the number of one-third of the total be allocated to the Soviet [Union] commencing about 1 February 1944, and as rapidly as they can be made available from their present employment in the Allied war effort'. This means that the Soviets would get about:

One or two battleships, two or three cruisers, three destroyers, six torpedo boats, six corvettes, 10 submarines.

5. We are alarmed at the new proposals which may well have the following effects:

(a) *Loss of the Italian Navy's co-operation*

Although no battleships are being employed in the war effort, four Italian cruisers and three escort groups, besides a number of individual vessels, are actively employed in the interests of the Allied cause in the Mediterranean. Further escort groups are being formed. Moreover, two cruisers are being used in Allied blockade runner patrols. Fourteen submarines are being scheduled for immediate anti-submarine training with both US and British Navies. More are expected to be employed in this valuable service in due course.

Should the transfer of Italian units to the Russians alienate the sympathies of the Italian officers and men thus serving the Allied cause, replacements could only be found at the expense of the build-up of the British Eastern Fleet and British Pacific Force. Moreover, this would occur at a moment when our combined Atlantic and Mediterranean naval resources would be very hard stretched to provide [for?] the needs of OVERLORD and ANVIL.

(b) *Indirect Assistance in Italian Dockyards, Ports, etc.*

The CCS are aware of the heavy congestion imposed on UK conversion and repair facilities by the needs of OVERLORD. This congestion is already delaying the modernisation of Britain's warships for the war against Japan, and the repair of damaged units. Moreover, the date of landing ships and craft from Mediterranean operations for OVERLORD is dependent on the refit and

---

[1]W Averell Harriman (1891–1986): railroads; National Recovery Administration 1934–5; US Amb to UK 1941 & 1946, USSR 1943–6; Sec Commerce 1946–8; special asst to Pres Truman 1950–2.

repair facilities both on that Station and at home, which are fully stretched. This state of affairs is accentuated by the recent decision to execute ANVIL. In the light of the foregoing the withdrawal of the willing Italian co-operation we are now receiving in Italian yards, particularly at Taranto, would be disastrous and would necessitate a complete recasting of the Mediterranean and UK refitting programmes. It would also throw a serious additional burden on our manpower resources in provision of dockyard labour in Italy.

(c) *Scuttling and Sabotage*

The ships to be turned over might be scuttled and the remainder sabotaged when the news became known.

6. It is not clear from the President's telegram what procedure is to be used for obtaining transfer of the ships. If, however, we proceed to enforce a transfer of Italian fleet units to the Soviet at the present time, we must be prepared to face some or all of the above consequences. We consider this risk inacceptable.

Given time and a tactful diplomatic approach, we do not however exclude the possibility of arranging transfer in due course, particularly if it is made plain that compliance with our proposals will stand them in good stead in the post-war settlement.

7. Once our armies and air forces are established ashore in France with consequential loss to the Germans of their main Atlantic and Mediterranean U-boat bases, the situation will alter and the consequences outlined in paragraphs 5 (a) and 3 (b) might be risked.

8. Even if the Italians willingly acquiesce in the transfer of naval units to the Soviet, this would involve the immobilisation of Italian naval personnel at a time when we ourselves are desperately short. Such a state of affairs cannot be beneficial to the war aim and could only be relieved by the transfer of certain unmanned vessels to the Italians in lieu, in order to maintain our naval effort at its maximum. This would create serious difficulties with our Allies.

9. No corresponding gain would result to the common war effort from the immediate transfer of the enemy ships or even to Soviet naval operations, since:

(a) without extensive alterations the Italian ships are quite unsuited for northern waters and they cannot be introduced to the Black Sea.

(b) proper maintenance of these ships in Soviet bases would, in any event, be impossible without adequate spares and ammunition supplies, of which there is no great quantity in Italy itself.

(c) it would be a considerable time before Soviet crews could work up the ships and, in the interval any ships now actively employed, if transferred, would be a dead loss to our naval resources.

10. Taking into consideration the above factors, we consider that the CCS should be invited to report in the above sense to the President and Prime Minister.

26.   *Churchill to Alexander*

[ADM 205/35]   10 January 1944

Radio Proximity Fuze.

1. Are you content with the situation in which the American Navy will have a good supply of VT fuzes, even for 4in guns by the Spring, while we shall have no such facilities during the war?
2. Is there any possibility of our obtaining an allocation from the US, or are you satisfied that our methods are good enough?

27.   *Alexander to Churchill*

[ADM 205/35]   21 January 1944

… The Navy is getting a satisfactory supply of VT fuzes of all types from America. It is true that it is not at present the intention to go into full production of British VT fuzes but sufficient production would be put in hand to ensure that our technique was satisfactory and that we should be ready to expand to meet our own requirements if necessary. While supplies from the USA are adequate our organisation in this country is in the nature of an insurance, and I suggest this is the most economical arrangement.

28.   *Noble to Cunningham*

[CAB 122/1140]   25 January 1944

Admiral King has now sent the following written reply:

'…

2. While I realise it is not desirable to immobilise the carriers of this task force and that they may not be required for the European operation, the demands for the naval support of these operations have, as you

know, increased materially since SEXTANT. At SEXTANT the British stated that they could provide naval forces for ANVIL only at the expense of the Eastern Fleet, and that they would then provide the naval force then requested for OVERLORD. Since that time the demands for naval support of these operations have increased to the extent that they would more than use up the cruisers and destroyers which the British propose to employ in the Indian Ocean. There are indications that with the increased scope of these operations even greater demands will be made for naval support. I cannot agree to the despatch of any British naval forces to the Pacific until the naval requirements of OVERLORD and ANVIL are firmly established and fully met. The demands already indicated to us would require withholding some of our naval forces already scheduled for the Pacific.

3. At the same time as the employment of British task forces in the Pacific was discussed at SEXTANT, it was assumed that there would be surface activity in the Indian Ocean to tie down in Malaya and the East Indies a reasonable amount of Japanese air strength. We were relying on BUCCANEER to do this and subsequently when BUCCANEER was cast overboard we were relying on other amphibious operations and air strikes which the British said they would carry out. If we now show no activity in the Indian Ocean or the Netherlands East Indies area, we leave the Japanese free to move all their aircraft into the Pacific. As a matter of fact, there are already indications that the Japanese are moving air forces from the SEAC and Netherlands East Indies [areas] to the Pacific. I have been considering the advisability of operating some of our carriers in that area should you be unable to do so.

4. With regard to the Admiralty's statement that there are no profitable targets in the Indian Ocean for such a task force, I submit that if this task force is used aggressively in that area against Japanese airfields, port installations, shipping concentrations, and oil installations, which it can reach, that the threat will tie down a very considerable number of Japanese aircraft and contribute more to the war in the Pacific than if the task force is moved at this time into that area. It would also provide training and an opportunity to measure the effectiveness of these carriers against Japanese shore-based air which any British task force must eventually face when it moves into the Pacific. I feel that it is essential to maintain pressure of this sort against the Japanese in the Indian Ocean, and that this task force should initially be employed in that area. Task forces can be moved into the Pacific subsequent to ANVIL-OVERLORD when more of your forces become available, and when we will be able to do so without complete relaxation of pressure in the Indian Ocean.

5. Should it become necessary to temporarily immobilize the carriers in question to provide light forces for OVERLORD-ANVIL, I suggest that this might be an opportune time to augment the close-in AA batteries of these ships, which are considerably below the standards we believe necessary for operations in the Pacific. I attach hereto our latest information on this feature [not reproduced].'

29. *King to Admiral Royall E. Ingersoll, US Navy, and others*[1]

[Op Arch, King 4]   28 January 1944

Word has come to me from the senior members of the British Staff Mission in Washington that they are receiving personal letters to the effect that British Naval Officers (associated with the US Navy) are being quite frankly 'reproached' by word and manner for the 'inactivity' of the British Eastern Fleet and, perhaps also, other seeming 'shortcomings'.

Since the said British Naval Officers are not, as individuals, responsible for Admiralty (or higher) policy and decisions, it is obviously undesirable (even unfair) to initiate comment to them on such matters – and/ or the results thereof – *unless* the British Naval Officers themselves advocate the said matters or should presume to criticize like matters involving our own Navy.

Please take appropriate steps – quietly – to ensure conformity with the views in the preceding paragraph.

Identical letters are being written to Admirals Nimitz, Stark, Halsey and Kinkaid.[2]

---

[1]Adm Royall E. Ingersoll, US Navy: USNA 1905; CNO staff 1917–18; NWC; Capt *Augusta, San Francisco*; Chf, War Plans 1935–8; RA & CruDiv 6, 1938; Asst CNO 1940; VA & C-in-C Atl F Jan 1941–Nov 1944; Cdr, W Sea Frontier 1944–5.

[2]FAdm William F. ('Bull') Halsey, US Navy (1882–1959): USNA 1904; Gt White F 1907–9; DD commands, incl Queenstown 1918; Capt 1927; N & Army War Colls 1932–4; pilot 1935; *Saratoga* 1935–7; Cdt, Pensacola NAS 1937–8; RA 1938; carrier sqdn cdr, Pac F 1938–43; Adm Nov 1942; C-in-C, S Pac 1943; 3rd F June 1944; F Adm Dec 1945; ret 1947. E. B. Potter, *Bull Halsey* (Annapolis, MD, 1985).

Adm T. C. Kinkaid, US Navy (1888–1972): battleships, 1907–13; ordnc eng 1913–17; Lt, attached Ady 1917–18; *Arizona* Europe & ME 1918–19; Naval Gun Factory, Washington 1925–7; Fleet Gunnery Officer *Texas*; NWC 1929–30; Bu Navigation; CO *Indianapolis* 1937–8; Des Sqdn 8, June–Nov 1942; RA, CruDiv 6, Pac F; Coral Sea & Midway; Cdr, TF 16, *Enterprise*; Guadalcanal Aug–Nov 1942; Cdr, N Pac Force, Jan 1943; VA June 1943; Cdr, Allied Naval Forces, SW Pac & 7th F Nov 1943; Adm April 1945; E Sea Frontier Jan–June 1946; ret 1950.

30. *Commodore E. G. N. Rushbrooke, RN, to Stark*[1]

[Op Arch. Stark A2]   30 January 1944

I am frequently being told by Directors of Technical Departments in the Admiralty, particularly the Director of the Signal Department and the Director of Torpedoes and Mining, that they are very anxious to see any available Japanese Navy captured documents concerning technicalities in the original as well as translated versions thereof.

2. Although many of the NID's opposite numbers in Washington realize this, particularly Op 20 G, whose activities make them also interested in such matters, there is a great dearth of captured material in the Admiralty.

3. I am wondering therefore if I could enlist your help and ask you to inform the necessary authorities of our great interest in captured Japanese Navy documents, particularly those of a technical nature, and to try to arrange that, if the originals themselves are not available, Photostat © copies of them should be sent to me, in addition to the valuable translations received at present.

4. I should be most grateful if you could take such action as you think fit in these connections. You will realize, of course, the value of original documents not only to the technical departments themselves but [also] to those working on the Signals Intelligence side of Japanese communications.

31. *Combined Chiefs of Staff: 149th Meeting*

[CAB 88/4]   Washington,
                                              10 March 1944

...

6. *The Pacific Situation – Statement by Admiral Nimitz.*

...

Admiral Nimitz said that he considered there were now enough experienced amphibians, carrier task forces and air group commanders to continue the further westward movement in the Pacific with confidence. Each operation had produced more information and from each lessons had been learned. In operations against the coral islands the defenders were unable to get away or disperse and it had been found wise to spend,

---

[1]Capt E. G. N. Rushbrooke: Capt 1936; *Guardian* 1939; *Argus* 1940; *Eagle* April 1941.

not one, but several days in preliminary air and naval bombardment. On Kwajalein it had been established that from 50 to 60% of the Japanese casualties had been due to such naval and air bombardment. However, the Japanese who remained were found to be still full of fight and in every case had put up stiff resistance.

Only some 10% of the Japanese Army was committed to the defence of the islands and the remaining 90% was presumably available for major land operations and were well trained and equipped. Wherever the terrain permitted, therefore, the Japanese preferred to draw us into battles in large land areas rather than to take us on in amphibious warfare in restricted areas. He felt it right, therefore, that our aim should be, whenever possible, to postpone land battles with the Japanese Army until such time as they were necessary to capture vital bridgeheads in, for example, Formosa or China.

The capacity of the Japanese Fleet to operate was limited by its losses in both tankers and destroyers. In the latter class, they were short because of sinkings and because of the necessity of using them to escort convoys. The US submarine fleet operating in the Pacific had, it is estimated, caused almost 70% of all damage and losses inflicted on Japanese shipping. It was these shortages which, in his view, had necessitated the Japanese withdrawal of their heavy units from Truk.

The Japanese positions in and around the Chinese ports south of the Yangtse could in many respects be likened to island strongholds. Their only communication was by sea, by which all maintenance had to be undertaken. Thus, operations against these strongholds approximated to island warfare. Around the perimeters of the Japanese positions were the Chinese, who though they might not much like us or General Chiang Kai Shek's regime, liked the Japanese even less.[1]

To sum up: He felt it essential to avoid as long as possible fighting the Japanese Army in any land area where they could delay our operations by avoiding our decisive sea and air superiority.

He considered that the Japanese remaining on the isolated islands of the Marshalls could not exist for long. No surface support could be given them, though key personnel had been evacuated by air and submarine.

Present operations were aimed at neutralising Ponape and Kusaie. Heavy bombers should be able to operate as from 10 March [1944] from Kwajalein against Truk. From photographs and captured orders and charts, the defences of Truk appeared to be less strong than had at first been thought. He considered it feasible to take Truk if that should

---

[1]Chiang Kai-Shek (1887–1975): Pres & C-in-C, China, 1924–49; deposed in Communist revolution 1949.

prove necessary, but it might be better to by-pass it and to take the Marianas and islands to the westward from which the flow of aircraft and supplies to Truk could be stopped. The Japanese aircraft losses on Truk had already been replaced and an attack had been made from Truk on our airfield at Eniwetok which had caused some damage, the exact extent of which was not yet known. Further attacks from Truk should be prevented as soon as the bombing of Truk by four-engined bombers commenced.

The further west we advanced the more difficult was the problem of supply and larger periods would therefore elapse between successive operations until additional combat loaders and landing craft were available. At present he was more concerned with the geography of the Pacific and the distances involved than he was with Japanese opposition. The US superiority in battleships and destroyers was very marked and even in cruisers was sufficient. The US submarine force was increasing at the rate of six to seven a month and was now operating from bases closer to the Japanese lines of communication. This increase of strength should produce greater sinkings of Japanese vessels, though the rate of sinking would drop when the targets became fewer and Japanese A/S measures more effective.

In general, he was extremely optimistic in regard to future operations in the westward drive through the Pacific.

In reply to a question, Admiral Nimitz said that the quality of the Japanese air fleet was 'iffy'. Certain formations, particularly of floatplanes, had continued to be very efficient but the carrier pilots were not as good as they previously had been, due largely, he thought, to the fact that many of the best carrier squadrons had to be employed ashore. Some of the Japanese carriers had been employed to transport aircraft and carry freight and even landing barges. This was an indication of the critical Japanese shipping problem.

In reply to a further question, Admiral Nimitz said that in the recent operations the ratio of airpower had been four to one in favour of the US forces.

32. *Blake to Cunningham*

[ADM 205/38]   25 March 1944

...

3. It would appear that he [Stark] has not been kept in the picture as regards developments which have been occurring over ANVIL. I have been unable to inform him because the particular Signals on that operation have been kept to a very narrow circulation.

4. On a previous occasion, a matter of this nature has reached a fairly advanced position without Admiral Stark being informed. ... During the planning for the North African landings, when matters of policy arose, Admiral Stark was invited to COS meetings.

5. If this is not considered politic, ... I suggest that the COS should either request Eisenhower to inform COMNAVEU or that it should be done by yourself directly, or through me. You will always find the Admiral only too ready to go down and have a talk with you, and I know he appreciates very much the mutual confidence which exists between you. On the other hand the invitation to the COS Committee puts the Admiral on a good wicket and brings his position as Commander, US Naval Forces in Europe, and Commander, 12th Fleet, on the right plane.

6. I have spoken to the Admiral about this. There is no doubt he would appreciate being in on such matters. Between ourselves, his information from Eisenhower has not proved satisfactory and he would much prefer to receive it from you or from myself.

7. Perhaps you might think this over. As you know, the Admiral is the last person in the world to push himself forward. His whole object is to ensure that he is well informed so that he can give the fullest co-operation. I also think his advice when dealing with the other side is valuable. He knows how they, or rather he, reacts!

33. *Cunningham to Blake*

[ADM 205/38]   28 March 1944

...

I think it is usual to show him all Admiralty signals, but I doubt if it is right that he should see signals between British COS and the US COS, even though they may contain some reference to the US Navy.

... When I was in Washington I was certainly not invited to the meetings of the US COS. ... In my opinion, there is no doubt that he should get his information about the US COS decisions from Eisenhower. I think it would be most unwise if I was to saddle myself with this responsibility. Some questions concerning the US Navy only may arise in the near future as you will have seen that COMINCH is unwilling to divert American ships to make up the bombardment force required for OVERLORD.

...

34. *Blake to Cunningham*

[ADM 205/38]   5 April 1944

[Enclosing extracts from a report by Rear Admiral Brushek, US Navy, to the [US] Director of Navy Yards].[1]

1. We were afforded every facility to carry out our inspection and everywhere the local British Naval Authorities were most cordial and cooperative.

2. In general, it is our opinion that British Dockyards are devoting most of their capacity to the repair and overhaul of active vessels of the Fleet. Some new construction is going on but is not being prosecuted very actively and serves more or less as a reservoir to fill the gaps in the repair load. As is probably well known, the Dockyards are old-fashioned, the equipment is out-of-date, and it surprising that they do so much with the facilities that they have.

3. While the Dockyards are under-manned and there has been considerable dilution in the quality of their personnel, conditions are not nearly so severe as in the US. As a whole, the workmen are much better skilled than ours. Their turnover is very small compared to our own, according to figures given me. However, their personnel has increased only about 33% over the 1939 figures.

4. The system of "payment by results", which is in use at all Dockyards and most of the private yards which we visited, in our opinion, has done a great deal to speed up production and counteract the lack of adequate supervision. This is a system which gives the employee incentive to perform his work quickly and efficiently. I am told that the plan is used on about 80% of the work undertaken, both repairs and new construction.

5. Because of the necessity for blackout, all shops have their windows painted out and, as a result, are dingy, poorly lighted and quite depressing. Very little is done in the way of showers, clean and sanitary washrooms, and lockers for the men. Small canteens, or cafeterias as we call them, have been provided but they are entirely inadequate.

6. The housekeeping in all Dockyards is extremely poor, with the possible exception of Chatham, where I was informed the Admiral Superintendent had insisted upon a clean-up and, as a result, this yard is fairly presentable. There is so much scrap and rubbish stored around all vacant areas and even at the waterfront at repair berths

---

[1]RA Brushek, US Navy: unidentified.

that it is difficult to move material expeditiously. In general, the crane facilities in the Dockyards are good, except that their capacity should be greater to keep pace with modern conditions. As a rule, the private yards are better equipped than the [Royal] Dockyards – the tools and equipment are more modern and better laid out.

7.   In our opinion, the Dockyards need a well-planned replacement program for both machine tools and buildings. The plans should be laid out to cover a period of years and should be followed even though administrations change.

8.   Bombing has caused much destruction, particularly at Devonport, but in spite of this fact morale is high and production good.

9.   Many new ships are under construction with personnel not available even for existing vessels. The question naturally arises as to how these ships are going to be manned. The *Ausonia* and *Artifex* are being converted to repair ships and presumably are intended for service in the Pacific Ocean.[1] The equipment is excellent and both vessels should be able to handle most any kind of a job.

10.   We find that one of the vessels overhauled in the US, the *Arethusa*, is having considerable work done in the UK because the repairs back home were not entirely satisfactory. The British officers, including the Captain of the ship, were painstakingly insistent that the Navy Yard did the best they could with the equipment that they had. Unfortunately, this vessel had gone to Charleston and the work was to some extent beyond their capabilities. Because of the heavy repair and conversion load in the US, it will be necessary in future to send British vessels to yards which are not always the best fitted to handle such work.

11.   Our tour of British repair activities in the UK has been most instructive and profitable, and it is believed we will take back with us a very clear picture of conditions as they exist over here.'

35. *Notes on Royal Navy by Admiral Stark*

[Op Arch, King 4]   [c. 6 April 1944]

British Naval Manpower

Admiralty have issued a Memorandum concerning Naval Manpower in 1944. It states that the nation's manpower is now fully mobilized. The numbers in the Navy on 31 December 1943 will therefore be the future manning ceiling for the Navy. Unfortunately the categories of personnel have become unbalanced; there is a deficiency among higher and

---

[1]*Ausonia*: heavy repair ship: 1922 (ex-Cunard), 20760t, 15.3k. To RN 1939.
Artifex: heavy repair ship: 1924 (ex-Cunard *Aurania*). 13948t, 15.5k. To RN 1942.

specialized branches of officers and enlisted men. In order to meet essential commitments the following action needs to be taken:

(a) Pay off: 5 Battleships (old 'R' Class and *Malaya*)

> 1 Carrier (*Furious*, due for extensive refit)
> 1 Fighter Catapult Ship (1914 program)
> 14 Cruiser types (oldest types – approximately 1918 program)
> 20 'Town' Class Destroyers (ex-American)[1]

(b) Abolish MNBDO
(c) Reduce Patrol Service by 3000 personnel
(d) Reduce Shore Establishments by at least 11,000.

British Main Units

It was stressed that the Admiralty had decided, for the time being, to make Battleships *Nelson* and *Rodney* non-operational in order to ease the manpower situation. Subsequent dispatches indicate however that the ships will not be paid off or destroyed.

Battleship *Royal Sovereign* is to be lent to USSR. It is expected that the Russian crew will arrive to man her on about 12 March. Orders have also been given for four submarines to be turned over to the Russians on about the same date.

New Type U-boat

NID reports that Germans have been experimenting with U-boats propelled submerged by internal combustion engines. It is believed that the Germans are likely to achieve success, and may bring the new type into service gradually without any indications being obvious to us. Estimated maximum submerged speed is 13 knots; submerged endurance seven hours at 13 knots, 25 hours at 8 knots.

German Economy

In connection with sinking of four German blockade runners during January, the effect on German rubber and tungsten production is estimated to be as follows:

Rubber

German annual minimum need   20,000 tons

---

[1]'Town' class: DD; ex-US, to RN in 'Destroyers-for-Bases' deal, Sept 1940; many unserviceable by 1943.

Amount sunk   21,500 tons
Amount arrived   6,500 tons.

Tungsten

German annual minimum need   4,000 tons
Amount sunk   815 tons
Amount arrived   nil.

German Morale

Prisoners from 'Elbing' Class destroyer sunk on 29 December in Bay of Biscay action fought without relish and were apathetic after capture.[1]

British Warships

New Construction – January

1 Fleet Destroyer
16 Frigates
6 Corvettes
1 A/S Escort
3. Fleet Minesweepers
4 Submarines.

Losses

1 Cruiser
2 Fleet Destroyers
1 Frigate

CVE State on 7 February was:

14 Operational
2 Working up
2 Undergoing modification
4 Refitting
3 Ferrying aircraft
2 Deck landing training
1 Trials

---

[1] 'Elbing' class: Ger: DE: named for place of building.

36. *Department of Scientific Research*

[ADM 116/5395]   12 April 1944

Proposals for Post-War co-operation in Scientific Research and Development between the US and British Navies.

... It is sincerely hoped the political atmosphere will permit and place high value upon continued co-operation between the US and Great Britain not only on Naval matters but [on] all other aspects of Defence. ...

...

vii. *Scope of Co-operating Authorities' Responsibilities*

In exchanges of Research and Development the responsibilities of the Admiralty and Navy Department would extend to all Research and Development work in hand...

viii. *Visits and Exchanges of Technicians*

Co-operation or liability which is effected only through correspondence, exchanges of written reports and blueprints can never be very vital. Experience during this war has shown how much more value can be obtained from visits by US and British experts to each other's laboratories and workshops than from mere exchange of printed material. ...

...

x. *Staffing of the Offices of British Naval Attaché Washington and US Naval Attaché London*

It is expected that if the machinery outlined under sections (iv) to (ix) is to work smoothly and efficiently the key liaison offices of the US Naval Attaché in London and the British Naval Attaché in Washington will have to be much more generously staffed than they were in pre-war years, that they will need to be fully representative of all branches of the parent Naval Service and must include a sizeable complement of experienced Naval scientists and technicians.

37. *US Naval Attaché, Moscow, to King*

[MRF 35]   8 June 1944

... Opinion [in] this office is that (a) Soviets go back on all their statements about urgent need for ship and how quickly they will get it into action on escort duty and attacks on enemy shipping; (b) Soviets have seen in British ships items not on *Milwaukee* and [are] anxious to request everything modern. In this respect they [are] understood to be driving British frantic in expressing dissatisfaction with British ships [and] demanding additional work and complete modernization. Recommendation [of] this office is that we take [a] very firm stand denying retention of ship for overhaul ...

38. *Combined Chiefs of Staff: 165th Meeting*

[CAB 88/4]

Cabinet Offices,
London,
14 June 1944

...

2. *War in the Pacific*

...

Base facilities were considered at some length, including the facilities of Indian ports. Other points considered were: the fact that India, including Ceylon, had no base that would take a battleship, whereas both Brisbane and Sydney can; the need of a British naval force for the facilities of Brisbane and Sydney; the remoteness of Sydney; the likelihood that, after the seizure of the Palaus, US naval forces in the Pacific would not be dependent on Australia and this might leave Brisbane and Sydney available for a British task force.

Sir Andrew Cunningham has outlined the British naval force that should be available towards the end of 1944. A short discussion took place as to the possibilities of operations in the Bay of Bengal, where it appeared that a small fleet should suffice as there was no major task for a main fleet to undertake.

During consideration of the British forces likely to be available to take part in the war in the South West Pacific, it was pointed out that, in the initial stages, British naval forces would expect to work under General MacArthur with Australian and New Zealand land and air forces. British forces in the South West Pacific would be built up from elsewhere as they became available. It would be for consideration whether any air forces would be released from SEAC.

Full consideration was given to the question of whether or not it would be possible, in view of the acceleration of US operations in the Pacific, for British forces to arrive in time to be of real value to the US operations envisaged. This included consideration of the importance of flexibility and of so placing the British effort that it would not be separated from the US effort, so that the British assistance might be called in as and when found necessary.

39. *Leahy: Diary*

[LC, Leahy]   29 June 1944

... This controversy [over ANVIL] is of long standing. It is caused by American all-out concentration on an early defeat of Nazi Germany, and a British intention to combine with a defeat of the Nazis the acquisition of post-war advantages in the Balkan States for Great Britain.

40. *Blake to Cunningham*

[ADM 205/48]   1 July 1944

...

I think he [Stark] feels very badly about King's lack of understanding but evidently King has been very blunt with him on the suggestion.

King is persistently temperamental as you describe it.

...

Having regard to the fact that we are doing our best to build up the Eastern Fleet in the shortest possible time it is invidious that we should not be informed fully of the progress which is being made.

41. *Chiefs of Staff to the Joint Staff Mission*

[CAB 88/4]   12 July 1944

We think it is important that the US Chiefs of Staff should be left in no doubt as to our attitude towards operations in the Mediterranean. The position is that neither HMG not the British COS consider that operation ANVIL is our correct strategy. The only reason why we gave way to the views of the US COS in this matter is because we did not wish them to think that we were trying to gain our point by delaying tactics. Nevertheless, having accepted the decision we will of course do our very utmost to make ANVIL a success.

42. *King to Vice Admiral Horne, VCNO*[1]

[NWC, King 7]   26 July 1944

Repair and Modernizing of British Naval Vessels in the USA.

1.   Please give me the following information, with comments as appropriate:

(a) HMS *Nelson.*

(i) Prospective date of completion.
(ii) Controlling (major) jobs.

(b) Actual commitments for doing work on other British Naval vessels.
(c) Tentative commitments for doing work on other British Naval vessels.

2.   The time has come to scan work, actual or proposed, on British Naval vessels from the point of view of questions.

(i) Is this work necessary to the efficient conduct of the war?
(ii) Is it to be expected that this work will be completed in time to contribute to the efficient conduct of the war?

43. *Admiralty Memorandum:*
Naval Issues in the Allocation of Western Zones of Occupation in Germany.

[ADM 116/5359]   3 September 1944.

...

2.   ... only one of the two Western Zones has a seaboard so that, unless special arrangements are made, either we or the US will be shut out from any participation in the enforcement of the Naval surrender of Germany. ...

3.   ... our first main principle should be that Naval responsibility in the North Western Zone must be British ...

---

[1]VA F. J. Horne, US Navy (1880–1959): USNA 1899; NA Tokyo 1915–19; c/o *Omaha* 1924–6; naval aviation; c/o *Wright*; W Plans 1927–9; *Saratoga* 1930; RA 1933; CruDiv 6, 1935; member Gen Board; VCNO 1941, a chiefly logistical role.

4. Our second principle should be that the US Navy are not to be shut out from all participation in Naval control ... Not only would it be extremely unreasonable to exclude the US Navy having regard to their considerable contact with the German Navy in the course of the last two years but we must look to our own position upon the surrender of Japan. Again, and this may be the most cogent argument, we would be glad to have our slender manpower resources supplemented by a quota of US personnel.

5. ... the appropriate proportion of US to British personnel would be that the US should have 25% of the total number of Naval personnel employed in the occupation of Germany. ... in order to bait the trap, we should offer the US the Flag Officer's post at Wilhelmshaven, keeping Kiel for ourselves.

44. *Combined Chiefs of Staff: 174th Meeting*

[CAB 88/4]   Château Frontenac,
                                                    Quebec,
                                                    14 September 1944

...

6. *British Participation in the Pacific (CCS 452/18, /25, /26, /27)* [not reproduced].

Sir Alan Brooke said that ... for political reasons it was essential the British Fleet should take part in the main operations against Japan.

Admiral Leahy asked if Sir Alan Brooke's point would be met by the elimination of the words [in JCS/CCS 452/27 – not reproduced]: 'They consider that the initial use of such a force should be on the western flank of the advance in the South West Pacific'. It might be that the British Fleet would be used initially in the Bay of Bengal and thereafter as required by the existing situation.

Sir Andrew Cunningham said that the main fleet would not be required in the Bay of Bengal since there were already there more British forces than required. He agreed to the deletion proposed by Admiral Leahy.

Admiral King also agreed to the deletion of these words which he felt were not relevant to the general case.

Continuing Sir Andrew Cunningham asked [for] the US views as to the meaning of the term 'balanced forces' in the first sentence of paragraph 1 of CCS 452/27. He said that the British COS had in mind a force of some four battleships, five or six large carriers, 20 light fleet carriers and escort carriers and the appropriate number of cruisers and destroyers. This he would regard as a balanced fleet.

Admiral King stressed that it was essential for these forces to be self-supporting.

Sir Andrew Cunningham said that if these forces had their fleet train, they could operate unassisted for several months provided that they had the necessary rear bases – probably in Australia. The provision of these bases would be a matter for agreement.

Admiral King said that the practicability of employing these forces would be a matter of concern from time to time.

Admiral Leahy said that he did not feel that the question for discussion was the practicability of employment but rather the matter of where they should be employed from time to time.

Sir Andrew Cunningham referred to the Prime Minister's statement that he wished the British fleet to take part in the main operations in the Pacific. Decision with regard to this was necessary since many preliminary preparations had to be made.

Admiral King suggested that the British COS should put forward proposals with regard to the employment of the British fleet.

Sir Andrew Cunningham said that the British wish was that they should be employed in the central Pacific.

Admiral King said that at the plenary meeting no specific reference to the central Pacific had been made.

Sir Alan Brooke said that the emphasis had been laid on the use of the British fleet in the main effort against Japan.

Admiral Leahy said that as he saw it the main effort was at present from New Guinea to the Philippines and it would later move to the northward.

Admiral King said that he was in no position now to commit himself to where the British fleet could be employed.

Sir Charles Portal reminded the CCS of the original offer made by the British COS which read: 'It is our desire in accordance with HMG's policy, that this fleet should play its full part at the earliest possible moment in the main operations against Japan wherever the greatest naval strength is required.'

When the British COS spoke of the main operations against Japan they did not intend to confine this meaning to Japan itself geographically but meant rather that the fleet should take part in the main operations within the theatre of war wherever they might be taking place.

Sir Andrew Cunningham stressed that the British COS did not wish the British fleet merely to take part in mopping up operations in areas falling into our hands.

Admiral Leahy said that he felt that the actual operations in which the British fleet would be involved would have to be decided in the future. It might well be that the fleet would be required for the re-conquest of Singapore, which he would regard as a major operation.

The CCS then considered paragraph 2 of CCS 452/27 referring to the use of a British Empire Task Force in the South West Pacific.

Sir Charles Portal said that the Prime Minister had offered the British fleet for use in the main operations against Japan. By implication this paragraph accepted a Naval Task Force for the South West Pacific, and was therefore contrary to the notion he had expressed.

Admiral King said that of course it was essential to have sufficient forces for the war against Japan. He was not, however, prepared to accept a British fleet which he could not employ or support. In principle he wishes to accept the British fleet in the Pacific but it would be entirely unacceptable for the British fleet to be employed for political reasons in the Pacific and thus necessitate the withdrawal of some of the US fleet.

Sir Charles Portal reminded Admiral King that the Prime Minister had suggested that certain of the newer British capital ships should be substituted for certain of the older US ships.

Sir Andrew Cunningham said that as he understood it the Prime Minister and President were in agreement that it was essential for British forces to take a leading part in the main operations against Japan.

Admiral King said that it was not his recollection that the President had agreed to this. He could not accept that a view expressed by the Prime Minister should be regarded as a directive to the CCS.

Sir Charles Portal said that the Prime Minister felt it essential that it should be placed on record that he wished the British fleet to play a major role in the operations against Japan.

Sir Alan Brooke said that, as he remembered it, the offer was no sooner made than accepted by the President.

Admiral King asked for specific British proposals.

Sir Charles Portal referred once more to the offer made in CCS 452/18 which he had previously quoted.

Admiral Leahy said that he could see no objection whatever to this proposal. He could not say exactly where the Fleet could be employed at this moment but there would be ample opportunity for its use provided it was self-supporting.

Admiral King said that the question of the British proposal for the use of the main fleet would have to be referred to the President before it could be accepted.

Admiral Leahy said that if Admiral King saw any objections to this proposal he should take them up with the President. It might not be wise to use the term 'main fleet'.

Sir Andrew Cunningham said that the British fleet had been offered by the Prime Minister and the President had accepted it. He was prepared to agree to the deletion of the word 'main' from paragraph 1 of CCS 452/27.

Sir Andrew Cunningham confirmed that there would be no objection to the British fleet working from time to time under General MacArthur's command.

...

The CCS:

(a) Agreed that the British Fleet should participate in the main operations against Japan in the Pacific.
(b) Took note of the assurances of the British COS that this fleet should be balanced and self-supporting.
(c) Agreed that the method of employment of the British fleet in these main operations in the Pacific would be decided from time to time in accordance with the prevailing circumstances.

45. *Extract of Minutes of Meeting between Admiral King and Admiral Cunningham*

[ADM 116/5359]   Quebec,
                                                    15 September 1944

...

7. *Occupation of Germany*

Admiral Cunningham ... was of the opinion that the tripartite military committee in Berlin should consist of nine officers – the Senior officers of the land, sea and air forces of the US, the UK and Soviet. Each Admiral on the committee would be responsible for naval disarmament in his zone. Whatever the decision as to the allocation of zones, it had never been the British intention to exclude the US Navy from taking part in the naval disarmament of Germany. Admiral King stated that he considered these proposals entirely appropriate.

Admiral Cunningham ... suggested that Flag Officers should be established at Kiel and Wilhelmshaven, who could conveniently control the ports in the vicinity.

Admiral King stated that he did not wish to establish any elaborate organisation in Germany which would be difficult to eliminate at a later Treaty stage. He wanted the US Navy to take part in the disarmament of German naval installations and also to take over such ports as were necessary for supplying the US forces of occupation. He would provide the necessary port parties for this purpose.

...

46. *Extracts from 176th Meeting of the CCS*

[ADM 116/5359]   Quebec,
16 September 1944

...

7. Allocation of Zones of Occupation in Germany

Admiral Cunningham suggested that any naval disarmament measures for US controlled ports should be under the US naval member of the Central Control Commission.

Admiral King agreed with this proposal. American control of the port of Bremen would have to include American control of a suitable area for disembarkation and staging.

Admiral Cunningham agreed. He suggested that the American area should also include Bremerhaven. Some 40 or 50 miles down the river, Bremerhaven was, he understood, the port where the large ships had to berth.

...

The CCS –

...

(b) Agreed that any naval disarmament measures for Bremen and Bremerhaven would be under the US naval Commander of the Central Control Commission.

47. *Assignment of American combat aircraft to the Royal Navy in 1945:*

Result of Negotiations.

[ADM 116/5347]   28 November 1944.

...

3. Negotiations with the Americans have been completed and the following table shows what they are prepared to release compared with the numbers ultimately bid for. ...

First half of 1945	Bid	Firm Assignment
Corsair	660	90/150
Hellcat	336	316

First half of 1945	Bid	Firm Assignment
Avenger	348	80
Wildcat	45	150.[1]

48. *BAD to the Admiralty*

[ADM 116/5341]   4 January 1945

...

'The US Navy has immediate urgent requirements for additional Fighter type aircraft which have been brought about by the decision to increase the number of Fighters aboard our aircraft carriers'.[2] It appears that the present requirements are greater than the present production programme can meet. ...

3. Decision by US Authorities to increase proportion of Fighters carried in the aircraft carriers has resulted from experience gained during recent operations in the Pacific. In spite of production for 1945 being increased by 1800 to a grand total of 14,456, this number is apparently considered insufficient to meet both US and British requirements and hence [the] proposed raid on [the] assignment to Britain.

...

Admiralty to BAD.

27 January 1945.

In our view, if there is to be any substantial reduction in our assignments this will be reflected in the scale of the effort we shall be able to bring to bear in the Pacific War.

...

It is readily admitted that our resources will not allow us at first to maintain a comparable sustained attack on Japan to that now built up after three years of experience by the US Navy, but our desire is to fight alongside them to the best of our ability. If our planning is to be yet again completely upset by a fluctuating policy on assignments we shall find it extremely difficult to pull our weight.

---

[1]Chance Vought Corsair: US; fighter-bomber; 1940; 1 engine, 1 crew, 446mph; 6mg; 2000lbs bombs/8 rockets.
   Curtiss Hellcat: US; fighter; 1942; 1 engine, 1 crew, 376mph; 6mg.
   Grumman Avenger: US; bomber; 1941; 1 engine, 3 crew, 271mph; 5mg; 2000lbs bombs/1 torpedo.
   Grumman Wildcat: US; fighter; 1940; 1 engine, 1 crew, 328mph; 4mg.
[2]Largely as a result of *kamikaze* (suicide) aircraft.

Admiralty to BAD.

2 February 1945.

...

B. Our First Line IE includes 282 Corsairs actual rising to 324 in August 1945 and 202 Hellcats rising to 270 in August 1945. If assignments cease no aircraft will be available to replace Corsair wastage after August 1945. This would adversely affect operations after that date. ... Hellcat shortage would be immediately apparent and existing squadrons would have to be maintained at the expense of new squadrons.

C. ... There are possibilities of increasing production of Seafire 45 in 1946. ... Seafire 45 in not [a] substitute for Corsair in its role of Fighter/Bomber.[1]

BAD to Admiralty.

20 February 1945.

There is obviously considerable pressure working somewhere in the Navy Department to reduce fighter assignments to Britain in view of urgent requirements for more fighters in [the] US Pacific Fleet consequent upon recent operational developments. ...

49. *Memorandum by First Sea Lord's Office*

[ADM 205/49]   10 January 1945

Conflicting Priorities of European and Far Eastern Theatres of War.
At OCTAGON, last September [1944], the COS undertook to deploy a balanced and self supporting fleet in the Pacific to take part in the main operations against Japan. This undertaking was made at a time when it was considered that the war against Germany would end in 1944. On [Cunningham's] return to London the build-up of the BPF was planned, and on 1 November [1944] a signal was made to the authorities concerned, including the Americans, giving the planned strength of the Fleet up to July 1945.
2. The British Government consider it essential that British Forces shall take an active part in the main operations against Japan, since it would be a most uncomfortable position if our lost possessions were restored as part of a purely American effort.
    The Americans, on the other hand, have always shown a desire to carry the full burden of Pacific operations and pressure had to be exerted on the

---

[1]Supermarine Seafire: 1941; 1 engine; 1 crew; 352mph; 2×20mm cannon; 4mg; 500lb bombs.

highest level before they were persuaded to accept the British offer. Thus the BPF has assumed marked political as well as military importance.

3. Since OCTAGON the American Fleet has had considerable losses in action off the Philippines, and it is believed that they may now feel the need for British help which hitherto they were reluctant to accept. Indeed, this is substantiated by the recent talks between Admiral Fraser and Admiral Nimitz, which not only show that it is intended to employ the British Fleet in the near future in the most advanced operations, but also assure the willing co-operation of the American Navy. It is, therefore, of primary importance both politically and for the British Navy's prestige, that the part played by the BPF shall be effective and sustained.

4. Against this background is the fact that the German war has become prolonged. ...

5. ... great difficulty is to be found in providing the necessary logistic support to enable it [the BPF] to operate with the same prolonged activity as the American Fleet, backed as this is by abundant resources. ...

...

7. It is therefore necessary to exercise the strictest economy in manpower and resources in European waters, releasing everything for the Far East that is not absolutely essential for the concluding of the German war.

50. *Combined Chiefs of Staff: 182nd Meeting*

[CAB 88/4]   Malta,
30 January 1945

...

9. *The U-boat Threat.*

Sir Andrew Cunningham explained that at present we were in a somewhat similar position to that of 1918. The ASDIC was proving less effective against present U-boat operations in shallow waters where tide affected the efficiency of the ASDIC. The Germans had discovered this and were working their submarines close inshore round the UK. At present they were operating principally in the Channel, the Irish Sea, and one had even penetrated the entrance to the Clyde. Our aircraft were also hampered by the extremely small target presented by the schnorkel. This relatively small object was normally only used some three feet above water and ASV aircraft could therefore only detect it in calm weather.

Further the Germans were fitting a radar device on their schnorkel which enabled them to detect the ASV emissions before the aircraft contacted the submarine.

In the last month there had been six sinkings in the Irish Sea, an escort carrier had been torpedoed in the Clyde, and at least four ships sunk in the Channel.[1] He hoped, however, that the position would improve, and, in fact, two submarines had been sunk in the Irish Sea in the last week and a further one sunk off Land's End.[2] The object was to force the submarine back into deep water where the ASDIC would be effective, and to achieve this deep minefields were being laid in order to shut the enemy out of the Irish Sea.

The Chief of the Air Staff explained that from the air point of view new devices were being brought into action, and included an infra-red device. It must be remembered, however, that with a submerged submarine using her schnorkel, the aircraft, even after it had contacted the submarine, found difficulty in sinking it since it could dive in some three seconds and left no swirl at which to aim.

Sir Andrew Cunningham explained that the Germans were building new types of submarine which were a vast improvement on those which had been used previously. There were two new types: one of 1600 tons with a speed of up to 18 knots submerged, and carrying 20 torpedoes; the other, a small coastal type, was capable of 13 knots submerged and carried two torpedoes. The larger boat had an extremely long range. It was thought that these new boats would be coming into operation about the middle or end of February.[3]

The CCS:

Took note of the foregoing statements.

51. *Combined Chiefs of Staff: 184th Meeting*

[CABB 88/4]   Malta,
                                                    1 February 1945

...

6. *U-boat Threat (CCS 774/1 and /2)* [not reproduced].
Bombing of Assembly Yards and Operating Bases:

...

---

[1]*Thane*: CVE: Irreparably damaged in Clyde by *U-482*, 15 Jan 1945
[2]U-boat losses: *U-105, U-1172*: Irish Sea. *U-1199*: off Land's End.
[3]Type XXI: Ger: 1945, 1595/1790t, 15.6/17.2k, 6×21in tt.
Type XXIII: Ger: 1945, 230/254t, 15/22k, 2×21in tt.

Sir Charles Portal ... felt that if persistent bombing of U-boat assembly yards was now undertaken the effect of this action on the attacks on the vital oil targets would be unacceptable. ...

...

Sir Andrew Cunningham said that the Naval Staff would have liked to see some additional emphasis being placed on the bombing of submarine targets. He had, however, been convinced that the attacks on oil targets would in fact pay a more valuable dividend.

52. *British Admiralty requirements from US Navy Department, 1945*

[ADM 116/5330]   22 May 1945

[Copy of minute (ref. COS 815/5) dated same day, from the Secretary of the COS Sub-Committee to the Minister of Production].

The COS consider that the unco-operative attitude now in evidence on the part of the Americans towards Lease-Lend supplies for stage II, revealed in JSM's telegram 826 [not reproduced], is primarily a production matter which you would wish to handle.

[Enclosed] *Draft Minute from the COS to the Prime Minister* [seeking the Minister of Production's agreement]

The JSM in Washington report a serious turn of events in the American attitude towards Lend-Lease supplies for stage II. The immediate issue concerns supplies of aircraft.

2. A wave of economy is said to be sweeping the administration and the Americans propose that we should receive only a small fraction of the aircraft we are counting on as a result of the negotiation between the Keynes/Sinclair Mission and the Morgenthau Committee.[1]

3. The effect of these proposals, if passed by Congress, would seriously prejudice our future operations, since the whole programme for the equipment of the RAF and FAA is designed on these ultimate expectations from American production.

---

[1]John Maynard Keynes (1883–1946): Cambridge economist; member, Bloomsbury set; Treasury 1915–18; Treasury advisor 1940–46; baron 1942. Most eminent economist of 20th century.

Sir Archibald Sinclair: Ldr, Lib party; SSt for Air 1940–45.

Henry Morgenthau (1891–1967): US: Chmn, Federal Farm Board 1933; US Treasury 1933; Sec Treasury 1933–45. Confidante of Pres Roosevelt.

4. The urgency of this issue lies in the information that the US War Department are tabling their requirements for the next proportions before the end of this month.

...

*Minute of Agreement between Admiral Sir James Somerville
and Vice Admiral F. J. Horne, US Navy, the Vice Chief
of Naval Operations*

10 November 1944

...

1. The Navy Department accepts the British requirements. ...
2. It is understood that the material is to be used to perform the role assigned to the British at the Quebec Conference [September 1944] subject to such modifications as may later be made by the CCS.

...

9. It is agreed that the British will accept combat service equipment of the type and kind suitable for re-issue to the US Navy for use against Japan with the understanding that spares will be furnished on the same scale as for the US Services.

53. *Memorandum for the Cabinet by the First Lord*

[ADM 205/54]   1 July 1945

Disposal of the Italian Fleet.

... The effective units of the Italian Fleet of importance are:

Two modern 'Littorio' class battleships
Three older 'Cavour' class battleships
Eight light cruisers
10 Fleet destroyers
22 torpedo boats
20 corvettes
28 submarines

2. The Russian demand for one battleship, one cruiser, eight destroyers and four submarines, first made in Moscow in October 1943, was agreed ... by the Prime Minister and President Roosevelt.

...

4. [after detailing the claims by France, Greece and Yugoslavia] ...

...

7. The problem, therefore, is to find a settlement which, without permanently estranging Italy, will meet inescapable Allied claims and reduce Italy's Navy to a size acceptable to her neighbours. The following is the policy proposed:
(a) Russia's claim to be met in full, i.e., one 'Cavour' class battleship, one 6-in cruiser, eight destroyers, four submarines.
[there follow the French, Greek and Yugoslav allocations].

8. ...

(a) We should claim both ['Littorio' class battleships] (or only one if the US also make a claim) in order to ensure that the ships do not fall into undesirable hands. We should persist in this claim at TERMINAL and until the Russian claim for a battleship has been liquidated by the provision of one of the old 'Cavour' class, as we have always stipulated.

54. *Memorandum for the Cabinet by First Lord*

[ADM 205/54]   7 July 1945

...

2. It is the fact that all the important German naval units surviving undamaged, including the cruisers *Prinz Eugen*, *Nürnberg* and *Leipzig* (collision damage only), 26 destroyers and torpedo boats, 147 U-boats, and a large number of auxiliary vessels have fallen into the hands of the British and US Navies. The Russians hold only damaged ships, including the battleships *Gneisenau*, *Schleswig-Holstein* and *Schlesien*, the pocket battleship *Lützow*, the aircraft carrier *Graf Zeppelin*, and about 10 damaged or incomplete U-boats.

...

3. The Americans, last November [1944], circulated to the European Advisory Commission a memorandum on the disposal of the German Navy in which they proposed a policy of wholesale scrapping, with the exception of:

(a) vessels of special design required for experimental purposes;
(b) vessels required for immediate operational purposes, e.g., minesweepers
(c) vessels capable of being converted to civilian use.

4. The Admiralty consider the scrapping of the combat units of the German Fleet to be in the best interests of the Royal Navy and of world peace. ...
5. The Admiralty, though in full sympathy with the American views, did not think it advisable that HM Government should come out in open support of their memorandum.

...

8. British requirements for German ships are for:

(a) Three destroyers, one torpedo boat and a large number of U-boats for experimental purposes; the U-boats are for extended explosives trials, which would be tantamount to scrapping them.
(b) A number of auxiliary vessels, such as naval tankers and depot ships for the Far Eastern war. Some of these ships are already being prepared for the Far East.
(c) Other specialised ships which would make valuable additions to our research and experimental resources.

The US have asked for two destroyers for technical experiment, and are keen to acquire some U-boats for the same purpose. They have not, however, yet tabled their detailed demands.

...

10. The Admiralty's aim is to satisfy British requirements and to keep U-boats out of undesirable hands, particularly Russian hands. It is believed that the Americans, also, will have the latter object. ...

(a) If the Americans are prepared to press for the scrapping of the German combat fleet, we should strongly support their proposals as being in the best interests of world security. We should be careful, however, to avoid stating that we are disinterested in acquiring units of the German Fleet.

...

11. The fact that the Soviet Navy lost 92 submarines compared with our own loss of 76 and the USA of 47 is the most troublesome obstacle to our policy of withholding U-boats from the USSR. On the other hand, the losses of the Royal Navy and US Navy in major surface ships are enormously greater than those of the Red Navy, and the Russians will be ill-advised to press losses as the yardstick for disposal if they wish to obtain any surface ships at all. The following is the suggested division of the German Fleet:

Russia	UK	US	France
Nürnberg *Leipzig* *Graf Zeppelin* *Lützow*	*Prinz Eugen* (for technical examination in US & UK)		
6 destroyers	4 destroyers	4 destroyers	4 destroyers
2 torpedo boats	2 torpedo boats	2 torpedo boats	2 t/boats
10 U-boats	65 U-boats	65 U-boats	6 U-boats
50 minesweepers	Naval tankers & Auxiliaries	?	m/sweepers Older depot ships & auxiliaries not required by US & UK.

If the above is insufficient to obtain a settlement, there would be no objection to offering the USSR two further destroyers and two torpedo boats, and *Prinz Eugen* in six months' time after completion of the technical examination in the UK and USA. We should be very loath to increase the figure for U-boats. The lowest possible number of U-boats should be given to the Russians which will secure a settlement. If the Russians contest the allocation of U-boats to the Royal Navy and US Navy, they should be reminded that:

(a) The Royal Navy and the US Navy have in two major wars borne a very heavy burden in defeating the U-boats and are entitled to insist upon their views prevailing concerning the disposal of U-boats.

(b) The Red Army announced the capture of 45 U-boats at Danzig. We know this to be untrue, but the Russians may find it embarrassing to go back on the Red Army's announcement.

(c) They have taken over the whole Romanian Fleet, including four destroyers, three torpedo boats, gunboats and other craft.

137 of the U-boats now lie in the UK, a potent argument.

...

15. I ask my colleagues to endorse the policy proposed in paragraph 9 and the suggested division in paragraph 11. American support is essential if we are to succeed in our aims; I propose that the First Sea Lord should therefore take an early opportunity of discussing the whole matter with Admiral King.

55. *Decisions of the Tripartite Committee on the Distribution*
of the German Navy

[CAB 99/38]   Potsdam,
                                                         1 August 1945

1. The tripartite Conference agreed upon the following principles for the
distribution of the German Navy:

(a) The total strength of the German surface navy, excluding ships sunk
    and those taken from other Allied countries, but including ships
    under construction or repair, shall be divided equally between the
    USSR, UK and USA.

   (1) The British representatives expressed the view that a portion of
       the German Navy should be allotted to France and that, there-
       fore, full agreement with the above principles must be subject
       to the final decision of the Plenary Conference.

...

(b) Ships under construction or repair mean those ships whose con-
    struction or repair may be completed within three to six months,
    according to the type of ship. Whether such ships under construction
    or repair shall be completed or repaired shall be determined by the
    technical commission appointed by the Three Powers and referred
    to below, subject to the principle that their completion or repair must
    be completed within the time limits above provided, without any
    increase of skill employed in the German shipyards and without
    permitting the re-opening of any German shipbuilding or connected
    industries. Completion date means the date when a ship is able to go
    out on its first trip, or, under peace time standards, would refer to the
    customary date of delivery by shipyards to the Government.

(c) The larger part of the German submarine fleet shall be sunk. The
    Committee are not able to make a recommendation as regards the
    number of submarines to be preserved for experimental or technical
    purposes.

   (1) It is the opinion of the British and American members that not
       more than 30 submarines shall be preserved and divided equally
       between the USSR, UK and US for experimental and technical
       purposes. Paragraph 1 (a) (1) also applies to submarines.

   (2) It is the view of the Russian members that this number is too
       small for their requirements and that the USSR should receive

about 30 submarines for its own experimental and technical services.

(d) All stocks of armaments, ammunition and supplies of the German Navy appertaining to the vessels transferred pursuant to sub-paragraphs (a) and (b) hereof shall be handed over to the respective Powers receiving such ships.

(e) The Three Governments agree to constitute a tripartite naval commission comprising two representatives for each Government, accompanied by the requisite staff, to submit agreed recommendations to the Three Governments concerning the German fleet. The Commission will hold its first meeting not later than 15 August 1945, in Berlin, which shall be its headquarters. Each delegation on the Commission will have the right on the basis of reciprocity to inspect German warships wherever they may be located.

(f) The Three Governments agree transfers, including those of ships under construction and repair, shall be completed as soon as possible, but not later than 15 February 1946. The Commission will submit fortnightly reports, including proposals for the progressive allocation of the vessels when agreed by the Commission.

56. *Report of the Joint Staff Mission*

[CAB 122/1579]   July, 1946
                                                                BOOK I.

...

US Views on Grand Strategy and Policy.

Strategy:

... The strategic offensive was to be aimed at Germany, minimum forces only to be used to safeguard vital interests in other areas. The JSM and others however had to remember that partly as a result of the 'disgrace of Pearl Harbor' and partly due to strong natural antipathy to the Japanese, certain sections of US opinion were urging strong action against Japan as soon as possible. Thus, whilst the basic strategy, outlined above, had been accepted, there was a constant tendency to divert larger forces, particularly air forces, to the Pacific theatres than might be considered necessary for a defensive policy. This tendency was mainly a naval one and the Army and Army Air Force generally joined the British in opposing it during the critical period in 1942 and 1943.

...

Attitude:

Considerable complication arose in the later stages of the war from three very pronounced American attitudes. In the first place there was a very marked Naval jealousy regarding the Pacific war. This had flourished when the British felt it necessary to curb in every possible way a tendency to regard it as the primary theatre. From 1943 onwards it took the form, not only of excluding the British from any discussion of strategy in that theatre, but also of denying them early and complete information. When it was repeatedly suggested in the US press that, after the defeat of Germany, the British would render as little help as possible in the extension of the war against Japan, the US JCS were none too ready to admit the unfairness of this and, to accept publicly, the powerful assistance which they had been promised repeatedly at Head of State Conferences and otherwise from Casablanca onwards.

    ... The determination to have no part in the re-conquest of British or Allied territory as such was understandable.

...

57. *Memorandum by Rear Admiral J. W. S. Dorling*

[ADM 199/1236]   July 1946

Naval Supplies in General (June 1941–March 1944).

Selected Production Items:

...

215. *Escorts.* ... the Escort programme was just coming to fruition and auxiliary carriers required for anti-U-boat duties were well advanced. The first British DE of our programme was delivered on 11 February [1943], a little less than 19 months from approval of the programme. Trials proved satisfactory and we looked forward to assignments of anything up to 90 vessels of this or similar classes before April 1944.
216. ... In the Autumn and Winter of 1943 the escort deliveries should have been massive, but the programme did not look like getting into its stride quickly enough. In co-operation with the Navy Department the pressure on escorts was maintained in all relevant departments of the US Administration and definite priorities were established.
217. On the assignment side discussion chiefly ranged on the proportion of slow to fast escorts that we should receive. Our own forces being largely composed of slow Corvettes we felt that we should receive

enough fast escorts to maintain the balance between our escort force and that of the US Navy. In the end though we did not get all for which we asked our proportion of fast ships was very reasonably satisfactory.

218. *Landing Vessels* in this period were starting to grow in numbers and after some teething troubles proved generally satisfactory, and in the event there was no particular difficulty for providing the ships for the assault on Sicily in the Summer of 1943. Pacific operations also required these ships and craft in increasing numbers.

219. *Auxiliary Carriers* were likewise coming forward satisfactorily.

...

221. The *Oerlikon* gun and ammunition assignments proved a running controversy throughout the period. We were never satisfied with our assignments nor with the manner in which our requirements were treated. We never felt that the relative needs of the two Navies were properly discussed in the light of probable scales of air attack, and too often we were the victims of unilateral decisions with no logical backing.

222. *Torpedoes.* It was not until February 1943 that the step, rather overdue, of transferring procurement action on British torpedo manufacture in USAS from BATM, Ottawa, to BAD, Washington, was finally taken. Large requirements had been stated and accepted by the US Navy, and finally a good rate of output was reached. Changes in the War situation intervened and in the end production had to be slowed down just when it had been organised satisfactorily.

223. In passing it may be noted that the process of adapting British torpedoes to US methods of manufacture did not entail less accuracy in manufacture of components; on the contrary, smaller tolerances were enforced to ensure inter-changeability and to cut out hand fitting.

224. *Proximity Fuses.* A good example of rapid co-operation was the provision of US proximity fuses for British AA ammunition to assist in the defeat of Flying Bombs attacking Southern England and London. A large production of the fuses had been developed in the USA and they were rightly regarded as essential to our gun defences in the event of Flying Bombs developing into a serious menace.

225. In co-operation with the Navy Department special measures were taken early in 1944 to pack and ship by special ships large quantities of these items.

Scale of Research during this Period:

226. The first year of the US war had led to intense research and in 1943–44 this reached truly large proportions in all fields. Gunnery, antisubmarine, Radar, synthetic training, to mention only a few subjects had

intensive study by large numbers of enthusiastic scientists on a scale far beyond anything of which we were capable.

227. Man for man our scientists were probably of higher grade, but they were relatively few.

228. Thus the output of new devices in the USA was most impressive, and in many fields the lead we had gained was rapidly disappearing. Not only this, but the period which elapsed from the inception of an idea to mass production was extremely small. This was largely due to the American method of spreading the manufacture among as many firms as possible; and, more important still, of placing the firms' designers alongside the scientists at an early stage so that the development and manufacturing drawings could be progressed while experiments were still in progress.

229. In the *Radar* field this was particularly impressive.

American Political Situation:

...

231. In mid-1943 the long-term effects of the Presidential election in November 1944 began to make themselves felt, and as time went on these effects became more marked in those quarters antagonistic to us.

232. The disruption manifested itself in various ways. At one time we were suddenly without warning told that the only US officer entitled to discuss US munitions production in relation to our requirements was Admiral Reeves.[1] This if taken literally would have meant an entire stoppage of the normal procedure by which the first discussions took place between our procurement officers and their opposite numbers in the Navy Department with subsequent confirmation or discussion of difficult cases by MAD (N). To imagine that Admiral Reeves, a man well on in years, could conceivably handle this mass of detail was fantastic, and yet it was laid down in all seriousness.

233. It was only by some very straight speaking in high quarters in the Navy Department that this truly ridiculous edict was revoked. Nevertheless, the fact that that this had once been the official attitude had its effect all down the line, and could only be overcome by cultivating friendly relations with those who were disposed to be friendly and being tough with those who were not so disposed.

---

[1] Adm Joseph M. Reeves, US Navy (1872–1948): USNA 1894; Capt *Oregon* 1915–16; *Maine* Atl F 1917–19; Naval Attaché, Rome, 1919–21; Capt, Mare Island NY, San Francisco, 1922–3; NWC 1923–5; Cdr, Air Sqdns, Battle F 1925–9; Gen Board 1929–30; Adm 1933; C-in-C, US F 1934–6; Chmn, Gen Board 1936; ret 1936.

234. It is reasonably certain that this attitude was inspired by the Cominch, Admiral King, US Navy, who knowing the Presidential election would make it difficult or impossible for the President to check him, he chose this way of gratifying his anti-British feelings. In fairness to Admiral King, it must be said that various Congressmen were not too helpful in the Congressional Committees of investigation and the Navy Department were equally hard put to it to justify their actions. However that may be, the Allied cause would have been better advanced if we had been taken more into the confidence of the Navy Department and allowed to make common cause with them rather than being forced into opposition.

...

248. ... at the Cairo Conference at the end of 1943 the question of a Fleet Train for the future British Eastern and Pacific Fleets was discussed. Agreement was reached that the US and British Navies would first discuss the matter to agree on the scale of equipment required. The provision of the requisite ships would then be decided by the Merchant Shipping operating authorities, namely the Ministry of War Transport and the [US] War Shipping Administration.

249. This agreement was followed by the dispatch of a Mission by Captains Friedburger and Bateson, RN, to discuss British draft requirements with the US Navy.[1] After much one-sided deliberation and no round-table discussion, US agreement as to the numbers and types of GF train ships for British forces in the Indian and Pacific Oceans was notified.

250. In communicating his agreement Admiral King stated, however, that only five repair ships could be made available from the USA, a matter which by the Cairo agreement was no concern of his but should have been decided between the MSA and WSA.

251. At this time information available in Washington showed that considerably more than these five ships could have been supplied from US sources without undue effect elsewhere.

252. However, this matter was not followed up and the five ship offer was accepted. ...

Programmes in Retrospect:

253. Looking back on our Lend-Lease programmes in the USA, as a broad statement I can safely say that all the particular classes of ships

---

[1]Capt W. Friedburger: PD Sep 1939; *Menestheus* Sep 1940; Capt Dec 1939; *Welshman* Sep 1941; BAD 1942–5; DoP (Q), *Braganza* India Sep 1945.

Capt Bateson: ent RN 1916; torpedo spist; *Repulse* Sep 1939; Capt Dec 1939; *Latona* Sep 1941; Naval Asst to 3 SL Nov 1942; *London* 1944; *Ajax*; RA & Dir Naval Elec Eng 1946–51.

we sponsored and persuaded the Americans to build justified themselves in action.

254. The escorts came into mass production rather late in the day and it turned out that we could not man as many as we at one time hoped. Nevertheless the holding of the U-boat menace in 1943–44 was to a great extent due to there being enough escorts. The latter day big troop convoys of 50 or 60 ships with 12 escorts were a great contrast to the meagre escorts of earlier years. The important counter-offensive by hunting groups also depended on sufficient number of escorts.

255. Then again the experience of the inshore 'snorting' U-boats in the last few months of the war showed the still existing need for more escorts, to counteract the decrease in effectiveness of air patrols against 'snorting' U-boats. A further factor was the increased speed submerged which made the hunt extremely difficult unless large numbers of escorts were quickly available.

256. Finally at the end of the war the new mass-produced U-boats were coming into action. Had the end of the war been delayed for any reason we should have been glad indeed to have had escorts available in quantity.

257. Thus it is felt that anything the British were able to do in Washington to press for large-scale [production] ocean-going escorts was amply justified by events.

258. Certain difficulties in maintenance, due to lack of spares, were anticipated, but as far as can be gathered once the ships' companies became accustomed to the American layout the ships were very well liked, on the whole have given very little trouble and have proved fully seaworthy and efficient units.

259. Of the auxiliary carriers it can be said that they have played their full part in all operations, whether on the wide oceans to back up the hunting groups or in the landing operations providing fighter cover. Our main effort in this class was to get them built less vulnerable to attack after our early sad experience when two ships were lost. Subsequent experience, however, seems to have been more happy, and as far as is known our forebodings were not fully justified.

260. The landing ships and craft which we were instrumental in getting built in the USA have it is believed fully proved their value in every part of the globe. In particular the LST (2), after early teething troubles, appears to have been an unqualified success.

261. The Fleet and Motor Minesweepers also appear to have given satisfaction on many operations, and there is little doubt that the practical experience of our minesweeper Officers helped to develop a satisfactory layout of the minesweeping gear. The same can be said of Rescue tugs and their ocean towing arrangements.

262. As regards engines, it is perhaps true to say that in the Gray Diesel, originally a powerful Truck (Lorry) Engine, used in large numbers for British-built landing craft, the Americans possessed an engine which had no counterpart in England. This engine was manufactured in the USA in large numbers by mass production, and it is understood that no British Diesel engine is available in similar quantities. Our later landing craft have, therefore, to return to Petrol engines with all attendant fire risks and other disabilities.

263. This is an instance where the enormous US domestic production was converted to war use.

264. In the Armament field the Americans owe us a debt of gratitude for introducing them to the 20mm Oerlikon gun, a favourite two-man close range AA weapon until the changes of war demanded the more powerful 40mm Bofors.[1]

265. As a makeweight the Americans developed for us methods of producing torpedoes of good quality by mass production (18in Aircraft Torpedo), methods which it is hoped will have proved valuable to our own factories.

266. In the Radar field the Americans owe much to our original discoveries and early experience freely given. Latterly we probably learnt more from them, particularly on methods of rapid production from the development stage. It is to be hoped that this co-operation thus started will continue at least until our own scientific effort can recover from the strain of long years of war.

267. In the Naval Landing pontoon and all its many and varied applications for building causeways, pontoons, docks and piers, the Americans made a major contribution comparable to our own Bailey Bridge or Mulberry Pier Heads.

268. Without this the problem of bridging the gap between landing ship and the shore would have been difficult to solve.

269. Taking the whole field of supply it is felt that on many subjects there was genuine pooling of ideas and brains, greatly to the benefit of the United Nations' war effort.

Results to time of leaving the USA:

270. In this account of my mission in the USA during nearly three years, much mention has been made of difficulties of co-operating with the Navy Department. On the other side of the picture some figures speak for themselves. For example, in 1943, the peak year of the programme, the following were estimated to be the tons of new ships to hoist the White Ensign:

---

[1]Oerlikon: Swiss 20mm AA gun.
Bofors: Swedish 40mm AA gun.

Built in UK	630,000 tons.
Built in Empire	52,500 tons.
US Lend-Lease Built to [for] Britain	804,000 tons.

271. During the whole period from 1 June 1941, to 8 April 1944, 813 ships and craft were taken over for the White Ensign, not counting small craft such as would be hoisted on davits.

272. Added to this were millions of dollars worth of stores, guns, ammunition and munitions of all kinds.

...

Conclusion:

277. Above all, in dealing with Americans: it is important to remember that they are not English, they are proud of being American; that they dealt in frankness and openness, they detest and suspect reserve or any hint of condescension; that they are very susceptible to generous praise and that a word of praise will pave the way for a helpful suggestion or comment; and, being not averse to a good bargain, if help is required one must try to help them. Lastly it is personal contacts and friendships that count most in the long run.

58. *Report by Rear Admiral J. W. A. Waller, BASR*[1]

[ADM 199/1236]   July 1946

Naval Supplies in General: April 1944-February 1946.

4. ... by April 1944, the rising tide of US production had reached such a level that the most critical period in the Board's history was over, and whilst a number of items were still in short supply, particularly Bofors anti-aircraft equipment, there was a steady flow of munitions going through the Munitions Assessment Committee (Naval) and the Board without dispute, which amounted to some $700m worth per month. While therefore the BASR (subsequently the BAM & SR) had to fight against what was virtually stonewall opposition on the items in critical supply, we were far from being cut off from Lend-Lease assistance altogether. The Bofors argument, as with certain other items in short supply, dragged on through 1944, however, and was only abandoned when the ships for

---

[1]RA J. W. A. Waller: Naval Asst to FL May 1941; Capt *Malaya* March 1942; RA July 1943; RA Red Sea & Suez Canal Area Oct 1943; BAD – Matériel & Supply June 1944–5.

which they had been intended had already sailed against the Japanese and there was no longer an opportunity to fit them if we had them.

...

8. After VE-Day the attitude of the Navy Department changed considerably... The White House, however, took other steps towards the curtailment of Lend-Lease, principally a Directive shortly after VE-Day restricting the total $ value of Lend-Lease which was to be made available to the various countries, and a further Directive issued in July that Lend-Lease aid was to be restricted to munitions which were to be used directly in the war against Japan. ...

59. *Report by Rear Admiral G. G. P. Burt*[1]

[ADM 199/1236]   July 1946

Refits, particularly the Engineering Aspect, January 1941–1944.

...

Training of Personnel

35. Almost all Lend-Lease craft were equipped with machinery unfamiliar to Royal Navy officers and ratings, and a big job we tackled was to arrange training courses for our personnel as they arrived in the USA. It is pertinent to remark that the US Navy is much more Diesel-minded than the Royal Navy.

...

44. Our relations with the Navy Department were with minor exceptions admirable, the latter due to lack of tact and in some cases lack of knowledge of the particular subject under discussion on the part of a few of our members and on the other side by, I suspect, anti-British feeling in a few cases.
45. Directness, with tact, always paid in dealing with the US Naval Officers. If you knew your subject whole-hearted co-operation was forthcoming. It was noticeable that US Naval Officers who had visited the UK[,] particularly those that had served some time there[,] were particularly co-operative and understanding.

...

47. US Navy Yards are far better equipped than our Dockyards, and we envied them their facilities. With exceptions they have not the general

---

[1]RA G. G. P. Burt (1888–1965): engr; Engr-in-C, BAD 1941; ret 1946.

all-round men that we have and concentrated rather on the one-man, one-job type.

48. Research work in the US Navy never lacks financial provision. It is hoped we have learnt our lesson, that it pays to divert money to research in peace. A concrete example is given by the greater endurance of US Ships compared with the Royal Navy. Had the money been available to the Admiralty to carry on research in the special materials and design of machinery necessary for higher steam pressure and temperatures we should have been able to meet the operational requirements found necessary in this war.

49. Private firms spend freely on research, an example to their British confreres. They believe in the dictum that 'money should make money'.

...

58. The organisation of the US Navy with its common root for all specialist officers merits study. We certainly appreciated the versatility of the Bureau of Ships, Bureau of Aeronautics and Bureau of Ordnance. There is much to be learnt from the US Navy and continued liaison is very desirable.

...

59. A visit was arranged for the Head of the Maintenance Branch of the Bureau of Ships (corresponding to our Director of Dockyards) and the Head of the Maintenance Division [of the Office of] Naval Operations to the UK to see our building and repair facilities. They returned with an understanding of our difficulties in the UK.

60. *Report by Captain E. M. C. Abel-Smith, Naval Air Representative*[1]

[ADM 199/1236]   July 1946

Aircraft Procurement, August 1944–1945.

Captain Abel-Smith relieved Captain Caspar John as NAR at the beginning of August 1944.[2] At the time negotiations for aircraft for the period 1 July–31 December 1944 had been concluded and consisted of:[3]

---

[1]Capt E. M. C. Abel-Smith (1899–1983): ent RN 1913; pilot; *Condor* Sep 1940; Capt June 1940; *Biter* Nov 1942; *Hermes* Sep 1943; Naval Attaché, USA Sep 1945; *Triumph* 1947; RA 1949; Naval Air & Eqpt, Ministry of Supply 1950; VA 1952.

[2]Capt Caspar John (1903–84): son of Augustus John, the artist; ent RN 1916; pilot 1926; *Hermes* 1925–7; technical posts 1930s; Naval Air Div 1937; A/Capt, Dir Gen, Naval Development & Production, MAP May 1941; Capt June 1941; Asst Naval Attaché (Air), USA June 1943; *Ocean* May 1945; IDC 1947; & Adm 1957; FSL 1960–63; AoF 1962.

[3]Curtiss Helldiver: dive bomber: 1940, 294mph, 2 cannon, 2mg, 2000lbs bombs/1 torpedo.

Hellcat	828
Corsair	702
Wildcat	336
Helldiver	306
Avenger	126

...

8. After somewhat protracted negotiations the Navy Department recommended to the US JCS the following assignments should be made for the period 1 January–1 July 1945:

Hellcat	316
Corsair	90–150
Avenger	80
Wildcat	150.

It was possible, however, to include a statement in which it was agreed that should the strategical consideration alter and thus justify a review of these assignments the British were free to request such a review.

9. Negotiations for aircraft for the Royal Navy from 1 July–31 December 1945, that is the last negotiations before the end of the war, followed much the same lines as above.

...

11. The negotiations for this period ended with an assignment of the following aircraft:

Corsair	120
Avenger	180
Avenger (reconditioned)	80.

61. *Report by Director of Airfields and Carrier Requirements,*
April 1943–1945[1]

[ADM 199/1236]   July 1946

...

---

[1]DACR: Capt E. O. F. Price: Lt Cdr 1933; FAA Aug 1939; Cdr Dec 1939; *Argus* May 1940; *Jackdaw* May 1941; *Victorious* May 1942; A/Capt, ACRD, May 1944; DACR, 13 Nov 1944.

3. On the helicopter side the USAAF were involved ...

4. It can be fairly stated that the vast majority of the US Navy did everything in their power to help and a more co-operative crowd would be difficult to find anywhere. Most of the information acquired was done by personal dealings with individual officers in the Bureau [of Aeronautics] ... At no time was any request to inspect US Naval activities of any sort ever refused.

5. Reciprocal information was obtained from the Admiralty but it must be admitted that there was little that we could tell the US Navy that they did not know already, particularly with regard to the operation of aircraft from carriers.

...

6. In January 1944 DACR (Washington) embarked in SS *Daghestan* with two Sikorsky R4 helicopters in order to evaluate them for use in ocean convoy work. The party consisted of RN, RAF, US Navy and US Coast Guard officers and ratings and much valuable experience was gained.[1]

...

9. In conclusion, this is one aspect which is considered of paramount importance. It cannot be stressed too highly that it is essential that Royal Navy officers who are sent over to the USA to work with the US Navy must be prepared to co-operate and understand the US viewpoint. This, at times, is not easy and friction can easily develop. However, with tact and understanding the average US naval officer is one of the best people in the world to get on with and will do everything in his power to help, By British standards some of them may appear somewhat uncouth but he [*sic*] knows his job and cannot be bothered to waste his time with anyone who obviously does not know what he is talking about. For this reason a line shooter is a bad selection. One misfit can undo the good work of many good officers.

62. *Report by Superintendent of Air Training*[2]

[ADM 199/1236]   July 1946

Survey of Air Training Activities in the USA, 1941–1945.

1. *Towers Scheme Training.* In June 1941 Admiral Towers, US Navy, then Chief of the Bureau of Aeronautics, informed the British Military

---

[1]Helicopters: developed by Igor Sikorsky 1939; trials & production 1943.

SS *Daghestan*: tanker: Hindustan SS Co, 1921, 5842t, 11k. All refs say ship sunk by *U-57*, 15 Mar 1940, off Orkney. True identity of trials ship is a puzzle.

[2]Supt of Air Trng: Cdr (A) A. E. Shaw: Lt 1935; *Raven* May 1940; *Heron* Sep 1940; *Victorious* 1942; A/Cdr, BAD 1943.

Mission that the US Navy had agreed to train some RAF and RN pilots. This offer was immediately accepted by both Admiralty and Air Ministry.[1]

...

C. *Numbers Trained.*

In the early stages, the Towers scheme was providing almost 30% of the RN requirements for pilots. This percentage has risen annually, and is now about 44%.

...

II. *Formation and Training of Squadrons in the USA.*

10. The Scheme allowed for a three months' working-up period and eventual deck landing qualification.

...

A. Alterations.

6. *Major Increases and Peak Figures.*

The original scheme allowed for a maximum of 93 aircraft and 675 officers and men in the USA at any one time. In January 1943 the Admiralty asked for a large increase, but this was not wholly accepted by the US Navy, who agreed only to provide facilities for 150 aircraft, 175 officers and 1000 men. This agreement still stands, but at present we are below these figures.

...

IV. *Helicopter Training.*

17. After various trials had been carried out in previous months, it was decided to form a Helicopter Training Unit in the USA.
18. In March 1944 six pilots commenced instruction with the US Coast Guard at Floyd Bennett Field, NY. Later some maintenance ratings commenced a course of instruction.
19. In June 1944 we set up our own training unit consisting of eight aircraft and 30 ratings. The instructors were picked from the first course

---

[1]Adm John H. Towers, US Navy (1885–1955): USNA 1908; pilot 1911; air cmds 1911–23; Bu Aeronautics 1925; c/o *Langley* 1925–8; NWC 1933; air cmds; *Saratoga* 1937–8; RA 1939; Chf, Bu Aeronautics 1939–42; VA 1942; Dep Cdr, Pac F; Adm 1945; 2 CTF 1945; Cdr, 5F; C-in-C, Pac F 1946–7; ret 1947.

which was trained by the US Coast Guard. Both the ratings and the instructors contained some RAF personnel.

20. It has now been decided to discontinue training and return the Unit to the UK in December 1945.

21. Three courses of pilots and two of maintenance ratings have been trained by this Unit.

...

V. *Approximate Numbers dealt with in USA by the Air Training Staff during the period covered.*

Training Scheme Students: 2100.
Squadron Forming, Helicopter Unit and Technical Training:

Officers	Ratings	Aircraft
850	6000	600.

VI. *Flying Hours carried out during the period.*

Squadron forming	52,700.
No. 738 Squadron	11,700
No. 732 Squadron	3,000
	67,400.

63. *Report by Mr A. J. Atkins, Director of Armament Supplies (Washington), August 1941–April 1946*[1]

[ADM 199/1236]   July 1946

...

Gunwharf – Gun Repairs, etc.

24. ... Spare guns and spare parts had to be sent out from the UK and storage accommodation had to be provided at a central point convenient for distribution. The storage question was discussed with the US Navy who allocated the required space at US Naval Warehouse, 35th Street Pier, Brooklyn, NY. This building was a covered commercial Pier taken over from one of the SS Lines and as the US Navy was operating there, the necessary labour, lifting and packing facilities were provided by them for our use.

---

[1] A. J. Atkins: BAD Mtc Representative; Senior Armament Supply Officer.

25. The facilities were admirable …

…

34. During the period 1941–1944 ships of all classes, from Battleships to Destroyers, were in hand and repairs, etc., work was undertaken on guns of all descriptions from 16in to light machine guns. Gun steel to approved specifications had to be provided for many repair jobs and in the case of others, e.g., conversion of two-pounder pom-poms from AHV to CHV the necessary parts were obtained from Canadian production or from stock.

35. In instances where additional AA guns were installed in HM Ships, arrangements were made to obtain them from either US Lend-Lease sources, e.g., Oerlikon, Bofors, etc., or from the UK or Canada, e.g., two-pounder pom-pom, etc.

36. In addition to the work carried out on gun armament, examination, etc., of DCTs in numerous small craft, e.g., Destroyers, Corvettes, etc., was undertaken.

…

New Construction Ships.

43. Whilst generally speaking Lend-Lease New Construction ships were delivered complete with US-type guns, and ammunition, owing to temporary US Naval allocation difficulties it was necessary from time to time to equip certain Lend-Lease craft with British-type guns and ammunition.

44. A particular case in point was a big delivery of LSTs which, owing to a shortage of 3in 40-calibre guns, had to be equipped with 12-pounder guns with appropriate outfits. About 200 12-pounders were obtained from Canadian production and distributed over many yards throughout the USA for installation in the LSTs. Ammunition to provide gun outfits had to be obtained in large quantities from the UK to meet this unforeseen requirement. Similarly, other craft were equipped with 2-pounder pom-poms from Canadian production as a result of a temporary production shortage of light, close-range US-type weapons.

45. In all cases Lend-Lease ships were supplied with British-type pyrotechnics, small arms, steel helmets and anti-gas gear. Taking account of the fact that these ships were building all over the country, the distribution of British-type stores to the various yards required considerable attention in order to ensure that outfits were on hand by the completion date.

…

FAA.

49. As part of the FAA training scheme, training squadrons were assembled at various US Navy Flying Fields on the east coast. Arrangements were made to provide for these training squadrons the necessary pools of ammunition for practice firings, also pyrotechnics and practice bombs, and to supply gun spares for the maintenance of the installed gun armament.

50. As the CVE building programme got under way, FAA squadrons were formed in the USA and embarked in these Carriers, which completed at yards on the east and west coasts. For the Squadrons it was necessary to provide outfits of Bombs, Pyrotechnics, Ammunition and Torpedoes, the latter being 22.4in obtained from Lend-Lease sources.

51. Distribution of bombs, torpedoes and FAA ammunition and pyrotechnics to meet the completion dates of these new CVEs was something of a problem in view of the vast distances to be covered. The formation of FAA pools at US Naval Ammunition Depots, however, overcame the difficulties.

64. *Report by Captain S. W. Roskill, Director of Naval Ordnance (Washington)*

[ADM 199/1236]   July 1946

Naval Ordnance (Procurement), May 1944–October 1945.

I arrived in Washington on 12 May 1944 and took over from Captain E. K. Le Mesurier.[1]

2. At the time of assuming the above duties we were in serious discussion with the Navy Department over a number of requisitions which had been placed prior to my arrival. The principal procurement items involved were:

(a) Mark 52 Directors, a further 100 of which had been requested by the Admiralty.

(b) Mark 14 Gyro Sights, of which 1500 more were required.

(c) Mark 15 Gyro Sights, of which a further 1000 had been asked for.

(d) Mark 37 Fire Control System for the 1944 Destroyer Programme (40 sets).

(e) Bofors Twin and Quadruple equipments.

---

[1] Capt E. K. Le Mesurier: TSD Sep 1939; A/Capt BAD Nov 1942; OD (F) Sep 1944; Capt May 1944.

The Navy Department was flatly refusing to accept Lend-Lease Requisitions for any of the above, and also for a considerable number of less important items.

We had also been refused release of a large quantity of manufacturing information which we had requested under the Patent Interchange Agreement. Missions from Vickers Armstrongs on welded gun mount structures and small VSG engines and from British VT fuze manufacturers to store American Rugged Tube and Reserve Battery manufacture had also been refused.[1]

In general, as regards Ordnance and allied items, the situation appeared extremely bad and relations with the Navy Department and MAC (Navy) on procurement matters were at this time and later very difficult.

3.   It may be worthwhile to assess, in the light of previous history and subsequent events, the reasons why we had got into this jam and why our requisitions and requests were being regarded with a good deal of scepticism and suspicion.

The primary reasons for the Navy Department's mistrust appear to have been:

(a) Doubts about the soundness of British advanced planning. Our requirements had been changed numberless times, e.g, in November 1943 the Admiralty had told the BAD that no more Bofors guns were required for the RN.

(b) Doubts over whether we were really playing fair over the share of American production which we claimed for our services. This undoubtedly dated back to the mishandling of the 20mm Oerlikon gun requisitions, where we persistently claimed half a share of American production whilst ignoring the current British production of the same gun. ... These protracted negotiations left a very nasty impression in the Navy Department, which we never succeeded in dispelling.

(c) The feeling that we were trying to use Lend-Lease to arm the post-war British Fleet. For example the Mark 37 system and some of the Mark 52 Directors were required for ships which could not possibly complete before 1947–1948 and the Navy Department did not believe that the war would last that long.

(d) Inability in many cases to provide accurate and up-to-date statistical data proving the military necessity for our requisitions.

---

[1] Vickers Armstrongs: a leading British shipbuilder & arms manufacturer.

That a very great share of the responsibility for the impasse in which we found ourselves in mid-1944 rested with ourselves cannot be denied.

On the other hand the Navy Department's own commitments had vastly increased as the war construction programme got into its full stride and they were determined to subordinate our needs to their own. Moreover there was an undoubted desire among a certain circle in the Navy Department to reserve to their own Service the entire credit for defeating the Japanese Navy and to treat the European and Mediterranean theatres as secondary to the Pacific.

4. In spite of protracted, and sometimes heated negotiations we never achieved success in getting acceptance of the Mk 37 system, Mk 52 Director and Mk 15 Sight requisitions. In the latter case our position was further undermined by the final discovery that even the 33 Mk 52 Directors and 500 Mk 15 Sights originally procured for our Service were not really wanted by the Admiralty. We did obtain a further 700 Mk 14 Sights but even lost these finally when, in 1945, the Admiralty failed to prove that they were really needed for the war against Japan. After a hard battle, we succeeded, in July 1944, in stopping reassignment to the US Navy of the 500 Mk 15 Sights for which a requisition had been accepted and it was with some bitterness that we finally learnt that, even for these, no vital service was envisaged by the Admiralty.

   By going to London to prepare the brief ourselves we finally convinced the Navy Department of our need for more Bofors twins and obtained very rapid delivery of 24 equipments early in 1945.

5. The only really important requisitions which we managed to get accepted in full during this difficult period were those placed to meet our VT fuze requirements. A very careful briefing proving 'military necessity' to the hilt secured full acceptance of the requisitions, which seemed to indicate that, when we could present one [our?] case properly, the Navy Department would not be unreasonable.

6. As Lend-Lease procurement tended, early in 1944, to die so did the refitting and repair of ships in the USA. Considerable difficulty was experienced in getting the required work, particularly Alterations and Additions, done. In the case of *Nelson*, in spite of acceptance of our original Defect and Alteration and Addition Lists, the Navy Department finally refused to do more than repair action damage and increase the AA armament. Our experience with that ship proved to be the death knell for refits of major treatment. In consequence by the end of 1944 the Repair side of this staff began to close down.

7. In the field of technical collaboration, which comprised the third part of this department's duties (the other two being Lend-Lease Procurement[,] and Ship Refit and Repair), matters went very much more smoothly. This was due to the personal willingness of American scientists and Service men to work with us and exchange ideas and information.

We finally obtained, through a direct approach to Admiral King, release to us of all manufacturing information on VT fuzes except the Rugged Tube made by Sylvania, and in July 1945 the Ministry of Supply and British manufacturers visited the American firms concerned.

In February 1945 an Inter-Service GM Committee was formed in Washington to pool all available service talent to cover this increasingly important subject. ... Its formation is an example of what can be done in the way of Inter-Service co-ordination and collaboration with the Americans. ... In July 1945, Dr Goodeve (ACR & D) and Mr C. S. Wright (DSR) came out to place before the Navy Department the Admiralty proposals for continued collaboration.[1]

---

[1]Sir Charles Goodeve (1904–80): b Canada; chemicals & metals; Cdr, RNVR; Dep Dir, Misc Weapons Development 1940–42; Dep Cntrlr Research & Development 1942–5.

C. S. Wright (1887–1975): b Toronto; Scientist, British Antarctic Expedition 1910–13; Royal Engineers 1914–18; DSIR 1919–39; Dir Scientific Research 1938–45; Chief, RN Scientific Service 1946–7.

PART II

THE ANTI-SUBMARINE WAR

The U-boats were defeated effectively before this volume begins, for on 24 May 1943, Dönitz, acknowledging the Allied victory, withdrew his U-boats from their main theatre in the Atlantic to re-configure their armament and electronic equipment and to reconsider their tactics and explore other seas where they might have more effect with sustainable losses.[1] Dönitz himself best expressed the nature of the defeat:

Events in May 1943 had shown beyond dispute that the anti-submarine organization of the two great sea powers was more than a match for our U-boats. Months would have to elapse before the latter could be equipped with the improved weapons which were being developed and produced and the new boats with high underwater speed could not be expected till the end of 1944.[2]

Allied success was due to a number of factors. By the spring of 1943, it is estimated that the Allies deployed over 2200 aircraft and more than 1000 vessels; thus the Atlantic was covered from shore to shore, the convoys assured of more or less continuous air cover (including escort carriers), while on the surface they were well protected by strong close escorts, which were strengthened by support or escort groups, which had the freedom to hunt submarines in the vicinity of the merchantmen [66, 76–8, 82, 83, 89, 93, 111, 114, 122]. Experiments were going on, meanwhile, with new detection systems, weapons and novel platforms such as helicopters. Tactics, organisation and training, shared information and experiences were now highly sophisticated. Captain F. J. Walker, RN, was a leading exponent of escort group anti-submarine warfare, while the American escort carrier groups were also extremely successful and it was noted that 'The hunter/killer groups' anti-submarine efficiency was high. Once contact was made it was rare for a U-boat to survive the attacks'[3] [73, 80, 89, 92, 98, 101, 102]. By this time, too, the escorting

---

[1]M. Milner, *The Battle of the Atlantic* (St Catharine's, Ont., 2003), p. 154; R. Overy, *Why the Allies Won* (London, 1996), pp. 56–61; C. M. Bell, *Churchill and Sea Power* (Oxford, 2013), pp. 280–82, argues that Churchill was less concerned about the 'Battle of the Atlantic' than is generally thought – he had a much wider range of concerns.

[2]K. Dönitz, *Memoirs: Ten Years and Twenty Days* (London, 2000), p. 406.

[3]D. W. Waters (ed. E. J. Grove), *The Defeat of the Enemy Attack on Shipping, 1939–1945* (Aldershot, 1997: NRS vol. 137), p. 122; W. Hackmann, *Seek and Strike: Sonar, Anti-Submarine Warfare and the Royal Navy, 1914–1954* (London, 1984), pp. 234, 254, 256; S. E. Morison, *History of U. S. Naval Operations in World War II*, X, *The Atlantic Battle Won* (Boston, 1990), pp. 19, 21, 45, 159–77; D. Hobbs, 'Shipborne Anti-Submarine Warfare', in S. Howarth and D. Law, eds, *The Battle of the Atlantic, 1939–1945* (London, 1994), pp. 393–4, 398–401, and D. C. Allard, 'A U.S. Overview', ibid., p. 567; W. F. Kimball, ed., *Churchill and Roosevelt: The Complete Correspondence*, II, *Alliance Forged* (Princeton & London, 1984), pp. 406–7, 513, 515, 564; W. S. Chalmers, *Max Horton and Western Approaches* (London, 1954).

forces were well organised, each of the three Atlantic nations having a defined area of responsibility – the Canadians controlling the North-West Atlantic, the British the Eastern Atlantic, and the Americans the Caribbean, the Central Atlantic, their own Eastern Seaboard and the crucial oil traffic [114, 123, 124]. The Americans had instituted a 10th Fleet, under the direct command of the Chief of Naval Operations, Admiral King, and dedicated to anti-submarine warfare. In Britain, there was already a well-honed Western Approaches Command, led by the redoubtable ex-submariner Admiral Sir Max Horton. A 'Bay Offensive' conducted by aircraft of several nations over the transit area of U-boats sailing to and from the Biscay ports was no longer cost-effective (even if it ever had been) by this time. It generated a good deal of heat, however, between Admiral King, who was (rightly) sceptical of its continued value and as an optimum use of Allied force, and the British high command, who were almost universally in favour of prolonging the Bay Offensive [65, 67–70, 72, 74, 75, 84, 85, 88]. Neutral Portugal was persuaded to allow an Allied airfield to be established in the Azores in October 1943, allowing the Allies to command the central Atlantic; in effect, the Azores became a moored aircraft carrier, helping to close yet another gap [81, 83, 86, 91, 97, 119]. Despite inter-national and inter-service arguments, co-operation between the nations and between the air forces and navies was by now highly effective [81, 94, 110, 123]. The anti-submarine forces were by 1943 extremely experienced. Training had been refined and the lessons of war absorbed; the leading physicist Professor P. M. S. Blackett (a former naval officer) conducted operational research analyses from 1942 and headed the Admiralty's Operational Research Department from January 1944.[1] Finally but most importantly, Allied shipyards (chiefly American) turned out 14 million tons of merchant shipping in 1943 and more than made up for all the shipping lost since the start of the war.[2]

A major source of victory was Ultra, information gained from cracking the German submarine code, though it was not responsible solely for success.[3] Of equally great importance was High Frequency Direction

---

Capt F. J. Walker (1896–1944): ent RN 1909; ASW spist, unfashionable pre-war; original thinker & successful practitioner ASW; late promotion to Capt.

[1]Hackmann, *Seek and Strike*, pp. 244–5

Prof P. M. S. Blackett (1897–1974): ex-naval officer, physicist (Nobel Prize winner); radar pioneer; Dir of Operational Research, Admy, Jan 1942.

[2]Morison, *Atlantic Battle Won*, p. 149.

[3]W. J. R. Gardner, 'An Allied Perspective', in S. Howarth & D. Law, eds, *Battle of the Atlantic*, pp. 531–2; D. Syrett, ed., *The Battle of the Atlantic and Signals Intelligence: U-boat Situations and Trends, 1941–1945* (Aldershot, 1998: NRS vol. 139), pp. xxxii–xxxiv; J. Rohwer, 'Afterword', in Dönitz, *Memoirs*, pp. 495–7, 507–9.

Finding (HF/DF), which enabled the Allies to identify specific U-boats and their commanders, interpret their mission and locate them. Centimetric radar was supplied to ships and aircraft to pin down targets and some aircraft were equipped with Magnetic Anomaly Detection (MAD), which enabled them to locate submerged U-boats. Leigh-Lights, two powerful aircraft searchlights which produced a converging beam, aided night-time attacks. Studies of the seas enabled scientists to devise equipment that could identify layers of dense water.[1] Sonar (or asdic) was further refined, the Types 144 and 147B appearing in the later stages of the war.[2] Perhaps the most significant organisations in signals intelligence were the Submarine Tracking Rooms located in London, Ottawa and Washington; by the autumn of 1943 they were functioning smoothly, their leaders meeting each other and arranging co-operation, and 'Throughout the war Britain and America held the technical initiative'.[3]

At sea and in the air, electronic advances enabled the better direction of existing weapons like the depth charge (itself refined during the war) and assisted a new generation of weapons to improve the lethality of attacks – notably forward-throwing weapons like the 'Hedgehog' and, later, the 'Squid'; whereas the 'kill rate' of depth charges was about 6 per cent; the 'Hedgehog' raised this to 20 per cent, while the 'Squid' elevated it to at least 50 per cent. Aircraft were equipped with acoustic torpedoes and especially effective were solid-shot rockets. 'There is no doubt', wrote Zimmermann, 'that the introduction of new ASW equipment was one of the decisive factors in the defeat of the U-boats.'[4] Mines, though used liberally, destroyed few U-boats and had no significant effect on U-boat movements. Bombing of submarine pens and assembly yards, though carried out from time to time, was not effective until late in the war, when improved navigation and heavier bombs, allied to a relative ineffectiveness of defences, had a major disruptive effect on production and transportation of parts and assembly of boats, while catching a number of boats in port [71, 105, 116, 118].

The co-ordination of a plenitude of force, able and unified direction, sophisticated electronic devices and lethal weapons led to the destruction of 341 U-boats in the last eighteen months of the war; a further 29

---

[1]Syrett, *U-boat Situations and Trends*, pp. x, xv; D. W. Waters, *Defeat of the Enemy Attack on Shipping*, p. 122; Hackmann, *Seek and Strike*, 240; D. Zimmermann, 'Techniques and Tactics', in S. Howarth & D. Law eds, *Battle of the Atlantic*, pp. 486–8.

[2]Hackmann, *Seek and Strike*, p. 238.

[3]Ibid., p. 240; D. Syrett, ed., *The Battle of the Atlantic and Signals Intelligence* (Aldershot, 2002: NRS vol. 144), pp. 3, 352–3.

[4]Zimmermann, 'Techniques and Tactics', p. 487; Waters, *Defeat of the Enemy Attack on Shipping*, pp. 154, 172; Hackmann, *Seek and Strike*, p. 310.

were lost through accidents or unknown causes. Thus of 784 U-boats lost throughout the war, 370 (or nearly half) were destroyed in the last eighteen months.[1] They had several successes, nevertheless, and U-boat crews were not alone in suffering and largely succumbing to the merciless, lonely sea and the sky [121].

When Dönitz withdrew his U-boats from their main theatre of operations, against North Atlantic convoys, he recognised that he had lost the 'tonnage war' – that is, his calculation that he could destroy more Allied shipping than the Allies could replace, and in doing so construct an effective blockade round the British Isles, thus starving Britain of food, fuel and raw materials and forcing her surrender. Now he concentrated on maintaining the submarine campaign and compelling the Allies to divert considerable air and naval forces and other resources to anti-submarine warfare – an effort which could have been applied elsewhere in the war – and he therefore delayed the Allied victory and relieved pressure on Germany. The U-boats would have to suffer heavy casualties for poor rewards, but they must hold the fort until new types of U-boats, representing significant advances on the conventional boats, could be deployed, giving him hopes of reversing the tide of defeat [89].[2]

These new boats would not be operational until at least the end of 1944. In the meantime, Dönitz had to re-equip his conventional boats, retrain them, devise new tactics, and redeploy them in areas allegedly more profitable and less dangerous than the North Atlantic The boats were re-equipped with better search radar, devices to block Allied radar, decoy buoys, acoustic torpedoes (GNATs) and improved AA batteries [68, 109, 112, 115, 118].[3] Their most far-reaching improvement, however, was schnorkel, a pipe breaking the surface and allowing the faster diesel motors to power the boats underwater while disposing of exhaust fumes. It had the effect of allowing boats to remain submerged for several days and, importantly, was difficult to spot, especially from the air. It was a device to which the Allies never found an answer, the First Sea Lord, Sir Andrew Cunningham admitting early in 1945 that 'the air is 90% out of business.' Schnorkel had its limitations, however, as it could be used only in moderate seas and caused sickness among ships' companies; moreover,

---

[1]The figures for U-boats sunk are taken from the most authoritative analysis, A. Niestlé, *German U-boat Losses during World War II* (London, 2014), supplemented by P. Kemp, *U-boats Destroyed: German Submarine Losses in the World Wars* (London, 1997).

[2]Dönitz, *Memoirs*, p. 402; Milner, *Battle of the Atlantic*, pp. 183–4, 217; W. A. B. Douglas et al., *A Blue Water Navy: The Official Operational History of the Royal Canadian Navy in the Second World War, 1939–1945* (St Catherine's, Ont., 2007), p. 351; G. H. & R. Bennett, *Hitler's Admirals* (Annapolis, MD, 2004), p. 184.

[3]J. Rohwer, 'Afterword', in Dönitz, *Memoirs*, p. 494; M. H. Murfett, *Naval Warfare, 1919–1945: An Operational History of the Volatile War at Sea* (London, 2009), p. 302.

it was only in 1944 that the Germans began to fit a device introduced by the Dutch before the war, and many submarines never received it [104, 112, 118].[1]

Dönitz sent the U-boats out into the Atlantic again in September 1943. He instructed them to travel in pairs on the surface through the Bay of Biscay and use their heavy AA armament to fight it out with aircraft. Though he claimed that Allied air losses mounted and caution was induced in aircrew, the exchange rate in dead crewmen and damaged or sunken U-boats was unsustainable and after a month of this aggressive defence, Dönitz called off the tactic. In attempting passages across the Bay of Biscay, the U-boat command lost 29 boats.[2]

Other areas were exploited by his boats [71]. The Indian Ocean realised 600,000 tons of Allied shipping but, as Dönitz acknowledged, the Allies were quick to reinforce weak areas [71, 73]. Only a few boats were lost in the Indian Ocean (eight) but several were intercepted in the Central and South Atlantic en route for Oriental seas [90].[3] The Mediterranean became an area of diminishing U-boat effort. The Straits of Gibraltar were effectively closed to reinforcements by Allied possession of both shores, a swarm of vessels and especially MAD-equipped aircraft. The successful, if prolonged, hunt for *U-392* reveals the overwhelming Allied strength on the sea and in the air; the excellent co-ordination of the services of different Allied nations; the deadly dovetailing of air and sea attacks; and the crushing Allied technical superiority [98]. As the war wore on, many Mediterranean U-boats were either laid up for repairs or bombed in port; some 41 boats were lost from various causes.[4] In the Baltic, while U-boats conducted operations against the Russians, the sea, largely inaccessible to the Western Allies, was the principal testing and training ground for the submarine arm. No less than 18 were lost for non-combat reasons, while 58 were destroyed in combat, many in the late stages of the war by Allied mining and bombing.[5]

The resumption of Arctic convoys to North Russia in November 1943 gave Dönitz another area to exploit. In addition to the submarines, the heavy ships *Tirpitz* and *Scharnhorst* were based in Norway, ready to

---

[1]Adm Sir Andrew Cunningham to Adm Sir Bruce Fraser, 19 Jan 1945, in M. A. Simpson, ed., *The Cunningham Papers*, II, *The Triumph of Allied Sea Power, 1942–1946* (Aldershot, 2006: NRS vol. 150), p. 251; Waters, *Defeat of the Enemy Attack on Shipping*, p. 123; Syrett, *U-boat Situations and Trends*, pp. 398, 478–9.

[2]Dönitz, *Memoirs*, p. 415.

[3]Ibid., pp. 416–17; Morison, *Atlantic Battle Won*, pp 278–80, & 159–77; Milner, *Battle of the Atlantic*, p. 181; P. Lundberg, 'Allied Co-operation', in S. Howarth & D. Law, eds, *Battle of the Atlantic*, pp. 362–3.

[4]Waters, *Defeat of the Enemy Attack on Shipping*, pp. 122, 141–5.

[5]Ibid., pp. 154, 228.

strike against the convoys. The *Luftwaffe* also had over 100 torpedo aircraft in Norway, together with some reconnaissance planes. The air force was much reduced from its strength in 1942, however, while *Tirpitz* was put out of action for six months in late 1943 by midget submarines and when she had been repaired, carrier aircraft immobilised her for a further three months in the spring of 1944. She became no more than a paper threat, at best a floating coast defence battery, being sunk by RAF heavy bombers in November 1944. Meanwhile, *Scharnhorst*, endeavouring to attack a convoy around Christmas 1943, was despatched by the Home Fleet.[1]

The Arctic convoys were heavily protected by a strong close escort, which included one or two of the new escort carriers. These flew ancient Swordfish biplanes, slow but rugged aircraft, with many of the characteristics of helicopters, and able to fly in almost any weather (conditions were particularly severe in the Arctic winter) and they led an offensive effort against the U-boats, sinking 23 of them, often with rocket fire. A fine example of the use of escort carriers and their aircraft is the report of the sinking of *U-277* [96]. British use of CVEs was often criticised by the Americans but the British ships lacked the more lavish manning of the American vessels, had obsolete aircraft and had to contend with more hostile weather, As Andrew Lambert has remarked, 'The U-boat was being hunted, with success'. More U-boats were destroyed in Norwegian waters (37, with another three accidental losses), especially after the U-boats had to retreat to Norwegian bases after being forced to leave their bases in western France in August 1944, when they were about to be over-run by Allied armies [106].[2]

The Allies had landed in north-west France on 6 June 1944 and the U-boat arm sought to play a major role in preventing a lodgement. The U-boats were deployed from their Biscay bases and sought to move up the English Channel. Most of them were not schnorkel-equipped. They had very modest success, as the invasion convoys were heavily screened. The Allied navies also mounted extensive escort group and air patrols at the entrance to the Channel. Attacks from the east by midget submarines, E-boats, aircraft and mines proved equally ineffective and the U-boats suffered major casualties, most of the 25 boats committed being either

---

[1] J. P. Levy, *Britain's Home Fleet in World War II* (Basingstoke, 2003), pp. 138–51.
[2] A. D. Lambert, 'The Arctic Convoys: Seizing the Initiative: 1944–1945', in N. A. M. Rodger, ed., *Naval Power in the Twentieth Century* (Basingstoke, 1996), pp. 160 & 151–4; K. Dönitz, *Memoirs*, pp. 423–4; Milner, *Battle of the Atlantic*, p. 211; Morison, *Atlantic Battle Won*, pp. 305–9; Douglas et al., *Blue Water Navy*, p. 185; M. Whitby, ed., *Commanding Canadians: The Second World War Diaries of A. F. C. Layard* (Vancouver, 2005), pp. 246–54.

sunk or so heavily damaged that they had to return to harbour [95, 99].[1] There were now no hiding places in the deep.

In the spring of 1944 Dönitz sought a new hiding place in the shallow waters around the British Isles. The U-boats were sent to lie close inshore, where they found some safety among underwater rocks, tide rips, water of high density and wrecks. They were not easily detectable – until they showed their hand by moving out to attack merchant shipping, now routed mostly through the Channel. Their ability to hide and the fact that many were equipped with the virtually undetectable schnorkel made it hard to locate and attack them, The Allied air forces were certainly frustrated but there were now numerous escort groups which could spend time hunting down contacts and pounding them to destruction with frequent and massive depth charge attacks. They were aided by new charts which pinpointed underwater 'non-sub' obstructions and by the skilful use of echo sounders. In the period covered by this volume, some 72 U-boats were destroyed by Allied forces. Of these, towards the end of the war, a few were blown up by bombing in harbour and others were destroyed by the liberally-sown mines, while three were the victims of accidental loss; most were destroyed by anti-submarine forces in the waters around Britain [95, 99, 100, 102]. The documents serve to demonstrate the scale of the resources in aircraft and ships that the Allies were forced to deploy and also how unproductive and frustrating many 'contacts' were in practice. The inshore campaign was a headache but hardly a source of major shipping loss, and it frustrated Allied forces, particularly in the air, but Dönitz judged it to be unsustainable and called it off in March 1945 [106, 107, 108, 110, 112, 114, 118, 122].[2]

By that time, the new U-boats were beginning to become operational, while over a hundred were building; the Allies had wind of these formidable boats by the autumn of 1943 and forecast a production of 30 per month by 1945, with about 100 operational by the spring. They were of two kinds. Type XXI was a large ocean-going boat of 1600/1790 tons, schnorkel-equipped, with a streamlined hull, enhanced battery power, and could carry 23 torpedoes. It had improved radar and detection

---

[1]Syrett, ed., *Signals Intelligence*, pp. 277–92; Syrett, ed., *U-boat Situations and Trends*, pp. 394–5; Milner, *Battle of the Atlantic*, pp. 196–201, 211; Chalmers, *Max Horton*, p. 216; H. Probert, 'Allied Land-Based Anti-Submarine Warfare', in S. Howarth & D. Law, eds, *Battle of the Atlantic*, p. 384.

[2]Dönitz, *Memoirs*, p. 425; Syrett, ed., *U-boat Situations and Trends*, pp. 444, 452, 484–5; Whitby, *Commanding Canadians*, pp. 109–15, 259–60; J. Showell, *Führer Conferences*, pp. 455, 457, 463, 480; Douglas et al., *Blue Water Navy*, pp. 349–51, 370, 389, 391, 406–7; W. S. Chalmers, *Max Horton*, p. 217; D. W. Waters, *Defeat of the Enemy Attack on Shipping*, p. 129; Hackmann, *Seek and Strike*, p. 238; C. Barnett, *Engage the Enemy More Closely: The Royal Navy in the Second World War* (London, 1991), pp. 852–3.

equipment and could undertake voyages of 70 days, with about 10 days at a time spent under water. Its chief advantages were that it could fire blind from a submerged position, dive faster and deeper, run more or less silently, and use its greatly increased speed (15.6/17.2 knots) to close and withdraw from targets. The Type XXIII was a much smaller boat of about 230/254 tons, designed for coastal waters, carrying just two torpedoes but with the same qualities of silence and speed. Dönitz referred frequently to these boats and clearly saw in them a means of clawing back the initiative.[1]

The new boats were expected to be in service by the end of 1944. They were plagued, however, by teething troubles, which delayed their appearance until the spring of 1945. They were further delayed by Allied bombing of their pens, parts, factories and yards, and by the Red Army's advance along the Baltic, which deprived them of major production facilities and training areas. In the West, the Allied leaders were much exercised by these new boats, about which they had very full information as to their characteristics, numbers and progress – and to which they had no immediate answer. Their aircraft found it hard to detect schnorkel-equipped submerged boats, while the submarines could outrun most Allied escort vessels. Their silence, elusiveness and speed – and their potential numbers – appeared to threaten a new 'Happy Time' in which merchant ship sinkings rose significantly, though it was calculated that losses would not reach dangerous levels. All the same, the Allies, led by the First Sea Lord, Admiral Cunningham, who felt the chief responsibility for the safety of Allied shipping, particularly the reinforcement and resupply of the Allied expeditionary force, were constrained to throw everything they could at this new menace – extensive mining, blanket escort vessel coverage (including half-lame ships), enhanced air patrols, more intense bombing, and urging the Red Army ever westward. In the event, only one Type XXI got to sea and had an unproductive (though undetected) patrol. Several of the smaller boats hung around coastal waters and, though they caused virtually no damage, they also went undetected. The war ended before these new boats could have the effect both Dönitz and the Allies predicted for them.[2]

Could they have reversed the tide of the anti-submarine war, running strongly in the Allies' direction since May 1943, or even caused major Allied casualties? Were the Allies right to be very concerned about the

[1]Dönitz, *Memoirs*, pp. 427–8; Showell, *Führer Conferences*, 384–5, 391, 420, 433–4, 445–8, 467.

[2]Showell, *Führer Conferences*, pp. 433–4; Morison, *Atlantic Battle Won*, pp. 60–62; Douglas et al., *Blue Water Navy*, p. 397; Syrett, ed., *U-boat Situations and Trends*, p. 483.

potential of the new boats? Were their tactics right? It is most unlikely that there would have been enough of these boats, even if their production and training had been unimpaired, to cause more than an embarrassment to the Allies, who had a sufficiency of merchant bottoms and a vast fleet of escort vessels, as well as an air armada to protect the shipping; even if they would find it hard to locate and destroy these new enemies, their presence and strength probably would have deterred most attacks, for the U-boats had become timid after the spring of 1943. The Allies were nervous about increasing losses – indeed, so habituated had they become to scarcely any losses at all that those ships they did lose, like the *Leopoldville*, were invested with a regret proportionately greater than the more severe losses of 1941–43.[1] As to tactics, they employed everything they had to hand – ships, planes, bombs, mines, intelligence, search aids and attack systems – but it was acknowledged both at the time and by later authors that they had no real, effective answer to the new boats.[2] Given the sensitivity of shipping losses and the enhanced use of merchantmen following the Allies' move to the offensive, with the greater responsibility on navies and air forces to protect the large armies' men and materials, it is not surprising that Cunningham, the Combined Chiefs of Staff, Horton, Churchill and his Anti-U-boat Committee should express concern and take what measures they could to throw a protective blanket over the waters.[3] They were perhaps even more fortunate that the Walther boat, powered by hydrogen peroxide and even more revolutionary than the Types XXI and XXIII, and a true submarine, experienced development difficulties and had to be replaced by these other types, which represented, in comparison, souped-up conventional boats [79, 108, 110, 120].[4]

When Germany surrendered on 8 May 1945, U-boats were commanded to turn themselves in. Many did so, but many others were scuttled and a couple voyaged to a supposedly friendly Argentina, there to

---

[1]*Leopoldville*: Compagnie Maritime Belge, 1929, 11439t, 16k. She was torpedoed on 24 Dec 1944, en route for Cherbourg, by *U-486*: Morison, *Atlantic Battle Won*, pp. 334–6. Over 800 men (mainly US soldiers) died.

[2]J. Buckley, *The RAF and Trade Defence, 1919–1945* (Keele, 1995), pp. 178–89; Milner, *Battle of the Atlantic*, pp. 218–9, 230–6; Douglas et al., *Blue Water Navy*, p. 391; Syrett, ed,. *U-boat Situations and Trends*, p. 483.

[3]Cunningham to Actg Adm G. C. Jones, RCN, 25 Jan 1945, in Simpson, ed., *The Cunningham Papers*, II, pp. 251–5; Murfett, *Naval Warfare*, p. 429; see also above, Part I, pp. 38–9 [Doc. 14], 61 [Doc. 35], 74–6 [Docs. 50 and 51].

[4]Prof H. Walther invented a hydrogen peroxide propulsion unit for U-boats in 1936 but it had many teething troubles and was not ready to be used in the war. See Dönitz, *Memoirs*, pp. 128, 235, 236, 265–6, 352–4. After the war, the Western Allies were anxious to acquire Walther and the Walther Werke and deny the Russians access to the research and development. The RN later built two experimental submarines using Walther's propulsion unit. See Simpson, ed., *Cunningham Papers*, II, pp. 262, 263, 265.

be interned. It was agreed amongst the three principal Allies that most U-boats should be scrapped or sunk in deep water but some 30 boats, including some of the latest types were apportioned between the Americans, the British and the Soviets for experimental use. Dr Walther and his technology were recruited by the West, but the (rather dangerous) hydrogen peroxide boat was quickly overtaken by the nuclear submarine.[1]

Thus ended the anti-submarine war, with a resounding Allied victory, first achieved in May 1943 and confirmed in the subsequent months, and with a final twist in the tail which was more promise than actuality. Victory was a matter of overwhelming force in the air and on the sea. It depended on clear divisions of responsibility between the Allies, efficient organisation and co-ordination, experience and careful training, subtle tactics, superior intelligence, a sustained lead in science and technology, and the shortcomings of German naval policy.[2]

[1]The three major Allies were entitled to 10 U-boats each, mainly for experimental purposes. See Part I, pp. 78–82 [Docs. 54 and 55].

[2]R. W. Love, Jr, *History of the U.S. Navy*, II, *1942–1991* (Harrisburg, PA, 1992), pp. 116–17.

65. *Admiralty to BAD*

[CAB 122/1510]   7 October 1943

... We accept the conditions attached to Cominch's offer in his despatch 072210 of August last [not reproduced] that it was 'contingent on our acquiescence in removal of US squadrons in the Bay on the orders of Cominch in the event of [changes?] in US strategic requirements' as being reasonable if somewhat peremptory. But we are not aware of any situation in any US strategic area calling for the withdrawal of these squadrons from the Bay before they are all in action.

66. *Attack on a U-boat by Sunderland J/423,*
RCAF, Castle Archdale

[ADM 199/1415]   10 October 1943

[The attack took place] on 8 October 1943 [at] 1938 [hours].

Weather Conditions: Wind 200°, 30 knots, weather poor, cloud 10/10, base 500 feet, sea very rough, visibility varying from 0–0.5 miles.

Depth of Water: Ocean depth.

Duty: Escorting convoy SC 143.

Nature of Initial Contact: Aircraft was carrying out 'Frog' patrol [at] 300 feet, [when] a wake and then a surfaced U-boat was sighted dead ahead at a distance of 100 yards.

Course and Speed of U-boat: Between 110° and 180°, 8–10 knots (in very rough sea).

Distance of U-boat from Convoy: 225°, 35 miles.

Direction of Approach: Aircraft flew straight over the U-boat, the rear gunner opened fire while the pilot turned to port a few hundred yards away to deliver his attack, reducing height to 100 feet. U-boat then opened fire with AA guns, turning to port at 8–10 knots, until it reached a point where it appeared to lose forward motion in a pivot. When 550 yards distant, aircraft opened fire with 0.5 in gun in nose of aircraft, hits were seen on the conning tower. Tracers from the U-boat's fire were numerous below aircraft, bursting approximately 300 yards behind.

At about 200 yards' range AA fire from the U-boat stopped and aircraft tracked straight over the conning tower and attacked from Red 30° to the U-boat's course.

Details of Attack: Three Mark XI Torpex depth charges, set to 25 feet depth and spaced 11 feet apart, were released from a height of 100 feet.

Time of Release: While U-boat was fully surfaced.

Failures: Four depth charges were selected, three released and functioned correctly, one hung up.

Estimate Position of Explosion: Nos. 1 & 2 on 30° angle to port of U-boat; No. 3 to starboard slightly astern of conning tower; No. 2 explosion was within 10 feet.

Surface Evidence: No. 2 depth charge explosion lifted the conning tower some 15 feet in the air; it was seen to roll heavily to starboard until it was completely obscured from view by plume of third depth charge. When this plume had subsided, the U-boat could not be seen and had obviously disappeared below the surface.

The Captain manoeuvred for the second attack and on arrival at the scene, at least 15 survivors of the U-boat's crew were seen swimming in a rapidly spreading oil patch. White foam was rising in the centre of the patch. A great deal of debris was floating all over the sea.

When the aircraft left the scene, the oil had spread steadily to approximately a quarter of a mile in length.

Subsequent Actions of Aircraft: 'J' circled over the wreckage for 20 minutes, dropping three flame floats and a marine marker.

SNO was informed on R/T. At 2005 aircraft set course for base having previously been recalled. Ten minutes later aircraft met destroyers to whom position of attack was given by R/T at their request.

Description of U-boat: U-boat was of German 517-ton type – either 'K.13' or '113' was painted in red on the conning tower. It was camouflaged black and grey. Jumping wires were seen running from stem to stern of the conning tower. One 4.7 in gun forward of the conning tower and numerous machine guns and cannon round conning tower.

Decision of U-boat Assessment Committee: From visual evidence of survivors in the water and a great many similar objects of wreckage and oil, the attack is assessed as 'Known sunk'.

U-boat Report

Addressees: DASW, Admiralty.
Station Submitting: Castle Archdale.
Camouflage: Arctic.
Pilot: F/O Russell, A. H. (Canada).

Crew: [5 Canadian, 5 British].
Whether he has previously attacked a U-boat: Yes.

Was aircraft: ... (ii) Escorting a Convoy: Yes. ...

....

Who sighted U-boat first?: 2nd Pilot.
Was his sighting with naked eye or binoculars?: Naked eye.
Ground speed of attack: 135 knots.
If [U-boat] was attacked by gunfire, estimate number of rounds fired at U-boat and were any hits obtained: 500 rounds of 0.303 in. from four guns in tail turret and 80 rounds from 0.5 in. in bow. Hits observed on conning tower.
Was ASV on, if so was it of any assistance?: On, no assistance.
Squadron Commander's Remarks: An excellent and most successful attack.

Wing Commander J. C. Frizzle, RCAF, to OC, 423 Squadron, RCAF.
12 October 1943.

On 8 October I was flying with the crew of 'J' as air escort of convoy SC 143. On contacting the convoy ... we had been ordered by the SNO to carry out a 'Frog' patrol. We had been doing this patrol for approximately 45 minutes with myself as pilot at the time and were flying on a course of 343°. The weather at this time, and for the past several hours, had been very low cloud and continuous light and heavy rain. Thus, flying at 500 feet, we could see the water 50% of the time, with visibility ranging intermittently from nought to one mile. The flying therefore was principally on instruments and as pilot, I was not able to act as a look-out to any great degree.

As we came out of a cloud, I noticed the second pilot, F/O Mensaul [RCAF], lean forward for a better look at something. At the same time I looked up and saw a prominent wake ahead with the object making the wake obscured by the bow of the aircraft, and almost immediately the 2nd pilot yelled 'It's a submarine'. We were flying with a very strong wind on our port side, and in a matter of seconds had drifted to starboard sufficiently for me to identify the conning tower of a fully-surfaced U-boat. I continued on approximately the same course, and in going away sufficiently far to turn in for an attack, I started to turn to port and told the second pilot to get F/O Russell to take over. In the meantime I believe F/O Russell had instructed the wireless operator to send out a '465', and instruct the galley to put the DC's out.

As F/O Russell took over control, we were at 500 feet, and not more than 700 yards on the U-boat's port [side, in a] fairly steep angle because of our proximity to the U-boat. I checked the position of the DC fuzing switches and circuit lights and watched the fire from the U-boat and from our forward guns. I noted that fire from the U-boat all appeared to be going below the aircraft, but I was not sure where the fire was coming from. I did not observe any personnel on the U-boat deck though it made no effort to submerge. Our own fire from the 0.5 in. gun appeared very accurate, and apparently direct hits were ricocheting in all directions.

The aircraft passed over the U-boat at approximately 100 feet, and as we climbed with a fairly steep turn to port the galley advised that only three DC's had dropped. The 2nd pilot got out of his seat and reset the DC Distributor, and we turned in for a second attack. However, as we approached for a second attack there was no submarine visible. There was in place 15 or more Germans who appeared to be looking up at the aircraft, and a considerable amount of debris floating around. The DC's were therefore not dropped. My instantaneous reaction at the time was that the submarine had been definitely destroyed.[1]

67.   *Noble to King*

[RG 38]   16 October 1943

May I refer to your 082213 of 9 October [not reproduced], in which you informed Admiral Syfret of your decision to move four Naval Liberator and one Naval Catalina Squadrons from the Bay Offensive.

2. I have been in communication with the Admiralty, who view your decision with considerable concern.

3. While agreeing that the results during the past two months have been less profitable than we hoped, we are confident that by increasing the flying effort by night we can force the U-boats again to surface by day.

4. Among the many factors which have militated against complete success is the shortage of Leigh Lights in your Squadrons, but the situation will greatly improve by the end of this month.[2]

---

[1]*U-610*: no survivors; sunk SW of Rockall.

Short Sunderland: flying boat; 1937; 4 engines; 10–13 crew; 231mph; 2980m; 10–14mg; 2000lbs bombs.

Castle Archdale: flying boat base, N Ireland.

F/O A. H. Russell, RCAF: unidentified.

W/Cdr J. C. Frizzle, RCAF: unidentified.

[2]Leigh Lights: a pair of searchlights suspended below an aircraft's fuselage, focused on the sea; invaluable for attacking U-boats at night.

5. We are unaware of assurances that winter weather would reduce the Bay Offensive and since the record of last winter shows no marked decrease in flying effort due to weather, we had hoped to maintain a vigorous offensive.

6. We are positive that in the Bay the hardest blow of our combined A/S war effort can be struck, as all operational U-boats must pass this area, but without the help of American Squadrons it cannot be decisive.

...

8. We therefore request that you leave these Squadrons where they are, at least until the end of the year, by which time our increased night offensive should have proved its effectiveness, and in any case I request you to withhold action until consideration of our views is possible.

68.   *Rear Admiral F. S. Low, US Navy, to King*[1]

[RG 38]   16 October 1943

1. The studies which justified the Bay offensive as an effective means of crippling the U-boat campaign estimated that with U-boat sightings at the rate of 40 flying hours per sighting, 260 planes could kill 25 U-boats per month and cripple more than that number additional. The best period of air operations in the Bay Offensive with over 200 planes operating gave approximately this result with about 70 hours of flying per sighting and 12 kills in the month of July.

2. However, since the U-boats have commenced using radar they have proceeded through the Bay almost unmolested by aircraft. There have been no U-boats sunk by aircraft since 2 August and there were 317 flying hours per sighting during August and September. During these two months, however, there were about 30 Allied planes lost on this offensive.

3. Until effective technology and/or tactical counter measures are devised to render our air attack effective again, it isn't even good hunting in the Bay. As U-boats must attack our main supply lines eventually or acknowledge defeat, employment of our VLR aircraft to further protect our supply lines is desirable.

[1]RA F. S. Low, US Navy (1894–1964): USNA 1915; s/m; NWC 1926; CO *Paul Jones* 1932–5; Cdr, S/m Sqdn 13, 1937–9; Atl F staff Dec 1940–Aug 1941; *Wichita* N Africa 1942–3; RA & CoS, 10 F May 1943–June 1945; CruDiv 16; Okinawa 1945; Cdr, Dd, Pac F 1945–7; Cdr, W Sea Frontier 1953–6; Adm & ret.

69.   *King to Noble*

[Op Arch, King 4]   19 October 1943

1. I have given careful and sympathetic consideration to the view presented in your letter of 16 October [no. 67] and the attached 'Appreciation of the Bay offensive' [not reproduced].

2. Without wishing in any way to complicate the record further, I feel that I must draw attention briefly to those matters on which we do not appear to see eye to eye.

(a) *Duration of US participation:* from the beginning of conversations as to US participation in the Bay Offensive, we have been given the impression by Air Marshal Slessor and others that it would be a matter of limited duration as far as the US Squadrons were concerned. All of our plans (of which we kept you fully informed) have been premised on this assurance. If, as you now state, it has been your intention from the beginning to maintain a vigorous offensive with continuing aid of our squadrons it appears to me unfortunate that this was not made clear at the outset.[1]

(b) *Absence of Leigh Lights:* In a communication of May 1943 [not reproduced] from the Admiralty it was stated in effect that Coastal Command could adapt to night work sufficient additional British aircraft to provide the appropriate night components of combined forces in the Bay. In support of this we intend to make searchlight installations in certain of our planes in the near future as improved lights become available.

(c) *Paragraph 6 of the 'Appreciation':* the statement is made in this paragraph that there is no evidence to substantiate that U-boats are equipped with AA radar. By this I assume is meant a radar that can detect our planes. We have unmistakeable evidence of the existence of such a radar. I make this point only because of the serious implications in the event this fact is not appreciated by those who are conducting the Bay Offensive.

3. From the beginning I have been well aware of the advantages that would accrue from an effective offensive in the Bay. Because of this feeling and with due regard to other responsibilities and commitments, I am now agreeable to the following modifications of my 082213 to Comnaveu [not reproduced].

---

[1]ACM Sir Philip Slessor (1897–1979): Air Staff 1939; 5 Group, Bomber Cmd 1941; ACAS 1942; AOC-in-C, Coastal Command Feb 1943–Jan 1944; AOC Med 1944; Air Staff 1945.

(a) There will be retained in the UK until 1 January 1944 for operations in the Bay Offensive, a PBY [Catalina] Squadron and two of the B-24 [Liberator] Squadrons now there. Steps will be taken forthwith to provide full US logistic support. It is estimated that this support will enable these three squadrons to operate at a materially higher degree of effectiveness than present maintenance standards permit.

(b) I shall direct that on 1 November 1943, two of the B-24 squadrons now [in] the UK proceed to the Moroccan Sea Frontier for the relief of the Army squadrons now there. I further propose at about this time to send a new B-24 Squadron from this country for temporary duty in the Moroccan Sea Frontier with ultimate destination the Azores.[1]

4. Extension of employment of three of our squadrons now in [the] UK until 1 January 1944 is made with the understanding that the Admiralty will make every possible effort before that date to provide reliefs for these squadrons which I anticipate may then be required in other areas.

5. May I request that you communicate the sense of the foregoing to appropriate British authorities at once. I shall advise Admiral Stark.

70. *King to Noble*

[Op Arch, King 4]   26 October 1943

1. I find in the 'Remarks on the Bay Offensive' of 23 October [not reproduced] a reiteration of arguments contained in previous memoranda. These arguments continue to be unconvincing because they persist in dealing with the past and not with the present. The Bay Offensive was profitable employment for aircraft engaged in killing U-boats and it may again be profitable but the fact remains that for a period of nearly three months, since 2 August, aircraft have not sunk U-boats in the Bay. I am, however, fully aware of the 'nuisance' value of present operations.

2. I note the repeated contention that the Bay project has always been considered by the British to be continuing. I have never taken exception to this premise but to the clear implication by Air Marshal Slessor and others that *United States* participation was to be on a short term basis, and my agreement to such participation was premised on this assumption.

[1]Consolidated Catalina (PBY): US flying boat; 1935; 2 engines; 8 crew; 179mph; 3100m; 5mg; 2000lbs bombs.

Consolidated Liberator (B-24): US heavy bomber; 1939; 4 engines; 12 crew; 300mph; 2100m; 10 mg; 5000lbs bombs.

3. Considerations applying entirely to US matters and having to do with release of Army A/S Squadrons for employment of high priority with their Bomber Command require that one Liberator Squadron proceed from [the] UK to [the] Moroccan Sea Frontier on 1 November for the relief of an Army Squadron there. I am agreeable to leaving the third Naval B-24 Squadron in the UK for the time being, pending the arrival of full, logistic support for the two other Naval B-24 Squadrons, which is to be provided in compliance with my signal 192156 to Comnaveu [not reproduced] and pending the more pressing need for this squadron in the Azores or elsewhere.

4. When I have relieved both Army B-24 squadrons in the Moroccan Sea Frontier and additional VLR Squadrons become available, I shall give further consideration to replacement of the fourth Liberator Squadron in the Bay, having due regards to our other commitments including the Azores.

5. I shall continue to examine the results of the Bay Offensive and I must make it clear at this time and request specific concurrence that if the effectiveness of aircraft in the Bay does not materially improve before 1 January 1944, I shall then remove US squadrons from the Bay to whatever extent they can be more profitably employed elsewhere in sinking submarines.

6. As to paragraph 5 of the referred memorandum, I suggest this is a matter for reference to the CCS.

71.   *Meeting of the Anti-U-boat Warfare Committee*[1]

[CAB 86/2]   27 October 1943

...

2. *U-boat Trend:*

[The VCNS[2] stated that] ... The effect of the bombing of U-boat bases and production centres is now having an undoubted effect, and it was estimated that the output of U-boats was now down by approximately one-third. There had been two main attacks on Atlantic convoys recently. In the first of these the Polish destroyer *Orkan* had been lost but the enemy probably lost three U-boats. In the second attack on an outward bound convoy, one merchant vessel had been sunk at

---

[1]Anti-U-boat Warfare Cttee: est by PM, who usually attended; mix of UK & US mil, civil & political members; regular meetings.
[2]VA Syfret.

the probable cost to the enemy of six U-boats. We had been lucky, however, in that in both cases a strong escort and air cover had been available.

It appeared that the enemy was moving his main concentrations South and West, away from Iceland, which had proved such a dangerous area to him. Arrangements for air cover from the Azores were proceeding satisfactorily. He mentioned the very good work which had been carried out by US aircraft in the area North of the Azores. The Bay Offensive had been kept up, and it was hoped to obtain better results when more Liberator aircraft equipped with Leigh-Lights become available. The enemy's campaign in the Indian Ocean appeared to be dying down.

...

72. *Chiefs of Staff: 268th Meeting*

[CAB 122/1510]   3 November 1943

...

7. *US VLR Squadrons:*

Sir Andrew Cunningham said ... it would be better dealt with through BAD. Our case was not a strong one, since we had raised no objection at the time the squadrons were provided to the suggested date of withdrawal put forward by Admiral King.

73. *Captain H. W. Morey, RN, to Rear Admiral F. S. Low,*
US Navy[1]

[RG 38/32]   5 November 1943

In our conversation the other day, you expressed an interest in items of information which I receive periodically from the Admiralty, and the following are a few extracted from a letter which I have had, dated 27 October.

Convoy Formation:

You will remember a little while back some trials taking place in the North Atlantic as to the formation of the columns and screening of the

---

[1]Capt H. W. Morey: ret; A/Capt *President*; SO (Trade), BAD.

convoy by smoke as an anti-U-boat protective measure. Unfortunately, the various claims made for different formations conflict in their requirements. Commanders dislike more than 12 columns on account of signalling difficulties, the scientists want as large a convoy as possible, and the 'V' formation does not allow for more than 42 ships, if the Commodore's wish is accepted. As North Atlantic convoys average in the neighbourhood of 60 ships each the question of formation has been allowed to lapse somewhat.

As regards smoke making, the fitting of CSA as an anti-U-boat protection has been turned down by the Admiralty.

Indian Ocean Convoys:

You may have seen C-in-C, Eastern Fleet's latest arrangement of convoy formation. It is fully realised that the scheme looks rather more impressive on paper than in fact, as it is accepted that the available escorts are both thin and inexperienced. It is hoped, however, that this situation will improve shortly.

74. *Chiefs of Staff to Joint Services Mission*

[CAB 122/1510]   7 November 1943

...

2. We have considered the recent telegrams on the subject of a proposal by Cominch to withdraw certain US Navy Squadrons from the anti-U-boat offensive in the Bay of Biscay.

3. We do press for the retention in the UK of the one squadron now due to leave for Morocco. We note with regret that orders for this move have already been issued and the move would have taken place on 1 November but for bad weather. But we urge that this squadron should be employed in the Bay Offensive from its new base in Morocco as soon as it is operational. We consider that the former US strength of 61 [almost certainly six] Liberator squadrons between the US and Morocco should be maintained, if necessary, at the expense of other areas which are at present unquestionably of less importance to the U-boat war.

4. We regret the misunderstanding which led Admiral King to form the impression that US participation in the Bay Offensive was on a short term basis. This may have arisen from CCS (W) 587 of 21 April [1943] [not reproduced] and subsequent discussions in which it was emphasised that US co-operation was required as quickly as possible to take advantage of the enemy's being unable to listen to centimetric ASV [radar].

The impression may thus have been formed that the aircraft would not be required in the winter. Air Marshal Slessor has never intended to imply an operation of short duration but only that it was very important to act quickly.

5. We realise that the reasons for Cominch's present proposals are mainly administrative. The strategic effects of the changes proposed will however be a serious reduction in our combined strength in the Bay and Gibraltar/Morocco areas. ... We regard the Bay Offensive as still being a key factor in the war against the U-boats and stress that ... we consider [it] to be of major importance. ... Since 2 August aircraft have been responsible for five kills in the Bay and its approaches, and a further 18 Leigh Light attacks have taken place the results of which cannot yet be assessed.

6. The A/S statistics for the month of September have a significant bearing on the suggestion that the Bay is less profitable and no more unsafe for U-boats than any other areas. In the Bay Offensive in September 14,404 hours were flown for 14 sightings and 12 attacks resulting in one kill and one damaged and interned in Vigo as well as nine Leigh-Light attacks not yet assessed[;] hours flown per sighting were 600.[1] On the basis of hours flown per sighting (the latter representing an opportunity for a kill) the Bay compares very favourably with other areas and the statistics for October which are not yet complete look like following similar lines. In the Bay Offensive therefore there were 13 sightings and 10 attacks (including five Leigh-Light unassessed) and one kill.

7. The Gibraltar/Morocco area is also extremely profitable, the figures there for September being 11 sightings and seven attacks (of which five were Leigh-Light and still unassessed) for 2831 hours of flying or one sighting per 257 hours[;] in October there were six sightings in this area and three attacks (all Leigh-Light, unassessed). This is excluding the hours flown from Gibraltar and [Port] Lyautey in the Bay approaches which are included in the figures in paragraph 3 above.

8. ... Since July U-boat attacks have changed and offensive patrols in the Bay and its approaches have had to be extended westwards and southwards to catch U-boats on passage in and out. Use of the Azores may well further extend [the] scope of the Bay Offensive.

---

[1] *U-760*: damaged by US Naval aircraft, 12 Aug 1943; interned Vigo 8 Sept 1943.

9. In view of the foregoing the strategic argument for maintaining the A/S offensive in the Bay and Gibraltar/Morocco areas at the greatest possible strength seem unanswerable to us.

10. ... we would entirely agree that the US squadrons and, we would add, British squadrons if required, should be moved away from the Bay ... when it is agreed ... that they could be more profitably employed elsewhere.

75. *The Chiefs of Staff to the Joint Services Staff Mission*

[CAB 122/1510]   7 November 1943

1. We have been considering the recent interchange of signals between the Admiralty and BAD and the representation by Noble and Welsh to the Admiralty and Air Ministry on the subject of Cominch's proposal to withdraw certain squadrons from the Bay Offensive.[1]

2. In order to avoid further misunderstandings and to clarify the responsibility for movements of anti-submarine forces in and out of the different strategic areas, we should look to establish certain agreed principles for the joint conduct of anti-U-boat operations in the Atlantic.

3. The principles are as follows:

(a) Any redistribution between British, Canadian and US areas of responsibility in the Atlantic will be effected in concert between the British, Canadian and US authorities concerned, reference being made to the CCS if necessary.

(b) The disposition of A/S units within any area of the North Atlantic will be a matter for decision by the British, Canadian and American authorities according to whether the area concerned is one for which Britain, Canada or the US are responsible in accordance with the conclusions of the authorities to whom the squadrons belong.

(c) The operational direction of all anti-submarine squadrons in a British, Canadian or American area of responsibility in the Atlantic shall be vested in the appropriate British, Canadian or American authority.

4. ... [We do not wish to go directly to the CCS] and antagonise King, who would feel he was being put on the spot. On the other hand it is held that unless King is made to accept these or similar principles we shall be

---

[1] AVM W. L. Welsh (1891–1962): Dir, Organisation 1934–7; Air Member, Supply & Organisation Sep 1937–40; AOC-in-C Technical Trng Cmd 1940–41; AOC-in-C Flying Trng Cmd 1941–2; TORCH 1942; head, RAF Delegation, US 1943–4; ret 1944.

perpetually liable to arbitrary action on his part resulting in disorganisation of our combined arrangements for anti-U-boat warfare.

5. We are content to leave it to you to decide what action is best calculated to achieve our object, which is to ensure the most efficient system of control of the combined anti-U-boat effort with minimum adverse effect on our relations with the American Chiefs of Staff.

76. *Memorandum from King to JCS*

[CAB 122/1510]   9 November 1943

Report on Recent and Prospective Developments in A/S Operations since QUADRANT.
1. *Operations – Availability and Employment of Surface Craft and Aircraft*

(a) In September, 17 merchant ships were sunk, in October 15. In September 11 U-boats were sunk, in October 32. For 1942, one submarine was sunk or probably sunk for every 9.3 merchant vessels lost. For 1943 to date this figure is 2.1 merchant vessels; for the past five months: 0.5.
(b) Enclosure (A) [not reproduced] indicates the status of Atlantic Fleet and Sea Frontier sections as of 1 August and 1 November. Significant are:

(i) The increase of 51 DEs in the Atlantic Fleet;
(ii) From 1 August to 1 November the decrease in the number of destroyers temporarily assigned to ComNav was 28 to 13.
(iii) There were still 16 Pacific Fleet DDs on temporary duty with Cinclant on 1 November.

(c) Matters of interest in the prospective escort situation are:

(i) Commencing with UGS 22 (about 25 October) a minimum escort strength of one DE division plus one DD division (10 ships) was established for these convoys. This will be raised to 12 as a standard and Cinclant plans to gradually increase this to 16 when more slow DEs become available.;
(ii) The number of escort groups for CU convoys is to be increased from one to four because of [a] reduced sailing interval.
(iii) DesDiv 57 (ODDs) now with 4th Fleet will be replaced by CortDiv 18. The four ODDs in Caribbean Sea Frontier and one ODD in Panama Sea Frontier will also be replaced by 327ft Coast Guard Cutters.
(iv) Eighteen acquired craft [in the] 100–150ft category in Sea Frontiers and Lant Fleet will be replaced by standard service designed craft, and four have been decommissioned without relief.

(d) Enclosure (B) [not reproduced] indicates the status of A/S aircraft as of 1 August and 1 November.

(i) The A/S aircraft available are adequate to cope with the anti-submarine position present and prospective. It should be noted, however, that the availability of PVs and B-24s until 1944 will not permit those squadrons to be built up to 15 planes as planned and that there is some question as to whether the eight B-24 squadrons can be maintained at a strength of 12 planes, unless B-24s not now in the program for the Atlantic are obtained. This plane shortage may adversely affect our ability to meet emergencies. (iii) The present CVE situation will remain unchanged until the end of the year when *Mission Bay* is scheduled to arrive in the Atlantic. Six additional CVEs are scheduled to arrive on the east coast during the first quarter of the calendar year 1944. The CVEs have continued the effective offensive operations against U-boats and only one ship has been sunk in convoys in the Atlantic that have been covered by a US CVE Support Group;

(iii) All Army aircraft in our Sea Frontiers were relieved from A/S duties with the Navy by 1 October with the exception of one squadron of B-25s in the Caribbean Sea Frontier equipped with 75mm cannon which were loaned to the Navy for anti-submarine use of that weapon.[1] The four Army B-24 squadrons on anti-submarine duties in the UK were relieved by Navy squadrons in October. The two remaining Army B-24 squadrons in anti-submarine operations in Morocco are in process of being relieved by Navy B-24 squadrons.

2. *Materiel*

(A) Surface Craft:

(i) A single towed parallel rod noisemaker is now issued to all US escorts to counter enemy acoustic torpedoes. Expendable devices actuated by explosives or air are under test and give promise of being superior to FIXER; (ii) A surface craft evaluation division of the A/S Development Detachment has been established, and in addition to conducting experiments will further develop coordinated air and surface anti-submarine tactics; (iii) Mark IX Depth Charges with proximity pistol [are] now being produced with quantity production commencing 1December; (v) Bearing Deviation Indicators to improve echo-ranging sound equipment [are] in quantity production;

---

[1]North American Mitchell (B-25): US medium bomber; 1940; 2 engines; 6 crew; 275mph; 1275m; 13mg; 4000lbs bombs.

(vi) Bathythermograph giving a water temperature depth curve is now to be issued to escorts to obtain more accurate information on the sound conditions;

(vii) 100-inch Dome being installed in new construction DDs will give improved echo-ranging performance at higher speeds over 20 knots;

(viii) Shipboard A/S Attack Teacher is to be issued to assist in shipboard training;

(ix) Prospective developments to be accomplished in the next six months are:

(a) Mark IX Model 2 Depth Charge with Döppler AC Proximity Fuse and improved sinking rate;

(b) Scatter Depth Charges to be projected from the usual projector;

(c) Mark XII Depth Charge – small fast sinking stern-dropped depth charges;

(d) The net result to be expected from improvements in depth charges is that effectiveness of patterns will be improved about six times.

(B) Aircraft:

(1) Rocket Projectile equipment to be introduced into service in both the Atlantic and Pacific Fleets; in the Atlantic as an A/S weapon;

(2) Interception receivers for enemy radar without DF and homing features are being installed in many Atlantic Fleet aircraft. A special test plane (B-24) is now in Moroccan Sea Frontier for purpose of obtaining data on German Radar wavelengths, etc., and when this is determined installed detectors will be made directional.

(3) Sono-radio Buoys and associated receivers are being installed in the Atlantic Fleet aircraft in limited numbers.

(4) Aircraft tactics to counter radar and use of intercept receivers by the enemy are being revised as new information is received.

(5) Increased forward firing power, additional armor and leak-proof tanks are being provided for all A/S aircraft to offset fighting back tactics of U-boats.

77. *King to Noble*

[Op Arch, King 4]   10 November 1943

Thank you for your letter of 5 November dealing with contemplated assignments and operations of British CVEs.

It would appear that with the shore-based and carrier-based aircraft available to each of us plus the advantage of the Azores base, we should be able to quite satisfactorily cover all important Allied shipping.

78.   *Meeting of the Anti-U-boat Warfare Committee*

[ADM 205/30]   11 November 1943

...

III. *American CVEs: Reports of Movements*

ACNS (UT)[1] informed the Committee of the recent case of a US carrier operating in the close vicinity of a UK/Gibraltar convoy without the Admiralty being aware of her exact position. He remarked [that] this might well lead to serious incidents and also, in this case, the carrier would have been of great assistance with the convoy, which had been attacked, if the Admiralty could have been given sufficient warning of her intended area of operation.

...

6. AOC-in-C, Coastal Command, stated that a Liberator had, in fact, unexpectedly encountered carrier aircraft on this occasion.[2]

7. Admiral Wilson [US Navy] said that he would raise this particular incident with the American Authorities with a view to improving exchange of information as to movements of carriers.[3]

8. ACNS (UT) then raised the point of American carriers operating with British convoys and vice versa, asking whether any difficulty was anticipated regarding operating procedure. C-in-C, Western Approaches, stated that he had already visualised such a situation and was investigating the matter.[4]

9. It was suggested that a meeting to discuss the matter between the Admiralty, American Naval Authorities, Western Approaches and Coastal Command would be the best solution. ACNS (UT) undertook to speak with Admiral Wilson about the best way to approach this problem.

---

[1]Adm Sir John Edelsten (1891–1966): ent RN 1913; Capt 1933; DDP 1938; SNO, Somaliland 1940; Cdre & CoS Med F 1941; RA & ACNS (UT) 1942; RA (D) BPF 1945; VA, 1 BS 1945; 4 CS 1946; VCNS 1947; Adm & C-in-C Med 1950; C-in-C Portsmouth 1950–52; ret 1954.

[2]AM Slessor.

[3]Rear Adm G. Barry Wilson, US Navy: unidentified.

[4]Adm Sir Max Horton (1883–1950): ent RN 1898; s/m; great success in E-9 1914; CO, s/m flotilla, Baltic 1919–20; Capt 1920; CoS to Adm Keyes, C-in-C Portsmouth; *Resolution* Med F; RA 1932; 2inC, Home F 1934–5; 1 CS, Med F 1935; VA 1936; Reserve F 1937–9; Northern Patrol 1939; FO S/M 1940; refused Home F because he wanted control of Coastal Cmd; C-in-C W Apps 1942–5; W. S. Chalmers, *Max Horton and the Western Approaches* (London, 1954).

79.   *Stark to Knox*[1]

[RG 13/24]   15 November 1943

... we can only assume that some of the best brains in Germany are working on plans, how to make the submarine weapon effective. We must never relax being on the look-out for counter-measures, new tactics, new weapons, etc. It is a case of increasing vigilance and pressure. ...

80.   *Syfret to Stark*

[Op Arch, Stark A2]   28 November 1943

... The policy in this paper [probably by Cdr Solberg, US Navy][2] is one inviting encounters with U-boats rather than evading them as in the past. The difficulty of finding convoys has been at the root of the U-boats' troubles in the North Atlantic, and direct routeing would remove this difficulty. This, it may be argued, is the main object of direct routeing in order to invite attack, but what is omitted in this argument is that the U-boats need not accept all of the invitations, and once the difficulty of sighting is removed, it is the U-boats who will decide where and what to attack, and in fact their whole behaviour during reconnaissance and attacking will be modified in their favour.

Under conditions of scattered routes and of evasive routeing the scarcity of convoy sightings make it a vital necessity for the U-boats to form into long reconnaissance lines and to make the maximum possible use of every sighting, even though the effort exposes them to serious counter attacks from the air and surface forces. Even with these exertions the U-boats have in the past not been able to put in more than about one attack per cruise, thus returning to port with a high percentage of torpedoes unspent. This is so in spite of long cruises involving re-fuelling, so that the U-boats have been severely opportunity-limited.

Under conditions of direct routeing the U-boats would have the following advantages:

1. They could form into more compact reconnaissance lines so that on making a sighting they could mass on the convoy more quickly and in bigger numbers, thus increasing the chances of success and of overwhelming the surface defences.

---

[1]Hon Frank Knox (1874–1944): Repub politician; newspaper publisher; VP candidate 1936; Sec of Navy 1940–44.
[2]Cdr Arthur Solberg, US Navy: unidentified.

2. There would probably be much less danger from the air because (a) the initial massing on to the convoy would be in a more advanced state before the arrival of strong air forces; (b) more convoys would be threatened and attacked, thus somewhat reducing the air protection available for any threatened convoy; (c) the compactness of the reconnaissance line would permit the U-boats to adopt maximum submergence while on patrol (should the area be covered by aircraft).

3. The greater opportunities for attack would reduce the necessity of taking risks.

4. The initiative as regards how many and which convoys to attack would lie largely with the U-boats.

The only certainty of direct routeing would be the 10% or so shorter route, but this is not thought great enough to balance the above disadvantages. It is likely that the greater assistance from support groups due to the closer proximity of convoys would be more than counter-balanced by the increase in the number of convoys under threat or under attack. In fact for this reason the surface protection as well as the air protection to threatened convoys would probably be less well directed than with evasive routeing.

It is considered therefore that direct routeing is nearly all in favour of the U-boats, and that it should not be adopted as long as the U-boats are operating in the North Atlantic.

81. *Alexander to Churchill*

[ADM 199/241]   1 December 1943

Joint Statement by the President and the Prime Minister, Cairo.

1. U-boat killings for November: 12 sunk or probably sunk; 6 other promising attacks under consideration.

2. Following is a draft statement:

'Anti-U-boat operations in November have been notable for the little the enemy has achieved for the great effort he has exerted. The number of merchant vessels sunk by U-boats in November is less than in any other month since May 1940.

'By means of aircraft operating from the Azores we have been able to improve the protection to our convoys and to diminish the area in which enemy U-boats were free from attack by our forces.

'The enemy has used long-range aircraft to assist in concentrating U-boats on our convoy routes, but in spite of this the hard blows we have delivered during the last few months have made him so cautious that his efforts have been ineffective.

'Due to this caution the number of opportunities presented to our forces for striking at the enemy U-boats has diminished; nevertheless the number of U-boats sunk in November has again exceeded the number of their victims.'

82.   *Meeting of the Anti-U-boat Warfare Committee*

[CAB 86/2]   1 December 1943

10. *MAC Aircraft Carriers*

...

Lord Cherwell asked what the position was regarding Helicopters.[1]

The First Lord of the Admiralty said that though experiments were going on they had been held up, chiefly by weather and that the project had not yet reached a stage where we could envisage the operational use of this type of aircraft.

Admiral Stark said that no reports had been received on this subject recently from America, and that his impression was that experiments were no more advanced over there.

83.   *Map Room Memorandum: White 89*

[MRF 17]   White House,
                                                  Washington, DC,
                                                  4 December 1943

...

Atlantic

ALUSNA Lisbon reports on 2 December that second interview with Salazar showed preservation of neutrality still paramount.[2] Without a cloak like the Anglo-Portuguese Alliance, he will not at present agree to granting any facilities directly to the US. He is also concerned with Portuguese participation in freeing Timor because of conviction that special

---

[1]Frederick Lindemann (Lord Cherwell) (1886–1957): Prof of Physics, Oxford; long-term friend of PM; chief of Admy statistics section; Lord 1941; Paymaster Gen 1942.

[2]Dr Antonio Salazar (1889–1970): PM & virtual dictator of Portugal 1932–68; neutral in war. Anglo-Portuguese Alliance: 1374 and later renewals.

German-Japanese arrangement exists which might produce German action in case of hostilities with Japan.

Salazar resists request for facilities on San Miguel because (1) it is the seat of government and is considered part of the Continent; (2) Portuguese Navy insists on exclusive use of harbor; (3) Portuguese Air Force must reserve field at Cablo de Peize for defence of islands, as provided in the British-Portuguese discussions.

It was suggested to him that the US construct, by private contractors or service contractors out of uniform, a field for Portugal at Santa Maria. Upon completion, if strategic situation warrants, the Anglo-Portuguese agreement would be enlarged to permit Allied military use, nominally British but actually largely American. This suggestion was not rejected and is believed under study.

Salazar is in full accord with maximum US use of Terceira provided use appears British so he can deny knowledge of US use. Believe British marking supplementary to US markings satisfactory.

84.   *King to Noble*

[CAB 122/1510]   13 December 1943

...

As to your statement that the Admiralty presume that I will discuss with them employment of our aircraft before withdrawing them from the Bay, ... I am unaware of any incident that would make it desirable at this time to circumscribe the employment of A/S Forces with machinery that up to now has not been necessary.

When we first assigned some of our US A/S Squadrons to British and Canadian operational control, this agreement was made with the clear understanding that if in my opinion it became necessary to shift the Squadrons, such shifts would be effected on the basis of my judgment of the situation within our area of responsibility.

...

Every action I have taken with respect to the deployment of our A/S Forces has been with due regard to the broad perspective of the whole Atlantic area. That we should have disagreed as to some deployments is natural, but that such an incident should now be made the vehicle whose effect would be to impede and delay action as to deployment of US A/S Forces is not, in my opinion, in the best interests of our combined effort.

85.   *Joint Staff Mission: 47th Meeting*

[CAB 122/1510]   16 December 1943

...

2. *Policy with regard to the employment of anti-submarine forces in the Atlantic*

...

Admiral Noble reminded the committee of the previous history of this question. Admiral King who had previously wished to withdraw all five US Naval squadrons from the Bay offensive, had been induced to retain all but one of them for this purpose,

London had felt, however, that it was essential to agree principles with regard to the employment of US and British A/S air forces in the Atlantic. Sir John Dill had written to Admiral King putting forward certain proposals. Admiral King had now replied to him (Admiral Noble) stating his view that the employment of A/S forces in the Atlantic could not be decided by 'Committee action' and taking the line that present arrangements were satisfactory.

It was wrong of Admiral King to maintain the position that he could take unilateral decisions with regard to A/S air forces, since it was obviously a matter of combined interest. In a signal from Admiral King it appeared that he did not, in fact, propose to remove the remaining squadrons for the present.

86.   *Rear Admiral Low, US Navy, to King*

[SPD 243]   23 December 1943

2. Cominch's intention to send B-24 squadron to Azores in mid-January [1944] holds.

3. Three squadrons in the Azores – [we] consider it acceptable at the present, but we may, at a later date, consider one more necessary.

...

9. Use of Liberators in emergency – ... the bald facts are that Air Marshal Slessor (probably from habit) has at least sanctioned an effort to get into the detailed administration of Hamilton's squadrons.[1] Ham-

---

[1]Hamilton, US Navy: unidentified.

ilton has successfully opposed him. In the one instance to which our attention has been called where the British state an emergency exists, and directed that some of Hamilton's planes go after Heinkels (to which Hamilton demurred), the facts seem to be that the emergency did not in fact exist, for a few hours later the British walked back on the cat.[1]

If the British state an emergency to exist and issue appropriate orders through the correct channels, our people should carry out the order. If subsequently it develops that the British position was unsupportable, we should take appropriate action up to and including, if necessary, removal of our squadrons.

87.   *Stark to Rear Admiral G. Barry Wilson, US Navy*

[SPD 243]   29 December 1943

[Attachment]

Escort Carriers

Admiral Blake asked me to get a list of the important changes made to our CVEs so that what we are doing might be compared with what the Admiralty is doing. Our list follows:

1. Catapult changes (to provide longer run).
2. Second catapult added (certain vessels only).
3. Flag quarters provided (flagships only).
4. Additional personnel accommodation for 200 men, 199 officers [?] (certain vessels only to be used for transport services).
5. Replace 5in 51 [caliber] guns with 5in 38 [caliber] guns.
6. Additional radar added.
7. Armament increased to 10 twin 40mm and 27 [of] 20mm.
8. CIC modified.
9. Bomb stowage [changed] to universal type.

Regarding 'Captain' class frigates, Admiral Horton wanted to know what we are doing on these. Cochrane is getting me a list. Cochrane states in general we are taking them, as well as the CVEs, off the pile and with very few alterations.[2]

---

[1] Heinkel He-177: Ger bomber; 1939; 2 engines; 6 crew; 295mph; 2260m; 2×20mm cannon, 4–6mg; 13225lbs bombs.
[2] Edward L. Cochrane, US Navy: Chf, Bu Ships 1943.

88.   *Air Marshal Sir John Slessor to Stark*

[SPD 243]   [n.d., December 1943]

...

2. ... our COS have, I believe, come to certain agreements with yours in Cairo on the despatch of US Navy Squadrons to Lagens. ... I saw Commodore McCanlish in Casablanca ... and understood from him that he is holding a PBY5A Squadron ready to go there.[1] As far as I know, Cominch's intention to send a Liberator Squadron in the middle of January [1944] still holds good, subject of course to satisfactory arrangement with the Portuguese being completed. I think myself that it would be very wasteful to have more than a total of three squadrons in the Azores because I do not believe there will be work for them. Our calculations are that our two Fortress Squadrons and one of yours could cover every single convoy at sea within range of the Azores throughout the hours of daylight; that represents a very substantial margin of safety because, as you know, we never do cover every convoy at sea, but only those that are in any way threatened.[2]

3. One point is very essential in the present circumstances. and that is that we must have more aircraft in the Azores with lights. We have told Cominch that we hope the Liberator Squadron he sends there in January will be fitted with new lights and I hope you will take that up strongly. If this cannot be arranged, then we shall have to keep a detachment of Leigh Light Wellingtons there, which will congest the accommodation and be an undesirable detachment from the Bay Offensive.[3]

...

5. ... I am sure I need not ask you to emphasise in Washington the importance of continuing to keep up the maximum pressure in the Bay, in spite of the present rather disappointing results in the shape of kills. Even now I am certain that our efforts are not being wasted, because they are forcing the Hun to creep through the Bay at the rate of 60 or 70 miles per day instead of 160, which he could make good if there were no air threat, and that, of course, reduces the useful time he can spend in the patrol areas in the Atlantic. Here again, however, it is of the utmost importance to get as many aircraft as possible fitted with lights. I have

---

[1]Cdre McCanlish, US Navy: unidentified.

[2]Boeing Fortress (B-17): US heavy bomber; 1935; 4 engines; 10 crew; 300mph; 1850m; 13mg; 1760lbs bombs.

[3]Vickers Wellington: British bomber; 1936; 2 engines; 6 crew; 255mph; 1325m; 6mg; 6000lbs bombs.

asked for all my Liberators to be fitted with the Leigh Light though it will inevitably take a longish time to put that recommendation fully into effect. But I think you will agree that our present experience shows that we ought to be able to transfer almost every aircraft at our disposal to night work, keeping only a token effort going during daylight hours. I understand that for the Moroccan Sea Frontier that the American GEC light is to be fitted first to the Mariners; I hope the programme of fitting can be accelerated to the utmost and that the Liberator Squadrons in Hamilton's Wing and those in Morocco can be fitted at the earliest possible moment.[1]

6. As regards Hamilton's Squadrons, I am not quite clear as to whether the Navy Department do want us to carry out major repairs for them in our Group 43 organisation. As you know, we are prepared to do that if required.

7. The question of spares is again an urgent one. … We are only too ready to provide your squadrons with spares through our own organisation, but the spares position is pretty tight. …

8. I should be interested to hear from you if you could let me know as soon as possible what the decision is as regards the takeover of Dunkeswell. … We are ready to hand it over as soon as you can make available the necessary US Naval personnel.[2]

9. Finally, I don't know whether you would think it desirable to mention in Washington the question of the use of A/S Liberators in an emergency to cover convoys against long-range air attack. You will remember the slight difference of opinion with Hamilton on this matter. I know Hamilton is full out to do all he can to co-operate in the protection of shipping, either directly or indirectly, but I think he is definitely unhappy about the prospect of being asked to help defend a convoy against attack by He-177s. We, of course, don't regard this as a normal job for Liberators, but if a convoy is seriously threatened by long-range bombers and no other type of aircraft can reach it, we don't hesitate to use the Liberator for this purpose, and I am sure that the action of our Liberators against [i.e., in defence of] the convoy on 22 November did save it from far worse damage and incidentally resulted in shooting down two He-177s. I was interested to find the Moroccan Sea Frontier did not hesitate to use the A/S aircraft for this purpose if necessary. …

[1]Martin Mariner: US flying boat; 1939; 2 engines; 198mph.
[2]Dunkeswell: airfield, S Devon.

89. *Comnaveu Memorandum*

[RG 38/24] 11 January 1944

German Submarine Situation

[Counter-measures] have restricted the operations of U-boats to the point that for the first time in the war there are no U-boats on distant patrol in the Atlantic area. ...

90. *Vice Admiral J. H. Ingram, US Navy, to King*[1]

[Op Arch, King 4] 11 January 1944

...

3. My boys in blue cheered me very much by dashing triple play on enemy blockade runners. I was certain that my barrier was well conceived and effective in spite of lack of much British support on the Eastern end of the line. Recent sinkings and our success in knocking a sub[marine] out as far East as Longitude 5°W was an eye opener to them.

91. *Sir Ronald Campbell to the Foreign Office*[2]

[ADM 199/1887] Lisbon,
3 February 1944

I have as already reported made two determined but not unsuccessful attempts to move Dr Salazar from [the] standpoint that he cannot agree to an American squadron operating as a unit. His reasons are, firstly, that the Germans have warned him that while recognising that he could not refuse [an] appeal to an ally, they would be obliged to take a very different view of any American participation; and secondly, that it would run counter to its whole policy. He would not object he said to American aircraft, if they wore British colours; nor to 'two, five or even 10 American pilots if they were incorporated in [the] RAF'.

---

[1]VA Joseph H. Ingram, US Navy (d 1952): cdr, 4 F South Atlantic; C-in-C, Atl F 1945; ret 1947.

[2]Sir Ronald Campbell (1883–1953): Asst USec, Foreign Office 1906–11; Minister, Paris 1929–35; Yugoslavia 1935–9; France 1939–40; Amb to Portugal 1940–45; ret.

92. *Admiral Sir Max Horton to the Secretary of the Admiralty*[1]

[ADM 199/241]   Western Approaches HQ,
                                                          Liverpool,
                                                    5 February 1944

...

4. *Flying Personnel*

... The CO of an American CVE, during his visit to Area Combined
HQ, Liverpool, stressed the importance of maintaining seven squadrons
to operate from five carriers. This ensured that two squadrons would
always be available for training in new weapons, training new personnel and giving leave. The scheme is facilitated by the American system
of establishing the maintenance personnel, stores, etc., in the Carrier.
It is therefore only necessary for the flying crews and their aircraft to
disembark.

93. *Rear Admiral F. S. Low to King*

[RG 38/32]   22 February 1944

...

2. In order that you may have all available information (some of which
amounts to no more than impressions), it is to be emphasised that the
British and ourselves have quite different philosophies as to breaking
off and independent sailings. There is constant pressure by their people
here to get us to accept the principle that, always with due regard to the
U-boat situation, ships of any speed should be broken off [from convoys]
or sailed independently when material benefit is to be anticipated. In a
conference yesterday afternoon the British representative admitted that
this despatch will be helpful, but we should not close our eyes to the fact
that, in spite of this, they may be expected to continue to exert pressure
looking towards further concessions.

94. *Admiralty to Cominch*

[ADM 199/2403]   29 February 1944

1. HMCS *Wetaskiwin* attacked a U-boat with 'Hedgehog' at 0203, 0225,
0247/24 in position 47° 19N, 26° 00W. DC attack at 0552/24 forced

---

[1]Sec of Admy: Sir Henry Vaughan Markham.

U-boat to surface. It sank at 0610/24. One officer and 19 ratings taken prisoner.[1]

2. Two US Navy Catalinas 14 & 15 and Catalina G/202 with *Anthony* sank a U-boat at 1747/24 in position 35° 57N, 06° 15W.[2]

3. HM Ships *Affleck* and *Gore* (EG1) sank U-91 at 0325/26 in position 49° 45N, 26° 20W by creeping attack. Sixteen survivors including Captain were picked up.[3]

4. Catalina M/210 attacked surfaced U-boat at 0925/25 in position 70° 26N, 12° 40E.

Survivors seen in water.[4]

95. *Meeting of the Anti-U-boat Warfare Committee*

[CAB 86/6]   15 March 1944

...

2. *Operation OVERLORD*

The Prime Minister enquired about possible U-boat activity during Operation

OVERLORD.

In the course of discussion on this point the following views were expressed:

(a) The enemy was unlikely to attempt to operate more than 20–25 U-boats on the Western Coastal Convoy route. Others might be operating on the main route, on the Eastern Coastal Convoy route, in the Bristol Channel and off the North Cornish Coast. His greatest difficulty would be the four hours at night during which U-boats must recharge their batteries. If we took the necessary precautions the threat of U-boats to OVERLORD should not be great. The threat by E-boats was greater.

(b) The enemy might well stage diversionary attacks by U-boats in the Northern Approaches and the Atlantic, as he would judge that we had withdrawn considerable escort forces from the Atlantic. It would be of the greatest help if the American escort carriers and their attendant

---

[1]*U-257*: sunk 24 Feb 1944; 30 casualties.
[2]*U-761*: 9 casualties W of Gibraltar; *Anthony* assisted by a US Ventura.
[3]*U-91*: 35 casualties.
[4]*U-601*: no survivors. Arctic.

destroyers could act as support groups in the Atlantic during the OVER-LORD period.

96.   *Report of an attack on a U-boat*
by Swordfish aircraft LS284[1]

[ADM 199/602]   2 May 1944

Pilot: Sub-Lieut (A) L. G. Cooper, RNVR.
Observer: Lieut (A) R. V. Barnes, RNVR.
Air Gunner: PO (A) K. Sutherland.

We were sent out to investigate a suspected U-boat ... At 1641 we turned on to vector 360° as directed, and almost immediately the whole crew sighted a U-boat fine on the port bow distant 5–6 miles. Course and speed estimated at 265°[,] 10 knots. The approach was made out of the sun and height was lost down to 1000 feet. At a range of half-a-mile we dived steeply and levelled out at 100 feet, 300 yards from the U-boat on a relative bearing of Red 90°. The aircraft tracked over the conning tower and a stick of three depth charges was dropped ... These charges were seen to straddle the U-boat and explode midway between the conning tower and the stern. After the attack we continued to shadow the U-boat from a position one-and-a-half miles upwind. The U-boat was seen to lose headway gradually after the attack, and was down by the stern. Ten minutes later she was stationary and began to disappear below the surface stern first. The bow canted upwards at an angle of 80° to the horizon, about 20 feet of the U-boat project-ing out of the water. It remained in this position for about 45 seconds before sliding slowly below the surface. On circling the area it was observed that air bubbles over an area approximately 50 feet across (precisely over the spot of submerging) continued to arise for a period of 45 seconds. No oil, survivors or wreckage was observed. Several explosions were heard about a minute later. These, however, sounded like those of a U-boat opening fire with 20mm ammunition, and it was at first thought that this was the case, but no apparent cause of their origin could be seen.

---

[1]Fairey Swordfish: British TBR; 1934; 1 engine; 3 crew; 138mph; 546m; 2mg; 1500lbs bombs.
  Fencer was a US-built CVE. Half the MV in RA/JW convoys were US.
  U-277: no survivors.
  On 1 May Cooper sank *U-959* & on 2 May another Swordfish sank *U-674*; there were no survivors from either submarine.

97.   *Captain A. J. Isbell, US Navy, to FX-01*[1]

[RG 38/36]   2 June 1944

11 May

… It is my impression, gained from the evasive answers of British officers contacted at the party, and substantiated by subsequent conversations
with British officers at other stations, that the British have no intention
whatever of letting us into the Azores. In general, their attitude to all
Americans is that of 'Hello Sucker'. … if … the British didn't watch
out, Salazar would get our squadron into the Azores in spite of them. …

17 May

   1000 – Conference at FAA Office with Rear Admiral Boyd, Captain
   Wright and other officers.[2] MAC boats and helicopters were discussed, and both dismissed as useless. … .
   1500 – Conference at Admiralty with Rear Admirals Brind and Edelsten on anti-submarine warfare. Discussed use of rockets, mines,
   carriers, and fighter affiliation. …

98.   *Anti-U-boat Division: Analysis*
of U-boat Hunt in the Strait of Gibraltar, 16 March 1944

[ADM 199/1491]   15 June 1944

The enemy detected (14 March):

From aircraft reports on the morning of 14 March and again on 15 March,
it was evident that a U-boat was attempting to close the Strait of Gibraltar
from the Westward. It was estimated that it would have to charge batteries
during the night of 15–16 March and that sometime during the morning of
16 March it would pass through the area between Camiral and Malabata
Points, the normal MAD patrol. An additional MAD Catalina was ordered
to patrol to the Eastward between Europa and Alamina Points … in case
the U-boat slipped through the MAD barrier during the night.

---

[1]Capt A. J. Isbell, US Navy (1890–1945): USNA 1920; aviation posts; CO, NAS Sitka
1942–3; CO *Card* CVE group Apr 1943; killed on *Franklin* CVA 19 March 1945.
[2]Adm Sir Denis Boyd (1891–1965): ent RN 1906; RAN 1926–8; Capt 1931; Capt (D)
4 DF, Med F 1936; *Vernon* 1938; CO *Illustrious* 1940–1; RA (A), Med F 1941; 5 SL
& Chief, Naval Air Eqpt 1943; VA June 1944; Adm (A) June 1945; C-in-C, BPF & FE
1946–9; ret 1949.
   Capt Wright, US Navy: unidentified.

2. Planes 8, 1 and 7 took off from Gibraltar at dawn on 16 March, the first two sweeping North of Malabata Point and the third to the Eastward.

First contact by MAD:

3. At 0853 Plane 8, on a course of 352°, obtained a MAD contact on a submerged U-boat which was on an estimated course of 090°. With Plane 1 the Catalina proceeded to track the U-boat and the float lights fired on nine successive contacts showed the target to be proceeding to the Eastward at a speed of 3–4 knots.

4. Plane 8 ran in to attack at 0905 but contact was lost, possibly due to evasive action taken by the U-boat on the appearance of a Free French sloop escorting a surfaced submarine. A spiral search was then carried out and after about half-an-hour Plane 8 regained contact about a quarter of mile to the Eastward and approximately two and a half miles from the original contact. Plane 7 joined in the tracking at 0938 and the float lights dropped on MAD contacts showed the U-boat to be continuing on an Easterly course.

The Aircraft Attack:

5. At 0939 24 contact retro bombs were dropped by Plane 8 who was followed five minutes later by Plane 1 with 23 bombs, one failing to fire. *Vanoc* had closed the position on receiving R/T reports and stood off while the aircraft attacked. She reported hearing explosions of three bombs a few seconds after each attack. Swirls in the water were also seen by Plane 7 after the first attack.

Vanoc *joins the hunt:*

6. The aircraft continued tracking and obtained contact indicating that the U-boat was still under way on an easterly course. Plane 7 prepared to make a bombing run but was ordered to withhold his attack so as not to interfere with the tracking for a surface craft attack.

7. *Vanoc* was informed at 1000 that the aircraft had a firm contact and she was requested to attack. The destroyer started to close while the Catalinas continued to indicate the U-boat's position by float lights and, at 1028, a 'Hedgehog' attack was carried out without result, the projectiles exploding on the bottom about 95 seconds after being fired. A thin film of oil spread to starboard of the ship's wake.

8. At 1030 a MAD contact was obtained by Plane 8 but the float light failed to fire and contact was then lost by all three aircraft. After flying in a trapping circle for 45 minutes without result, they proceeded to search further to the Eastward.

Surface Patrol strengthened:

9. The 1st Escort Group (SO in *Affleck*), which had been ordered to the area by FOGMA then arrived from the Westward with *Kilmarnock* and *Kilbirnie*. Marine markers had been dropped in the estimated position of the U-boat and the ships were informed of its probable course and speed. They swept to the Eastward in line abreast and at 1145 *Affleck*, when within one and a half miles of the most recent aircraft marker, obtained asdic contact. This was classified as 'submarine' but was lost six minutes later in the wake of *Kilbirnie*, who was manoeuvring to clear the area.

'Hedgehog' attack by Affleck:

10. The echo was regained at 1200 and, after warning the aircraft to stay clear, EG1 decided to carry out a 'Hedgehog' attack. Contact was held up to the moment of firing and five seconds after the bombs had struck the water three distinct explosions were heard, followed by several unexplained noises. Almost immediately pieces of wood broke surface accompanied by a number of bubbles; about a minute after firing time a violent underwater explosion and other noises were heard. From the moment of the first 'Hedgehog' explosion contact, which had been fine, faded completely. A subsequent search revealed a quantity of oil and wreckage spread over a wide area, some of which was recovered.

No further contact:

11. A North–South A/S patrol was then carried out by all ships and the Catalinas continued their search. At about 1300 a MAD barrier was established between Acobuche and Leona Points to prevent any possibility of the U-boat escaping into the Mediterranean. This patrol, though maintained until last light, produced no sign of the enemy.

CONCLUDING REMARKS:

12. A total of seven MAD aircraft were used to ensure that the U-boat did not escape and it is of interest to note that it was detected by one of them within two hours of the time anticipated.

13. The Catalinas successfully tracked [the U-boat]. [Planes] 8 and 1 may have caused slight damage, since three explosions heard by *Vanoc* occurred only a few seconds after each attack, thus precluding any possibility that the bombs exploded on the bottom.

14. *Vanoc*'s 'Hedgehog' attack missed the target, possibly owing to avoiding action taken by the U-boat, as the aircraft lost contact immediately afterwards. In a depth of 325 feet the projectiles would take about

95 seconds to reach the bottom. *Vanoc* states that during this attack asdic conditions were poor with tide and fish echoes.

15. The attack by *Affleck* appears to have been extremely accurate; the U-boat was probably hit by three projectiles which exploded at a depth of 125 feet. This was followed by convincing breaking up noises and surface evidence, including diesel oil used by U-boats and wooden wreckage, some of which was picked up later by *Garlies* and has been identified as locker lids, freshly splintered and broken, with pieces of human flesh embedded in them.

16. A high standard of co-operation was achieved by the air and surface forces, as shown by the following extract from the reports of the CO, *Vanoc*, and the CO, Squadron VP-63.

17. 'MAD Catalinas were a pleasure to work with and co-operation appeared to be entirely satisfactory. Aircraft continued to mark the contact throughout *Vanoc*'s attack up to the moment of firing and the manner in which the dropping position of each smoke-float agreed with the asdic bearing and the range was remarkable.'

18. 'Coordination between aircraft and ships was excellent. The teamwork displayed between the three aircraft and *Vanoc* during the 40 minutes prior to *Vanoc*'s attack was *particularly* outstanding.'

19. The MAD recorder traces show the initial contact obtained by Plane 8 at 0853, followed by the signals caused by the U-boat during the subsequent tracking and bombing run.

20. This successful operation has been assessed by the Admiralty Assessment Committee as follows:

'German U-boat probably sunk by US MAD Catalinas 8, 1 and 7 of VP-63, HM Ships *Affleck* and *Vanoc*. All forces taking part were held to share in the credit for this success, with the exception of *Vanoc*, who contributed less than the other units. The Assessment Committee notes that Catalina 7 reinforced the search after the commencement of the hunt but withheld his retro bomb attack on the orders of the SO in order to enable *Vanoc* to deliver an attack.'[38]

99.   *Report of Proceedings by HMCS Statice*

[ADM 199/1460]   5–6 July 1944

[Position:] 50° 32N, 00° 23W.
Weather Conditions: Wind SE, force 1; sea 10; visibility 10.
Statice: Escorting Channel Convoy.
Escort Group 11: A/S patrol.
Narrative: At 1955 SS *Glendinning*, in convoy, reported a violent explosion. *Statice* commenced an asdic search, and gained contact

astern [at] 2001, bearing *Glendinning* 130°at 1700 yards.[1] This was classified as 'possible' submarine and counter-attacked. The submarine classification was then confirmed and a series of attacks was carried out until 0033/6. On completion of a 'Hedgehog' attack at this time contact was lost. An all-round sweep was carried out, followed by box searches. At 0600 *Ottawa* and *Kootenay* joined, and at 0738 *Ottawa* obtained an asdic contact. She held the contact while *Kootenay* gained a contact, and at 0750 *Kootenay* attacked. Three more attacks by *Kootenay* followed, and at 0859 *Ottawa* attacked with 'Hedgehog', obtaining an explosion at about 100 feet [deep]. Some oil was observed.

The target appeared to have bottomed after *Ottawa*'s attack, and at 0918 *Statice* attacked with 'Hedgehog'. Two distinct explosions were heard, and it was assumed that some projectiles had hit the target, the rest detonating on the bottom. Wood and oil resulted from this attack.

At 0959 *Kootenay* attacked again, with depth charges and a large amount of wood, clothing, books and oil resulted.

The wreckage was then recovered by *Ottawa*'s whaler, while *Ottawa* passed over the target, obtaining an echo sounding trace showing the target on the bottom with oil pouring from her.[2]

At 1939 an attack was delivered by *Ottawa* with a towed depth charge, which exploded against the U-boat's hull – two prongs found to be straightened when the grapnel was recovered, it was assumed that it had hooked the U-boat.

As there was no sign of survivors it was decided to hold the contact and attacks were made at intervals, which only produced further oil.

Between 2001/5 and 2047/6, 34 attacks were made by three ships of which 11 were delivered by *Ottawa* before she lost contact at 0033/6. Of these, it is considered that those by *Ottawa* at 0859/6, *Statice* at 0918/6 and *Kootenay* at 0959 were lethal. The towed charge at 1030, and many of the subsequent attacks were on the target.

Surface Evidence: Wood, oil, clothes and books.

Commodore (D), Western Approaches, Opinion: U-678 was hit by *Ottawa*'s 'Hedgehog' at 1059/6, *Statice*'s 'Hedgehog' at 1120, and by *Kootenay*'s depth charges at 1159/6. The U-boat must have been killed by 1200.[3]

---

[1] *U-392*: no survivors.
[2] Probably *Glendene*: Dene Shipping Company, London; 1929; 4500t; 10k.
[3] *U-678*: no survivors.

C-in-C, Nore's, Opinion: As 10 attacks were carried out by *Statice* during the night 5–6 July, without results it seems likely that these were 'non-sub' contacts and that *Ottawa* obtained the genuine submarine contact, approximately 10 miles away, the U-boat being killed by *Statice*'s 'Hedgehog' attack at 0918/6, and it is thought that her attacks before 0033/6 were probably on a 'non-sub'.[1]

It is considered that the initial contact was made with the U-boat by *Ottawa* at 0738/6, and in her attack at 0859 the 'Hedgehog' projectiles probably hit and caused damage.

There is evidence from the plot, however, that the U-boat continued under way until attacked by *Statice* at 0918. This attack appears to have been accurate and it is almost certain that the U-boat bottomed after it.

Many attacks were made subsequently on the bottomed U-boat which caused a quantity of wreckage to surface; from among this wreckage there was evidence to identify the kill as being U-678.

100.   *Senior Officer, Escort Group 11, to C-in-C, Portsmouth*[2]

[CAN 51/520–8440/EG11, Vol. 2]   14 July 1944

Brief Narrative: [on EG11's destruction of U-678].

    …

8. *Lessons Learned:*

(a) The value of echo-sounder.

(b) The difficulty of damaging a bottomed submarine with 10 charge patterns.

(c) The necessity for holding the contact continuously with one or two assisting ships while it was being attacked by another ship.

(d) Following from this the necessity for attacking in slow time.

(e) The effect of tide on Asdic conditions.

(f) The necessity for a maximum amount of perseverance and patience when attacking a bottomed U-boat.

---

[1]C-in-C Nore: Adm Tovey.
  U-247: no survivors. Cdr A. F. C. Layard: M. Whitby, *Commanding Canadians: The Second World War Diaries of A. F. C. Layard* (Vancouver & Toronto, 2005).
  [2]Cdre F. J. Prentice: prob Cdre A. St.J. Prentice.
  C-in-C Portsmouth: Adm Little.

9. (a) The use of towed charges and delayed action charges in connection with the echo sounder to ensure destruction of a bottomed submarine.

(b) That no ship should carry out an attack till the second ship is firmly in place.

(c) Flares should not be used in a tideway as they are most deceptive.

(d) That even Dan buoys unless very carefully anchored will drag and that these give deceptive Radar echoes in calm water, and therefore they should be used with caution. ...

101. *Horton to Admiralty*

[81/520–8440 CAN] Western Approaches HQ,
Liverpool,
14 August 1944

The present situation off the French coast coupled with the possibility of a successful campaign against U-boats returning to Norway calls for the formation of the maximum possible number of hunting forces.

2. The following proposals are put forward with a view to making the best use of the available Western Approaches and Royal Canadian Naval Forces:

(a) Close support of mid-ocean convoys on a new cycle to be provided by three B groups and eight C groups. ...

(b) B and C groups, including the four B groups employed on the Gibraltar convoys, to consist of a paper strength of eight ships apiece. In the case of B groups, the normal group composition would be two fast ships and six corvettes.

(c) Fast ships thus saved to be organised in support of hunting groups for service where most needed.

3. To implement this scheme two additional C groups would be required in late September and mid-October respectively. It is anticipated that RCN could provide these from present resources and new construction.

4. It is calculated in this way the following additional support or hunting groups could be formed during September and the early part of October.

(a) Two or three Western Approaches groups;

(b) One Royal Canadian [Navy] group.

5. It is further submitted for consideration that ships now allocated to the Eastern Fleet from my command should be retained in these Waters for the present and organised for support or hunting duties.

102.   *Report of Proceedings: 9th Escort Group, 31 August–11*
September 1944

[ADM 199/1644]   [c. 15 September 1944]
31 August

0900: EG 9 slipped and proceeded to [area] Z 243.

1250: Received C-in-C's [Plymouth] 311111 [not reproduced] ordering Group to search along Convoy route to Hartland Point.

1845: When approaching Land's End *St John* gained contact in position 081°, Wolf Rock five miles. Contact was lost but *St John* considered it promising and worth an organised search.

1955: Instructed *Monnow* to continue along convoy route with Second
Division and *Swansea* with First Division remained with contact.

2115: *Swansea* picked up contact and dropped one charge, thinking it
might be fish. *St John*, following along behind, reported that depth
charges had produced a slight oil trace.

This contact was very difficult to hold as echoes could only be picked
up from one direction. *St John* then attacked with 'Hedgehog' which
considerably increased [the] patch of oil. A second 'Hedgehog' attack
was carried out just before 2300 after which contact was completely lost
and it was too dark to see the oil patch.

2400: Started a parallel sweep from the Datum Point, down tide,
which was to the westward.

1 September

0107: Altered course to 080° to pass west of the Wolf.

0143: Altered course to the east to sweep back to south of the Wolf
towards Datum Point.

0210: *St John* gained contact, in position 200°, Wolf Light three
miles, and reported that she got echo sounder trace which might
be a bottomed U-boat. She attacked and the result was a considerable quantity of oil. *Swansea* was unable to gain contact and after
carrying out a second attack *St John* could only obtain very occasional and faint echoes. The oil however remained a good mark
until daylight.

0230: Received C-in-C's 010119 [not reproduced], instructing Group
to remain with contact until further orders. At daylight, in spite of
assistance which the oil patch gave, only an occasional and very
unconvincing echo could be obtained. Even *St John* who was the

most successful, found it impossible to attack as recorder trace was too poor and target could not be located by echo sounder.

0930: All three ships moved to investigate the position of last night's contact, 080° five miles from the lighthouse. Some traces of oil were still visible but nothing but fish echoes could be picked up by ships' Asdics.

1200: Returned once more to the oil patch. *Swansea* was just about to drop a pattern by eye, when *St John* reported having obtained a good echo sounder trace at last. At 1400 she ran in and dropped a five charge pattern, on passing over, by echo sounder. The result was startling. Vast quantities of oil came up and when boats were lowered, various articles such as: letter, photographs, certificate, German technical books and part of an engine room register marked U-247, clothing and a mass of splintered woodwork, were picked up all indicating very plainly the presence of a U-boat.

After hoisting [in] sea boats, the northerly tide showed clearly the position from which the oil was rising, but as no contact could be obtained, *St John* dropped an 11 charge pattern and *Swansea* a 10 charge pattern by eye at 1628 but without much result.

1742: Left *St John* with *Assiniboine* who had now appeared on the scene to continue with the hunt and *Swansea* with *Port Colborne* proceeded in accordance with C-in-C's orders north of Trevose Head.

The entire credit for this possible success must be attributed to the skill and persistence of *St John*, who in spite of the meagre evidence, always seemed confident in all his signals that we were on to something 'worthwhile'. The skilful operation of his A/S and E/S, under very difficult conditions, was outstanding. It must regretfully be admitted, that but for the C-in-C's instructions to remain on the contact and *St John*'s insistent optimism, I would have given up the hunt in disgust long ago.

2108: Sighted *Monnow* and Second Division in position 11 miles from Trevose Head. *Monnow* reported that they were on to what they considered was a good contact and made several attacks but without any results.

2125: When within about two miles of the other ships, *Swansea* obtained a very good A/S contact and immediately carried out a 'Hedgehog' attack. The result was most promising. The time intervals of explosions indicated that the bombs were detonating at different levels and before the ship even reached the disturbed water, a couple of black objects were seen to rise to the surface. Without waiting to examine the wreckage the second attack was carried out, but this was not so accurate. It was now nearly dark, with a very heavy rain squall and blowing quite hard and it was found impossible to find and pick up any conclusive evidence. From the number of dead fish in the vicinity, however, and what could be seen by searchlight of the floating objects, it appeared probable that the target attacked was a wreck.

2400: *Meon* and *Stormont* were left in contact and in compliance with C-in-C's 012021 [not reproduced], *Monnow* and *Port Colborne* were ordered to patrol Convoy [route]. South of Trevose Head and *Swansea* went off by herself to sweep in the vicinity of the original Aircraft sighting.

2 September

[0000–0900]: Patrolled area between Trevose Head and northern edge of QEX during the night.

[0900–2200]: [Reformed Group, investigated contact].

3 September

[0710–1245]: [Sweeps, patrols and investigations].

4 September

[0800–2324]: [More of the same].

5 September

[0145–1304]: [Attacks on suspected contacts – no results].

2015: *Stormont* reported having lost contact and *Swansea* closed her to assist in regaining the target, which was easily done with the aid of QH at 2100. The value of this navigational aid for pin-pointing the position of wrecks, contacts, submarines, etc., in tidal waters out of sight of land, cannot be over stated.

2350: *Meon* relieved *Swansea* on the contact, *Swansea* and *Stormont* rejoined the Group, as they swept past to the north east.

6 September

0042: The Group had hardly gone any distance, when *Swansea* obtained A/S contact in a position 002° from the other target. It was a poor echo and difficult to hold but on running over with E/S showed presence of an object on the bottom. *Port Colborne* was ordered to remain and assist *Swansea* while *Monnow* continued sweep with remainder of Group. At 0400 fairly firm contact was obtained and held until daylight.

0300–0430: [Ships were ordered by turn into Falmouth to restock with 'Hedgehog' bombs and depth charges, most of the Group going on to the convoy route while *Swansea* and *St John* remained with the contact].

0750: *Swansea* and *St John* started attacks on target which had been held throughout the night. ... One such attack by *St John* brought up a quantity of muddy discoloured water but absolutely nothing else.

1200–2245: [Relief by EG 6, EG 9 reforming and joining convoy EE 97].

9 September

0150: *Monnow* rejoined from Falmouth and a sweep to north west was carried out along convoy route from Trevose Head to Hartland Point. On this and succeeding days, the patrol of this route proved most exhausting. The area was littered with wrecks and at time contacts were made almost hourly, each of which had to be investigated, plotted, probably attacked and finally classified. The many occasions on which this occurred day after day are not mentioned in detail in this report, but by the end of four days patience and temper were nearly exhausted.

[1105–2215]: [Whole Group on convoy duty].

10 September

[0015–0525]: [Convoy and patrol duties].

11 September

[0235–0525]: [Convoy and patrol duties].

1200: *Monnow*, *Stormont* and *Meon* detached to proceed to Plymouth for short layover, while *Swansea*, *St John* and *Port Colborne* remained on patrol.

[1530–2337]: [Convoy duty].

12 September

[0411–2400]: [Convoy duty, getting somewhat mixed up with *Rodney* and her screen].

13 September

[0000–2153]: [Convoy and patrol duty].

14 September

0100: When abreast of Pendine, Group altered course to 313° and detached from convoy and continued patrol.
1500: Turned over convoy to *Monnow* and proceeded to Plymouth with *St John*.
2030: Arrived Plymouth.

103.   *Horton to Admiralty and others*

[CAN 81/520–8440]   26 September 1944

I have had under consideration the most effective employment of the fast escorts allocated to reinforce my command.

2.   Excluding (R) those operating under C-in-C CAN [Canada] there are at present the following 19 Support Groups either formed or in process of formation:

(a)   14 RN Groups, namely Groups 1, 2, 3, 5, 10, 14, 15, 17, 18, 19, 20, 21, 30 and 31.
(b)   5 RCN Groups, namely Groups 6, 9, 11, 25 and 26.

3.   There are two alternatives for the employment of replacements:

(a)   To form three additional RN Support Groups.
(b)   To bring the strength of RN Support Groups up to six ships apiece.

4.   The following are reasons against forming additional Support Groups:

(a)   Training facilities would be overstrained.
(b)   The provision of additional senior officers and Group staffs is difficult in view of the need to economise manpower. However, owing to the recent increase in the number of Support Groups, there is a lack of experienced officers available for such duties, and this fact would tend to impair the efficiency of any additional Groups formed.
(c)   Intensive operations in Winter conditions are likely to reduce a paper strength of five to a running strength of three ship per Group.

5. I intend, therefore, to bring the paper strength of RN Support Groups up to six ships per Group.

6. With regard to RCN Support Groups, groups 6 and 9 are up to strength, and a paper strength of five should suffice groups 25 and 26 for the present, as these groups are composed of new ships.

104. *Comnaveu Memorandum for Captain Kline, US Navy*[1]

[RG 38/24] 28 September 1944

... our first priority and primary consideration is THE SAFETY OF OUR CONVOYS – this is paramount. ...

... the present German use of the so-called 'schnorkel' which unquestionably, due to the inability of radar to detect submarines when this schnorkel is in use, has greatly minimized the effectiveness of our aircraft and surface craft in anti-U-boat warfare. We have got to solve this latest German move as we have solved former ones, and we have got to solve it by research and by actual training at sea against it and how best to combat it and overcome it, which is one of the very important things entering into every phase in this area.

105. *Stark to Cunningham*

[Op Arch, Stark A2] 29 September 1944

On my trip to Ike HQ, I strongly urged bombing of the new U-boat pens in process of construction in the Norwegian ports. To me the great thing is to hit them and demolish them during this process of construction and while they are vulnerable, with an occasional return visit to keep them demolished. I believe you feel exactly the same way and I do hope we can get this done.

106. *Cunningham to Stark*

[Op Arch, Stark A2] 2 October 1944

Thank you for your letter of 28 September [probably similar to Document 104], I hasten to assure you that our A/S policy has never wavered from its true object of putting the safe and timely arrival of the convoys

[1]Capt Kline, US Navy: unidentified.

first, and the destruction of U-boats second. This policy is reiterated in C-in-C, Coastal Command's A/S plan [no. 107].

2. The fifth sentence of his plan may require explanation. In the days of the 'Bay Offensive' the main concern was in the South. Now that the U-boats have been shifted to the Norwegian coast it follows that our offensive effort must shift to the North.

3. This does not mean that the Southern Approach channels for our convoys will be neglected and, in fact, adequate provision has been made to provide air cover in this area, having regard to the U-boat threat there.

4. If the threat increases, the AOC-in-C, Coastal Command has plans to move squadrons back to South West England at short notice. We can move our anti-U-boat squadrons there more quickly than the enemy can move his U-boats. Hence, provided we maintain a flexible outlook, we should always be able to oppose him with maximum forces.

5. Coastal Command will be much stretched if the U-boats operate in strength around our inshore routes in addition to maintaining U-boat concentrations in the Atlantic Ocean, and I welcome any reinforcement to Coastal Command's strength.

6. I consider, however, that these reinforcements should be based in the UK, operating from airfields in South West England and under the control of Coastal Command. By so doing we shall avoid dual control, maintenance facilities and accommodation problems will be simplified.

7. I am averse to areas of responsibility and it would be impractical to divide the South Western Approaches into an American and a British sphere. I consider it essential for efficient and economical operation that an air effort round the waters of the UK against U-boats be co-ordinated under one control.

107.   *C-in-C, Coastal Command:*

Memorandum on the Trend of the Anti-U-boat Campaign[1]

[Op Arch, Stark A2]   2 October 1944

Introduction

1. On the conclusion of the first phase of OVERLORD, when the Biscay ports were becoming rapidly untenable to the enemy, an Appreciation of

---

[1]ACM Sir W. Sholto Douglas (1893–1969): fighters, RFC 1914–18; commercial aviation; RAF 1920; AVM 1938; DCAS 1940; AOC-in-C Fighter Cmd Nov 1940; ACM & AOC ME; AOC-in-C Coastal Cmd Jan 1944; MRAF 1946.

the possible development of the U-boat war was made. This Appreciation envisaged in the first place a period during which the U-boats formerly based on the Biscay ports would be on passage to Norway, possibly operating in the Atlantic against the ocean convoys on the way. It was expected that after that the U-boats would operate from Norwegian bases, devoting their main effort to the attack of the Atlantic convoys, but at the same time retaining sufficient U-boats in the South West Approaches to the British Isles and to the West Coast of France, with object of containing our A/S as far as possible in this area. To put such a plan into operation, the enemy would have to maintain the continual passage of U-boats from the Norwegian Coast through the Northern Transit Area, i.e. between Iceland and the Faeroes and perhaps to some extent between the Faeroes and Shetlands.

2. In order to meet this situation there were broadly speaking two courses open to us – namely, (1) to concentrate entirely upon a defensive policy of providing close cover to the convoys wherever they were within operational range of shore-based aircraft, and (2) to provide for the direct protection of our convoys in the Atlantic and South West Approaches whenever they were threatened with attack, and to use the remainder of the A/S forces offensively in the Northern Transit Area. Since the provision of continuous cover to convoys would involve much abortive flying where no U-boats were present, the first of the two courses outlined above was considered to be uneconomical and likely to be unprofitable. It was therefore decided, while giving the protection of convoys <u>first call</u> on Anti-U-boat forces, to concentrate the rest of our effort in the North to cause the maximum interference with the passage of U-boats through the Northern Transit Area. The success of this policy naturally depended upon the continued receipt of accurate information as to the movement of U-boats, since only by this means is it possible to confine the protection of convoys to periods when they are threatened and thus to avoid wasted flying over areas where no U-boats are present. It was felt that we had every reason to hope for such a state of affairs, and so far our hopes have been justified.

3. Accordingly, in the Directive issued under reference TS/134 on the 10 August [not reproduced], arrangements were made to transfer the bulk of the A/S forces then operating in 19 Group to the operational control of 18 Group in Scotland, and to retain in the South West Approaches and Western Approaches only sufficient aircraft to guarantee the provision of close cover to threatened convoys and to provide against the smaller number of U-boats operating at that time in the English and St George's Channels. It was however emphasised in the Directive that our plans must remain flexible, and that in particular the reinforcement of No. 16 Group in Northern Ireland might become necessary, either during the preliminary phase of the transfer of the U-boats from Biscay to the Norwegian ports or in

the later stages when the concentration of effort in the Northern Transit Area might for various reasons prove inadequate to prevent the passage of U-boats in large numbers to the Atlantic. To provide for this flexibility, arrangements were made to retain full operational facilities in the 19 Group Stations vacated in the plan outlined above and also to increase the facilities then existing in the 15 Group area.

The Present Situation

4. The trend of events as they have developed so far has to a great extent conformed to the Appreciation outlined above. The enemy has however added to our responsibilities by the establishment of U-boat patrols in three restricted areas not provided for in our original plan, namely, the Moray Firth, the area off Cape Wrath and the Minches and the Approaches to the North Channel. At the same time the expected move to the Norwegian ports is in full swing and there are now 20 U-boats inward bound passing through the Northern Transit Area, and seven also inbound in the North Atlantic.

5. Owing to the concentration of U-boats off the Approaches to the North Channel, it has been found necessary already to apply the principle of flexibility and reinforce 15 Group by basing five more Squadrons in this Group. In addition, 15 Group has been given first call upon the aircraft of both 19 and 18 Groups in order to provide for the protection of threatened convoys under the 'Stipple' procedure, as well as for the flooding of the immediate Approaches to the North Channel and to the Minches. The Admiralty have assisted by the loan of certain disembarked FAA squadrons. Plans have also been made for the establishment in Northern Ireland of two further squadrons which are being returned from the Mediterranean. These squadrons will however have to undergo re-equipment and considerable training, and will not be operationally effective for a month or more. The reinforcement of 15 Group has had to be made largely at the expense of the intended reinforcement of 18 Group, with the result that the very wide area of the Northern Transit can only be covered to a limited extent.

6. The U-boats operating in St George's Channel have now been withdrawn, but there are indications that, as a result of the routeing of inward convoys to the South of Ireland, the U-boat operations in the North West Approaches are becoming unprofitable, and the enemy may well transfer his attentions once more to the South West Approaches. It is therefore not considered wise at this stage to make any further moves Northward from the 19 Group area, and it may indeed be necessary again to exploit the flexibility of our plans by returning some of the squadrons now in 15 or 18 Groups to the South West Approaches.

7. From the above it will be seen that the squadrons now available for Coastal Command are insufficient to cover all the U-boats operating in the wide area for which the Command is responsible, and many U-boats are now proceeding free from molestation by our A/S aircraft. The addition of American A/S squadrons would therefore be welcomed in that it would make possible the transfer of British squadrons to areas where U-boats are not now being hunted, thus filling the present gaps in our Anti-U-boat cover.

Location and Operation of American Squadrons

8. Should it be decided to operate American squadrons in the Coastal Command area, it is considered that they could be most profitably employed on the escort of convoys in the South West Approaches. For this purpose they could be based in the West of England or on the West Coast of France, preferably the former. In either event it is considered that the most efficient way to operate them would be to place them under the operational control of AOC 19 Group. Requirements for convoy escort should be controlled by the normal 'Stipple' procedure. This will reduce unprofitable flying to a minimum and may make possible on occasions the allotment of more than single cover to threatened convoys.

108. *Stark to King*

[Op Arch, Stark A2]   22 October 1944

... This week I had a talk with Max Horton and also Admiral Edelsten on the U-boat picture. Both are apprehensive about the situation, and I gather from a few minutes' talk with Admiral Cunningham that he also does not feel comfortable about it. This results from inability to locate or pick up submarines due to their use of 'schnorkel'. ...

Admiral Horton say he is doing all he can in the way of drills and plans, but that he is not getting much of anywhere. Should the submarines start operating in convoy waters with determination and guts, he thinks it is possible they might have considerable success.

109. *Cunningham to Stark*

[ADM 205/48]   2 January 1945

In reply to your letter of 29 December 1944, a Soviet broadcast from Moscow on 22 October 1944 announced that the Soviet Baltic Fleet had successfully salvaged a German U-boat which had previously been sunk by them in the Gulf of Finland.

2. Enquiries were made by our Naval Mission in Moscow, as the result of which an officer from the staff of SBNO, North Russia was allowed to make a two-day visit to the raised German U-boat at Kronstadt at the beginning of November.

3. Only in so far as the Gnat torpedo is concerned was this U-boat found to be of particular interest and now, just recently, the Russians have agreed to our sending a team of experts from this country to examine the torpedo on the spot. The DTM, Admiralty, has been in touch with your Readiness Division on this subject and has kept them thoroughly informed throughout.

4. DTM is fully aware of the delicacy of the situation in which our experts will find themselves, and these officers are to be particularly warned that the greatest care must be taken against any kind of indiscretion which might give the Russians knowledge as to the existence in Allied hands of a similar torpedo. Captain Missis, US Navy, is attending their final briefing.[1]

110.   *Stark to King*

[Op Arch, Stark A3]   3 January 1945

… The submarine picture has quietened down temporarily … there is much confidence on the subject, particularly with regard to routeing.

Saw Max Horton yesterday on his end of the submarine picture, he continues to be worried about it. He was early to recognise the potentialities [of the new Type XXI and Type XXIII submarines] and to do all he could. I had a pretty thorough review of the situation [on] Tuesday with Admiral Cunningham, and we again talked it over this noon.

111.   *Commodore Flanagan, US Navy, to Stark*[2]

[Op Arch, Stark A3]   Navy Department,
                                                          Washington,
                                                          5 January 1945

…

18. The people here are still pushing the subject of the bombing of the submarine bases, and Admiral King has just signed a letter to the JCS

---

[1]Capt Missis, US Navy: unidentified.
[2]Cdre Flanagan, US Navy: unidentified.

asking them to recommend higher priority for the project to the CCS. He hopes that Admiral Cunningham will assist you more strongly in stressing this point over there.

112. *Memorandum to Stark from Captain Ingram, US Navy[1]*

[Op Arch, Stark A3] 11 January 1945

Coastal Convoys in Waters of UK, Escorting of.

1. The above subject was discussed at the second meeting of DASW's sub-committee of the [Anti-]U-boat Warfare Committee on 9 January during a consideration of the sinking of seven ships while under escort in British Waters since 18 December [1944].

2. Convoys in British Waters may include as many as 29 ships. These are usually accompanied by only two escorts which act primarily as shepherds, the COs knowing little about A/S intelligence or tactics. As an example of this it was stated that in a recent attack on a coastal convoy the two escort vessel commanders did not know who was the SO, and that when one of the escorts attempted to hunt down the attacking submarine its commander did not know how to conduct operation SCABBARD – a recently adopted searching procedure for 'bottomed' U-boats.

3. Most of the escort vessels are trawlers based at Milford Haven, Plymouth or The Nore.

They are in these ports for only 49 hours, except for occasional five-day boiler cleaning periods. The crews of these escorts have been trained particularly for E-boat warfare and have shown little knowledge of A/S activities.

4. The Committee expressed its surprise over the existence in British home waters of a situation that would be understandable only in regions such as the African West Coast areas. It is agreed that the present escort situation was most unsatisfactory and DASW undertook to take up the matter of sending experienced A/S officers to the ports mentioned to acquaint escort commanders with recent intelligence on U-boats and to indoctrinate them in modern ASW tactics.

5. The possibility of increasing the number of escort vessels in each convoy was not considered by the Committee and there was no discussion as to the desirability of saturating the convoy areas with air patrols as was done during operations on and after D-day.

---

[1]Capt Ingram, US Navy: unidentified.

113.   *Admiral J. H. Ingram, US Navy, to King*

[Op Arch, King 3]   15 January 1945

...

2. Very recent U-boat activity has pointed to the fact that they must have a new technique and are going to be increasingly difficult to hunt down. The fact that one submarine in the swept channel very close to the Harbor of Halifax, in less than 36 fathoms of water, was successful in sinking three vessels is an indication of what we may be called upon to face if they get out their new stuff in any numbers. To combat this menace, it is my opinion that surface craft in increasing numbers are going to be necessary in conjunction with all the aircraft we can muster. I seriously recommend that the Atlantic Fleet small craft only be not further decreased, but also that consideration be given to augmenting my forces with the Destroyer Squadron now in the Mediterranean, ...

114.   *Stark to Edwards*[1]

[Op Arch, Stark A3]   19 January 1945

The CSTC has issued the priority list of Naval targets for attack by Allied bombers, dated 11 January, as follows:

Group 1: U-boat Assembly and Fitting Out – Hamburg, Bremen, Danzig.
Group 2: U-boats and Midget U-boats: Kiel, Vegesack, Ymuiden.
Group 3: U-boat Shelters: Bergen, Trondheim.

[An enclosure, apparently from C-in-C, Western Approaches]:

C-in-C considers that sinkings in the Irish Sea during the last few days, and attacks off the Clyde, make it apparent that A/S forces require reinforcement and readjustment. The blow directly against our inner focal points must be countered before those further afield. Outside narrow waters there is at least some possibility of evasive routeing which is not possible at the inner focal points.

He intends therefore to institute, as soon as possible, continuous local patrols in order to cover the vital areas. The object of these patrols will be to attack and harass the enemy directly incidents are reported and to carry out rescue work.

The areas covered by these patrols will be:

---

[1] Adm Edwards, US Navy.

(a) North Channel and Clyde Approaches.
(b) St George's Channel.
(c) Belfast Lough and approaches.
(d) Approaches to Liverpool.
(e) Minches and approaches to the Minches.

In addition to mounting local patrols, C-in-C considers that ML Flotillas should be available at suitable bases to back up the patrols, and to carry out sorties, in sheltered waters where U-boats may be Schnorkelling.

115. *Stark to Commodore Flanagan*

[RG 38/32]   22 January 1945

The present U-boat threat is so great that I feel I should personally attend the Prime Minister's Anti-U-boat [Warfare] Committee meeting.

116. *ACNS (UT) to Cunningham*[1]

[ADM 205/44]   24 January 1945

Intended Bombing of U-boat sheltered building slips and installations.

…

2. After discussion with myself and ACNS (H), Captain Terrell has arranged for Hamburg and Bremen to be bombed with Admiralty Concrete Piercing Bomb as soon as possible by the US Army 8th Air Force. General Doolittle expects to attack with about 150 aircraft, carrying a total of 300 bombs, and expects a high proportion of hits on the target. He will give relative priority to Hamburg and Bremen according to the weather, but he has been informed that while Bremen is more important on a long-term basis (the first U-boats from the Bremen shelters are not expected to be in operation before early autumn, 1945), the less pretentious shelters at Hamburg, containing as they do, many U-boats now being assembled, are of primary importance for the immediate future.

I think we can expect both yards to have received heavy attention within the next month.[2]

[1] Adm Edelsten.
[2] Capt Terrell: unidentified.

117.   *Anti-U-boat Warfare Committee*

[CAB 86/7]   26 January 1945

2. U-boat Campaign of 1945

The Prime Minister welcomed Mr Macdonald, the Canadian Minister of Defence for Naval Services and said that the Committee knew what a large part the RCN had played in the Battle of the Atlantic.[1]

Mr Macdonald thanked the Prime Minister for his remarks and said the RCN were readily engaged in the present U-boat Warfare, which included several attacks on merchant and naval vessels off Halifax. To some extent the immediate escort problem would be eased by the closing of the St Lawrence by ice which persisted, 1 April. Well over 1000 RCN ships were engaged on anti-U-boat operations in the Atlantic and Mediterranean areas.

...

118.   *CCS774/3: The U-boat Threat during 1945: Directive*

[CAB 88/35]   2 February 1945

The CCS consider that the current German U-boat programme, if not countered, will present a serious threat to our North Atlantic shipping lanes.

It is therefore directed that the following counter-measures be taken by all appropriate commanders.

(a) Build up as much as practicable the strength of surface hunting groups and anti-U-boat air squadrons.

(b) Maintain, and if possible increase 'marginal' bomber effort on assembly yards, concentrating as far as practicable against Hamburg and Bremen.

(c) Maintain 'marginal' effort against operating bases, be ready to increase this when bases become crowded beyond the capacity of concentration pens.

(d) Increase by 100%, if possible, the air mining effort against U-boats, including the training areas.

(e) Mine waters beyond the range of (d) by using surface minelayers and carrier-borne aircraft.

[1]Macdonald: unidentified.

(f) Intensify operations against enemy merchant ships.

(g) Maintain and intensify operations against the enemy shipping used
     to supply U-boat bases.

119.   *H. B. Miller, US Navy, to Stark.*[1]

[Op Arch, Stark A3]   18 February 1945

Geographic Relationship between Coastal Command at Gibraltar
and Fairwing 15.

1. The A/S activities based at Gibraltar are British, under the control of
Coastal Command. The US aviation A/S activity in this area is based at
Port Lyautey and consists of FW 15, which is controlled by Commander,
Moroccan Sea Frontier. The operating area of each of these A/S activi-
ties overlap considerably ... In view of this overlapping, close volun-
tary coordination between AOC at Gibraltar and Commander, Moroccan
Sea Frontier is maintained through an Area Combined HQ at Gibraltar.
A representative of Commander, Moroccan Sea Frontier is stationed at
Gibraltar and coordination of flying activities between the two Com-
mands is thus achieved.

2. The two Commands work in close harmony. However, the British
and US have two different concepts of ASW. The British belief is that a
threatened convoy should be covered, and is derived from a basic shortage of aircraft available to them. The American concept as outlined by
Cinclant is that convoys should be provided with air coverage at all times.

...

4. ... The Azores patrols depend more or less on the convoy routeings,
and in general, cover the area north of the Azores. However, their accepted
operating line lies between 20° and 40° W and from 26° to 48° N. The
Gibraltar and Port Lyautey planes operate in approximately the same
area, but since some of the Gibraltar planes are equipped with lights they
concentrate on night work and the Mediterranean Approaches, whereas
the US planes carry on the major part of their work in the daytime.

5. Rear Admiral Brind stated to Rear Admiral Wilson [US Navy] and
myself today that the British are moving two squadrons of Hudsons from

---

[1]Capt Henry B. Miller, US Navy: unidentified.

Cmdr, Moroccan Sea Frontier: unidentified.

AOC, Gibraltar: unidentified.

Gibraltar to the UK in order that the crews may be used in airlift operations. They have also requested that the US provide two squadrons of
PVs from Port Lyautey to operate from Gibraltar. He stated, however,
that even if this request is not granted the US planes could still cover the
necessary area reasonably satisfactorily from Port Lyautey.[1]

120.   *Stark to King*

[RG 38/24]   3 March 1945

Saw Admiral Cunningham yesterday. Max Horton has been pressing
him to get some surface groups to assist him in A/S defense. Admiral
Cunningham told me that he is making some changes in the Mediterranean whereby he will get something from there in view of the fact that
some of the new types of submarines may be headed toward the Atlantic
seaboard. Knowing how Horton feels, I think Cunningham has been very
fair about the picture.

121.   *Experiences of Survivors following the sinking
of HMCS Guysborough*[2]

[CAN DHH 81/520/8000]   [March 1945]
                                            [Story told by CPO Maurice Benoit]

I was one of the lucky ones. I was just coming from the chartroom onto
the bridge when the torpedo struck and I was thrown about 40 feet away
from the ship by the explosion. I swam for about half an hour – I must
have been the first one into the water. Then I came to a Carley float which
was supporting 40 men. Some of them were on it, some were in the water
holding onto ropes attached to it. There were four other floats in the water,
lashed together. This one had drifted away from the rest and they couldn't
reach it. When I got to the float it made 41 men on a float intended for
10. A little later we heard someone calling for help and Joseph Marcel
Bodeaux and I swam out and brought in one of the officers who was badly
wounded. He died a few moments later. It was getting darker and colder;
it had been pretty cold all the time. We got organised a bit – told the mar-
ried men with children to get right next to the float where they would have
the best chance of surviving. When it got dark a cold wind came up; some
of the injured men began to say they couldn't hold out much longer. We

---

[1]RA Brind: ACNS (H).
[2]HMCS *Guysborough*: 1942; m/s; 675t; 16.5k; 1×3in.

did what we could for them but there was almost nothing you could do. When a man went he went very quietly. One minute he would be talking to you – the next minute he wouldn't be there any more. Our morale was pretty good, we sang quite a bit at first. Then we got too cold and weak for it. We didn't have any feeling of time passing. Coder Gleason had a watch that was still working. He sang out the time once in a while. Finally we told him not to do it. It made the time seem longer. The worst times were when the Carley float turned over. It did that twice. The wind was strong and the sea was rough. The first time it turned over eight of the fellows who were lashed to it couldn't get loose and were drowned. The second time five men were drowned. By one o'clock in the morning only 20 of us were left. The waves were breaking over our heads and no matter what you did you couldn't help swallowing a lot of water. We couldn't hold on to each other by this time. Our hands were so cold they were almost useless. Nobody seemed frightened – everything was just a long, grey blankness with the sea and sky and the wind. Nothing mattered. More men were going. Dawn came but it didn't help any – the waves were still breaking around us, over our heads. It seemed impossible that anyone would ever find us. Then – suddenly, it seemed – a ship was alongside us. It was a Royal Navy ship – they lowered lifelines – helped us on board; we could hardly do anything for ourselves. There were only six of us left by then: A/B Guy Mercier, Stoker P.O. Ben Walker, A/B Maurice Olchewesky of Port Arthur [B.C.], Coder Gleason, A/B Gauthreau and myself. They did everything for us in the British ship. They were wonderful. I think the best thing was when we got ashore to hospital and met 30 more of our ship-mates from *Guysborough*. It all seems like a dream now. It was a tough experience, but I guess no tougher than thousands of other men have gone through; and we were among the lucky ones. I feel sure that you will agree that spending 19 hours in the water watching 36 of your shipmates die one after the other without knowing whether or not you would be the next is an experience that nobody would like to go through twice.

...

... One thing it does make you realise is that war is wicked and wrong and it is up to those of us who have come through to make very sure that this kind of thing never happens again.

122. *Cunningham to Stark*

[RG 38/24]   [6?] April 1945

... Will you please thank Admiral King for his offer of blimps? They will be a most useful contribution to the war against the U-boat in the inshore waters of the UK. Apart from being able to use their special equipment, they will release some long-range aircraft for operations further afield. ...[1]

123.   *Cominch to Admiralty OIC.*

[ADM 199/2403]   27 April 1945

1. Beginning 0550/26 *Micka* and *Gustafson* made repeated attacks on sound contacts 56° 12 N, 72° 49W.
    0200/26 PBM had disappearing radio contact 34° 43N, 76° 15W.
2. 2025/25 RAF had disappearing radio contact 25° 35N, 76° 38W.
3. Canso aircraft had sonobuoy indications following sighting oil slick at 2040/25 in 45° 08N, 65° 20W.
4. USS *Lorain* attacked sonar contact 42° 57N, 36° 39W.
5. MV *Zanesville Victory* sighted surfaced U-boat 31° 55N, 31° 05W, course 180°.[2]

124.   *A/Cdr J. B. McDiarmid (SB), RCNVR, to Officer-in-Charge, OIC, NSHQ, Ottawa.*[3]

[Pte: M. Whitby]   11 July 1945

1943

...

17. In October Lieut P. Beesly, RNVR, of the Admiralty U-boat Room visited OIC.[4]
18. In November Lieut-Cdr McDiarmid visited Cominch F21.

1944

19. In April and May Lieut-Cdr McDiarmid again visited the Admiralty U-boat Room. One of the chief objects of discussion was the use of Operational Intelligence in routeing and diverting convoys. It was discovered that, contrary to the original intentions of NSHQ, the arrangements in Canada were not the same as those in England. This fact was

---

[1]Blimp: US airship.
[2]*Zanesville Victory:* unidentified. Canso: RCAF Catalina.
[3]Lieut-Cdr McDiarmid: unidentified.
[4]Lieut P. Beesly: author of *Very Special Intelligence: The Story of the Admiralty's OIC, 1939–1945* (London, 1977).

brought to attention of NSHQ, but it was considered that no change could be made at that time.

20. On 29 April 'Cancon' was brought into effect. This was a system for controlling the movement of ships in the Canadian Coastal Zone. This area was sub-divided into several parts which were declared 'Open', 'Restricted' or 'Closed' as the U-boat situation required. The normal procedure was that the Staff Officer, OIC 5, reported to DOD whatever changes seemed necessary in the controls, and on this advice DOD promulgated a 'Cancon' signal. The signal was usually sent out in the evening in order to be available for use by the NCSOs the following day.

21. There were no organisational changes in OIC 5 in 1944.

1945

22. On 14 May the last NSHQ Sighting and Attack Summary was issued and on 2 June the last U-boat estimate, and [on] 14 June the last Otter.

Memorandum: Lieut-Cdr McDiarmid to Joint RCN-RCAF Anti-Submarine Warfare Committee.

1. The purpose of this paper is to examine and evaluate U-boat activities and A/S counter-measures in several different areas in the North Atlantic, with particular reference to the Canadian Area. The following areas are considered:

A. The Canadian Area. (North of 40°N and west of 40°W).

B. The Caribbean Area. (The Caribbean Sea Frontier plus the Panama Sea Frontier).

C. The Freetown Area. (The coastal strip to east of a line from 16°N, 28°W to the Equator, 20°W).

D. The North East Atlantic. (North of 40°N and east of 40°W, but excluding the Faeroes–Iceland transit area and the Biscay Area).

E. The remainder of the Atlantic north of the Equator (including the Biscay Area, the English Channel, and the part of the Faeroes–Iceland transit area west of the Greenwich meridian).

2. Areas A, B and C are similar in the type of U-boat patrolling them, the type of patrol carried out, and their accessibility to land-based aircraft. Areas A and D have in common the passage of convoys to and from the UK, and similar weather. Area E includes the invasion coast in the Channel and one or two American coastal forces Areas in which patrols have been occasionally made, but in general it may be considered a transit area.

3. The unit employed in making evaluations is the 'U-boat day', i.e., the presence for one day of one U-boat in a given area. The measure of the effectiveness of U-boat operations is provided by the quotient U-boat days over ships sunk. The measure of effectiveness of A/S operations is provided by the quotient U-boat days over contacts, attacks and kills respectively.

U-boat Operations

4. Figure 2 shows the Allied losses in ships and the efficiency of U-boat operations in the different areas. It will be noted that no merchant shipping losses occurred in Area E. The three coastal areas accounted for two-thirds of the total merchant shipping tonnage lost. If the three coastal areas are taken together and compared with Area E, it will be found that in the coastal areas the enemy's expenditure was 84 U-boat days per merchant vessel and 19 days per 1000 tons [of] shipping sunk, while in Area E it was 600 and 81 days respectively.

5. The low efficiency of the U-boats in Area D reflects the complete failure of the enemy's latest anti-convoy campaign in the past winter. This failure is made more striking by a comparison between the effectiveness of U-boat operations in the Western Approaches in March 1943 and January 1944, which were the months of greatest activity against convoys in the two years respectively. In March 1943 54 merchant ships were sunk at the expenditure of 45 U-boat days per ship and eight U-boat days per 1000 tons [of] shipping. In January 1944 two ships were sunk at the expenditure of 797 U-boat days per ship and 97 U-boat days per 1000 tons of shipping.

6. The utter lack of success against merchant shipping in Area E is interesting chiefly as an indication of the comparative uselessness of the U-boats in hampering Allied operations in the invasion area. In the parts of Area E, poor results were to be expected because U-boats would encounter shipping only by chance when on passage to or from patrol.

7. The fact that the number of warships sunk in Areas D and E was greater than in the coastal patrol areas A, B and C, is due probably to the greater scale of surface A/S activity in the former two areas. Even so the expenditure per warship was only 380 days in the three coastal areas taken together, while it was 720 in Area D and 1025 in Area E. The indifferent success against warships in Area E is particularly significant because A/S operations in this area included not only the intensive patrols in connection with the invasion but also the numerous searches by US CVE groups in the vicinity of the Azores and to the southward.

8. It is impossible to explain fully why the U-boats were less efficient in Area A than in Areas B and C without more detailed information than

is available on the shipping and A/S forces in the latter two areas. The extreme weather off the Canadian coast in winter and the fog and ice in spring were certainly important factors. Another partial explanation may be the lack of operational experience among U-boats in this area. From prisoners of war it is known that at least four of these U-boats were on their first war cruise. The reason for this is probably that the Canadian coastal area is the only coastal area within economical range of 740-ton U-boats leaving the Baltic on their first [war] cruise.

A/S Operations

9. Figure 3 shows the effectiveness of A/S operations in the different areas and the effectiveness of the different kinds of A/S forces. Contact is taken as meaning a sighting or mechanical contact, and only those contacts are considered in which there was no reasonable doubt of the U-boat's presence. Kills include probable as well as certain destructions.
10. In terms of the ratio of kills to U-boat days, i.e., to available targets, Area D was the most favourable, Areas A and E being in second position with the same ratio. Since, however, contacts and attacks that are not followed by kills have a definite value in estimating the enemy's operations and in causing damage, they must be taken into account in the assessment of the overall effectiveness of A/S operations. By this criterion Areas D and E were roughly between two and three times more favourable than Areas A, B and C. Contact was made with U-boats more than twice as often in Area B as in Area A, and nearly twice as often as in C.
11. The chief reason for the success of the operations in Areas D and E was the use of support groups both as additional escort and on independent operations. In the former area they accounted for more than one-half. The remaining kills in Area E were made by aircraft – chiefly by the Coastal Command in Biscay and the Channel. The remainder in Area E were divided about equally between aircraft and close convoy escorts.
12. As regards offensive surface operations the five areas are roughly comparable. U-boats are usually as accurately located in coastal areas as they are in Area D. The part of Area D south of 40°N may be compared with the approaches to the coastal areas, and A/S operations off the invasion coast are in many ways similar to those off ports such as Halifax. The only explanation for the poor results in the coastal areas appears to be poorer effort.
13. The high rates of contacts, attacks and kills to U-boat days obtained by aircraft in Area E are due in part to special conditions, namely the concentration of U-boats in the narrow transit areas in Biscay and north of the Faeroes. Area D is however comparable to the coastal areas in not possessing these special conditions. In fact the accessibility of the coastal

areas to land-based aircraft and the fairly restricted movement of U-boats in coastal patrols give A/S operations in the coastal areas a decided advantage over those in Area D. But Area B was the only coastal area in which aircraft were more successful in even locating the enemy than in Area D. In this respect Area A was less than one-third as successful, and Area C less than one-fifth.

Details of A/S Operations in Canadian Area

14. In the six month period Canadian ships spent 285 days on A/S patrol in Area A. American patrols in the area occupied 188 ship days commencing 20 March [1944]. Canadian ships obtained one contact. Both U-boats sunk in the area were sunk by US forces, one by *Croatan*'s Group and one by the escort of CU 21.[1]

15. In addition American CVE groups sank one U-boat about five miles to the east of Area A, and two in Area A since 30 June [1944]. In the area north of 40°N and west of 39°W, therefore, US forces sank five of the 10 U-boats at a rate of one kill for 31 U-boat days, i.e., at a rate of about three times as high as that obtained in the North East Atlantic.

16. The reason for this success is clear. The Americans used co-ordinated groups of CVEs, destroyers and DEs, while out of the 285 Canadian ship days only 70 were by destroyers or frigates. Thirty per cent of the Canadian effort was spent on short or incidental patrols, or sweeps on passage; only 14% of American patrols were of this sort. Because of the lack of ships most of the Canadian operations were hurriedly organised with whatever ships were available after the U-boat had been located, whereas the American operations were planned ahead and executed on the basis of tracking data. The U-boat sunk in the area by *Croatan*'s group was killed after nine days' patrol totalling 125 ship days. The longest sustained Canadian ship patrol was 53 ship days.

17. In the six month period 7765 aircraft hours were spent base to base on A/S operations in the Canadian area. One certain and one doubtful sighting were made. If these be given the value of 1.5 sighting the number of hours flown per sighting was 5177. The number of hours flown by Coastal Command in the period January to May 1944 was 583. Undoubtedly the main cause of the lower success in the Canadian area was lack of sufficient night flying. In the air operations against a U-boat from 1 May to 17 June [1944] only 12% of the patrols were flown by night. The proportion of night flying done by Coastal Command is not known but it may be guessed at from the flying time per sighting and from the fact

---

[1] *Croatan*: US CVE & escorts.

that 63% of the Coastal Command sightings in the period mentioned were made by night.

The Enemy's Appreciation

18. There are several factors that may make the enemy's estimation of the situation in the Canadian Area different from that obtained above.

19. It has already been noted that the Canadian Area is only one of three coastal areas within economical range of as 740-ton U-boat leaving the Baltic for her first [war] cruise. This fact gives the Canadian Area a special value for the enemy, for while convoy attacks are in abeyance, his only choice is to send the new 740-ton U-boats to the Canadian Area or to waste them on operations that could be done by shorter range boats. As a training area for all new U-boats, therefore, the Canadian Area need not yield so much shipping as the others to be considered successful.

20. Because the Canadian Area is nearer also to the Biscay ports than the other two coastal areas the enemy can accept a lower return for each U-boat day on patrol. On an average cruise of 105 days the time spent on passage to and from the coastal areas is 40 days in the Canadian Area as it is in the Caribbean, and the return in shipping sunk per U-boat day in the Caribbean must be twice that in the Canadian Area if the cruises are to have the same value.

21. From prisoner of war statements and German Communiques it appears certain that the enemy considers his operations in the Canadian Area to have been much more successful than they actually were. Probably his estimate of the ships sunk is more nearly eight than the actual three, i.e., that the expenditure of U-boat days per ship sunk was about 34 instead of 92.

22. It is known from prisoner of war statements that the enemy does not consider the defences in the Canadian Area to be very dangerous.

23. These considerations, although important, must now be secondary in the enemy's mind to the question of U-boat operations after the Biscay Ports are taken. When this situation does arise and the U-boats are able to operate only from Norway and the Baltic, patrols in the Caribbean and off the African coast will then become impossible.

Conclusion

24. The conclusions this survey points to are as follows:

(a) Because of the strengthening of the [escorts of] transatlantic convoys, particularly by support groups, losses in convoy have become negligible. The ratio of shipping losses to enemy patrol activity has been higher in the coastal area because the local forces have not been correspondingly strengthened.

(b) The high ratio of kills to targets available has been due chiefly to the use of support groups. The success in Area A was due about equally to support groups and aircraft. By comparison the general A/S effectiveness in the coastal areas cannot be considered to have been satisfactory. Apart from the two kills made by American forces, the effort in the Canadian Area was least satisfactory of any of the areas considered. The success of the American operations however indicates what might be achieved from similar Canadian operations.

(c) The enemy probably regards that rate of ship sinkings in Area A as very satisfactory in comparison with the rate in other areas, and A/S measures have not been strong enough to discourage future operations. In the present circumstances, therefore, U-boat operations off the Canadian coast are not likely to fall during the first six months of the year. If the U-boats are compelled to operate solely from Norway or the Baltic, activity in this area is likely to increase rather than decrease as long as distant patrols are maintained. And since such patrols are now by far the most profitable to the enemy, they are likely to be maintained as long as the U-boats take an active part in the war, unless the U-boats are forced away from the coast by more effective A/S operations.

PART III

THE INVASION OF NORMANDY

The British, evicted from Europe in the spring of 1940, vowed to return but it was clear that they could not do so alone, nor, they felt, could an invasion of Nazi-held mainland Europe take place for several years and until Germany had been severely weakened by attacks elsewhere, notably round the periphery of her conquests. In the end, an Allied return to the continent owed much to Soviet pressure on Germany from the east; the bulk of the German army was held on the eastern front. The Allies – chiefly Britain, the United States and Canada but also including elements of the occupied European countries – achieved a return to the continent in June 1944.

The date of the landings was a matter of dispute in the Combined Chiefs of Staff. The Americans, true to their military tradition, advocated an early and direct assault on Europe. They had argued for a diversionary landing in 1942 to draw pressure from the eastern front, where the Germans threatened to force the Soviet Union to surrender. The British Chiefs of Staff held firm against the Joint Chiefs of Staff. Not only did they wish to promote their own traditional indirect strategy, based on the Mediterranean, they felt that a descent on Europe in 1942 would be premature. Command of the surface of the Channel could not then be assured, while the Allies did not have overwhelming supremacy in the skies over the sea and Normandy. American troops in Britain in 1942 were very few and the majority of Britain's own soldiers were occupied mainly in North Africa, Burma and Madagascar. Moreover, the major bottleneck, never satisfactorily cleared throughout the war, was the lack of sufficient landing craft [129–30, 133–4, 144]. Even after the troops had been got ashore, much would depend on Germany's army being stretched by operations elsewhere and its means of reinforcement in Normandy effectively blocked. Moreover, as important as the initial landings was the capability to reinforce and supply the army quickly and steadily over many months. Planning for the great expedition, the assembly of much specialised equipment, the gathering of intelligence, elaborate deception and secrecy schemes, not to mention the training not only of the common soldiery but also numerous specialised units, would take many months. The JCS, somewhat chastened and chagrined after losing the argument over a 1942 invasion, proposed 1943. That, too, proved unacceptable to the COS. They wished to capitalise on their Mediterranean successes in clearing North Africa and Sicily with a descent on Italy and later a 'leapfrog' landing near Rome (Anzio, in January 1944). They were understandably nervous about tackling a substantial and capable German army in territory they recalled as bloody stalemated ground in the First World War; in this they had the support of Churchill and other politicians and most of the public. Britain had no wish to engage in another long-drawn-out bloodbath. Their experience of amphibious operations, though overlain by success in the Mediterranean, was coloured by the blood-red waters of Gallipoli in 1915–16.

Real movement towards an invasion began in August 1943, with the appointment of Lieut-General Sir Frederic Morgan as the Chief of Staff to the Supreme Allied Commander (COSSAC).[1] Morgan began the long process of planning – it was to take nine months – but major progress was slow until the appointment of the Supreme Commander, General Dwight D. Eisenhower, U. S. Army, on 3 December 1943. Eisenhower had experience in the role as Supreme Allied Commander in the Mediterranean from the autumn of 1942 and had overseen three successful invasions there – North Africa in November 1942, Sicily in July 1943 and Italy in September 1943. Eisenhower, a noted staff planner, was a shrewd Supreme Commander, handling the forces of at least two nations, their three services and powerful subordinates ('insubordinates' might have been a better word on occasion);[2] he had the confidence of both British and American forces, which he treated even-handedly.

The Americans suspected the British of not wishing to face the German army in north-western Europe and thus of dragging their feet over an invasion. The British insisted that they were committed to an invasion – when the time was right. At the TRIDENT conference in Washington in May 1943, the British COS agreed with the American JCS that an invasion should take place in May 1944 but momentum was really secured at Tehran in November 1943, when Stalin insisted that a Supreme Commander be appointed forthwith. Eisenhower was called back from the Mediterranean to resume the role he had taken up in February 1942, that as commander of U.S. ground and air forces in Britain, building up strength, supplies and fighting skills. He was no advocate of a precipitate invasion, recognising that the landing craft bottleneck would govern its date; in the event, the invasion was postponed until June 1944 to obtain a further month's production of landing craft. Apart from his high reputation as a result of Mediterranean successes and his skill at handling a somewhat unruly team of commanders, Eisenhower reflected the American insistence on a U.S. Supreme Commander; as

---

[1]Lt-Gen Sir Frederic E. Morgan (1894–1967): COSSAC Mar 1943; DCoS, SHAEF Feb 1944.

[2]Among these self-willed commanders were Lt-Gen George Patton, US Army; Lt-Gen Mark Clark, US Army; and Gen Sir Bernard L. Montgomery, a soldier's soldier, whose somewhat idiosyncratic dress contrasted with the immaculate and traditional Gen Sir Harold Alexander.

they would provide the bulk of the forces (and much of the equipment of other Allies), the British acquiesced readily, especially as his Deputy was British (Air Chief Marshal Sir Arthur Tedder),[1] the commander of all ground forces for the landing and subsequent Normandy campaign was the leading British General, Sir Bernard Montgomery, and, most relevantly, the Allied Naval Commander of the Expeditionary Force was Admiral Sir Bertram Ramsay, RN, who was appointed ANCXF in October 1943 and started work in January 1944[2] [126, 128, 137, 150, 158, 160].

Ramsay was a veteran of major amphibious operations, though his first experience was conducting the successful withdrawal of British and French forces from Dunkirk and other Channel ports in May and June of 1940. He had acquired a formidable reputation as a disciplinarian, a successful junior officer in First World War Channel operations, and as a thoughtful and capable organiser, steadfast and clear-sighted. Although he was noted for his sternness, he was also patient, calm, urbane, cheerful, considerate and amusing. Paul Kennedy has termed him as 'rather modest' and certainly Ramsay got on with the job of organising operation NEPTUNE, the naval preliminary to the invasion itself (OVERLORD), unobtrusively. 'You understand us soldiers', said Montgomery, and he had the ability to see the Army's point of view and requirements.[3] He led the planning for the TORCH operation in North Africa in November 1942 and commanded a major part of the assault on Sicily in July 1943.

During his time as Commander-in-Chief at Dover (1940–42) he had worked closely with the Prime Minister, who came to repose great confidence in this calm, assured, efficient naval officer; Ramsay's achievement in the Dunkirk operation was one of the foundations of Churchill's (and the country's) survival in 1940. Thus when the First Sea Lord,

---

[1]MRAF Lord (Sir Arthur) Tedder (1890–1967): RFC; Sqdn Ldr 1919; AVM & Air Officer, FE 1937; Dir Gen, Research & Development 1940; Dep AOC-in-C, Mid E Dec 1940; AM & AOC-in-C, Mid E, May 1941; ACM & VCAS May 1942; Cdr, Med AF Feb 1943; Dep Supreme Cdr OVERLORD Dec 1943; MRAF Sept 1945; CAS Jan 1946; V. Orange, *Tedder: Quietly in Command* (London, 2004).

[2]Adm Sir Bertram H. Ramsay (1885–1945): ent RN 1898; sig spist; Naval War Coll 1913; Grand F 1914–15; *M25* 1915; *Broke* 1917; Capt 1923; *Weymouth, Danae*; NWC 1927–9; *Kent* China 1929–31; IDC 1931–3; *Royal Sovereign* 1933–5; RA & CoS to C-in-C, Home F, Adm Sir Roger Backhouse Dec 1935 but, feeling redundant, resigned & ret 1938; VA Dover 1939–42; Chf planner, Med landings 1942–3; ANCXF 1944–5; died in plane accident 2 Jan 1945.

[3]Montgomery to Ramsay, Oct 1943, in W. S. Chalmers, *Full Cycle: A Biography of Adm Sir B. H. Ramsay* (London, 1959), p. 182. P. M. Kennedy, *Engineers of Victory* (London, 2013), p. 251.

Admiral of the Fleet Sir Dudley Pound, nominated the C-in-C, Portsmouth, Admiral Sir Charles Little, as ANCXF, Churchill turned down the suggestion and installed Ramsay instead, as he was a proven amphibious commander and well known to the Prime Minister. Ramsay, he said, had 'natural abilities and unique experience' – for once a fine judgment of a senior commander.[1]

Ramsay recognised the enormity of the undertaking and the need to get it absolutely right the first time (there might well be no second chance). He was a meticulous planner, considering all aspects of the expedition and providing for all eventualities. This meant an enormous investment in planning, production of materials, logistics, training and the provision of supporting forces. Ramsay's preparations were certainly elaborate and incredibly detailed. The Americans, less used to such precision, felt that he over-insured. Ramsay, however, "got on well with the Americans and thought highly of their Commanders".[2] He seems to have approved of most of them – Rear Admirals Bieri, Glassford, Hall and Moon in particular – but there are reservations about his relationship with the principal U.S. naval commander, Rear Admiral Alan G. Kirk. Ramsay's diary is full of uncomplimentary references to Kirk. He felt Kirk was not big enough for the job and they had numerous disagreements on proposals. Ramsay termed him 'A poor fish'.[3] Kirk wanted a massive prior bombardment, a suggestion Ramsay turned down and Love, who called his appointment 'an unfortunate choice', feels that Ramsay was slow to ask Bomber Command to attack the troublesome naval base at Le Havre, home of a nest of E-boats and other motorised craft[4] [147, 157]. To his credit, Kirk paid him a warm posthumous tribute, acknowledging his natural courtesy and patience and calling him a 'big man'.[5]

Ramsay seems to have been quick to take offence and was highly strung. That intensity worried Churchill, who asked the First Sea Lord, Admiral of the Fleet Sir Andrew Cunningham, to keep an eye on him. Cunningham, who had worked with Ramsay in the Mediterranean and shared a mutually respectful and jocular friendship with him, also had

---

[1]C. Barnett, *Engage the Enemy More Closely: The Royal Navy in the Second World War* (London, 1991), p. 754.

[2]Chalmers, *Full Cycle*, p. 211; R. W. Love, jr, & J. Major, eds, *The Year of D-Day: The 1944 Diary of Adm Sir B. Ramsay* (Hull, 1994), pp. 13 (23 Jan), 40 (8 Mar), 41 (10 Mar), 56 (14 Apr), 57 (17 Apr), 71–2 (18 May), 105 (14 July), 129 (1 Sept).

[3]Love & Major, eds, *Year of D-Day*, pp. 7 (14 Jan), 61 (29 Apr), 64 (6 May), 65 (7 May), 70 (15 May).

[4]R. W. Love, jr, *History of the US Navy, 1942–1991* (Harrisburg, PA, 1992), p. 156. This remark is not explained.

[5]Chalmers, *Full Cycle*, p. 212.

occasional differences with him. Cunningham heeded the Prime Minister's request but he had his own reasons for supervising Ramsay. This was a largely Royal Navy show, most of the ships were British and the expedition sailed from British Channel ports; Cunningham realised that he bore the ultimate responsibility. He sought both to temper Ramsay's demands and to keep the Prime Minister from his well-known penchant for interfering in operations. By great good fortune, Cunningham's home was at Bishop's Waltham, an easy drive from Ramsay's headquarters at Southwick House, and on several occasions Ramsay drove over to dine with the Cunninghams, the quiet country atmosphere offering a release from the burden of responsibility.[1]

When Ramsay took over the planning of NEPTUNE in January 1944, he found that much research and planning had been undertaken already, under Morgan's supervision [125, 128, 131, 133–8]. Ramsay's task was to draw up the naval plans and oversee the assembly of all the elements required for a successful landing – and he was determined to leave nothing to chance. He ignored suggestions that his planning was over-generous, too elaborate and far too detailed; such was his reputation that he got almost everything for which he asked and, shielded by Cunningham, he was able to operate with a free hand. Fortunately, he got on well with the Supreme Allied Commander, Eisenhower, the general commanding the landing forces, Montgomery, the air commander Air Marshal Sir Trafford Leigh-Mallory, and his fellow-planner, Morgan.[2] In his plans, he had to accommodate Montgomery's insistence on broadening the initial landing from three to five divisions [137, 139]. In view of the breadth of invasion areas, the beach profiles, access to the country beyond, the tides, and the level of German resistance to be expected, it was decided to land in the Bay of the Seine. As it was likely that the major harbours of Cherbourg and Le Havre would be rendered unusable by the Germans, it was proposed to build two 'Mulberries' – floating harbours which consisted of many components, to be protected from

---

[1]The Cunninghams lived at The Palace House, Bishop's Waltham. Southwick House, a few miles nearer Portsmouth, was SHAEF HQ from Apr 1944. M. A. Simpson, ed., *The Papers of Admiral of the Fleet Viscount Cunningham of Hyndhope*, vol. II, *The Triumph of Allied Sea Power, 1942–1946* (Aldershot, 2006), diary, 10 June 1944, p. 205; 2 Sept 1944, p. 216. Love & Major, eds, *Year of D-Day*, diary for 7, 11, 13, 20 & 27 May 1944, pp. 65, 67, 69, 73, 77.

[2]AM Sir Trafford Leigh-Mallory (1892–1944): RFC; RAF 1919; AVM, 12 Group, Fighter Cmd, 1938–40; AOC-in-C, Fighter Cmd, Nov 1942; AM, Allied Expeditionary Air Force Dec 1943; AOC-in-C, SEAC Nov 1944; killed in plane crash on way out E.

heavy seas by a line of old vessels sunk as a breakwater. Fuel was to flow through 'Pluto' – Pipeline Under The Ocean.

Ramsay, like all the other senior commanders, had considerable Mediterranean amphibious experience; while they had specific differences, they formed an integrated team, well aware of their responsibility of ensuring that NEPTUNE/OVERLORD was a success.

The operation, says Kennedy, 'had an Allied Combined Operations command under Admiral Ramsay that had been brought, through earlier experience, to remarkable standards of coordination of planning'.[1]

Apart from his experiences in the field of combined operations, Ramsay brought to NEPTUNE a capacity for keeping control of a vast enterprise. Despite clear personal dislikes and confrontations, revealed bluntly in his diary entries, he endeavoured to get on with a variety of senior figures of varying temperaments and points of view; his criticisms, though sharp, remained private.[2] He had a knack of appreciating the standpoints of other nations and services; he was, in one of Churchill's more colourful and apt words, 'triphibious'. Despite an overwhelming burden of detail, he contrived to see the larger tactical and strategic picture. He identified early and precisely the major problems confronting him – the need for a calm sea and a prosperous voyage; the co-ordination of many different elements of land, sea and air power; the deception and diversion of German defenders; the utmost secrecy surrounding the operation; the colossal extent of the forces required in all three realms; the requisite production and training (the worst event of the whole process occurred during an American training exercise at Slapton Sands in south Devon, when an E-boat attack cost several hundred American lives)[3] [156]; the weeding out of inefficiencies and shortages; the vital issue of timing and the dovetailing of the armada's numerous convoys; the defence of the invasion armada from threats by sea and air and the destruction of obstacles and strongpoints on the beaches. After a deep study of amphibious operations, he approached his task with logic, keen analysis, a sense of initiative and an ability to delegate responsibility.

As Ramsay neared the end of his vast planning task, he remarked that he was 'more confident as regards the purely naval aspects but I view with less confidence our ability to establish the Army firmly onshore

---

[1]Kennedy, *Engineers of Victory*, p. 251.

[2]Diaries were often a way of relieving stress & judgments are therefore hasty & likely to be revised in the cool light of day.

[3]At Slapton Sands, S Devon, on 28 Apr 1944, E-boats created havoc with a US practice landing, causing some 700 US casualties. It was a tragic indication of the surface threat to the invasion armada.

in face of the increasingly stiff defences'.[1] Though Ramsay deserves praise for seeing and managing many aspects of NEPTUNE, two insights were of especial importance. In the first place, he was clear that the whole NEPTUNE/OVERLORD operation should serve the Army's needs. Secondly, he was equally convinced that his part did not cease with putting the soldiers on the beaches; of equal importance to a successful landing was a rapid and substantial build-up of men, munitions, weapons and a vast volume of other supplies.

Ramsay's plan and orders to the various forces engaged in NEPTUNE, issued on 7 April 1944, ran to 579 pages (with 22 annexes, which raised the total to over 1100 pages) and involved 2700 ships and 1900 landing craft, together with additional orders for communications and transport, to support the landing of 130,000 men, 2000 tanks, 12,000 vehicles (and their fuel) and mountains of munitions and other supplies. It was, says Barnett, 'a never surpassed masterpiece of planning and staff work'[2] [150, 153, 158].

The specifically naval demands of this great enterprise expanded over the planning period of nine months. At first, the British felt that the Royal Navy, with the assistance of the Royal Canadian Navy and the 'refugee' navies of Free France, the Netherlands, Norway and Poland, could cope with the demands but the enlargement of the beachhead from three to five landing places increased the demands on the Royal Navy by 60 per cent and involved the British asking for the support of a substantial proportion of the U.S. Navy, in addition to the forces escorting and landing American troops at their two beaches. Admiral King was slow to agree to furnish more support and Americans felt, not unreasonably, that the British kept too many ships in the Home Fleet, based several hundred miles north of the Channel, and which faced an emasculated, not to say timid, German surface threat[3] [125, 131–5, 138–43, 146, 148–9, 152–5, 157, 160, 162].

The beaches were to be covered by a substantial bombarding force of older battleships, cruisers, destroyers and monitors. They were to engage the shore defences and their gunfire was to reach some 15 miles inland [125, 139–40, 143, 145, 148–9]. The vast convoys of landing craft were to be escorted by flotilla craft and motor launches of different kinds; they would be required also to accompany the rapid and enormous build-up

[1]Love & Major, eds, *Year of D-Day*, p. 36 (1 Mar).

[2]C. Barnett, *Engage the Enemy More Closely*, pp. 779–80.

[3]Love, *History of US Navy*, pp. 155, 156, 158, 160–61; S. E. Morison, *History of US Naval Operations in World War II*, vol XI, *The Invasion of France & Germany, 1944–1945* (Boston, 1957), pp. 50–67; S. W. Roskill, *The War at Sea*, vol III, pt 2, p. 11.

[150]. Submarines and motor launches would act as beach markers. In the western approaches to the Channel, escort groups were withdrawn from the battle of the Atlantic to guard against expected U-boat attack. Off the Brittany coast were small groups of destroyers (British, Canadian and Polish), taking care of German flotilla craft and coastal convoys. RAF Coastal Command also blanketed the western seas, patrolling against U-boats.

It had been a costly lesson of earlier campaigns that ships of all kinds and sizes were vulnerable to air attack and British and American fighters covered the Channel, which was within their operational range. Bombing of defences, communications, U-boat and E-boat pens and army concentrations was also a vital element, especially in places beyond the range of naval guns. An airborne drop was to precede the seaborne landings [147, 153, 157–8, 185].

Of particular importance were minesweeping forces. Ramsay reckoned that mines were the enemy's principal threat; his other naval forces were weak. 'There is no doubt', Ramsay confided in his diary, 'that the mine is our greatest obstacle to success'.[1] Numerous flotillas of minesweepers were deployed, especially along the convoy lanes and the approaches to the beaches [125, 131, 140, 148, 150, 153, 158]. A second line of static enemy defence was the use of a large number of beach obstacles of various kinds, cunningly laid below the high-tide line. Small parties of brave men surveyed possible beaches and destroyed many obstacles before the landings took place but many more remained; army commanders insisted on landings at mid-tide, so that these lethal defences would be below the shallow landing craft's keels and thus avoided.

Ramsay was clear that the navies' principal role was to facilitate the landing, build-up and continued support and supply of the armies [158]. As it was unlikely that enemy ports of any size would be captured in the first few weeks, landing and subsequent reinforcement would have to arrive over the beaches. The troops would have to take their ports with them. Thus were born the Mulberry harbours, developed from an idea by Captain Hughes-Hallett in 1942 and seized on by Churchill, always on the look-out for novel and potentially influential schemes; he had a schoolboyish fascination with unorthodox ideas and used his position to foster them and foist them on conventional military authorities, often to his secret delight and their exasperation and chagrin. The Mulberry harbours consisted of massive components, largely of concrete, which had to be towed hundreds of

---

[1]Love & Major, eds, *Year of D-Day*, p. 48 (24 Mar).

miles from their construction sites and assembled on a hostile shore. They were protected from the sea by lines of old ships sunk as breakwaters.[1]

The Mulberries were a British idea and are remembered with great pride and as an ingenious indigenous idea to solve a major problem but they excited no love among many Americans. They found them expensive, wasteful and unnecessary.[2] Their scepticism seemed justified after the American (westerly) Mulberry was virtually destroyed in the 'Great Storm' of 19–22 June. It was decided not to rebuild it and to beach landing craft on the sands and supply the army directly; 'More supplies actually came over the beach using LSTs than the Mulberries could have handled', said Love.[3] On the other hand, Morison pays homage to British inventiveness: 'The novel, not to say colossal, solution is a tribute to British brains and organisation'.[4] The British Mulberry, placed further to the east and thus less subject to the storm's fury, though damaged, was reparable. Ramsay (who else?) organised emergency assistance and soon the British Mulberry was actually out-performing the rate of supplies achieved before the gale. 'Thus was swiftly overcome a crisis that could have endangered the whole campaign,' wrote Barnett[5] [136, 139, 165, 167, 174, 177, 184].

Though the problems of minesweeping, escort, patrol, air cover, beach defences, bombardment and build-up were real and present dangers, the major headache was the supply of landing craft. Their production, though substantial, represented a bottleneck in Allied operations worldwide and throughout the war. Many different types were employed, from simple platoon-strength infantry landing craft, to larger landing ships (mostly for armoured vehicles, guns and motor transport), rocket-launchers, specialised craft for many other functions, and parent landing ships with small landing craft hung from their davits. The shortage for the Normandy operation involved the cancellation of other Allied landing plans in the Pacific and Indian Oceans and a delay in the launching of the invasion of southern France (ANVIL-DRAGOON) [134, 138–9, 141–2, 146, 148]. On D-day itself, Ramsay had at his disposal over 1200 warships, 229 LST, 245 LCI, and over 3500 LCT and other small landing craft, together with over 700 auxiliaries and some 900 merchant vessels.

---

[1]The Mulberries were based on an idea in 1942 by Capt J. Hughes-Hallett (1901–72): *Lion* 1918; Norway 1940; Dieppe 1942; *Jamaica* 1943; *Vernon* 1946–8; V-Cntrlr 1950–52; MP (Con) E Croydon 1954–65; Parl Sec, Ministry of Transport 1961–4.

[2]Love, *History of US Navy*, p. 173–4.

[3]Morison, *Invasion of France & Germany*, p. 24.

[4]Barnett, *Engage the Enemy More Closely*, p. 837.

[5]Morison, *Invasion of France & Germany*, pp. 28, 162.

The margin was tight, however, and in the following weeks the toll of landing craft through enemy action, accidents, and the effects of the great gale strained resources (and staff officers' stress levels) even further. The problem of providing sufficient landing craft was well summed up by the Prime Minister: 'The destinies of two great empires ... seem to be tied up in some God-damned things called LSTs'.[1]

A vast armada was gathered together from harbours all along the south and east coasts of England and Wales. 'Every available berth was filled in every port from Felixstowe on the North Sea to Milford Haven in Wales, and many vessels for which no room could be found in these harbours were moored in the Humber, Clyde and Belfast Lough', as Morison graphically described it.[2] From these creeks they funnelled into a broad maritime highway known as 'The Spout'. Just to the south-east of the Isle of Wight, passing through the all-important swept channel, they fanned out again to approach their designated beaches. Though there was a slight variation between landing times, it was planned to reach the beaches one to three hours after low tide, and between about a quarter of an hour and an hour and a half after sunrise. The seaborne troops were not the first to land in France, as American and British airborne forces had been landed inland in the early morning. All the while, a protective umbrella of fighters roared overhead, while other aircraft attacked targets on and beyond the beaches; yet more planes patrolled the sea lanes, on the alert for enemy naval forces, especially U-boats. Flotilla craft and motor boats roamed the Channel and then the heavier ships, with the aid of some destroyers, provided a bombarding force.

Even with these massive and elaborate arrangements, problems still arose. The weather, though much calmer than on the day before, was still grey, cloudy and whipped up the sea to cause much seasickness. Though guidance was carefully arranged, some craft ended up on the wrong beaches, while others were carried beyond their landing points by wind, tide and current; others broke down and simply drifted. Most troops and supplies, however, landed when and where they should, sliding over reefs, rocks and man-made obstacles. For the most part the troops got ashore without serious opposition. The Germans were expecting an invasion, they had many carefully sited obstructions, hidden machine-gun and concreted artillery emplacements, and, though their air and naval

[1] Kennedy, *Engineers of Victory*, p. 252.
[2] Roskill, *War at Sea*, vol III, pt 2, p. 52; Morison, *Invasion of France & Germany*, pp. 168–9; R. Overy, *Why the Allies Won* (London, 1996), p. 160; G. H. & R. Bennett, *Hitler's Admirals* (Annapolis, MD, 2004), pp. 198–9; *The Führer Conferences on Naval Affairs* (London, 1990), p. 397; Barnett, *Engage the Enemy More Closely*, p. 825.

resources were weak, they were not negligible; finally, there were abundant mines, quickly renewed when swept up.

On the whole, however, the Germans were ill-prepared to meet a major landing in the Bay of the Seine and certainly not on 6 June 1944 [159, 185]. There was division within the German high command as to where the invasion would take place, with Hitler and some others believing that the main assault would be in the Pas-de-Calais, the nearest point to England; even after the landings had taken place well to the westward, these leaders believed that they were a diversion and expected the principal thrust to come near to the BEF's hasty departure in the spring of 1940. To that end, largely at Hitler's behest, they kept back much of the German armour and many of the army's best troops. Even those, like von Rundstedt and Rommel, who took the Bay of the Seine invasion much more seriously, differed on the tactics for defeating the invaders. Rommel wished to confront them as they landed but his superior, von Rundstedt, preferred to tackle them inland.[1] Even had these strategic and tactical differences been resolved, the Germans would still have been in the dark and misled. Their radar was often out of action or jammed, they could not conduct adequate air reconnaissance over Britain because of blanket Allied air cover, they had no reliable agents in Britain (where a remarkable security was maintained), and they were fooled by a phantom American 'army', lodged supposedly in Kent and 'commanded' by the Allies' most aggressive general, Patton, whose 'obvious' route to the Continent lay across the Straits of Dover.[2] While the Allies were understandably anxious about the one element they could not control, the weather, and even on 6 June it was not ideal, they were much better served by a wide-ranging, deep and accurate meteorological unit. The Germans, lacking adequate weather reports from the Atlantic, the source of most Channel weather, concluded that the weather conditions early on 6 June were highly unfavourable to a landing and literally went to sleep; they were understandably slow to react when the Allies came ashore. Rommel was assured by his forecasters that 'in present weather conditions there could be no invasion within the next fortnight'.[3] As Murfett has noted, 'German ignorance of what was afoot on 5 June was almost total'[4] [185].

[1]Bennett, *Hitler's Admirals*, pp. 193–7; Morison, *Invasion of France & Germany*, pp. 87–8, 107; Kennedy, *Engineers of Victory*, pp. 258–61; K. Dönitz, *Memoirs: Ten Years and Twenty Days* (London, 1990), pp. 391–7.

[2]Chalmers, *Full Cycle*, p. 220.

[3]M. H. Murfett, *Naval Warfare, 1919–1945* (London, 2009), p. 342.

[4]Morison, *Invasion of France and Germany*, p. 152.

The landings, therefore, went more or less according to plan; what confusion there was on the beaches was quickly put right by well-trained and experienced beach parties, excellent interservice and international co-operation, good communications and the services of dedicated command ships. At the British and Canadian beaches, on the eastern side of the bay, and at the more easterly of the two American beaches (Utah), the forces established a firm lodgement by the end of D-day. At the other American beach (Omaha), conditions were much more unfavourable. The geography of the area, notably a high bluff to the west, was much more challenging, while the sea was rougher, and obstacles were more substantial. A capable German division in the area had not been located by reconnaissance or intelligence, and the defences on land enfiladed the beach and were well hidden. The Americans added to their own difficulties by inadequate planning and erroneous landing and bombardment tactics. Their landing craft and especially their 'amphibious' tanks were launched too far out and their bombardment started at a late hour and was less effective than elsewhere. At the end of the first day, the Omaha landing was successful but the day was saved by the utmost bravery of the Rangers (the American version of the Commandos) and 'the resourcefulness of the American sailor' (Kirk). Destroyers risked grounding by moving into the shallows and engaging the shore defences at close range. Even so, Omaha suffered more casualties (2400) than the other four beaches put together. 'It seems a miracle', wrote an American naval officer quoted by Morison, 'that this beach was ever taken'[1] [159–60].

Though the overwhelming majority of the forces were American and British, it should not be forgotten that the Canadians played a substantial and important role, in the air, on the ground (a division was in the first flight of invaders) and at sea. Canadian patrol aircraft were active in the western approaches to the Channel, where Canadian 'Tribal' class destroyers were deployed alongside British and Polish vessels to interdict the German flotilla craft based on the Biscay ports. On the beaches, most Canadian troops got ashore safely but some landing craft were wrecked and the Canadians suffered over 1000 casualties. Of particular value were the Canadian minesweepers and Canadian escort groups, drafted from the Atlantic battle to hunt Biscay-based U-boats seeking to interfere with the invasion[2] [161–2, 171].

[1]Morison, *Invasion of France & Germany*, quoting Lt W. L. Wade, USNR, p. 142.
[2]Douglas, *Blue Water Navy*, pp. 184, 231–3, 255, 257, 260–7.

For two weeks after the initial landings, bombarding ships were in action. The Allies had two years of experience in how to organise a shoot and had perfected their techniques of fire and communications. The ships ranged from rocket-firing landing craft, through destroyers and cruisers to monitors and battleships. Their guns ranged from 4in to 16in. Their ranges were up to 15 miles. Thousands of rounds were fired. Direction was by spotter aircraft and observers on the ground. Their targets varied from coastal defences to troops and vehicles on the move. Some spectacular results were achieved but it was difficult to hit moving targets or stationary ones that were well concealed and heavily protected. Both the Allies and the Germans claimed that naval bombardment was very effective. There is a feeling that the German defenders attributed more success to the naval gunnery than it deserved to cover their own defensive failures. It is likely that it destroyed few targets permanently but it probably exercised a strong morale boost for the invaders (who often called for more of it) and equally demoralised the German forces, interfering with their reinforcements in particular. One German admiral claimed that 'we were taken by surprise by the efficiency of naval gunfire of the invading force, both by their multiplicity and by their accuracy even at extreme ranges', a conclusion echoed by Rommel and Hitler[1] [170]. Air power was vital, both blanketing the western approaches to the Channel and providing an impenetrable umbrella over the invasion fleet and its target beaches. While aircraft were often less effective in dealing with hidden fixed defences, their strafing and bombing roles crippled the German counter-attack; reinforcements were held up by blown-up bridges and railways, wrecked vehicles blocking roads, and the loss of supplies, especially oil (already in very short supply).[2]

The Germans were relatively well prepared to meet the invasion on the beaches. Under Rommel's energetic leadership, they had constructed an elaborate multilayered line of 500,000 beach obstacles and their inland defences consisted of well-concealed guns, in concrete housings, which were difficult to locate and hit. 'A casemated gun', wrote Morison, 'is exceedingly difficult for a rapidly moving warship to destroy with a direct hit.'[3] They sowed an abundance of mines and renewed these

[1]Barnett, *Engage the Enemy More Closely*, pp. 810, 816–18, 825; Morison, *Invasion of France & Germany*, pp. 142–8, 168–9; Bennett, *Hitler's Admirals*, pp. 198–9; *Führer Conferences on Naval Affairs*, p. 397; Douglas, *Blue Water Navy*, pp. 236, 241, 257, 258, 261; Roskill, *War at Sea*, vol III, pt 2, p. 52.

[2]Kennedy, *Engineers of Victory*, p. 252; Barnett, *Engage the Enemy More Closely*, pp. 787–91; Chalmers, *Full Cycle*, pp. 192, 203, 224, 232.

[3]Morison, *Invasion of France & Germany*, p. 212.

after they had been swept, a difficult process as there were several types of mine. Their most potent mine was the pressure mine but it was held in reserve due to concerns for its secrecy, which was good news for the Allies, as it was virtually unsweepable. They had some good divisions to hand, too – but that was about as far as their defensive effort went. Their major land forces were held back from Normandy by a combination of Allied bombing destroying communications and Hitler's conviction that the main assault would come in the Pas-de-Calais. Though they possessed numerous divisions in the vicinity of the beaches, most of them were static and of mediocre quality. They lacked intelligence and awareness about the location of the landings and the nature and extent of the total Allied effort[1] [185].

The Luftwaffe was weak and short of pilots and fuel. It was up against heavy odds and extensive anti-aircraft fire, backed by effective warning systems. It made some sorties to strafe and bomb and much of its effort went into minelaying. One of its novel weapons was the glide bomb, which had a serious morale effect on Allied seamen, as there seemed no effective counter-measures against it [159–60, 171].

The German Navy also played an insignificant part in repelling the invasion. This was due in part to careful and blanket Allied defensive efforts, interdicting coastal convoys and patrolling off the Biscay ports to prevent German flotilla craft from interfering with the landings. German forces were in any case very limited; there were only eight destroyers and torpedo boats available – 'meagre forces', said Dönitz – and, although there were numerous E-boats, S-boats and other motorised craft, their numbers were not substantial enough to penetrate Allied screens and elude the Allies' air cover except on a few occasions.[2] Ramsay persuaded Bomber Command to attack the German E-boat lair at Le Havre, an operation which had a spectacular success. A number of new mini-submarines sortied but achieved nothing while suffering grievous losses.[3] Dönitz acknowledged, ruefully, that the odds lay with the Allies. 'They encountered no effective minefield', he wrote, 'and no patrol craft were in the area.'[4] [147, 153, 157–9, 162]

The most potent German weapon was the conventional U-boat, based on the Biscay ports and normally targeting Allied shipping in the Atlantic.

[1]Barnett, *Engage the Enemy More Closely*, p. 830; Morison, *Invasion of France & Germany*, pp. 39–49, 169–76; Dönitz, *Memoirs*, pp. 391–7.
[2]Dönitz, *Memoirs*, p. 394.
[3]Barnett, *Engage the Enemy More Closely*, pp. 798, 845–6; Morison, *Invasion of France & Germany*, pp. 190–94; Love, *History of US Navy*, I, p. 171.
[4]Dönitz, *Memoirs*, p. 395.

Like most German forces, they were caught napping and failed to challenge the first landings. Dönitz had some 36 U-boats available, mostly equipped with Schnorkel. Twenty of them were lost in the Channel by the end of August. In addition, several boats not fitted with Schnorkel were employed; they, too, suffered severely at the hands of elaborate Allied air and sea counter-measures. Even most of the boats reaching their home ports were damaged. The U-boats sank 22 Allied warships, merchantmen and landing craft (about 70,000 tons in total), which was a very poor rate of return for the U-boat arm.[1]

After the initial landings, it was vital that the Allied follow-up should be rapid and substantial. The early availability of the Mulberries helped; construction of floated parts began on 7 June and they were operational by 16 June. They were supplemented by some small harbours and the PLUTO oil pipeline, and, importantly, by the successful experiment of beaching supply-carrying craft on the sands.[2] Though vast quantities of men, materials, munitions and motors were landed, the Allies always struggled to keep up to schedule. In the week following D-day, more than 325,000 men, 54,000 vehicles and over 100,000 tons of supplies came ashore. After 10 days, the Allies had 19 divisions in Normandy.[3] The large ports of Le Havre and Cherbourg, though taken quickly, took weeks to clear of obstructions. Cherbourg was ready to receive ships only on 16 July but thereafter it speedily resumed full capacity and indeed exceeded its targets. Brest, the most important harbour on the Biscay coast, took some three weeks after its capture in August to resume activities[4] [137, 157, 165, 167, 170].

Apart from isolated pockets of strong resistance, some confusion on the landing beaches and the inevitable tangle of rapidly arriving troops and equipment, the follow-up operation went smoothly. There was one major issue of Allied dissension. Admiral King, who had tardily placed American bombarding vessels at Ramsay's disposal (but actually contributed more than he was asked for), gave what Ramsay described as 'peremptory

---

[1]Dönitz, *Memoirs*, p. 422; *Führer Conferences on Naval Affairs*, p. 398; H. Probert, 'Allied Land-based Anti-submarine Warfare', in S. Howarth & D. Law, eds, *The Battle of the Atlantic, 1939–1945* (London, 1994), p. 384; M. Milner, *The Battle of the Atlantic* (St Catharines, Ont. 2003), p. 197; Morison, *Invasion of France & Germany*, pp. 319–25.

[2]Morison, Invasion *of France & Germany*, pp. 165–6; Chalmers, *Full Cycle*, pp. 235, 240; Overy, *Why the Allies Won*, p. 147; Barnett, *Engage the Enemy More Closely*, pp. 839–43.

[3]Barnett *Engage the Enemy More Closely*, pp. 827–9.

[4]Morison, *Invasion of France & Germany*, pp. 195, 216–18; Love & Major, eds, *Year of D-Day*, p. xl.

instructions ... to surrender all US vessels'.[1] King was understandably keen to bring forward the invasion of southern France (ANVIL), originally projected as a parallel landing to complement those in Normandy, creating a second front for the Germans and affording another supply route via Marseille and the Rhône valley; shortage of shipping, particularly landing craft, had caused its postponement. King ordered American ships off Normandy to leave by 19 June, much to Ramsay's fury, for he wanted a maximum bombardment force to stay on station until Operation NEPTUNE was over in late August. Cunningham wrote to the Prime Minister that 'The unilateral action taken by Admiral King amounted to the withdrawal of the bulk of the American forces in OVERLORD and allocating them to ANVIL, without consultation with the Admiralty or the CCS, before the Supreme Allied Commander had stated his requirements'.[2] King felt that the British (who had little liking for ANVIL) had 'overreacted' and had already proposed to consult Eisenhower and the CCS. In the event, substantial American forces remained, mostly engaged on bombarding the defences of Cherbourg (with limited effect)[3] [163, 166–8].

Far more serious than this squabble between the principal Allies, which owed much to the way in which it was conducted and misunderstandings, were the effects of the 'Great Storm'.

The worst storm seen in the Channel for 40 years, it struck on 19 June and continued for four days. It blew in from the north-east, reaching force 8, with 30 mph winds. It produced high seas with short, steep waves and heavy surf. Vessels were driven ashore and many smaller ones were left as splintered wrecks; larger ships dragged their anchors. Unloading was halted and the already difficult supply and reinforcement programme was totally disrupted.[4] Neither the British nor American Mulberries were complete when the storm struck but the more exposed American harbour was more in the path of the gale, with its blockships ill-positioned, and was effectively wrecked; it was said that its structure was 'poorly sited and improperly erected'.[5] Ashore, 'the Omaha beaches were a shambles of stranded and wrecked craft, coasting vessels, barges and Mulberry

[1]Love & Major, *Year of D-Day*, p. xxxix; Simpson, ed., *Cunningham Papers*, II, p. 208 (diary, 21 & 22 June 1944), p. 209 (Cunningham to Churchill, 22 June 1944).

[2]Simpson, ed., *Cunningham Papers*, II, pp. 208–9 (Churchill to A. V. Alexander, & Cunningham to Churchill, 22 June 1944).

[3]T. B. Buell, *Master of Sea Power* (Boston, MA, 1980), pp. 435–6; Morison, *Invasion of France & Germany*, pp. 168, 195–218.

[4]Morison, *Invasion of France & Germany*, pp. 176–9; Barnett, *Engage the Enemy More Closely*, pp. 834–8; Chalmers, *Full Cycle*, pp. 238–9; Overy, *Why the Allies Won*, pp. 147, 165.

[5]Murfett, *Naval Warfare*, p. 345.

fragments'.[1] The Americans had been sceptical about the Mulberry concept and, now that their artificial harbour was thoroughly wrecked, decided not to repair it but to carry on with the already-proven scheme of beaching craft. The British Mulberry, although damaged, was reparable and, following emergency action headed by Ramsay, the reception of troops and supplies was resumed; within three days, the shortfall had been made up. When OVERLORD ended on 22 August, over 700,000 troops, more than 100,000 vehicles and in excess of 250,000 tons of supplies had reached France.[2] The millionth soldier came ashore on 5 July. Were the Mulberries cost effective? Clearly the American one could not fulfil its potential, but the British artificial harbour functioned well. It was an ingenious idea, well-planned and efficiently carried out but, while it supplied about 15 per cent of the armies' needs, it could not be considered crucial to the enterprise[3] [165, 167, 174, 177, 184].

Within three months the Allies had conquered Normandy and were into Belgium. There were hiccups, the most substantial of which was Caen, which should have fallen to Montgomery on the first day, but held out for a month. The major ports on the coast of the Pas-de-Calais were unusable for some weeks but one large and undamaged port, Antwerp in Belgium, fell on 4 September. By that time the armies were racing ahead of their port and beach supply facilities; it seemed vital to the sailors, among whom Cunningham and Ramsay were the most insistent, that this good fortune should be exploited quickly to stave off a potential supply crisis. The trouble was that Antwerp lay some 70 miles inland on the Scheldt River, both sides of which were still held by German forces, who had also mined the river liberally. The need, as Ramsay and Cunningham saw clearly, was to gain control of both banks and then sweep the mines. Otherwise, as Barnett states, 'The Allied supply position remained hideously precarious'.[4]

Montgomery, still in charge of the coastal strip, had his sights fixed on a parachute drop in the Arnhem area, with the object of taking important bridges across the Rhine, and refused to acknowledge the pleas of

---

[1]Morison, *Invasion of France & Germany*, p. 178.

[2]Barnett, *Engage the Enemy More Closely*, pp. 827–30, 834–8.

[3]Morison, *Invasion of France & Germany*, pp. 165–6, 178; Chalmers, *Full Cycle*, pp. 238–9; Overy, *Why the Allies Won*, p. 147; Barnett, *Engage the Enemy More Closely*, pp. 758, 795–6; Love, *History of US Navy*, pp. 173–4.

[4]Barnett, *Engage the Enemy More Closely*, p. 847; Simpson, *Cunningham Papers*, II, pp. 216–17 (diary, 2 Sept & 4 & 6 Oct 1944), pp. 218–19 (Cunningham to Churchill, 15 Nov 1944), pp. 219–20 (Ramsay to Cunningham, 1 Jan 1945); Simpson, *Cunningham*, p. 192; Love & Major, eds, *Year of D-Day*, pp. 135 (10 Sept), 141 (21 Sept), 143 (22 Sept), 151 (5 Oct), 160 (21 Oct), 167 (1 Nov), 201–2 (30 Dec), 203 (31 Dec); Chalmers, *Full Cycle*, pp. 248, 251, 256.

Ramsay, Cunningham, the COS, Eisenhower and Tedder (Eisenhower's Deputy) to concentrate on clearing the Scheldt and opening Antwerp. 'It is extraordinary', wrote Cunningham, 'that the generals will pay no attention to our warnings.'[1]

Ramsay, still ANCXF, expressed his anxiety to get the Scheldt cleared of troops and mines as early as 10 September. A month later, he 'lambasted' Montgomery for his faulty strategy and by 21 October complained that Montgomery was 'six weeks late' in recognising the importance of Antwerp and launching an attack; it was not until 1 November that an assault on Walcheren, at the Scheldt's mouth, led by Ramsay himself, took place. The campaign lasted three weeks and over 150 minesweepers were engaged in clearing the river. The first convoy reached Antwerp only on 29 November. The Royal Marines and Canadian troops spearheaded the landings, meeting stiff resistance and suffering heavy casualties as the Germans had reinforced the area[2] [173, 176, 178, 179].

By the end of 1944, Ramsay was still concerned that the north bank of the river was insecure and wrote to Cunningham on 1 January 1945 that he intended to fly to the region from his headquarters in northern France on the next day. Tragically, Ramsay and all his party were killed when their Hudson crashed on take-off. Thus it came to pass that the greatest exponent of amphibious operations the world had known perished on the cusp of his final triumph[3] [180, 185].

One final natural barrier remained to be crossed – the broad Rhine – and landing craft and naval engineer units assisted the armies in doing so from 11 March 1945. Within six weeks, after nearly six years of war, Germany surrendered.[4] The three major allies had plans for the occupation of Germany and in particular the division of naval vessels, supplies and installations and the administration of German ports [182].

[1]Simpson, ed., *Cunningham* Papers, II, pp. 216–17 (diary, 2, 5 & 7 Sept, 4 & 6 Oct),. pp. 219–20 (Ramsay to Cunningham, 1 Jan 1945); Love & Major, eds, *Year of D-Day*, pp. 151 (5 Oct), 160 (21 Oct).

[2]Love & Major, eds, *Year of D-Day*, pp. 167 (1 Nov); Chalmers *Full Cycle*, pp. 248–50, 253–6.

[3]Simpson, *Cunningham Papers*, ed., II, p. 221 (diary, 2 Jan 1945).

[4]Morison, *Invasion of France & Germany*, pp. 317–30; Chalmers, *Full Cycle*, p. 266.

125. *Rear Admiral B H. Bieri, US Navy, to Assistant Chief
of Staff (Operations)*[1]

[SPD 243]   24 October 1943

Naval Requirements for OVERLORD.

1. Requirements for OVERLORD as given in COSSAC's approved outline calls for the following vessels:

3 BM
6 Expendable Cruisers[2]
2 AA Cruisers
59 DD (Fleet and 'Hunt'; 11 for HQ ships)
20 ODD
6 PE
60 Corvettes or Frigates
64 A/S Trawlers
72 AM

Other minesweeping craft depending on situation at the time.

48 Trawlers
72 PT
100 Aircraft Rescue Boats
204 MGB and ML (48 Navigation Leaders, etc.)
5 LCG (L)
33 LCF (L)
13 LCG (M)
8 LCS (S)
15 LCS (L)
80 LCS (M)
36 CT (R)

Plans [Division] sees no objection to the use of some 'expendable' cruisers but believes that this operation should be supported by some cruisers with modern fire control so as to afford the same measure of support afforded in critical periods by the US Navy at Gela and

---

[1]RA B. H. Bieri, US Navy: TORCH plans 1942; DCoS, Atl F 1942–3; Principal Plans Officer, CNO, 1943; Supreme Cdr staff 1944; VA & C-in-C, 6F (Med) 1946–8.
[2]'Expendable' probably means over 20 yrs old.

Salerno. It is believed that the British similarly should have some modern cruisers employed in addition to the 'expendable' type. This operation is so critical that it will warrant the risks of possible damage to modern cruisers. Accordingly, US cruiser support is listed below.

2. These forces are expected to be furnished by the British with augmentation from the US. In advance of detailed plans from US NTF Commander, it is estimated that the US requirements to provide adequate support and escort for US forces will be as follows:

1 OBB	36 SCs (110 ft)
4 CL	18 YMS (136 ft)
36 DD	12 AM (220 ft)
8 ODD	18 PTs
18 PCs (173 ft)	3 CM

3. The British are providing the following for which the US is furnishing crews:

5 LCG (L)	11 LCF (L)
48 LCP (L) (for laying smoke)	12 LCT (R)

P.S. [to Captain Moon[1]]: I feel that our OBB *New York*, *Texas* and *Arkansas* should be used if we undertake this. What is possibility of them loading with HC 14in and 12in and telling them to have a field day? They have contributed little to the war so far in my opinion.

126.   *King to Stark*

[SPD 243]   27 October 1943

Task Forces: Directive for Establishment and Command of.

1. Effective from the date of reporting of Rear Admiral A. G. Kirk, you will establish a Task Force of the 12th Fleet of those forces to be assigned to his immediate command for the purpose of training for and participating in operations for the invasion of Western Europe, and inform me of its designation.

---

[1]Capt D. P. Moon, US Navy (1894–1944): USNA 1916; *Arizona* 1917–18; gun spist, Bu Ordnance; DesRon 8, Atl F 1941; N Af 1942; CNO staff 1943; Med 1943; RA Jan 1944; Utah beach 6 June 1944; died by own hand 5 Aug 1944.

2. You will direct him to report for duty to the Supreme Allied Commander when that officer is appointed, and prior to that time, you will direct him to report to the Chief of Staff to the Supreme Allied Commander for duty under the Allied Naval Commander-in-Chief.

3. The 11th Amphibious Force, and Landing Craft and Bases, Europe, will be assigned to the above Task Force upon its establishment. Additional US Naval Forces for this operation, as allocated and made available in the future, will be assigned to this Task Force.

4. ... The Commander of this Task Force, having reported either to the Chief of Staff to the Supreme Allied Commander or to the Supreme Allied Commander himself, will operate under this chain of command. ... For the embarkation, and during the joint operations of the US forces, the command of the US Army and Navy forces will be in accordance with the principle of unity of command. The shift of command from the NTF Commander to the Army Commander will be arranged by those officers in accordance with the normal US procedure. ...

127.   *Joint Chiefs of Staff: Meeting 121*

[RG 218/196]   2 November 1943

...

6. *Provision of Tugs for OVERLORD and for artificial harbour purposes.*

Admiral Leahy said that in CCS 307/3 [not reproduced] the representatives of the British Chiefs of Staff had examined the availability of tugs for OVERLORD and had concluded that there would be a deficiency of 40 tugs in the immediate requirements which could not be provided from UK resources. The British COS had expressed the belief that unless this shortage of 40 tugs [was] provided, OVERLORD would be prejudiced and suggested an immediate examination of US resources to provide the 40 tugs still required.

In JCS 552 [not reproduced] the Joint Logistics Committee had thoroughly examined the availability of tugs and found that a large number had already been sent to the UK, which apparently had not been considered by the British COS in their examination of the position.

The Committee concluded that the US commitment of 25 sea-going tugs or towing vessels for OVERLORD was now being met and that, moreover, an additional 235 tugs, many of which could be temporarily diverted for OVERLORD, had been allocated to the European theater of operations. Further, that 25 sea-going tugs or towing vessels were now scheduled for delivery to the British prior to 1 April 1944 under Lend-Lease.

The Committee therefore concluded that the problem could be solved by a well-thought out distribution of all tugs and towing vessels in the UK area and by the acceptance of a temporary interruption of normal services in that area.

128.   *Rear Admiral A. G. Kirk, US Navy, to Admiral Sammy Cooke, US Navy*[1]

[SPD 243]   16 November 1943

...

(c) *Committees:* There are six Sub-Committees for representation and some 15 smaller ones. This is the present bill of goods but I hope to cut down if possible.

...

(f) *Flagship:* Have recommended that *Ancon* go as Flagship of 11th Amphibious Force.

Going afloat was something of surprise to COSSAC and Naval Commander. My position was, that being responsible, I must be there. If all went well, Hall would have a free hand. If there was trouble, I would have to step in and must thus be on the spot.[2]

(g) *US Navy Combatant Types:* I have carefully and studiously refrained from any intimation that we would provide such. However, it seems to me inevitable, particularly as our ships know how to use their guns on targets deep-in from the beach. ... I would like to have Hall's views, especially after Salerno, before reaching even a tentative recommendation.

(h) *General:* There has been considerable confusion here because of a lack of a directive head. As soon as the Supreme Allied Commander is

[1]Adm C. M. ('Savvy') Cooke, US Navy (1886–1959): USNA 1910; b/s 1910–14; s/m 1915–20; WPD, ONO 1938–41; *Pennsylvania* Feb–Apr 1942; ACoS (P), C-in-C, Flt Apr 1942–Oct 1943; DCoS Oct 1943–Oct 1944; CoS Oct 1944–Aug 1945; Cdr, 7 F Dec 1945–Jan 1947; Cdr, Naval Fcs, W Pac Jan 1947–Feb 1948; ret May 1948.
[2]RA J. L. Hall, US Navy: Cdr, XI Amph Force, Omaha beach, 6 June 1944.

appointed, many things will 'jell'. Judging from experience in TORCH and HUSKY, initial plans for the assault area are very likely to be altered radically, once the supreme commander gets to work.

... There are still too any functions. I have no objection to eating dinner with a small group and talking business afterwards. However, these large affairs get out of hand, waste time, and are bad for the digestion. ...

129. *Roosevelt to James F. Byrnes[1]*

[MRF 17]   Cairo,
                                                            23 November 1943

Extremely important and urgent that I know at once whether the present schedules for production and completion of landing craft can be increased during January, February, March, April and May. On the assumption that landing craft takes precedence over all other munitions of war will you let me know how many additional landing craft by types can be delivered during the months of January, February, March, April and May. List each month separately. Call conference of all interested departments. Very urgent.

130. *Byrnes to Roosevelt*

[MRF 17]   24 November 1943

Based on BuShips Predictions, Program 'C' LST can be increased in January 0, February 2, to total of 447, March 5 to total of 477, April 15 to total of 517, May 28 to total of 570; LCIL increase in January 0, February 3 to total of 508, March 0 to total of 547, April 20 to total of 597, May 38 to total of 665; LCT7, no increase in months specified; LCT5 and 6, increased in January 0, February 10 to total of 724, March 21 to total of 785, April 35 to total of 860, May 50 to total of 950; LCM 3, increased in January 0, February 300 to total of 6079, March 300 to total of 6829, April 300 to total of 7629, May 300 to total of 8469; LVCP, increased in January 0, February 200 to total of 9646, March 200 to total of 10596, April 200 to total of 11546, May 200 to total of 12486; LVT, no increase considered feasible before June; any increase

---

[1] James F. Byrnes (1882–1972): Dem Reprv, SC 1911–25; Sen 1931–41; Associate Justice, Supreme Court 1942; Dir War Mobilization, Oct 1942–5; SSt July 1945–Jan 1947; Govr, SC 1951–3.

in LCPL and LCSS would be at the expense of and in equivalent reduction of LVCP. HQ ships AGC can be increased 1 [in] April delivery, 2 [in] May.

Above figures result of conference of all interested agencies based on assumption that landing craft take precedence over all other munitions including Russian protocol. Dates represent different tidewater ports [in] US. Will affect army truck, naval construction and to some extent high Octane [fuel]. Deliveries depend upon promptly directing priorities. Should I proceed?

131.   *Kirk to Cooke*

[SPD 244]   28 November 1943

… The C-in-C Portsmouth held a meeting [on] Thursday. General Bradley and I attended. We settled a few remaining points. In general, I indicated that the US Navy would want to increase its participation just as fast as ships and landing craft become available. The need to minesweep and escort will be a British Naval obligation for some time, and it is so understood. ….[1]

132.   *Preliminary Outline of Naval Forces – Operation NEPTUNE*

[ADM 199/628]   9 December 1943

…

1.   No attempt has been made to differentiate between British and US requirements, or to show which commitment can be best met by the Royal Navy and which by the US Navy. Such division of responsibility is, however, considered necessary and desirable, and it is felt that this can best be done by the ANC-in-C in the light of his special knowledge of the requirements. …

2.   At a very rough estimate it is considered that approximately one-third of all cruisers, destroyers and frigates (or equivalent) should be provided by the US Navy and that the remainder including all minesweepers and coastal craft should be provided by the Royal Navy.

[1] Adm Sir C. Little.

133.   *Kirk to Captain Donald P. Moon, US Navy*

[SPD 243]   23 December 1943

...

7. *British Support Craft manned by US Naval Personnel.*

A few British special support craft have been received and have been manned by the US Navy. Captain Sabin is organising this group now and training is in hand.[1]

...

14. *Hospitalization and Evacuation.*

We are going ahead with this subject and have suggested to the British that they should make as many of their LSTs equipped for this as practicable, including the supply of needed equipment.

134.   *Noble to King*

[SPD 244]   BAD, Washington,
                                      28 December 1943

It was planned to withdraw from the Mediterranean for OVERLORD 45 British LCT (3) and (4) in two flights of 24 and 21 respectively.

19 of the first flight arrived in England, five having been lost on passage in bad weather. The second flight left Gibraltar on 10 December but were recalled on account of weather, and in view of our experience with first flight it has been decided to cancel their sailing and return them to the Mediterranean.

It is anticipated that 14 of these LCT will be operationally available for ANVIL thus increasing the planned ANVIL lift by this amount over the SEXTANT allotment.

To compensate for this diversion from OVERLORD it is suggested that two US LST each carrying one LCT (5) or (6) of the 26 LST planned to proceed to the Mediterranean be diverted to the UK for OVERLORD. This would add the equivalent lift of the 14 LCT for ANVIL to OVERLORD making a net gain of the equivalent of nine

---

[1]Capt L. S. Sabin, US Navy: Close Gunfire Support Grp, TF 125, Utah beach.

LCT to OVERLORD while the ANVIL lift remains unchanged at its original planned figure.

I would be grateful for your concurrence in this suggestion.

135.   *Rough Notes on COMNAVEU 031448 [not reproduced]*

[SPD 243]   4 January 1944

... The desire is to limit US commitments to permit employment of US resources in other theaters, and to take advantage of British proximity to fully employ their resources.

136.   *COSSAC to Secretary of the Admiralty*

[ADM 199/1614]   12 January 1944

Staff Requirements

General

The requirement is for two harbours, 'B' for the British, 'A' for the Americans, which must be sited to suit Naval requirements and to conform to the Military operational plan. Each harbour is to be so constructed that:

(a)   Sheltered water is provided by D+2 day.
(b)   The harbour and equipment can be completely established by D+14 day.
(c)   The harbour remains effective for at least 90 days.

2.   The erection of the harbour and its equipment must not interfere with the assault and the immediate follow-up. It must be so planned as to involve the minimum interference with the existing beaches.

3.   The components of the harbour and its equipment, e.g, Bombadon, Phoenix, Blockships, Pier Units, must be capable of being towed at least 100 miles – in winds up to force 4 (inclusive) during spring tides.

...

Sheltered Water

6.   Sheltered water in winds up to force 6 (inclusive) must be provided at all states of the tide:

(a)   To enable ships at anchor or alongside to discharge into landing craft and small craft.

(b) To allow loaded landing craft and small craft to operate between ships and beaches.

Size

7. There must be inside *each* harbour sufficient sea room at all states of the tide and in winds up to force 6 (inclusive):

(a) For ships ('Liberty' ship type) up to 450 ft in length and drawing 25 ft to take up and leave their moorings.

Note: Moorings for eight such ships are required in 'B' – seven in 'A'.

(b) For ships (Coaster type) up to 360 ft in length and drawing 17 ft maximum, to proceed alongside piers, to leave piers or to anchor.

Note: There will be about 20 coasters in 'B', and 15 in 'A' at any one time.

137. *Kirk to Vice Admiral R. S Edwards, US Navy*[1]

[SPD 243]   13 January 1944

With the arrival of General Montgomery things have begun to move. ...

The General feels very strongly that originally OVERLORD was weak and narrow. He wants a five-division front, three British and two US, and [this] extends the beach front accordingly to eastward and westward. The two new beaches are feasible from the naval point of view.

He wants Cherbourg captured in much quicker time than OVERLORD [initially projected]. His plan is for the US Army to take Cherbourg, and then swing westward and take Brest. The British Army is to cover our Army until these objectives are seized.

Of course all the above is contingent upon CCS approval of Montgomery's plan – and naturally General Eisenhower must agree, too.

There have been many meetings of the different C's-in-C and staffs involved, with representation from CTF 122 where appropriate. Our lash-up with the US 1st Army is excellent, and also with the II and VII Corps. Hall is hand-in-glove with the Army Divisional Commanders.

We likewise are getting on well with the 9th [US] Air Force, and Lewis Brereton is being helpful and receptive.[2]

---

[1] VA Richard S. Edwards, US Navy.
[2] Gen Lewis Brereton, USAAF (1890–1987): USNA 1911; pilot 1913; AEF 1918; Maj & Air Attaché, Paris 1919–22; Brig-Gen 1939; Cdr 3 AF July 1941; Cdr FE AF Nov 1941; Cdr 10 AF, India, 1942; Cdr, ME AF June 1942; Cdr, 9 TAF & Maj Gen 1944; ret 1948.

With Ramsay our relations are entirely satisfactory. Under Montgomery's plan, which all recognise now creates two distinct sectors, Ramsay has decided to pull Vian out of Force J and place him over the three British assault forces and the follow-up force. Vian will be afloat, and Ramsay said that of course this new plan would require me to be afloat, too. This suits me.[1]

Personally, I think the proposed changes are a large improvement on the original. We must have power, and since our speed of attack is slow, the only way to increase the power is to enlarge the mass.

I realize these proposed alterations mean headaches to Admiral King. On my part, I will keep my own requests as low as [is] consistent with ensuring success. But we can't get back in the Continent without power.

138. *King to Noble*

[SPD 244]   15 January 1944

… In general I plan to make available US Naval Forces for operations in the Europe-Mediterranean Theater by withdrawing them from other Atlantic employment for that purpose. Further, I consider that the major portion, if not all of the US Naval Forces so made available should be used in ANVIL, in order, first, to simplify the use of the US Forces, and second, because present plans contemplate the initial assault divisions in ANVIL will be composed entirely of US troops.

Accordingly, it is my view that the British plan for providing all of the Naval Forces for OVERLORD should continue, and that the US Navy should make available Naval Forces for making good deficiencies for ANVIL. …

139. *Stark to King*

[Stark A2]   26 January 1944

Have just had a talk with Admiral Cunningham, the substance of which follows:

1.   Bombarding vessels in close support of landing forces – The British are ready to furnish all the combatant ships for this, both for their landing[s] and ours. Admiral Cunningham states that if you would prefer to assign US Naval vessels to TF 122 such vessels would be very welcome. He

---

[1]AoF Sir Philip Vian (1894–1968): Lt 1916; Jutland; gun spist; Capt 1934; 1 DF, Spanish Civil War 1936; *Arethusa* 1937–9; convoys 1939–40; 4 DF 1940; rescued British PoWs from *Altmark* May 1940; RA July 1941; Liaison Officer, USSR; Force K, Spitzbergen Aug 1941; 15 CS, Med Oct 1941; Malta convoys; Sicily 1943; E TF June 1944; 1 CV Sqdn, BPF Nov 1944; VA 1945; 5 SL 1946–8; C-in-C, HF 1950–52; Adm & AoF 1952.

is neither proposing nor asking that you do this, but simply wants you to know that it would be perfectly agreeable to him and he would welcome our ships. I told Admiral Cunningham that if we had the ships to spare our people would naturally prefer them, but I doubted we had them, and felt you were counting on him to supply them.

2. OVERLORD-ANVIL – As you know, General Eisenhower feels strongly he should not have less than five divisions in the OVERLORD assault. If this should occur ANVIL may become problematical. There is, of course, no question as to the very great desirability of ANVIL; nevertheless, OVERLORD must go over even if ANVIL has to be sacrificed. Ways and means are being studied as to how it would be possible to keep ANVIL in the picture, even to the possibility of delaying the starting date a month with a view to getting the necessary landing craft should they become a controlling factor. Admiral Cunningham mentioned 26 LST and 26 LCT originally slated for ANVIL but which will have to be transferred to OVERLORD if the OVERLORD assault is now to be carried out on the larger scale. He feels just like Ike does about doing everything possible to do both, but agrees, as noted above, that the success of OVERLORD must be assured at all costs.

3. MULBERRY and GOOSEBERRY[1] – Thought is generally shaping up here that early reliance must not be placed on the MULBERRY Phoenixes; I have always felt this way and expressed this opinion while home. All agree that GOOSEBERRY should be set up as quickly as possible and that the MULBERRY Phoenixes may be placed later when things have settled down, followed by the other elements of the MULBERRY harbor, such as the Lobnitz Pierheads, boarding, etc., etc. You will recall my statement that we must be prepared, in the last analysis, to just go in and put stuff on the beaches without any artificial help. Admiral Cunningham agrees with this and of course Kirk is studying this from all angles and in other details with which I will not burden you.

4. Outer breakwater – Regarding the formation of a breakwater by mooring an outer line of Liberty ships (probably 12 in all) which I mentioned to you when I was home and which I thought should be placed to advantage about 700 yards outside the line selected for the Phoenixes or Lilos – this proposal is growing in favour among our own people.[2] Kirk has already sent a despatch home regarding this. It is new to Admiral Cunningham and until he has had a chance to

---

[1]GOOSEBERRY: breakwaters for the MULBERRY harbours, formed of old ships.
[2]Liberty ships: US-built standard freighters; 7126t, 11k. 2710 built, often completed in a month or less.

look it over in detail, he prefers not to comment. The lee such a line could give might prove invaluable in the early stages for the unloading of MT and stores ships onto barges as well as for craft of all types unloading directly on the beach. Time element is an important factor. These ships should be able to steam right over, when desired and on short notice, and form their line quickly; in addition to their primary function as a breakwater they would have (at least so long as they were afloat) other outstanding advantages in that they could provide a concentration of AA fire; they offer opportunity for storage of fresh water and fuel, and food and ammunition, and quarters, and facilities for feeding, or at least giving a hand out to the crews of small craft, they might even provide some first aid, etc., etc. I realize they may be targets for the submarines, and of course they may also be targets for bombs and E-boats, etc., etc. They will be moored in about six fathoms (minimum low water) to which about four fathoms must be added for tide, total 10 fathoms at high water. I have not stated in detail how much of a breakwater these ships might afford if they are sunk, but my guess is that they should afford considerable [protection]. For example, take the 10 fathoms just mentioned, which happens to correspond to the beam of a Liberty ship. I haven't measured up the Liberties for the variable heights from keel to main deck, bridge structure, etc., should they be sunk and remain upright.

5.   Admiral Cunningham asked me about how I felt regarding the repair of each other's craft during this operation. My reply was that my own mind was perfectly clear on it – *other things being equal*, we would prefer to repair our own craft and our own craft would prefer to have us repair them, and that I assumed the same held with regard to his, but that, *if other things were not equal*, and either of us were jammed and the other were slack, of course every facility either possessed should be utilized to the utmost to repair *all* craft, taking care of the picture as a whole. He said that he was in entire agreement. ...

140.   *CCS 486: Memorandum by Representatives*
of the British COS:

Provision of Naval Forces for OVERLORD

[CAB 88/24]   10 February 1944

1.   The following revised naval requirements for OVERLORD have been prepared by the Admiralty and agreed to by General Eisenhower and the Naval C-in-C:

Battleships or Monitors	4–5
Cruisers	18
Fleet Destroyers, 'Hunts' and A/S Sloops	78
Old Destroyers, Frigates and Corvettes	88
A/S Trawlers	50
Fleet Minesweepers (flotillas)	10
Motor Minesweepers	42
Minesweeping Trawlers	45
Motor Launches	114
MTBs and MGBs	120
Gunboats	2

2. All the above forces for OVERLORD, with the exception of the two gunboats which are Dutch, can be found from British resources in time for a May or June [1944] date.

3. In providing the forces for OVERLORD, besides reducing Atlantic escorts, Home Fleet and [other] Commands to a minimum, and absorbing all new construction, it will be necessary to draw on British Mediterranean Forces to the extent of five cruisers and 20 destroyers.

4. In consequence it will be necessary for the British Mediterranean Forces to be reinforced by US Forces to meet their deficiencies and, in accordance with the general policy proposed by COMINCH, to an extent dependent on what operations are carried out in the Mediterranean during the OVERLORD period.

5. The maximum American contribution, i.e., assuming ANVIL on the scale of a two-divisional lift will be – four cruisers, 44 destroyers or destroyer escorts, one or two escort carriers.

6. This contribution will be in addition to the US Forces at present in the Mediterranean, and would require to arrive on the station about D-28 to relieve the British forces required for OVERLORD.

7. The British forces remaining in the Mediterranean for ANVIL and station duties would amount to one 6-in cruiser, one 5.25-in cruiser, four AA cruisers, two FDS, three gunboats, 82 destroyers and destroyer escorts, in addition to trawlers, coastal and minesweeping forces. In addition, seven escort carriers will be made available from British resources if required.

8. We suggest that the provision of the necessary naval vessels should be discussed between the British and US Naval Staffs.

141.   *Commodore A. W. Clarke to Rear Admiral Charles M. Cooke,*
US Navy[1]

[SPD 243]   18 February 1944

When we had our talk the other day you gave me the impression that you felt the Admiralty were possibly being parsimonious in the allocation of British naval forces for the forthcoming major European operation, or alternatively that necessity for maximum sea bombardment support was not fully appreciated and that consequently insufficient British naval forces would be provided.

2. I am quite certain that the authorities at home are fully alive to the necessity of laying on the maximum sea effort. Indeed, only just lately the British COS have themselves said that heavier support than that contemplated to date should be given to OVERLORD, and it was for that reason that to meet this desirable quantity the British found themselves on the debit side in respect of cruisers in particular. You suggest, in addition to other steps, that we ought to meet this further bill by accepting drastic reductions in the Home and Eastern Fleet strengths over and above those already contemplated.

3. The Home Fleet will be reduced to two fast battleships, two fleet carriers (one old), three 8in cruisers, three 6in cruisers (one of which is running on three shafts only and will in any case be spare for OVERLORD in case of casualties) and 12 fleet destroyers (in practice a paper strength). We know that the Germans are rapidly bringing all their available ships up to full operational efficiency, and apparently the information goes to show that the *Tirpitz* may be fit for limited operations, and shows no sign of going south at present. To her, therefore, can be added two pocket battleships, two 8in cruisers and four 6in cruisers, all potentially a threat to Atlantic communications if they can see any opportunity of trying it on. It seems to me, consequently, difficult to suggest that the strength of the Home Fleet during OVERLORD could be reduced any further. Indeed the margin is very fine. We all know that an ample balance over a raiding force is the only sure means of providing for early interception and destruction. As I see it, it would not be sufficient to have all or part of this minimum distant cover diverted to the scene of OVERLORD, even if it was understood that they would be withdrawn if the enemy main forces were taking any offensive steps. It will always

---

[1]Cdre A. W Clarke: *Sheffield* Sep 1941; *Aurora* Nov 1942; Malta Sep 1943; Cdre 1st class, Sep 1944; Asst Naval Attaché & BAD.

be necessary to have the ships required to counter the enemy throughout fully fuelled up and ammunitioned all the time.

4. As regards the Eastern Fleet, apart from the 25-year old capital ship, there will only be the French fast battleship *Richelieu*, two carriers (one USA), four 8in cruisers (one of which is on three shafts), five 6in cruisers, one 5.25in cruiser and 24 destroyers. We are all agreed that the Japanese strength which has moved to Singapore is there for defensive and administrative motives, but even so it cannot be unreasonable to say that if they felt they could, they certainly would be tempted to strike into the Indian Ocean. If they did, I would be inclined to go so far as to say that temporary Eastern Fleet strength in that theatre would have great difficulty in dealing with such action. I confess that the Admiralty's apparent desire to get out there our other two modern battleships as soon as practicable, seems a proper one. One must go fairly soon as the argument is that the *Richelieu* should return to take part in the liberation of France. Meanwhile two of our four modern fast battleships must therefore go ahead with their modernization and tropicalization, and in the interim I have a feeling that the naval situation in the Indian Ocean is nothing to feel comfortable about. Apart from the capital ship issue, the cruiser and destroyer strength is nothing to write home about in view of the Japanese potentialities. One could after all compare the Eastern Fleet strength on one side of the Japanese main Fleet with the US Fleet strength on the other.

5. After cruiser requirements for the Home and Eastern Fleets, and for OVERLORD and ANVIL have been met, there is nothing left in the bag. All refits have been postponed where they would have prevented the ships taking part and the remainder are undergoing action repairs and cannot be ready in time.

6. The only possibility that would appear to remain is an endeavour to man up those old battleships that are not now in commission.[1] I am quite sure that the Admiralty would like to do this if it were at all practicable, but no doubt you will have heard a great deal, one way or another, about our manning situation these days. We have reached the upper limit and the Government in reviewing the manpower situation as a whole, is not prepared to help us further. The fact is we have not got any more men, and the intake of youngsters is only, full and bye, sufficient to cover ordinary losses and wastage. In order, therefore, to ensure that the Navy could man up the increased number of escort vessels and the FAA, it was

---

[1]Manning was the first major problem faced by Cunningham when he became FSL in Oct 1943. Simpson, ed., *Cunningham Papers*, II, pp. 175–92.

decided, reluctantly, to pay off some of our older battleships. They could only be re-manned by a reduction in other classes of ships, and I conclude that they have, so far, decided against this, what might be called, retrograde step.

7. I am personally hoping that the outcome of yesterday's CCS Meeting may prove fruitful. Evidently, if ANVIL is separated in time from OVERLORD as now proposed, many ships can be switched from one operation to the other, thereby creating weight at each. By this means, the mutual desire of both of us to see even greater naval strength applied, could be met, and at the same time that the Admiralty's considered minimum requirement for distant cover and the maintenance of the security of the supply routes would be ensured.

8. I hope the above may go some way to show you that the Admiralty are not trying to hold back forces. It is unfortunate that we have quite a number of ships out of action for one reason or another, but age does tell and, apart from action damage, four years of sea keeping has had its inevitable result. Long term repairs have become essential in some cases and in others breakdowns have just appeared.

142.   *Memorandum by Captain L. E. Porter, RN, and Captain*
D. R. Osborn, US Navy[1]

[SPD 244]   1 March 1944

Transfer of LSTs from the Mediterranean to OVERLORD
(for JCS/CCS).

1.   US COS agree with [British] COS (W1035) [not reproduced] with the exception of paragraph 2 (d) which is under separate discussion. They would prefer, however, in view of the fact that the bulk of the ANVIL assault will be US troops and also because it is desired to have as many 6-davit LSTs as possible, that the 12 US LSTs now scheduled to sail for OVERLORD in the latter part of January be retained in the Mediterranean and 12 more British LSTs proceed to OVERLORD in their stead, if this can be arranged without prejudice to SHINGLE or OVERLORD. The British LSTs referred to may already have been mooted for SHINGLE. The arrangement proposed will provide more British LSTs for OVERLORD with a corresponding reduction in US

---

[1]Capt Donald R. Osborn, US Navy (b 1898): USNA 1919; c/o *Lassen* 1942; plan staff, CNO 1943–4; c/o *Duluth* 1944–5; ND 1945–9.

LSTs and more US LSTs for ANVIL with a corresponding reduction in British LSTs, thereby increasing the national lift for each operation.

2. If the above proposal is agreeable to the British COS, a recapitulation of the manner in which the 68 LSTs due for OVERLORD from the Mediterranean will be withdrawn, is as follows:

US	10	ex-BUCCANEER
UK	5	" "
UK	53	Mediterranean
Total	68	

3. It is recommended that the CCS inform C-in-C, Allied Forces, Mediterranean, requesting his views on the matter.

143. *Marshall to Eisenhower*

[SPD 243]   19 March 1944

Smith asked Handy to approach Cooke in an effort to obtain more fire support for your assault – battleships especially. Cooke states that all US battleships except one have been directed to the Mediterranean and that there is some difficulty about suitable ammunition for the one remaining.[1] Furthermore, Cooke feels that it is not advisable for us to send these ships to you when there are sufficient British battleships available. He states that he did all the missionary work he possibly could do while he was in London, that he agreed fully with you that naval support fire is insufficient, but that he now feels that the only way in which this additional support can be obtained is for you, as the Supreme Commander, to ask for it from the British. Cooke's idea is that this is not strictly a naval matter, but is both Army and Navy, and that you, as the responsible commander, should state the fire support you consider you need, based on the requirements of the Ground Forces, and then it is up to the naval authorities to provide as much of it as they can. The foregoing outlines what our naval people believe is the practicable approach to this problem. I concur with their view and suggest that, if you are unable to get any help this way, you present the matter to the CCS.

---

[1]Smith: prob Gen W Bedell ('Beetle') Smith, US Army (1895–1961): AEF 1917–18; Lt Col Apr 1941; Maj Gen Dec 1942; Lt Gen Jan 1943; CoS to Eisenhower 1944–5; Gen 1951.

144. *Stark to Secretary Knox*

[Stark A2]   20 March 1944

... About a month ago I made a swing round our South coast bases checking up on this, that and the other thing, and really it was an inspiration. The way our people took hold, the way they do things, and their cheerfulness, just the entire spirit of all hands, are just great. I felt refreshed and invigorated and highly encouraged from everything I saw. For example, we set a goal of a minimum of 95% of our [landing] craft being ready on D-day, or rather that was the official mark, the British generally put the figure considerably lower. However, our aim is 100%, and I honestly believe we will come pretty close to it. My only concern, if any, in all that I saw was the seven days a week of long hours, but there certainly was no sign of weariness anywhere. On the contrary, they were just 'rarin' to go'.

145. *Extract from a letter written to Stark by Rear Admiral Hall, US Navy*

[Stark A2]   20 March 1944

... I have written Kirk that I realize the evil in comparisons of gunnery standards of US and British ships. It is a delicate subject to discuss at all generally. But I can't discourage my gunfire liaison officers, who have observed both in action, in their professional discussions, nor can I silence Army artillery officers who have seen our new cruisers and destroyers in action in Sicily and Italy. British fire control equipment is not equal to ours. British ships have need of intensive training in bombardment, including its communications and air support, to be prepared to give the support we need. Those British officers who have seen our ships at Scapa would agree, I believe. I still hang on to a slight hope that when we land US soldiers we'll be able to give them the support of modern US naval gunfire. But I now realize it seems a groundless hope, and I will do all I can to promote the training of British ships that are assigned to us, and also to bolster the confidence of our people.

146. *King to Noble*

[SPD 242]   23 March 1944

... The Admiralty has requested for ANVIL on a two-divisional scale the following additional US Forces:

4 Cruisers
44 Destroyers or Escorts
1 or 2 CVEs

These have been made available, plus three old Battleships, one cruiser and four DEs.

The need for battleship bombardment for ANVIL has been strongly presented by the NTF Commander for the operation. The slight additional escort strength which has been provided is due to uncertainty in regard to the escorts which will be available for the seven CVEs which the Admiralty might allocate. The US Forces which have been assigned for ANVIL are not considered in excess of the requirements for that operation.

It is possible, of course, that the ANVIL operation may be delayed or reduced in scope. If it is reduced in scope, the requirements of naval support forces will be substantially the same, with possibly some reduction in regard to the need for escorts.

I strongly concur in the Admiralty view that additional bombardment forces should be allocated for NEPTUNE. However, in view of the fact that the Atlantic Fleet has been stripped of combat and escort forces in order to make available the US vessels which have already been provided, the additional requirements for NEPTUNE must come from British sources. With the improved situation in the Atlantic, I believe that these can be found without too much risk. Also, as NEPTUNE-ANVIL, by agreement of the CCS, are not to be interfered with by other operations, it should be practicable to provide the additional necessary supporting naval vessels required by withdrawal from the Eastern and Home Fleets and by pointing up the refitting of vessels in preparation for this all-important operation.

Use *Lorraine* if you wish extra US battleships allocated; suggest two French cruisers can stay Mediterranean and [a] British 5.25[in cruiser] go to NEPTUNE, which will also have *Augusta*, leaving cruiser deficit at three.

147. *Stark to Cooke*

[Stark A2]   25 March 1944

... I still maintain one of the heavy threats to us during the big move across the Channel will be the German E-boats. Admiral Cunningham is in complete accord with this. I saw him again the day before yesterday, asking him in view of our previous conversations if it had been possible to get some determined air offensive, particularly against the additional heavy concrete pens and shelters being built for these E-boats, and any other offensive we can get towards their destruction. Admiral Cunningham said he was hopeful. I remember so well the reports concerning the effort that was made to get the Air Force to bomb the big concrete structures that protected the U-boats in the Biscay ports. As I understand it, the first bombings were not made until after the structure was complete. Then it was found the structures were too heavy for the bombs to crack, so – why bother to bomb them? We should have kept them from being erected if possible.

148.   *Cunningham to King, via Noble*

[SPD 242]   30 March 1944

1.   BAD has sent me your reply to Admiralty requests for US assistance in NEPTUNE and ANVIL. I note that you can provide a proportion of Minesweepers and Escorts additionally required for NEPTUNE but that you will not be able to find the six Cruisers and 14 Destroyers to make up numbers which the Supreme Commander now considers necessary for [the] bombardment force. Because of *Lorraine*'s limited supply of ammunition I would have preferred to include a US Battleship in [the] NEPTUNE bombardment force, but if you do not wish to provide one *Lorraine* will be used.

2.   Your suggestion that Supreme Commander's requirements can be met by further withdrawal from Eastern and Home Fleets and by speeding up refits is not practicable. These two Fleets are already reduced to minimum strength I consider necessary for tasks they are required to perform. All speeding up of refits has already been done. British forces remaining in Mediterranean will comprise one 6in Cruiser, one 5.25in Cruiser and 13 Fleet Destroyers. I could not agree to any further reduction of British force in this theatre, and it for this reason that I consider that two French Cruisers should be withdrawn for NEPTUNE.

3.   However, if ANVIL is now postponed, as is now probable, I presume extra force which you assigned to Mediterranean in your 161805 [not reproduced] … will be available for NEPTUNE, since they will have time to return [to] Mediterranean for the postponed operation. This arrangement would solve all outstanding difficulties

4.   I shall be glad to have early confirmation that this is your intention, for if it is not so, the Supreme Commander must be informed to what extent his bombardment requirements for NEPTUNE cannot be met.

149.   *Noble to King*

[SPD 242]   1 April 1944

…

2. Admiral Cunningham assumes that after seeing my letter NO28/44 of 20 March [Document 147 refers], you will obtain the approval of the

CCS for the use of two French 6in cruisers in NEPTUNE. The Supreme Commander's requirements for bombardment will then be met with the exception of four cruisers. (He presumes that the *Augusta* would not be available for bombarding).

3. To meet possible casualties in any theatre between now and D-day we shall have a 5.25in cruiser now employed as Flagship of assault carriers, and a 6in cruiser in the Home Fleet, whose steaming efficiency is affected by a defective turbine. These are the only British reserves.

4. Subject to your confirming that no further US cruiser can be allocated to NEPTUNE, the First Sea Lord proposes that the Supreme Commander should be informed by the CCS that the forces required for NEPTUNE can be met with the exception of four cruisers in the worst circumstances, and two cruisers in the best.

150.   *Admiral Ramsay: Operation NEPTUNE*

[ADM 199/1586]   10 April 1944

Naval Orders.

...

16. The object of the Naval C-in-C is the safe and timely arrival of the assault forces at the beaches, the cover of their landings, and subsequently the support and maintenance and rapid build-up of our forces ashore.

Intention

17. The intentions of the Naval C-in-C are:

(a) to provide adequate surface covering forces to protect the flanks of the routes of our assault, follow-up and build-up convoys

(b) to provide adequate close escort for all our convoys, both coastwise along the English coast and across the Channel

(c) to route our forces prior to the assault so far as possible to avoid disclosure of their intended location

(d) to make full use of counter-measures against enemy Radar

(e) to provide minesweeping forces to sweep our forces into the assault, to sweep the convoy anchorages, and later to establish swept channels from the assault area and captured continental ports to England, and coastwise along the French coast

(f) to provide the maximum possible gun support for our landings

(g) to establish a shuttle service of LST, LCI (L) and LCT between England and France, in which, in addition to personnel ships, MT ships and coasters, will be carried the build-up of our forces

(h) to employ a proportion of the available LCT and all available minor landing craft off the French coast to ferry vehicles and stores ashore during the build-up

(j) [i is missing] to provide adequate forces for the protection of the anchorages off the enemy coast

(k) to support the advance of our land forces with naval bombardment

(l) to make preparations to re-form one assault force at short notice to carry out another assault if so ordered by the Supreme Commander

(m) to provide adequate administrative, repair, salvage, and rescue facilities off the French coast

(n) to provide five areas of sheltered water off the beaches by sinking lines of old merchant vessels

(o) to provide two artificial harbours on the French coast for the unloading of stores

(p) to provide petrol and oil in bulk on the French coast by establishing –

　　(i) submarine pipelines across the Channel
　　(ii) tanker discharge points off the French coast.

…

Weather

21. Quiet weather is required for the initial passage and assaults; absence of fog is necessary to enable air operations to be undertaken. Meteorological forecasts cannot be relied upon for more than 48 hours ahead and a decision will be made about H-24 whether to confirm D-day or to postpone it. No further signal will be made unless it is necessary to postpone D-day.

…

Assembly of Forces on the South Coast

23. The assembly of such a large concentration of shipping on the south coast prior to the assaults necessitates the most careful berthing of all forces. Instructions for the assembly are given in ON4 [not reproduced]. Every endeavour is to be made by all COs to take up the appointed berths accordingly; this applies particularly to ships and craft returning to the anchorages after landing.

Landing of Assault Forces and Follow-up Forces

24. The detailed plan for the landing and assembly of the naval assault and follow-up forces is included in ON4.

This may be summarised as follows:

Load	Assemble

Force L:

1 Brigade Group Tilbury	Southend & Sheerness
2 Brigade Groups Felixstowe	Harwich

Force S:

2 Brigade Groups	Portsmouth	Portsmouth & Spithead
1 Brigade Group	Newhaven & Shoreham	Newhaven & Shoreham
Force J	Southampton & Portsmouth	Southampton, Solent & Spithead
Force G	Southampton	Southampton, Solent & Spithead
Force O	Weymouth & Portland	Weymouth, Portland & Poole

Force U:

1 RCT	Torquay, Brixham & Dartmouth E	Torquay, Brixham & Torbay
1 RCT	Dartmouth W	Brixham
1 RCT	Plymouth	Salcombe

Force B:

1 RCT	Plymouth W	Plymouth
2 RCT	Falmouth	Falmouth, Helford R, Fowey

…

Sailing of the Forces to the Assault

26. The sailing of all forces for the assaults is the responsibility of the Cs-in-C, Home Commands and FOSIC, in accordance with the detailed requirements of Task Force and Assault and Follow-up Force Commanders so far as their own forces are concerned. Bombarding ships will proceed independently of the assault forces; fleet minesweepers will accompany each assault force. …

…

Covering Forces

28. Four divisions of destroyers will be employed as surface cover on the flanks of the operation, two divisions in the Plymouth Command, one division in the Portsmouth Command and one division in the Dover Command. Coastal Forces patrols will also operate off the enemy coast. …

The Assaults

32. The following simultaneous main assaults will made at H-hour:

Approximate Location	Division	Naval Force	No. of Brigades/ RCT Assaulting
Ouistreham	3 Div	S	1
Corseulles	3 Can	J	2
Asnelles	50 Div	G	2
St Laurent	1 US	O	2
	29 US		
Varreville	4 US	U	1

[There were assaults by Commandos and US Rangers simultaneously or shortly afterwards]

...

Clearance of Shipping and Craft from the Area

36. The rapid clearance of ships and craft from the assault area after discharge is of the greatest importance, both so as not to expose them unnecessarily and so as to make them available for further service during the build-up. ...

Follow-up and Build-up

37. Of equal importance to weight and violence of the assaults is the speed with which our subsequent military formations and stores are landed. In order that the Expeditionary Force may be sustained, and so that its rate of reinforcement can match that of the enemy, a great volume of shipping and craft must be discharged without delay continuously throughout the first few weeks of the operation. ... The Build-up comprises a complex and extensive convoy programme which permits of little variation, and which necessitates a high degree of efficiency from all concerned. ...

...

Escorts

39. It is intended to operate escorts in the same groups as far as possible throughout the operation. MLs, however, will be formed into pools at the escort bases and will not always operate with the same escort groups. Escort groups will be allocated to the Cs-in-C, Home Commands. ... Some escorts will, however, be lent to the Naval Force Commanders for the period of the assault. ... Task Force and Assault Force Commanders are to ensure that all escorts return to the UK as soon as possible after the assaults as they are required for early build-up convoys.

...

Artificial Harbours

46. An essential part of the plan is the construction of two prefabricated ports (code word MULBERRIES), one in the British Sector at Arromanches (MULBERRY 'B') and one in the US Sector at St Laurent (MULBERRY 'A'). These ports are required to enable the unloading of stores to continue should the weather prevent discharging over open beaches. The towage across the Channel of the units of which these ports are constructed will begin a.m., D-day. Task Force and Assault Force Commanders are to render every assistance in the progressing of this work, as the Expeditionary Force can have no real security until these ports are working. The construction of the ports may take any time from 14 to 42 days, but so far as possible use will be made of the shelter provided by the outer breakwaters once these are completed insofar as this can be done without prejudice to the completion of the work.

Craft Shelters – GOOSEBERRIES

47. It is all planned to form five small havens (code word GOOSEBERRIES) to provide sheltered water for the discharge of ferry craft off the enemy coast if an onshore wind gets up, and a refuge for small craft. Two of these will be in the US and three in the British sectors. They will be numbered from 1 to five from west to east. GOOSEBERRIES nos. 2 and 3 will be formed by 60 to 70 old ships (code word CORNCOBS) which will steam across the Channel arriving p.m. on D+1 and subsequent days, and which will then be sunk near the two-fathom line. A limited number of small coasters may be able to take advantage of the shelter for discharging in rough weather.

151.   *Memorandum by Admiral Little*

[Stark A2]   11 April 1944

Meeting held at Admiralty House, Portsmouth.

At a meeting with Rear Admiral Wilkes [US Navy] at Admiralty House today, the following was discussed:[1]

---

[1]RA John Wilkes, US Navy (1895–1957): USNA 1916; s/m 1920–33; Cdr, s/m Sqdn 14, 1939–41; Cdr, TG 51.1, SW Pac, 1941–2; *Birmingham* 1943–4; Sicily; Cdr, Landing

1. The general set-up and chain of command for the 'Turn-round' organisation in the Portsmouth Command. While C-in-C, Portsmouth, was responsible generally under ANXCF for the Turn-round in the Portsmouth Command it was clear that the representation of the US Navy on TURCO organisation and also at hards and in all other activities where US landing craft were involved was essential in order to help out with this complex problem.

    At Portland where the US activities predominate, the hards and other facilities relating to the landing craft would be handled by the US Navy, and would co-operate in the 'Turn-round' organisation which includes British LCT.

2. Commander Anderson, US Navy, would represent Rear Admiral Wilkes on the Portsmouth TURCO with three assistants. Commander Anderson would join the Command now and work out, with C-in-C's staff, exactly what US representation there would be on the other activities in which the US Navy were interested.[1]

3. The C-in-C stressed the importance of having this personnel in place as soon as practicable and certainly not later than the end of April for exercise FABIUS. Although US landing craft are not taking part in FABIUS this would be the best opportunity for US staffs to become acquainted with local set-up and conditions.

4. The C-in-C hoped it would be possible to provide additional US officers to assist piloting the US LST to Southampton, having acquired local knowledge previously.

5. The Isle of Wight area charts with the assembly areas superimposed were examined and explained. A general discussion took place regarding the Mulberries and these being primarily a British Army commitment it was considered the exact position of the US Navy in relation to the different types could best be got out with RANP (Rear Admiral Tennant).[2]

6. Rear Admiral Wilkes will be represented at the meeting at Admiralty House, 1100 tomorrow, when the TURCO organisation is

Craft & Bases, Amph Fcs, Eur Aug 1943–July 1944; RA & Cdr, Bases, France July 1944–Mar 1945; Cdr Admin, Amph Fcs, Pac F 1945; Cdr s/m Atl F 1945–7; Cdr Naval Fcs, Ger 1948–51; Cdr E Sea Frontier 1951; VA & ret 1951.

[1] Cdr Anderson, US Navy: unidentified.

[2] Adm Sir Willian Tennant (1890–1963): ent RN 1905; nav 1912; N Sea & Med 1914–18; Nav Officer *Renown* & *Repulse*; Staff College; Capt 1932; IDC 1934; *Arethusa*; CSO to FSL; SNO Dunkirk May–June 1940; Capt *Repulse* May-Dec 1941; RA 4CS, EF Feb 1942; RA i/c Mulberry; Actg VA & FO Levant & E Med Oct 1944; FO Egypt; C-in-C NAWI 1946–9.

being explained to the representatives of ETOUSA, the War Office and other British Naval Commands concerned.

152. *King to Noble*

[SPD 242]   11 April 1944

[King agrees] with the request that two French 6in cruisers of the 'Montcalm' class be used in NEPTUNE and will take the necessary action to implement this. It is understood that these French cruisers will be returned to the Mediterranean in time to participate in any future operations there.

The *Augusta* which was assigned for duty as Flagship of Commander, TF 122, is to be used for bombardment purposes as well.

No US cruisers in addition to the *Augusta* and *Tuscaloosa* can be allocated to NEPTUNE. However, in view of the fact that the requirements of the Supreme Commander cannot be met with regard to cruisers, [King] will now assign to Commander, TF 122, the *Texas* and *Arkansas* and nine additional destroyers, which it is considered will more than make up for the deficiency in cruisers for NEPTUNE. Nine fleet minesweepers will also be assigned to TF 122 to assist in overcoming the shortage over minesweepers mentioned in your letter of 20 March. This allocation is made possible by changing conditions in the Mediterranean and on the understanding that the British forces will not be decreased but will be increased to the maximum extent possible.

153. *Memorandum by ANXCF*

[ADM 199/873]   13 April 1944

General Outline of Operation NEPTUNE.

...

9. *Naval Forces taking part*

...

4 Battleships, 2 Monitors, 20 Cruisers, 79 Destroyers (58 Fleet, 21 'Hunts'), 15 AA Sloops, 141 Escorts (17 Destroyer Escorts, 43 Frigates, 69 Corvettes), 12 Patrol Craft (US), 50 A/S Trawlers.

Minesweeping: 10 Minesweeping Flotillas, 4 BYMS, 7 Motor Minesweeper Flotillas, 16 LL Trawlers, 18 YMS.

Coastal Forces: 139 ML, 42 HDML, 64 'D' class MTB, 6 'C' class MGB, 6 SGB, 32 71ft 6in MTB, 52 70ft MTB, 32 RML, 18 SC (US), 3 PT (US).

...

11. *Enemy Forces Available*

(a) Enemy surface forces likely to be used against the assault are as follows:

Destroyers	3
TB (including 'Elbings')	9–11
E-boats	50–60
R-boats	50–60
M-class Minesweepers	25–30
Miscellaneous small local craft	60

(b) A further six destroyers and 10 torpedo boats might be sent from the Bight or the Baltic, but if so the enemy's heavy ships would have no screen should they put to sea.

(c) 130 U-boats operating from Biscay ports might, between D+4 and D+14, be reinforced to a total of about 200. They could work for a short time at a ratio of 60% at sea, losses up to a rate of 30 a month being made good from the partly trained Baltic reserve.

...

(e) Up to 25 short-range U-boats (300 tons or less) could in addition to the above, be sent from the Baltic to operate off our East and South East coasts.

12. *Enemy Naval Reaction*

(a) Once it is clear that invasion is taking place, it must be expected that the enemy will expend his forces ruthlessly to meet it. His cruisers and larger ships may make diversionary sorties into the Atlantic, but their use in the Channel is unlikely except as a desperate measure. His light surface forces will probably be used as directly as possible against the assault. They will probably be concentrated in the Channel and Southern North Sea area. These forces will probably restrict ruthless attacks to the dark hours and periods of low visibility, operating on the flanks.

(b) His U-boats will probably be concentrated rapidly in the Channel and its approaches and operated without regard to losses. In order to maintain the threat to the Atlantic shipping routes, U-boats from Norway and the Baltic could relieve those moved into the Channel by about D+14.

(c) Evidence of midget submarines or fast submersible craft is accumulating and (March 1944) a small number may have reached the operational stage.

(d) Offensive and defensive minelaying by enemy surface vessels and aircraft is probable. New types of mine may be used.

13. *Preliminary Measures*

(a) The general air offensive prior to the operation will be directed towards the destruction of the enemy's air forces, particularly his fighter force, and the interruption of his communications. This will reach a climax immediately before the assaults and a heavy air bombardment of the beach area and defences will be carried out before the landings.

(b) Air and naval anti-U-boat and anti-E-boat operations will be intensified in the Channel and in the Bay of Biscay during the weeks prior to the operation. Air bombardment of the enemy's bases will be carried out.

(c) Offensive minelaying will be carried out off enemy bases and elsewhere in accordance with the minelaying plan.

154. *Noble to King*

[SPD 242]   13 April 1944

The First Sea Lord has seen your messages 102104 and 111641 [see Document 152]. He wishes me to inform you that the additional ships you intend to assign to CTF 122 are most welcome. He now considers that adequate naval forces have been allocated to NEPTUNE.

He asks me to assure you that all available British forces will be used.

155. *Cunningham to BAD for King*

[SPD 244]   27 April 1944

SCAEF has asked for as many spare bombarding ships as can be made available.

2. As pointed out in my 28153 of 5 March [not reproduced] arrangements have been made to reduce Home Fleet to minimum strength, and am only able to offer *Sheffield* who has one shaft out of action.

3. I am also considering making *Nelson* available for this purpose if she can be prepared in time.

4. *Nelson* is at present manned with reduced crew and is due to sail at end of May for Philadelphia for modernization. If she can be worked up in time can you accept a delay of two or three weeks in arrival of *Nelson* in USA? If so, is her date of completion likely to be extended by much more than this period?

156.   *CTF 125 to COMINCH, CTF 122, CTF 127*

[SPD 244]   1 May 1944

[COMNAVEU summary]

Accompanying my 2914088 [not reproduced] convoy T-4 was proceeding independently as a follow-up convoy for exercise TIGER to arrive at Slapton beach latitude 50° 17' N, 3° 38.5' W at 0730B 28 April. At the time of the attack it was approximately 33 miles from this destination.

Force U after landing division 4 of VII Corps in assault on 27 April at nightfall had under protection in transport area Slapton beach 1 APA, 21 LSTs, 28 LCIs, 65 LCTs, 14 miscellaneous and 92 small landing craft of total 221 awaiting unloading and sailing empty at daylight.

Representative [of] C-in-C Plymouth informs [me that] all available escorts had been assigned to assault force convoys[,] patrols and screens.[1]

Four special patrols totalling 3 MTBs[,] 2 MGBs and 4 'O' class destroyers were stationed on a patrol line from Start Point to off Portland Bill. A fifth patrol of 3 MTBs was stationed off Cherbourg to intercept any departing E-boat.

HMS *Scimitar*'s suffering slight damage although still operational resulted in [a] mix-up in Plymouth command in regard to orders and she was not sailed with convoy leaving corvette HMS *Azalea* as only escort.

This was unknown to anyone in authority until discovered by Plymouth command too late to provide an additional escort before [the] attack.

Saladin proceeding to reinforce as a result of C-in-C Plymouth action after discovery arrived in time to pick up survivors but not assist in repelling attack. E-boats penetrated the screen and operated freely in Lyme Bay until convoy was picked up and attacked. Timely reports of E-boat movement from radar plot were made by C-in-C Plymouth. Cdr Skahill[,] convoy commander[,] now in Plymouth

---

[1]C-in-C Plymouth: Adm Sir Ralph Leatham (1886–1954): ent RN 1900; CO *Yarmouth,Durban, Ramillies, Valiant*; RA; 1BS 1938–9; C-in-C, EI, 1939–41; VA, Malta, 1942–3; Adm 1943; C-in-C, Plymouth, 1943–5; Govr & C-in-C Bermuda, 1946–9.

contacting scattered LST commanders and senior survivors in preparation of reports.[1]

157. *Kirk to Ramsay*

[ADM 199/156]   4 May 1944

...

9. In my opinion the E-boats must be destroyed, or driven from the Cherbourg area, prior to D-day. The only successful defense against the E-boat is to sink it before it can reach an attack position.

10. It is my understanding that the responsibility for covering the movement of the Western Task Force to its assault area (south of 49° 40' N) lies with the C-in-C Portsmouth, except for routes which are within the Plymouth Home Command. It is further understood that C-in-C Portsmouth has eight destroyers, plus Coastal Forces, attached.

11. It is my considered opinion that it is vital to the success of the initial phase of Operation NEPTUNE that the following steps be taken:

(a) Bring the port of Cherbourg under heavy bombardment, both by the heaviest naval guns and by the heaviest aerial bombs, at such prior time to D-1 as will destroy the port as an operational base for German E-boats and destroyers.

(b) Strengthen the covering force of the Plymouth and Portsmouth Home Commands by naval types capable of dealing with the E-boat menace, to such degree as will destroy all E-boats which attempt to interfere with our entire cross-channel movement and subsequent deployment in the Bay of the Seine.

12. To implement the above I propose, for (a), the following:

(1) A bombardment force of two modern battleships, with destroyer screen and minesweeping flotillas, [should] attack the Port from separated areas, using air-spotting.

(2) A heavy bomber striking force of appropriate strength.

(3) Fighter cover for the naval forces.

(4) I offer to make available the USS *Nevada* with destroyer screen, as one of the two modern heavy ships required. The *Nevada* to be returned to Force U for her assault duties at H-hour.

(5) I offer a US Flag Officer and Staff to conduct this operation.

---

[1]Cdr Skahill: unidentified.

(b)   as to 11 (b), I have no ships to offer for this task; and they might be obtained elsewhere for this most important addition to our common security.

13.   In my view we are faced with a critical situation on D-1/D-day in this respect, and I recommend that every means be employed to overcome and crush this threat to our success.

158.   *Force G: Orders for Operation NEPTUNE*

[ADM 199/1558]   20 May 1944

Outline of the Operation.

Object of the Operation

The object of Operation NEPTUNE is to secure a lodgement on the Continent from which further operations can be developed. This lodgement area must contain sufficient port facilities to maintain a force of 26 to 30 divisions and to enable this force to be augmented by follow-up formations at the rate of from three to five divisions a month.

General Plan

The operation is combined British and US undertaking by all services of both nations.

3.   The general intention is –

(a)   To carry out airborne landings during the night of D-1/D-day.
(b)   To assault on a five divisional front with three British and two US divisions in landing ships and craft, between Ouistreham and Varreville on the Bay of the Seine, early on D-day.
(c)   To land two follow-up divisions, one British and one US, later on D-day and on D+1.
(d)   Thereafter to build up our forces at the average rate [of] one and a third division per day.

Home Command

4.   The Supreme Commander Allied Expeditionary Force is General Dwight D. Eisenhower.
   Under him, and exercising their command jointly, initially there are three Commanders:
   Naval – ANC, Expeditionary Force: Admiral Sir Bertram Ramsay.
   Army – C-in-C, 21st Army Group: General Sir Bernard Montgomery.

Air – Air C-in-C, Allied Expeditionary Air Force: Air Chief Marshal Sir Trafford Leigh-Mallory

Principles of Naval Command

5. The Allied Naval C-in-C will exercise general command and control all naval forces other than those providing distant cover, and over all naval operations forming part of the general plan. He will exercise direct command within an 'assault area' off the French coast which is defined below.

The Cs-in-C, Home Commands, will continue to exercise command of their own forces, and later will exercise operational control within the 'assault area', subject to the necessity to give effect to the plan of the ANCXF.

6. The Naval Task Force and Assault Force Commanders will initially exercise command of their own forces, and later will exercise operational control within the 'assault area'.

The Assault Area

7. The Assault Area is bounded on the North by the parallel of 49° 40N and on the West, South and East by the shores of the Bay of the Seine. This are is sub-divided into two Task Force areas. The boundary between them runs from the root of the Port en Bessin Western breakwater in an 025° direction to the meridian of 0° 40W, and thence Northwards along this meridian to latitude 49° 40N. To the Westward of this dividing line is the US, or Western Task Force Area, in which Forces O, U and B will operate. To the Eastward is the British or Eastern Task Force Area.

Naval Command in the Eastern Task Force

8. The command of the Naval Assault and the Follow-up Forces in the Eastern Task Force will be exercised as follows –

Force	Area	Sectors	Naval Cdr.	Corresponding Mil. Formation
Eastern TF			V Adm Vian	2nd Army
G	Gold	How, Item, Jig, King	Cdre Douglas-Pennant	50 N'humbn. Div.
J	Juno	Love, Mike, Nan	Cdre G.N. Oliver	3 Canadian Div.

(Continued)

(Continued)

Force	Area	Sectors	Naval Cdr.	Corresponding Mil. Formation
S	Sword	Once, Peter,	R Adm A. G. Talbot	3 [British] Div.
		Queen, Roger		
L			R Adm W. E. Parry[1]	7 Armoured Div.

...

Unity of Command

10. Until the Army is firmly established ashore, the command of each Task Force and Assault Force, and of the military formations embarked, will be exercised by the respective naval commanders.

Air Support and Cover

11. The operation will have the support of powerful British and US air forces based in the UK. The following table gives an indication of the air forces likely to be available:

Heavy Duty Bombers	1,407
Heavy Night Bombers	1,150
Medium & Light Bombers	835
Day Fighters	2,230
Fighter-Bombers	565
Night Fighters	170
	6,357

Naval Forces

12. Naval forces, including battleships, cruiser, destroyers and escort vessels, have been allotted to the Assault Forces. The Naval Forces allotted to Force G for the assault are –

---

[1]RA Douglas-Pennant: *Despatch* June 1940; NSO to C-in-C, Home Fcs, Apr 1942; RA 1944; CNSO, SAC, SEAC, Nove 1944.

    Adm Sir Geoffrey Oliver (1898–1980): ent RN 1915; gun spist; destroyer cmds 1934–6; Capt 1939; SD 1939–40; *Hermione* 1940–42; N Af Nov 1942; NOIC Bône 1943; Sicily, Italy; W Af 1944; RA & EIF 1945; Adm (Air) 1946; ACNS 1946; Pres RNC Greenwich 1948; VA 1949; C-in-C EI 1950–2; Adm 1952; C-in-C Nore 1953–5.

    RA A. G. Talbot: Capt June 1934; *Furious* Dec 1940; *Formidable* Aug 1942; RA July 1943; *Lothian* July 1944.

    RA W. E. Parry: Capt Dec 1934; *Achilles* (RN NZ Div) June 1939; River Plate Dec 1939; Cdre 2nd Class, 1 Naval Member, NZ June 1941; Cdre 1st Class, *President,* Oct 1942; *Renown* Jan 1943; RA Jan 1944; 2 i/c, RN Control Commission, Ger May 1945.

(a) Bombardment

Cruisers	*Orion, Ajax, Argonaut, Emerald*
Destroyers	*Grenville* (D25), *Undaunted, Ulster, Urchin, Undine,* *Urania, Ulysses, Ursa, Jervis,* ORP *Krakowiak,* *Cattistock, Pytchley, Cottesmore*
Gun Boat	HMNS *Flores*

(b) Escort

Destroyers	*Blankney, Hambledon*
Sloops	*Hind, Magpie, Redpole*
Frigates	FFS *La Decouverte, La Surprise*
Corvettes	*Campanula,* HHMS *Kreizis,* HHMS *Tompazis*
A/S Trawlers	*Bombardier, Sapper, Grenadier, Lancer, Fusilier,* *Victrix*

(c) 18th and 6th Minesweeping Flotillas will sweep the channels for Force G prior to the assault.

13. The cruisers and *Flores* allotted to Force G for bombardment will be known as Bombardment Force K. The two 'Hunt' [class] destroyers allotted for escort may also be used for bombardment.

…

Scale of Enemy Naval Attack

15. It must be expected that the enemy will expend his forces ruthlessly in the attempt to defeat invasion. It is unlikely that he will employ his larger ships in the Channel but his light forces will probably be used as directly as possible against the assault and subsequent convoys, restricting their attacks to darkness and low visibility, and operating on the flanks.

16. U-boat attacks on our coastal and cross-channel convoys must be expected.

17. Evidence of midget submarine or fast submersible craft is accumulating, and a number may have reached the operational stage. Attacks by such craft must be expected in the anchorages.

18. Offensive and defensive minelaying by enemy surface craft and aircraft is probable. New types of mine may be used.

…

Scale of Enemy Air Opposition

20. The enemy bomber force will operate mainly at night, but in the early stages a few daylight operations must be anticipated. Attacks at dawn and dusk are very probable. The bomber force has had no experience of

day operations and its efficiency in any such operations will be low. The morale of German bomber crews is gradually deteriorating.

21. The single-engined fighter force will mainly be used defensively, and as escorts to fighter [bombers] and day bombers, but a proportion of both single and twin-engined fighters may operate as fighter bombers and ground attack aircraft by daylight and possibly by moonlight.

22. Attacks on landing craft and shipping may be carried out by single-engined fighter with rocket mortars, but the pilots will probably be lacking in experience.

23. Glider, rocket bomb and air torpedo attacks are also to be expected.

Naval Object

24. The object of the Naval Force Commander is the safe and timely arrival of his assault forces at the beaches, the cover of their landings and subsequently the support, maintenance and rapid build-up of our forces ashore.

Method of Execution

25. D-day will be the day on which the assault will be carried out. H-hour will be the time at which the first landing craft should hit the beaches. D-day will be communicated by the Allied Naval C-in-C by signal to those authorities holding his orders.

Time of H-hour

26. H-hour will be related to morning civil twilight and to the time of local High Water. Thus, if postponement is necessary, H-hour will alter. H-hour on the first suitable day will be about 85 minutes after morning civil twilight and approximately three hours before High Water. This should allow a minimum period of 70 minutes good daylight for observed bombardment before H-hour, and sufficient time for the clearance of beach obstacles before they become submerged.

159.   *NEPTUNE: Summary of Operation from information*
[at] SHAEF and COMNAVEU's HQ

[SPD 250]   6 June 1944

D-day: 6 June 1944.
Tabulation of Naval Information

Losses and Damage

US

Ship or Craft	*Remarks*
1 Destroyer (*Corry*)	Sunk by shore battery
1 PC	Sunk – reported by Force U
1 LCI (L)	Sunk – reported by Force U
6 LCT	Sunk – 2 off 'Utah'; 3 off 'Omaha'; 1 capsized
2 AMs	Damaged

Operating with British, safely towed to port

40–50 LVCB   Broached in landing

British

1 Destroyer (*Svenner*) Norwegian	Sunk
1 Destroyer	Damaged (mined)
1 Corvette or AM	Sunk
1 HQ Ship (*Bulolo*)	Damaged slightly; bomb on morning of D+1

No data on landing craft

...

General Remarks

Apparently Germans were surprised as to exact time and locality. Naval H-hour varied from 0630 to 0745. Deception measures by Air Force BJ Units were successful.

No German reaction with surface forces until 0430 when three destroyers and some trawlers from Havre were encountered. One trawler was sunk, one damaged.

The landing of the airborne divisions was very successful. They apparently landed in the right places and suffered only a 2% plane loss. None of these losses were due to friendly AA fire. There had been some concern in Force U as to the possibility of friendly fire at returning transport planes because of the closeness of the plane tracks to Force U's assault area.

Many of the DD tanks were swamped due to rough water and about 80% of the first wave of LCVP broached.

Less mines were encountered than anticipated. Most of the channels were clear by 0640.

Later report indicated that only seven lines of mines existed. These were presumed located and swept.

Naval bombardment proceeded according to plan and return fire from German batteries was weak. Admiral Kirk's report at 0646 was: 'Happy landing, no enemy gunfire encountered in either transport area, everything according to plan.'

Later, however, considerable trouble was had with a strong battery in the 'Omaha' area. Air help was called for and the *Texas* moved closer to bombard.

No reports were received concerning difficulties in overcoming beach obstacles. However, later reports indicated retracting landing craft suffered from encountering Teller mines or Naval beach obstacles, which apparently had not been removed, and over which they were probably forced to move later on as the tide came in.

No German air opposition was encountered until late in the evening when there was one attack which caused slight damage.

Reports indicate that by 0945 two bridges across the Orne River were captured intact (British area) and that fighting was occurring in Caen at 1330.

Considerable congestion occurred on the 'Omaha' beaches during the day. More difficulties were encountered by this force than the others. The above-mentioned German battery and then difficult beach exits are presumed to have been the cause. Later information indicates that a German Division was holding manoeuvres in this area on D-day and consequently was more difficult to overcome. One statement of US 1st Division estimated casualties were approximately 5000 men.

160. *Admiralty Reports*

[SPD 250]   7 June 1944

Weather Forecast, Wednesday and Thursday, 7 and 8 June: Winds NW force 4, veering slowly northerly during Wednesday and decreasing. Fair to good. Visibility good. Sea waves 3ft decreasing slowly.

Outlook for Friday, Saturday and Sunday [9–11 June]: Light variable winds increasing from WSW [on] Sunday. Mainly fair weather with moderate to good visibility.

2227/6 [June]: Admiral [Ramsay] with General Eisenhower in *Apollo* will visit beaches. Arriving at 1130/7[,] returning [to] Portsmouth p.m.

2230/6: General Montgomery in *Faulkner* will close *Augusta* at 0600 Wednesday, 7 June, afterwards proceeding to 'Juno' section of N beach.

0023/7: Cosintrep No. 8 – Landings on beaches now proceeding satisfactorily except in 'Omaha' sector where little progress is being made. Warships are beginning to return to re-ammunition. First build-up convoys are approaching the anchorages and the first flights of empty landing craft are returning to UK to re-load. Weather has not favoured the operations of minor landing craft and has caused some slowing down in rate of discharge.

2400/6: 3 Canadian Division has reached immediate objectives and [is] continuing to advance. Unloading of LSTs progressing slowly owing to weather.

2101/6: Aircraft report seven U-boats leaving Brest and two U-boats leaving St Nazaire between 1900–2000.

1927/6: From NWCYF, Colleville taken. St Laurent partially occupied. Considerable mortar and artillery fire falling on beaches. Foot elements of approximately four regiments ashore. Many stranded landing craft due to surf and obstacles not initially cleared. DDs giving close gunfire support. Good progress on 'Utah'.

161. *Report of Proceedings: Lieut J. C. Davis, RCVNR,*
(Temporary) CO, HMCS Prince Henry *528th Flotilla*[1]

[ADM 199/1659] 9 June 1944

528th Flotilla lowered away at 0655 on 6 June and formed up, proceeding to a position off the bows of HMS *Queen Emma* where we rendezvoused with 516 and 526 Flotillas. 526 Flotilla (*Queen Emma*) proceeded on from QQ without waiting for group 315(a) and for three-quarters of the run-in remained about a mile away from 528 and 516 Flotillas, on our starboard bow. 528 and 516 Flotillas followed 315(a) according to orders until *MGB 324* arrived from shore. At this point group 315(a) turned out to sea again, apparently to fill in time, and *MGB 324* led 528 and 516 Flotillas to where 526 Flotilla was waiting and gave us all the course to the beach.

I consider that *MGB 324* should have led us behind group 315(a) as she did not apparently intend to lead this group in as laid down. Instead, she led us to a position just off the junction of Mike Red and Mike Green where 526 Flotilla was waiting. Three Flotillas of minor landing craft in this position appeared to make it difficult for group 315(a) to manoeuvre to deploy. Furthermore, I think it is most probable that *MGB 324* could have led us in behind group 315(a) had 526 Flotilla been in position, behind group 315(a).

At 0827 the Flotilla deployed and beached at 0830. Fire was moderately heavy in places and beach obstacles with Teller mines and a type

---

[1] Lt J. C. Davis, RCNVR: unidentified.

of bottle mine attached proved much more difficult and closer together than had been anticipated. At 0830 the water was just over some of the stakes and at the top of the tetrahedras. Several craft were holed and one blown up by a mine. Lifelines were rigged from all craft to enable the troops to get ashore.

Reports on the beaching and subsequent movement of craft are contained below:

LCA 856 (Lieut Davis, RCVNR): Beached, as all craft, in between obstacles, and went as far as possible before being stopped by a mined beach obstacle which did not explode. A badly wounded Winnipeg Rifles corporal was found in an abandoned landing craft belonging to SS *Canterbury* some yards on our left and was brought into *LCA 856* and given first aid. We came off the beach and discovered we were holed and taking water fast.

The casualty was transferred to *LCA 850* and *LCAs 1372* and *925* came alongside and took us in tow. The engine room was flooded and the forward bulkhead had to be closed off. Five men bailed with buckets continually in the well until we reached HMCS *Prince Henry* and at one time we had to stop bailing *LCA 856* to bail out *LCA 925* which was filling with water owing to the heavy seas. I should like to commend the spirit and endurance of those men who thus enabled the craft to be saved.

LCA 1033 (Sub-Lieut J. A. Flynn, RCVNR) went in as far as the beach obstacles permitted. The troops took approximately 15 minutes to clear the craft, leaving part of their equipment behind. ... The craft came off the beach some 25 minutes after beaching and returned independently to the ship, one propeller being fouled by a large piece of canvas. AB Payne was wounded by shrapnel at about 0845.

LCA 736 (Lieut C. Hendery, RCVNR) beached amongst obstacles and as the door went down the craft swerved onto a mined beach obstacle. The mine did not explode as the door lay on top of it and the troops went over the door into waist high water. On coming off the beach, the kedgewarp tangled with obstacles and had to be cut. The craft came off on engines alone and after surveying the beach for any of our craft that were damaged proceeded to *Prince Henry* on one engine, a heavy piece of rope having fouled the port propeller.

LCA 1021 (Ldg Seaman D. Townson) beached and disembarked troops. A tracked vehicle came off an LCT and fouled the kedge as well [as] pushing the craft broadside onto the beach. The kedge was cut and the craft was coming off well when a mine exploded on the starboard quarter and filled the engine room with water, badly wounding the Stoker. L/S Townson, wounded by shrapnel just before landing, went aft and put out a fire in the engine room, while ABs McQueen and Smith removed

L/Stoker Bialowas from the engine room and the three of them dug him into the beach as the mortar fire was heavy. L/S Townson contacted a doctor and left the casualty in his charge. He then brought his craft back to the ship via an LCTT that was sunk and a Canadian LCI (L). I recommend this rating for a mention in despatches for leadership and devotion to duty.

LCA 1371 (AB R. Mellway), *LCA 925* (L/S H. Moody), and *LCA 850* (L/S P. Duchnicky) ran in as far as possible amongst the mined obstacles, got the Army personnel off, and came away from the beach skilfully, using engines to avoid hitting mines. *LCA 950* with one propeller fouled, came alongside *LCA 856* and took my casualty to HMS *Stevenstone*, returning from there to HMCS *Prince Henry*. *LCAs 1371* and *925* took *LCA 856* in tow and brought the craft back to *Prince Henry*.

The report I received from *LCA 1372* (Lieut G. E. Nuttall, RCNVR) was verbal and given to me just before he left to report to D/SOAG, Mike Red. His craft touched down just before some mortar bombs exploded in front of it. The troops left the craft very quickly, but Lieut Nuttall estimates that one-third had shrapnel wounds. AB D. Tennant was wounded in three places by shrapnel and refused to stop working until finally ordered to by Lieut Nuttall. I recommend this rating for mention in despatches for devotion to duty. *LCA 1372* had two holes in her bottom which were repaired before she left the ship for the second time.

I should like to commend the work of Lieut (E) W. J. Scarlett, RCNVR, and his maintenance staff who got all the Flotilla's damaged craft back.

Extracts from the Report of Proceedings of HMCS Prince Henry.
14 June 1944.
HMCS *Prince Henry* proceeded to landing berth No. 37 at Southampton on 2 June 1944 and embarked 362 Military Officers and other ranks. These included 227 personnel from the Canadian Scottish Regiment with Major C. Wightman as CO. Embarkation was completed by 1800 and the ship returned to area 18, berth 7, at 2000.

Orders were given to LST Group J 1 to weigh at 2110, 5 June and the Group was formed astern of HMS *Lawford* (Captain Group J 1) south of West Ryde Middle Buoy at 2125.

The signal to deploy to starboard was received from Captain Group J 1 at about 0540.

At 0700, 227 Officers and other ranks were disembarked by the 528th Flotilla. Craft were lowered at 0645 and formed astern of *MGB 324* for the run in to the beach.

At 0720, 44 survivors and one casualty (wounded) from *LCT (A) 2039*, 109th Flotilla, ... were embarked from *ML Q297* for passage to the UK.

At approximately 1155 108 Officers and other ranks were disembarked in an LCI (L) for Mike Red Beach.

At about 1155, *LCT K 02–2044* was ordered alongside *Prince Henry* as she had reported herself to be in a sinking condition. She was found to be taking in water through the stern tube due to defective glands. Assistance was rendered by the ship's engine room staff and *Prince Henry*'s portable salvage pump was transferred to *LCT 2044* and put into immediate operation. Hot meals were provided for the crew and after a short period alongside, *LCT 2044* was able to proceed.

All craft of the 528th Flotilla with the exception of *LCA 1021* which struck a mine, were hoisted by 1230. Lieut J. C. Davis is commended for the manner in which he led his Flotilla to the beach and brought it back with so little loss despite heavy seas and enemy mortar fire. Lieut Davis's own craft was badly holed in the stern and had to be towed back from the beach.

The Flotilla Engineering Officer and his staff lost no time in effecting repairs and by 1330, [an?] LCA under the command of Lieut G. W. Nuttall was lowered and proceeded to the beach for ferry craft duties.

All LSI were reported to be ready to proceed by 1445 and at 1453, *Prince Henry* took LSIs of Group J 1 under her orders and the Group proceeded under destroyer escort to Cowes, Isle of Wight, anchoring in Cowes Road at 2320.

162.   *C-in-C Plymouth to Admiralty: Destroyer Action:*
Night of 8–9 June 1944.

[ADM199/1644]   18 July 1944.

...

2. On 7 June, photo reconnaissance of Brest had shown there two destroyers pf the 'Seetier' type, and the ex-Netherlands ship of the *Tjerk Hiddes* type, as well as one 'Elbing'. PoWs have established that these ships were the *Z32*, *Z24*, *ZH1* and *T24*.

3. The threat to our convoys and A/S patrols by this division of powerful destroyers was considerable. They might operate from Brest or from Cherbourg, but it seemed most possible, in order to operate against the convoys carrying the build-up forces to Normandy.

4. On 8 June, the 10 DF was disposed on east and west patrol about 30 miles south of Mounts Bay and in the course of routine refuelling. *Tartar* and *Ashanti* left the Flotilla during the forenoon to return to Plymouth.

...

6. The 10 DF, at full strength, [consisted] of *Tartar* (Cdr. B. Jones, SO), *Ashanti*, *Haida* and *Huron* (19th Division), *Blyskawica* (Capt Naimien-dorski), *Eskimo*, *Piorun* and *Javelin* (20th Division). ...[1]

...

9. The 10 DF carried out the orders given, and on the second sweep to the west at 0114, *Tartar* made contact by radar with four units, directly ahead of her.

10. At this time, the 10 DF was in staggered line ahead formation, on a course of 0255°, speed 20 knots, with 20th Division bearing 000° two miles from the 19th Division, being thus some 15° abaft *Tartar*'s starboard beam.

11. The weather was overcast with intermittent rain, with a light SW wind and calm sea. The visibility varied between one and three miles.

12. Preliminary interrogation of PoWs captured after the action, reveals that the enemy force was in a diamond formation, *Z32* leading, *ZH1* on her starboard quarter, *Z24* on her port quarter and *T24* astern.

13. *Tartar*, when the contacts were confirmed, increased to 27 knots, by signal, and then turned both divisions by white pendant 35° to starboard, and then by blue pendant 50° to port to comb possible torpedo tracks. By 0127 the enemy were in sight, turning to port, at a range of about 4000 yards and fire was opened by the 19th Division

14. The wisdom of the turn to comb tracks of possible torpedoes was soon apparent; reports a few minutes later showed that torpedoes had been fired; the 19th Division passed the tracks on an opposite course at about 0130.

15. It seems that the enemy were somewhat confused and taken by surprise – the leader turned about 90° to port, but his consorts appear to have turned 180°. Consequently, *Tartar* passed astern of *Z32*, and leaving him to be dealt with by the 20th Division, he himself engaged number two, *ZH1*. *Ashanti*, who was second in the line, also engaged *ZH1*, who was slowed down and temporarily hidden in a thick black screen of smoke.

16. Meanwhile, *Blyskawica*, leading the 20th Division, had seen the enemy illuminated by the 19th Division, and estimated he was turning north to get behind. He consequently led his Division round to a northerly course, and engaging *Z32*, who replied with a heavy volume of fire.

17. The report that torpedoes were being fired unfortunately caused *Blyskawica* to make an evasive turn away to starboard and her Division followed her.

[1]Cdr B. Jones: Naval Ordnc Dept Sep 1940; *Isis* Nov 1940; A/Capt *Tartar* Sep 1944; Capt Sep 1945.

18. Meanwhile *Z32* whose fire enveloped *Blyskawica* until she turned away to avoid the threat of torpedoes, opened fire on *Tartar* at 0138 from the northward. *Tartar*, who had shifted fire from *ZH1* (when the latter was covered in smoke) to the third ship, returned *Z32*'s fire and silenced her, but not before she received three hits herself, one of which caused a considerable fire just abaft the bridge, and another wrecked her radar and wireless.

19. *Ashanti*, on seeing *Tartar* hit, shifted fire to *Z32* for a short time, but the volume of smoke from *Tartar* obscured her target – a few minutes later she sighted an enemy ship at the edge of the smoke, steaming slowly, and fired four torpedoes at her at a range of 1500 yards. Two hits were observed, one forward which blew off her bow and the other aft. The ship was *ZH1*, [which] however, did not sink at once. *Ashanti* remained in the vicinity, firing at her as visibility through the smoke permitted.

20. While these events were proceeding, *Haida* and *Huron* had left the two right hand enemy ships, *Z32* and *ZH1*, to *Tartar* and *Ashanti*, and were chasing the other two, *Z24* and *T24*, to the westward.

21. The fire in *Tartar* was severe enough to force her to reduce speed to six knots in order to get it under control: the situation, therefore, at about 0145 was as follows:

The leading enemy ship had disappeared to the northward, heavily hit by *Tartar*, reduced to six knots, steaming slowly northwards. *Ashanti* circling her crippled enemy, *ZH1*, who was seen intermittently through heavy clouds of smoke, and *Haida* and *Huron* chasing *Z24* and *T24* to the northward.

...

24. By 0215, *Haida* and *Huron*, who had altered to the northward slightly to avoid our own minefield when the enemy entered it, had lost contact with them at a range of about 19,000 yards, and now turned back towards *Tartar*, who was estimated to bear about 040°.

...

27. About this time, *Haida* and *Huron*, returning from the westward, obtained radar contact with a ship moving slowly, which they thought was *Tartar*. Reply to their challenge was unintelligible, but they still thought the ship was *Tartar* with signal apparatus and radar out of action, and passed within a mile of her. She made smoke and made off to the SW, and just at this time, 0237, a 'terrific' explosion occurred bearing 140° from *Haida*. This was *ZH1* blowing up, and shortly after *Ashanti* was sighted and told to join. She was unable to do so, owing to *Haida*'s subsequent movements, and later joined the 20th Division at 0430.

28. But by now *Haida*'s suspicions of the strange ship were fully aroused, and she and *Huron* increased speed and altered to the SW to chase the suspect.

29. At 0255, *Haida* and *Huron* opened fire and illuminated a 'Narvik' [class] destroyer bearing 135° at 6900 yards. The enemy fought back with accurate fire, and soon altered course to the eastward, passing through our minefield.

30. *Haida* [followed by *Huron*] continued the chase to the eastward, the range (which our destroyers had been forced to open while avoiding our own minefield) remaining at 18,000 yards, closing slowly.

31. Meanwhile, at 0247, the 20th Division had made contact with *Tartar*, who took station astern, as she had neither wireless nor radar in action, and very soon after they sighted the action being fought by *Haida* and *Huron* to the southward and proceeded towards it.

32. Thus, once more, the 20th Division knew where the remainder of the 19th Division were, but themselves were too far to the north and west to be able to join in the action.

33. The enemy, who was making towards the Channel Islands at full speed, at 0432 for some quite unaccountable reason, turned to the southward evidently to try to break back to Brest or possibly Morlaix.

34. The range closed rapidly, and *Haida* led her consort towards the enemy, opening fire again at 0445 when the range was down to 7000 yards. The enemy again replied with accurate fire, shifting later to *Huron*, but neither side seems to have made hits at this period.

...

36. From 0500 the action continued, but the attempt of the enemy ship to break back was frustrated, and by this time, it was too late for her to escape. At about 0515 she was seen to be heavily hit, and at 0517 she ran ashore on the rocks on the NW corner of the Ile de Bas. In this position she was again heavily hit, and left on fire at 0526. Reconnaissance has shown her to be a total loss.

37. *Haida* and *Huron* then rejoined the remainder of the Flotilla, and the whole force returned to Plymouth, arriving at 0830.

Remarks

40. This action, one of the very few which has been fought between large and fast modern destroyers at night during this war, effected the destruction of half of the enemy's force and inflicted damage on at least one of two who escaped. It was thus a not inconsiderable success and a useful contribution to the safety of our invasion convoys.

...

44. *Haida* and *Huron* correctly appreciated the enemy's movements after the opening clash and acted accordingly. ...

Cdr H. G. De Wolf, HMCS Haida: *Report of Proceedings, 9 June 1944.*[1]

...

27. At 0255 opened fire with Star Shell on end destroyer bearing 135° at 6900 yards. Careful watch was still kept for identification signals and a good view of the enemy left the impression of a single funnel but on comparing silhouettes after the action I am convinced [that] what I saw [was] the foremost funnel of a 'Narvik' class destroyer.

28. The enemy fought back with accurate fire, HE shell bursting overhead and in the water, often very close to the ship.

29. At 0311 enemy altered to the eastward through QZX 1330.

30. At 0315 course was altered to the north-eastward and for the second time it looked as if an enemy would escape through the intervention of the minefield. Fire was checked at about 0320 when range reached 10,000 yards.

...

33. At 0342 when clear of the minefield, course was altered to 090°, the enemy then bearing 126° at 10 miles. Radar contact was made with forces bearing 360° at six miles (five echoes showing IFF). Radar contact with the enemy was lost at this time and it was thought he had escaped to Morlaix. Contact was regained shortly afterwards and plot reported enemy's course 070° and later 060° and course was altered towards.

...

35. At 0412 the enemy bore 090° at nine miles and course was altered to 070° parallel with the enemy. At this time the range was closing very slowly.

36. At 0432 plot reported range closing, enemy altering to southward.

37. ... Course was altered to the south and south-west to close the enemy who first appeared to be making towards Morlaix and then attempting to return to the westward. ...

38. At 0445 opened fire with Star Shell and engaged the enemy at 7000 yards' range.

---

[1]Capt H. G. De Wolf, RCN: RNC Canada 1921; Staff 1935–7; SO (O) 1 CS 1937; CSO, Halifax 1939–42; HMCS *Haida*, 1943–4; ACNS 1945–6; Washington 1952–6; CNS 1956–60.

The enemy returned our fire and his first salvo fell very close ahead. Subsequent salvoes all appeared to burst or splash close, but the enemy's rate of fire was not rapid. His fire was later directed at *Huron*. Our own fire and *Huron*'s appeared to converge at the right point but few hits were observed.

...

40. From 0500 to 0525 the action was continued to the southward, the enemy passing through QZX 1298 and finally beaching herself on the ledges north of the Ile de Bas at 0517. He was observed to be heavily hit a few minutes before this and again after he stopped and was finally left burning and considered fixed at 0526. As *Haida* and *Huron* returned northward the fire appeared to increase in intensity. The enemy commenced firing distress signals, white and red flares, as soon as he grounded. ...

41. *Haida* and *Huron* rejoined the remainder of the Flotilla at 0600. ...

163. *King to Stark*

[NWC, King 8]   15 June 1944

Release of Forces from OVERLORD.

1. CCS to SACMED and SCAEF.
2. 'Plans for the release of assault shipping and support forces from UK and their movements to the Mediterranean must therefore be taken in hand at once.' ...

164. *Action Report by Commander, Cruiser Division 7: Assault Phase, Operation NEPTUNE (3–17 June 1944)*[1]

[ADM 199/1661]   10 July 1944

...

II. Chronicle of Events

17. *Black Prince* was narrowly missed many times by the larger batteries. ... *Tuscaloosa* and *Quincy* were also taken under fire and received

---

[1] RA Morton L. Deyo, US Navy (1887–1975): USNA 1911; NWC 1932–3; DD Sqdn 11 1941–2; RA 1942; Cdr, DD Force, Atl F 1943; Cdr, Bombardment Grp, TF 125, *Utah*; Dragoon, 1944; Cdr, CruDiv 13, Pac F; Cdt, 1 Naval District 1946–9; VA & ret.

close misses from time to time. Enemy batteries appeared to be 170mm and 155mm. ... Prior to the time that the enemy could accurately apply their spots, the batteries were taken under effective fire and were soon neutralised. On two occasions prior to H-hour, effective smoke screens were laid by smoker planes between the fire support area and the shore. In laying the second screen one plane was shot down.

18. The beach drenching fire was extremely effective. All firing proceeding according to plan, with secondary batteries of *Nevada* and *Quincy* and main batteries of *Enterprise, Hobson, Shubrick* and *Herndon* all concentrating on the landing area for 10 minutes prior to H-hour. In addition *Nevada* and *Quincy* main batteries were used for the period H-15 to H-5 minutes to breach the seawall which was done in five places. Very little opposition was encountered by the troops in landing.

...

20. Ships in close support stations on the north Flank of the beach, *Fitch* and *Corry*, came under the fire of medium and lighter batteries as they arrived on the station. *Fitch* withdrew temporarily, but *Corry* was hit in the machinery spaces and immobilised. (Note: Her CO has since reported that she hit a mine but no such report was received on D-day). She continued with heavy fire from her batteries as long as possible while *Tuscaloosa, Quincy, Nevada* and *Black Prince* took under fire suspected batteries. It was not until after *Corry* commenced to sink with, seemingly, a broken back that the batteries were silenced. Upon [the] sinking of *Corry, Fitch* was ordered to rescue survivors, which she did very gallantly and was able to remain and hold her own without damage thereafter.

21. By early afternoon the known heavy batteries had been silenced except three, 8, and A, and 14. These had a tendency to come to life unexpectedly and to fire a few rounds when ships were in the vicinity, but caused no obstacle to work on the beaches.

22. The destruction of batteries, concentrated as many of them were in casements or pillboxes heavily protected with several guns separated from one another, is a very difficult problem. Direct hits observed by spotting planes did not permanently disable the batteries, which within a few hours or a day, were able to resume fire, though at greatly reduced volume and effectiveness. Never before has it been attempted to silence with naval gunfire so extensive and elaborate a system of coast defences as found here. The surprising thing is that more losses were not sustained by our force in this stage of the operation.

(a) *Tuscaloosa* – Since initial difficulty was experienced in contacting her spotting plane, her first three targets, one of which was fired [on] to protect *Corry*, were largely unobserved. At establishment of communications, *Tuscaloosa* delivered effective counter-battery fire on some 14 targets, including battery no. 8 and battery no. 7A. This latter battery caused some difficulty throughout the early stages of the operation by periodically coming to life and dropping a few scattered salvoes in the vicinity of the fire support ships. It was silenced regularly and by D+9 apparently became entirely discouraged. *Tuscaloosa's* fire was well placed and accurate. At 1931 on D-day, *Tuscaloosa* took under fire target no. 86 which was suspected of firing into the beach and transportation areas. For this fire *Butler*, on close supporting station provided effective spotting, using TBS for the purpose.

...

(c) *Nevada* – ... The Shore Fire Control Party which requested her fire reported that with a total of 68 rounds she destroyed (1) a group of enemy tanks in one locality, (2) an enemy troop concentration in another locality, (3) a concentration of field artillery and tanks in another area, and (4) an assembly point in still another area. Her SFCP reported that a dangerous counter-attack had been destroyed by this fire. All of these last missions were carried out between 2129 and 2230.

(d) *Hawkins* – *Hawkins* opened fire promptly when directed, and her spotting plane reported 18 hits out of 110 rounds on target no. 5. Thereafter she took under fire target no. 16 using air spotting and reported 24 hits out of 57 rounds. These batteries were neutralised and thenceforth caused no trouble. For the remainder of D-day *Hawkins* fired on target of opportunity as requested by air spotting plane and by SFC Parties. *Hawkins's* area was in territory which was to be captured by 5th Corps troops. ...

(e) *Enterprise* – ... Her firing was timed carefully on coordination with the expected advance of the initial assault troops and she carried out all missions assigned, reporting successful results, and a total expenditure of 645 rounds for D-day.

(f) *Erebus* – Her fire appeared on all occasions to be highly effective. It is unfortunate that at 1701 *Erebus* split her left gun, mounting and cradle, thus preventing her from firing on any more targets. The service of *Erebus* as a long range counter-battery ship was missed considerably in later stages.

(g) *Black Prince* – ... Her work was always spirited and she gave the impression of being an efficient, smart, and trim ship.

7 June

23. The firing on D-day carried on into the night from the anchorage nearer the transport area. There were, on the night of D/D-1, air and

E-boat alarms, and enemy planes were overhead, though not in great strength. Some bombs were dropped in the 'Utah' area, though fire support ships were not seriously endangered. There was no AA fire observed from ships of this group. Use of radio-controlled bombs was reported in the area.

...

165. *Kirk to Stark*

[Stark A2]   USS *Augusta*,
                                                                           22 June 1944

We had no forecast of winds of such violence, and anyway our construction [Mulberry A] was only half complete. So, we took a beating from winds offshore [of] 35–40 knots; waves 8–9 feet high and on a lee shore.

The Phoenixes just disintegrated under the impact – 16 destroyed out of 23, making a break in the center about where the 40mm gun was. Many ends are sticking up.

The Bishops are breaking up and slewing around and so the nice adjustment you saw last week is now destroyed. There is no harbour for small craft and the beach is covered with them.

The Bombardons are all broken and many adrift. We wonder if the line of moored ships will have fared any better.

Clark's piers are badly damaged and smashed.

Wind and sea continue high and boating is impossible. We are beaching some Ammunition Coasters, accepting the loss if necessary. Some coasters are going to Issigny. Ammunition in transport aircraft and preloaded DUKWs in LST, I have asked for.

Opening Cherbourg is now of vital importance. I fear, however, the harbour will not be usable for some time.

Complying with ANXCF orders, we have directed Deyo to form an Attack Force for Cherbourg.

166. *Cunningham to Churchill*

[ADM 205/57]   22 June 1944.

... The unilateral action by Admiral King amounted to ordering the withdrawal of the bulk of the American forces engaged in OVERLORD and allocating them to ANVIL without consultation with the Admiralty or the CCS, and before the SAC, Mediterranean, had stated his requirements.

167. *Stark to King*

[Stark A2] 23 June 1944

The old saying, 'Man proposes, God disposes', certainly seems appropriate at the present time. As Admiral Cunningham says, 'Once in a while the elements have to tell man how puny he is'.

The Phoenixes are badly busted up, a number of the Gooseberry ships with broken backs, the old battleship *Centurion* being among them, and in many spots the lee originally provided is gone. Twelve foot waves were washing over them and simply knocked things about. We will patch the Gooseberries by an additional 12 ships and eight on the British [Mulberry harbour]. We were in great fettle over being so much further along than the British in getting our harbour going. However, the British have some of theirs safely on this shore and it can now be sent over, or shortly, because the wind is still out of the North East.

Lobnitz pierheads are damaged and the runways from them to the beach pretty well wrecked. Just prior to the blow we were unloading LSTs alongside these piers and getting the material ashore in something over an hour.

I have no definite word yet about the Rhino ferries, causeways, etc., except that someone who came over said they were likewise pretty well knocked about. ...

In other words we've got a job on our hands, but 'twas one of those contingencies we had thought about, although not happening so soon, it being contrary to all weather predictions for this time of year – (first NE gale in June in 20 years).

Thank God, Ike, when he had fairly bad weather and made his decision to go, didn't delay it. Delay would have meant two weeks. Had this been made we would have been caught on the way over, because all weather predictions were fair and we had tows on the way when this thing broke – last weekend. ...

Meanwhile we are strengthening our repair groups in the beach harbors, surveying the situation, and endeavoring to get things going. ...

I saw Admiral Cunningham again today and he says while Ramsay is General Eisenhower's advisor on naval questions, he himself (Cunningham) would not employ naval gunfire at Cherbourg and that he had so informed the Prime Minister, this was in response to my saying that with the Army so close to Cherbourg, and with the air force we had available, I questioned employing naval gunfire.

Mine situation continues to be menace and we are still having casualties even with constant sweeping.

I spent yesterday on the South coast trying to put a little fire under the repair, landing and turn-around situation, particularly on the British end. Hope the foundation has been laid for considerable improvement.

P. S. The former naval person may have taken exception to what some of the British called your unilateral action.[1] Last time this remark was made to me I invited attention to the fact that it was your unilateral action which sent the considerable support force over here and not action by the CCS, that the CCS's decision was that the British should furnish all the combatant ships and that you voluntarily had supported this, etc., etc. I have also pointed out that it is not a case of unilateral action in any case because of your perfectly plain statement in your paragraph 2 calls for '*plans* being taken in hand', and your paragraph 4, that their directive to execute the plans awaited final CCS decision.

I asked him [Syfret] to please read paragraphs 2 and 4 of your memorandum and, as it had been discussed by the CCS, to set them right on it. Also called Eisenhower's HQ and Bedell [Smith] said it was perfectly plain to them and always had been, and that they fully realized that the memorandum was reasonable. ...

168. *King to Stark*

[NWC, King 8]   23 June 1944

Former Naval Person sent message to White House stating that he was much upset at information reaching him about my memorandum to you date 15 June [the subject of which was] release of forces from OVER-LORD. Seek earliest opportunity to show him original of said memorandum and invite his particular attention to paragraph 4 thereof.

169. *Memorandum for F-1*

[SPD 250]   24 June 1944

Availability of LSTs for European Operations.

1.   According to information available to date the LST situation in the UK is as follows:

	US	British	Total
In area	167	61	228
Estimated operational	152	50	202

---

[1] 'former naval person': Churchill.

2. As of 1 August the Mediterranean situation will be as follows not counting any which may be sent from the UK:

	US	British	Total
In area	53	10	63
Estimated operational	52	7	59

3. The LSTs from the US which could now reach the Mediterranean by 1 August would have to come from the 27 which are shaking down and getting ready for movement to the Pacific as indicated below:

Gulf Area

The larger proportion of these should be ready about 30 June. These vessels are assigned to 7th Fleet.

4. In addition to the above there are 24 LSTs assigned [to] PhibTraLant which are in full use for training.
5. 7th Fleet has stated their requirement to be 108 LSTs beginning August. The 27 LSTs mentioned above should arrive late August and would give that fleet a total of 75.

170.   *Stark to Cunningham*

[Stark A2]   5 July 1944

It is just possible you have missed the following: ...

Extract from Weekly Intelligence Report No. 225 (30 June 1944).

Re: bombardment of Cherbourg ... it is interesting to note the remarks of the German Army publication *Militarische Korrespondenz* [of] 16 June ... on the efficacy of the Allied Naval gunnery:

> 'The fire curtain provided by the Navy's guns has so proved one of the Anglo-US invasion armies' best trump cards. It may be that the Fleet's part was more decisive than that of the Air Force's, because its fire was better aimed and, unlike the bomber formations, it did not have to confine itself to short bursts of fire. ... It would be utterly wrong to underestimate the firepower even of smaller vessels. ... Of particular advantage to the invasion troops was the great mobility of the vessels, by which artillery concentrations could be achieved at any point of the coast and the place could be changed according to the exigencies

of the situation. The attackers have made the best possible use of this opportunity. Strong formations of battleships and cruisers were repeatedly used against single coastal batteries, thus bringing an extraordinarily superior firepower to bear on them. Moreover, time and again they put an umbrella of fire over the defenders at the focal points of the fighting, compared with which very heavy waves of air attacks have. had only a modest effect. It is no exaggeration to say that the cooperation of the heavy naval guns played a decisive part in enabling the Allies to establish a bridgehead in Normandy. … At present, however, fighting at many points has been taking place for several days on the periphery of the range of the heavy and very heavy naval guns.'

Cunningham to Stark.

5 July 1944.

… While I agree in general with the description given by the writer, I think that the Germans are now trying to find in the heavy Naval gunfire an excuse for their failure.

There is no question, however, in my mind that the gunfire is more accurate if the air spotting is good and certainly more persistent than bombing.

I have never been able to make myself believe that accurate spotting can be undertaken from a single seater plane travelling at about 250 mph, but I am assured that is so. I still remain doubtful.

171. *Report of Proceedings of 9th Escort Group, 15–22 July 1944*

[ADM 199/1644]   8 August 1944

Narrative of Events:
15 July
1330: HM Canadian ships *Matane*, *Swansea* and *Stormont* sailed from Moville and proceeded southward [at] 16 knots.

2330: On arrival at K2 buoy [EG 9] was joined by HMCS *Meon* from Liverpool.

…

2055: When in position 48° 14N, 05° 33W an explosion occurred astern of *Matane* which at first was believed to be caused by a Gnat, action alarm gongs were rung and shortly afterwards aircraft were sighted and it was realised that air attack was imminent. Conditions were ideal with high clouds, and having no air warning radar we were taken entirely by surprise. An aircraft, angle of sight about 60°, was seen approaching from fine on the starboard quarter at a height of about 10,000 feet. Almost as soon as sighted a glider bomb was seen to detach itself, hover for a few seconds under the aircraft, and then dive down onto the ship. The starboard Oerlikons immediately came into action and the engines were put to full ahead, but almost before this order could take effect, the bomb arrived, hitting the ship a glancing blow just before Y gun and bursting in the water close alongside. There was a large escape of smoke and steam, which made further observation of the attack very difficult. It is considered however that the attacking force consisted of three aircraft, each carrying two bombs. Two were seen to fall astern of *Matane*, one appeared to get out of control and fell a very long way short of *Swansea*, a second fell close to the port side of *Matane* and one between *Swansea* and *Stormont*. During the attack the aircraft were free to manoeuvre as they wished, well out of range of our 4in guns and the only hope was to hit the bombs with Oerlikon fire as they approached. *Swansea* claims to have hit and deflected one which was heading for her.

On examination it was found that the damage was not so serious as at first anticipated. The bomb which came in at a very steep angle from the starboard quarter (estimated at about 70°) hit the edge of the Carley float on the roof of Y gun ammunition hoist, passed through the combing of the gun deck on the port side, through the ladder onto the quarter deck through the small bulwark at the break of the upper deck, into the water where it burst close alongside. The effect was to blow a large hole in the port side abaft the after end of the engine room which immediately flooded, luckily both bulkheads remained intact which confined the flooding to one compartment only. In the circumstances casualties were extremely light; two men who were standing in the path of the bomb on the port side of the ammunition supply shelter were never seen again. Everyone in the engine room suffered more or less seriously from steam scalding and one man was either killed or trapped and drowned and his body was recovered on return to harbour. The fact that the bomb burst under water, undoubtedly saved the lives of all [of] the after gun crews and supply parties, as there was no blast or splinter effect at all. As it was the Officer of the Quarters at Y gun was the only casualty, with a very severe foot wound.

As soon as it was apparent that the attack was over, the Medical Officers of *Swansea* and *Stormont* were transferred to attend the wounded, and *Matane* was taken in tow by *Meon*. Steps were taken to shore up the foremost and after bulkheads of the engine room. In a very short time the diesel dynamo was running, and lighting and general electric services were re-established throughout the ship and it was not long before the galley was again in working order and hot meals were able to be obtained. ...

In reply to the 'Help signal' sent out by *Swansea*, fighter cover was on the spot about 20 minutes after the attack and remained until dark. Towing proceed without difficulty or incident in flat calm water throughout the night.

...

21 July

0630: Stopped while further medical stores and equipment were transferred from *Swansea*. The weather now started to deteriorate with a wind and sea from the north-east and though there was no sign of the bulkhead yielding, small anxiety was felt on account of the weakened upper deck which began to work badly. In order to increase the freeboard aft all upper deck depth charges were jettisoned.

1000: *Meon* reported shadowing aircraft which did not respond to her Type 242. This was reported to C-in-C [presumably Plymouth] and shortly afterwards fighter cover arrived; about this time the tug *Recovery* arrived but was of little use as she reported her engines defective and unable to steam more than five knots. *Matane* remained in tow of *Meon* until about 1500 when the tow parted. *Stormont* was then ordered to pass her towing hawser, which was done extremely smartly and quickly and the tow was once more resumed. The weather now changed again with very heavy rain, but decreasing wind and sea. No further incident occurred.

2145: When just past the Eddystone, the tow was transferred to the tug *Retort*, and later on, on passing through the gate [at Plymouth] at 2308 a Dockyard Tug took over and berthed *Matane* at No. 1 Jetty, South Yard.

All officers and men behaved with great coolness and steadiness both during the attack and afterwards, although in many cases it was their first experience of action.

172.   *Little to Stark*

[Stark A2]   11 August 1944

Captain Moran, USNR, has now left us on his return to the US. You may remember he joined the Tug Control, Lee-on-Solent, on 18 May and took over his duties as Tug Controller on 22 May. Captain Moran's experience with tugs and towing has proved to be of inestimable value in Cross-Channel Operations. He was the only officer we had in a position to advise on suitable tugs for the various tows and also on the most suitable method of towing.[1]

Captain Moran has also been able to visit other ports and 'parks' from which equipment had to be taken and to advise on towing requirements at these places.

Being known personally to the Captains of most of the American tugs, he had their confidence from the start and he quickly won the confidence and respect of the British tug captains. This assisted greatly in keeping tugs running in arduous conditions.

Under his command all the resources of Tug Control have been used impartially and this fact has largely contributed to any success that has been achieved by the organisation of which he was the head.

Although Captain Moran's services will also be the subject of official report I would like to take the opportunity of paying this tribute to him and to thank you for having made him available at such an important period.

His charming personality goes without saying, and we are indeed sorry to part with him on this score alone.

173. *Commodore H. A. Flanagan, US Navy, to Stark.*

[Stark A2]   15 August 1944.

...

I guess we are in for a lot of annoyance from Ramsay from now on. ...The sum total is that Ramsay's job has passed out of existence. However, he is going to hold on to it and with a staff of 600 people is going to move to France with Eisenhower. ... with nothing to do I presume Ramsay will be constantly interesting himself in our affairs. Moreover, since Eisenhower told him that he would like to have him stay on as Naval C-in-C and go into Berlin with him he has been more and more throwing his weight about.

174. *NOIC, Arromanches, to Flag Officer, British Assault Area.*[2]

[ADM 199/1614]   19 August 1944

Situation Report – MULBERRY 'B' at Arromanches.

The enclosed report on MULBERRY 'B', some 10 weeks after the construction of the harbour was started to be submitted for information and record.

---

[1]Capt Moran, USNR: Tug Cntrlr 1944.
[2]NOIC Arromanches: unidentified.

In the words of the Prime Minister after his recent visit:

'This miraculous port has played and will continue to play a most important part in the liberation of Europe.'

The provision of 'sheltered water', a Naval responsibility, upon which everything has depended, has been achieved by the skilful handling and placing of Blockships and Phoenix[es] as breakwater.

…

As regards the organisation and operation of the harbour as combined Naval and Military port, its success may be measured in terms of discharging which today averages over 9,000 tons per day and aggregates a half million tons of stores, 120,000 personnel and 12,000 vehicles.

…

175. *Report of Proceedings of HMS* Mauritius
(Captain W. W. Davis), with HMS Kelvin *and HMCS* Iroquois[1]

[ADM 199/1645]   25–29 August 1944

…

26 August

…

5. Choosing *Iroquois*, who might reasonably produce French[-speaking Canadian] Citizens capable of a wider range of communication than other ships, I instructed her to land a party with portable W/T set to gather what information they could with regard to the strength and intentions of German Forces on the mainland.

6. The party landed in a fishing vessel with the Captain of the Port and the Acting Mayor. On landing they were accorded a tumultuous reception by the inhabitants, and were promptly invited to solve almost every problem from domestic farm disputes to the re-provisioning of the island, disposal of collaborationists, etc. Lieut Saks, RCNVR, the officer-in-charge of the party, evidently conducted himself with rare tact and discretion. Full reports of the information obtained have already been forwarded, and the party were re-embarked on the following day in accordance with your orders.[2]

---

[1]Capt W. W. Davis: OD (F) Sep 1941; PD Nov 1942; *Mauritius* Sep 1943; DTM Sep 1945.
[2]Lt James Saks, RCNVR: unidentified.

The Acting Mayor presented the SO, Force 27, with a bottle of the produce of the country in recognition of his gratitude for the services rendered by Force 27.

176.   *Stark to King*

[SPD 250]   13 September 1944

US Naval responsibilities in the European Theater of Operations.

1. Under the plans now in force or being developed under the direction of the Supreme Commander, Allied Expeditionary Force, US Naval responsibilities on the Continent in the European Theater of Operations can be placed under four headings:

(a) Port operating groups.
(b) Port liaison groups.
(c) Naval missions in liberated countries.
(d) Naval control missions in enemy countries.

2. It has been planned that the US Navy will furnish the naval port operating groups in all ports occupied and operated by the US Army. We now have such groups on the assault beaches, in Cherbourg, and in certain small ports on the east and west side of the Cotentin peninsula and on the north side of the Brittany peninsula. It was part of the original plan that we would abandon the beaches and the small ports on the Cotentin peninsula about 1 October, turn over Cherbourg to the British about the same date, and establish ourselves with the Army in ports from Brest southward to the Spanish frontier. The rapid advance of the army on the Continent has resulted in recent decisions by the US Army that it will:

(a) Not occupy ports from Brest to Bordeaux inclusive;
(b) Retain Cherbourg as a cargo and personnel discharge port;
(c) Occupy Le Havre;
(d) Occupy Antwerp or Rotterdam or both; (not yet finally approved by the Supreme Commander)
(e) Abandon the beaches when Le Havre and Antwerp and/or Rotterdam are able to handle all cargo lift other than that entering through Cherbourg and its satellite ports.

The necessary cargo lift for the US Army which is now approximately 42,000 tons per day and which was estimated would gradually rise to over 60,000 tons per day, will probably stabilize at a little over 40,000 tons per day, owing to reduced demands for certain materials. Cherbourg should be able to handle about 15,000 of these tons per day.

3. The US Navy will continue to furnish the groups at Cherbourg and expects to furnish the groups at Le Havre, Antwerp and/or Rotterdam, and at any German ports that the US Army might possibly operate. Sufficient officers and men are now available in this theater, earmarked for port duties, to cover all these commitments. It is to be noted that the Admiralty has informed ANCXF that it will be British policy in the occupied ports of the liberated countries to use the nationals thereof to as great an extent as possible in port operation. Presumably we will do the same and it is to be expected that our initial personnel commitments in the ports of the liberated countries will gradually reduce.

4. It has been planned that the US Navy will place port liaison groups in all liberated countries and in all enemy country ports operated by the British where the volume of American shipping warrants the presence of such groups. One port liaison group is already established on the British assault beaches. Three others are formed and ready to go into ports which the British may occupy and develop for the reception of large ocean going ships. Sufficient officers and men for liaison are available in the theater for any additional British operated ports, including Norwegian ports.

5. Both the port operating groups and the port liaison groups are and will be logistically under ComNavEu, and administratively and operationally under the Senior U. S. Naval Officers in their respective countries. In those liberated and enemy countries where SCAEF is in military control, the Senior US Naval Officers in the country, the port officers and the port liaison officers will receive their operational orders from SCAEF through ANXCF. This point has been thoroughly discussed with the Chief of Staff to the Supreme Commander, and the latter is firm regarding it. US Naval Port Officers and port liaison officers will receive directions as to the movement of merchant shipping and of escorts from the Admiralty in the same way that the Admiralty issues these directions to the home commands, and to the British port officers and port liaison officers.

6. It is the Supreme Commander's intention to set up naval missions in liberated countries and steps are already being taken to form the missions in France and Belgium. In regard to the French mission, the Admiralty are considering what form their representation will take but have reached no decision as yet. It is considered that Admiral Kirk can include the duties of the US Naval mission with his duties as Commander, US

Naval Forces in France. In both capacities, Admiral Kirk will be responsible to the Navy Department through ComNavEu in policy matters; to ComNavEu for administrative and logistic matters, and to SCAEF through ANXCF for operational matters. In this connection it should be restated that the US Flag Command over ports and bases in France is a sub-command of ComNavForFrance.

7. It now appears, as noted in paragraph 2(d), that we will have major shipping interests in the Low Countries. For this reason it is considered that a rear admiral or a commodore heading a small mission with Headquarters perhaps at The Hague, would best serve our interests.

8. No plans have yet been developed for Denmark and Norway and definite recommendations regarding these two countries will be made later in conformity with the directives and wishes of the Supreme Commander.

9. The plans for Germany as they have developed through several stages of discussion now envisage parallel Royal Navy and US Navy control missions in Berlin. The British intention is that until SCAEF relinquishes control, ANXCF will be their representative; who it will be after that, has not yet been decided. Inasmuch as Rear Admiral Hall is not available for the US Naval mission, it is recommended [that it should be] Vice Admiral Glassford.

10. SCAEF also plans for subordinate control missions at Kiel and Wilhelmshaven, and perhaps a third at Hamburg, to exercise control over German naval ships, German naval headquarters and German naval shore activities.

11. For the sub-missions, the British are thinking along the line that a possible solution might be to have them joint or integrate RN and US Navy with one headed by a U. S. Flag Officer, the other by a British Flag Officer. If SHAEF has to continue to command for a considerable period of time with Germany in a chaotic condition and before tri-partite government begins, he will necessarily have to take some post-hostilities steps. ComNavEu does not recommend the joint or integrated missions as it might result in there being no direct and clear-cut U. S. Naval opinion as to the advisability of steps contemplated or undertaken; the same applies to the British. It would also mean that we would probably come in contact with Russian naval missions as a joint US-British team, which is considered highly undesirable.

12. Originally, our thought was for us to have parallel missions with the British at Wilhelmshaven and at Kiel, but it might be equally well to have an American mission at Wilhelmshaven and a British mission at Kiel, or vice versa, each with adequate liaison from the other service. In the first case (parallel missions) we would recommend a flag officer for each of the sub-missions; in the second case (separate missions with liaison) we

would recommend a flag officer for only one of the sub-missions, that is at Wilhelmshaven or at Kiel; this latter (need for only one flag officer) would also apply to integrated missions. An alternative would be for the British to have both sub-missions and for us merely to furnish liaison; this is not recommended.

13. The US control mission and the U. S. sub-missions will be responsible to the Navy Department through ComNavEu for policy, ComNavEu for administrative and logistical matters and to SHAEF through ANXCF for operational matters. SCAEF has stated that the head of the control mission may always approach him and present the US Navy viewpoint regarding any post-war matters.

14. These control missions and sub control missions are the nuclei of the missions which will ultimately become the agencies of the tri-partite government. However, the planning for that government and for the post-war period is already in progress and the steps now being taken and the plans now being made will necessarily influence the actions of the tri-partite government. It is therefore important that the heads of our missions be appointed and their staffs formed so that they can take part in the planning for both the immediate and post-war periods.

15. It will not be possible to furnish from this command the flag officers to head missions in liberated and enemy territories other than Admiral Kirk and Admiral Glassford. As to the rest of the personnel, as much as possible will be furnished from here but a number may have to be requested from home.

16. Early decisions as to the set-up to be employed, and as to the flag officers to be made available is requested, so that plans may be made accordingly.

177.   *Commander W. M. Passmore, RN, to CO,*
US Navy Advanced Bases, 11[1]

[ADM 199/1614]   15 October 1944

State of MULBERRY 'A'.

1. A tracing has been prepared showing the extent of damage to Phoenixes and Blockships as a result of the gale in June and later after a NE wind of lesser strength and duration of 6 October.

2. From intersected rays into the cross-trees of selected blockships obtained by theodolite at triangulation stations ashore, it has been

---

[1]Cdr W. M. Passmore: *Princess Victoria* Sep 1940; *Gulmore* Nov 1942; *Hathi* Sep 1945.

ascertained that there has been no lateral displacement. This also applies to the Phoenixes with the exception of the extreme eastern one (B1204), which has slewed about 30° on account of its eastern half being exposed and the rest [lying in?] in sheltered water.

3. The sea bottom is soft (fine sand), and there appears to be no rocky foundation, as for instance at Arromanches; and from the changing angles of heel and trim of both blockships and Phoenixes is considered to shift to a certain extent after ground swells and spring tides.

4. During the June gale most of the damage was done on the second and third days when the units were bedded or anchored; the maximum settlement of a Phoenix [was?] noticed [to be?] about 10ft, that is from one to two feet below its top to the level of the gun platform. Twenty 'A' units had been wrecked, and three 'B' units in the western breakwater had broken their backs. Seven blockships, including the *Centurion*, had broken their backs, and other had taken up different angles of heel and trim. An extreme example was that of the *Galveston* whose propeller blade was visible and forecastle almost covered at low water springs; now, after the strong wind of 6 October her stern has settled and she has recovered her normal trim.

5. After the June gale comparative soundings were taken alongside the draft marks of the *Olambaja* (broken back) and her bow [was] found to have settled four feet and stern seven feet. Similar readings are now being taken alongside certain Phoenixes and blockships where the draft marks are still legible.

6. During the storm of 6 October the few remaining Phoenixes of the outer breakwater were destroyed, leaving only a few portions showing which cover at high water, as well as five Phoenixes partly destroyed which were breaking up the Gooseberry. Four of the 'breaking up' blockships had broken their backs, and movement in heel and trim of most of the remaining units was to be seen.

178.   *Memorandum on Supply Situation*

[Stark A2]   Autumn 1944

Ports, Shipping, etc.

...

9. Antwerp ... is practically in perfect condition. A couple of sunken ships along the river quays and the blowing of some of the lock gates are about the only casualties. We are fortunate, however, that [only] in No. 1 lock were all the lock gates blown. The port should be in perfect operating condition when river access is accomplished. There are about

60 mines in the rivers and locks, but their position is known and as soon as the minesweepers can reach the points they will be swept. Meanwhile, some of them are being blown by pulsator and some are being removed by divers. It is difficult to forecast when the Scheldt will be open. The British NOIC at Antwerp and the Admiralty agree that three to four weeks of sweeping will be needed before the river can be cleared for vessels of 25-foot draft, though coasters might reach there a little earlier. A guess on operations at Antwerp is somewhat between 1 and 16 December, and it is estimated that about 15 days after starting, the port should be handling 15, 000 tons for the British and 15,000 tons for us.[1]

10. The port will be British operated with the British NOIC in charge, a US Army Port Commandant on equal level under him. Our port party will assist the Army and perform its usual duties for armed guard crews and merchant ships. The actual operation of the port will be handled by the Belgians, whose organisations are pretty well intact. Latest reports indicate only about 5000 Belgian stevedores [are] available instead of the expected 15,000. Some concern is expressed regarding rocket bombing, 26 of which landed in three days last week, and this matter slowed down the Belgian port parties.

179. *Stark: Diary*

[Stark A1]   3 November 1944

[In north-west Europe] … at last the Army had woken up to the critical supply question.

… The Army had finally realized that they had been dazzled by the thought of the great port of Antwerp, not realizing that it would be a long time before it would be usable. Now they had finally realized that Rouen and Le Havre could be utilized more and more every day. They had concentrated on them with excellent results.

180. *Cunningham to Alexander*

[ADM 205/43]   7 January 1945

The Prime Minister has remarked on the appointment of a Flag Officer as relief for the late Admiral Sir Bertram Ramsay, in the post of ANXCF. …

It does not appear that the importance of the position held by ANXCF is fully realised. This officer is in command of all British and American

---

[1]NOIC Antwerp: not identified.

naval forces, and other Allied units, directly employed in connection with operations on the Continent. The Senior US Naval Commander, Vice Admiral Kirk (Comnavforfrance) and Rear Admiral Wilkes (CTF 125) are directly under his orders. Since being in direct command of the main cross-Channel naval assault and operations in connection with the opening of deep-water ports, Admiral Ramsay has acted as principal adviser in naval affairs to the SAC. If this appointment is now allowed to lapse, General Eisenhower will receive his advice from an American Admiral on naval matters, including the operation of units of the Royal Navy in British waters.

...

... the Navy's high standing at Supreme Headquarters will be lost, and the conduct of naval operations on the Continental seaboard will pass into the hands of the US Navy. This I feel could not be contemplated after the major part taken by the Royal Navy in the planning, provision and conduct of operations leading to the successful invasion of the Continent.

...

181. *Operation NEPTUNE: Admiralty Summary*
of Lessons Learned

[ADM 199/1663]   7 March 1945

...

V. *Bombardment:*
Scale and Effect of Bombardment –
Counter-Battery Fire

...

5. Helped by accurate fixing and aircraft spotting, ships were able to neutralise open batteries for a comparatively small expenditure of ammunition. Against casemented batteries a much heavier scale of bombardment was required ... The fire of Capital Ships or monitors is considered necessary. ... If insufficient heavy ships are available cruiser fire against casemented batteries is justified since temporary neutralisation may result, or at least the enemy's fire may be drawn. When it is known that Cruisers' piercing shell cannot penetrate the thickness of protection, the use of HE shell is recommended as being more likely to do incremental damage to control arrangements or cause splinters to enter the embrasure. ...

Beach Drenching Fire

6. The beach drenching concept has been justified and the technique now developed for use of destroyers and support craft has proved satisfactory. ...

Effect of Bombardment

7. As was to be expected with the type of bombardment employed, naval fire support of the landing achieved little destruction but evidently had considerable moral effect. ...

182.   *Kirk to King*

[Op Arch., King 5]   16 March 1945

I feel you should know the trend of thinking in regard to the Command set up over here after Operation ECLIPSE.[1]
    ... I offer the following suggestions from the US Naval point of view:

(a) Turn over Naval affairs in France, Belgium, Holland, to the Naval Attachés – possibly leaving a small Task Group in Paris, because of its being only remaining Communication Center on the continent.
(b) Under the Commander (undoubtedly Army), assign a Flag Officer of rank, designated as 'Commander, US Naval Forces Continent'.
(c) Shift the logistic and administrative support of US Navy Continental forces to this officer, using Le Havre as base initially.
(d) Diminish the London command, close out the British bases, and eventually restore to Naval Attaché status.
(e) Insure strong US Naval representation on the European Advisory Council.

One reason for shifting the center of gravity of US Naval weight to the continent from England is to get away from dependence upon the British Admiralty. In this important transition from Allied operations against a common enemy, to control by National Forces of areas allocated to the four Powers occupying Germany, it seems to me important that the US set up be divorced from outside influence, and in direct contact with the Navy Department.

---

[1] ECLIPSE: not identified.

183. *Commander [US] Amphibious Bases, Plymouth:*[1]
A History of the US Naval Bases in the UK:
US Naval Advanced Amphibious Base, Falmouth, Cornwall

[ADM 199/691] [n.d., 1946]

Arrival in Falmouth

... On 5 September [1943], after assembling 325 men and 20 officers, the FOXY-29 unit departed from New York harbour following a two-day detour at Pier 92. First stop overseas was Base 2, Roseneath, Scotland. Here, at the mammoth receiving and assessment area for the US Fleet, disclosure was made of the ultimate destination of this group of FOXY-29. Commander [James E.] Arnold, USNR was to become CO of a US Naval Advanced Amphibious Training Base in Falmouth, health and holiday resort of the Duchy of Cornwall. Described as 'the Gem of the Cornish Riviera', Falmouth from a historical point of view, does not claim to be old. Because of the shipping and commercial possibilities of the harbor, the idea of building a town around the simple fishing village was born to the Killigrew family in 1613.

...

... the bathing beaches were scarred and ugly, not from enemy action but from the intricate barriers erected by the British to thwart the German invasion which never came. There were palm trees, tennis courts and golf courses. But the tropical shrubs were few, and the golf courses were overrun with Quack grass and weeds. And British manufacturers had long since diverted production from tennis rackets to munitions. Bananas hang on trees? Yes, one ancient resident had a small patch of the tropical fruit trees, but nature had been unkind to his herbaceous plants and the connoisseur of fruitage had turned to apples instead. With mixed visions and an air of expectancy the FOXY group on 5 October [1943] – one month from the date of departing New York- arrived in Falmouth.

...

Nearby, at St Mawes, a sub-base of Falmouth, the establishment of a landing craft training base had begun under Lieut Cdr Frank A. Varney, USNR. St Mawes was 20 minutes from Falmouth by ferry, and considerable of the personnel working at Falmouth were billeted at the adjacent

---

[1]Cdr, US Amph Bases, Plymouth: Cdre J. E. Korns, US Navy.

fishing village. Meanwhile, at Fowey, another sub-base 35 miles away on the south [English] Channel coast, a small contingent of men under Lieut Hemingway Merriman, USNR, were establishing a similar base for landing craft.

US Naval HQ was established at the Greenbank Hotel where the bulk of the officers had been quartered. The more than 300 enlisted men attached to the base were billeted at the King's Hotel across town near to Prince of Wales Pier.

The major undertaking which confronted the pioneer Falmouth Navy group was erection of the hut camp on Beacon Hill. Next in importance was a suitable location for the Maintenance unit which would repair and overhaul the large amount of craft and ships scheduled to pass through Falmouth harbour in the coming months. Before long the Maintenance shop was constructed adjacent to Taylor's garage in mid-town. Four dry docks were available and a broad harbor entrance permitted many ships to anchor near the repair headquarters. Lieut Hagerty was officer in charge.

A suitable hospital location was found by Lieut-Cdr Ray T. Holden, [Medical Corps,] USNR, in St Michael's Hotel, an up-to-date building with central heating, spacious grounds and excellent location.

Lieut J. V. Keogh [USNR] completed a survey and inventory of all motor vehicles at Falmouth, Fowey and St Mawes and established a transportation center at the Town Quay, a short distance from the King's Hotel. The pace continued. HQ was shifted from the Greenbank Hotel to 4 Stratton Place, across the street. CBs living in two requisitioned buildings, Polltair and Wrekin, moved to Beacon Hill [site of Quonset huts].

The Ships Arrive

On 28 October [1943], the first amphibious ship, the LST 30 (proudly carrying the LCT (6) 527 in its bosom) steamed into Falmouth harbour for repairs. A month later the initial flotilla of LSTs, under Cdr William D. Wright, Jr, US Navy, arrived from combat service in the Mediterranean with stimulating tales of glider-bomb attacks by the enemy aircraft off the Bay of Biscay.[1]

...

In the face of extremely difficult road transport – at a time when troops en route to receiving ships for embarkation was the number one priority – the

---

[1]Cdr James E. Arnold, USNR: unidentified.
Cdr W. D. Wright, jr., US Navy: unidentified.

supply department serviced the same number of ships as indicated above [200]. Supply accomplished this feat by travelling from Falmouth to Exeter on short notice over narrow roads which were impractical for large truck transports.

...

Two unforeseen problems were encountered when the base was established, and had to be constantly faced throughout its tenure. One was the impractical landscape of the average English town. There was very little centralization, and activities were scattered over a wide area. This was a major concern in Falmouth, where the Beacon Hill, living area for the men, was nearly two miles from Maintenance HQ and from the Hydro Staff Building. The other problem was to maintain our official function – to exist as an Advanced Amphibious Base – and yet actually to perform as a Receiving Ship. Like Fowey, which was established as an Advanced Amphibious Training Base, Falmouth, which was never designed to be anything but an Advanced Amphibious Base, was forced to function as a receiving base for certain periods of its existence.

...

Prior to D-day the sole function of the base was to serve the forces afloat. Every effort was bent toward this end. LST and LCT flotillas operated from here, and a month before the invasion the base had been requisitioned and in use for billeting establishments. There were numerous stores and buildings throughout town for storage and supplies.

...

Falmouth, as a target for flying bombs was never in 'doodlebug alley' nor, because of its geographic location, was it ever as serene as Wheeling, W Va. Shortly before D-day, on 31 May [1944], the enemy struck from the sky in a vain effort to destroy or impede the ships and craft in the harbor waiting to strike at the Normandy coast. For the Luftwaffe, which according to all modern military standards, must have been instructed to hit at the invasion fleet, the attack on Falmouth was however, little more than a hasty flight from Berlin to Land's End – and back again. Total destruction of the US 'invasion fleet' in Falmouth harbour was three hotels, and an oil dump.

On 1 October 1944 the principal function of US Naval Advanced Amphibious Base, Falmouth was repair and maintenance of Landing Ships and Craft. This department was still fully occupied in routine maintenance and the repair of battle and storm damage.

184. *Report by Sir Walter Monckton to the Chiefs of Staff*[1]

[ADM 199/1616]   18 January 1946

...

II. Sum of Conclusions

10. ... No prudent plan could have admitted the measure of security afforded by the artificial harbours. Indeed the operation could not rightly have been undertaken without that insurance. As events turned out is probable that we could have achieved a successful invasion without the MULBERRIES and this conclusion is to some extent confirmed by the American experience at MULBERRY 'A'. But this in no way conflicts with the conclusion that the provision of an artificial harbour could not properly have been omitted.

11. If sheltered water was to be provided, Phoenix, i.e., concrete caissons, and the GOOSBERRY breakwater, consisting of CORNCOBS, i.e., blockships, were essential. ...

12. Sheltered water would not have been enough without the provision of means of discharge of men, tanks, other vehicles and stores. For this purpose the LST Pier, in spite of its later completion, was an important and perhaps essential feature. ...

13. ... There is striking evidence that in the storm that raged between D+13 D+16 hundreds of small craft from beaches on the Normandy coast outside MULBERRY 'B' came into the harbour and were sheltered by the GOOSEBERRY and such of the Phoenix units as had been planted. It is further clear that, during the period of the storm, which was a crucial period in the building up of the concentration of force, unloading continued at MULBERRY 'B' when it was not possible on unprotected beaches. ...

14. The view of the Admiralty is that the contribution of Bombadon, the floating breakwater, to the build-up as a whole was not very large but that it was a useful addition to the sheltered area in the crucial first few days of the landing. Subject to this, the evidence is that the Bombadon, though it stood up to the test which in the plan it was required to satisfy, did not yield a useful dividend and turned out to be a menace to the rest of the harbour and the shipping making use of it. ...

---

[1]Sir Walter Monckton (1891–1965): business & finance; govt service; Solicitor-Gen & Con MP 1945; Min Labour 1951–5; Paymaster Gen 1956–7; Visct Monckton of Brenchley.

15. It is not clear that the Stores Pier was an essential component in the artificial harbour. It was undoubtedly a great convenience and was substantially used. It was of special value for its use with awkward and heavy loads; and was of some value for the discharge of the express coaster which regularly brought stores urgently demanded and mail. ...
16. ... The overall cost in money for the two harbours was in the neighbourhood of £20 million, of which £9m is attributable to Phoenix, £7m to Whale and £1.25m to Bombadon. The evidence does not suggest that a diversion of labour or materials or facilities made any significant difference to the war effort, but the use of docks, carpenters and welders must have constituted a substantial diversion from shipping repair and the repair of bombed houses. ...

185. *Supreme Commander's Dispatch on Operations in North West Europe*

[ADM 199/1664]   11 February 1946

The Assault

...

On D-day the wind had, as forecast, moderated and the cloud was well-broken, with a base generally above 4000 feet. ... The sea, however, was still rough, and large numbers of our men were sick during the crossing. The waves also caused some of the major landing craft to lag astern, while other elements were forced to turn back.

As events proved, the decision to launch the assault at a time when the weather was so unsettled was largely responsible for the surprise which we achieved and more than offset the difficulties which we experienced.

The enemy had concluded that any cross-Channel expedition was impossible while the seas ran so rough ... and, with his radar installations rendered ineffective as a result of our air attacks, his consequent unpreparedness for our arrival ...

The weather was not the only circumstance surrounding the Allied landings which was contrary to the enemy's expectations. He had, apparently, assumed that we should make our attempt only when there was a new moon and on a rising tide, and that in choosing the place of main assault we should pick upon the neighbourhood of a good harbor and avoid cliffs and shallow, dangerous waters. In point of fact, we assaulted at low tide, when the moon was full; we landed away from large harbors and at some point below sheer cliffs; and the waters through which we approached the shore were so strewn with reefs and subjected to strong currents that the German naval experts had earlier declared them to be impossible for landing craft.

While our assault forces were tossing on the dark waters of the Channel en route for France, the night bombers which were to be the harbingers of our approach passed overhead. ... The seaborne forces bore witness to the inspiring moral effect produced by this spectacle of Allied air might and its results as they drew in towards the beaches.

...

As the night bombers were finishing their work in the early hours of 6 June, the Allied sea armada drew in towards the coast of France. The crossing had, as Admiral Ramsay reported, an air of unreality about it, so completely absent was any sign that the enemy was aware of what was happening. No U-boats were encountered, the bad weather had driven the enemy surface patrol craft into port, the German radar system was upset as a result of our air attack and scientific counter-measures, and no reconnaissance aircraft put in an appearance. Not until the naval escort fleets had taken up their positions and commenced their bombardment of the shore defenses was there any enemy activity, and then, taken unprepared as the Germans were, it was mainly ineffective. We achieved a degree of tactical surprise for which we had hardly dared to hope. The naval operations were carried out almost entirely according to plan. ... [The enemy] was still uncertain as whether he had to deal with invasion or merely a large-scale raid while our first assault was plunging shoreward to discover the truth about the vaunted Atlantic Wall.

The layout of the defenses which the Allied armies had to breach in order to establish their beachheads on French soil had been largely determined by the German experience at the time of the Dieppe raid in 1942. This raid convinced the enemy that any attempt at invasion should be destroyed on the beaches themselves, and the defense system subsequently constructed on this principle was in consequence lacking in depth.

Appreciating that one of our chief objectives would be the capture of a port, the enemy had developed heavy frontal defenses during 1943 at all of the principal harbors from Den Helder to Brest; and as the invasion threat grew, Cherbourg and Le Havre were further strengthened, while heavy guns were installed to block the entrance to the Bay of the Seine. Between the ports stretched a line of concrete defense positions, coastal and flak batteries, each self-contained, heavily protected against air bombing and lavishly equipped. These positions were designed for air-raid defense, their frontal approaches were mined, and where possible artificial flooding was used to guard rear approaches. Static heavy and medium guns, intended to bombard approaching shipping, were sited well forward at the rear of the beaches ...

The assumption of command in France by Field Marshal Erwin Rommel during the winter of 1943–44 was marked by a vigorous extension and intensification of the defensive work already in progress, and this continued up to the very day on which our landings took place. While the coastal guns were casemated and the defense posts strengthened with thicker concreting against the threat of air attack, a program was commenced in February 1944 of setting up continuous belts of underwater obstacles against landing craft along the entire length of all possible landing beaches. It was intended by this means to delay our forces at the vital moment of touch-down, when they were most vulnerable, and thus to put them at the mercy of devastating fire from the enemy positions at the rear of the beaches. The obstacles – including steel 'hedgehogs', tedrahedral, timber sticks, steel 'Element C' curved rails and rafts – were developed to cover high and low tide contingencies, and most of them had affixed mines or improvised explosive charges. The program was not, however, completed by 6 June, and the obstacles which our men encountered, though presenting considerable difficulties, nevertheless fell short of current German theory. Few mines were laid on the actual beaches. ...

Despite the massive air and naval bombardments with we prefaced our attack, the coastal defenses in general were not destroyed prior to the time when our men came ashore. Although naval gunfire proved effective in neutralising the heavier batteries, it failed to put them permanently out of action, thanks to the enormous thickness of the concrete casements. ...

The defenses on the beaches themselves were also not destroyed prior to H-hour as completely as had been hoped. ...

Nevertheless the naval and air bombardments combined did afford invaluable assistance in assuring the success of our landings, as the enemy himself bore witness. Although the strongly protected fixed coastal batteries were able to withstand the rain of HE, the field defenses were largely destroyed, wire entanglements were broken down and some of the minefields were set off. The smoke shells also blinded the defenders and rendered useless those guns which had escaped damage. ... The terrible drum fire of the heavy naval guns especially impressed the defenders, and the moral effect of this bombardment following a note of hell from the air was perhaps of greater value than its material effects. Such return fire as was made from the heavy batteries was directed mainly against the bombarding ships, not the assault forces, and it was generally inaccurate.

The close support fire from destroyers, LCG (L), SP artillery and LCT (g), which deluged the beaches during the 'free for all' bombardment covering the infantry as they waded ashore, was particularly effective. In this connection, it may be noted that the first assault waves generally had fewer losses in landing than had succeeding ones. The aim of the gunners was to demoralize the defenders by a general barrage rather than to destroy particular targets. ...

The high seas added enormously to our difficulties in getting ashore. Awkward as these waters would have been at any time, navigating under such conditions as we experienced called for qualities of superlative seamanship. Landing craft were hurled onto the beaches by the waves, and many of the smaller ones were swept before they could touch down. Others were flung upon and holed by the mined underwater obstacles which the men called 'Rommel's asparagus'. Numbers of the troops were swept off their feet while wading through the breakers and were drowned, and those who reached the beach were often near exhaustion. It was, however, impossible on every beach to swim in the amphibious DD tanks upon which we relied to afford fire support for the infantry clearing the beach exits. These were launched at SWORD, UTAH and OMAHA beaches, and, although late, reached land at the two former; at OMAHA, however, all but two or three foundered in the heavy seas and those which got through were speedily knocked out on shore. At the remaining beaches the tanks had to be unloaded directly [on]to the shore by the LCTs, which were forced, at considerable risk, to dry out for the purpose. Fortunately the beaches were sufficiently flat and firm to obviate damage to the craft.

Despite these difficulties, the landings were duly carried out, and on all but one sector the process of securing the beachheads went according to plan. ...

...

The seaborne assault on the British-Canadian sector was carried out according to plan, and despite the rough approach substantial bridgeheads were established on D-day. ... Though met by considerable shelling and mortar fire, the troops succeeded in clearing the beaches by 1000 hours and pushed inland towards Caen.

In the 30 Corps sector, 50th British Division landed on GOLD beach, near Asnelles-sur-Mer. Although troops on the left flank caused some trouble, the enemy opposition as a whole was found to be less than anticipated, and the defenses at the rear of the beaches were successfully overcome. During the day Arromanches, Meuvaines and Ryes were occupied and a firm footing was obtained inland.

It was in the St Laurent-sur-Mer sector, on OMAHA beach, where the American V Corps was launched, that the greatest difficulties were experienced. Not only were the surf conditions worse than elsewhere, causing heavy losses to amphibious tanks and landing craft among the mined obstacles, but the leading formations – the 116th Regiment of the 29th Division at Vierville-sur-Mer and the 16th Regiment of the 1st Division at Colleville-sur-Mer – had the misfortune to encounter a German Division, the 352nd Infantry, deployed on manoeuvres along the coast. Against the defense offered in this sector, where the air bombing had been largely ineffective, the naval guns, hampered by the configuration of the ground which made observation difficult, were able to make little impression. Exhausted and disorganized amid the pounding breakers, the Americans were pinned to the beaches for some hours but regrouped under a murderous fire from the German field guns along the cliffs and, with extreme gallantry, stormed the enemy positions. The cost was heavy – when the beaches were cleared some 800 men of the 116th had fallen and a third of the 16th were lost – but by their unflinching courage they turned what might well have been a catastrophe into a glorious victory.

The American 4th Division (VII Corps) assault on the UTAH beaches in the Varreville area of the Cotentin [peninsula], west of the Vire estuary, met with least opposition of any of our landings. Moreover, an error in navigation turned out to be an asset, since the obstacles were fewer where the troops actually went ashore than on the sector where they had been intended to beach. The enemy had apparently relied on the flooding of the rear areas here to check any force which might attempt a landing, and the beaches themselves were only lightly held. Complete surprise was achieved and a foothold was obtained with minor casualties, although it was here that we expected our greatest losses.

PART IV

THE MEDITERRANEAN

It can be argued that the 'great days' of naval warfare, encounters between battle fleets, in the Mediterranean were over for good when our story opens in October 1943; it saw the close of two centuries of major warship engagements, culminating in Admiral Sir Andrew Cunningham's command of the Mediterranean Fleet between June 1939 and March 1942, with its high peaks of Taranto (November 1940) and Matapan (March 1941). His leadership of a battle fleet from Alexandria against the sizeable and balanced Italian fleet was paralleled by the command of Force H from Gibraltar by his friend and contemporary Admiral Sir James Somerville (June 1940 to February 1942). In our period the only capital ships in the middle sea were superannuated dreadnoughts of British, American and French navies (used solely for bombardment of shore targets), for the Italian fleet was, in the words of Cunningham's famous signal, 'under the guns of the fortress of Malta'; it was defeated, much of it was disarmed and reduced to a care-and-maintenance basis, and a handful of its light forces supplemented those of the Allies in the continuing fight against the Germans.[1] It was, though, a diplomatic football, as President Franklin Roosevelt, eager to establish good relations with the Soviet dictator Josef Stalin, ahead of post-war diplomatic arrangements, had promised rashly to hand over one-third of the Italian fleet to the Soviet navy. He appears to have done this without adequate consultation with Prime Minister Churchill or the Combined Chiefs of Staff; much time and effort was spent trying to row back from this over-hasty commitment [187, 190–91, 194, 201].[2] In the event, the Soviets were fobbed off with obsolete British and American vessels, pending the end of hostilities worldwide; the Russians received Italian vessels after 1945. Roosevelt's cavalier offer did not take into account Italian pique at the proposed transfer without their consent, the current co-operation of the Italian Navy, the use of its light forces and its dockyards and its mercantile marine, nor the unsuitability of vessels designed for the Mediterranean for service in the Soviet Arctic.

The modern battleships and aircraft carriers may have departed many months before this story opens and there may have been no actions between surface ships in the last eighteen months of the Mediterranean war but it is not to say that the naval contribution to the fighting was not considerable. The purpose of the naval war changed and so did the instruments of naval power. Whereas between the entry of Italy into the war (June 1940) and the final relief of Malta (November 1942), the Allied

---

[1]Cunningham to the Admiralty, 11 Sept 1943, in M. A. Simpson, ed., *Cunningham Papers*, II (Aldershot, 2006: NRS vol. 150), p. 128; W. F. Kimball, *Forged in War: Churchill, Roosevelt and the Second World War* (London, 1997), p. 217.

[2]Churchill to Roosevelt, 16 Oct 1943, in W. F. Kimball, ed., *Churchill and Roosevelt: The Complete Correspondence*, II, *The Alliance Forged* (Princeton, NJ, & London, 1984), pp. 438–9.

navies (chiefly the Royal Navy) had been one of the main elements in the war against Mussolini and his later reinforcement by Hitler, enduring much loss of ships and men, now the naval forces were the handmaidens of a series of Allied landings. This change had been prefigured by the invasions of North Africa (November 1942), Sicily (July 1943) and Italy proper (September 1943). In the latter part of 1942, the maritime war had moved inexorably from that between ships of the line to that of the little ships. As the fighting moved from the African shore to that of the European beaches, it underwent a subtle change, for it was no longer a contest between imperial powers over colonies or client states in North Africa but now a struggle between democracy and dictatorship, a transformation unacknowledged, at least consciously, in official communications.

The period witnessed the gradual evaporation of British power in a region the nation had long regarded as its own *mare nostrum*; almost two hundred years of domination of the inland sea slid quickly to an end, marked by the advent of greater American naval power, much to the chagrin of Admiral Sir John Cunningham, the Allied Naval C-in-C.[1] The Admiralty's Director of Plans pointed out in April 1944 that the Americans would have shortly some 49 destroyers to 13 British – an 'undesirable American preponderance' [205]. Despite this naval 'preponderance', the American high command, both civilian and military, remained convinced that the British – scheming, devious, perfidious Albion – intended to resume their historic domination of the great sea after the war [192–3, 196, 205, 223].

American fears on these grounds, already stirred by the British campaign against Italy from June 1940, were strengthened considerably by a purely British venture, again largely at Churchill's instigation, in the Aegean. This was an attempt to capitalize on the Italian surrender by amphibious landings on several Dodecanese islands, culminating, it was intended, in an assault on Rhodes, the gateway to the area and much the largest island in that sea. In October and November 1943, fierce battles were fought for control of these Italian islands. The Germans responded with unexpected vigour and force, disarming the dispirited Italian garrisons, exercising air superiority and running men and supplies by sea. The British suffered humiliating and costly defeats everywhere, while Rhodes remained inviolate. It was a fiasco and Churchill himself was largely to blame for this hasty, ill co-ordinated, overambitious, inadequately resourced series of landings.[2]

---

[1] Adm Sir John Cunningham to AoF Sir Andrew Cunningham, Naples, 4 Mar 1944, & A. Cunningham to J. Cunningham, 6 May 1944, in Simpson, ed., *Cunningham Papers*, II, pp. 283–4, 286–7.

[2] Simpson, ed., *Cunningham Papers*, I, pp. 81–2, 86–98, 121, 169.

Churchill's aims were laudable. He hoped to consolidate Britain's historic influence in the Balkans, lure Turkey into the war on the Allied side, and supply the Soviet Union via the Bosphorus and Black Sea, turning the German flank in south-east Europe. It was in many ways a mirror of the equally ill-fated Dardanelles campaign of 1915–16 – and as much of a costly failure [189]. The Americans refused to divert forces which they had recently (and with some reservations) invested in mainland Italy and Britain found her means too limited to achieve Churchill's objective. Eisenhower explained to the CCS midway through the campaign that 'our resources in the Mediterranean are not large enough to allow us to undertake the capture of Rhodes' [186]. Thus the Americans, who regarded the Mediterranean, quite rightly, as a strategic dead-end, were convinced of Albion's well-known and long-term imperial ambitions and, for political as well as military reasons, wished to have no part in them. They now had an increasing preponderance of power in the middle sea, were increasingly wary of British enthusiasm for further adventure in that area, and exercised their growing primacy in the Western Alliance.

The remaining ships of the Italian Navy were governed by an agreement between the Italian Minister of Marine, Admiral de Courten, and the Naval C-in-C of Allied forces in the Mediterranean, Admiral of the Fleet Sir Andrew Cunningham.[1] The Cunningham-de Courten Agreement was modified on 17 November 1943, in the light of a new general armistice, but was again dependent on Italian good behaviour and gave the interim Italian government, despite its support of the Allied cause, only limited control of its vessels and facilities [187, 190–91, 201, 222].

The other conquered nations in the Mediterranean fared rather better. The French Navy had been divided in its loyalty to the post-armistice French government, headed by Marshal Pétain, and the continued resistance of France, led by General de Gaulle. Some French naval forces had switched allegiance from Pétain to Free France in 1942–43 (notably the force at Alexandria, neutralised by unprecedented Cunningham diplomacy in June 1940).[2] In the campaign of landings in the latter part of the war, the old French battleship *Lorraine*, a squadron of cruisers and a handful of *contre-torpilleurs* (large destroyers) took part in bombardments [188, 195, 202, 204, 206–7, 217, 220–21, 224]. The only other substantial Allied navy was that of Greece; it had played an honourable part in Allied operations but, politically, Greece was polarised, reflected

---

[1]T. B. Buell, *Master of Sea Power: A Biography of Fleet Admiral Ernest J. King* (Boston, 1980), pp. 436–8.
[2]M. A. Simpson, ed., *Cunningham Papers*, I, (Aldershot, 1998; NRS vol. 140), pp. 83–97.

in the navy, where mutinies occurred in April 1944, suppressed blood-
ily by loyal Greek sailors. At the beginning of 1945, Britain interfered
in the more-or-less inevitable Greek civil war, but it required American
landing craft to transport men and vehicles to Greece. Admiral King felt,
rightly, that this was a war in which Americans had no part but was pre-
vailed upon to allow American craft to be used [223].[1] Dutch and Polish
combatant ships and mercantile transports completed the Allied line of
battle, while a number of Canadian landing craft were drafted into the
ANVIL operation after their service in the Normandy landings.[2]

The Allies had landed in the Italian peninsula in September 1943, at
Taranto in the heel and at Salerno on the western coast, just south of
Naples. Their descent upon mainland Italy was characterised by haste (to
take advantage of the Italian armistice), divisions among the politicians
and also their commanders, hazy aims, and inadequate land forces. The
German defence was stout and wily (led by a consummate tactician, Field
Marshal Kesselring). The Allies failed to appreciate that peninsular Italy
was prime defensive ground and had almost no harbours on the east coast
and few of any consequence on the west, save Naples and in the far north,
in the Gulf of Genoa. The land campaign soon became bogged down
due to a combination of skilful German defence, unusually cold and wet
weather, and the rugged, mountainous, heavily-wooded spine of Italy.

It was to break this logjam in central Italy that a bold plan was devised
to land at Anzio, on the west coast and within easy reach of Rome, a clas-
sic outflanking manoeuvre exploiting the mobility and flexibility of sea
power and using the Allies' considerable experience of, and expertise
in, amphibious operations. It was yet another of the daring, not to say
reckless, operations that Churchill had pressed for and 'he had imposed
his will on the generals and admirals and their better judgment,' wrote
Morison, going on to conclude, 'Either it was a job for a full army, or it
was no job at all'.[3] Anzio came to represent for the Royal Navy a long-
term commitment in support of the stalled landing [198–200].

The major event in the Mediterranean was the invasion of southern
France on 15 August 1944. This was yet another indication of America's
increasing domination of Western strategy. The Americans viewed the

[1]S W. Roskill, *The War at Sea*, III, pt. I (London, 1960), pp. 297–300; Kimball, *Forged in War*, p. 258; C. Barnett, *Engage the Enemy More Closely: The Royal Navy in the Second World War* (London, 1991), pp. 687–90; S. E. Morison, *History of United States Naval Operations in World War II*, IX, *Sicily-Salerno-Anzio* (Boston, 1960), pp. 317–79, esp. pp. 328, 336.
[2]Roskill, *War at Sea*, III, pt. 1, pp. 193–211; S. W. Roskill, *Churchill and the Admirals* (London, 1977); Kimball, *Forged in War*, pp. 226–7.
[3]R. W. Love, Jr, *History of the U.S. Navy*, II, *1942–1991* (Harrisburg, PA, 1992), pp. 75–7.

invasion as a way of diverting German forces from the fundamental campaign in Normandy which opened in June and of increasing Allied supplies through the captured ports of Marseille and Toulon and along the Rhône valley, of vital importance as the ports of northern France could not deliver the volume of supplies needed [195, 206, 217]. British preference was for a continued push up the spine of Italy and they resisted the diversion of resources to the southern French venture. Roosevelt, backed by America's growing and superior might, and having made promises about the invasion of Europe to Stalin at Tehran in November 1943, was well aware of British desires but stood firm [197]. The British knew the stakes were loaded against them but persisted in trying to divert ANVIL to an attack on Trieste, in the Adriatic, to within a few weeks of ANVIL's launch. The Americans knew they had the measure of them, however, Eisenhower informing Marshall that the British (specifically Churchill, whose eyes were on Vienna, and Brooke, who wished to preserve British army control in Italy) would 'not permit an impasse to arise' and would fall in with America's wishes, if with some reluctance [210]. Cunningham, by then First Sea Lord, thought that the British COS 'did not come out of it very well'; he was always ambivalent but felt that the Navy should take a back seat to the soldiers.[1]

Once the British had accepted the American wishes on ANVIL, discussions thereafter were on the provision of forces. As the troops were to be American and French, the Royal Navy was required to provide bombardment and escort forces and air cover. Much wrangling took place over the extent of the forces, how long they should stay on station, and who should provide them [195, 197, 202–7, 211–20, 224]. The Americans, who had a low opinion of British ships and capabilities, provided many ships – over and above requests, according to King, who was anxious to relocate American forces to the Pacific as soon as possible. As in the case of NEPTUNE, King urged the British to furnish additional forces; most American senior officers believed that the Home Fleet was too large for its tasks and that the Eastern Fleet was underemployed, but Cunningham was adamant that he could not withdraw forces safely from either fleet [202, 204–5, 213]. The American Admiral H. Kent Hewitt, an experienced Mediterranean and amphibious commander, stressed the need for 'adequate naval support' and a considerable force was collected [195, 202, 206–7, 211]. He need not have worried – the assault was 'a

---

[1]Roskill, *War at Sea*, III, pt 2, p. 104; Roskill, *Churchill and the Admirals*, p. 243; Morison, XI, *The Invasion of France and Germany* (Boston, 1957), pp. 221–92; M. A. Simpson, *A Life of Admiral Andrew Cunningham: A Twentieth Century Sailor* (London, 2004), p. 171.

well-nigh perfect co-ordination of our three Services'. Little opposition was encountered on land, in the air, and at sea [218–20].

The launch of ANVIL in August 1944 represented the last major naval activity in the Mediterranean, though light forces and coastal craft continued to be active in the Adriatic and Aegean until the close of the war in the spring of 1945.

186. *Eisenhower to CCS and COS*

[Map Rm 33]   10 October 1943

I held a meeting at La Marsa today attended by the C-in-C Mediterranean, Air C-in-C Mediterranean, C-in-C Middle East, C-in-C Levant, Deputy AOC-in-C Mideast.[1] The Mideast situation was exhaustively explored in an effort to find means to restore the situation in the Aegean by the assault and capture of Rhodes. Our combined resources were reviewed and the effects on the Italian campaign considered, together with the effects of a pause in Italy while Rhodes was secured. The following report represents the unanimous views of all C's-in-C.

2. *Present situation in the Aegean.*

Operations against Dodecanese were originally designed to take full advantage of the Italian armistice and to exploit it to the maximum possible extent. Because of enemy anxiety in this theatre he reacted even more strongly than expected and brought reinforcements of GAF from Russia and France, which at once resulted in giving him almost complete control of the air and, consequently, of the sea in the Aegean.[2] Cos with its airfields was lost, and as a result it has been impossible to build up our garrisons with adequate weapons. This situation has been aggravated by the poor fighting spirit of the Italians and the inadequacy of their fixed defences and equipment. This has placed the garrisons of the islands remaining in our hands in imminent danger and they cannot be reinforced without incurring prohibitive Naval losses. Owing to the remoteness of our air bases as well as deterioration of the weather, we have been unable to remedy the air situation even with the considerable

---

[1]C-in-C Mediterranean: Adm Sir John Cunningham (1885–1962): ent RN 1900; navig spist; Med F & Grand F 1914–18; Cdr, Navig School 1922–3; Master of F 1923; Capt 1925; staff cdr, Naval War Coll; DP; *Adventure, Resolution*; RA & ACNS 1936; ACNS (Air) & 5SL 1937–9; RA, 1 CS, Med F 1939; VA & 1 CS, Home F 1939–40; Naval cdr, 'Menace', Dakar, 1940; 4SL 1941–3; C-in-C Levant & then Med & Adm 1943; FSL 1946–8; AoF 1948; Chmn, Iraq Petroleum Company 1948–56; M. H. Murfett, 'Adm Sir John Cunningham', in Murfett, ed., *The First Sea Lords* (London, 1995).

C-in-C Levant (temp): Adm Sir A. U. Willis (1889–1976): ent RN 1903; torpedo spist; Grand F 1916–18; Capt 1929; Naval War Coll 1930–2; *Kent* China 1933–4; *Nelson* Home F 1934–5; *Vernon* i/c 1935–8; *Barham* Med F 1938; Cdre & CoS Med F 1939–41; RA 1840; A/VA & C-in-C S Atl Sep 1941–Feb 1942; VA, 3BS & 2inC, Eastern F Mar 1942; FOIC Force H 1943; C-in-C Levant, 1943; Adm 1944; Adm 1944; 2SL 1944–6; C-in-C Med 1946–8; C-in-C Portsmouth 1948–50; AoF 1949. VA Sir Bernard Rawlings succeeded as FO, E Med, 28 Dec 1943.

C-in-C Middle East: Gen Sir Henry Maitland Wilson.

C-in-C Mediterranean Air Force: ACM Tedder.

Deputy Air C-in-C Mediterranean: AVM H. E. P. Wigglesworth.

[2]GAF: German Air Force (the 'Luftwaffe').

air fields which have been allocated from MAC within the last few days.[1] Consequently, maintenance is limited to such small tonnage as can be infiltrated by small craft or by arrangement through Turkey. All of us are agreed that if Rhodes is not captured and held there is no chance of restoring the local air situation sufficiently to allow surface forces and maintenance shipping to defend and maintain the islands we still hold.

3. *Requirements for Aegean operations.*

View is firmly held that if the operation for the capture of Rhodes is to be mounted, [it is] most important that it should be on scale to make reasonably certain of success. First essential would be establishment of high degree of air mastery in Aegean; for this it would be necessary to employ bulk of Mediterranean bomber forces to attack air fields in Athens-Salonika-Crete-Rhodes in order to neutralize enemy air forces before the assault. This preliminary action, in view of break in weather, would take a period of three weeks before the assault to ensure its accomplishment. Thereafter there would be a period during which this effort must be sustained in order to get our ground and air forces firmly established ashore.

To provide even limited cover over our convoys and assaults (at the rate of eight aircraft a time) it would be necessary to employ all P-38 (Lightning) aircraft in the Mediterranean.[2] Even adding carrier-borne aircraft which might be made available, we consider this cover quite inadequate. This conclusion is based upon experience, the most recent notable example being at Salerno.

...

6. *Effect of undertaking Aegean operations on campaign in Italy.*

While ground forces could be provided from formations which cannot, at the moment, be placed in Italy, yet provision of landing craft, if taken from pool intended to be left in Mediterranean, would react most seriously upon continued build-up and maintenance in Italy. Moreover this would preclude amphibious operations that are an integral part of Alexander's plan. The CCS may decide to call upon craft intended for return to UK and defer their date of departure. This might not be serious in case of LSTs but would prevent dispatch of LCTs before weather conditions make passage to UK impossible.

7. To sum up, we are agreed that our resources in the Mediterranean are not large enough to allow us to undertake the capture of Rhodes and at

---

[1]MAC: Mediterranean Air Command.
[2]Lockheed P-38 (Lightning): 1939; 2 engines; 1 crew; 414mph; 2260m; 1×20mm cannon, 4mg.

the same time secure our immediate objectives in Italy. We must therefore choose between Rhodes and Rome. To us it is clear that we must concentrate upon the Italian campaign.

We therefore recommend that ACCOLADE be postponed until such time as weather conditions and availability of forces make the operation a reasonable undertaking.[1] We venture to suggest that the CCS examine the situation as it will exist after we have captured Rome.

187. *King to Noble*

[Op Arch, King 4] 16 October 1943

Employment of Italian Vessels.

1. The recent declaration of war by the Italians against the Germans changes their status and may modify some of recommendations of reference (a) [in a BAD memorandum of 12 October – not reproduced]. This change in the situation indicated the maximum use of Italians in managing their own vessels. Further comments are given below.

Specific Comments on Reference (a)

2. (a) *Littorios*: US facilities are being fully employed and there is no excess available for the overhaul of these vessels. Manufacture of ammunition would be required to enable the ships to be actively employed. The battleships have poor defensive characteristics which make them undesirable for active Pacific operations. Until the Italians declare war on Japan there is further objection to their use in the Pacific. Recommend against proposed employment.

A possible use appears to be in the Mediterranean, using [their] own crews with Allied liaison personnel, for supporting miscellaneous operations, and for transport purposes in emergency.

(b) *Cavours*: The Italian declaration of war changes the position of these ships. It is considered these ships should be re-militarised and employed for the support of operations and for transport purposes in the Mediterranean.

3. *Cruisers*: Information upon which recommendation is based is not available. Their use in the Mediterranean under control of C-in-C Allied Fleet as fast transports and for the support of minor operations appears desirable.

4. *Submarines*: Concur.

---

[1] ACCOLADE: the Aegean landings.

5. *Miraglia*: The employment should be under CCS control and be based on relevant needs. The US need for the transport of Army aircraft by carrier to the UK and elsewhere is urgent.

6. *Saturnia*: This ship should be operated in the general shipping pool. There are inadequate personnel shipping facilities in the Pacific. It seems desirable that she be used with [an] Italian crew and Allied liaison officers on board in an Atlantic run for UK build-up of US Army personnel. A shift of equivalent lift to the Pacific would then appear to be in order.

7. *Eritrea*: Consider this ship to be used to best purpose at the discretion of the Supreme Commander, SEAC, the Italian crew to be employed as practicable in view of the manpower shortage.

188.   *King to Noble*

[Op Arch, King 4]   25 October 1943

1.   I have received Admiralty dispatch 232254A [not reproduced] concerning an agreement between the C-in-C Mediterranean and Admiral Le Monnier providing that for the present, one of the three French cruisers is to be kept in the Mediterranean and the other two at Dakar (6). I also note that the C-in-C Mediterranean considers that all three cruisers may be required in the Mediterranean at a later date; while the Admiralty takes the view that this will have to be considered with respect to the existing situation at the time.[1]

2.   I concur in the Admiralty opinion. I should be grateful if you will so inform the Admiralty.

3.   With regard to future cases of similar nature within the Mediterranean-African region, I suggest that the Admiralty take for granted my concurrence in such detailed allocations of French naval vessels as may be agreed upon by the French Naval Command, General Eisenhower (or the C-in-C Mediterranean, acting for him) and the Admiralty. I should expect to be kept informed of changes as they are planned, but I do not think it necessary … that you and I be consulted. …

189.   *Stark to King*

[Stark A2]   3 November 1943

I have just seen Admiral Cunningham. In substance he gives the following in support of what the British are doing in the Aegean.

---

[1]Adm Le Monnier: FFN; Fr cruisers: FFN *Montcalm, George Leygues, Gloire*.

1. From the long range standpoint the war will be much shortened if conditions get bad in the Balkans. By Spring the Russians should be in Romania. The effect of the British holding the Dodecanese may have a stiffening effect on Turkey, and in any case, Turkey will feel more comfortable with the British in those islands than the Hun. He rather expects when the Russians get into Romania, and in the general direction of Bulgaria, that Turkey is likely to come in. In general, the all-round effect (on Turkey and the Balkans) of holding these islands is good. Conversely, the effect of losing them, while in no sense disastrous, would be harmful.

2. ... if these islands could be securely held, Crete and Rhodes, instead of dominating the entrance to the Aegean, would fall of their own weight. The position is not too secure now. It's a good deal of a question who holds on. If the Aegean can be cleared, the route to the Black Sea and to Russian seaports would be enormously shortened, in fact several thousand miles shorter than the Persian route.

3. Mistakes was originally made and showed up in the loss of Kos by not putting sufficient strength there. Damage to the cruisers can be afforded because it is doubtful if the cruisers employed in the Aegean would have been employed anywhere else. The loss of the destroyers is, of course, keenly felt because they are so much in demand everywhere.

4. He hopes to be able to secure the Aegean without paying an overprice for the advantages which would accrue.

190. *Amended Cunningham-de Courten Agreement*[1]

[Map Rm 35]   17 November 1943

A new Armistice having been signed between the head of the Italian Government and the Allied C-in-C under which Italian warships and the Italian Mercantile Marine were placed unconditionally at the disposal of the United Nations, and HM the King of Italy and the Italian Government having since expressed their wish that the fleet and the Italian Mercantile Marine should be employed in the Allied effort to assist in the prosecution the war against the Axis Powers, the following principles are established on which the Italian Navy and Mercantile Marine will be disposed.

It is understood and agreed that the provisions of this agreement as to immediate employment and the disposition of Italian warships and merchant

---

[1]Cunningham-de Courten Agreement: in M. A. Simpson (ed), *The Cunningham Papers*, II, pp. 131–3.

ships do not alter the right of the United Nations to make such other dispositions of any or all Italian ships as they may think fit. Their decisions in this
respect will be noted to the Italian Government from time to time.

A. Such ships as can be employed to assist actively in the Allied effort
   will be kept in commission and will be used under the orders of the
   C-in-C Mediterranean as may be arranged between the Allied C-in-
   C and the Italian Government.
B. Ships which cannot be employed will be reduced to a care and maintenance basis and be placed in designated ports, measures of disarmament being undertaken as necessary.
C. The Government of Italy will declare the names and whereabouts of
   warships, [or] merchant ships, now in their possession which previously belonged to any of the United Nations, these vessels are
   to be returned forthwith as may be directed by the Allied C-in-C.
   This will be without prejudice to negotiations between the governments which may subsequently be made in connection with replacing losses of ships of the United Nations caused by Italian action.
D. The Allied Naval C-in-C will act as the agent of the Allied C-in-C in
   all matters in connection with the operation of the Italian Fleet, and
   matters concerning the employment of the Italian Fleet or Merchant
   Navy, their disposition and related matters.
E. It should be clearly understood that the extent to which the terms of
   the armistice are modified to allow the arrangements outlined above
   and which follow, are dependent upon the extent and effectiveness
   of Italian co-operation.

Method of operation

The C-in-C Mediterranean will place at the disposal of the Italian Minister of Marine a high ranking naval officer with the appropriate staff
who will be responsible to the C-in-C Mediterranean for all matters in
connection with the operation of the Italian Fleet, and be the medium
through which dealings will be carried out in connection with the Italian Merchant Marine. The Flag Officer acting with these duties (Flag
Officer, Liaison) will keep the Italian Minister of Marine informed of
the requirements of the C-in-C Mediterranean, and will act in close co-
operation as regards issuance of all orders to the Italian Fleet.

Proposed disposition of the Italian Fleet

A. All *battleships* will be placed on a care and maintenance basis in
   ports to be designated and will have such measures of disarmament

applied as may be directed. These measures of disarmament will be such that the ships can be brought into action again if it so seems desirable. Each ship will have on board a proportion of Italian Naval personnel to keep the ships in proper condition and the C-in-C Mediterranean will have the right of inspection at any time.

B.   *Cruisers*: Such cruisers as can be of immediate assistance will be kept in commission. At present it is visualised that one squadron of four will suffice and the remainder will be kept in care and maintenance as for the battleships but at a rather greater degree of readiness to be brought into service if required.

C.   *Destroyers and Torpedo Boats*: It is proposed to keep these in commission and to use them on escort and similar duties as may be requisite. It is proposed that they should be divided into escort groups working as units and that they should be based in Italian ports.

D.   *Small craft, MAS, Minesweepers, Auxiliaries and similar small craft* will be employed to the full, detailed arrangements being made with the Flag Officer (Liaison) by the Italian Minister of Marine for their best employment.

E.   *Submarines*: In the first instance submarines will be immobilized in ports to be designated and at a later date these may be brought into service as may be required to assist the Allied war effort.

Status of Italian Navy

Under this modification of the Armistice Terms, all the Italian ships will continue to fly the Italian flag. A large proportion of the Italian Navy will thus remain in active commission operating their own ships and fighting alongside the forces of the United Nations against the Axis Powers.

The requisite Liaison Officers will be supplied to facilitate the working of the Italian ships in co-operation with Allied Forces. A small Italian Liaison Mission will be attached to the HQ of the C-in-C Mediterranean to deal with matters affecting the Italian fleet.

Mercantile Marine

It is the intent that the Italian Mercantile Marine should operate under the same conditions as the merchant ships of the United Nations. That is to say, all merchant shipping of the United Nations is formed into a pool which may be employed as may be considered necessary for the benefit of all the United Nations. In this will naturally be included the requirements for the supply and maintenance of Italy. The system will be analogous to that used in North Africa, where the North African shipping board controls all US, British and French shipping under certain agreements which will have to arranged in detail in so far as Italian ships are concerned. While it may be expected that a proportion of Italian ships will be working within the Mediterranean and to and from Italian ports, it must be appreciated that this will not always necessarily be the case and ships flying the Italian Flag may be expected to be used elsewhere as is done with merchant ships of all the United Nations. Italian ships employed as outlined in this paragraph will fly the Italian Flag and will be manned so far as possible by crews provided by the Italian Ministry of Marine.

191.   *Meeting of the President with the JCS, Harry L. Hopkins and Admiral Wilson Brown[1]*

[Map Rm 29]   USS *Iowa*,
                                                              19 November 1943

...

Dodecanese: The President asked why Leros, why Kos? He said the Prime Minister had been upset as regards the US attitude regarding the Dodecanese. He asked whether we knew of the details of the British operations in the Dodecanese initiated by the Middle East command before those operations began? The general consensus of opinion of the JCS was that the US had not been informed in advance of the proposed operations in the Dodecanese. However, General Marshall said he believed possibly he had seen a British despatch regarding their movements against the islands. He added that the British always regarded the Dodecanese as of greater importance than have we in the US.

South East Asia: [King says the British say without any more American aid, they can only do the Andaman island operation] which is certainly a case of marking time.

...

Italian Fleet: [King said] he did not believe the Soviets were in a position to *demand* Italian ships. The President thought that as a matter of goodwill and without transfer of title, it was as well to let Russia have one-third. The Italians should be considered, they would not have a Navy but might get a few ships back.

---

[1] Adm Wilson Brown, US Navy: Pres Roosevelt's Naval aide; carriers, Coral Sea 1942.

192.   *The President, the JCS and Harry L. Hopkins*

[Map Rm 29]   American Legation,
                                                    Tehran,
                                                    28 November 1943

Britain, the Mediterranean and the Indian Ocean: ... [Marshall said] the British COS are in an embarrassing position with regards to giving up BUCCANEER.[1] ...

... He [Marshall] believed the Prime Minister would use every wile to cut out BUCCANEER. ...

... [The President] felt that the British would probably say after Rhodes was taken, 'Now we will have to take Greece'. ...

General Marshall said the Prime Minister believes he could control the Mediterranean if he could get his own man, General Alexander, in as C-in-C.

The President observed that we must realize that the British look upon the Mediterranean as an area under British domination.

General Marshall said the British were wedded to committeeism. Unity of command would expedite operations. ... He pointed out while the US perhaps does not do committee work as well as the British, nevertheless they (the British) have certainly had a very serious time in the Middle East due to the lack of unity of command.

193.   *Stark to Admiral G. B. Wilson, US Navy*

[SPD 243]   23 December 1943

...

4. The Planners made a very careful study of the Mediterranean set-up, were familiar with the objections of our Naval people to the set-up (and with which I assume Kirk is familiar) and the Joint Planners' charts eliminated what they regard as the Mediterranean's objectionable features. For example, down there, as I understand it Hewitt could not go beyond Cunningham. Cunningham had no American Navy officer on his staff. Without going into further detail, this means in the last analysis, complete British domination and insufficient representation for us. Also in the Mediterranean there is no liaison between the US Naval Forces and US Ground and Air Forces. These and similar discrepancies the Joint Planners have taken care of.

---

[1]BUCCANEER: a proposed descent on the Andaman Islands.

194. *Memorandum for the President and Prime Minister*
by Admiral William D. Leahy, US Navy

[Map Rm 35]   28 December 1943

Assignment of ships surrendered to the Allies by Italy.

1.   The CCS have been considering the manner and timing of the deliv-
     ery of captured Italian vessels to be transferred to the USSR. In
     the examination certain conclusions have been reached which are
     presented for your consideration.

2.   There are grave military objections to the transfer of Italian vessels
     at this time because of the probable effects that this will have on
     pending operations. These effects are as follows:

(a) *Loss of Italian Naval Cooperation*

Valuable assistance is now being obtained in the Mediterranean from
four Italian cruisers and three escort groups. Other escort groups are
being formed. Submarines are scheduled for immediate and important A/S training with the US and British Navies. Two cruisers are
now being used on Atlantic Blockade Runner Patrols. Should the
transfer of Italian units to the Russians alienate the sympathy of the
Italian officers and men thus serving the Allied cause, replacements
could only be found at the expense of the build-up of the British
Eastern Fleet and British Pacific Force. Moreover, this would occur
at a moment when our combined Atlantic and Mediterranean naval
resources would be very hard stretched to provide the needs of OVER
LORD and ANVIL.

(b) *Indirect assistance from Italian dockyards and ports*

The UK and US are receiving important assistance from Italian yards.
The withdrawal of this willing assistance, particularly at Taranto, would
throw a serious additional burden on repair and manpower resources
and in proved dock-side labor in Italy.

(c) *Scuttling and Sabotage*

The ships to be turned over might be scuttled and the remainder sabotaged when the news became known. Apart from the material loss,
the psychological effect of such an act would be far-reaching.

(d) *Merchant shipping*

The most important merchant ships consist of one 24,000-ton pas-
senger ship shortly to be employed in Allied trooping, and two 9000-

ton hospital ships, all of which are urgently needed.[1] Most of the Italian ships presently employed on the Italian coast and in neighbouring waters are supporting the Italian economy. These are mostly small coasting vessels. In general, their condition is poor and precludes movement far from their own repair facilities. Removal of this shipping from the Mediterranean at present would leave the Allied C-in-C with a shortage which could not be made up from other sources without detriment to other operations. It is understood this merchant shipping is desired for employment in the Black Sea, the entry to which is now denied.

(e) *Loss of Italian Army Troops*

At the present time Italy, acting as a co-belligerent, is furnishing valuable assistance, including labor and security troops, along our lines of communication in Italy. Some Italian troops have already engaged in action and there is a possibility of further assistance from this source. It is considered that this valuable assistance may be lost to the Allies if the transfer of Italian vessels is enforced at this time.

3. In brief, to initiate transfer of Italian ships to Russian control at this time may cause serious harm to the war effort without compensating gain to the Russian effort since:

(a) Without extensive alterations the Italian ships are quite unsuited for Northern waters and they cannot yet be introduced into the Black Sea.

(b) Proper operation of these ships in Soviet waters would in any event be impossible without Italian type spares and ammunition supplies, of which there is no great quantity in Italy itself.

(c) It would be a considerable time before Soviet crews could work up the ships and in the interval any ships now actively employed, if transferred, would be a dead loss to our naval resources.

4. It is recommended the USSR be informed that:

(a) The present time is inopportune for effecting the transfer of captured Italian ships because of pending Allied operations.

(b) To enforce the transfer at this time would remove needed Italian resources now employed in current operations, and probably result in loss of Italian cooperation, thus jeopardising OVERLORD and ANVIL.

---

[1] *Saturnia*; other vessels unidentified.

(c) At the earliest moment permitted by operations, the implementation of the delivery of Italian vessels will proceed.

195. *Meeting held with Admiral Hewitt, US Navy,*
by Navy Department committee dealing with Atlantic Theater,
Mediterranean and UK

[SPD 244]   8 January 1944

Admiral Hewitt: ... The attack area is Toulon. According to our best information it is very heavily defended with coast defense guns and additional defences which the Germans have and are still constructing. There are tanks, traps, pill boxes and mobile artillery – so we anticipate the need for very heavy gunfire support. We have here in order to meet that an estimated requirement of three or four old battleships, six light cruisers, and 12 to 24 destroyers. I am not quite sure about the old battleships. It is something that I would like to discuss. I don't think they would be of much value against fixed defences – I mean fixed coastal artillery. They might have great value against beach defences and they may be of great value at long range, but on the other hand, if we have them, it means additional escort requirements and additional AA requirements, so I am not quite sold on the idea. We would like to get all the US cruisers that we can – 6in because they have better batteries and are better equipped than anything the British or French can furnish. Of the seven light cruisers the British can make available there is only one of them that amounts to anything – that is the *Mauritius* with 12×6in guns. The other have a small number of 6in or lighter guns and except for the *Mauritius* none of these ships is capable of a high volume of medium caliber support. The French cruisers – only about three of them are worth very much. They have no radar and as far as I can make out they haven't any bombardment ammunition.[1] Besides the gunfire support requirements there is the AA requirement. There are something like 70 airfields within reach of that attack area, and our experience has been [that] even though we have a fair fighter cover we can't help some planes breaking through. Besides the actual assault area to provide any aircraft protection for[,] there are the various convoys. There will be about 170 merchant ships brought in[to] that area between D+1 and D+5, all of which require AA protection. They are using rocket glider bombs against escort vessels and merchant ships and the high level radio controlled armor piercing bombs against combatant ships like the

[1]*Gloire, Montcalm, George Leygues.*

Savannah are very effective.[1] We want to get all the AA protection we can. The British have two good AA cruisers.[2] They will be available but you can't stretch them too far. My Plans Officer would like to have four US AA cruisers. As far as I know they don't exist so naturally we have to get along without them, but the fewer cruisers the more we'd like additional destroyers for AA protection. We could use some DEs in place of some destroyers but the DEs are not as good for AA protection. There will only be about 11 [German] submarines in the Mediterranean and C-in-C Mediterranean doesn't believe more six can be operated at any one time, so he doesn't feel greatly concerned about the submarine menace. You can never tell where the submarines are going to be and we have to protect all our convoys on the basis that they may encounter submarines. I don't think we can cut down our requirements for A/S protection.

The proposed landing is inside islands that are defended and in order to get the assault craft inside[,] these islands have got to be seized and neutralized. The proposal is to land commandos and rangers on them. We have to have something to land the rangers. We have a couple of fast small British LSIs but we would like some APDs. Two are in the Atlantic Fleet and could help. The *Dallas, Cole* and *Bernadou* would be fine except they don't carry landing boats. If they could be fitted to carry LCVPs they would be fine. I would like to find out what could be done about that.

196.   *Rear Admiral D. P. Moon, US Navy, to Rear Admiral
B. H. Bieri, US Navy*

[SPD 244]   15 February 1944

[Report on North Africa and Italy prior to taking command there].

Bizerte: [Admiral Dickens in command]. [He] feels his job is not big enough and would like to return to the UK.[3] US set-up is far superior to the British though it is a supposed British port.
Naples: Called on Admiral [Sir John] Cunningham who was temporarily in Naples. His major concern at the moment was setting up training facilities in Salerno and unloading supplies for the Army forces in Italy

---

[1] *Savannah* was hit by a guided bomb.
[2] Probably converted 'C' class light cruisers with 8–10×4in, and *Delhi*, rearmed in US with 5×5in.
[3] Adm Sir Gerald Dickens (1879–1962): ent RN 1894; Dardanelles 1915; ID; Capt 1919; DDP 1920–22; *Carlisle* 1922–4; IDC 1926–9; *Repulse* 1929–31; RA 1932; DNI 1932–5; Res F 1935–7; VA 1936; ret 1938; Naval Attaché The Hague 1940; SNLO Allied Navies 1940; FO Tunisia 1943; FO Netherlands 1945.

at the same time. This appears questionable to me, but will be tried out in accordance with the existing directives. Admiral Hewitt does not think the two can be done at the same time in view of the exceedingly small port capacity.

Called on Admiral Morse, who has his HQ in Naples as FO Western Italy. He seemed very pleasant, a well-informed and active officer.[1]

197.   *The President and the JCS*

[Map Rm 29]   21 February 1944

ANVIL: … The British say that Wilson is having hard going in Italy and therefore we should cancel ANVIL now, We say ANVIL should not be cancelled.

General Marshall said the British say ANVIL cannot be maintained with sufficient strength to justify the means which might be added to strengthen OVERLORD.

…

[The President] did not feel willing to take up the abandonment of ANVIL with that third power [the Soviet Union] at this time in that we had made previous promises to the Russians which we had not been able to meet. He felt that we have given up promises in the past and had better not do it again.

198.   *Naval Commander, Force P: Operational Order No. 1 –*
SHINGLE Amphibious Naval Operation

[ADM 199/873]   29 December 1943

Scope of the Operation

Force P is part of a joint British and American Assault Force which is to land on the West Coast of Italy in rear of the German 10th Army, sever their communications, and draw off enemy forces opposing the US 5th Army.

2. Two main landings will be made:

(a)   Peter Sector: North of Anzio, by the British 1st Division in the area Torre San Anastasio–Torre San Lorenza.

---

[1]RA J. A. V. Morse: Capt 1934; *Neptune* & F Capt & CoS to C-in-C Africa 1937; CSO *Pyramus*; NOIC Kirkwall June 1940; MNBDO (1) May 1941; NOIC Syria & Lebanon Ports July 1941; *Hannibal* Nov 1942; RA July 1943; FO W Italy Sep 1944; FO N Area Med Oct 1944.

(b) X-ray Sector: East of Anzio, by the US 3rd Division, in the area Nettuno–Torre Asturia.

3. The first objectives are the port of Anzio, and a beachhead extending from Torre Foce Verde along the Musso Canal for seven miles, and thence to Torre del Padiglione and west to Torre San Lorenza.

The former objective is assigned primarily to a US Ranger Force landing close [to the east] of the port.[1]

Object of Force P

4. The initial object of Force P is the capture of the western half of the beachhead referred to in paragraph 3, and the development of the port of Anzio.

5. Command:

The Naval Commander, Force P, is R Adm T. H. Troubridge. The Army Commander is Maj Gen W. R. C. Penney, Commanding the British 1st Division.

These Task Group Commanders are subordinate to the US Navy and Army Task Force Commanders. R Adm F. J. Lowry, US Navy, Commanding 8th Amphibious Force, and Maj Gen J. P. Lucas, US Army, commanding VI Corps.[2]

...

Forces available for the Assault

10. In Peter Sector: Assault Ships and Craft –

1 Flagship: *Bulolo*.
3 LSI (L): *Glengyle, Sobieski, Derbyshire*.
4 LST (US 6-davit): 1, 381, 326, 351.
24 LST (British Mk 2): 1st & 2nd Flotillas, part of 8th Flotilla.
2 LST (Greek).
3 LST (Mk 1): *Boxer, Bruiser, Thruster*.

---

[1]Rangers: US equivalent of Commandos.
[2]Maj Gen W. R. C. Penney: unidentified.
RA F. J. Lowry, US Navy (b 1888): USNA 1911; *Raleigh, Pittsburgh* 1917–18; Mare Island NY 1919–22; NWC 1925–6; CO *Minneapolis* 1940–42; RA 1942; Cdr, Morroccan Sea Frontier 1943; Anzio Jan 1944; Pac amph ops; Eur 1945; VA & ret 1950.
Maj Gen J. P. Lucas, US Army: unidentified.
RA T. Troubridge (1890–1949): ent RN 1902; Lt, Jutland 1916; staff spist; Capt 1934; Naval Attaché Berlin 1936–9; *Furious* 1940; *Nelson* Force H 1941; *Indomitable* EF & Malta convoys 1942; Cdre CTF N Af Nov 1942; RA Sicily 1943; Anzio Jan 1944; CVE force 'Anvil' Aug 1944; 5SL May 1945; Adm (Air) Sept 1946; 2CinC MF & FO (Air) Jan 1947–8.

17 LCT (US Mk V).
1 LCT (US Salvage).
2 LCT (British Mk 2 Repair).
2 LCI (H) (British).
27 LCI (L) (British): 251 & 252 Flotillas, part of 258 Flotilla.
2 LCI (L) (US Salvage).
2 LCG.
2 LCF.
1 LCT (R)

Screen, etc.

2 Cruisers: *Orion* (CS 15), *Spartan.*
8 Fleet Destroyers: *Laforey, Loyal, Jarvis, Janus, Grenville, Ulster, Urchin, Faulknor.*
3 'Hunt' [class] Destroyers: *Tetcott, Beaufort, Brecon.*
1 AA Ship: *Palomares.*
1 Submarine: *Ultor.*
11 Fleet Sweepers: *Fly* (M/S 12), *Acute, Cadmus, Circe, Espiegle, Albacore, Mutine*; *Rothesay* (M/S 13). *Stornoway, Bude, Brixham, Polruan.*
4 YMS (US).
3 PC (US).
6 SC (US).
8 ML (British Fairmile).
3 Salvage Tugs: *Edenshaw, Evea, Weasel.*
1 Fleet Tender (Balloon).
4 Trawlers (British).

11. In X-Ray Sector: Assault Ships and Craft–

1 Flagship: *Biscayne.*
3 LSI (L): *Circassia, Ascania, Winchester Castle.*[1]
2 LSI (M): *Royal Ulsterman, Princess Beatrix.*
10 LST (US 6-davit).
41 LST (British).
6 LCI (H) (US).
48 LCI (L) (US).
6 LCI (L) (British).
4 LCI (L) (US Salvage).
7 LCT (US Mk V).

---

[1]*Winchester Castle*: Union-Castle; 1930; 20,012t; 20k; troop transport 1941–5.

25 LCT (British Mks 3 & 4).
2 LCT (US Salvage).
2 LCG.
2 LCF.
2 LCT (R).

Screen, etc.

1 Cruiser: *Brooklyn.*
1 Cruiser: *Penelope.*
7 Fleet Destroyers (US): *Woolsey, Edison, Mayo, Ludlow, Trippe, Plunkett, Niblack, Gleaves.*
2 Destroyers (US): *Davis, Jones.*
3 'Hunt' [class] Destroyers: *Croome* (British), *Crete, Themistocles* (Greek).
2 Gunboats (Netherlands): *Flores, Soemba.*
1 AA Ship: *Ulster Queen.*
1 Submarine: *Uproar.*
7 Fleet Sweepers (US): *Prevail, Sustain, Symbol, Sway, Portent, Pilot, Dexterous,*
Strive.
15 MS (US).
9 PC.
14 SC.
2 Air Rescue Boats.
1 Tug: *Prosperous.*

199.   *Report of Proceedings of Naval Commander, Force P*

[ADM 116/5459]   24 February 1944

…

3. The passage to the assault was uneventful. …

…

5. There was no evidence during the approach of any alarm or any activity ashore, except at 2225 when there was a single explosion from the direction of Anzio.

…

6. Landing craft were lowered from the LSI and 6-davit LST according to timetable. The sea was flat calm and there was no wind, and although

the submarine subsequently reported that the ships and craft were clearly visible and audible to her, there appeared to be no alarm ashore, although enemy radar activity was described as 'feverish'.

...

9. ...although all beaches were heavily mined there was little active opposition from the defences. ... At 0645 the first LCT were accepted.

...

13. At 0830 *Palomares*, acting as AA and standby FDS, struck a mine and began to settle by the stern. ... arrangements were made to tow *Palomares* to Naples as soon as the area had been swept.

I ordered shipping to close the beach to facilitate discharging, but there continued to be a certain amount of sporadic shelling of the inshore anchorage, and ships not immediately required to beach were later again anchored further offshore. LST 320 and 362 were both hit by shellfire but received only superficial damage. Several shoots were carried out by Cruisers and Destroyers at these guns, but without much apparent effect. They were evidently on mobile mountings, and were apparently between 88 and 150mm calibre.

...

15. During the forenoon Generals Alexander and Lucas visited the Sector and came aboard the *Bulolo* for discussions. I went ashore with the former and visited the beaches.

16. At 1600 there was a sharp attack on the beaches by five FW 190 fighter-bombers, escorted by some FW 190 fighters. LST 363 was near missed, and there were a few casualties from splinters and cannon fire.

...

20. Due to the slow rate of discharging of LST over PETER beaches, and to continued shelling, I decided during the afternoon to send all LST and LCI (L) carrying 3rd Infantry Brigade to unload in X-Ray Sector. These ships and craft proceeded at 1600.

21. By 1800 the discharging situation in PETER Sector was as follows:

All infantry and vehicles of the 2nd Brigade landed.
All infantry and about one-third of the vehicles of the 3rd Guards Brigade landed.

22. ... Anti-E-boat patrols were maintained at night to the NW of the anchorage by the two PC and the two LCG, and by the Fleet Sweepers anchored round the perimeter of the shipping.

D+1 (23 January [1944])

23. ... The discharging of all LST of the 24th Guards Brigade was completed by 0930, and the discharging of the remaining LST in PETER Sector, with the exception of two LST (2) and *Boxer* and *Bruiser*, was completed before dark. These ships were later sailed to X-RAY Sector in view of the adverse weather reports. The Commander [of the] 1st British Division, Major-General Penney, disembarked from *Bulolo* and landed with his staff during the forenoon.

24. There was an attack at dusk by torpedo-bombers and glider bombers on PETER Sector shipping. At about 1745 *Janus* was hit by torpedo and sank within a few minutes. Shortly afterwards *Jervis* was hit forward by a glider bomb, but escaped with a few feet of her bow missing and no casualties. Eighty-two survivors from *Janus* were picked up by *Jervis* and taken to Naples. Eleven more were recovered by *PC 621* and by three DUKWs sent out from the beach. The remainder of the ship's company was lost mainly in the explosion of the forward magazines. It seems highly probable that this torpedo-bomber was shot down by *LCF 16*.

25. After this night attack I suggested to CS 15, who is my senior, that he took *Orion* and *Spartan* to Naples.[1] ... From Naples the cruisers could return within 14 hours or less in the event of a large-scale attack developing on the beachhead. To this CS 15 agreed, and he sailed with his two ships soon afterwards.

26. The weather got rapidly worse during the night, and all small craft were sent round to Anzio for shelter.

D+2 (24 January)

27. By daylight, both pontoons had broached onto the beach, and conditions had become too bad for any further discharging in PETER Sector. The two 'Liberty' ships and all LCT were consequently sailed to X-RAY Sector, and from that time came under the orders of CTF 81 (Rear-Admiral Lowry, US Navy). The 'Liberty' ships, using LCT and DUKWs, had already discharged about 1700 tons of stores over the PETER beaches.

28. The C-in-C Mediterranean visited the area in *Kempenfelt* during the day, for discussion with the Naval Force Commanders. It was decided that now unloading was confined to the US Sector my presence was no longer required, and accordingly at 1645, on orders from Rear Admiral Lowry, US Navy, I sailed in *Bulolo* for Naples. *Bruiser* joined at 1750, and *Brecon*, *Beaufort* and *Tetcot* formed the A/S screen at the same time.

29. While *Bulolo* was proceeding down the swept channel there was a severe dusk air attack in which the USS *Plunkett* was hit. In addition,

[1] RA J. M. Mansfield.

attacks were made on all three hospital ships, which had left the anchorage shortly after *Bulolo* and were fully illuminated. *St David* was sunk, *Leinster* damaged, and *St Andrew* near missed. ... [Two splashes] were thought by *Grenville*, in company, and an expert in these matters, to be dud glider bombs. No doubt this form of attack will soon be mastered, but [in the] meantime it is uncomfortable to have radar reports of unidentified aircraft passing by, turning round and passing again at a range known to be favourable for such attacks. There are times 'what the Radar don't pick up the heart don't grieve after'.

30. *Bulolo* arrived at Naples at 0945 on 25 January.

31. A number of British Naval Personnel was left to assist in unloading in the US Sector under the orders of Captain A. N. Grey, RN, and in Anzio under Captain Errol Turner, RN.[1] ...

200. *Rear Admiral T. H. Troubridge to Admiral*
Sir John Cunningham

[ADM 199/873]   24 February 1944

I have the honour to submit herewith my report on operation SHINGLE in which British and US Naval Forces under US Command landed a mixed US-British Army Corps in the vicinity of Anzio-Nettuno on 22 January 1944.

2. The landings were carried out in two sectors. In the Northern sector, under my command, British and US Naval Forces landed two British Brigade Groups of the 1st Division and a Commando Force. One Brigade Group (2 Brigade) assaulted and the other (24 Guards Brigade), together with the Commandos, followed up.

3. The landing, though up to time and well conducted, was made slightly to the southward of the planned position, the marking folboats having difficulty in picking up the exact position on an almost featureless coast. In the event this made almost no difference since opposition was negligible, being limited mostly to mines both in the Approach Channel and on the beaches.

4. After daylight there was sporadic gunfire from mobile enemy guns aimed at ships in the anchorage, and one well conducted air attack on the beaches which happily did no important damage.

---

[1]Capt A. N. Grey: ND Sept 1940; *Sultan,* Singapore Sept 1941; *Lanka* Nov 1942; A/ Capt, *Excellent* Sept 1943.

Capt Errol Turner: *Active* Sept 1940; A/Cdr *Hydon* Sept 1941; A/Capt *Glenearn*; *Glengyle* Sept 1943.

5. The actual beaches with their shallow approach and offshore sandbars were the worst in my experience, and after landing the 24 Guards Brigade the Naval Force Commander, Rear Adm Lowry, US Navy, decided to concentrate further follow up landings in the port of Anzio and in the more favourable beaches in the US Sector to the South of that place. The move was foreseen in the planning stage of the operation, but was dependent upon Anzio being captured undamaged. Fortunately this had been achieved by the US Rangers under the gallant leadership of Colonel Darby, US Army, landing in British Assault Craft, a happy combination first carried out at Arzeu during Operation TORCH.[1]

6. The Northern (British) Sector was accordingly closed down, and the men and gear having been transferred to the US Sector I was directed by Rear Adm Lowry to return to Naples.

7. Operations of 'peculiar complexity and hazard' of this nature seldom go as planned. SHINGLE was an exception, a result I attribute largely to the fact that Naval Force Commanders have at their disposal nowadays a large body of officers and men who are familiar with every aspect of the business and for whom the process of landing troops and their impedimenta on an unknown hostile shore on a pitch black night is no longer any novelty. This is not to say that the organisation is by any means perfect. Every Combined Operation raises its own special problems and usually reveals shortcomings that call either for modification of existing organisation or for better training, or both. It is my experience that such faults as are found to exist can nearly always be traced to weak links in the chain of command which have prevented the team of experts from functioning as an expert team. ...

201. *Hewitt to Commodore Ziroli.*[2]

[Map Rm 35]   13 March 1944.

Prime Minister and President have agreed following communication from CCS for confidential information of Italian officer at your discretion. Begins:

'At Tehran it was agreed that ships of the Italian Navy should be used where they could be employed most effectively against the common enemy. It was also agreed in principle that Russia is entitled to her share in the increase of Allied Naval strength resulting from the

---

[1]TORCH: The invasion of North Africa in Nov 1942.
[2]Cdre Humbert W. Ziroli, US Navy (1893–1979): USNA 1916; c/o *Simpson* 1933–4; c/o *Narwahl* 1934–6; *Brooklyn* 1943; Allied Control Commission 1943; RA & ret 1947.

surrender of the Italian fleet. Russia is now in urgent need of additional naval strength. For the present Great Britain and the US will lend some of their ships to Russia to compensate for the help they are receiving from the Italian Navy. It is not intended to transfer any Italian ships to Russia at present.'

202. *King to Noble*

[SPD 242]   23 March 1944

… The Admiralty has requested for ANVIL on a two-divisional scale the following additional US Forces:

4 Cruisers.
44 Destroyers or Escorts.
1 or 2 CVE.

These have been made available, plus three old Battleships, one cruiser, and four DEs.

The need for battleship bombardment for ANVIL has been strongly presented by the NTF Commander for the operation. The slight additional escort strength which has been provided is due to uncertainty in regard to the escorts which will be available for the seven CVEs which the Admiralty might allocate. The US Forces which have been assigned for ANVIL are not considered in excess of the requirements for that operation.

It is possible, of course, that the ANVIL operation may be delayed or reduced in scope. If it is reduced in scope, the requirements of naval support forces will be substantially the same, with possibly some reduction in regard to the need for escorts.

I strongly concur in the Admiralty view that additional bombardment forces should be allocated for NEPTUNE. However, in view of the fact that the Atlantic Fleet has been stripped of combat and escort forces in order to make available the US vessels which have already been provided, the additional requirements for NEPTUNE must come from British sources. With the improved situation in the Atlantic, I believe that these can be found without too much risk. Also, as NEPTUNE-ANVIL, by agreement of the CCS, are not to be interfered with by other operations, it should be practicable to provide the additional necessary supporting naval vessels required by withdrawal from the Eastern and Home Fleets and by pointing up the refitting of vessels in preparation for this all-important operation.

Use *Lorraine* if you wish extra US battleships allocated; suggest two French cruisers can stay [in the] Mediterranean and British 5.25[in cruiser] go to NEPTUNE, which will also have *Augusta*, leaving cruiser deficit at three.

203. *Rear Admiral R. H. Bieri, US Navy, to Vice Admiral*
A. G. Kirk, US Navy

[SPD 242]   24 March 1944

1. In view of the prospective delay to ANVIL,

(a) the British are withdrawing four British cruisers and 20 destroyers from the Mediterranean for OVERLORD. Admiralty … indicates their desire to withdraw two French 'Montcalm' class in addition.

(b) Ships in Cominch 161805 [not reproduced] are now under orders to the Mediterranean in types, numbers and arrival details as follows:

Type	Nos.	Arrival Dates
OBB	3	3 May
CA	2	"
CL	3	"
CVE	2	"
DD	33	"
DE	8	"
APD	4	"
YMS	6	"

In order to continue the support of current operations indicated in paragraph 1 (a) above after withdrawal of British forces and to be available for a later ANVIL, it is recommended that the following go to the Mediterranean as now scheduled:

Type	No.
CA	1
CL	3
AM	10
DD	18
APD	4
YMS	6

(c) Admiral Noble's letter of 20 March requests US assistance for OVERLORD as follows: one OBB, six cruisers, 14 destroyers, for bombardment; 10 escorts, 24 fleet minesweepers, 32 YMS.

(d) Of these, Cominch 161805 has assigned to 12th Fleet one CA (*Augusta*), 18 SC, 14 YMS. Cominch's letter 00939 [document 208] to Admiral Noble states that the additional requirements for OVERLORD must come from British sources.

(e) In view of the prospective delay of ANVIL, it is considered feasible to provide some US naval support for OVERLORD from forces now allocated to ANVIL, and after the OVERLORD assault to send them to the Mediterranean. It is recommended that this support consists of the following, to arrive in the UK by 3 May:

Type	No.
OBB	1 (*Nevada*)
CA	1 (*Tuscaloosa*)
DD	13 (one squadron + one division)
PC	12

To send a larger force to support OVERLORD would result in such a depletion of bombardment ammunition as to jeopardize proper support for ANVIL.

(f) The prospective delay in ANVIL makes it reasonable to delay the arrival of the remainder of the ships listed in Cominch 161805 in the Mediterranean until 12 June, i.e., two OBB (*Texas, Arkansas*), two CVE, 9 DD, 6 DE … .

204. *Cunningham to King, via Noble*

[SPD 242]   30 March 1944

1. BAD has sent me your reply to Admiralty requests for US assistance in NEPTUNE and ANVIL. I note that you can provide a proportion of Minesweepers and Escorts additionally required for NEPTUNE but that you will not be able to find the six Cruisers and 14 Destroyers to make up numbers which the Supreme Commander now considers necessary for bombardment force. Because of *Lorraine*'s limited supply of ammunition I would have preferred to include a US Battleship in bombardment force, but if you do not wish to provide one *Lorraine* will be used.

2. Your suggestion the Supreme Commander's requirements can be met by further withdrawal from Eastern and Home Fleets and by speeding up

refits is not practicable. These two Fleets are already reduced to minimum strength I consider necessary for tasks they are required to perform. All speeding up of refits has already been done. British Fleet remaining in Mediterranean will comprise one 6in Cruiser, one 5.25in Cruiser and 13 Fleet destroyers. I could not agree to any further reduction of British forces in this theatre, and it is for this reason that I consider two French Cruisers should be withdrawn for NEPTUNE.

3. However, if ANVIL is now postponed, as is now probable, I presume extra force which you assigned to Mediterranean in your 161805 [not reproduced] ... will be available for NEPTUNE, since they will have time to return [to] Mediterranean for the postponed operation. This arrangement would solve all outstanding difficulties.

4. I shal be glad to have your early confirmation that this is your intention, for if that is not so, the Supreme Commander must be informed to what extent his bombardment requirements for NEPTUNE cannot be met.

205. *Memorandum by the Director of Plans:*
Fleet Destroyer Dispositions after OVERLORD[1]

[ADM 205/37]   12 April 1944

...

Mediterranean

7. At the time of OVERLORD our paper strength in the Mediterranean will be 13 British [destroyers]. The Americans on the other hand will have 27 (nine already on the Station and 13[?] arriving on 3 May). A further 22 arrive as soon as they are released from OVERLORD. Thus by about the end of June there would be 49 American destroyers in the Mediterranean and 13 British.

8. This seems an undesirable American preponderance which, however, may in part be adjusted if the American OVERLORD force (22) does not in the event go on to the Mediterranean. They are unlikely to do so unless a definite amphibious operation has been planned for the period shortly after OVERLORD has been launched.

---

[1]DP: Capt Guy Grantham: Capt 1937; Ady 1939; NA to FL 1940; CO, *Phoebe* June 1940; Capt & CSO 15 CS, *Naiad*, *Cleopatra*, March 1942; *Indomitable* & COS, Home F Carriers Aug 1943; *Cormorant* Gibraltar 1943; DPD April 1944; FO (S) 1948–50; 2 i/c Med 1950–51; VCNS 1951–4; C-in-C Med 1954–7; NATO C-in-C Channel 1957; C-in-C Portsmouth 1959; ret 1959. See also Doc. 149.

9.   In any case it seem desirable to increase the British numbers – which
will incidentally allow us to enjoy the unusual experience of inviting Cominch to withdraw an equal number and transfer them to the
Pacific.

206.   *Naval Outline plan – ANVIL.*
(Vice Admiral Hewitt, C-in-C, US Naval Forces,
North West African Waters)

[SPD 250]   15 April 1944

Information

1.   An amphibious operation, code name ANVIL, is to be launched
in the Mediterranean against Southern France in support of operation OVERLORD launched from the UK against Northern France.
Operation ANVIL will be mounted from Italy, Corsica, Sardinia,
Sicily and North Africa. The assault area in Southern France is
the St Tropez-Fréjus area. The immediate objective is the capture of the ports of Toulon and Marseilles with subsequent movement through the Rhône Valley towards Lyon and Vichy. This
broad plan is designed to contain the maximum enemy forces in
Southern France, thereby rendering effective support to Operation
OVERLORD.
2.   The date of D-day has not been fixed but in any case it will be
subsequent to the launching of OVERLORD, and will not be before
1 June 1944.
3. The military assault forces have not yet been nominated but they are
expected to be of the order of two US Infantry Divisions (reinforced)
with a subsequent build-up of American and French Army forces to
eight Infantry Divisions and two Armored Divisions.

Naval Tasks

. . .

9.   The Naval Tasks are briefly as follows:

(a)   Preliminary bombardment of enemy defences which threaten
the landings.
(b)   Close escort of the convoys to their destinations.

(c) Screening of assault convoys against interference by enemy surface forces.

(d) Landing of troops on the selected beaches.

(e) Close support of the landings by naval gunfire.

(f) The maintenance by sea of the forces landed, including the protection of shipping off the beaches.

(g) Augmenting the scale of fighter protection to assault shipping off the beaches.

(h) Opening of captured ports and the installation there of Port Parties.

Allocation of Shipping and Craft

10. The following ships and craft have been allocated:

(a) US:

3 flagships (amphibious)
3 XAP (converted assault transports)
6 AXA (assault cargo carriers)
4 APD (high speed transports)
100 (approximately) MT/store ships
46 LST (2)
63 LCI (L)
39 CT (5)
26 LCT (6)

(b) British:

1 LSH (flagship)
8 LSI (L)
1 LSI (M)
1 LSI (H)
1 LSP
100 (approximately) MT/store ships
3 LST ('Killer' type)
3 LST (2)
48 LCI (L)
5 LCT (2)
30 LCT (3)
38 LCT (4)

The above tabulation indicates the allocation of craft for the operation. The numbers of each type will be somewhat below the quantities shown.

Allocation of Combatant Ships

Type	British	French	US	Total
OBB	–	1	3	4
CA	–	–	2	2
CL	3	5	5	13
CL (AA)	4	–	–	4
CVE	7	–	2	9
DL	–	3	–	3
DD, Fleet	8	6	50	64
DD, 'Hunt'	21	–	–	21
DE	–	7	10	17
PC	–	–	29	29
SC	–	–	31	31
AM	14	–	21	35
YMS	6	–	30	36
LCG	6	–	–	6
LCF	7	–	–	7
PT	–	–	41	41
LCT (R)	6	–	–	6
ARSC	–	–	20	20
FD Ships	3	–	–	3

Allocation of Auxiliaries

11. The following ships have been allocated:

Type	British	French	US	Total
LSG	2	–	–	2
LSC	1	–	–	1
LSD	2	–	–	2
ML	6	–	–	6
AT, Fleet	1	–	3	4
At, Medium	4	–	2	6
VT	6	–	6	12
ATR	3	–	1	4
ARS	3	–	3	6
ARS, Cargo	1	–	1	2
ARL	1	–	1	2
AO	4	–	4	8
AO, Medium	4	–	–	4
YOG	1	–	3	4

Trawlers, M/S	4	–	–	4
2-Balloon Trlrs	2	–	–	2
YW	4	–	–	4
YF	4	–	–	4
AC	2	–	–	2

207. *SACMED to the COS.*

[CAB 88/29]   24 July 1944

[Enclosure]

COSMED 156

1. Reference MEDCOS 152 [which outlined forces required for ANVIL and not available on station]. Provision of extra forces over and above those required by your 2211944 June [not reproduced] has been investigated by the Admiralty and Cominch and the following will be allocated – one US battleship, one British monitor, four US cruisers, two British cruisers.

2. The final allocation of battleships, monitors and cruisers will therefore be as follows:

   (a) Battleships and monitors: British: *Ramillies, Abercrombie.*
   American: *Nevada, Arkansas, Texas.*
   French: *Lorraine.*

   (b) Cruisers: British: *Aurora, Orion, Ajax, Achilles, Dido, Black Prince, Argonaut, Sirius.*
   American: *Brooklyn, Philadelphia, Augusta, Tuscaloosa, Quincy, Omaha, Marblehead.*
   French: *Montcalm, George Leygues, Gloire, Emile Bertin,* and either *Dugay Trouin* or *Jeanne D'Arc.*

3. In addition the British battleship *Malaya* may become available for the later stages of ANVIL if then required depending on the future requirements and casualties of NEPTUNE.

208. *AFHQ: Supreme Commander's Despatch:*
The Italian Campaign, 8 January 1944–10 May 1944

[ADM 199/120]   16 April 1945

...

ANZIO

Preparations

...

The successful breaking up of enemy blockade running in the Atlantic released cruisers of 15 CS to return to the Central Mediterranean. The return from the Levant of *Phoebe* resulted in our having the entire British Mediterranean cruiser strength available for use in time for the amphibious operation.

On 20 January, *Orion, Spartan, Jervis, Janus, Laforey* and *Faulknor* bombarded enemy coastal batteries in the area of Terracina; the 12th Minesweeping Flotilla being employed to ensure safe passage for the bombardment forces through the unswept Gulf of Gaeta. On the following night, in accordance with the Cover Plan, *Dido,* FS *Le Fantasque* and *Inglefield* carried out a diversionary bombardment near Civittavecchia and coastal forces carried out dummy landings following Naval fire. At daybreak the naval force was withdrawn southward and given the task of bombarding the coast in the area of Formia and Terracina in order to check any reinforcements to the enemy's troops at Anzio from his southern front.

...

The Anzio Landings

Under perfect weather conditions and with a forecast that these favourable conditions would hold, the Assault Task Force, under the command of Admiral Lowry, US Navy, set sail from Naples at 0500 hours on 21 January. The convoy was made up of 243 warships, transports, landing craft and various other vessels of the US and British Navies, supported by Netherlands, Greek, Polish and French craft. The assault forces, under command of Major-General Lucas, US Army, consisted of some 50,000 US and British troops and more than 5000 vehicles.

On leaving port the convoy turned south, sailed around the south coast of the Isle of Capri and well out into the Mediterranean before turning north onto a direct course to Anzio. This strategy was adopted to mislead the enemy and to avoid minefields. MACAF gave air protection to the ships during the first half of the voyage after which this responsibility was assumed by XII Air Support Command.

The voyage was uneventful and no interception was made by the enemy. The convoy arrived off Anzio at 0005 hours on 22 January under cover of darkness. HM Submarines *Ultor* and *Uproar* acted as beachmarkers for the beaches on either side of the point and Naval Scout parties were sent ashore to locate and mark the points of landing, while minesweepers of the 12th and 13th M/S Flotillas, assisted by US minesweepers, cleared the approaches to the landings. It was planned to have our landing programme well advanced before moon-rise at 0255 hours.

Ashore all was quiet and the assault craft were assembled and despatched towards the beaches. At 0150 hours two LCT (R) laid down a rocket barrage lasting for five minutes on the two divisional beaches; the third rocket ship did not fire. At 0200 hours the first assault troops touched down.

Off the eastern beach, where the US 3rd Division landed, USS *Biscayne*, *Frederick C. Davis* and *Brooklyn* and (HMS) *Penelope* hove-to to give covering fire support, while similar Naval assistance was given by *Orion* and *Spartan*, where the British 1st Division went ashore. The two gunboats *Flores* and *Soemba* of the Royal Netherlands Navy stood by to lend additional fire support as it might be needed.

3rd US Division overran a few patrols and was able to quickly clear the beaches which contained no anti-invasion obstacles and advanced towards the first objective. The Rangers landed at the port of Anzio and captured the dock area which the enemy had not had time to destroy, and proceeded to mop up the weak enemy defences in the town and its neighbouring seaside resort of Nettuno. On the Western beach the assault elements of the 1st British Division immediately ran into minor difficulties; the beach was lightly mined and DUKWs were delayed in the initial stages of landing; beach conditions were worse than estimated and even LCTs required pontoons for unloading because of the offshore bar so that troops had to wade 300 yards to shore; and enemy mobile guns trained on this landing point caused some slight interference with the unloading. Despite these difficulties, however, the assault elements of the division secured a beachhead with few casualties.

By 0445 hours, LSI (L)s had completed unloading and were under way on the return trip to Naples. With the bulk of the infantry ashore, progress towards the consolidation of the beachhead had been made satisfactorily. AA units were ashore and in position to give protection to beach dumps and unloading areas. Anzio and Nettuno were completely in our hands in the early afternoon and, before last light the channel had been cleared of mines and the port opened to landing craft.

Throughout the day, opposition had been negligible, both divisions advanced to their initial objectives four miles inland and consolidated their gains. On the Eastern beach the bulk of the US 3rd Division was ashore, while on the Western beach the 1st British Division had one Brigade Group ashore complete with guns and tanks and a portion of second Brigade Group. At Anzio, 304 Parachute Infantry Regiment was landing to be followed by a regimental combat team of the 45th US Division and am armoured group of the 1st US Armored Division. As beach conditions were so bad on the Western beach it was decided not to land the 3rd Brigade Group of the 1st British Division at this point but to divert it to the port of Anzio.

The unloading of supplies followed immediately on the landing of the assault force. On the Eastern beach LSTs unloaded on to LCTs and also on to a tandem of three pontoons reaching from the anchorage to the beach, whence supplies were transported to dumps situated beyond the dunes. Rehabilitation of the port was carried out so expeditiously that Anzio was ready to receive four LSTs and three LCTs almost as soon as the town had been taken. On the Western beach, because of the offshore bar, the poor gradient and bad surface, unloading was entirely unsatisfactory. The beach was closed therefore, on the completion of the unloading of the assault troops and their equipment.

The construction of the beach exits was quickly accomplished, but the clay soil between the beaches and the main road soon became so badly rutted that matting, corduroy and rock had to be laid down in order to make this area passable. ... By 1600 hours on 23 January the entire British 1st Division and the 3rd US Division ... had been landed. Loading facilities had been so improved that 60 LSTs could be unloaded per day so long as the weather remained favourable.

On D-day enemy air attacks were slight but on 23 January they increased in intensity and, during an air raid at dusk the two Hospital Ships *St David* and *Leinster* which were lying in the roads off Anzio, fully illuminated, were wantonly attacked. *St David* sank and *Leinster* was damaged. *Janus* was sunk by a glider bomb and an LCI (L) was also hit by a bomb and lost. Losses from mines were slight, *Palomares* struck a mine on D-day and had to be towed back to Naples on the following day; USS *Portent* was mined and sunk.

...

... Yet on 24 January enemy opposition was still slight in the beachhead area, undoubtedly the effect of blocking the Formia–Terracina road on the previous day through the continuous bombardment from *Dido*, *Kempenfelt*, *Inglefield* and FS *Le Fantasque*. *Kempenfelt* continued to bombard this road in the early morning of 24 January on receipt of a report that transport was passing north through Formia. Later in the day *Inglefield* and FS *Le Malin* covered this area and FS *Le Malin* was replaced by *Mauritius*. This road was kept under fire throughout the following night. ... Now that the beachhead was established we planned to co-ordinate our operations there and on 5th Army main front very closely. ...

209. *Memorandum for F-1 [Navy Department]*

[SPD 250]   24 June 1944

Availability of LSTs for European Operations.

1. According to information available to date the LST situation in the
    UK is as follows:

	US	British	Total
In area	167	61	228
Estimated operational	152	50	202

2. As of 1 August the Mediterranean LST situation will be as follows
    not counting any which may be sent for the UK:

	US	British	Total
In area	53	10	63
Estimated operational	52	7	59

3. The LSTs from the US which could now reach the Mediterranean by
    1 August would have to come from the 27 which are shaking down
    and getting ready for movement to the Pacific as indicated below.

Gulf Area

The larger proportion of these should be ready about 30 June. These vessels are assigned to 7th Fleet.

4. In addition to the above there are 24 LSTs assigned [to] PhibTraLant
    which are in full use for training.
5. 7th Fleet has stated their requirement to be 108 LSTs beginning
    August. The 27 LSTs mentioned above should arrive late August
    and would give that fleet a total of 75.

210. *Eisenhower to Marshall*

[Map Rm 33]   29 June 1944

It is my belief that the Prime Minister and his COS are honestly convinced that greater results in support of OVERLORD would be achieved
by a drive towards Trieste rather than to mount ANVIL. They are aware,
of course, of the definite purpose of the US COS to mount an ANVIL

and I have been even more emphatic in my support of this operation than have your telegrams on the subject. I have the further impression that although the British COS may make one more effort to convince you of the value of the Trieste move, they would not permit an impasse to arise, and will, consequently, agree to ANVIL. ...

211.   *General Sir H. M. Wilson to COS*

[Map Rm 33]   2 July 1944

The plan for naval supporting fire in ANVIL is developing along lines which will make rather heavier demands than had been thought and will be required for a prolonged period probably until D+60 during which time it may be necessary to reduce the defences of the two major ports with heavy bombardment.

1. In order to provide this support it is estimated that three battleships and four cruisers 5.25in or above will be required to replace ships in the original allocation whose guns will almost certainly become worn during the initial phase. Additional ammunition reserves will be required accordingly to the following extent:

Battleships	2 outfits per ship	60% HE; 40% AP.
Cruisers	3 outfits per ship	75% HE; 25% AP.

2. It is a matter of great concern to me that there be adequate naval support for ANVIL should I be directed to execute that operation and in that event I strongly urge that my requirements as stated above be given full consideration.

212.   *King to Hewitt*

[SPD 244]   8 July 1944

A. Sufficient ships and craft now allocated to 8th Fleet will remain in Mediterranean until success of battle of France has been assured. Combat vessels needing regunning and vessels now being withheld from Pacific (*Quincy* and six DEs) will be withdrawn when assault phase of ANVIL completed.

...

C. When situation in France permits ships and craft including excess shipborne type landing craft will be returned to US for complete overhaul and repair prior to deployment to other theaters. ...

The situation as it develops may require a change in the above.

213. *Noble to King*

[SPD 244] 8 July 1944

...

2. In considering this matter you will remember that at your request all NEPTUNE are now being supplied from British sources. Naval supporting fire may be required for a long time to come, and provision must be made for replacement of bombarding ships. In this connection you will note that of the four British battleships employed in the OVERLORD bombardment, two (*Nelson* and *Warspite*) have already received such damage as to put them temporarily out of action. In view of the menace of the new German mine in the Channel, the Admiralty consider that they must retain adequate insurance against such risks. In addition the British forces are containing German main naval units, and the Admiralty cannot call on the Home Fleet beyond a certain limit.

3. For these reasons the Admiralty suggest that General Wilson's extra requirements should be met on an equal basis. They therefore suggest that one further US battleship should be provided for ANVIL, and that the monitor *Abercrombie* should be allocated in lieu of a battleship in addition to the British battleship already detailed to augment *Texas*.

4. As regards cruisers, they suggest that *Quincy* should be counted towards the extra requirements in MEDCOS 152 [not reproduced], and that one more US cruiser should be allocated. For their part the Admiralty propose to allocate two extra cruisers.

214. *King to Noble*

[SPD 244] 9 July 1944

... It is presumed that the above ships [extra battleships and cruisers for ANVIL] are wanted after the initial assault phase to provide naval support fire to carry the Army along the coast and into the major ports. I believe all concerned are in agreement to support the initial establishment of the beachhead. However, the length of usefulness of some of the US ships assigned will probably be short because a considerable portion of their gun life has been expended on NEPTUNE.

... I consider that the requirement of MEDCOS 152 [not reproduced] should be met to the extent of two battleships and three cruisers in addition to those firmly allocated.

As you know, the US naval support originally intended for ANVIL was diverted to support NEPTUNE after considerable exchange of correspondence between us on the subject and with the knowledge that a good deal of the gunlife of the major ships might be used up. I have allocated to ANVIL an additional cruiser, the *Quincy*, and the *Texas*, until her gunlife precludes further usefulness, which allocations are in effect in excess of those which it might have been expected I would make. In so doing, every ship of the above categories available from US sources has been assigned and it is my view that the extra requirements of MEDCOS 152 should be met by the Admiralty.

215.   *King to Noble*

[SPD 244]   10 July 1944

… I consider the urgency for continued support of ANVIL outweighs present needs in Eastern waters, and since no additional battleship can be spared from the Home Fleet or from the US, it would appear that a heavy ship from the Eastern Fleet is the only recourse. In this connection, I agree that a slower ship than the *Richelieu* would be satisfactory.

216.   *Noble to King*

[SPD 244]   13 July 1944

… The Admiralty note that you can provide *Texas* and *Quincy* which, with *Abercrombie* and two Cruisers which we can provide leaves a deficit of one Battleship and one Cruiser.

As regards your suggestion that a Battleship should be provided from the Eastern Fleet, the Admiralty observes that the Japanese Fleet has not been disposed of and is still capable of operating in the Indian Ocean. Unless these circumstances change they are not prepared to consider any depletion of Eastern Fleet Battleship strength in favour of ANVIL. They consider that the withdrawal of one old Battleship from the Pacific would appear to be more reasonable.

Malaya is being brought forward from reserve as a stand by in case *Warspite* cannot be made fit for service, and as an insurance against further battleship or monitor casualties in NEPTUNE. If she is not required for these reasons by ANVIL [D-day] date, the Admiralty would consider sending her to the Mediterranean. If *Malaya* can be brought forward from reserve [we] suggest that consideration might be given to bringing

New York forward for service. *New York* may even be in better condition for this than *Malaya*.

As regards cruisers, the Admiralty is now faced with finding a relief for *Dragon*. Mine and torpedo risks in the Channel are serious and we must be prepared for further casualties. The requirements of NEPTUNE are also a first charge on British naval resources, and therefore the Admiralty cannot promise more than two additional Cruisers for ANVIL.

217. *Outline of Operation DRAGOON*

[ADM 205/57]   14 August 1944

Object

The object of Operation DRAGOON is the capture of St Raphael, St Maxime, St Tropez, Toulon and Marseilles from which, by exploitation of the Rhône Valley, to assist with Operation OVERLORD.

Command

...

Naval – Vice Admiral H. Kent Hewitt, US Navy, with his flag in *Catoctin*.

Forces Employed

The assault is to be carried out by US troops with large French reinforcing formations, supported by Naval Forces of the US, Great Britain, France, Greece and Portugal and the Mediterranean Allied Air Force.

Fighter Protection

Fighter protection over the Assault Area will be given from the escort Carrier Force under Rear Admiral Troubridge until the RAF are able to operate from captured bases ashore.

Summary of forces taking part

Battleships	5
CVEs	9
Cruisers	22

AA Ships	3
Gunboats (2) & Monitor (1)	3
Destroyers & DE	109
Coastal Craft	60
Minesweepers	8
Assault ships and major assault craft	380
Personnel & MT ships	131

No Allied submarines will be at sea in the area of Operations.

D-day is 15 August and H-hour is 0800.

C-in-C Mediterranean is establishing an Advanced HQ in *Largs* at Ajaccio.

Naval Covering Forces not including Minesweepers or CO ships and craft

Task Force 80:

HQ ship   *Catoctin*
Relief Destroyer   *Plunkett*

Special Operations Group
TF 80.4:[1]

Destroyer   *Endicott* (Captain Johnson, US Navy)
Gunboats   *Aphis, Scarab*
FD ships   *Antwerp, Ulster Queen*
            + 13 ASRC, 8 PT, 8 ML.

A/S & Convoy Control Group
TF 80.6:   (Capt Clay, US Navy)[2]
Desron 7
Desdiv   13 Desdiv 14
Jouett (SO)   *Madison* (SO)
Benson   *H. P. James*
Niblack   *G. F. Hughes*
Desron 18
Desdiv 35   Desdiv 36
Frankford (SO)   *Baldwin* (SO)
Carmick   *Harding*
Doyle   *Satterlee*
McCook   *Thompson*

[1]Capt Henry C. Johnson, US Navy: head of a Special Ops Grp (deception unit).
[2]Capt James C. Clay, US Navy: Cdr, DD Sqdn 8.

5 DF	18 DF	59 Div
Aldenham (SO)	*Farndale* (SO)	*Bicester* (SO)
Beaufort	*Atherstone*	*Liddesdale*
Belvoir	*Brecon Oakley*	
Whaddon	*Calpe*	*Zetland*
Blackmore Catterick	*Crete*	
Lauderdale	*Clevedon*	*Themistocles*
Pindos	*Haydon*	
Escorts		
[Es]Cort Div 57 (DE)	French Escorts	
3 Div	2 Div	
Tatum (SO)	*Fortune* (SO)	*Morocain* (SO)
Haines	*Forbin*	*Tunisien*
Runels	6 Div	5 Div
Hollis	*Trombe* (SO)	*Hova* (SO)
Marsh	*Simoun*	*Algérien*
Currier	*Tempête*	*Somali*
L'Alcyon		
H. C. Jones	10 Div Avisos 6 Div Avisos	
F. C. Davis	*Cdt Domine* (SO)	*Cdt Bory* (SO)
	La Maquesse	*La Gracieuse*
	Kilmarmock	*Cdt Delage*
		La Boudeuse

ALPHA Attack Force:
TF 84:

HQ ship	*Duane* (R Adm Lowry, US Navy)
FD ship	*Stuart Prince*

Transport Div 1
Escort Sweeper Group
Auxiliary Group
Gunnery Support Force

Battleship	*Ramillies*
Cruisers	*Quincy, Orion* (CS 15), *Aurora, Ajax, Black Prince, Gloire*
Desdiv 21	*Livermore* (SO), *Eberle, Kearney, Ericcson, Terpischore, Termagant*

(carrying 3rd US Infantry Division (reinforced))
DELTA Attack Force

TF 85:

HQ ship	*Biscayne* (R Adm Rodgers, US Navy)[1]
	LSF 13

Transport Div 5
Escort Sweeper Group
Auxiliary Group
Gunfire Support Group

Battleships	*Texas* (R Adm Bryant, US Navy), *Nevada*[2]
Cruisers	*Philadelphia, Georges Leygues, Montcalm*
Destroyers	10 Div Contre-Torpilleurs
	Le Fantasque, Le Malin, Le Terrible

Desron 10

Desdiv 19	Desdiv 20
Elyson (SO)	*Forrest* (SO)
Hambleton	*Fitch*
Rodman	*Hobson*
Emmons	
Macomb	

(45th US Infantry Division)
CAMEL Attack Force
TF 87:

HQ ship	*Bayfield* (Cdre Edgar, US Navy)[3]

Transport Div 3
Escort Sweeper Groups
Auxiliary Group
Gunfire Support Group

Battleship	*Arkansas*		
Cruisers	*Tuscaloosa* (R Adm Deyo, US Navy), *Brooklyn, Omaha, Argonaut, Dugay-Trouin, Emile Bertin* (Contre Amiral Aboyneau)[3]		

---

[1]RA Bertram J. Rodgers, US Navy: NA 1916; s/m; blimps 1928–34; DD cmd 1939–40; NWC; CNO staff 1941–3; CO *Salt Lake City* Pac; SEAC; Cdr CTF 85 DRAGOON; Iwo Jima; Okinawa 1945; cdr Amph Fcs, Pac F 1948–50; Cdt, 12 N Dist 1950; cdr, N Fcs in Ger 1954.

[2]RA C. F. Bryant, US Navy (b 1892): USNA 1914; gun spist; CO *Chareleston* 1939; *Arkansas* 1941–3; N Af 1942; Normandy & S Fr 1944; VA 7 ret 1946.

[3]Cdre C. D. Edgar, US Navy: Sgn RA Sept 1940; 'Neptune' June 1944; ret Sept 1945.

[4]Contre Amiral Aboyneau, FFN: unidentified.

Destroyers	Desron 16		
	Desdiv 31	Desdiv 32	Desdiv 25
	Parker (SO)	*Boyle* (SO)	*Woolsey* (SO)
	Kendrick	*Champlin*	*Ludlow*
	MacKenzie	*Nields*	*Edison*
	McLanahan	*Ordronaux*	

(36th US Infantry Division (reinforced))
(French Army units as assigned)
Support Force
TF 86:
Gunfire Support Group

Cruiser	*Augusta* (R Adm Davidson, US Navy)[1]
Battleship	*Lorraine*
Cruiser	*Dido*
Destroyers	*Somers, Gleaves, Lookout*

Gunfire Support Reserve

Cruisers	*Cincinnati, Marblehead, Jeanne D'Arc, Sirius*
	+ Gunfire Support Units released from other forces.

SITKA Assault Ships and Craft

Princess Beatrix, Prince Henry, Prince David, Prince Baudouin, Prince Albert

Transport Division 13
Escort Sweeper Group
US Army and French Army units as assigned.

Aircraft Carrier Strike Force

Cruiser	*Royalist* (R Adm Troubridge)
CVE	*Khedive, Emperor, Searcher, Pursuer, Attacker, Stalker, Hunter* ([USS] *Tulagi* (R Adm Durgin, US Navy), *Kasaan Bay*[2]

---

[1]RA Lyle A. Davidson, US Navy (1886–1950): USNA 1910; engr posts; CO, DD Div 9, 1934–6; CO, *Omaha* 1939–40; NWC; CO, CruDiv 8; 1942; N Af 1942; Sicily & Italy 1943; Normandy June 1944; S Fr 1944; ONO 1944–6; ret 1946.
[2]RA Calvin T. Durgin, US Navy: CO *Ranger* 1942; dd sqdn, Sicily 1943; carriers, Pac 1944–5.

AA Ships	Colombo, Delhi, Caledon
Destroyers	Troubridge (D24), Tuscan, Tyrian, Teazer, Tumult, Tenacious, Garland, Navarinon
	Desdiv 33: Murphy, Jeffers
	Desdiv 34: Butler (SO), Gherhardi, Herndon, Shubrick

Naval Aircraft in CVEs	Khedive	20 Seafires
	Emperor	20 Hellcats
	Searcher	20 Wildcat V
	Pursuer	20 Wildcat V
	Attacker	20 Seafires
	Stalker	20 Seafires
	Hunter	20 Seafires
	Tulagi	20 Hellcat, 2 Avenger
	Kasaan Bay	24 Hellcats (day), 8 Hellcats (night), 2 Avenger.[1]

218. ANVIL-DRAGOON: *The Invasion of Southern France, August 1944*

[ADM 199/120]   17 March 1945

...

The Assault Landings

The Navy prepared and executed in remarkably short time a complicated schedule of loading and assembling the vast armada which carried the invasion forces. ...

...

The approach was excellently conducted by all groups of ships and craft which reached the final assault destinations according to plan, and

---

[1] Supermarine Seafire: 1942; 1 engine; 1 crew; 352mph; 465m; 2×20mm cannon, 4mg.
Grumman Hellcat: 1942; 1 engine; 1 crew; 376mph; 1090m; 6mg.
Grumman Wildcat: 1937; 1 engine; 1 crew; 328mph; 1150m; 4mg.
Grumman Avenger: 1942; 1 engine; 3 crew; 271mph; 1020 m; 5mg, 1 torpedo/2000lbs bombs.

the commando operations were begun on schedule shortly after midnight. ...

...

The carefully synchronised programme of naval and air bombardment which preceded the assault landings achieved the almost complete neutralisation of shore batteries. Observers described naval gunfire as heavier and more effective and during any previous operation in the Mediterranean Theatre. In the preliminary bombardment and subsequent gunfire support of the landings, the Navy fired 19,000 shells of minimum 5in calibre, of which 12,500 were of 12in calibre or above. In all three areas the gunfire support ships fired on the assigned targets during the hour preceding the landings between 0700 and 0800 hours, lifting their fire periodically for the waves of bombers attacking the same targets. ...

So effective was the combined naval and air bombardment, that opposition to the landings was in most cases confined to small arms and mortar fire ...

... the landings of the 36th Division on the extreme right of the assault area encountered little opposition. By noon of the day following both Fréjus and St Raphael had been captured by an advance from west, north and south, and the St Raphael beaches were in operation.

In the centre 45th Division landed on the beaches of St Maxime against very light mortar fire which caused no damage or casualties, and captured the town by 1700 hours. Before midnight all personnel and vehicles had been unloaded from LCTs, LSIs and combat loaders and unloading of merchant ships had begun. Early the next day the Division assisted the 36th [Division] on its role in the capture of Fréjus and then proceeded north-west in two columns. ...

On the left the first eight assault waves of the 3rd Division landed on schedule on beaches in the bays of Cavalaire and Pamelonne with only slight hindrances from enemy mines, enemy fire, and underwater obstacles. Unloading, hindered in the early stages by shallow water mines, was later accelerated with the development of additional landing ports. ...

There was neither naval nor air resistance on any scale worthy of mention to counter-act the well-nigh perfect co-ordination of our own three Services in the assault, and consequently our own losses were relatively slight, and the enemy's correspondingly heavy. ...

Our shipping losses were also light on the day of the assault, a US LSGT and two LCVPs sunk by glider bombs, about nine LCT damaged by mines and shell-fire and about a dozen smaller craft damaged in the same way. ...

219. *Admiral Sir John Cunningham to the Admiralty*

[ADM 199/864]   26 September 1944

Be pleased to lay before Their Lordships the attached report of the Tactical Deception operations. ...

2. Except for feints of a purely local character, such as diversionary bombardments in conjunction with raid operations on the Dalmatian Coast, and a minor feint against the north coast of Elba during the assault on that island, these two operations are the only occasions during the last six months in which tactical deception methods have been employed.

3. The organisation of both these operations was greatly assisted by the fact that Lieut-Cdr Fairbanks, USNR, whose whole time in the Mediterranean has been devoted to deception schemes, and particularly to tactical deception, was available to the Force Commander.[1]

4. In any extensive deception plan such as that carried out in operation DRAGOON, the closest possible co-operation with the Air Forces is essential. For this operation, great assistance was given by representative sent out to this theatre by Admiralty, Navy Department, Air Ministry, TRE and Allied Expeditionary Air Force.[2]

A planning Committee for DRAGOON was formed in which these officers and those on the staffs of the C-in-C Mediterranean, Commander, 8th Fleet and expeditionary Allied Air Force, were represented. The only serious handicaps experienced were due to the very short time available to complete the Radar Counter-Measure plan, fit the ships concerned with the type of equipment which they would require, and tune the apparatus to the frequencies revealed by radar intelligence.

5. Experience has shown that if the best use is to be made of modern devices for the purpose of tactical deception a special SO for the purpose is essential in any theatre of maritime operations. The fact that one of the operations under report appears to have failed in its object, and that there is yet no conclusive evidence that the other was successful, must not in any way be taken to suggest that future operations of this nature may not prove to be of decisive importance to battles on land.

[1]Lt-Cdr Douglas E. Fairbanks, USNR (1909–2000): a well-known film star; Lt (jg) 1941; Lt Cdr 1943; Cdr 1945.
[2]TRE: unknown.

220.   *Invasion of Southern France:*
Report of the Naval Commander, Western Task Force

[ADM 199/865]   29 November 1944

12 August 1944
Operations

At 1230 LCI assault convoy of 115 LCI and 30 other vessels divided into sections SF-2, SF2A and SF-2B and departed Naples for Ajaccio via route one, speed 11 knots.

At 1530 LST assault convoy of 69 LST and 63 other vessels divided into sections SM-1, SM-1A and SM-1B under tactical command of CTF 85 in *Biscayne* and departed Naples for the assault area via route one, speed 8 knots.

At 2000 'Sitka' gunfire support group composed of one CA, one CL and three DD under tactical command of CTF 85 in *Augusta* departed Naples for the assault area via route one ...

Aircraft carrier force composed of four AACL, eight CVE and 13 DD under tactical command of CTF 88 in *Royalist* departed Malta for the carrier assault operating area via the standard westbound Mediterranean Secret Convoy Instructions route to the Tunisian war channel then along route two. The Aircraft Carrier Force consisted of seven carriers of the Royal Navy and two of the US Navy. Aboard each were 24 aircraft: Seafires, Hellcats and Wildcats in the Royal Navy carriers, and Hellcats in the US Navy carriers. Fighter, fighter-bomber, tactical reconnaissance, spotting, photo and rocket projectile aircraft were included. The latter type was only in the USS *Tulagi* and USS *Kassam Bay*.

Thirty-six additional spare aircraft were based at Malta, Casablanca, in Corsica, as well as five Avengers for ferry operations and A/S operations. Five night Hellcats were based at Solenzara, Corsica, for night carrier cover.

HMS *Ulster Queen*, standby FDS, sailed with convoy SF-2B.

The air sea rescue service ranging from Leghorn to Toulon reported the rescue of three airmen.

A channel 2000 yards wide through the Straits of Bonifacio was swept with 'Oropesa' minesweeping gear, with negative results.

...

22 August 1944

Operations
Sixty ships arrived in convoy and 21 vessels departed.

One DD was established on each wing of the screen to maintain communications with night searching aircraft and DD hunting groups.

Naval bombardment covered the area from Giens to Marseille in the third day of the action to reduce Toulon. USS *Augusta* fired 54 rounds; FS *Gloire* answered urgent calls from the Army in the St Marcel area; HMS *Aurora* fired 78 rounds at Cape Brun scoring two direct hits' and USS *Philadelphia* neutralized targets near Giens. Coastal defence guns replied vigorously, shells from St Mandrier landing near the *Augusta* at a range of 16 miles. A white flag was seen on one battery on the Giens peninsula, but the battery on Cap de l'Esterel continued to be active.

Bombardment of Porquerolles was continued, and a white flag was raised twice. At 1130 CTG 86.3 in USS *Omaha* accepted the surrender of the enemy garrisons except isolated stragglers. Later, USS *Eberle* destroyed batteries, barracks, and ammunition dumps, and removed 58 prisoners. USS *Blackaby* landed 190 Sengalese troops and USS *Tattnall* removed 150 more PoW (100).

In Golfe de la Napoule, cruisers and destroyers successfully engaged numerous targets with the aid of shore and plane spotters, including 170mm batteries, armored vehicles, pillboxes and railroad guns. One cruiser had a near miss and two DD suffered personnel casualties.

A four-foot surf impeded the program of unloading.

Unloading figures were:

	Personnel	Vehicles	Tons
Alpha Beaches	123	568	2696
Delta Beaches	7364	1604	4229
Camel Beaches	1703	871	2394
Total	9190	3043	9319
Total to Date	127,890	22,822	63,245

25 September 1944

Summary Statistics
Ships and Craft in the Assault: 2250
Our losses were:

Sunk or destroyed: one US LST, one HM M/L, two US YMS, two US PT, five US LCVP, two HM LCM.

Damaged: 1 US DLCM (3)D, 3 US SC, 10 US LCI (L), 5 US LCT, 3 HM LCT, 1 US AM, 1 US ATR, 2 US ARS, 2 HM M/L, 1 US YMS, 1 HM BYMS, I US LGC, 1 US PT, 8 US LCVP, 5 HM LCM (3).
Enemy losses were:
Sunk or destroyed: 1 DD, 1 TB, 13 EV, 5 MAS, 1 M/V, 5 inactive S/M, 3 M/S-type craft, at least 5 small craft, 16 explosive motor boats, 13 human torpedoes.

Damaged: 2 EV, 2 M/V, 2 M/V-type craft, an unknown number of small craft.

Captured: 1 fishing vessel, 2 motor boats.

Movement into Southern France, 15 August–25 September 1944

	Personnel	Vehicles	Tons (dry)	Barrels (wet)
Alpha Beaches (closed 9 Sept)	81,573	15,675	67,353	
Delta Beaches (closed 16 Sept)	119, 954	25,176	121,692	
Camel Beaches	66,888	18,229	146,974	
Marseille	50,569	6,711	99,171	10,000
Toulon	5,085	2,628	24,252	76,130
Point de Bouc	- -	- -	30,795	239,600

For the beaches the quantity of supplies in barrels (wet) was included in the tonnage.

221. *Admiral Sir John Cunningham to Rear Admiral*
J. A. V. Morse

[ADM 199/864]   30 November 1944

As from October 1944, DRAGOON Area will revert to your operational control.

...

2. From that date the title of FO, Western Italy, will lapse and you will be known as FO, Northern Area, Mediterranean with the short title of FONAM.

3. You will be responsible for the control of naval forces operating in support of the 5th and 6th Armies and for the maintenance of communications in your area. Allied Naval forces will be placed under your command to enable this control to be exercised.

4. Under your direction the Préfet Maritime (Premar 3) will assume responsibility for those duties on the Southern French coast normally performed by an FOIC, including the administration of the ports and anchorages in his area, local defence policy, coastal defence, lights and navigation aids, maintenance of swept channels and minesweeping clearance. *He will under your direction control coastwise shipping movements and will, with the assistance of COMLAB, initiate Allied and neutral shipping movements and co-ordinate and acquire all other shipping movements, except those of the Flank Force. He*

*will assume operational control all ships and craft allocated to him
for escort and local defence duties.*

5.   Under the Préfet Maritime, French Naval Officers in charge at Toulon and Marseilles will assume operational responsibility for those
operational functions at present being exercised by the US Navy at
these ports, including general port duties, local patrols, maintenance
of swept channels, and the sailing of purely French traffic (French
controlled coasters, etc.), as required by the Préfet Maritime. They
will also sail merchant shipping by coastwise routes as required by
the Préfet Maritime and as arranged by NCSOs.

6.   *Under your direction the Flag or SO Flank Force (short title Flan-
For) will assume operational control of bombarding ships and all
other ships and craft allocated to him for the protection of the Eastern Flank from Enemy surface and submerged attack and for the
support of the 5th and 6th Armies by Naval Bombardment.*

7.   The organisation under the control of a Commodore, US Navy, Commodore Liaison American and British (short title COMLAB), will
liaison with the Préfet Maritime (in which the French Navy is to be
represented), *assist the Préfet Maritime to co-ordinate and arrange
offshore movements (except those of the FlanFor) and to initiate
Allied and neutral sea movements;* supervise the minesweeping programme and keep you informed of port activities, and minesweeping
progress as it occurs. In addition COMLAB is to administer and supply British and US ships and personnel on the South Coast of France.

222.   *CCS to Eisenhower and Wilson*

[Map Rm 35]   4 December 1944

1. CCS agree with your proposals for the handling of Italian warships
and merchant vessels captured in ports of Southern France. This is to
say these ships will be dealt with under the surrender instrument and the
Cunningham-[de] Courten agreement, being turned over to the Italians
for operations of care and maintenance pending ultimate settlement concerning the Italian fleet and merchant shipping.

223.   *Despatches relating to American LSTs used in Greek crisis*

[Map Rm 88]   8 December 1944

King to Commanders of 8th and 12th Fleets.

CCS authorised transfer 10 LST to Britain.

Hewitt to King. 8 December 1944.

In view Greek situation and reported attitude [of] State Department, attention invited [to the] fact US LSTs currently employed ferrying troops and material Taranto to Piraeus.

King to Hewitt. 8 December 1944.

US LSTS are not to be used for ferrying troops and military equipment to Greece.

Hewitt to King. 9 December 1944.

Present situation as follows:

A.   Five LSTs unloading or about to unload in Greek ports.
B.   Two LSTs loading vehicles at Taranto due to sail.
C.   Need for reinforcement to preserve order reported to be urgent.
D.   Unloading of Libertys at Piraeus reported to be impracticable due to lack of facilities and stevedore strikes.
E.   Exclusive of US LSTs there are only four LSTs (three Greek, one British) in Mediterranean. Of these only two Greek are operational.

Position of C-in-C Mediterranean and SAC Mediterranean, is that withdrawal of resources though to be available during progress of war operation is unfortunate. Urgent dispatch to be addressed [to] CCS seeking confirmation and requesting instructions. The two LSTs at Taranto are being loaded pending clarification of situation.

King to Hewitt. 9 December 1944.

My 091605 [above, top] provides for the transfer of 10 US LSTs in the Mediterranean to the British. This transfer can be effected immediately.

With reference to your statement in your 091430 [above] 'position of Cincmed and Sacmed is that withdrawal of resources thought to be available during progress of war operation is unfortunate', the 'war' referred to does not appear to be war in which the US is participating.

Unloading of US LSTs now in progress can be completed. LSTs loading are not to move forward to Greek ports under US flag.

Allied Forces HQ to Marshall. 9 December 1944.

A message is to be dispatched today to CCS protesting Cominch directive prohibiting further sailings [of] American LSTs to Greek ports. This message is sent at my suggestion in hope of clearing up unsatisfactory situation here. ...

If highest level decisions are not involved, recommend message referring LSTs be used as a vehicle to prevent further weakening this theatre at the moment we are about to resume the battle, unless concurred in by the CCS.

King to Hewitt.   10 December 1944.

Suspend action on my 082146 and 091913 [above] except transfer of 10 US LSTs can go ahead.

224.   *Lieut-Cdr P. F. Brine, USNR, to Hewitt*[1]

[NWC, Hewitt 1]   27 February 1945

... I want you to know how fine has been your work with the French Navy. You are considered their staunchest friend and their devoted ally. They have a complete confidence in your wisdom and have at all times expressed their admiration for the delicacy with which you handled a difficult task.

---

[1] Lt-Cdr P. F. Brine, USNR: unidentified.

PART V

THE FAR EAST

H. P. Willmott called his book on Britain's war in the Far East *Grave of a Dozen Schemes* and the title is most appropriate.[1] Britain faced several major problems in defending – and winning back – her extensive Imperial territories in the period 1921–45. In the 1890s, it became apparent to British statesmen and naval chiefs that the extent and scattered nature of the Empire would be difficult to defend against a major foe, especially one who was much closer to Imperial territories than the 'mother country'. Furthermore, the 1890s witnessed the rise to maritime 'great power' status of several new contenders – the United States, Japan and Germany – all of whom were ambitious to establish their own empires and were of doubtful friendliness. These new world powers were ranged alongside Britain's traditional colonial rivals, France and Russia (allied to each other since 1893). Despite a steady enlargement of the Royal Navy after 1889, it was recognised in Britain that the country could not hope to defend its Empire without defusing what had become a highly dangerous situation, with all the great powers, old and new, seemingly ranged against her, each with their own aims and, worse, disputes with Albion. It was necessary to solve these disputes peaceably and, if possible, to make alliances or at least tacit understandings with some of them.

In 1895, a dispute with the United States (and its client Venezuela) over territory in South America was resolved peacefully; Britain thereafter consistently appeased the United States (often to Canada's mortification). In 1902, Britain made an unprecedented move in signing a defensive alliance with Japan; if either power found itself at war with two or more countries, the other was treaty-bound to come to its partner's aid. Japan was a country of yellow-skinned people, not normally treated with respect by Europeans at that time. Moreover, she was at the beginning of her rise to 'great power' status and Britain was taking a real risk in going into an alliance with her. The alliance was to last 20 years and Japan fought on Britain's side in the First World War, effectively protecting the Empire's extensive Asian territories. In 1904 and 1907, settlements were made with France and Russia. They were much less binding and rather vague but they defused colonial disputes. Of the major world powers, only Germany remained immune to Britain's overtures.

After the First World War, Britain and France were considerably weakened, while Germany was decisively eliminated as a threat. Both Japan and the United States had profited from the war. In the Five-Power Treaty of Washington, negotiated in 1921–22, the United States set the agenda for ending a putative naval race in major warships, and Britain

---

[1] H. P. Willmott, *Grave of a Dozen Schemes* (Annapolis, MD, 1996).

was compelled to bow to America's new-found capacity to out-fund and out-build all other nations. France and Italy were compelled to sign, too. The Japanese, though they sought parity with Britain and the United States in naval terms, had to be satisfied with a warship ratio of five for the British and the Americans and a mere three for themselves. This gave them, however, local superiority in the Eastern Pacific and into the Indian Ocean. This local dominance was increased by two other treaties of the same date. The Nine-Power Treaty recognised China's independence and internationalised the American 'Open Door' policy – but there was little will to defend Chinese sovereignty, reform the ancient country, or safeguard Western interests; the scene was set for further Japanese domination of her neighbour, a position staked out with increasing control since 1894. The Four-Power Treaty agreed that the Pacific islands should be unfortified but there was again no provision for its enforcement. China was a land divided between the Nationalists, the Communists, warlords, brigands and pirates (some of them wearing at least two hats); it was a sleeping giant, ripe for exploitation by its aggressive and ambitious neighbour. Years of Japanese exploitation culminated in an undeclared but very real Sino-Japanese war in 1937.[1] By 1941, Japanese ambition, economic need, irritation at the disapproval of Western powers (who were unwilling to face Japan militarily or to unite in effective sanctions) and a government fully under military sway, led to a sudden strike by the Rising Sun against the Western powers, their imperial territories and their local defences. After six months of warfare, Japan had secured not only much of China but also the Philippines, other Pacific islands, Malaya, Burma, French Indo-China, and the Dutch East Indies, as well as putting out of action the major naval vessels of the Western powers, notably the American fleet at Pearl Harbor in Hawaii, deep into the western Pacific.[2]

The Western powers, led by the United States and including Australia and New Zealand, managed to stabilize the position in mid-1942 and went over to a gradual offensive later in that year, a process hastened only slowly in 1943. Informal and secret discussions between Britain and America had taken place in 1938–39 and there was local co-operation on the great rivers of China, for both nations became increasingly alarmed at Japanese expansionism, carving deep into the carcass of a seemingly

---

[1] G. Hudson, *The Far East in World Politics* (London, 1939); R. Mitter, *China's War with Japan: The Struggle for Survival* (London, 2013).
[2] G. W Prange et al., *At Dawn We Slept: The Untold Story of Pearl Harbor* (Harmondsworth, Middx, 1981). A. Boyd, *The Royal Navy in Eastern Waters: Linchpin of Victory, 1935–1942* (Barnsley, 2017).

moribund China and threatening the commercial and missionary interests of the two Western powers.[1] When war with Japan broke out in December 1941, hasty military co-operation between the British, Australians, New Zealanders, Dutch, Free French, Chinese and Americans attempted to defend their Far Eastern and Pacific interests, to no avail; the Japanese swept all before them in the Pacific, setting up a defensive shield of islands within which they exploited the natural resources of conquered imperial territories. When the advance of the Rising Sun was stemmed in June 1942, these nations continued to co-operate, ships of several nations serving with the American fleets in the Central Pacific and the South West Pacific Area, and the British Eastern and East Indies Fleets.[2]

The American-led counter-offensive against Japan's ring of island conquests, which shielded the larger islands and the Japanese homeland, began immediately after the Americans halted effectively the Japanese advance across the south and western Pacific at the Battle of Midway in early June 1942. The Allied advance, slow at first but gathering pace in 1943, was about to enter the central Pacific. After a series of bloody tit-for-tat blows, the central Pacific campaign 'really picked up steam during the first eight months of 1944', by-passing islands and thus allowing a thousand-mile advance in four months, en route to a direct assault on the Japanese home islands[3] [228, 230, 237, 239, 243–4, 273–4, 335].

At this point, the Royal Navy re-entered the Pacific scene in some strength. With the Italian surrender, the decisive victory in the war against the U-boats and the elimination of the German surface fleet, the British were able to reinforce the Eastern Fleet from the beginning of 1944. At last Admiral Somerville was able to go over to the offensive. In collaboration with the veteran American fleet carrier *Saratoga* and her escorting destroyers, a series of bombardments and carrier air attacks were made on targets in the southern Indian Ocean. These gave the British useful practice in carrier operations (learning much from the Americans) and hammered their objectives, though by themselves they were sideshows in the grand strategy rather than decisive.[4]

In fact, British Far Eastern strategy in the latter stages of the war was the battleground for a fierce struggle between Churchill and his Chiefs of

---

[1]M. A. Simpson, ed., *Anglo-American Naval Relations, 1919–1939* (Aldershot, 2010, NRS vol. 156), pp. 247–8, 252–60, 279, 284–5.

[2]S. E. Morison, *History of U.S. Naval Operations in World War II* (Boston, 1948–75), vols. III–VIII, XII, XIV.

[3]D. Rigby, 'The CCS and Anglo-American Strategic Cooperation in World War II' (unpub. PhD, Brandeis U, 1997), p. 75.

[4]M. A. Simpson, ed., *The Somerville Papers* (Aldershot, 1996, NRS vol. 134), pp. 513, 521, 523, 536–7, 544–60.

Staff in 1943 and resolved in the latter's favour only on the eve of the second Quebec conference (QUADRANT) in September 1944. The Prime Minister, an old imperial lion, wished to restore Britain's Far Eastern Empire, much as it had been before the war. This meant not only denying India its independence but assuming that Australia and New Zealand would submit meekly to the mother country's post-war Imperial dominance. To that end, Churchill wanted a concerted Commonwealth effort to regain lost colonies – Burma, Malaya, Singapore, Hong Kong, and many Pacific islands, while restoring Britain's pre-eminent position in China. There was to be a major British effort centred in the Indian Ocean and spreading out into the lost territories. Churchill appeared content to leave the Americans to focus on the defeat of Japan proper. Cunningham fumed at the politicians' strategic blindness – they 'prefer to hang about outside and recapture our own rubber trees'.[1]

This was a strategy of dead-ends and a misuse of Britain's scarce resources, argued the Chiefs of Staff, led by the new First Sea Lord, Admiral of the Fleet Sir Andrew Cunningham. Since the Royal Navy had the flexibility and strength to take the lead in that watery maze, he was the main driver of a strategy that called for British participation in the direct assault on Japan, in association with the Americans, though it was acknowledged that the United States would be the major player and would dictate both strategy and tactics. The COS argued that such a strategy was not only correct militarily but that it would aid British retention of Hong Kong and thus renewed penetration of China's illimitable markets. It would give Britain also a voice in the post-war occupation of Japan. Australia and New Zealand would regain confidence in the mother country's willingness to defend them. Britain's extensive but scattered colonies would fall back into her lap with defeat of Japan by direct means. Furthermore, the Royal Navy would learn much about the new forms of naval warfare, centred on carrier task forces, supported by a dedicated fleet train [233, 235, 241, 247–8, 250, 264–70, 272, 275–6, 280, 282, 285, 289, 327, 333]. The provision of a substantial British force depended on the near-conclusion of the war against Germany in late 1944. Naval forces would be largely free of that incubus, while land and air forces would be heavily involved until victory was complete. The COS had agreed with American Chiefs in November 1943 to provide a British Pacific Fleet in about a year's time. The COS were thus 'firmly of the opinion that we should put in our maritime effort in the Pacific on the

[1]Cunningham, diary, 14 July 1944, in M. A. Simpson, ed., *The Cunningham Papers*, II (Aldershot, 2006; NRS vol. 150), p. 320.

left of the American forces' in the central Pacific[1] [229, 236, 247–8, 250, 264, 269, 285]. 'The advantage of a Pacific strategy, in their view, was that it offered the best means to hasten the defeat of Japan by strengthening the main and decisive thrust in the Central Pacific.'[2] There followed an almighty row between the Prime Minister and the COS, exploding in January 1944. The COS even contemplated resignation. General Sir Alan Brooke, chairman of the COS, noted in his diary that 'dear old Cunningham was [so] wild with rage that he hardly dared let himself speak'.[3] The impasse continued until 8 March, when the two sides agreed on a compromise 'Middle Strategy', which would see British forces moving into the East Indies and driving up to China from the south. The Chiefs had agreed to this compromise with some reluctance and continued to press the Prime Minister to adopt their preferred more direct Central Pacific policy. The matter was still unresolved in August 1944. Churchill did not answer the Chiefs directly but by the time the QUADRANT conference opened on 13 September 1944, he had come round to their view. In a sudden gesture, the Prime Minister offered a British Pacific Fleet to the President; Roosevelt was equally quick to accept the offer. The CCS were taken by surprise at this political expression of their view[4] [247–8].

In general, the American civil and military leadership welcomed the British offer. For Roosevelt, it would sweeten the pill which he would compel Churchill to swallow over post-war policies. It would reassure America's sceptical public opinion that Britain would play a full part in the final victory over Japan. American forces were finding it tough going to winkle the Japanese out of their defensive strongholds and were suffering heavy casualties in men and ships from the new Japanese tactic of *kamikazes*, or suicide bombers. A substantial British force to take the heat off the US Navy (literally) would be welcome, particularly the British armoured-deck fleet carriers, largely immune to crippling damage by Japan's suicide armada.

King objected strongly to the British offer. At the meeting at which the Prime Minister had offered a British Pacific Fleet, to be accepted with alacrity by the President, King, like the other members of the CCS, had been stunned by the seemingly casual interchange between the two war leaders. By the morrow he had recovered his wits and steamed angrily into battle. King was by then the all-powerful head of the US Navy; even

---

[1]Cunningham to Noble, 8 April 1944, *Cunningham Papers*, II, p. 314.
[2]C. M. Bell, *Churchill and Sea Power* (Oxford, 2013), p. 296.
[3]Gen Sir Alan Brooke, diary, 8 March 1944, in A. Danchev & D. Todman, eds, *War Diaries, 1939–1945: Field Marshal Lord Alanbrooke* (London, 2001), p. 530.
[4]Cunningham, diary, Quebec, 13 Sept 1944, *Cunningham Papers*, II, p. 160.

senior admirals trod the quarterdecks in fear of him. He was efficient, ruthless, ambitious, innovative, had a broad appreciation of both technology and logistics and had formulated an impressive global maritime strategy. He was a fierce nationalist, somewhat contemptuous of the Royal Navy, under-impressed by Churchillian bluster and FDR's apparent willingness to humour the old warrior, and harboured deep suspicions about British motives and strategies. By October 1943, he was up against Andrew Cunningham, as crusty an old sea dog as himself, equally given to straight speaking; their relationship, though frequently tempestuous, was founded on mutual respect. The two navies dovetailed efficiently and amicably all over the world, though Cunningham wrote of King, 'I can't bring myself to like that man'[1] [239, 241, 260, 262, 275, 279, 299, 305, 344].

King had legitimate doubts about a BPF serving in the central Pacific. It could not become operational until spring 1945 and he had not considered his strategy for that time, though he thought it unlikely that the British could offer substantial assistance and was unsure that he could find useful tasks for them, unless he withdrew American forces to make space for them – a path which he refused to follow. He understood that American supply chains were already at full stretch and he had no wish to add the burden of a British presence upon them [226, 231, 233–5, 240, 255, 282, 285, 289, 298]. Furthermore, America's sweeping Pacific triumphs in 1943–44 had endowed King and the US Navy with assurance and pride; he and his fleets had no wish to share the glory of victory with anyone else (the US Army included).

King launched his broadside on the morrow of Churchill's sudden offer and the President's ready acceptance of it. His legitimate arguments were obscured by his smoke and fury. 'King flew into a temper,' recorded Cunningham. The BPF 'couldn't be allowed there. He wouldn't have it and so on.' Moreover, he suggested that the President hadn't meant what he said.[2] After several more days of talks, during which King found himself isolated within the CCS, the CNO became 'more or less resigned to having the British fleet in the Pacific'.[3] Thereafter, there is no strong indication that King did not accept the BPF's presence in the central Pacific, though Cunningham continued to mutter darkly that the Americans in general and King in particular wished to divert British forces into the Indian Ocean and the South West Pacific Area, to regaining their lost colonies[4] [225, 233, 235, 238, 246, 249, 334].

---

[1]Cunningham, diary, 9 June 1944, *Cunningham Papers*, II, p. 158.
[2]Cunningham, diary, Quebec, 14 Sept 1944, *Cunningham Papers*, II, p. 160.
[3]Cunningham, diary, Quebec, 15 Sept 1944, *Cunningham Papers*, II, p. 161.
[4]*Cunningham Papers*, II, pp. 157, 160, 161, 164, 170.

King having accepted, somewhat grudgingly, the presence of a BPF, the British government had to find its commander-in-chief, naval strength, supporting fleet train, and rear and forward bases. The Commander-in-Chief selected himself. Admiral Sir Bruce Fraser had 'won his battle' – the sinking of the German battlecruiser *Scharnhorst* in the Arctic in December 1943. He was not on particularly good terms with Cunningham but the First Sea Lord realised that there was really no alternative [245, 250–53, 256–7]. The spearhead, the Fleet itself, was of little concern. The Royal Navy had sufficient modern ships, newly released from European waters, to provide a task force. There were six war-built fleet carriers, though they had very small aircraft capacities compared with the Americans – a consequence of their armoured decks, which limited the size of their hangars; typically, they carried 54 to 60 planes, whereas the (much more numerous) American fleet carriers, unarmoured and therefore less capable of standing up to the Japanese *kamikaze*, held around 100 aircraft each, and even their light fleet carriers took on board 45 planes. There were also four recent fast battleships, a score of cruisers and flotillas of destroyers, together with frigates and minor warships. The warships, though modern, were designed more for European conditions than the Pacific, which had always been a lesser concern of the constructors; thus a large programme of installing air conditioning was undertaken. British ships also had inadequate AA armaments and control systems. They were short-legged, relying on a chain of well-equipped bases – entirely absent in the Pacific. British servicing capacity, on shore and at sea, fell far below American standards. The Americans also lacked suitable bases but made up for it by instituting a fleet train of fast, rangy, capacious, specialised vessels of largely wartime construction. The British lacked sufficient ships of speed, endurance, equipment and capacity. Such British, Commonwealth and Allied merchantmen as were available were required also for the myriad other tasks still being performed in the Atlantic, Arctic, Mediterranean and Indian oceans and seas. Lord Leathers, the Minister of War Transport, was especially resistant to Admiralty requests for ships from his over-burdened merchant fleet; it took an intervention from the Prime Minister to force him to disgorge enough ships.[1] Even when the Fleet Train was finally assembled, it was a rag-bag of vessels, most of which lacked one or more of the attributes required for their new role, chief among them lack of speed. The BPF

---

[1]Lord (Edward J.) Leathers (1883–1965): ship and mine owner; shipping advisor to Govt in both wars; friend of Churchill pre-war; baron & MWT May 1941; SSt Transport, Fuel & Power 1951–3; Visct 1954.
Cunningham, diary, Yalta, 8 Feb 1945, *Cunningham Papers*, II, p. 169; see also pp. 302–3.

put to sea with an antiquated and inadequate Fleet Train, and it was only by a supreme effort that it served its purpose, often by the skin of its teeth [229, 232, 256, 259, 262–3, 265–6, 268, 281, 303]. The shore base situation gave concern, too. The principal rear bases were in Australia, distant by thousands of miles from the BPF's area of operations. Admiral Fraser based himself in Sydney [251, 268, 270, 300, 330, 349]. Australia lacked manpower, a sophisticated economy, and a docile dock labour force. The Australian government and people were war-weary, though the BPF enjoyed a fine reception from the host nation. The South West Pacific Area's bases were located in Australia, too, and the BPF had to compete with and also bargain with the SWPA and its often-awkward Supreme Commander, the American General Douglas MacArthur.[1] There was much dispute with the Americans over forward bases; the British pressed for a base in the American possession of the Philippines, a request politely turned down by the Americans, who offered instead Manus, an island in the British Admiralty Islands – itself hardly handy for operations and with a foul climate. The Americans based there, however, took a most liberal view of self-sufficiency and provided the BPF with generous assistance, which would have met with King's wrath had he been informed of it [268, 270, 277, 283–4, 287–90, 293, 295–6, 298–301, 306–7, 311, 313–20, 322–3, 330, 344, 349].

The BPF grew out of the Eastern Fleet, which had been strengthened since January 1944 by over 150 ships. Admiral Somerville, in command of a truly offensive and multi-national force in the first half of 1944, struck at targets in Sabang and Surabaya in carrier-led operations. Somerville left the Eastern Fleet for BAD in Washington and Fraser inherited the command. When he moved eastwards, the residue of his force, chiefly older vessels and escort carriers, formed the East Indies Fleet. Fraser was induced by the Americans to carry out heavier carrier air attacks on oil refineries at Palembang in the Dutch East Indies before proceeding to the Pacific. The Americans asked for diversionary attacks to distract Japanese attention from landings in the Pacific but it is at least as likely that they wished to test the mettle of the BPF and assess whether it could undertake modern carrier-based assaults of the kind they had pioneered in the Central Pacific. These were successful but still of minor importance in the wider strategic picture[2] [231, 234, 238, 264, 267, 325, 348–9].

[1]D. Hobbs, *The British Pacific Fleet: Britain's Most Powerful Strike Force* (Barnsley, 2013), pp. 63–107.
[2]FAdm Chester W. Nimitz, US Navy (1885–1966): s/m; RA 1938; Chf, Bu Navigation 1939; Adm & C-in-C, Pac F Dec 1941; FAdm Dec 1944; CNO Nov 1945. E. B. Potter, *Nimitz* (Annapolis, MD, 1976).

King and his entourage were sceptical that the BPF would make a significant contribution to the defeat of Japan and extended no favours to Fraser. Cunningham and Fraser, however, felt that a smooth operational relationship could be built up with the Supreme Commander in the Central Pacific, Admiral Chester W. Nimitz, whose headquarters at that time were at Pearl Harbor. He was an amenable man, and lived up to the First Sea Lord's and Fraser's hopes that he was a man with whom they could work; King slipped from the equation. Much hung on Fraser's meeting with Nimitz at Pearl in mid-December 1944. The two men saw eye to eye at once and enjoyed a happy relationship[1] [251, 253, 256–8, 261, 264, 267–8, 272, 278–9, 286, 291, 294, 296, 300, 305, 309–10, 319, 328, 341, 349]. This was confirmed by the welcome given to the BPF, which was comanded at sea by Admiral Sir Bernard Rawlings, by the leaders and personnel of the US Pacific Fleet, notably Admiral William F. Halsey (3rd Fleet) and Admiral Raymond A. Spruance (5th Fleet).[2]

The BPF did not see action until late March 1945, largely, it seems, because the American Supreme Commanders, MacArthur in the SWPA and Nimitz in the Central Pacific, were unable (or unwilling) to decide their next steps [258, 264, 282, 285, 289]. Finally, Nimitz asked the BPF to support the American invasion of Okinawa by neutralising the airfields in the island chain of Sakishima Gunto [304–6, 321].[3] In subsequent operations, it carried out bombardments and carrier strikes against similar shore targets [309–10, 319, 328, 337–8, 342, 346–9]. It defended itself against the *kamikazes* though its carriers suffered extensive damage and casualties. Their armoured decks, however, proved their worth, for they were all back in action within an hour or two, much to the admiration of the Americans [279, 304, 308, 321, 345, 349]. Their fighter direction was also superior to that of their hosts but in other respects – modern carrier aircraft and their efficient operation from their carriers, radar, anti-aircraft defence, servicing productivity, refuelling at sea, ships'

---

[1]FAdm William F. ('Bull') Halsey, jr, US Navy (1882–1959): USNA 1904; Great White F 1907–9; Lt 1909; DD cmds; Queenstown 1918; Capt 1927; N & A War Colls 1932–4; pilot 1935; *Saratoga* 1935–7; Cdr Pensacola NAS 1937–8; RA 1938; carrier sqdn cmds 1938–43; Adm Nov 1942; C-in-C, S Pac 1943; 3 F June 1944; FAdm Dec 1945; ret 1947. E. B. Potter, *Bull Halsey* (Annapolis, MD 1985).

Adm Raymond A. Spruance, US Navy: USNA 1907; CO *Bainbridge* 1913; Asst Engrg Officer, NY 1917–18; CO *Mississippi* 1938; Cdr 10 N Dist (San Juan) 1940–41; RA CruDiv, TF 16, Pac F; CoS & DC-in-C, Pac F; C-in-C 5 F 1943–5.

[2]Adm Sir Bernard Rawlings (1889–1962): ent RN 1904; Military Mission to Poland 1918–21; Capt 1930; *Active*, *Delhi*; NA Tokyo 1936–9; *Valiant* 1939; RA & 1 BS Jan 1941; 7 CS 1941; ACNS (F) 1942; A/VA & FO, W Af 1943; VA Nov 1943; FOIC, E Med Dec 1943; 2inC & 1BS, BPF Dec 1944; Adm & ret 1946.

[3]Gen Douglas MacArthur, US Army.

propulsion and fleet train support – they lagged behind the US Navy. It was a stiff lesson in modern warfare, and the BPF learned quickly and well [233–4, 239, 255, 262, 272, 275, 304, 308, 325, 344–9].

The BPF exercised a useful supporting role but it was hardly a vital element in the defeat of Japan. It earned American praise for its efforts on the front line and in the ability to stay at sea for lengthy periods (often two months). Rawlings, who commanded the BPF at sea, told Fraser with relief that the fleet had passed American muster [293]. It may not have been the deciding factor in Japan's eventual defeat but it was a template for the post-war Royal Navy [236, 327, 333]

225. *Memorandum from C. T. Joy for ACOS (P)*[1]

[RG 38]   20 September 1943

...

2. (a) Use the British Fleet in the South East Asia area in a campaign
         against Burma initially, and later against Singapore. After the
         Straits of Malacca have been opened, employ the Fleet in a cam-
         paign against Hong Kong, followed by joint British-American
         operations to reduce Formosa.
    ...

3. (a) In line with QUADRANT:
    (b) exert pressure on Japan from two directions;
    (c) simplify logistics;
    (d) require full use of British Fleet for BULLFROG and then
         Singapore.

226. *King to Noble*

[Op Arch, King 4]   27 October 1943

I note from your letter of 27 October [not reproduced] that the Admiralty
regrets it is not possible to lend a Dutch submarine to General MacArthur for the period between the departure of O21 and the arrival of K15.
I understand that this is based on certain requirements relating to the
operations of the Eastern Fleet.

I should be grateful if you will ask the Admiralty to give further consideration to this matter. It is important that General MacArthur maintain
communication with the Netherlands East Indies and the only effective
way he can maintain communications is by using Dutch submarines which
are particularly well suited for this work and are manned by personnel
familiar with the waters in which they have to operate. I hope it can be
arranged that one operational Dutch submarine be kept always at General
MacArthur's disposal as discussed at the 123rd meeting of the CCS.

I recognise that this will cause some inconvenience to the Eastern Fleet
but I hope that this can be accepted as part of the general give-and-take
that is a necessary part of the collaboration between our two Navies. As
you will recall I loaned some of our new submarines to the Royal Navy

---

[1]RA C. Turner Joy, US Navy (1895–1956): USNA 1916; CO *Litchfield* 1933; *Louisville*
1942–3; PD, Pac F 1943; CruDiv 6, 1944–5; Amph Grp 2, Aug 1945; Yangtze 1945–6; VA
1949; Cdr, Naval Fcs, FE 1949–52; CO, USNA 1952–4; Adm & ret 1954.

for service in European waters at a time when the loan made it necessary to reduce the Pacific Fleet below its minimum requirements in submarines. I think that on further examination we may find that this instance is one of equal importance to our combined war effort, particularly in view of the lessening need for all submarine operations in the Mediterranean.

227.   *Admiral Lockwood, US Navy, to Nimitz*[1]

[Nimitz 1/121]   26 November 1943

Proposed Submarine Operations in the Gulf of Siam.

1.   It is considered that the subject operation could be carried out by submarines of the South West Pacific forces plus those of the British available at Colombo.
2.   On 1 January 1944 there will be 27 US submarines in the South West Pacific and I am informed unofficially from a memorandum issued by the Flag Officer Submarines [in] London that there will be 17 British submarines at Trincomalee on the above date. These latter could be operated from Freetown, Exmouth Gulf or Darwin, depending on the enemy air power situation existing at that time.

228.   *Cdr F. H. E. Hopkins to Rear Admiral H. Pott*[2]

[ADM 199/117]   15 December 1943

Information Bulletin No. 35: Fleet and General Operations.

A. Central Pacific.

1.   With the occupation of the Gilbert Island bases completed, the major units of the Central Pacific Force have returned to their harbours at Pearl Harbour and Efate.

A small cruiser force is operating from Funafuti in the Ellice Islands, in support of the Gilbert bases, but air support is being provided by land-based aircraft from Makin, Tarawa and Apamana themselves (Gilbert Island bases), as well as from Funafuti.

---

[1]VA Charles A. Lockwood, US Navy (1890–1967): USNA 1912; s/m; Naval Attaché London 1941–2; CO, S/m, S W Pac 1942; Cdr, S/m, Pac F 1943; VA 1943; Cdr, S/m, SWPA.
    [2]Cdr F. H. E. Hopkins: Lt (O) 1933; *Peregrine*, Ford, Sussex, May 1934; 816 Sqdn, *Formidable*, Nov 1940; Matapan; Lt Cdr, 830 Sqdn; Malta, Nov 1941; BAD, July 1942; Cdr, Nov 1944; NLO, US Pac F, Jan 1945.

2. The bomber strips at the Gilbert bases are not yet completed, but work is progressing rapidly as is also the case with fortifications, radar installations and the blasting of entrances through the coral reefs which surround the islands, in order to provide suitable surface ship bases.

3. The enemy made a few bombing attacks on the Gilbert Islands since the capture, but these raids have been small ones and very little damage has been done.

The first defence against these bombing raids are our own air strikes against the enemy bases in the vicinity. The air strike from a strong carrier force against the Marshall Islands on 4 December, the air and surface bombardment of Nauru Island on 8 December, and many raids by aircraft from Funafuti, are instances of this policy, which is apparently having good results.

...

5. *Distribution and Movement of Major Units.*

On 14 December, ships in the Central Pacific were distributed as follows:

BB   *Pennsylvania, New Mexico, Idaho, Tennessee, Maryland, Colorado, Mississippi* – Pearl Harbor.

CAV   *Yorktown, Essex, Enterprise, Cowpens, Belleau Wood* – Pearl Harbor.
Lexington (damaged – at Pearl Harbor but will shortly go to coast).
Independence (damaged – en route Pearl Harbor).

CA   *Minnesota, New Orleans, San Francisco, Baltimore, Portland* – Pearl Harbor.

Note: The Escort Carriers are becoming so numerous and they move about so much, transporting aircraft to different parts of the Pacific, that they will not be included in this bulletin.

       Indianapolis – en route [to] West Coast.

CL   *Santa Fe, Mobile, Oakland* – Pearl Harbor.
Birmingham – Pearl Harbor (damaged).
San Juan, San Diego – en route [to] West Coast.
Louisville – West Coast.

CA   Away from Pearl Harbor on Operations: *Chester, Salt Lake City, Pensacola.*

B. South Pacific:

1. In the South Pacific the operation on Bougainville continues.

    The object of this operation is not so much the capture of the island, which owing to the difficult country and strong enemy forces at the northern and southern ends would be very costly, but to establish air and surface ship bases in the vicinity of Cape Torokina, from which to operate against the main enemy base at Rabaul, and in addition to cut off the strong forces in Bougainville itself.

2. Airfields at Torokina are already in operation, and the forward naval base is in use, and our ground troops are in the process of enlarging our beachhead and defending these bases.

    The function of the Navy in this operation, of which the larger units operate from Guadalcanal, is to deliver supplies and reinforcements to Bougainville, prevent interference by enemy surface forces and to harass enemy shipping and barge traffic.

    This is also the function of our land-based air forces, with the additional and continuous task of striking against the enemy air bases in the vicinity. In this latter task, great success is being achieved, and a number of enemy air bases are at present unserviceable.

3. *Distribution and Movements of Major Units.*

    On 14 December ships in the South Pacific were distributed as follows:

    BB   *Washington, South Dakota, North Carolina, Massachusetts, Indiana, Alabama.* – Efate.

    CAV *Bunker Hill, Monterey* – Efate.

    CL   *Montpelier, Cleveland, Colombia, Denver* – Purvis Bay, Guadalcanal.

          Honolulu, St Louis – Espiritu Santo (for training).

C, North Pacific:

1. *Distribution and Movement of Major Units*

On 14 December ships in the North Pacific were distributed as follows:
CL *Raleigh, Richmond, Detroit* – operating from Adak.

Owing to the bad weather conditions, very little is happening in the North Pacific except reconnaissance, and occasional air strikes on the Kurile Islands by shore-based aircraft

II. *Submarine Activities*

… the CoS to the Admiral Commanding Submarines, Pacific, informed me today that the results against enemy shipping continue to be good and that the tonnage of enemy shipping sunk during November 1943 was 358, 000 tons.

2. *Areas of Operations*

On 14 December submarines were distributed as follows:

Off Japan	4
Off Formosa	3
In the vicinity of the Caroline Islands	4
In the vicinity of the Solomons	1
In the vicinity of the Marshalls	6
In the vicinity of Midway	4
En route Pearl Harbor from West Coast or patrols	6

III. *General Intelligence:*

1. *Operations from our own Bases*

The most striking feature to a new arrival in the Pacific area, is the grand scale on which operations are carried out in the Central Pacific area.

The huge distances which are involved are undoubtedly the cause of this, and directly related to 'Distance' are:

(a) The supply problem.
(b) The fuelling organisation.
(c) The very large combatant forces involved.

The number of ships and aircraft employed have to be such that success will be achieved certainly and quickly, and not only must the supply problem be on a large scale, but it must NOT fail. Any failure through delay or lack of reinforcements, stores or fuel can immediately be taken advantage of by the strong enemy forces in the vicinity, who have the advantage of nearby major bases.

As examples of the large numbers required, in the recent operations in the Gilbert Isles, 19 aircraft carriers were employed.

Twelve battleships were available in the event of interference by enemy forces and the number of cruisers and destroyers present was almost unbelievable to an officer who has seen most of the war from the Eastern Mediterranean.

In order to maintain the Fleet at sea, a large number of tankers were employed, and a carefully planned routine for fuelling the various forces at sea was followed.

The supply department and the Fleet tankers are manned and operated by naval personnel.

2. *South Pacific Operations:*

In the South Pacific, where all forces are operating from nearby bases, the situation is more comparable to the Mediterranean in the later stages of the Tunisian campaign, when fighter protection was available, and smaller forces in conjunction with land-based fighter protection were available, and smaller forces in conjunction with land-based aircraft are more the order of the day.

3. *Realism of American Naval Officers:*

American naval officers are realists, and if war experience shows that certain things are desirable, they act at once and do not take too much heed of past customs.

As examples:

(a)   All ships in the Pacific Fleet are entirely free of paintwork between decks, ornamental woodwork and other fire hazards, such as cortisone and carpets.

(b)   With regard to uniform, the fact that you do manual work in a modern ship you will probably get dirty, the necessity for having the limbs covered to reduce the chances of being burnt, and a colour scheme which does not stand out for the benefit of low-flying aircraft, have been considered, and uniforms have been evolved for officers and men which are suitable for both harbour and sea. With regard to the ratings, sufficient numbers of each item of the uniform are issued so that a man can always appear in clean working rig, and as he is expected to do so, properly equipped laundries are fitted in the ships.

(c)   Harbour defence nets for all major units are provided, even in remote bases, and the Executive Officer's nightmare of having his ship bumped by rat-infested lighters is obviated. ...

229.   *Cunningham to the Chiefs of Staff*

[CAB 122/1140]   22 December 1943

Directive to the Special British Naval Mission to Washington.

It has been agreed in principle by the CCS that, for the war against Japan, the main effort of the United Nations shall be in the Pacific. The strategy will necessitate the British naval and amphibious forces operating in both the SEA and SWP theatres.

2. It has been agreed with the US, particularly in the early stages, the logistic support of the British Pacific Task Force would be a US naval commitment, excepting for the provision of personnel and naval stores necessary to maintain British equipment and services about which the US Navy would have no specialised knowledge.

3. The size of the British Pacific Task Force would be small initially but would be increased according to the phase reached in the war against Germany.

(i)   After European operations planned for mid-1944, certain vessels of escort carrier and cruiser types and downwards could be sent to reinforce the original force. Certain major fleet units could be sent if the British navy manning conditions permit.

(ii) After the defeat of Germany there would be a considerable increase which would also include the elements for amphibious assault.

Complementary with the elimination of Germany, the increase in both the SEA and SWP theatres would depend on the state of British naval manpower, and it should be borne in mind that this consideration would govern all negotiations with the US Navy Department.

4. The support of the forces in both areas will require a fleet train. It has been agreed by the CCS that the MWT and WSA shall be called on to provide the ships for this fleet train to the scale agreed by the First Sea Lord and COMINCH. The task of the British Naval Mission is to get agreement with [the] US Navy Department on this requirement and to submit it to [the] First Sea Lord and Admiral King for approval.

Thereafter the Controller and a representative of the MWT will probably visit Washington to arrange with the Americans how this requirement is to be provided.

5. In view of the above, the discussion on the Pacific must open with a decision on the area in which the naval task force and the amphibious assault 'lift' would be based; the main consideration being whether an Australian port or US bases in the SWP islands would be the main base area, with advance bases in the Solomon or Bismarck Islands area. The chief points governing this decision would be the fact that from 1944 onward the FAA would require the US Navy to provide considerable and increasing shore facilities for aircraft maintenance, and in 1945 similar shore facilities would be needed for the maintenance of landing ships and craft; the necessary installations for these purposes being placed on a supply route which would continue to be used during advances from 1944 onwards.

6. Complementary to this would be the consideration of the probable line of communication between the UK and the SWP area. Doubtless

for warships, landing craft and ammunition this would be via the Suez Canal, whereas for stores it might well be via the Panama Canal, and for personnel via the US.

7. Having reached some broad agreement on these points, it would be necessary to define what equipment and services the US would provide for the logistical support of the Pacific task force and amphibious assault 'lift', bearing in mind that until Germany is defeated, the British contribution would be a minimum because of the British manpower shortage.

8. Finally, agreement should be obtained on the quantity and types of ships that should be provided to form a British fleet train to be ready to support the British naval and amphibious forces that could be sent to the Indian Ocean and Pacific after the defeat of Germany. The latter might well be planned progressively to take over some of the services previously performed for the British by the US Navy. This agreement will be submitted to [the] First Sea Lord and COMINCH for approval on behalf of the CCS.

...

10. Early action by signal with the US Commander in the SWP area or with the Australian Commonwealth Navy Board as agreed with the US Navy Department, might be necessary before return to [the] Admiralty.

230.   *Mountbatten to Nimitz*[1]

[Nimitz 13/121]   24 December 1943

I am giving this letter to Captain Tufnell[2] who will be coming to your staff in Pearl Harbor as British Naval Intelligence Liaison Officer.

It would be of immense help to me and to Admiral Somerville, the C-in-C of our Eastern Fleet, if we could have early news of the experiences of your forces after any operations which have taken place in the Pacific.

I feel that a short summary of the forces which you have employed and the opposition put up by the Japanese together with the results, casualties

---

[1]VA Lord Louis Mountbatten (1900–79): son of Prince Louis of Battenberg, FSL 1914; *Lion* 1916; Capt 1937; Capt (D), 5DF, *Kelly* 1939–41; *Illustrious* June 1941; A/Cdre, Combined Ops, Oct 1941; VA & Chf, Combined Ops, Apr 1942; A/Adm & Supreme Cdr, SEAC, Oct 1943; Viceroy, Gov-Gen & Earl 1947–8; RA 1CS 1948; VA 1949; 4SL 1950; C-in-C, Med 1952; SACMED 1953; FSL 1954; AoF 1956; CDS 1959–65; assassinated, IRA 1979. I. McGeoch, *The Princely Sailor: Mountbatten of Burma* (London, 1996).

[2]Capt Tufnell: unidentified.

and any immediate lessons learned from a tactical point of view, is the sort of information which would be of immediate value.

After the attacks on the Gilbert Islands, the Japanese put out such fantastic claims of the damage to your Force that a true picture of what really happened would ease our minds considerably. At present we are very much in the dark.

If, therefore, you could allow Captain Tufnell to have such information, which he could signal to me after submitting it to you for your approval, I would be most grateful and we in this area would be better able to appreciate the difficulties and the effort required for any specific operations which we are planning from now on.

231.   *Capt L. E. Porter to Capt Charles Lambe*[1]

[CAB 122/1140]   8 January 1944

... We are more and more forming the impression that the Americans are lukewarm upon the question of British forces operating in the Pacific, [in] at any rate only the latter half of 1944, and I think this is the polite way of telling us so.

2. The reason for this may be Admiral King's well-known dislike of mixed forces and the fact that with their growing fleet and the large forces necessary for late 1944 they are stretched logistically.

3. Admiral Bieri seemed keen on the employment of this task force on raiding operations in the Indian Ocean, partly as a useful diversion, but I think mainly, as I gathered today when I cleared the signal with him, as this would be a most useful opportunity to work up the task force as a whole in actual operations before proceeding to an active combat zone in the Pacific. At the time of our first meeting I knew that PIGSTICK was off and he didn't, which made asking about the employment of the Eastern Fleet rather difficult. He envisaged the task force as supplementing PIGSTICK and produced this as one of the arguments for its later arrival.[2]

4. I pointed out our probable dislike of using heavy carriers in virtually restricted waters such as the Mediterranean and that they would be of no use to OVERLORD. Admiral Bieri's main preoccupation

---

[1]Capt Charles E. Lambe (1900–60): ent RN 1914; torpedo spist; pilot; *Vernon* i/c 1935; Capt 1937; *Dunedin* 1939–40; ADP, DDP & DP 1940–4; *Illustrious* 1944–5; RA & ACNS (A) & FO, Flying Trng 1947–9; RA 3 CV Sqdn 1949–51; VA 1950; FO (A), Home 1951–3; C-in-C, FE 1953–5; 2 SL 1955; C-in-C Med 1957; FSL May 1959; AoF 1960; ret, ill 1960.
[2]PIGSTICK: proposed descent on Burma coast.

however was Admiral Kirk's report on the forces that Admiral Ramsey apparently requires for OVERLORD and the size of this bill, to fill which Admiral Kirk suggests some American destroyers. It did not seem logical to Admiral Bieri that they may have to withdraw forces from the Pacific to augment European operations, quite apart from the disadvantage again of mixed forces, while we withdrew forces from Europe to work in the Pacific, which I gather they are not really pro- posing at this early stage. Admiral Noble gathered from Admiral King that this was the main reason for the proposal to postpone the arrival of the task force.

5. Finally Admiral Bieri said it was his understanding of his discussions with you and the First Sea Lord at SEXTANT that the arrival of the force would be about the middle of the year [1944] rather than in the Spring, and everything considered he regarded August a good date, or Autumn if some of the force are required for OVERLORD or ANVIL.[1]

232.   *Joint Planning Staff, Washington, to Joint Planning Staff, London*

[CAB 122/1140]   10 January 1944

... The means now available to the US Navy in the Pacific are in general only sufficient to support its own forces now present or projected. This is taken to mean that the SEXTANT promise that we need only provide specialist personnel with knowledge of equipment peculiar to our ships would not be implemented even for an eastern task force, as we would have to furnish our own civilian stores personnel at an Australian base. There is also no doubt that our main base must be in Australia.

2. Perhaps the actual wording used by Admiral McCormick in a recent minute would be useful to you[2] [:] 'British task forces arriving prior to the defeat of Germany in the Pacific Ocean should be prepared to maintain their own service of supply (food, clothing, stores) and be self-sustaining except that the US Navy will:

(a) share such excess facilities as it may have afloat or ashore in forward areas;

(b) initially maintain harbour defences, harbour control posts, a Naval base commander, and other minimum port facilities and personnel (the

---

[1]SEXTANT: conferences, Cairo, Tehran, Nov–Dec 1943.
[2]RA Lynde D. McCormick, US Navy: Pac F 1942–3; b/s & Batdiv cmds; trng unit, Pac 1945.

sharing and maintenance of facilities shall not prejudice the move-ment of such facilities forward if later developments so determine the necessity);

(c) render emergency and battle aid to British fleet units on the same basis as it renders like aid to US vessels in the same area;

(d) make available such airfields as may be under its control adjacent to the British fleet anchorage, for British carrier aircraft. The US Navy is not prepared to undertake the support of such planes, their routine over-haul, or maintenance by US personnel while on shore or afloat.

As to fuel, this requirement is pooled and can be handled by expand-ing present arrangements. This, in general, will require that tankers now supplying British fleet units be made available to the Pacific Ocean tank-ers' pool.'

233. *Memorandum by Admiral C. M. ('Savvy') Cooke, Jr, US Navy*

[RG 38]   24 January 1944

[There are] three undesirable aspects:

1. We are not in a position to reject the offer of the use of British fleet units in the Pacific without very bad reactions against our continued building program.
2. If we send them down there without improving their AA, their useful-ness will be impaired, and if they are sent into forward combat areas, probable damage will add to the load on our repair facilities.
3. If we undertake to improve their AA armament, we would throw workloads on our Navy Yards that we would prefer to avoid.

234. *King to Noble*

[RG 38]   25 January 1944

I cannot agree to the dispatch of any British forces to the Pacific until the naval requirements of OVERLORD and ANVIL are firmly established and fully met.

With regard to the Admiralty's statement that there are no profit-able targets in the Indian Ocean for such a task force, I submit that if it is aggressively employed in that area against Japanese airfields, port installations, shipping concentrations, and oil installations, which it can reach, the threat will tie down a very material number of Japanese air-craft and contribute more to the war in the Pacific than if the task force was moved at this time into that Area. It would also provide training and an opportunity to measure the effectiveness of these carriers against Japanese shore-based air which any British task force must eventually face when it comes into the Pacific. I feel that it is essential to maintain pressure of this sort against the Japanese in the Indian Ocean ... [The British need to] augment the close-in AA batteries of these ships, which are considerably below the standards we believe necessary for operations in the Pacific.

235. *Noble to Cunningham*

[CAB 122/1140]   25 January 1944

...

3. King's remarks fall into line with his general criticisms of our failure to achieve results in the Indian Ocean-Burma area.

4. I have just found out that there is a strong under-current of similar thought in the Pacific Fleet, criticising what they call our lack of effort in the East generally.

5. Yesterday I had a frank discussion with King on this subject which brought out the fact that this is, in truth, the opinion generally held throughout the [US] Navy, if not by the other services. King added that he had expressed himself in this sense to the late Admiral Pound on more than one occasion.

236. *Nimitz to King*

[RG 38]   31 January 1944

...

2. The force described would constitute a valuable augmentation of available naval strength in the Pacific and the logistic difficulties involved can be overcome.

...

4. It is considered that this force would contribute most effectively to the prosecution of the war against Japan by vigorous operations in the Indian Ocean including attacks on vulnerable and vital objectives in Java and Sumatra. Such operations would inflict damage on enemy forces and on the resources upon which they depend, would extend the pressure on the enemy defensive perimeter, and would reduce his capacity simultaneously to resist the advance of our forces through the Central Pacific and along the New Guinea Coast.

...

5. If the British Task Force is sent into the Pacific, it is recommended that it be placed under the command of CINCPOA. It is contemplated that it would then be assigned to the 3rd Fleet until it becomes desirable or expedient to assign it otherwise.

237. *Nimitz to Mountbatten*

[Nimitz 13/121]   26 February 1944

It is a pleasure to have with us Captain Tufnell who arrived today and gave me your letter of 24 December 1943 [no. 235].

You may be assured that we shall give him full information such as you have requested, and will provide facilities for his passing the information to you.

Our recent operations in the Gilberts, Marshalls, Carolines, Marianas have had some considerable degree of success while our losses have been very slight. The extravagant claims made by Japanese spokesmen as to damage inflicted upon us are apparently for propaganda or face-saving purposes.

238. *Memorandum for King by Cooke*

[RG 38]   [n.d., spring 1944]

British Proposals to send CTF to Pacific in April 1944.

...

6. ... Now they propose to move out the only weapon [Eastern Fleet] they have which could tie down Japanese airfields. We already see the Japanese moving aircraft from the Netherlands East Indies to the Marshalls. An aggressive carrier force properly used in the Indian Ocean could find effective targets.

239. *Vice Admiral Denis Boyd to Admiral C.E. Kennedy-Purvis*[1]

[ADM 205/36]   2 May 1944

---

[1]RA Denis Boyd: Capt 1931; Capt (D), 4 DF 1936; *Vernon* i/c 1938; *Illustrious* 1940; A/ RA (A), Med F Apr 1941; RA July 1941; RA (A), EF 1942; 5 SL & Chf, Naval Air Eqpt 1943; VA June 1944; Adm (A) June 1945; C-in-C, BPF June 1946.

Adm Charles E. Kennedy-Purvis (d May 1946): Capt 1921; RA 1933; Pres, RNC, Greenwich 1938; Asst to DCNS (A. Cunningham) 1938; C-in-C NAWI Apr 1940; DFSL 1942.

Tactical experience of operating large numbers of aircraft.

1. Our own experience is negative in that we have never been able to fly off a large strike.

    Taranto: two ranges of 10.
    Other Mediterranean strikes; maximum of 15 (larger than Taranto as L. R. tanks were not fitted)
    North Africa: maximum of 15.

TUNGSTEN: *Victorious*: two ranges of 12 + 10 fighters each team.
           Furious: two ranges of 10.
COCKPIT: *Illustrious*: 17 + 13 fighters.
           (*Saratoga*: 29 + 24 fighters).[1]

2. The US experience was however positive at Midway, Coral Sea and Bismarcks. It was clear that large strikes were overwhelming and small strikes of little value such as their mis-timed and unco-ordinated torpedo attacks which resulted in 40 being shot down out of 44 without apparent results, and the Japanese attacks on *North Carolina* and *Enterprise*.

3. Since they [the US Navy] have rebuilt their carrier fleet they have carried out many operations such as Rabaul, Marshalls, Gilberts, Truk and New Guinea, in each of which they have developed the maximum effort from every large carrier using smaller carriers only for defence. In none of the operations could they have developed such strength without the use of their open hangars and deck edge lifts (*vide* reports from Naval Observer).

4. For the attack on Guadalcanal and Tulagi, the *Hornet*, *Wasp* and *Saratoga* made over 250 sorties each in the course of the day. Our best effort in comparison was 68 sorties from *Indomitable* on the first day of the attack on Diego Suarez. On neither occasion were large strikes used and the *Hornet* and *Wasp* were of less tonnage than *Indomitable* but being built for the efficient operation of air-craft as their primary function they were able to achieve this remark-able performance. It would have been quite out of the question, with the best will in the world, to have done more than about 120 sor-ties from *Indomitable* in one day (had the number of aircraft car-ried permitted it) owing to delays in striking down, stowing and

---

[1]TUNGSTEN: CV op v *Tirpitz* 3 Apr 1944, put out of action for 3 months.
COCKPIT: CV op, Sumatra, EF (Adm Somerville), 16–19 Apr 1944.

re-ranging, with our arrangements of lifts and hangar. Quite apart from the inability to develop the maximum single impact against the enemy the proposed design [of 1943 Fleet Carriers] imposes a delay in operation of aircraft which reduces the offensive and defensive value of the ship.

5.   TUNGSTEN: The experience of Operation TUNGSTEN shows the ability to flow off the strike in one bite is indeed a requirement as it will be recalled in planning this Operation, the Admiralty staff urged that the striking aircraft should be flown off to strike in one formation, but that on reviewing the capabilities of the Carriers concerned, it was realised that this was not possible, with the result that the attack was carried out in two waves, separated by an interval of one hour. Had there been any available fighter opposition, the time lost might well have made a second strike abortive. It is to be noted that with two large carriers and four CVEs a force of only 21 strike aircraft only, plus defence could be flown off on each range. A comparable effort in one strike could have been achieved by one 'Essex' class and two CVEs.

240.   King to General MacArthur

[Op Arch, King 4]   Pearl Harbor,
                                                    21 July 1944

... an account of the discussions that took place in London in June between the US [JCS] and the British COS on the subject of full British participation in the war in the Pacific.

These discussions were general in character, and involved no commitments or decisions. The discussions were particularly sought by the British in order that they could plan for the future, with particular regard to basing facilities. The British consider that the expansion of military facilities in India must be limited. They recognise the barren prospects of logistic support on the West Coast of Australia. They appear to feel, therefore, that it will be necessary for them to make use of basing capacity on the Australian East Coast.

As you probably already know, the British are now giving special consideration to operations through the Arafura-Banda Sea Area directed at Amboina, and later against Borneo. They had previously given special thought to an advance down through the Strait of Malacca toward Singapore, but now appear to have given up this questionable project.

The US [JCS] request the British to submit concrete proposals as to British operations – objectives, forces involved, timing, and specific supporting measures (logistics). In this connection the British may propose certain extensions in the South East Asia Theater to include most of the Netherlands East Indies, in order to provide for British operations in that area after the South West Pacific forces have become established in the Philippines.

Major reorientation of the British effort, with particular relation to amphibious resources, cannot take place until after the conclusion of the European war. By that time we hope you can be at least well on the way to the establishment of a firm foothold in the Philippines. We did, it is true, manage to get six British combat loaders moving your way in the immediate future to meet some of your urgent needs.

241.   *Noble to King*

[RG 38]   22 July 1944

... the ability of the British to play an active part at an early date in the war against Japan depends on whether British needs of certain types of Landing Ships and craft can be met from US production.

2. If we rely on British and Canadian construction only, we shall only be able to provide two Naval assault forces each lifting one division by autumn 1945, and a further Naval assault force lifting one division by spring 1946. If, however, you agree to provide the ships and craft shown ... dates could be advanced to May 1945 and September 1945 respectively. ...

242.   *Memorandum by Cunningham*

[CAB 122/1140]   26 July 1944

*Dispatch of a British Submarine Force to operate
from Freemantle under US Naval Command.*

The number of British submarines now available for the war against Japan now exceeds that which can usefully be operated against targets in the Malacca Strait.

2. In order to operate the additional submarines against Japanese shipping in the South China and Java Seas, the Admiralty has made arrangements with COMINCH for a force, consisting of three 'T' class, six 'S' class submarines and the Depot Ship *Maidstone*, to be based at Freemantle. The final composition of the force will be adjusted in the light of experience.

...

4. ...the Admiralty has ... agreed to place this submarine force under the operational control of the Commander, South West Pacific. This unity of command is necessary to ensure complete co-ordination of effort against the enemy and to protect Allied units from chance encounter with other Allied submarines and aircraft.[1]

243. *Leahy: Diary*

[LC, Leahy]   Hawaii,
                                                         29 July 1944

... [Leahy believed] that Japan can be forced to accept our terms of surrender by the use of sea and air power without any invasion of the Japanese homeland.

244. *King to Stark and Hewitt*

[SPD 244]   16 August 1944

Transfer of Assault Craft from European Waters to the Pacific.

1. Availability of amphibious assault craft is the controlling factor at present in PACIFIC operations. If adequate amphibious lift were available now, operations would proceed at a much faster pace. Prospects are that the present shortage will be further aggravated by slippage in new construction.
2. Obviously it is necessary, in order to continue with our war in the Pacific and quicken the pace if possible, to make maximum use of all amphibious assault craft that can be made available. Therefore, it is highly desirable that as many of these craft as practicable, now in European or Mediterranean waters, be transferred to the Pacific as early after completion of contemplated amphibious operations as is compatible with assured success of the operations.
3. Following is the total of amphibious assault craft, other than shipborne types, now in European or Mediterranean waters.
    APA 7; AKA 7; XAP 6; LST 232 less 35 that may be transferred to the British = 197; LCI (L) 189 less 52 that may be transferred to the British = 137; LCT 94; LCT (6) 174; AGC 4.

---

[1] VA Thomas C. Kinkaid, US Navy.

...

5. It is desired that COMNAVEU and COMNAVNAW keep constantly in mind the necessity of releasing subject craft promptly as they become available for release, and that they notify COMINCH when it appears that any units are no longer required. Preference of types in the order listed is:

    APA; AKA; LST; AGC; XAP; LCT; LCI (L).

6. In general accordance with the foregoing, it is desired that COM-NAVEU and COMNAVNAW proceed with detailed plans, coordinating with British authorities and their commanders concerned. COMNAVNAW should inform COMNAVEU as well as COMINCH of the craft he is prepared to release in order that COMNAVEU may have full information at hand in coordinating with the Admiralty. ...

245. *King to Marshall*

[Op Arch, King 4]   17 August 1944

Naval Command in the South West Pacific Area.

1. ... the present C-in-C, British Eastern Fleet, is Admiral [Sir] Bruce Fraser, who would be 'automatically' senior to Vice Admiral Kinkaid, now commanding 7th Fleet under General MacArthur. Making Kinkaid an admiral would not remedy the seniority situation.

2. I think we can all agree – and that MacArthur will concur – that it is preferable that the senior naval commander in the SWPA should be US. On this premise I have to propose that Admiral Royall E. Ingersoll (now C-in-C Atlantic Fleet) be sent out – at the appropriate time – to relieve Kinkaid. Ingersoll's seniority date as admiral is 1 July 1942 whereas Fraser's is at least some months later. Ingersoll, as you know, is an outstanding officer in every way.[1]

---

[1]Adm Royall E. Ingersoll, US Navy: USNA 1905; Naval Operations, 1917–18; ONI; Capt, Dir, WPD 1935–8; mission to UK 1938; RA 1938; Asst CNO 1940; CoS, Atl F (King) 1941; VA & Cdr, Atl F, Jan 1942; Adm July 1942.

246. *Memorandum for Admiral Duncan, US Navy,*
by Captain M. M. Dupre, Jr, US Navy[1]

[RG 38]   18 August 1944

British Participation in Far Eastern Strategy.

[The British and the Dutch should regain their own territories].

Advantages:

(a) Maintains our own forces' homogeneity and under our close control.
(b) Avoids the complication of combined operations.
(c) Puts the British and the Dutch on their own logistically, and stops that ever-increasing drain on our own resources.
(d) Gives the British and the Dutch definite incentives not only to stay in the war but to keep the heat on. (If they want their pre-war territories back, it is up to them to do something about it).
(e) Avoids criticism from our own people that our armed forces are supporting British, Dutch and French Imperialism.

Disadvantages:

(a) Perhaps does not make as full use of British battleships and aircraft carriers as we might.
(b) Gives the British first access to and thus possible control of such critical raw materials as rubber, tin and petroleum that may be found available in the Netherlands East Indies, Malaya and French Indo-China.

Advantages outweigh disadvantages.

247. *Joint Chiefs of Staff: 173rd Meeting*

[RG 218/196]   8 September 1944

...

2. British Participation in the War against Japan.

Admiral Leahy reviewed the fact that that in CCS452/18 [not reproduced] the British COS proposed a British fleet being employed under US command in the main operations against Japan, or alternatively that a TF of British, Australian and New Zealand land, sea and air forces be

---

[1] Adm Duncan, US Navy: unidentified.
Capt. M. M. Dupre, US Navy: unidentified.

formed to operate under the SAC, South West Pacific Area. The JSPs have reported on these proposals in JCS 992/3 [not reproduced].

Admiral Leahy said that the planners' recommendations open up the question of whether any assistance will be given by the British in the face of the questions which it is proposed to direct to them. He felt that it was understood that the British will render the maximum possible assistance after the war with Germany is over. He recommended that their offer of a fleet be accepted with alacrity and without conditions. This acceptance will put the offer of British forces on record. The British may well be expected to make qualifying demands later, which can then be discussed, but we should accept this proposal before there is any change of mind. He recommended that a memorandum be presented to the CCS accepting the British proposal in paragraph 10 of CCS 452/18 [not reproduced] which would note that this proposal would still enable the British Fleet to be well placed to reinforce the US Pacific Fleet if this should later be desired.

General Marshall recommended that the memorandum to the CCS should be presented as suggested by Admiral Leahy. The matter could be discussed at OCTAGON, where the US COS may state their assumption that the assignment of British Empire TF to the SWPA will not interfere with General MacArthur's plans to include operations against Luzon. The acceptance of the proposal will thus be protected by commitment for the record. The British offer should be accepted now and problems of logistical support may be brought up later.

The JCS:

Agreed to reply to the British proposals in paragraphs 9 and 10 of CCS 452/18 as follows:

'The US COS accept the British proposal in CCS 452/18 for the formation of a British Empire TF under a British commander, consisting of British, Australian and New Zealand land, sea and air forces to operate in the South West Pacific Area under General MacArthur's supreme command. It is noted that this will enable the British fleet to be well placed to reinforce the US Pacific Fleet if this should later be desired.'

248.   *Joint Chiefs of Staff: Meeting 175*

[RG 318/196]   13 September 1944

...

6. *British Participation in the War against Japan.*

Admiral Leahy said that JCS 9992/6 is a report by the JSP, prepared on their own initiative, as a formal expression of the views of the US

COS on the British preference for the employment of the British Fleet in the main operations against Japan. He felt that the British should be informed immediately that the US COS would be pleased to have the assistance of any force that they could provide in the Pacific. The necessary details, including its size and maintenance, could be discussed later. He felt that the British had very likely intended that such a force would be used in connection with their operations, presumably against Bangkok, Rangoon, Singapore and beyond. He felt that the last sentence of the second paragraph might give them the impression that their forces were not desired, especially in regard to the mention of being self-supporting logistically.

General Marshall said that Admiral Cunningham had indicated to the Prime Minister that the TF would consist of some 50 vessels instead of approximately 100 that had been previously indicated and except for major repairs could maintain itself independently for six to eight months. ... After further discussion,

The JCS:

Approved the draft memorandum proposed by General Marshall, as amended during discussion, and directed that it be presented to the CCS (subsequently circulated as CCS 452/27) [not reproduced].

249. *Memorandum by Capt M. M. Dupre, Jr, US Navy,*
for Assistant Chief of Staff (Plans)

[RG 38]   18 September 1944

... We may rest assured that they [the British] will not be backward in their demands for compensation, territorial or otherwise, for their token participation when the war is over. ...

250. *Movement of a British Fleet to the Pacific*

[ADM 205/39]   24 October 1944

1. *Command and Administration of the BPF.*

The operations to be carried out could not be decided before Admiral Fraser had visited Admiral Nimitz at Pearl Harbor. The First Sea Lord stated that it would be important when talking to Admiral Nimitz to stress that the War Cabinet would insist on the BPF taking part in the main operations against the islands of Japan. Subject to this requirement, it would probably be as well for the fleet to operate initially in the South West Pacific theatre. ...

251.   *Cunningham to Fraser*

[NMM, Fraser 20]   11 November 1944

The Prime Minister has now sent to Mr Curtin a message on the command, movements, building up and maintenance of the British Pacific Fleet in which the following points are made:[1]

(a) Your appointment in command.
(b) Your intended early arrival in Australia for discussion with Mr Curtin on maintenance of Fleet and that you would give him date of arrival.
(c) Your intended visit to Nimitz at Pearl Harbor on conclusion of talks in Australia.

2.   The following additional information was included:

(a) Fleet will operate under control of Nimitz.
(b) Numerical strength of Fleet which will arrive in Australia towards end of December and total in July 1945 including number of RAN and RNZN ships. AM 012006 refers [not reproduced].

3. *Administration in Australia.*

(a) VA (Q) to be your and Admiralty's permanent representative at Melbourne and to work in close association with ACNB.
(b) He will communicate with Australian Government through Minister of Navy.
(c) He is administrative authority for RN Personnel on shore in Australia.
(d) Under him would be FONA and Commodore in command of *Golden Hind* at Sydney (NSM).[2]

4. Following has been made to C-in-C US Fleet:

You have no doubt already been informed by Admiral Somerville of the strength and composition of the British Fleet which will arrive in the Pacific in January and build up during the first six months of 1945. Admiral Fraser, the C-in-C of the British Pacific Fleet, will visit Australia in near future to discuss administrative arrangements with Australian Authorities, to make best arrangements regarding a forward Base for his Fleet and for operating in best way in support of US Pacific Fleet. I suggest Admiral Fraser should visit Admiral Nimitz about mid-December at Pearl Harbor

---

[1]Rt Hon John Curtin (1885–1945): Aus industrialist, Trade Union Ldr; Lab MP 1928; Ldr, 1935; PM 1941–5.
[2]*Golden Hind*: RN barracks, Sydney, 1944–5.

and discuss all relevant questions. If you agree it is requested that you will inform Admiral Nimitz of strength and build up of BPF and ask him if Admiral Fraser's visit will be convenient. I will then instruct Admiral Fraser to make detailed arrangements directly with Admiral Nimitz.

252. *King to Cunningham*

[NMM, Fraser 20]   12 November 1944

I note that your 110146A [above], confirmed by your 101700A [not reproduced], designates Admiral Fraser as the 'C-in-C of the BPF'. This action sets up two C-in-Cs in the Pacific, which is an action not carried out in any other Naval Area or Theater of action, notably in the Mediterranean and in British Home Waters.

2. At Quebec the agreement was 'that the method of employment of the British Fleet in these main operations in the Pacific would be decided from time to time in accordance with the prevailing circumstances'. The method of employment that appears to be contemplated by the command set up of your despatch is, in my opinion, not workable.

3. As indicated in the Memorandum to Admiral Somerville of 11 November, I contemplate initial employment of British Fleet Units under Vice Admiral Kinkaid, the Allied Commander of Naval Forces in SWPA. Subsequently employment to be under Admiral Nimitz and/or Vice Admiral Kinkaid as operations may indicate. To accomplish this employment I agree that a Commander (not a C-in-C) of the BPF can be set up in East Asia from which British units can pass for operational control to Nimitz or Kinkaid when and as the use of forward bases can be made available. We have not as yet arranged for the establishment of such forward bases. The designation of Admiral Fraser for the duty given in this paragraph is wholly acceptable to me. I am taking up with Admiral Nimitz the question as to the best time for Admiral Fraser's visit to Pearl Harbor.

253. *Captain Wheeler, US Navy, to Nimitz*[1]

[Nimitz 13/121]   Colombo,
13 November 1944

...

Admiral Fraser arrived here on 10 November and told me quite frankly that owing to recent developments in the Philippines and the consequent

---

[1]Capt C. J. Wheeler, US Navy (b 1895): USNA 1916; CO *Waters* 1931–4; CO *Mobile* 1943–4; NLO, BPF 1944–5; NWC 1946; RA & ret 1948.

narrowing of the combat area, it appeared to him that due to his orders complications might arise in the matter of command in the case of joint operations. He spoke of two possible alternatives, one consisting of setting up his own HQ on shore, with a more junior Flag Officer in command of the British Task Force and the other alternative of working within General MacArthur's command.

He is, of course, aware of Admiral King's opposition to joint operations but visualizes the possibility that if both fleets operate in the Pacific unforeseen developments might cause the two fleets to converge unless they are widely separated initially.

...

Entirely apart from the subject of command, I believe the strongest argument arguing against joint operations, at least for the present, is the fact that the British Fleet is not sufficiently trained to keep up with the standard of performance maintained in our fleet, either in combat operations or refuelling at sea. The obvious solution therefore, as Admiral King has already stated, is to assign them a special objective where they can operate more or less independently of our principal naval forces.

I made a point of stressing to Admiral Fraser, Admiral King's insistence that the British Fleet in the Pacific must be self-supporting in whatever area it operated [in]. He said that was his intention but come what may, it appeared to him that the BPF might have to depend on us to a certain extent in the matter of supplies. Of course, the truth of the matter is, that the British are years behind us in the organization and administration of a fleet train, and furthermore until the Torres Strait or Netherlands East Indies Barrier are opened up, the distances from their sources of supply (except, of course, provisions which can be obtained in Australia) will be staggering.

All of this emphasises the obvious fact that the logical theater of operations for the British Fleet is in the Burma-Malaya-Netherlands East Indies area, but it has taken me less than three weeks to arrive at the conclusion that with the exception of 'hit and run raids' and occasional minor amphibious operations, nothing of any consequence is going to be accomplished here until at least nine months after the war in Europe is over. In that connection Admiral Fraser told me that the Admiralty is opposed to Admiral Mountbatten's plan for the capture of Mergui or Hastings Bay next spring, as the Admiralty feels it will be too difficult to maintain satisfactory communications with the forces of occupation in either place during the monsoon. I know that Admiral Mountbatten will be very disappointed to give up that operation as he was most enthusiastic about it – in fact so much so that when he heard that Admiral King had spoken to me of his particular interest in it, he asked me to send the despatch regarding it, which I recently sent to you and Admiral King.

...

254. *Somerville to Cunningham*

[NMM, Fraser 20]   13 November 1944

[Text of message from King to Somerville].

I assume that, in accordance with the Prime Minister's views as expressed at OCTAGON and the terms of the original offer by the British COS in the matter these forces will be operating under US Command. It is required therefore that they be directed as they arrive in the Pacific to report to me for assignment. It is my present intention to employ them initially under 7th Fleet Command with the view of facilitating basing arrangements and developing operational procedures during the build-up period. Subsequently as future operations require, their employment will be in the SWPA under General MacArthur or in the Pacific Ocean areas under Admiral Nimitz.

255. *Somerville to Cunningham*

[NMM, Fraser 20]   13 November 1944

Should be grateful for your views on following matters which arise from COMINCH's 12137 and my 13435 [above]:
  2. Are you willing that Fleet should be under

(a)   King
(b)   Nimitz and/or MacArthur
(c)   Nimitz only [?].

I understand from General Lumsden that MacArthur would welcome dealing directly with British Admiral and not through King.[1]
  3. Have you any stipulations about British forces being employed

(a)   As unit attached to American task forces on arrival
(b)   As a number of task forces attached to US Fleets

---

[1]Gen Sir Herbert Lumsden: Royal Artillery; 2nd Lt 1916; W Front 1916–18; Capt 1925; Maj 1931; staff appts; Lt Col 1938; Brig 1940; PM's personal reprv, MacArthur's staff; killed on *New Mexico* 6 Jan 1945, Philippine landings. (Adm Fraser escaped unhurt).

(c) On build-up being completed, as separate force under Nimitz or MacArthur but otherwise under British Admiral [?].

4. To what extent do you consider Fleet should have a say in planning and execution of operations in which British Naval Task Forces take part [?].

256. *Cunningham to Somerville*

[NMM, Fraser 20]   15 November 1944

...

2. I consider that the proposed visits by Fraser to both MacArthur and Nimitz will of themselves clear up the many points of detail concerning the command and operation of the BPF. I am not anxious to prejudice these visits by a prior discussion with COMINCH.

3. In fulfilment of the OCTAGON decisions, it is expected that Fraser will serve under Nimitz and under MacArthur if the British Fleet is detached by Nimitz to serve in the SWPA. Fraser may detach forces to serve under Kinkaid or other US commander senior to the British officers concerned. But it should be clearly understood that Fraser is directly under Nimitz or, from time to time, MacArthur, and not under any other American naval or military commander. On the other hand in operations for which the larger part of the Naval Force will be British I should expect the Naval Command to be given to a British Admiral of suitable seniority just as the command of the operation DRAGOON was given to Hewitt. In normal circumstances I do not consider there need be any change from the existing practice that in a mixed force British and American officers take command and precedence by their rank and seniority.

4. From the administrative and supply point of view it will be easier to operate the British Fleet in complete units. In this way the best use will be made of the Fleet Train and the balance of the Fleet will not be upset. I do not preclude the detachment of one or two ships to complete an American force for a period during which those ships could be self-supporting. Of the alternatives in your paragraph 3, (a) and (c) are preferable; (b) is undesirable for any extended period.

5. In order that Fraser may accept his responsibility to the Admiralty and to the British and Dominion Governments for the operations of British ships I should expect him to be kept fully informed of plans and

operations in which his ships will take part. Only so could he express his opinion that a British ship should or should not be employed on any particular service. In order to give effect to this it may be found necessary for him to maintain representatives at the Headquarters of Nimitz and MacArthur. That, however, can await the outcome of Fraser's talk with Nimitz.

257. *Cunningham to King*

[NMM, Fraser 20]   15 November 1944

...

2. I can confirm that, in accordance with the Prime Minister's views expressed at OCTAGON and the terms of the original offer by the British COS, British naval forces in the Pacific will operate under the command of Admiral Nimitz or from time to time as circumstances dictate under General MacArthur.

3. For administrative and logistic purposes and to retain their entity as a balanced force it is desirable for British units normally to operate as one force, but this does not preclude detachments being made from one theatre to the other to meet operational requirements.

4. I think some misconception may have arisen due to the difference between British and American interpretations of the title 'C-in-C'. Admiral Fraser will be the C-in-C of the British Fleet operating in the Pacific with its supporting organisation both ashore and afloat. This title in no way implies that he has operational control of the area nor of any of the forces in it but is warranted by British naval custom, and by the size and importance of his command. It should not, I feel, cause confusion or lead to misunderstanding regarding the C's-in-C of US theatres of operations or the Commanders of US Fleets.

5. The British Fleet and its C-in-C will doubtless be given a convenient local title and number by Admiral Nimitz, and I suggest that this and details of command as, for example, the employment of certain units under Vice Admiral Kinkaid, might be settled by Admiral Fraser as my representative when discussing basing arrangements and operational arrangements with Admiral Nimitz and General MacArthur.

6. As you request, forces will be directed to report to you on arrival in the Pacific. I very much hope that it will be practicable for Admiral Fraser to pay his visit to Admiral Nimitz before the first units arrive, as many details will require settling if active participation in operations is not to be delayed.

258.   *Cunningham to Fraser, repeated to Somerville*

[NMM, Fraser 20]   [n.d., but probably 15 November 1944]

Text of reply from Admiral King:

Although I should prefer [otherwise] in [light] of your despatch of 15th I accept title of C-in-C BPF for Admiral Fraser for purposes within British Force which you have outlined.

2. For operations with US Forces he or such other Commander as may be designated will be assigned an appropriate title and number by the Fleet Commander under whom operating.

3. I agree that for administrative[,] logistical and other purposes it is desirable for British Units to operate as one force when practicable.

4. I am unable to confirm a date for Admiral Fraser's visit to Admiral Nimitz but shall do so at an early date.

259.   *JCS to President Roosevelt*

[PSF 7]   18 November 1944

Existing and prospective demands for cargo shipping are beyond the prospective allocations to the War and Navy Departments. A reassignment of shipping must be sought whereby existing American and British resources can be applied more effectively to the military effort.

The increased tempo of operations in the Pacific together with increasing demands for shipping to handle civilian supplies for occupied countries has produced deficits in sailings necessary to support the military effort during coming months. The most recent request for additional shipping to support the movement of more tonnage to Siberia on Russia's account had accentuated these deficits to a degree which requires a decision on the highest level as to the use of American bottoms, and a request to the UK for other shipping to support American resources.

...

It is essential, if the war against our enemies is to be driven home with all the force at our command, that all of the war powers available to the Executive be used to man the yards of the Maritime Commission with due regard for other important military programs, and that urgent representations be made to the British Government to secure the additional assistance needed. ...

260. *Memorandum by Vice Admiral R. S Edwards, US Navy*

[Op Arch, King 4]   23 November 1944

Canadian Naval Participation in the Pacific War.

1. Rear Admiral Reid tells me that plans for the employment of Canadian vessels are still in the stage of staff consideration.[1] The Naval Staff has not yet made any concrete suggestion to the Canadian Government.
2. At the present time the Naval Staff is tentatively considering the idea that Canadian vessels that may be assigned to the Pacific will be placed in Admiral Fraser's command, and will be considered as part of the British forces for operational control, supply and repair.
3. He offered the suggestion that they had a number of corvettes and escort craft which would be available after the defeat of Germany, which he thought the Canadian Government would be glad to put at our disposal for escort work at advanced bases if you wanted them. He is, however, of the opinion that because of similarities in supplies and repair parts, it would be best for Canadian and British ships to work together from bases controlled by the British.
4. Rear Admiral Reid says that they expect to have two Light Fleet Carriers, two cruisers, and a number of destroyers and escort craft in the Canadian-manned forces for service in the Pacific. He thinks none of them will be ready before February.

261. *Nimitz to Fraser*

[RG 38]   25 November 1944

I concur strongly in your idea that operations of your force against Sumatra objectives this winter is more important than your early arrival in Pacific.

---

[1] RA Howard E. Reid, RCN (b 1895): ent RCN 1912; service in RN 1914–34; Dir Naval Ops & Trng 1934; CO, *Skeena, Fraser* 1936–8; NOIC, Halifax DY 1938–9; Capt Atl Coast 1939; DCNS Oct 1940; Cdre, Newfoundland 1942; RA, Canadian JSM, Washington 1943; VA, CNS 1946–8.

262. *Assignment of American Combat Aircraft to
the Royal Navy in 1945:
Result of Negotiations*

[ADM 116/5347]   28 November 1944

...

3. Negotiations with the Americans have been completed and the following table shows what they are prepared to release compared with the
numbers ultimately bid for: ...

First half of 1945	Bid	Final Assignment
Corsair	660	90/150
Hellcat	336	316
Avenger	348	80
Wildcat	45	150[1]

263. *King to Nimitz*

[Nimitz 13/117]   29 November 1944

To effect efficient employment [of] tankers in Pacific Ocean areas and
utilize world-wide sources of petroleum supply [it is] essential that providing these products be the responsibility of a single agency through
existing area operation organisations. ...

Your future requirements submitted via area petroleum office should
include increased quantity necessary for RN units. ANPB will be
responsible for delivery [of] these requirements by commercial tankers
into areas where RN will furnish sufficient oilers to service RN units.

264. *Admiralty to Fraser*

[NMM, Fraser 20]   6 December 1944

Prime Minister has pointed out that end of war in Europe will have significant effect on Far East forces. Need to provide higher standard of

---

[1]Chance Vought Corsair: US; 1940; 1 engine; 1 crew; 446mph; 6mg; 2×100lb bombs or 8 RP.
Grumman Hellcat: US; 1942; 1 engine; 1 crew; 376mph; 6mg.
Grumman Avenger; US; 1941; TB; 1 engine; 3 crew; 271mph; 5mg; 1 torpedo or 2000lbs
bombs or 8 RP.
Grumman Wildcat (FAA: Martlet): US; 1937; 1 engine; 1 crew; 328mph; 4mg; 2×100lb
bombs.

welfare to ensure high morale against Japanese and standards as near US as [British forces] can get. Especially leave [facilities?].

265. *King to Nimitz*

[NWC, King 7]   13 December 1944

Following for your information in connection [with] discussion with Admiral Fraser. At OCTAGON we received the assurance of the British COS that the British Fleet in the Pacific would be balanced and self-supporting. At OCTAGON and in subsequent communications I have pressed the British as to the necessity of their providing the supporting elements required for their combatant forces both shore based and afloat.

The suggestion has now been made by the British that we 'pool resources' in the Pacific. I do not agree with the use of this term in describing the manner in which the British and US forces will be supported. I desire it to be understood that the British Fleet shall be supported by British forces and that they should put into the Pacific such supporting elements as are required for the combatant forces sent into the theatre. This does not imply that US supporting elements cannot be used for the British nor that British cannot be used for the US. This will be done wholly at the discretion of the area commander.

The point I wish clearly made is that the term 'balanced and self-supporting' shall be realistic and not REPEAT not mere words. A good example lies in their preparations for the OVERLORD operation in which we provided the complete support afloat and ashore for US forces including repair, supply, manning and equipment of bases, etc. The British likewise made provision for their forces. These provisions having been made, allocation of facilities from one service to the other, as from time to time became necessary and feasible, followed.

266. *Nimitz to King*

[Nimitz 13/117]   13 December 1944

I do not need Paul Revere (with three lanterns) to tell me the British are coming. ...

I enclose a copy of 'Agenda for Conference with C-in-C, BPF' [not reproduced], which is self-explanatory. I will keep the discussions on an exploratory bases and will make no commitments beyond directives you have already issued.

I will encourage operations against Japanese-held oil installations in Sumatra, which lies within the British areas. I will encourage any operations which they propose against objectives in the SWPA, but will of course expect such operations to be referred to, and controlled by, C-in-C, SWPA if and when the BPF is [allocated?] to Kinkaid's fleet for operations.

267.   *Brief for C-in-C British Pacific Fleet (copy to CINCPAC)*

[NMM, Fraser 20]   [n.d., December 1944]

Subjects for Discussion at Pearl Harbor
Part I: Strategic Function of BPF
Method of Operation of BPF

There are two possibilities:
(a) Separate American and British Strategic Areas
Advantages –

(i) Full operational control by C-in-C BPF.
(ii) Easier for the British Fleet to operate.

Disadvantages –

(i) BPF can hardly expect to get anything but an insignificant area.
(ii) We are not entirely self-supporting as regards shore facilities and harbour defences.
(iii) It is uneconomical in overall Naval power.

(b) Combined American-British Strategic Areas

In this case the British Fleet would operate as a tactical unit on special missions as designated by American High Command.
Such missions might be for example:

(i) A Strategic Mission –

(for example, operating from Manila to cut the Japanese North-South supply route in the South China Sea)

combined with

(ii) A series of Specific Operations –

(for example, a Highball or XE attack on the Japanese Fleet).

1. I favour alternative (b) and it is particularly desired that the British Fleet should operate as near the heart of the enemy as possible. At the

same time I want to emphasise that it is placed unreservedly at the disposal of the American Command for the purpose of bringing the war to a conclusion at the earliest possible moment.

Part II: Advanced Base for BPF

Fleet Base

The Admiralty policy has been to provide an operating force and a fleet train adequate to support it at an advanced base. Balanced components of the force and its train are proceeding to the Pacific now and the remainder should have arrived and be deployed by July.

2. The aim is to operate, fully self-supporting, from an advanced base as soon as possible and not call upon the Americans for any support.

3. The first force to arrive and be ready to operate in an advanced area early in March [1945], will be balanced:

(a) Operating force of two Battleships, four Carriers, five Light Cruisers, three Destroyer Flotillas.

(b) Fleet Train of two Repair Ships, one Aircraft Repair Ship, six Fleet Attendant Tankers, one Air Components Repair Ship, one Air Stores Issuing Ship, two Hospital Ships, about 15 Ammunition and Store Ships.

(c) Mobile Naval Air Base.

4. It may be, however, that the various later components of the BPF will not arrive in precisely the planned order and that for some time before the arrival of the whole force in July, parts of it may be unbalanced. (This seems particularly likely in the case of the Shore-based facilities). In this case it may be necessary to ask temporarily for American assistance.

5. No provision has been made by the Admiralty for the defence of advanced bases in the Pacific other than ship-borne defences.

6. Consequently the first advanced base from which the BPF operates would most conveniently be one also used by the US Navy.

7. We would like to know now what base this will be, in order that we may arrange for the necessary British shore-based facilities.

Submarine Base

8. One Flotilla of British Submarines (10 boats) is already operating in the Pacific from Fremantle under CTF 71 (not under BPF). Depot ship *Maidstone*.

9. A second Flotilla (depot ship *Adamant*) can sail for a Pacific Base from Ceylon in January [1945] and a further Flotilla (Accommodation

ship *Oranje*) is due to arrive in the Pacific in March or April. These two Flotillas will form part of the BPF.

10. It is suggested that these three Flotillas should be operated by the American Admiral (Submarines) from an advanced base or bases in the Pacific moving as follows:

(a) The *Maidstone* Flotilla moving forward with CTF 71.

(b) The *Adamant* Flotilla sailing from their present location (Ceylon) in time to join up with CT F 71.

(c) The *Oranje* Flotilla when they are ready.

11. Advanced base will be ready for Submarines by mid-February. If not, we must delay the sailing of *Adamant* and her Flotilla.

12. *Base for Midget Submarines*

The following considerations govern the choice of a base for the Midget Submarines –

(a) There are very few of them (only six).

(b) The chances of getting away after an attack are small.

Consequently they should be used only against the most important targets, i.e., main units.

(c) Their training tends to be critical.

(d) It takes a long time to launch an operation with them.

Consequently they are best employed against a static target (e.g., floating dock or damaged main unit).

(e) Their own range is limited (60 miles approximately before attacking).

(f) They are towed by submarine.

Consequently a base from which the submarines can operate as near to the target as possible is desirable.

(g) They are carried in a depot ship (*Bonaventure*).

(h) They should train with the submarines they operate with.

Consequently the training base can be the submarines' own training base. This may be qualified by the fact that it is best for them to train in the same climatic conditions as those in which they will be operating.

13. *Bonaventure* and her six XE craft are expected out in March and a decision in due course is required on the choice of their training and operational bases.

Part III: Position of C-in-C BPF and Staff.

The broad alternatives are:

(A) At Sydney where C-in-C would be primarily an Administrative authority supplying and repairing the Fleet and sending it forward to the operating area. (VA(Q) already carries out the function as C-in-C's representative at Melbourne).

(B) At an advanced base, where C-in-C would be either:

(a) an advanced administrative authority acting as a link between VA (Q) and the operating part of the Fleet. (RAFT should fulfil this function admirably).

(b) commanding the Fleet at sea in person in which case his administrative and planning functions would cease periodically for a month or so at a time. (VA, BPF, would normally perform this function).

(c) with CINCPAC at his Headquarters, advising on the strategic plans in which the BPF takes part and issuing directives as necessary to VA, BPF, in operational matters and VA (Q) in administrative matters.

(a) *Administrative Staff*

VA (Q) acting as the C-in-C's main Administrative Staff with RAFT as an advanced echelon at the advanced base.

Note: RAFT's directive would have to be slightly amended to bring this into force.

(b) *Operational Staff*

The PF main Headquarters and the C-in-C's main Operational and Intelligence Staff to be situated at the British Advanced Base, preferably ashore; alternatively in one of the ships of the Fleet Train.

The C-in-C himself to work with a small Operational Staff (on the Montgomery model).

Either (a) with CINCPAC
or (b) at the advanced base.
or (c) at sea
depending on the situation at the time.

Part IV. First BPF Operation in the Pacific

Operational Availability of First BPF Forces

Assuming:

(a) That the Palembang Operation takes place as planned in mid-January, and the force reaches Sydney late in January or early in February.
(b) 15 days for reforming the Naval Air Squadrons in Sydney (it is expected that losses will be sustained at Palembang)
(c) 15 days on passage to the operating area.

A Task Force comprising
    two Battleships, four Carriers, five Light Cruisers, three Destroyer Flotillas
    should be available in the operating area late in February or early in March.

HIGHBALL

...

2. One of the first operations could be a HIGHBALL attack on the Japanese Fleet. The operational range of the HIGHBALL Mosquitos is about 600 miles.[1]
3. Two possible administrative programmes have been planned as follows and a decision is required now.

Programme A

(a) 22 December [1944] – two Escort Carriers arrive at Melbourne. They then

  (i) disembark 28 Mosquitos
  (ii) dehibit their aircraft and work up.

They then move to an airfield at Sydney where they:

  (iii) complete their deck landing training
  (iv) embark in the Fleet Carriers.

(b) Assuming that:

  (i) the Carriers arrive in Sydney as planned late in January (after the Palembang operation in mid-January). The Mosquitos

---

[1]De Havilland Mosquito: 1940; 2 engines; 2 crew; 400mph; 4×20mm cannon; 4000lbs bombs;

should be embarked and the carrier force ready to sail by
mid-February

(ii) 15 days on passage to the operating area,
the HIGHBALL force should be able to carry out an attack in
early March.[1]

Programme B

(a) 22 December [1944] – two Escort Carriers arrive Melbourne and are
re-routed on to an advanced base (Manus?) where they:

   (i) disembark their Mosquitos. (Certain special facilities are
   required).
   (ii) dehibit their aircraft and work up
   (iii) complete DLT and embark on the Fleet Carriers on arrival.

(b) Assuming:

   (i) the Escort Carriers go straight on from Melbourne and reach
   the advanced base [by] 10 January (approximately) and there
   dehibit and work up
   (ii) that the Palembang operation goes according to plan (mid-January) and the force arrives in Sydney late January and moves
   straight to the advanced base
   (iii) 10 days on passage to the advanced base (mid-February)
   (iv) 15 days for DLT
   (v) Five days on passage to operating area.

Advantages and Disadvantages

4. Programme A

Advantages

   (i) plans have already been made and the disembarking facilities (which
   are tricky) are known to exist at Melbourne
   (ii) the aircraft are officially inhibited for five weeks only
   (iii) facilities for dehibition exist at Melbourne.

Disadvantages

   (iv) once the Mosquitos are embarked we are committed to a HIGH-
   BALL attack or else a lot of time will be wasted

---

[1]HIGHBALL: proposed CV-borne op using 618 Sqdn, RAF, Mosquitos.

Consequently, as Sydney is so far from the theatre of operations we shall be committed to an attack nearly a fortnight earlier than we need be

(v) the Carrier Force may be kept hanging about Sydney waiting if the Japanese Fleet is not suitably placed for a HIGHBALL attack

(vi) The Naval aircraft displaced by the Mosquitos would be separated from their parent carriers for an unnecessarily long time even if they were promptly ferried up to the advanced base.

5. Programme B

Disadvantages

(i) Although 618 Squadron are very fully equipped, they will require the assistance of some American facilities or the advanced base

(ii) Supplies of special gasoline (150 Octane) will have to be transported to the advanced base (arriving Sydney 19 January by present arrangements)

(iii) subsequent training aircraft will have to be transported to the Advanced Base instead of Australia (Fleet delivery would do)

Advantages

(iv) increase in tactical flexibility (see 4(iv) and (v) above

(v) increase in morale of the aircrews through being in an advanced rather than a rear base.

6. The following considerations have no marked advantages in either direction:

(a) security

(b) the date of the earliest possible attack.

Conclusion

7. There would be a considerable operational advantage in having the Mosquito Squadron close at hand rather than having to fetch them from way back in Sydney.

On the other hand this might involve some administrative problems for the American Airfields.

Minelaying Operations

8. Subsequent operations might include minelaying by –

(a) FML

(i) *Ariadne* is already in the Pacific. It is assumed that she will be attached to the BPF (decision is required).

(ii) *Apollo* and *Manxman* can also be sent to join the BPF if required (decision is required).

(b) By carrier-borne aircraft. Some notice of this would be required as the aircrews have not yet been trained in minelaying.

Part V: Repair Facilities

Major Refits and Major Battle Damage

Admiralty policy is:

(a) To send ships to the BPF which are new or which have recently been refitted
(b) Not to keep individual ships in the Pacific for more than two years.

2. Consequently major refits should be unnecessary and if they should become necessary, or in the event of major battle damage, the ships concerned will be sent elsewhere.

Minor Refits and Minor Battle Damage

3. It was intended that the BPF policy should be –

(a) To carry out as many minor refits and repairs as possible using the repair ships of the Fleet Train thus avoiding sending the ships concerned far from the operating theatre.
(b) To carry out what is left over in the repair bases in Australia.

Repair Ships

4. For the purposes outlined in paragraph 3 above, seven Repair Ships and two Hull Repair Ships were planned.
5. The construction of five of them was assigned to the US by the Joint Assignment Board, and the British Repair plans and dispositions were framed accordingly.
6. Just recently the US authorities have withdrawn three of the ships assigned to the British Navy and have designated these to the US Navy in the Pacific on the quite understandable grounds that the US Navy in the Pacific was being subjected to greater battle damage than the British Fleet elsewhere.
7. Now that the British Fleet is to take part in the war in the Pacific it is to be presumed that –

(a) The overall battle damage will not be increased in consequence.
(b) That the British Fleet will share the battle damage with the American Fleet.

8. The reduction in assignments of repair ships to the British Navy may, however, make it difficult for us to repair all the battle damage that the BPF may be expected to sustain.

9. Consequently it is suggested that repair facilities should to some extent be pooled as soon as the British repair facilities are unable to compete with our battle damage.

VI: Fuel

Requirements

The following approximate quantities of fuel will be required. The exact figures are subject to confirmation after a more detailed study has been made of the operational commitments.

(a) Oil Fuel

Assuming the number of operational days per month of the various fleet units to be:

(i) Battleships – 12 days}
(ii) Carriers – 18 days} at an average of 17 knots
(iii) Cruisers – 18 days
(iv) Destroyers – 24 days

And allowing for a margin for time in harbour and for movement of non-operational units, it is estimated that the oil requirements will be approximately –

January	–	10,000 tons
February	–	75,000 tons
March	–	100,000 tons
April	–	100,000 tons
May	–	140,000 tons
June	–	140,000 tons

And subsequently about 160,000 tons per month.

(b) Aviation Gasoline (100 Octane)

Very rough estimate –

500,000 gallons per month to start with, rising to one million gallons per month from July onwards.

Location of Supply

2. Depending on the schedule for moving to an advanced base, a proportion of these supplies will be required in Australia and a proportion in advanced bases.

Origin of Fuel

3. It is understood that bulk supply will be made from American resources. This requires confirmation. Assuming that this is confirmed, a description is required of the general method of supply intended in order that the British methods of reception may be matched.

VII: Co-ordination of Intelligence Arrangements

Day to Day Intelligence

In order to operate the Fleet to the best advantage the C-in-C will require to receive intelligence on the same scale as CINCPAC receives at his base.

This intelligence will be required by the operating authority at the Advanced Base.

Note: If the BPF main Headquarters is at the advanced base this would be considerably simplified.

Intelligence Liaison Officer

2. It would be most desirable for British Naval Intelligence Officers to be allocated to *certain American Headquarters in order to help in sifting and selecting the intelligence* required by the British Forces. US ILOs would also be welcomed in the British Headquarters.

3. The Headquarters which would be most useful in this direction are thought to be

(a) on the staff of CINCPAC
(b) on the staff of 7th Fleet
(c) CIC, Pearl Harbor
(d) JIC Pacific Ocean Area (JICPOA).

Supply of Target Maps, Models, etc.

4. While operating under the US Navy, the BPF is relying on American sources for the supply of operational maps, models, photographs, etc. It seems far better that such services should be centralised and the BPF

does not wish to set up its own services of this kind. Within the SWPA, these facilities are to be provided at Melbourne. Presumably similar services will be available for the Central Pacific Area from Pearl Harbor.

5. The BPF could help any centralised organisation in various ways (provided the requirements were stated in advance), for example –

(a) Photo Reconnaissance

>   (i) One quarter of all the fighters in the Fleet Carriers are fitted to carry cameras capable of photo reconnaissance, but not survey.
>   (ii) Three Mosquitos of 618 Squadron are fitted for photo reconnaissance.
>   (iii) If survey were a requirement it would be necessary to ask the Admiralty for a special survey unit. (Decision required).

Model Construction

There are a few officers and ratings in the BPF who have qualified in the construction of models.

VIII: Co-ordination of Signalling Arrangements

Tactical Co-operation

The BPF is at present equipped to carry out –

(a) Strategic Co-operation. A British Squadron can work in support of a US Force.
(b) Limited Tactical Co-operation. A British Squadron can work within sight of a US Squadron but must operate as a separate entity.

2. If Liaison personnel could be provided on a generous scale the British Forces would be able to operate in closer co-operation (i.e., within the same squadrons, etc.) after a comparatively short period of training.

Space of the Ether for British Broadcasts

3. It will be necessary to reduce considerably the volume of American traffic of the Australian area broadcasts in order to allow for the BPF traffic. ACNB has already raised this point with Commander, 7th Fleet, but no reply has yet been received.

Communication Liaison Officer

4. It is suggested that a US Communication Officer should be attached to BPF staff as Communications Liaison Officer.

268.   *Cunningham to Fraser*

[NMM, Fraser 20]   14 December 1944

General Lumsden reports conversation with General MacArthur in which latter made following suggestions:

a)   If BPF allotted to SWPA he would prefer you to take over from [Vice] Admiral Kinkaid and establish your headquarters permanently in his area.
b)   All naval resources in SWPA would be placed under your control and with [this?] base in Australia, logistic support would be facilitated.
c)   Despatch of a British force for special operations would not be precluded.

2. As General MacArthur is directly responsible to US COS, no action can be taken at this stage, but I feel you should know that this suggestion may be put to you in forthcoming conversations.

3. Such arrangements might be considered convenient in future, but unwelcome at present since it might result in British forces being excluded from taking part in operations in Pacific. You should therefore neither discourage it, should it be brought up in discussions in Australia, or with Admiral Nimitz, but refer exact terms of any proposal to Admiralty.

269.   *Memorandum of Understanding Reached in Conference, 17–19 December 1944, Concerning Employment of BPF*

[NMM, Fraser 21]   20 December 1944

…

Command Relationships

4. It is understood that to the maximum practicable extent the British ships will constitute a separate task force with no more direct tactical co-ordination with US forces than the situation requires.

Operations

5. It is planned that the first combat operations of the British ships after entering the Pacific Ocean Area will be as a FCTF operating in the Philippine Sea and the approaches to the [Japanese] Empire during the Central Pacific operations for the occupation of the Nansei Shoto. The tasks assigned will involve attack on enemy shore-based airfields, shore installations and shipping.

6. The 8th Submarine Flotilla (*Maidstone*) is expected to continue operations with the SWP forces. It will be proposed by CINCPAC that the *Adamant* Flotilla, now at Ceylon, will likewise be allocated to operations with the SWP forces. Decision concerning deployment of submarines after the arrival of the *Aorangi* Flotilla will be deferred for the present.

7. The *Bonaventure* and XE craft will be held at rear base as designated by C-in-C BPF.

8. The Mosquito squadrons will be held in Australia for the present and will be moved forward when needed.

9. The C-in-C BPF will inquire into the feasibility of forming a fast minelaying division. It may consist of *Ariadne*, *Apollo* and *Manxman*.

Bases

10. In accordance with arrangements made by the British Admiralty, the principal base of the BPF will be at Sydney. … Espiritu Santo will be available also, but the US facilities present will be moved forward to the Philippines as rapidly as possible.

11. Arrangements will be made by CINCPAC for the use of Manus by the BPF for anchorages and carrier aircraft as rapidly as circumstances permit.

12. Anchorages in the Central Pacific Forward Area will be assigned for the use of British combat units and fleet train as required by specific operations as they occur.

Logistics

14. …

(g) Aeronautical Material:

The monthly requirements for aircraft to support combat operations will approximate 20% of the operating strength.

Pilot replacement will approximate 10% per month.

Replacements at advanced anchorages are effected directly by transport Escort Carriers which are loaded with replacement crews and combat-ready aircraft from pools maintained in the rear area. Espiritu Santo and when circumstances permit, Manus will be available for replacement pools and have ample airfields and pier facilities for that purpose.

A minimum of one month's supply of aircrews and pilots should be maintained at the intermediate base and the forward anchorage should be sufficient to provide continuous support for the Carrier Task Force contemplated.

Aircraft engine replacements will approximate 15% per month.

All overhaul and major repair should be accomplished in the rear area, preferably Australia. Facilities for minor repair and for accessory overhaul may be required to maintain the forward pool of aircraft.

Floating storage should be provided for aeronautical supplies at advanced anchorages. Two AKS should be sufficient, one on station at all times and one in process of replenishment at the main supply base or en route.

270. *Mountbatten to Hewitt*

[NWC, Hewitt 1]   23 December 1944

... As you know, things are going slowly out here and we are all waiting anxiously for the war in Europe to end so that additional resources can be realised for this theatre. However, things are not going so badly on land in Burma and I have great hopes that we shall be allowed to carry out an amphibious operation before the year 1945 is through

271. *Fraser to Admiralty*

[NMM, Fraser 20]   30 December 1944

The Pearl Harbor Meeting.

Part I: American Organisation

The following salient features of the American Naval Organisation in the Central Pacific which may be already known to the Admiralty are relevant to the agreement reached between Fleet Admiral Nimitz and Admiral Fraser at Pearl Harbor.

2. All combatant American Naval Forces under CINCPAC are organised into one fleet which is alternatively called 3rd Fleet when operating under Admiral Halsey or 5th Fleet when operating under Admiral Spruance. While one of these two 'Command Teams' is operating the fleet the other is planning its next operation.

3. The fleet is flexibly divided into a number of 'Task Forces', for example:

(a) A 'Fast Carrier Task Force' comprising most of the Fleet and light fleet carriers and fast battleships.

(b) A 'Close support task Force' comprising the old battleships and assault escort carriers.

(c) An 'Amphibious Assault Task Force'.

4. Once an operation has been launched, the Fleet remains in the 'Combat Area' (i.e., within air striking range of the objective) for several weeks and is kept supplied by a 'Service Force' which brings up, fuel, ammunition,

fresh provisions and also reserve aircraft and air crews (in escort carriers) from the advanced base.

5. An 'Advanced Base' (such as Ulithi at present) used for the service and supporting forces required for the specific operations in progress, for example:

(a) For the accommodation of 'Reserve Air Groups'. (A carrier which has suffered losses may be sent back to exchange her entire air outfit).

(b) As terminal for the Commercial Tankers and bulk supply ships who discharge their [oil and freight] into the Fleet Tankers and issue ships for forward transport to the Fleet in the 'Combat Area'.

(c) As an advanced repair or salvage base.

6. 'Intermediate Bases' (such as Manus at present) are used for more general uses such as:

(a) For advanced training.

(b) For mounting operations.

(c) As a supply dump.

(d) For recreation.

(e) As a repair base.

(f) As a pool for Fleet personnel.

Conclusion

7. The whole organisation is designed to enable the Fleet to keep the sea in a manner which has not previously been attempted since the advent of steam. This outlook differs greatly from our existing ideas whereby a fleet returns to a shore base for replenishment of stores, ammunition, etc.

Part II: The Agreement

8. Status and Command:

(a) The C-in-C, BPF, will have the same status under CINCPAC as the Commanders of the 3rd and 5th Fleets.

(b) As the constitution of the combat portion of the BPF is equivalent to a 'Fast Carrier Task Force' it will be operated as such; the 3rd (or 5th) Fleet will then have two FCTFs, one British and one American.

(c) The Flag Officer operating the BPF at sea will normally do so under COM 3rd or 5th Fleets.

9. Bases:

(a) The rear fleet base will be in Australia.
(b) Initially there will be an intermediate base at Manus. Espiritu Santo may also be used if required. Subsequently the intermediate base will be moved forward as occasion offers.
(c) Advanced bases (within the meaning of paragraph 5 above) will be allocated for specific operations.

Operations:

The BPF will take part as a 'FCTF' in the most advanced operations of the Pacific Fleet. Initially it will be allotted specific tasks which will not entail close tactical co-operation with American units. These operations will take place shortly after the arrival of the first contingent.

11. With the present eclipse of the Japanese Fleet, the principal enemy with which the Fleet will contend is the Japanese shore-based air force. Offensively the main objective will be the neutralisation of the enemy air forces and airfields. Defensively the main task will be to defeat the suicide bombers. *Note:* For this purpose the Americans are equipping their Fleet and light fleet carriers with a proportion of Fighters to TBR and Dive Bombers of 2:1.

12. Special weapons whose proper target is the enemy main units will be held in reserve pending a change in the strategic situation. Consideration will also be given to their use against lesser targets.

13. Minelaying by surface vessels does not form a part of the immediate strategy but is visualised as part of the future strategy of cutting Japan off from the mainland. The Fast Minelayers will be required at a later date.

14. It was agreed as a best policy that all British Submarines should operate together. Initially it appeared that the SWPA would be the most profitable for them and consequently the British Submarines have been offered to the COM 7th Fleet.

15. Minesweeping requirements will increase as the Allies approach Japan. Some minesweepers will be required shortly but it is doubtful whether British ones can be used as they will initially be needed as escorts.

16. Escorts for supply convoys are required from Manus onwards. The recent re-appearance of enemy submarines off the Australian coast may also make convoys necessary in this area.

Signal Communications

17. It was agreed that the BPF should turn over entirely to American signalling methods and procedures and cryptollogical systems with the

exception of ECM. The latter will be initially supplied to Flag Officers with a special operating team. Adequate American signal staffs are to be attached to each ship and unit.

18 It is quite evident that Logistic support is the limiting factor in the Pacific and not the number of available operating units. For this reason it was made abundantly clear that the BPF must be self-supporting in every respect.

19. This does not mean that the Americans would not be prepared to pool resources for the sake of efficiency, provided that we were supplying our proper quotas. Nor does it mean that they would withhold essential support to get a unit into operation, provided the equivalent British support was available elsewhere or was on its way.

20. It does mean however that the Americans are fully occupied with the supply of their own forces and have little to spare for us.

Action Required

21. I intend to operate the BPF to the best possible effect in the most advantageous operations in the Pacific and Fleet Admiral Nimitz has agreed that I should do so, but this will not be possible until the Fleet has adequate logistic support. Without such support there is no doubt I cannot carry out prolonged operations and take part in the same manner as the Americans.

22. From the information available to me, I consider that the logistic support already planned is not adequate to meet the new strategic situation involving as it does:

(a) The institution of an intermediate base between Australia and the advanced base (see paragraph 6 above).
(b) Support at sea in advance of the advanced base.
(c) Operations of a considerably more sustained nature than were originally contemplated.

23. It is requested that these problems should be given further urgent consideration in the Admiralty in the light of the strategic situation outlined above, and a fresh estimate of requirements made. Certain of the more prominent and urgent needs will be signalled as they become apparent. Also any further information that may be required on American methods of operating, or on their experience of the scale of operational requirements will be signalled if you need them.

24. Apart from the factual aspect, I believe that a basis of mutual good will has been laid and that CINCPAC and his Commanders are prepared to co-operate generously.

272. *Nimitz to Sir Philip Mitchell*

[Nimitz 13/121]   [n.d., December 1944?]

Last December [probably 1943], the Port Director, Suva, Fiji, forwarded to you my request for the establishment of Loran transmission stations on Gardiner and Atafu Islands, Phoenix and Unity Groups. In your reply, you kindly granted your approval for the Gardiner Island installation, and informed [me] that Atafu Island came under the jurisdiction of the New Zealand Government. In January, that Government was contacted and their approval obtained for the Atafu Island installation.

…

Details of proposed installation, Gardiner Island.

2. Installation – will consist of seven Quonset huts, each 20ft x 48ft in size which, together with necessary antenna[,] masts and ground systems, will require a plot of ground 900ft x 900ft in size.

…

11. The British local representative will be notified when construction begins so that suitable rearrangement of land ownership and recompense for coconut trees cut down at the Loran site may be made.

273. *Leahy: Diary*

[LC, Leahy]   1 January 1945

The Japanese are facing an inevitable defeat, but because of their fanatical savage resistance to death, there is little prospect of obtaining from them an unconditional surrender within the year that lies before us.

274. *British Admiralty Delegation to the Admiralty*

[ADM 116/5341]   4 January 1945

'The US Navy have formed urgent requirements for additional Fighter type aircraft which have been brought about by the decision to increase the number of Fighters aboard our aircraft carriers. It appears that the present circumstances are greater than the present production program can meet. ...'

[From Admiral Fitch, US Navy, Deputy Chief
of Naval Operations][1]

2. Decision by US Authorities to increase the proportion of Fighters carried in the aircraft carriers has resulted from experience gained during the recent operations in the Pacific. In spite of production for 1945 being increased by 1800 to [a] grand total of 14,456, this number is apparently considered insufficient to meet both US and British requirements and hence [the] proposed raid on [the] assignment to Britain.

Admiralty to BAD.

27 January 1945.

...

In our view, if there is to be any substantial reduction in our assignments this will be reflected in the scale of the effort we shall be able to bring to bear in the Pacific War.

...

It is readily admitted that our resources will not allow us at first to maintain a completely sustained attack on Japan to that now built up after three years of experience by the US Navy, but our desire is to fight alongside them to the best of our ability. If our planning is to be yet again completely upset by a fluctuating policy on assignments we shall find it extremely difficult to pull our weight.

Admiralty to BAD

2 February 1945.

...

B. Our First Line IE includes 282 Corsairs actual rising to 324 in August 1945 and 202 Hellcats actual rising to 270 in August 1945. If assignments

---

[1]VA Aubrey W. Fitch, US Navy: Cdr, CV Force, Coral Sea; Cdr (A), TF 33, S Pac 1942–3; DCNO.

cease no aircraft will be able to replace Corsairs wasting after August 1945. This would adversely affect operations after that date. ... Hellcat shortage would be immediately apparent and existing squadrons would have to be maintained at [the] expense of new squadrons.

C. ... There are possibilities of increasing production of Seafire [Mark] 46 in 1946. ... Seafire 45 is not [a] substitute for Corsair in role of Fighter/ Bomber.

BAD to Admiralty.

20 February 1945.

There is obviously considerable pressure working somewhere in the Navy Department to reduce fighter assignments to Britain in view of urgent requirements for more fighters in US Pacific Fleet consequent upon recent operational developments.

275.   *Stark to Admiral R. S. Edwards, US Navy,*
enclosing Admiralty to BAD, 8 January 1945

[Stark A3]   11 January 1945

In view of the movement of British Naval Forces to the Pacific we have had under review present arrangements for provision to Admiralty of information concerning US Fleet organisations and dispositions. Information is at present received from three sources, namely:

(a) Weekly signal from COMINCH: This is only a very rough guide to the dispositions of Pacific Fleet and does not indicate whether or not a warship is damaged.
(b) US Navy publishes 'Assignments of vessels and aircraft in the organisation of sea-going forces of US Navy': This document shows total number of warships assigned to the Pacific, administrative organisation of Fleet and names of Commanders. It does not assist in estimating composition of Task Forces which form basis of Fleet when organized for operations.
(c) Reports from British Naval Intelligence Officers and British NIOs in the Pacific: These reports usually contain latest known disposition of major units together with Task Group organization, but none of them can be received in less than a week, and in case of Officers at sea, a month or more must elapse before a report reached Admiralty.

2. Consequently, we have no method of ascertaining:

    (a) In which areas of Central Pacific main units are operating.
    (b) Of what Task Forces 3rd or 7th Fleet are constituted when at sea, and of what units Task Forces are composed.
    (c) Direction in which warships are proceeding.
    (d) Numbers of destroyers and smaller craft accompanying Main Fleet.
    (e) Whether units are damaged or returning to refit.

3. As our main fleet will shortly be operating in Pacific theatre it is most necessary for Admiralty to keep in close touch with strategic position there which is not possible under existing arrangements. To enable this to be done we understand from COMNAVEU Admiralty will require following additional documents:

    (a) US Pacific Fleet Operations Plan.
    (b) Pacific Fleet Weekly Operational Sheet.
    (c) Signals relating to Task Force assignment.

4. Request COMINCH now be asked to furnish Admiralty with 3 (a), (b) and (c) above. Previous approaches to Navy Department for similar information have not been successful and you may wish to consider mentioning matter personally to COMINCH.

5. It should be observed that US Navy are supplied with Pink List.[1]

276. *Fraser to Nimitz*

[Nimitz 13/117]   12 January 1945

Intend sailing *Swiftsure* flying flag of Rear Admiral Brind (Commanding Cruisers)[,] *Howe* flying flag of Rear Admiral Fisher (commanding fleet train) and three destroyers so as to arrive Manus AM 19 January.[2]

I would like Rear Admiral Brind in *Swiftsure* to go on for a few days to Ulithi to gain experience there and have instructed him accordingly.

277. *Fraser to Admiralty*

[NMM, Fraser 21]   17 January 1945

This is a list of four signals [following] on my visit to SWPA. Each signal contains a separate section and subject.

---

[1]Pink List: weekly state & positions of HM Ships.
[2]RA Douglas Fisher: Capt Dec 1932; *Nelson* Apr 1938; *Warspite* Apr 1940; RA, *President* July 1942; RAFT BPF Oct 1944.

Section I: Conversations with American Commanders

I have seen General MacArthur and Admiral Kinkaid and accompanied the American Fleet in the *New Mexico* to witness the Lingayan landings.
2. The general said that he would welcome the British Fleet in his area but indicated a probable intention of turning south to North Borneo at the same time as Admiral was pressing north.
3. I stated that we were already committed to Admiral Nimitz and could not do both at the same time, but if it was possible to do so we would always consider assistance in bombardment support. In such a case it would be necessary for him to provide logistics which he quite understood, He said I could write my own ticket concerning command, but in viewing the situation it would obviously be impracticable for a British Admiral to take over the area bound up as it was with American supply, transport, amphibious forces and air.
4. I emphasised the reason for delay in arrival of our forces necessitated by Admiral Nimitz's wish to strike at Sumatra and he seemed fully to understand and agreed with the project.
5. He regarded the capture of North Borneo as a most important objective not only to help our fuel supplies but, with Palembang knocked out, to cripple the Japanese.
6. The meeting with both the General and Kinkaid was most cordial and I received the utmost consideration from all members of the staff.

...

Section II: Description of Luzon Operations

8. Naval operations in the Lingayan Gulf were carried out for three days prior to the landings.
9. On the first day the minesweepers went in covered on each flank by the supporting force which totalled

  6 Old Battleships
  6 Cruisers (including *Australia* and *Shropshire*)
  12 Escort Carriers providing fighter cover from seaward
  47 Destroyer-type escorts.

10. On the second day as no mines had been found, the force proceeded to the head of the Gulf and plastered the beaches from stopped positions about 7000 yards from the shore. The beach obstruction parties went in in boats and swimming about they cleared obstructions.
11. On the third day this continued but by that time the Japanese had obviously abandoned the beaches and on 'S' day the Army landed with

negligible opposition touching down at 0921/2 compared with a planned time of 0930.

12. By the afternoon three aircraft tenders had arrived and 24 Catalinas were lying at their moorings laid in the Gulf for A/S patrol, and courier services.

Section III: Suicide Bombers

13. From 'S-5' to 'S-2' the fleet was subject to continuous air attack by day from small groups. The following damage occurred:

Sunk – 1 Escort Carrier
2 Minesweepers
2 AFDs with beach clearance parties

Damaged – 3 Battleships
2 Cruisers
1 Escort Carrier
6 Destroyers

Superficially Damaged –
1 Cruiser
1 Escort Carrier
3 Destroyers

14. *Australia* was hit six times and provided an interesting example.

(a) Horizontal bomber clipped the top of the centre funnel. 12 killed, 35 wounded.
     1 × 4in gun and air warning set out of action.
(b) Horizontal bomber hit ship's side. No.1 Boiler Room out of action, nearly lost steam but after 15 minutes ready for 22 knots.
(c) Dive bomber aft: slight damage and steering gear temporarily affected.
(d) Bomber hit on the bridge structure, slight damage.
(e) Hit by fragments from shore batteries.
(f) Horizontal bomber took away after funnel. On the night of 'S' day, having completed her task as a one-and-three-quarter funnel cruiser with only 30% of her AA in action and speed of 22 knots [she retired].

15. In no case did the damage prevent ships from carrying out their tasks although casualties were fairly heavy, e.g., in battleships one suicide bomber usually averaged 30 to 40 killed and 100 wounded.

16. Suicide bombers adopted two methods of attack:

(a) A dive in over the Fleet from the sun.
(b) Diving down to the surface three or four miles away and coming in as for a torpedo attack.

17. The Fleet's AA was perhaps a little wild but of good volume and many aircraft were crashing into the sea close to the ships.
18. Fighter direction has not been developed in these older ships. On the first day there were 100 fighters as cover but the numbers hampered any form of direction.

Cover was reduced later on and better results were obtained.

19. On the last two days Japanese air was negligible except at dusk and dawn due I think to Army and 3rd Fleet attacks on Luzon airfields and better protection from our fighters.
20. The following points need again emphasising during air attacks:

(a) Unnecessary personnel must not be on upper deck or concentrated on bridges.
(b) Alternative positions for controlling the ship must be permanently manned.
(c) Arrangements for fire-fighting and dealing with wounded on upper decks and bridges must be frequently practised.

Section IV: Fleet Tactics and General Remarks

21. The Fleet moved in two groups some 10 miles apart and each group had three tankers for rapid refuelling of destroyers. The tankers occupied the centre of the formation and manoeuvred with the Fleet, the centre one being the guide of the Fleet.
22. On 'S-5' all the destroyers were fuelled from the tankers.
23. On 'S+1' the ships were re-ammunitioned from LSTs, two going alongside each battleship.
24. Submarines were disregarded and indeed none appeared. The Fleet stopped for about three hours to transfer survivors during the night of 'S-4' and average speed made good was about 13 knots.
25. The Navy's own Catalinas arriving on 'S' day for immediate recon-naissance, courier service, and transport, makes one envious of the

American Naval Air Service after the difficulties experienced in finding one of our own aircraft to take one about.[1]

26. Such operations involve a considerable strain on personnel principally because of the suicide bomber. Everyone however seemed cheery although in the *New Mexico* no one had been ashore since 20 November.

27. The provision of amenities on board is of great importance, soda water fountains, ice, ice cream, water coolers and movies are all in abundance together with much literature and mail was delivered at sea on 'S-5'. There seemed to be ample resources.

28. Altogether a well-planned operation and carried out with determination, boldness and courage and the experience has proved of much value.

278.   *Fraser to Nimitz*

[NMM, Fraser 23]   22 January 1945

I am sending this letter by Hopkins and I am most grateful to you for allowing him to remain so long. His knowledge has been of great assistance to us in making our plans and I believe that he too will now be much better posted regarding our affairs.

2. I had a short but very pleasant talk with MacArthur and Kinkaid. I told MacArthur that as far as I knew I was pledged to you, but that if at any time we could assist in his operations by individual ships, he should ask; subject to your concurrence we would always endeavour to help.

3. I had a most interesting experience in the *New Mexico* watching the preliminaries to, and the actual landing [in the Philippines]. We had every help on board, and I thought everything was conducted with much boldness, courage and determination. Though we suffered some casualties, everything seemed to go according to plan, and except for ships sunk the damage did not prevent ships from carrying out their allotted tasks.

4. I felt that Fighter Direction might be improved, but as the older ships were not fitted up, I was really unable to judge how it was being done.

5. I have in mind that Hopkins should now start discussion with your staff on the question of Future Strategy and employment of the BPF. When these have reached a suitable stage it may be convenient for me or my Chief of Staff to pay a further visit to your HQ.

---

[1]Consolidated Catalina (RCAF: Canso): US; 1935; amphibian or flying boat; torpedo bomber, depth charges, freight, etc.; 2 engines; 8 crew; 179mph; 5mg.

6. I now have news that subject to the European War not being unduly prolonged some resources will be coming available about May 1945 for the establishment of shore base facilities for the Fleet and the equipment of aerodromes. It is necessary to plan where these should be established to the best advantage. Since it seems unlikely that we shall be able to establish more than one such base, it becomes a matter of considerable importance that it should be rightly placed.

7. I am not yet aware, of course, of your future plans, but it appears to me that there are great advantages in establishing this base at a harbour in Luzon if such could be made available together with near-by aerodromes.

8. A general collapse of the Japanese position in the Indies seems certainly a possibility at any rate in the air and events may well make it possible later this year to establish a much more direct line of supply from the Indian Ocean to the Philippines through the Moluccas.

9. If I have touched mainly on questions of supply and maintenance because, as we are so fully aware, these must condition the extent of the support we can give in the forward operations against Japan, which it my desire shall be on the largest possible scale.

10. Concerning HIGHBALL and Midget Submarines, I feel that after ICEBERG we might well bring these into operation. I sent a note on the Midget operational capabilities and I think you have data re-HIGHBALL.[1] The latter might well prove a suitable operation for the carriers while replacing any casualties they may have in Europe.

11. Subject to your concurrence I would like to push on with arrangements for these as early as practicable.

12. Wishing you the best of New Year's and again thanking you for all the kindness and help American forces are giving us.

279. *Fraser to King*

[Nimitz 13/117]   27 January 1945

A Carrier Task Force designated TF 118 will be ready for operations at an advanced anchorage on 15 March.

2. TF 118 will consist of two BB, four CV, two CL, three CL (AA) and 16 DDs.

---

[1]ICEBERG: Cape Bonin & Ryukyu Islands.

3. To support the above the following escorts and units of the Fleet Train designated TF 117 will be available[:] 8 DE, 16 PCE, 4 CVE, 1 ARB, 1 ARV, 4 AF, 2 AH, 4 ATA, 8 AO, 3 AKS, 1 AD, 1 AW, 1 ARH, 1 AM, 13 AE.
4. Names of ships are to be forwarded by airmailgram.
5. Additional forces are expected which will be communicated as they become available for operations.

280.   *CTF 77 to King*

[Nimitz 13/117]   30 January 1945

C-in-C, BPF, has requested immediate release HMS *Lothian* (LSH) for use as his flagship and release of six LSI of British force X to his control at earliest practicable date. With approval of C-in-C, SWPA, recommend modification release date proposed by my 041222 [not reproduced] as follows. Release HMS *Lothian* immediately to C-in-C, BPF. Release *Empire Arquebus* to C-in-C, BPF, about 15 February and remaining five LSI about 1 March. Your concurrence requested.

281.   *King to Nimitz*

[Nimitz 13/117]   31 January 1945

… I await your request to allocation to you of BPF units required by you for a specific operation to include your reasons why you need such units. I have now confirmed my intention to keep operational control of BPF units in my own hands.

Nimitz to King.

2 February 1945.

…

2. Request allocation of available carriers, battleships, cruisers and destroyers of the BPF together with British Fleet Train to operational control of C-in-C, Pacific, for ICEBERG operation. Contemplated employment is attack on enemy forces and possessions south of Okinawa and other operations as may be required. Augmentation of US Pacific Fleet by British carrier TF is not absolutely necessary but will

expedite campaign and by more complete neutralization of enemy Air Force will reduce our losses.

282. Kinkaid to MacArthur

[Nimitz 13/117] Leyte,
8 February 1945

An increasing volume of requests are being received directly by Commander 7th Fleet [and] Commander Allied Naval Forces, SWPA, and by his subordinates, particularly Commander Naval Base, Manus, from C-in-C, BPF, for facilities and services. Among these are requests for provision at Manus for HQ for C-in-C, BPF, of [an] airfield and facilities and the allocation of ground areas for the construction and installation of accommodations for 14,000 men[,] supply and fuel depots [,] barracks [,] docks [,] etc. It is requested I be informed [at] earliest practicable [date] of status of BPF with respect to Commander Allied Naval Forces and Commander 7th Fleet. Proper communications and correspondence channels and extent of my responsibility and authority with respect especially to provision of naval shore facilities in SWPA.

The present land on Manus for support of SWPA naval and naval air activities requires early decision with respect to nature and extent of transfer to BPF of existing facilities or of new construction to be undertaken for or by BPF.

283. MacArthur to Kinkaid

[Nimitz 13/117] 9 February 1945

Service involving BPF as an independent entity in its relationship to SWPA should deal directly with C-in-C, SWPA, in all matters of policy such as those presented in your 080121 [above]. None of the matters to which you refer has been submitted to this HQ and the C-in-C has no previous knowledge of them. The only information possessed by this HQ was conveyed in [a] verbal statement by C-in-C POA to effect that BPF when operating as part of the US Pacific Fleet would avail itself of anchorage facilities at Manus with all logistic support being provided by BPF train and that same facilities would be provided at Espiritu Santo. When operating as part of the US Pacific Fleet the BPF will use facilities at Manus on same basis as US ships, logistic support being as arranged by C-in-C Pacific. Commander Allied Naval Forces or Commander 7th Fleet will not provide personnel or material for construction or for other facilities nor allocate land areas unless specifically authorised by this HQ.

284.   *Cunningham to Fraser and Somerville*

[ADM 205/58]   12 February 1945

I have discussed employment of BPF with Admiral King and was disappointed to find that he would not assign BPF to first phase of ICEBERG. Reason he gave was uncertainty of MacArthur's plans.

2.   King inferred that BPF might be working under MacArthur if its decided that the latter is to swing left-handed and undertake further operations in the near future. I think this is rather unsatisfactory but there seems to have been some difference of opinion between American Authorities as to what operations, if any, were to be undertaken by MacArthur.
3.   I pointed out to him most strongly undesirability of Fleet remaining idle, with which he agreed. If not required for MacArthur's operation it will certainly take part in Phase II of ICEBERG.
4.   I expect to hear from Admiral King shortly. Meanwhile he is fully aware of my views which are in line with yours.

285.   *Fraser to Nimitz*

[SPD 155]   15 February 1945

. . .

4. My only object is to try and bring BPF into action on the dates you desired, but am beginning to feel a little frustrated. Time is getting short, the Fleet is in Sydney, and have as yet no airstrip allocations at Manus.
5. Can you help and advise me if we are doing wrong[?] It hardly seems to me to be practical to be based in the command of C-in-C SWPA without having communication on local matters.

286.   *Fraser to Nimitz*

[Nimitz 13/117]   20 February 1945

The position with regard to the BPF base in the forward area is that Admiralty –[?], bulk loaded, and in the process of sending material for a base of the following proportions:

A. Amenities and welfare facilities for 5000 liberty men daily.
B. Transit camp for 500 officers and men.
C. 200-bed hospital.
D. Covered storage to scale of one victualling store [to] one Naval issuing ship.
E. Mining unit and torpedo unit.
F. Minor W/T station.
G. Total complement including Royal Marines Engineering company (maintenance and 500 Asiatic pioneers would be 3000).

2. The material stores and boats for the above base are being shipped in four freight ships due Manus at monthly intervals from early May.
3. Two construction battalions (approximate total of 3000 RM Engineers) are being sent to build the base. The first contingent of 750 RM Engineers are due Sydney [in] May, June, August respectively.
4. With this construction party it is expected that some facilities would be available after five months but that the base would not be fully operative for nine months.
5. It is not thought that a base on the above scale would meet the full requirements of the BPF and consequently base facilities on a larger scale have been asked for from the Admiralty, but the prospect of getting anything larger depends mainly on our ability to obtain the facilities locally in Australia.

287. *Fraser to Nimitz*

[Nimitz 13/117]   20 February 1945

...

2. A MONAB was designated to Manus in the belief that the COMINCH's acceptance on NF 1 [not reproduced] carried with it an acceptance in principle of paragraph 2 of NF 1.
3. The present position of this MONAB is as follows:

A. Its equipment in *Clan Macaulay* is on its way via Panama and is due at Manus on 11 March.[1]
B. Its personnel are due in Sydney on 19 February and are planned to take passage in *Empire Arquebus* [due] to arrive in Manus by 11 March.

---

[1]*Clan Macaulay*: Clan Line; 1936; 10492t; 16k.

4. If the MONAB equipment cannot now be landed in Manus it will be necessary to divert this ship to Australia where her cargo must be off-loaded. This will entail a considerable delay in the final establishment of the MONAB.

5. It is believed that the early establishment of air facilities in Manus will considerably increase the operational effectiveness of the BPF in whichever area the latter may eventually be assigned.

288. *King to Nimitz*

[NWC, King 7]   21 February 1945

I am at a loss to understand why there should be any confusion as to status of BPF. All arrangements for basing BPF are in the hands of CINCPOA including CINCSWPA['s] concurrence where appropriate and always bearing in mind that said fleet is to be self-supporting.

Allocation of units of BPF for operations remains in my hands. I can't commit units of BPF to ICEBERG (involving two to three months) or any other operation until JCS decide what operations are to be carried out other than those already approved. Prospects are that such decision will be reached by middle of March.

289. *Fraser to Nimitz.*

[Nimitz 13/117]   26 February 1945

...

2. My detailed requirements for berths and shore facilities at Manus are as follows:

A.   During the period 6 March until the fleet moves forward for opera-tions. To berth the BPF and Fleet Train in the anchorage. During this period fleet training including air training will be carried out using own and as many resources as may be made available. Air-craft will require to be disembarked under circumstances outlined in paragraph 7 below.

B.   Certain units of the Fleet Train will require semi-permanent berths in the anchorage.

C.   From 6 March onwards. To augment the American pools and their personnel with British personnel consisting of four officers and 131 maintenance ratings for the purpose of maintaining reserve aircraft to a maximum of 50 and the forward staging of replenishment aircraft.

D. On about 9 March to start the establishment of MONAB on an existing air strip. To be completed about the end of April with a view to establishing shore facilities for refresher training for carrier pilots, and for aircraft maintenance and repair.

3. … semi-permanent berths will be required for 2 AKS, 3 AF, 1 AH, 1 AW, 1 ARH, 1 AN, 3 AE, 2 ATA.

4. The MONAB will be manned by 45 officers and 450 ratings, and when fully established will be required to accommodate 90 disassembled aircraft, 50 reserve aircraft and about 1600 officers and men.

5. The construction required for the establishment of this MONAB depends upon the air strip released for BPF purposes. This construction and assistance will be as follows:

A. If Mokareng is selected –

    1. Clearance of site for and erection of a tented camp to meet requirements in 4 above.

    2. Jetty for landing aircraft (use of pier and cranes at air centre would also be necessary).

    3. Arrangements for supply of fresh water and avgas.

B. If Ponam or Pityili is selected no construction is required if existing hutted camp and facilities are made available.

C. In either case a construction group of about 150 men [is] required permanently to maintain air strip and camp

D. Assistance in landing MONAB equipment (pontoon lighters for LCI).

6. Of these air strips Pityili is preferred.

7. In the event of BPF not moving forward as at present planned from Manus on the 13 March facilities for disembarking one carrier group of 80 aircraft and 500 officers and men would be required on a lodger basis from 6 March until the MONAB would be able to take them.

8. Quarters, messing and office accommodation will be required from 20 February for the liaison officer with COMNAVBASE and his staff. A total of nine Quonset huts are required. The party consists of one Captain, 10 other officers and 66 ratings.

9. Common requirements are being sent by separate dispatch.

Nimitz to Fraser.

27 February 1945.

The establishment of BPF MONAB at Ponam is authorized. …

290.   *Fraser to Nimitz*

[Nimitz 13/117]   7 March 1945

The following BPF movements are planned:

ATF (Fast Carrier TF) accompanied by a tanker group consisting of 4 AO, 2 CVE, 1 AZF – 6–13 March at Manus; 16–19 March at Ulithi.

BTF 112 (Fleet Train): 1 March onwards – units of the Fleet Train arriving at Manus; 19 March onwards – certain units of the Fleet Train arrive Leyte, where it is planned to replenish the fleet after its first period of operations.

291.   *Nimitz to King*

[Nimitz 13/117]   9 March 1945

Recommend assignment of 4th and 8th British Submarine Flotillas to 7th Fleet as of 1 April.

292.   *Rawlings to Fraser*

[NMM, Fraser 23]   9 March (from Manus), 4 April,
                                                     and 28 April 1945

… My own feeling, for what it is worth, is that the really important side of what we do here is to end up with the White Ensign still looked up to by the Americans. I cannot help feeling that it will do more for us than anything else.

Limba will tell you Vian has been difficult – as he saw for himself. … The trouble is due to two causes – 1. an intense resentment that he is not in command and 2. that he is neurotic.[1] This latter leads to petulant abruptness and exhibitions of boorishness that are a little trying. I'm not going to be staved off by him and he has got to be one of a cheerful party. 'wishes to be centre stage'. 'I have no complaint at all when we are in the forward area – indeed I suspect it is only when his nerves are stimulated by excitement that he becomes more balanced.'

'The American method of conducting business in most odd – in so far as the chances of our joining the 7th Fleet was concerned (and it seemed likely) as we hadn't been definitely assigned and they wouldn't

---

[1]Limba: unknown.

let us have any Intelligence, etc., to start. <u>Until</u> – they sent off a gent who wanted info about our speeds and [–?], etc. – after which we got down to barter! But I like them they' re fine.'

...

... for quite longish periods I have had but one anxiety – and that was never under any circumstance must we fail to keep our undertakings and appointments with the Americans. For me that mattered far more than who won any battle or whether ships got hit or no – looked up to, respected and admired, that if we gave any part of the Americans any opportunity to say 'The British have quit' or 'can't take it' – then something must be lost that could never perhaps be regained. I believe that was right and that we carried a destiny immeasurably more important to our race than any campaign.

293.   *Rawlings to Nimitz*

[Nimitz 13/117]   15 March 1945

I hereby report TF 113 and TF 112 for duty in accordance with orders received from C-in-C, BPF. I have recalled ships from sea exercises and am embarking air squadrons from shore training. Anticipate TF 113 with complementary units of TF 112 will be ready by 1200 17 March to sail from Manus as you may direct. I would add that is with a feeling of great pride and pleasure that the BPF joins the US naval forces under your command.

294.   *Fisher to Fraser*

[NMM, Fraser 23] *Lothian*,
Manus,   18 March 1945

...

On arrival at Manus I found Captain Waight, the SBNO, firmly installed and functioning at high speed. He and the Commander of the Naval Base (Commodore Boak, US Navy) spoke very highly of each other and get on excellently. This has been confirmed on several 'levels' here.[1]

---

[1]Capt Waight: A/Capt (ret); *Fortitude*, Ardrossan, Sept 1940; *Stag*, Red Sea, Nov 1942; *St Angelo*, Malta, Sept 1943; NOIC, Tripoli, Jan 1944; *Cochrane*, Rosyth, Sept 1944; *Camperdown*, Sept 1945.

Waight has got, and continues to get, a good many things out of the Commander of the Naval Base, without which we should have frequently been in considerable difficulties. Examples are – big fenders for fuelling carriers, water boats, etc.

I must stress that Waight has done <u>really</u> well and has shown great tact and initiative and drive.

I know my mandate is not to ask for help from the Americans, but we simply have to get assistance like this.

Commodore Boak has been most helpful in every way, and his staff have taken their line from him. I can really say that the relations between the US and us have been excellent.

...

The Americans had an 'at home' to all the British officers at their club ashore on Saturday, and that did a lot of good as regards 'mixing'.

295. *Fraser to Admiralty*

[RG38]   21 March 1945

Have [had] most cordial meetings with Nimitz and staff.

...

3. Main points are:

(a) Logistic situation of US Fleet is such that we can expect little help in that way but it is not on account of any unwillingness.
(b) Nimitz has obtained concurrence from C-in-C US Fleet for our use of Manus as a base on the same basis as his ships.
(c) He has promised participation of BPF in his most advanced operations as soon as it is ready to do so.
(d) I have decided to turn over to American signalling in the BPF as it seems the only practical solution.

...

4. The BPF will operate normally as a separate TF under Admirals Spruance or Halsey and I shall keep in touch with planning as it proceeds.
5. When practicable the Americans will develop Leyte as an advanced base which will relieve the overload on Manus.

Cdre Boak, US Navy (1891–1956): USNA 1914; CO *Morris* 1920–21; *R-18* 1924–6; CO *Gilmer* 1931–2; Cdr, Espiritu Santo 1943–4; Cdre, Manus 1944–5; 4 N Dist 1947; ret.

6. With the vast distances involved and after studying American procedure, there is no doubt that our logistical resources are of the slenderest nature, and we shall be unable to provide at present for any prolonged operations. We shall require the fuel supply to be cleared up and more ferry carriers and training carriers to keep reserve pilots in training.

296. *King to Kinkaid*

[Nimitz 13/117]   21 March 1945

In any conversations you have had or may have with representatives of Submarine Flotillas BPF assume you have not and will not make any commitments for British submarine bases in the Philippines. This is not intended to curtail present operational commitments for services and replenishment on occasion by tenders in presently established advanced bases furnishing similar services to US submarines of TF 71.

297. *King to Nimitz.*

[Nimitz 13/117]   22 March 1945

In view of the magnitude of the project and the time involved Manus will be too far from the combat areas when the facilities become available. My view is that minimum temporary facilities should be installed at Manus but for the main base consideration should be given to a location further forward such as Brunei Bay. Final decision in this matter depends on the future operations to be conducted in the Pacific Theater which matter is now under consideration by the JCS. Concur as to shore facilities in the Philippines.

298. *Fisher to Fraser*

[NMM, Fraser 23] *Lothian,*
Leyte,   27 March 1945.

...

15. This morning, by arrangement, I landed and called upon:

(a) Rear Admiral Davis, who is Commander of the 13th Amphibious Group. He is under Admiral Nimitz, is in 5th Fleet, and is therefore our BPF's head representative here. He should be afloat and awaits his flagship.[1]

(b)   Vice Admiral Kinkaid, who is Commander of the 7th Fleet under General MacArthur.

(c)   Rear Admiral Kauffman, who is Commander of the Philippine Sea Frontier.[2]

16.   Rear Admiral Davis is a very fine fellow, took pains to point out the difficulties of his position *vis-à-vis* Kinkaid and Kauffman. Stressed the fact that I should deal directly with himself over all matters, realised that whatever was agreed 'on high' about the BPF being self-supporting, there were some things we must need, and volunteered to help to the fullest extent.

17.   This was our first, and therefore semi-formal, meeting, and I have much confidence in our future relationships with each other.

18.   Vice Admiral Kinkaid is a tired old man – very nice – but quite played out, and he really ought to go back home (this view is supported by my Flag Captain, who knew him a year ago and says Kinkaid has aged incredibly). He was more outspoken about MacArthur than I would have expected, and brought out such remarks as, 'all MacArthur likes is to land from a ship, get his feet a little wet, and then wait for the photographers'.

19.   Rear Admiral Kauffman is an alert and very pleasant little man, but I did not see very much of him. ...

20.   They are all scared stiff of MacArthur, and [Captain Julian] Wheeler will expand on this, and tell you how the US Navy can get nothing out of him.

21.   My own instinct, which is <u>uninspired</u> and probably worthless, is that although the US Navy-Army feud is very real, it by no means follows that MacArthur would treat the British Navy as he treats the US Navy.

22.   In other words, if we could get [to] MacArthur direct, instead of through the US Navy, we could get all we want. To go to him behind the backs of the US Navy would however be as unthinkable as it would be unwise.

...

---

[1]RA Ralph L. Davies or Davis, US Navy: Cdr, 13 Amph Grp.

[2]RA Joshua Kauffman, US Navy (b 1887): USNA 1908; NWC 1933–4; CO *Memphis* 1936; DD Sqdns 1940–1; RA, Iceland 1941; Chmn, Allied A/S Board 1943; Pac F Sept 1943; Cdr, DD, Marshall Is 1944; VA & Cdr, Philippine SF 1945.

299.   *Fraser to Nimitz*

[Nimitz 13/122]   30 March 1945

...

2. I felt a bit anxious about the argument which started in the press, but it all arose from the fact that three pressmen flew out from England in a great hurry to join the Fleet, and then had to be told they could not go. They then said that everybody understood that the British Fleet was not ready. I told them that it was ready, and that is how it all happened. Fortunately, two American Naval Officers were present so I felt I was on firm ground, and I was not fighting the Americans but only trying to fight the Japanese!

3. We have been extending our admiration for all your forces which have been so heavily engaged and done such a big job of work; no odds seem to stop them, I hope you will be able to use the British Fleet in due course in equally worthy tasks.

4. On the question of forward bases, I know you will agree with me that if we are going to work efficiently far forward we must have shore facilities in the Philippines. It is perhaps a pity that we ever used the word 'bases' and I feel that if you could consider authorising us to put up British shore facilities in or near the Pacific Fleet Base we could go ahead and no one would object, although I fully realise the difficulty doing this in the area of another command.

5. Actually, I have referred the question now to the Admiralty to take action with Washington, as it seems that a decision is only likely to be made on the highest plane. I should be very grateful however for any action which you could take with Washington to back up the action I have taken with the Admiralty. I have specifically asked for 'British Shore Facilities' only.

6. I have just got Captain Wheeler back from Leyte where I think things are now settling down and Admiral Davies has been most helpful. I am afraid that we have put a great deal of work [in] on the [facilities], but you will realise that as we were not allowed to go forward until the time that the Fleet left Manus, we could not make any advance arrangements, and I do not think it was our fault. The Fleet was very relieved that they were finally assigned to you, and left Manus in very good heart and full of enthusiasm for the job.

...

8. In Sydney it seems a long way from the war, but it is communications and intelligence staff which tie me down, and shipping is so

scarce that I cannot get a HQ ship, or shore facilities further forward as yet.

...

I see that you have recently asked to keep the three ferry carriers which were going to be released to me. This will I am afraid hamper us a bit, but I think for the common effort it will probably be best for you to retain them and I have signalled the Admiralty suggesting that you should keep them at any rate until 1 July, when the question will be further considered.

(PS) Just received Spruance's signal and your communiqué which has bucked us up a lot, and many thanks. I feel now that we are ready for tough jobs.

300.   *Somerville to King*

[RG 38]   30 March 1945

...

The Admiralty ... request that a very early assignment of a suitable base to the BPF may be made in order that preliminary work may start at once.

301.   *Kinkaid to King*

[Nimitz 13/117]   31 March 1945

It is intended to operate British submarines from British tenders stationed only at those advanced bases from where submarines of TF 71 are operating. ... No commitments have been or will be made for British submarine bases in the Philippines. Present plan for operations of British submarines under Commander TF 71 is for tender *Maidstone* and accommodation ship *Arrange* to arrive about 22 May at Subic Bay where two US submarine tenders are now stationed. Submarine base Brisbane is being rolled up and will be re-established at Subic. Approximately 14 British submarines depart Fremantle for patrolling Java Sea en route to Subic to begin arriving about 27 May. Remaining British submarines at Fremantle based on *Adamant*. When submarine base Fremantle ready for roll up and movement to advance base (possibly Tutu Bay) *Adamant* and accompanying submarines plus dry docks from England to be moved forward for operations from advance base. Estimate only shore facilities required by British submarines will be possible torpedo and ammunition storage.

302. *Overall Logistic Plan US Navy: Quarterly Issue*

[Nimitz 13/122]   1 April 1945

...

9. The BPF operating in US strategic areas will be balanced and self-supporting except as indicated below:

(a) Bulk petroleum products.
(b) Packaged petroleum products.
(c) Spare parts and material of a particularly American type.

303. *Vian to Rawlings*

[ADM 199/595]   7 April 1945

The object set the British TF in ICEBERG was the neutralisation of the Nansei Shoto Group of Airfields; that is, to deny the airfields to enemy aircraft who might be staging through from China and Formosa to attack the Okinawa Invasion Forces.
2. The report which follows covers the operational periods 26 and 27 and 31 March, 1 and 2 April. It has been necessarily drawn up without viewing the reports from Aircraft taking part.
3. During these periods there is no evidence that the enemy was able to carry out this intention during daylight hours, and to this extent our object was achieved.
4. For the most part, the airfields were apparently dead and, after the heavy bombing and strafing effort made initially, it became a matter of mounting a CAP over the Islands, searching for heavily camouflaged aircraft and delivering bombing strikes against airfields and installations.
5. Aircraft for the most part were widely dispersed and camouflaged with care and intelligence, while the sites were well defended by flak of all kinds; strafing required good discernment in order that losses should not be incurred strafing camouflaged duds.
 In general, an unsatisfactory type of operation from the air point of view – much flak and few worthwhile targets.
6. From analysis of reports received, it is apparent that the Kamikaze force which attacked the Fleet on the morning of Easter Sunday was led in by a twin-engine ASV airplane, which itself retired at 3000 metres.
7. It was found that an operational period of three consecutive days imposes undue stress on aircrews and maintenance personnel which continues in the case of the latter, through the fuelling period.

The stresses imposed vary, in part, accountable to under-bearing of aircrews, to shortages of supplies, which implies lengthy improvisation, and to the heavy seas encountered, which involve a mass of man hours in lashing, and in draining overload drop tanks and oleos.

8. The stress has been felt particularly in *Illustrious*, whose Corsair Squadrons are overdue for relief, and whose Engine-Room Department has steamed long periods at full power to maintain the speed of the Fleet.

9. *Indefatigable* remains operationally efficient, although short of air-craft; the speed with which the ship dealt with action damage and was again ready to operate aircraft – 37 minutes – reflects high credit on the CO, Captain Q. D. Graham, and all officers and men concerned.[1]

10. The flying off positions used varied between 100 and 80 miles from the target area.

11. The wind during both periods of report has been ENE-ly, varying from force 3 to force 6. A heavy easterly swell persisted and it has been necessary to operate aircraft in heavier sea conditions than carriers have been accustomed to; there have been few crashes … and the general standard of deck landing in a seaway has steadily improved.

12. At the time of writing the Carrier Squadron is without the services of the Squadron Commanders: T/A Lt Cdr (A) C. T. Tomkinson, RNVR, 1836 Squadron, has been killed or is missing in action; T/A Lt Cdr (A) W. Stuart, RNVR and A/Lt Cdr (A) F. C. Nottingham, RNVR, of 857 and 858 Squadrons respectively, are in USS *Kingfish*, the lifeguard submarine.

13. The unsuitability of Seafires for operations of this type becomes more apparent from day to day. It has been a prime disadvantage during air attack to be forced to steady into wind to fly on Seafires running low on petrol; at time of writing, after seven days of operations and as many flying CAP, about 50% are serviceable, although six aircraft Replenish-ments have been received. Of those unserviceable, a few are in this con-dition, due to lack of spares, but the great majority are accidents.[2]

The inevitable result is that Seafires bear less and less of the weight, the additional work being undertaken by Corsairs and Hellcats. The prospect looms ahead of operating two Seafire carriers in one group.

14. Necessary night missions have been flown in this period under report by Hellcats, which are not fitted ASH and therefore dependent on

---

[1]Capt Q. D. Graham: *Baldur*, Reykjavik, Sept 1941; *President*, Nov 1942; *Unicorn*.
[2]Supermarine Seafire: 1941; 1 engine; 1 crew; 352mph; 2×20mm cannon, 4 mg; 1×500lb bomb.

moonlight. This is, of course, an added liability to *Indomitable*, who has to work her way by day.

In periods of darkness, the lack of night fighters must be severely felt; it is urged for this reason that one of the 'Colossus' class should be fitted as a Night Flying Carrier, equipped with night Fireflies and Avengers.[1]

304. *Nimitz to Fraser*

[Nimitz 12/122]   9 April 1945

I am very happy to have your letter of 30 March, and happier still to tell you that TF 57 is doing its job very well indeed in the ICEBERG Operation. Things seem to be going very well in the Ryukyus; so much so that I am now hopeful that we can finish up on that job earlier than we originally expected.

...

The argument that resulted in the press about the adequacy of the BPF was occasioned by an article written in the US where such articles are not censored, by a news correspondent called McMurtry who had been in the Pacific Ocean Areas. It was an unfortunate article; and during my visit to Washington in early March, at a press conference I was forced to hold, I did my best to indicate to the press that the BPF was completely adequate for our operations. I privately believe we could do without a lot of the publicity which I am told the public needs to have about our operations.

I believe you are correct in your statement that the word 'facilities' is a better one than 'bases' Whenever detachments of the BPF operate with the US Pacific Fleet I shall of course do everything I can, both at sea and in port, to facilitate these operations; and I would expect the Senior US Naval Officer Present to aid your detachments by extending the use of facilities wherever practicable.

I look forward to a visit from your CoS, and will welcome a visit from you at my Advanced HQ at a time to be determined by appropriate exchange of dispatches.[2]

---

[1] Fairey Firefly: 1941; 1 engine; 2 crew; 316mph; 4×20mm cannon; 2×1000lb bombs or 8 RP.

[2] Cdre Daniel De Pass: Capt 1934; *Cossack* 1937; Patrol Services, C Depot, Apr 1941; ret Jan 1944; CoS to Fraser 1944.

305. *ICEBERG: British and American Action Reports:*
Cdr Michael Le Fanu[1]

[ADM 199/591]   19 April 1945

...

5. The first preliminary actions in ICEBERG were strikes by aircraft of the Fast Carrier Task Force against Kyushu airfields and warships in Kure harbour. The former found comparatively few aircraft for the enemy have become adept at withdrawing their machines from area under attack. At Kure, although many ships were hit, the damage done was not commensurate with the gallantry with which the attacks were delivered in the face of fierce AA fire. The enemy reacted sharply to these attacks with suicide bombers, one of which damaged the carrier *Franklin*; only magnificent damage control saved the ship. It was significant in covering the crippled carrier the Force was able to prolong to nearly four days its stay within 300 miles of all major Japanese air bases without incurring further major casualties. The *Wasp* and *Enterprise* did however have to be sent back for battle damage repairs. The rapidity with which these repairs were accomplished was later a factor of great importance.

...

13. Meanwhile opportunities for offensive air action are being taken as they arise. As instance the long range fighter sweeps over Kyushu by TF 58 and the BPF strikes against Northern Formosa. Admiral Spruance was genuinely pleased with success of the latter, particularly as it was achieved without damage to our ships.

...

14. With regard to the BPF operations against Sakishima Gunto, Commander 5th Fleet was always convinced of the importance of this target. The justice of this operation must have become increasingly apparent to our aircrews as the operation developed and the evidence of staging accumulated. The results achieved by TF 57 were regarded as most valuable and CTF 57's ability to scrape the bottom of the bomb barrel

---

[1]Cdr Michael Le Fanu (1913–70): *Warspite* Aug 1939; *Aurora* Jan 1940; *Excellent* 1942; *King George V* 1942; *Howe* May 1944; Cdr Dec 1944; *Golden Hind* June 1945; *Eagle* 1957–8; 3SL 1961–5; C-in-C Med 1965–8; FSL 1968–70.

and remain in the combat area for three extra strike days was warmly welcomed.

15. The Commander 5th Fleet shows a keen appreciation of the British logistic difficulties which entail an effort less than the maximum on some strike days and periodical return to an advanced anchorage. Though TF 58 have now been away for five weeks they are not without their own problems, particularly as regards transport CVEs, aircraft and aircrews, and both pilots and planes.

...

16. This report would be incomplete without reference to the most impressive single feature of the operation, namely the cheerful and rugged determination displayed by the individual officers and men. This is particularly true of those who serve in the picket ships. Their work has been beyond praise.

17. In conclusion I am pleased to report that throughout the 5th Fleet there is a genuinely co-operative and appreciative feeling towards the BPF. As the CoS has said to me more than once, 'I feel we are completely "en rapport"'.[1]

18. Finally I should add that this cordial atmosphere is particularly pronounced in the new Fleet Flagship, the *New Mexico*, where the impression left by the last British officer to visit the ship has ensured a warm welcome for all other officers of the RN.

306. *Fisher to Fraser*

[NMM, Fraser 23] *Lothian*,
Leyte,   21 April 1945

...

Americans

... we continue to get on very well indeed with whom we come in contact, officially and otherwise. As I told you in my last letter [above], my dealings are primarily with Commander, Amphibious Group 13 (Rear Admiral Davis), and under him Commander, Service Squadron 10's representative (a Captain, US Navy, in the USS *Argonne*). These two could not be more helpful, and we get more things done by them which

---

[1] CoS to 5 F: unidentified.

would cause a flutter if heard of in Washington, (possibly also officially in Sydney).

...

307. *Vian to Fraser*

[NMM, Fraser 23] At Sea,   22 April 1945

Owing to our slow rate of taking in fuel and avgas our operational days over this period have been considerably less than the US carriers, i.e., we operate for two days and oil for two days, their figures are usually two and one. ... our closed in hangars are the devil in this climate and I don't believe our maintenance crews could stand up to the two and one cycle; also our pilots are pretty well done in after two days striking, and I don't believe they could change to two and one either; their average flying hours are higher I believe than US pilots because we are underborne in numbers.

Another unfavourable comparison between us and US Carriers is that, although we do all we can, we do not achieve the same number of ranges in the day – and therefore strike relatively less – than they do. The explanation to this is I think that (a) our handling parties are small compared to theirs (and we have no room for more), and (b) our rate of refuelling aircraft is pathetic compared to them, because we have low pressure supply and not enough fuelling points, this latter can be put right presumably.

Our plus side – our armoured decks and our fighter direction. The latter has been quite outstanding, and the American observers recognise it. It hangs on rather a thread this, as it is all wrapped up in the genius of Lewin and the fighter direction teams in *Indomitable* and *Victorious*.[1]

308. *Nimitz to King*

[RG 38]   26 April 1945

...

I consider that greatest contribution of the British carrier force to the war against Japan in the near future will be in continued participation in ICEBERG at least until additional airfields are activated in Shima ...

---

[1]AoF Lord (Sir Terry) Lewin (1920–1999): ent RN 1939; Capt *Hermes* 1966–7; VCNS 1971–3; C-in-C, F 1973–5; C-in-C, Naval Home Cmd 1975–7; FSL 1977–9.

309. *Nimitz to Fraser*

[NMM, Fraser 23]   27 April 1945

I thank you very much for your letter of 12 April [not reproduced] which was brought to me by your CoS, who also brought with him a case of stimulants, for which I am very grateful to him. ...

Admiral Spruance and I were extremely well pleased with the performance of TF 57, and particularly with energy and initiative being displayed by the task force commander who is apparently animated with but one thought – to keep engaged with the enemy as often as possible, and as long as possible. Your officers, men and ships have our complete confidence and great admiration, and I hope that nothing will prevent their continuing with us shoulder to shoulder until Japan is crushed.

...

Your CoS has presented very completely your needs for some shore facilities, and he will bring back with him a story of our present situation.

310. *CCS 847: Memorandum by Representatives of the British Chiefs of Staff:*

Naval Base for the British Pacific Fleet

[CAB 88/37]   28 April 1945

1. At the 190th meeting [19 April 1945] of the CCS, the US COS told us of their intended operations against Borneo.
2. We repeated these home to the British COS and explained that the objectives of the operation were:

(a) Primarily to secure a naval base for the BPF at Brunei in North Borneo; and
(b) Secondly to secure a source of oil.

3. The British COS have taken note of the intentions of the US COS and fully appreciate that it is for the US COS to say what operations should be co-ordinated in a US theatre. Nevertheless, they would like to lay before the US COS their views on the subject, particularly as British Commonwealth troops are being used in the operations and the

operations themselves are designed to provide a base for British naval forces.

4. The British COS feel that Brunei is unsuitable as an intermediate base for the BPF for the following reasons:

(a) It is too far from the main theatre of operations against Japan.
(b) It is unlikely that the development of a base could be completed before the beginning of 1946 which will be too late.
(c) It is a long haul from the main base in Australia, compared with other possible sites at the same distance from Japan.

5. What the British COS would prefer as a base for the BPF is a suitable anchorage, with facilities at least partly developed, much nearer Japan than Brunei Bay. They suggest that such an anchorage might be found in the Philippines in which case immediate action might be taken to set up an intermediate base organisation. If this is impossible they would prefer to continue using the existing facilities at Manus rather than establish a base in Brunei Bay. Operating from Manus the BPF might use such advanced anchorages as become available in the main area of operations.

6. In the light of the above views the British COS invite the US COS:

(a) To consider whether the allocation of resources to the proposed Borneo operations for the main purpose of establishing a fleet base is, in fact, justified at the present time.
(b) To consider whether a suitable anchorage, with facilities at least partly developed, can be provided for the BPF nearer Japan than Brunei Bay, preferably in the Philippines.

7. In regard to paragraph 6 (a) above, we fully appreciate that in reaching their decision to carry out these operations the US COS may have been influenced by other considerations than those described in paragraph 2 above, and that it may be considered undesirable and perhaps impossible, to make any change at this late stage. However that may be, the British COS do invite the earnest consideration of the US COS to the matter of the alternative base for the BPF.

CCS 847/1: Memorandum by the US Chiefs of Staff:

Naval Base for BPF.

12 May 1945.

1. The US COS have now examined the views of the British COS as set forth in CCS 847 relative to the establishment of an advanced naval

base for the BPF and the Brunei Bay operation, and offer the following comment:

2. The US COS consider that the main theater of naval operations against Japan extends in the Western Pacific from the Kuriles to the Malay Barrier. Both US and British forces may be employed in any part of this area. There will be naval operations required in the South China Sea in support of operations in the Netherlands East Indies and the Malay Peninsula. It is considered that such operations can be best supported from an advanced base in Brunei Bay.

3. The setting up of an advanced base at Brunei Bay is not intended to preclude the employment of the BPF in any part of the theater of operations or influence necessarily the locations in which it may be employed. The question is rather one of utilizing to the best advantage the base facilities which the British Admiralty is providing for the Pacific.

4. There are no available sites in the Philippines, partly developed or otherwise, at which to install the British base, and it is felt that Manus is too far from the theater of operations to be suitable.

5. The seizure of the Brunei Bay area is considered a desirable operation whether or not it is utilized for an advanced British naval base. In view of the fact that it should be in our hands within a month, and in light of the foregoing comments, the US COS ask that the British COS reconsider their views in the matter of installing base facilities at Brunei Bay.

311.   *Vice Admiral Sir Bernard Rawlings: Report on ICEBERG Phase I, 26 March to 20 April 1945[1]*

[ADM 199/555]   9 May 1945

14 April 1945.
Tribute to the Late President of the USA.

0630. Made contact with TU 112.2/5 and Tanker Group consisting of five tankers in position Cootie Island 21° 12'M, 128° 44'E.

HM Ships *Formidable*, *Kempenfelt* and *Wessex* were also met and joined TF 57.

Fuelling was commenced in fine weather and proceeded with less delays than usual.

Illustrious was sailed for Leyte at 1755 screened by *Urania* and *Quality*.

As from today the US Fleet was ordered to half-mast colours, and I gave orders that British ships in harbour, or near thereto, should conform.

---

[1] Adm Sir Bernard Rawlings commanded BPF at sea.

Since US ships do not, I understand, fly their colours in the operational areas and the half-masting of our colours at sea in war is I believe only done when conveying or burying the deceased, the position was not clear as regards TF 57. I felt it fitting, however, and in keeping with what I knew to be the feeling of the Fleet for this great leader and sincere friend of the British Empire, to mark the occasion irrespective of precedent; therefore I ordered colours to be half masted for the last hour before sunset today.[1]

The Fleet disengaged from the Tanker Force for the night.

312.   *Nimitz to Fraser*

[RG 38]   22 May 1945

Careful consideration has been given to the probable future requirements of the BPF for base facilities in view of the developments to be expected in the war against Japan. …

2. It would appear that the base facilities prospectively available for the support of the BPF would contribute more to the overall base structure in the Pacific if located at Brunei Bay rather than Manus. The establishment of an advanced base would not preclude the employment of the British CTF wherever needed. It would permit its employment in an area where base facilities will otherwise be lacking.

313.   *CCS 847/2: Memorandum by Representatives of the British Chiefs of Staff.*

Naval Base for BPF.

[CAB 88/37]   25 May 1945.

1. In accordance with the request of the US COS in CCS 847/1 [above], the British COS have re-examined the question of the suitability of Brunei Bay as an intermediate base for the BPF.

2. The British COS agree with the US COS that the main theatre of operations against Japan extends from the Kuriles to the Malay Barrier, and that both US and British forces may be employed in any part of the area.

---

[1]Pres Roosevelt died on 11 April 1945.

3. They cannot foresee, however, any operations in the South China Sea which would require in Borneo more than an advanced anchorage with very limited shore facilities.

4. They consider that to develop Brunei Bay as an intermediate base would be a waste of constructional resources at our disposal, especially in view of the fact that the base would not be completed until the end of the year, by which time Singapore may well have been captured.

314. *Stark to King*

[RG 38]   28 May 1945

Admiralty reply: Experience has shown the need for all the CVEs that we can provide.

Indeed C-in-C BPF has lately signalled an urgent request for more CVEs with which to support his fleet. Four LFCs are shortly to be sent to the Pacific. They must be supported by CVEs and spare air groups and the ferry work will increase proportionately.

2. The situation is aggravated by (a) the continued absence of an inter-mediate base in the Philippines for which we have asked; (b) by the increased tempo of operations in a sea where the assault operations are to a large extent beyond the range of support by shore-based aircraft; (c) the small assignments of US aircraft which make it more than ever necessary to reduce the time spent in transferring aircraft to operational carriers. ...

3. In view of the foregoing it is much regretted that no British CVEs can be made available to the US Pacific Fleet and that it now necessary for us to ask for the return of *Atheling, Rajah* and *Tracker* ...

315. *King to Nimitz*

[RG 38]   28 May 1945

First Sea Lord feels that unless BPF can base in Philippine Islands it cannot function as fully as it is otherwise capable of doing. ...

316. *Capt M. M. Dupre, Jr, US Navy: Memorandum for F-01*

[RG 38]   29 May 1945

It is obvious that the accumulating pressure ... is a well-worked out scheme correlated in the Admiralty with the political side of the British government

to put the British in a position to consummate a horse trade or two after the war. It is equally obvious that the horse trade that all this jockeying is leading up to is swapping the broken-down, toothless nag that will be the British base in the Philippines for a healthy spirited three-year old that is Manus.
2. Toughness and bluntness seems to me to be indicated.

317. *Nimitz to King*

[RG 38]   30 May 1945

… I see no need for a British base in the Philippines for either category of operations [i.e., operations with the US 3rd Fleet against metropolitan Japan, or re-opening the Malacca Strait and liberating South East Asia]. If it later develops that British ships operate against Japan with a line of supply through Malay Straits[,] Ulithi and Leyte can be used as advanced anchorages.

318. *Fraser to Nimitz*

[ADM 199/594]   4 June 1945

Provided no unforeseen difficulties in making good battle damage become apparent when the Fleet is inspected on arrival at Sydney I expect TF 37 to be ready to sortie from either (a) Manus on 2 July or (b) Leyte on 8 July.
2. Information would be appreciated on the next combat and servicing areas to be allocated to TF 37 in order that consideration may be given to the best anchorage from which to operate.
3. If these areas are to be in the neighbourhood of Hokkaido or North Honshu there would be much to be said for operating from Manus rather than Leyte. Advantages would be (a) the haul from Manus to Leyte would be saved (b) the typhoon area would be avoided (c) some British air facilities are already established at Manus (d) British air facilities would not require to be established at Leyte for the present.
4. The main disadvantage would be the rather longer haul from Manus to the probable servicing area which would be at present just beyond the capacity of my tanker resources. If the previous rates of striking are to be maintained, this disadvantage however would be offset if some of my tankers could occasionally draw from bulk supplies from Guam and Saipan.
5. Early advice on paragraph 2 would be appreciated as in the event of operating the fleet from Manus it will be necessary to divert to Manus

the aircraft pools at present planned to be established for the next operation at Samar.

6. On receipt of your reply I would like to send my assistant CoS Captain Brown[1] to your HQ at Guam to discuss implications (such as that referred to in paragraph 4) of long range operations to the northwards.

Nimitz to Fraser.

12 June 1945.

At present time consider you should plan to sortie from Manus as early in July as repairs to battle damage permit. Will keep you informed of any change of date.

2. Details of service areas have not yet been promulgated by Commander 3rd Fleet but initial combat area will be NE of Tokyo.

3. It is not (R) possible to draw bulk fuel supplies from Marianas but Ulithi could be used.

4. Concur with your proposal to send Captain Brown to my Advanced HQ. Captain Ewen [US Navy] will shortly be leaving Guam to visit you and after conferring with you I would like him to confer with Commander 3rd Fleet and CTF 38 before rejoining CTF 37.[2]

319. *Fraser to Nimitz*

[RG 38]   6 June 1945

... I would like to say how grateful I am for the great assistance that we have always had from Comnavbase and his staff at Manus. I fully realise that we are asking a great deal, but there is not time to build our own base if our additional ships are to operate this summer.

320. *Rawlings to Spruance*

[ADM 199/1041]   6 June 1945

I have the honour to forward for your information and in continuation of my 1092/4 of 9 May 1945 [not reproduced] the attached narrative and report of proceedings of TF 57 during the second phase of Operation ICEBERG; insofar as the BPF is concerned it terminates their contribution thereto.

---

[1]Capt Brown: unidentified.
[2]Capt E. C. Ewen, US Navy: Liaison Officer to Rawlings.

2. The object throughout was to prevent the enemy making use of the airfields in the Sakishima Gunto group.

3. Over the whole period TF 57 was at sea for 62 days, broken by eight days re-storing at Leyte, maintaining an intermittent neutralisation, we also attacked one of the airfields by day. During its absence an American TG took over this duty and, in the latter stages, aircraft based in Okinawa also took part. Whilst the latter's contribution is not known in detail their work at night was particularly welcome.

During this time the TF flew 4852 sorties, dropped 875 tons of bombs and rocket projectiles, destroyed 100 enemy aircraft and damaged 70 others; various other targets such as shipping, W/T stations, etc. Our own losses were 33 aircraft from enemy action; in all 92 were lost operationally.

4. The decisive factor governing the ability of the TF to continue operations was the armour of the carriers; details of the damage they sustained have been forwarded to the C-in-C, Pacific Fleet, and to the C-in-C, BPF.

These decks have proved their worth against the specialised form of Kamikaze attack, but the damage caused was nevertheless severe. The carriers were in every case able to continue operations in spite of this.

In this respect it is interesting that at one stage of the war (1941) when opinions were expressed in some quarters that we had 'wasted' a great deal of weight in armouring decks and so limiting the number of aircraft carried. This was in the days of high level and dive bombers.

…

12. The assistance of the US Authorities at Leyte was greatly appreciated, and I must once more express my admiration and gratitude for the excellent arrangements for ASR by means of Lifeguard submarines and Dumbo aircraft.

…

Appendix No. 1

…

23 April [arrived at Leyte].

Practices: Owing to the lack of local facilities [at Leyte] and the work in hand, few harbour exercise were carried out. US instructors were lent to the Fleet and instructor classes in aircraft recognition [were held], and a US Avenger was provided for daily height finding exercises.

…

Admiral Kingman:[1] On arrival at Leyte I waited upon Admiral King-man, and with him met Vice Admiral J. L. Kauffman, Commander, Philippines Sea Frontier and Rear Admiral R. O. Davis, Commander, Amphibious Group 13. They all lunched on board my flagship. Commodore E. M. Evans-Lombe, Captain (S) J. R. Alfrey, [respectively] CoS and Secretary to C-in-C, BPF, after most useful discussions with Flag Officers of the TF, left Leyte by air for Guam: Captain E. C. Ewen, US Navy, Liaison Officer with TF 57, travelled with them.

4 May.

Formidable *hit.*

There were no bandits on the screen when at 1131 a Zeke was seen diving from a great height on to *Formidable* and engaged by gunfire.[2] AC1 thereupon manoeuvred his force under wheel at high speed by successive emergency turns. Though repeatedly hit by close range weapons by his target, the Kamikaze crashed onto the flight deck of *Formidable* near the island structure and started a large fire in the deck park of aircraft. AC1 manoeuvred the formation to keep in close touch with the damaged ship, whose speed was temporarily reduced to 18 knots.

The Kamikaze appeared to release his bomb just before his aircraft hit the deck, causing the following damage: eight killed and 47 wounded, one Corsair and 10 Avengers damaged beyond repair; all radar except Type 277 put out of action, both barriers two feet square and two feet dead past the centre; armoured deck splinter passed through hangar deck; horizontal partition between down takes, escape hatch which was shut, and so to the central boiler room where it caused slight damage and loss of steam, and finally pierced the inner bottom.

Formidable *recovers.*

Meanwhile the fires in *Formidable* were soon under control, and by 1254 the ship was capable of 24 knots. It was estimated that one barrier could be in operation by 1600, and that the flight deck would be patched up by then.

... Aircraft from the *Formidable* were landed on the other carriers.

---

[1]Adm Howard F. Kingman, US Navy (1890–1968): USNA 1911; NWC 1932; Asst Naval Attaché, London, 1928–30; Cdr, DesRon 19, 1939–41; *Nevada* 1942–3; Cdr, 15 N Dist, PCZ; Cdr, SE Pac 1944–5; Cdr 3 F, 1945–6; ret 1947.

[2]Mitsubishi A6M Zeke (Zero): Japan; fighter; 1939; 1 engine; 1 crew; 351mph; 2×20mm cannon, 2mg; 700lbs bombs.

5 May.

Victorious *hit*.

From 1650 onwards the Fleet was radically manoeuvred by emergency turns at 22 knots. One minute after such a turn of 60° to starboard was executed, a suicider made a 10° angle dive onto *Victorious* from her starboard quarter. The enemy was hit by close range weapons but crashed onto the flight deck near the forward lift. The resulting fire was quickly brought under control, but the bomb explosion holed the flight deck, put the accelerator out of action, rendered one 4.5in. gun mounting unserviceable, and damaged one lift hoisting motor.

At 1656 another Kamikaze made a shallow power glide from astern on *Victorious*. Though hard hit by gunfire, and well on fire, it hit the flight deck aft a glancing blow, and burning furiously passed over the side. Damage to the ship was confined to one arrester unit out of action, a 40mm gun directly destroyed, and four Corsairs on deck damaged beyond repair.

Casualties from both these attacks were three killed, four seriously injured, and 15 wounded.

At 1705 a fourth Kamikaze approached *Formidable* and then *Indomitable*, being engaged by both ships without apparent result. It then turned and dived into the after deck park of *Formidable*.

There was a large explosion and fire and a great deal of smoke. Speed was reduced to 15 knots to aid control of the fire which was extinguished at 1720. Six Corsairs and one Avenger were destroyed by fire on deck. The explosion blew out a flight deck rivet and thus allowed burning petrol to fall into the hangar which had to be sprayed. As a result a further three Avengers and eight Corsairs were damaged. The total replacements required were therefore four Avengers and 14 Corsairs, of which three Avengers and seven Corsairs were flyable duds.

Casualties were fortunately light: one killed and a few injured.

At 1755 *Formidable* reported fit to land on aircraft and that during the engagement she had definitely shot down one enemy by gunfire.

Decision to withdraw.

The state of the Carrier Squadron was as follows: *Formidable* and *Victorious* could operate but the former had only four bombers and 11 fighters serviceable, and also had two pom-pom mountings out of action. *Victorious* could operate a few aircraft at a time, but damage to her lift seriously reduced her speed of handling. In the circumstances I agreed with the recommendation from AC1 that the Fleet should withdraw to fuel, sort out and make good the damage, etc., and return to strike on 12 and 13 May. In my signal 0911/5 I informed Commander 5th Fleet of this intention, and at 1950 course was set for area COOTIE.

…

321. *King to Stark*

[RG 38]   9 June 1945

… [If the COS] do not desire to meet our wishes for the establishment of shore facilities to support a fleet anchorage at Brunei Bay, I have no further suggestions to offer as to the employment of the resources involved.

322. *British Pacific Fleet War Diary*

[ADM 199/1457]   9 June 1945

…

Manus is an amazing example of what the Americans accomplish when they set out to 'plan big'.

After making full allowance for unlimited manpower and an open cheque book, the fact remains it was conceived and carried out by men with great minds and drive. In passing one might mention that Manus at this time of year possesses one of the most objectionable climates that I have ever known: it appears to improve but little at any time. I find myself wondering therefore under what circumstance and by whose whimsical conception these unpleasant islands should have been named in honour of Their Lordships.

323. *Vian to Fraser*

[ADM 199/594]   12 June 1945

To provide night fighter section and photographic unit in *Formidable* intend following arrangements:

2. Reduce *Formidable* to 12 Avengers.
3. Two PRU Hellcats and four Hellcats with appropriate pilots and maintenance ratings from *Indomitable* to *Formidable*.
4. Transfers to be effected as convenient before sailing.

324. *Operation MERIDIAN: Destruction of Oil Refineries
in Sumatra.*

[ADM 199/555]   13 June 1945

Note by Director of Air Warfare and Flying Training.[1]

Suitability of Aircraft

The lesson that endurance for Naval fighters is of great importance is
again evident from this report, not only that they shall be able to accompany the strike as escort but also that the Fleet does not suffer from the
restrictions of having to turn into wind at short intervals to relieve the
CAP. The Seafire has not got this valuable attribute, and further, falls
short of its American contemporaries in other matters of performance
and ruggedness. There is no escaping the fact that it falls short by a long
way of what is required, as AC 1 aptly puts it, for Ocean Warfare.

325. *Halsey to Fraser*

[ADM 199/594]   15 June 1945

Captain Brown sends:

TF 37 will in effect be a group of TF 38. Commander 3rd Fleet requests
early visit to Leyte of Staff Officers from Fleet (Commander level) to discuss tactical air operation, fighter direction and surface tactical co-operation.

326. *Joint Chiefs of Staff*

[RG 218/196]   18 June 1945

...

In connection with British participation in the Pacific, General Marshall
said that the President would find the Prime Minister very articulate.[2] He
is interested in showing that the British Government has played a full
part in the defeat of Japan and that it had not been necessary for them
to wait for the US to recapture Singapore for them. The Americans, of

---

[1]Capt G. Willoughby: Dir of Air Warfare & Flying Trng, 13 June 1945.
[2]Pres Harry S. Truman (1884–1964): Sen, Dem, Mo, 1935–44; Chmn, Sen Cttee on war
effort; VP, Jan–Apr 1945; Pres 1945–9 & (in own right) 1949–53.

course, were glad to have any real help or any assistance that would help in striking a real blow, but that British participation in some ways would constitute an embarrassment. However, the British were under American overall command in the Pacific.

327. *Fraser to Nimitz*

[ADM 199/594]   20 June 1945

Formation of Task Force for First Operation.

BB   *King George V*
CV   *Formidable* (Flagship, AC 1), *Victorious, Indefatigable, Implacable.*
CL   *Newfoundland* (Flagship, CS 4), *Achilles, Uganda, Gambia.*
CL/AA   *Black Prince, Eurydice.*
DD   *Barfleur* (Flagship, RA(D))
'   *Quality, Quadrant, Quiberon, Quickmatch, Queenborough*
        Troubridge (D24), *Tenacious, Termagant, Terpischore, Teazer*
        Grenville (D25), *Undine, Ulysses, Urania, Undaunted, Urchin*
        Napier (D7), *Nepal, Norman, Nizam*

2. *Maximum likely additions in July:*

BB   *Duke of York*
CL   *Bermuda* (Flagship, CS2)
CL/AA   *Argonaut*
DD   *Wrangler, Wakeful*

3. *Maximum likely additions in August:*

CVL   *Venerable* (Flagship, AC11), *Vengeance, Colossus*
DD   *Tuscan, Tyrian, Tumult*
        Kempenfelt (D27), *Wager, Whelp, Whirlwind*

328. *Memorandum for King by Admiral Edwards, US Navy*

[RG 38]   23 June 1945

…

2. … I think Admiral Fraser has some ground for being displeased by the US failure to get clear of bases he might use in Australia. While the British have been extremely unreasonable as to Brunei, nevertheless I

think it would be well to offer them something to cheer them up. Sherman suggests that it might be desirable to tell Fraser that he can use all the means at his disposal to build a British base in the Admiralties, provided he keeps clear of US installations.[1] This has some disadvantages which are obvious, but since the British appear to be building up a list of grievances, it might be [wise?] to offer something, and I know of nothing they are likely to regard as acceptable except a base of their own at Manus or in the Philippines, and the latter is certainly out of the question.

329.   *Fraser to Nimitz*

[RG 38]   23 June 1945

I do not think I can effectively support the BPF later in the year unless I can now get on with the facilities asked for at Manus and the use of Eagle Farm, Brisbane.

2. From the examinations we have made I do not believe that we should in any way be hampering the American war effort by using these places and I am now in the position of endeavouring to carry out your operational requirements whilst at the same time I do not seem to get the necessary support in my logistical arrangements.

3. I cannot see what action to take next and would be grateful for your advice and assistance as my operational C-in-C.

330.   *Fraser to Admiralty*

[ADM 199/594]   27 June 1945

Following is allocation of ships to TF commanders at outset of July operations:

A. To CTF 113.

DD	Depot Ship *Tyne*
DD	add *Wrangler*, *Wakeful*
B.	To CTF 113, who has detached them to CTF 112:
DD	*Napier*, *Nizam*, *Nepal*, *Norman*, *Queenborough*

---

[1]Adm Forrest C. Sherman: CO *Lexington* 1941; Gilberts; Carrier Task Grp 1943; Truk, Leyte 1944; Chf Staff Planner, CINCPOA.

C.
To CTF 112:

Depot Ships	*Montclare, Lothian, Empire Spearhead*
Transport	*Glenearn*[1]
Repair	Ships *Artifex, Resource*
Aircraft	Repair Ships *Pioneer, Unicorn, Deersound*
Escort Carriers	*Stalker, Speaker, Ruler, Arbiter, Chaser, Slinger*
Escort Maintenance	*Kelantor, Flamborough Head*
Escorts	*Pheasant, Woodcock, Whimbrel, Crane, Redpoll, Parrett, Findhorn, Avon, Usk, Barle, Odzam, Derg, Helford, Plym* and

all ships of 21 and 22 MSFs

Radar Repair	*Arbutus*
Deperming	*Springdale*
Tugs	*Wezel, Empress Josephine, Lariat*

Fleet Auxiliaries and Merchant Ships of Fleet Train.

331. *Fraser to Nimitz*

[ADM 199/594]   4 July 1945

I hereby report TF 37 for duty with 3rd Fleet. We are much looking forward to our first operation under your orders.

332. *King to Forrestal*

[LC, King 11] Potsdam,   22 July 1945

The major issue of the day in the CCS was the British bid for full participation in determining the strategy of the campaign against Japan proper. This, of course, the JCS opposed. After discussion in closed session, it seems likely that the outcome will be that we will inform and *consult* the British but that *we will decide*.

[1]*Glenearn*: Glen Line; 1938; 9784t; 18k.

333.   *Captain J. M. Creighton, US Navy, to Nimitz[1]*

[Nimitz 13/122]   24 July 1945

1. 'Face' has a great effect all over the Orient, and this effect powerfully influences business relations as well as social, diplomatic and all other relations.

2. Whether we like it or not, the Chinese have been convinced for a hundred years that the 'First Chop' foreign people were the British and the latter have gone to every possible contrivance to continue and fortify this 'impression'.

3. The swank location in Shanghai is on the Bund, and here you will find the British Consul-General, the British banks and the British (Shanghai) Club. Our counterparts are all down in the back streets.

4. The man-of-war buoys in front of the Bund mark 'Battleship row'. The leading berth (right in front of the Shanghai Club and all the big business houses) was reserved for the British flagship. It was also the only berth of the lot, the buoys of which were far enough apart to get a cruiser into. The results were, not only was the British man-of-war always at the head of the column with the rest of us tailing out behind up towards the slums of the native city, but a big cruiser with the British flag on it displayed its magnificent bulk to the world in contrast to a little gunboat or a couple of destroyers, which was all we could install in our 600 feet buoy span.

5. We made repeated efforts from 1933 onwards to get the British berth moved forward so that we could spread out our buoy and get the *Augusta* into the line. The British, through their instrumentalities the Harbor Board and the Shanghai Municipal Council said:

(a)   To move the British berth forward would interfere with traffic in and out of Soo Chow Creek.

(b)   To extend the rear (or upstream) buoys farther would interfere with the commercial traffic of the wharves up there.

(c)   (unsaid) The present situation was carefully planned and suits our purposes perfectly. Too bad.

To assist our future in China, to contribute to the primacy of our business, and to support all our diplomatic and service life in the area, I suggest that it be carefully planned that the first Allied men-of-war to enter this harbour will be OURS, and that they include a cruiser which can

---

[1]Capt J. M. Creighton, US Navy (1891–1957): USNA 1914; s/m 1915–20; CO, *Preston, Leary* 1928–31; Cdr, DD Div 12, Bat Force 1939–40; Naval Attaché, China 1940–41; staff appts; ret 1945.

take that front berth AND KEEP IT. If, for two or three years, we have a relief cruiser ready to slip into that berth whenever occupant departs, I think we will have it nailed down.

There is no longer any British-dominated Harbor Board or Municipal Council to be brought into play, and if it gets to a Chungking decision we should have more influence there than anyone else. But I bet my bottom $ that the British, fully aware of the great importance of these things throughout Asia, will employ every nimble, persuasive trick in or out of the book to get into the harbour first and get right smack into their old berth.

One scheme you may have presented to you is this:

The Japanese used to have a berth. Throw them out. Enlarge the upstream berths and then the French and Americans can get a cruiser into the line, but in the same sequence we used to lie [in].

...

334. *Leahy: Diary*

[LC, Leahy]   Potsdam,
                                                          8 August 1945

... The lethal possibilities of such atomic action in the future is frightening, and while we are the first to have it in our possession, there is a certainty that it will in the future be developed by potential enemies and that it will probably be used against us.

335. *Fleet Admiral Nimitz to ALPOA*

[ADM 199/594]   10 August 1945

The public announcement by the Japanese of counter proposals for the termination of the war must not be permitted to affect the vigilance against Japanese attacks. Neither the Japanese nor the Allied forces have stopped fighting. Take precautions against treachery even if local or general surrender should be suddenly announced. Maintain all current reconnaissance and patrols. Offensive actions should continue unless announced specifically.

336. *Rawlings to Halsey*

[ADM 199/594]   11 August 1945

The British Fleet is proud to have fought under your command in these great days.

337.   *Rawlings to Vian*

[ADM 199/594]   12 August 1945

On parting company I can speak for the whole fleet in saying how much we admired the gallantry and persistence of the aircrews and stout hearted work of the carriers.

2. You have written a new chapter in naval flying, which has been rewarded by helping to write finis to Japan and her fleet.

3. Not less valuable for our future are the links you have helped to forge between us and the US Fleet.

338.   *Atlee to Fraser[1]*

[NMM, Fraser 21]   12 August 1945

I have designated you as British representative to accompany General MacArthur in order to receive the Japanese surrender.

339.   *Cunningham to Fraser*

[NMM, Fraser 21]   13 August 1945

I am so glad that you have been selected as British Representative. You probably have already considered sending Vice Admiral, BPF, to Guam where he will be in best position to control movements of BPF for you in your absence and be in closest touch with CINCPAC HQ.

If you agree no doubt you will place TG 38.5 under another Flag Officer.

340.   *Nimitz to Fraser et al.*

[ADM 199/594]   12 August 1945

...

On 10 August 1945 Admiral Fraser, on behalf of HM King George VI invested Fleet Admiral Nimitz with the Order of Knight Grand Cross of the Bath. The ceremony was witnessed by a gathering of 50 officers and 200 enlisted men of the US forces. *Duke of York* was accompanied

---

[1]Clement R. Attlee (1883–1967); Maj, 1914–18; lecturer, London School of Economics 1913–23; Lab MP; Chancellor, Duchy of Lancaster, 1930–31; Paymaster Gen 1931; Ldr, Lab, 1935–55; Lord Privy Seal 1940–42; Dep PM 1942–5; PM 1945–51; Earl 1955.

by HM Destroyers *Wager* and *Whelp*. At a press conference on board Admiral Fraser revealed that HMS *Anson* and new light aircraft carriers were now in the Pacific as part of his fleet. He also stated that the combined strength of the BPF and Fleet Train was more than 400 ships and 200,000 men.

341. *Halsey to all Task Group Commanders*

[ADM 199/594]   15 August 1945

During the period 26 May to 15 August 3rd Fleet forces with British Carrier Task Force in company from 16 July to 12 August attacked 260 airfields in Nansei Shoto, Kyushu, Shikoku, Honshu [and] Hokkaido. 290 enemy aircraft were splashed, 1301 destroyed and 1374 damaged on the ground for a total of 2865 planes out of action. Of this total [?] were shot down, 131 destroyed on the ground and 217 damaged by TF 37. Recapitulation of shipping losses for the same period: Warships: sank 1 BB, 2BB-XCV, 1 CA, 1 CL, 1 CA, [–] DD, 12 various types [of] escort, 7 SS, 15 LC, [–] PTs and small naval craft. Damaged: 1 BB, 3 CV, 2 CVL, 3 CVE, 1 CA (probably sunk in shallow water), 18 DD, 44 [of] various types [of] escort, 15 SS including [–] midgets, 13 LC, [–] PCs and small craft. Merchant: sank 8 AO, 6 Train Ferries, 49 AP/AK under 1000 tons, 366 tugs, dredgers, luggers [and] miscellaneous small craft. Damaged: 27 AO, 5 Train Ferries (possibly 2 of these included under sunk), 101 AP/AK over 1000 tons, 193 AP/AK under 1000 tons, 643 tugs, dredgers, luggers [and] miscellaneous small craft. Some duplications undoubtedly exist between sunk and damaged in merchant vessels also possible minor duplication in late combat [–]. In addition to damaging very vital Okinawa ground targets during air support missions devastating strikes were made throughout [the] home islands against industries, railroads, warehouses, airfield installations, [and] dockyards. Destroyed 195 and damaged 109 locomotives of which TF 37 scored 8 destroyed [and] 5 damaged.

As part of Okinawa operation bombardments by surface units directed against Japanese positions [on] Okinawa [and] adjacent islands plus Okino Daito and Minami Daito. Subsequently major bombardments [were] carried out against industrial targets in the home islands at Muroran, Kamashi, Hitachia [and] Hamanatsu with British units joined in the last three. Day and night sweeps [were] conducted along coast of Japan.

From 28 May through 14 August TF 38 flew 14,304 offensive and 7708 covering sorties dropping 4780 tons of bombs and firing 21,713 rockets. TF 37 from 16 May through 12 August flew 1483 offensive [and] 969 covering sorties dropping 517 tons of bombs and firing 56 rockets. During these last three major air attacks against [the Japanese] Empire namely 9, 10 and 13 August a decisive blow was dealt [to] the Japanese air force with over 1100 of [the] enemy's jealously hoarded strength being put out of action.

342. *BPF: Task Organization*

[ADM 199/593]   19 August 1945

TF 37 (Vice Admiral H. B. Rawlings)

Make demonstration in force in Sagami Wan when directed. Reinforce, support and cover TGs 30.1, 30.2, TFs 31 and 35 when directed. CTF 37 arrange for own logistics in Tokyo Bay Area keeping Commander 3rd Fleet and CTF 35 advised of required movements.

TG 30.2 – British Flagship Group (Captain A. D. Nicholl).[1]

TG 30.1 and 30.2 operate as directed by Commander 3rd Fleet.

343   *Report by Rear Admiral Portal*[2]

[ADM 199/119]   August 1945

…

Part IX
Section 11
Report on the arrival of Nabaron *at Ponam Island*

8. (f) … it is an Army commitment to unload stores, a MONAB does not, except for the Coles Crane, carry the necessary equipment – cranes, grabs, slings, nets, etc. Nor does the *Clan Macaulay*. The Seebees came to the rescue with an assortment of fearsome machines and the finest crane driver it has been my [good] fortune to meet. Without them, it is doubtful whether the heavier stores could have been landed at all.[3]

…

---

[1]Capt A. D. Nicholl (1896–1977): Capt June 1929; War Cab, *President* Aug 1939–41; *Penelope* May 1942; DOD (F) 1942; *Duke of York* Mar 1944; Cdre, RN Barracks, Portsmouth, 1946–7; RA 1948; NATO 1948–51; ret 1951.
[2]RA Portal: RA & ACNS (A), Sept 1943; *Golden Hind, 1944–5*.
[3]Seabees: US Navy Construction Battalions.

Remarks and Recommendations

10. Some of the supporting requirements are mentioned below.

11. They are all provided by the Seebees, a magnificent corps, composed mainly of men who in civilian life engaged in the various skilled jobs required of them in war. The spirit, ingenuity and skill of those assisting us are beyond praise. It is strongly recommended that representatives of the corresponding Units forming to support the Royal Navy should be sent to study the Seebee organisation, methods and equipment; and to tap their unrivalled expertise.

Clothing

19. Some minor points:

(a) Coral boots are essential; ordinary boots and shoes fall to pieces in a few weeks. The US pattern coral boot is excellent.

...

(c) Some sort of light cap or hat is badly required. ... The US Navy white linen hat or their baseball cap are both light and practical. ...

...

21. In spite of (or perhaps because of) the very hard work they had to do, the party appeared thoroughly to enjoy the Robinson Crusoe existence. They were most cheerful and their behaviour was excellent.

344. *Report of Experience of the BPF, 1–8 August 1945*

[ADM 199/1457] August 1945

I. Fleet Organisation Lessons

...

(c) *Bombardment*

8. The US Fleet do not normally embark a bombardment liaison officer in a ship carrying out a bombardment. This is difficult to understand in the face of European experience, and it is of interest that when American bombardment liaison officers have embarked as has happened with US ships supporting Australian landings, the American ships and commanders have themselves reported in glowing terms of the very great help that the bombardment liaison officers have been.

(d) *AA Fire*

...

12. The towing arrangements in US aircraft were most efficient and considerably superior to our own.

...

14. The use by the Americans of small Drone aircraft was noticeable. This was the most common form of target at their shore AA ranges, which were set up at all their Pacific base, where excellent training was given to large numbers of men without unduly straining US resources of aircraft. Drone targets were also successfully operated from US combat ships, particularly cruisers, and it is recommended that some form of target be introduced.

...

(c) *Submarines*

The US submarines, with their high speed, long distance, good habitability and efficient radar, were more suited to Pacific operations than the British 'S' and 'T' classes. It was, in fact, only in the later stages of the war, when the enemy was forced into coastal crawling in shallow water, that the British submarines had an advantage over the American. It was however for this very purpose that British submarines were designed.
2. Submarines played a very definite part in the air-sea rescue organisation. British submarines were not generally employed on this duty. It is one however which they might well be called upon to perform in this type of ocean warfare.

...

(g) *Communications*

...

3. It is recommended that the British adopt in plan the basic principles of the organisation used by the US Navy, so that, should complete tactical co-operation be required again, it can be done quickly and with less effort.

345.   *Halsey to Nimitz*

[Halsey 37]   September 1945

Report on Operations of the Third Fleet, 16 August 1945 to 19 September 1945.

1. Early in August estimates of the situation indicated that the collapse of Japanese resistance might occur within a matter of days. ... Orders were issued by the Commander 3rd Fleet to keep the logistic pipeline full in case it might be necessary to indefinitely prolong operations in [Japanese] Empire waters; ...

2. By 10 August planning was well in hand to meet by emergency measures the contingency of surrender; ...

3. The forces afloat were called upon to organise marine and bluejacket landing force components and to assemble groups of specialists and artificers to permit the establishment of temporary emergency shore facilities and to operate seized Japanese facilities and equipment.

...

11. Satisfied with the minefield information, the advance units of the 3rd Fleet led by the *Missouri* and including *King George V*, flagship of Admiral Sir Bruce Fraser, C-in-C British Pacific Fleet, approached selecting anchorages in Sagami Wan (27 August, Yokohama). ... At sunset from the *Missouri*'s anchorage the sun appeared to descend into the crater of Fujiyama; the symbolism was obvious.

...

17. On 2 September, aboard the *Missouri*, the final surrender of the Japanese was received by General of the Army MacArthur (Supreme Commander) and by representatives of the Allied Powers. ... . The period of preparation was finished; the occupation of Japan had begun.

	British	American
No. of Fleet Carriers used	4	10
No. of LFC used	0	6
No. of Strike Days	8	13
No. of Complement Aircraft	255	1191
Total Sorties on Strike Days	2615	18163
Total Offensive Sorties on Strike Days	1595	10678
Offensive Sorties as % of Total Sorties	61.0	58.8
Total Sorties per complement aircraft per Strike Day	1.39	1.39
Tons of bombs dropped per offensive sortie	0.30	0.43
Nos. of enemy aircraft destroyed & damaged	447	2408
Nos. destroyed & damaged per offensive sortie	0.28	0.22
Tons of enemy shipping destroyed and damaged	356,760	924,000

Tons of shipping destroyed and damaged per sortie	224	90
Combat losses as % of offensive sorties	2.38	1.61
Operational losses as % of offensive sorties	2.00	0.55
RPs fired per offensive sortie	0.04	2.06

346.   *The BPF in Operations against Japan*

[ADM 199/118]   15 October 1945

…

XIV. *Comparison of British and American Carriers in the July-August Operations.*

138. The following table compares British and American Carrier effort and achievements during the July-August operations:

139. The above table is intended to give only a general picture. The report of the Commander, 2nd Carrier Task Force, does not go into detail, and it is therefore impossible, with the data at present available, to break the figures down by type of aircraft, by type of sortie, and targets.
140. Nevertheless the material is adequate to show that the British Carriers proportionate and total effort was almost exactly the same as that of the American Carriers. British Carrier aircraft dropped 30% less bombs per sortie than American aircraft owing to the fact that Seafires and Fireflies could not carry bombs over the long distances required. Only 56 RP were fired by Fireflies, compared with 22,036 HVAR by the Americans.
141. The ratios of enemy aircraft destroyed and damaged to offensive sorties (of all types) were roughly comparable between the two forces. On the other hand, the British interpretation of 'damaged' appears to have been more liberal than the American. Despite the similar average loads of bombs carried by British aircraft, and the fact that RPs were not used against shipping by any British aircraft, 2.5 times as much shipping per offensive sortie is claimed as sunk or damaged by the British as by the Americans. British claims of sinking compares more closely, however – 19 tons per offensive sortie as against the American claim of 24 tons per offensive sortie.
142. British combat losses were some 48% higher than American combat losses, though on the whole the Americans probably attacked the more heavily defended targets. This was probably due

(a) to the smaller average size of British sweeps and strikes (see #109) [not reproduced].

(b) to the fact that the British had no VT-fuzed flak-busting bombs to drop.

(c) to the fact that the British did not employ radar-jamming nor radar counter-measures.

Combat losses are further analysed in #100–102 [not reproduced].

143. British operational losses were nearly four times as high as American losses. The Seafire and Firefly, with loss ratios of 2.3% and 3.3% respectively, were only partly responsible for this. Even Corsairs and Avengers showed high operational loss rates compared with the Americans – 1.9% and 1.7% respectively, as against the overall American operational loss rate of 0.55% . . .

XV. *Conclusion.*

144. On eight days during July and August 1945, TF 37 of the BPF undertook air operations against Japan which proportionately, in effort involved and results achieved, compared favourably with the American TF 38, with which TF 37 was in company.

145. For the loss outright of 100 aircraft and 32 crews, and without damage to any Carrier, 133 enemy aircraft were destroyed and a further 215 damaged, over 30,000 tons of shipping were claimed as sunk and a further 300,000 tons damaged, and a large number of airfield installations and other important land targets were destroyed or damaged.

347. *Admiral Sir Bruce Fraser: The Royal Navy*
in the Pacific

[NMM, Fraser 21]   11 October 1945

No one is more thankful than I that the sudden end of the Japanese war made it unnecessary for us to deploy the full naval strength of the BPF. But, for the accuracies of the naval histories which may be written in the future, I think it should be known that, had the invasion of Japan been necessary, we had the warships and logistical support to enable two British Carrier Task Groups to take part.

As events turned out, we had little more than the opportunity to prove that we could assemble, train, support and put into action, in the short space of four months, a formidable task force capable of operating at sea for long periods in conjunction with similar forces of the US Pacific Fleet.

I arrived in Australia in December 1944, to set up my command. After the loss of Singapore and Hong Kong, Sydney was virtually the only suitable base left to us. It had many advantages – a magnificent harbour, a recently completed graving dock capable of taking our largest ships, ample food resources, and skilled dockyard labour, although in limited quantities. Its greatest disadvantage was its distance from what was to be the scene of operations. But there was no other choice.

One of my first tasks – and a very pleasant one it turned out to be – was to confer with Fleet Admiral Nimitz at Pearl Harbor. It was from Admiral Nimitz that I learnt that not only was the BPF welcomed by him and his Command but that there were many tasks awaiting it – tasks very different from those 'minor roles' which political observers and others had been hinting at. I and my staff officers returned to Sydney, determined to have the Fleet ready, and have it ready in record time.

On 17 December, HMS *Howe*, the first of our four battleships, steamed into Sydney Harbour. For some weeks she was the only major unit east of Ceylon. At this time, ships of what was ultimately to become the BPF were scattered over the oceans and seas of the world. We were still required to maintain powerful forces in the Home Fleet, the Atlantic, the Mediterranean and the Indian Ocean. Most of the ships which we had been able to withdraw had to be refitted and 'tropicalised' for what was then thought to be the long war ahead. But if anyone thinks that the BPF was our 'second team', I would remind him that of four battleships, 14 carriers, nine cruisers and 32 destroyers which later arrived in Sydney Harbour, only one cruiser had been built when the war began.

By mid-January, four of our Fleet Carriers – *Indomitable*, *Indefatigable*, *Illustrious*, and *Victorious* – were ready to move forward from Ceylon. They had been 'battle training' for some weeks, attacking targets in Java, Sumatra and the Andaman and Nicobar Islands. On the way to Australia, under the command of Vice Admiral Sir Philip Vian, they made a most successful and damaging attack on the Japanese oil resources at Palembang in Sumatra. They arrived unscathed in Sydney early in February.

Meanwhile, the assembly of the Fleet Train under the command of Rear Admiral Douglas Fisher was going ahead, and arrangements had been completed to enable us to use Manus in the Admiralty Islands as a forward staging point and anchorage. But each day it became clearer that distance was to be our main adversary, and logistical support our biggest problem. Throughout these difficult weeks of planning and organizing, the accumulated experience that the US Pacific Fleet had gained in three years of ocean operations was of tremendous help to us, and it was readily and generously made available.

It had already been agreed that the British forces should be under American operational control, and while this relieved us of much of the detailed work of operational planning, it also, in some ways, increased our difficulties in that we had no long range picture of the exact operations we must plan to support. We had, in fact, to plan for all eventualities.

By mid-March, our first task force was assembled at Manus, and I was able to announce it as 'ready for action'. It consisted of two battleships, four carriers, six cruisers and elements of four destroyer flotillas. It was commanded by Vice Admiral Sir Bernard Rawlings, flying his flag in HMS *King George V*, with Vice Admiral Sir Philip Vian in command of the carriers in HMS *Indomitable*. A few days later, designated as Task Force 57, under the operational command of Admiral Spruance, it sailed for Ulithi.

On 27 March, TF 57 struck at Japanese airfields in Sakishima Gunto in support of operation ICEBERG – the landings on Okinawa, which began at dawn on 1 April.

Through April and most of May the attacks went on – two days striking, three days replenishment – with a bombardment to lend variety to an unspectacular task. But the job was done, and went a long way in neutralising the Japanese air movements on the American left flank.

It was during this phase of the operation that the British task Force received its first baptism of *Kamikasi*. Three of our carriers – *Indomitable*, *Formidable*, and *Victorious* – were hit but none was out of operations for more than a few hours, and damage and casualties were mercifully light. A destroyer – HMS *Ulster* – was seriously damaged but successfully towed back to Leyte.

By mid-July, the British Task Force, replenished and reinforced, reported back for duty. This time it was assigned to Admiral Halsey's 3rd Fleet and designated Task Force 37. In conjunction with Task Force 38, under the command of the late Vice Admiral McCain, it took part in those culminating attacks against the Japanese home islands which did so much to bring Japan to her knees.[1] Fliers from the British carriers accounted for 600 Japanese planes and more than 250 Japanese ships of all sizes. Battleships, cruisers and destroyers bombarded targets on the mainland of Japan on several occasions. TF 37 continued in action until the cease-fire sounded.

No account of the Royal Navy's activities in the Pacific would be complete without reference to the work of our submarines which were

---

[1] VA McCain, US Navy: Cdr, Fast Carrier TF, 1944–5; Cdr, TF 38; died 6 Sept 1945.

operating under Admiral Fife from Fremantle and Subic Bay. One of them – HMS *Trenchant* – torpedoed and sank a Japanese cruiser in most difficult circumstances in the Java Sea. One of our midget submarines entered Singapore and blew up another Japanese cruiser lying at anchor inside the net defences. And day after day, they nibbled away at the Japanese resources, sinking junks and merchant ships, shelling railways and bridges right and left.

On 16 August, Admiral Nimitz signalled to me: 'The close cooperation and support provided by the BPF have been of great assistance in beating Japan'.

We are proud to have been in at the kill.

348.   *Admiral Sir Bruce Fraser's Dispatches, November 1944 to July 1945*

[ADM 199/1457]   23 November 1945

Report on the British Pacific Fleet

Section I: Purpose.

...

3. On purely strategic grounds it is clearly the best policy to employ the largest forces possible against the centre of the enemy's power, and it would be uneconomic to dissipate one's total forces in areas away from that centre. Furthermore, the BPF has, in fact, materially increased the striking power of the naval forces engaged against Japan and in doing so has in no way detracted from the efforts of the American fleet by absorbing their resources.

4. From a national point of view, it was of the utmost importance that the BPF should engage in the most modern form of naval warfare yet evolved, and to do so by fighting in company with its originators and prime exponents. In no way could we have learned the technical lessons which this type of warfare teaches. Had we not operated our striking forces in this manner we should have finished this war with only second hand knowledge of this revolutionary form of naval warfare.

5. ... Without the incentive that was added by the constant urge to emulate the US Fleet it is doubtful if these lessons would have been learnt. ...

6. Finally from a point of view of national prestige, it has been of the utmost importance that our Dominions should see the British Navy engaged, if not in equal numbers, at least on an equal footing, with American forces in the Pacific. ...

Section II: Special Features of the Pacific War.

...

9. With the decline of the Japanese Fleet, the Japanese Air Force [emerged] as the principal objective of the naval war. ... the best method of defeating the Japanese Air Force is to destroy its means of production and to harass its centres of training. ...

10. A second important part of the Fleet's task is to neutralise the Japanese Air Force in the area of amphibious assault. ...

11. Distances: ... In the BPF's first operation (ICEBERG), its target was distant 780 miles from its advanced anchorage at Leyte. ...

12. Bases: One most noticeable feature of the Pacific War is the very small number of permanent bases. Of these there is nothing nearer to Japan than Pearl Harbor, a distance of 3700 miles, and Sydney, distant 4300 miles. Even more remarkable, however, is the speed with which the Americans have improvised temporary bases, starting from nothing and often in the most unpromising country. ... The Americans have been able to accomplish all this by means of their naval corps of CBs (known as 'Seabees') who have grown up during the course of this war and have established themselves as an integral part of the US Navy with a remarkable *esprit de corps* and a reputation of being able to undertake absolutely anything.

...

14. Intense rate of striking: The US Fleet has evolved a method of operating its vast fleet more or less continuously off the enemy coasts. This rate of striking and length of time that all its units remain in the operating area are considered beyond anything that had previously been contemplated in the British Naval Service.

15. In order to do this, they have established a large logistics organisation which ensures adequate supplies for the operating Fleet. They have also evolved and are perfecting a system of replenishing their operating forces at sea, and have thereby restored to naval warfare something of the mobility and ability to keep at sea for long periods which the fleet possessed in the days of sail. ...

16. Fighting Qualities: ... this type of warfare has imposed hard living conditions on the American Fleet engaged in it. Personnel of these Fleets are seldom able to go ashore. ... These hardships are increased by extremely crowded accommodation of the American ships and the trying climatic conditions in most of the advanced bases.

17. All these circumstances have imposed a very heavy strain on the officers and men, the psychological effect of which has been carefully studied by the US authorities. As a result of these studies it has been

found that men are able to keep up this hard type of life for long periods at a time provided certain simple expedients are adopted ... :

(a) Good food, which includes, for the Americans, ice creams.
(b) Good entertainments, which primarily consists of universal cinemas, with a constantly changing programme.
(c) Rapid and reliable meal service.

All of these might have been regarded by us as soft and slightly ridiculous, had it not been found by experience that men fight harder and longer when so treated.

18. The principal strain of this continuous effort naturally falls on the carrier air crews who are liable to be operating in combat with the enemy, over enemy territory, almost daily for months on end. Experience has shown that aircrews' efficiency falls off rapidly after being engaged for a certain period of time in this type of operation, and to combat this the Americans have adopted the system of changing their combat carrier air groups at the end of four or six months, it having been found more profitable to have on board a relatively untrained air group rather than a highly trained one which is suffering from operational fatigue.

19. I was confident that this would apply equally to our own forces as soon as they became engaged in this intensive type of operation, and furthermore it would be unreasonable to expect our own air groups to engage in the same type of warfare unless they were given conditions at least comparable to those of the Americans. For these two reasons one of my first ambitions was to ask for the establishment of a separate air group policy, although I realised that it was essentially in conflict with the established custom of the FAA and the Royal Navy, which relies to a large extent on the close union between air squadrons and the ships to which they belong.

20. Conclusion: It was quite clear that, in the intensive, efficient and hard striking type of war that the US Fleet was fighting, nothing but the inclusion of a big British force would be noticeable and nothing but the best would be tolerated.

Section III: Problems.

...

22. Self-Sufficiency: ... The US logistic plan had been carefully worked out and their supplies, bases, etc., had been designed on a scale considered necessary to keep their Fleet operating at the intense rate indicated above, and no more ... Furthermore, the American system of rolling up

their bases as the war advanced ... meant that it was not even possible to follow behind the Americans using the facilities that they left in their wake.

23. On the other hand self-sufficiency must undoubtedly be looked upon as one of the BPF's chief difficulties and particularly at the start. It would also have been clearly more economical from an overall point of view for facilities to be pooled. This however was in many cases mechanically impossible. Ammunition, naval stores, and even food are of types not common to the two services and the American aircraft which form so large a part of the FAA are not interchangeable on account of the numerous modifications which have to be made to 'bring them up to British standards'.

24. In general the rule of self-sufficiency has been strictly adhered to, although in many particulars the American authorities have been most helpful in supplying the BPF needs when these have been an operational necessity and when they could not be obtained from British sources. Such breaches of the general rules have only been possible when an appeal to a higher authority has not proved necessary.

25. Distance from the UK: The great length of lines of communication from the UK has made the support of the Fleet a difficult problem, firstly because the shortage of shipping has made it necessary to reduce supplies to the bare minimum for foreseen operations, and secondly when such requirements have changed owing to a change of operational plan a very long timelag is inevitable before the arrival of the additional supplies called for.

26. Australia as a base: ... The preliminary arrangements ... had been worked out in advance by Vice Admiral Daniel, ... Australia found it difficult to make adjustments to meet these needs ...[1]

27. In the first place Australia possessed a very small industrial capacity ... not capable of any great or rapid expansion. The majority of this output had already been taken over by the US Forces in the SWP.

...

33. Advanced Bases: ... American experience had shown that it was uneconomical in overall resources to operate the Fleet more than 2000 miles ahead of its foremost shore base, since beyond that distance the cost in Fleet Train ships becomes disproportionately high.

---

[1]VA Charles S. Daniel: Capt 1934; Capt (D) 8 DF; DP 1940–41; Flag Capt & CSO, 2 BS, *Renown*, Aug 1941; RA June 1943; A/VA (Q), BPF, 1944–5; 1 BS, June 1945; 3 SL & Cntrlr Sept 1945.

...

38. The two main advantages in the establishment of an intermediate base of this type were –

(a) The Fleet would be able to remain more continuously in operation since it would not require to return to Australia for replenishment.
(b) A considerable economy would be effected in the Fleet Train whose function would then largely be to support the Fleet in advance of this intermediate base.

...

40. ... It was immediately apparent that the Philippine area would serve the purpose far better than anywhere else in the Pacific. It had the advantage of being reasonably close to Japan and it was also the geographical focus of lines of communication from the US and Panama from the east, from Australia and New Zealand from the south and from the UK and India via the Moluccas from the west. Furthermore after the capture of Singapore, it would also be on the direct route which the East Indies Fleet would take in advancing from that base to Hong Kong or Japan itself.

41. [This did not happen because:]

(a) ... it became clear that there were definite American political objections to the establishment of a British base in the Philippines.
(b) ... the length of time necessary to construct a base on the scale required would mean that it would be of little value to the BPF until a much later stage in the war, when the pattern of naval war in the Pacific may well have been altered, rendering the requirements for such a base obsolete.

...

43. ... [The lack of] the base and thence of an intermediate base and the consequent need for the Fleet to return to its main base in Australia for periodical replenishment has had a considerable effect in reducing the length of time for which the Fleet can remain off the enemy coast ...

...

45. The general pattern of operations is tending towards stability, with the 3rd Fleet comprising the FCTFs operating to the eastward of Japan based on Eniwetok, Guam, Saipan and Ulithi while the 5th Fleet, comprising the amphibious assault forces, operates on the westward based on Leyte, Okinawa and finishing in Japan itself.

46. ... it will be natural for the BPF ... to remain to the eastward with its bases and lines of communication through Sydney, Manus and Eniwetok, while the Eastern Fleet which is primarily an amphibious fleet, would join up with the 3rd Fleet after it has broken through the Singapore Strait with its lines of communication through Singapore, the Philippines and perhaps Okinawa.

...

48. In any case there is clearly no plan in this scheme of things for a base at Brunei Bay ... and one can only assume that the American idea of capturing it expressly for the purpose of a BPF base, must have been founded on political rather than strategic reasons.

49. Command in the Pacific: A great number of the problems that have faced me in the Pacific would have been greatly simplified or might indeed never have arisen had it not been for the confused state of higher command in the Pacific area.

50. There is no doubt that a principal cause of this confusion has been the attempt to amalgamate the two previously independent Area Commanders without appointing a Supreme Commander over them.

...

52. ... COMINCH retains for himself the right to re-allocate naval forces within the Central and South West Pacific areas. Up to date, although the BPF has been assigned to the Central Pacific Area, this has been so only on the understanding that it may be moved at seven days' notice to the SWP Area. Such a change in fact very nearly took place shortly after the BPF had become engaged in ICEBERG and it was only the combined representation of both Area Commanders that prevented the Fleet from being switched right in the middle of an operation.

53. Numerous difficulties have occurred through the necessity of operating the BPF in Admiral Nimitz's area, in the Central Pacific, and basing it in General MacArthur's area in Leyte, Manus and Australia ...

54. The problems that have arisen out of this have been mainly connected with bases. For example Admiral Nimitz was at first unwilling to allow the BPF to establish facilities at Manus ... since he was uncertain that it might not [at] any time be transferred to the SWPA.

...

57. C-in-C's HQ: ... It was clear that the Fleet would operate under US Control and that command at sea would be exercised by the Vice Admiral second-in-command. It was also clear that the logistic side would be organised by the Vice Admiral (Administration) with his HQ

at Melbourne, and it appeared in general that that the function of the C-in-C would be to co-ordinate these two sides of the Fleet's activities.
58. [Other prospects having proved impossible, HQ were established in Sydney]. ... experience has now led me to believe it was in any case the best choice. In this position I am quite clearly able to carry out the function of co-ordination of operations with logistics, and as the latter has proved by far the most difficult problem, it is better that I should remain in the closest touch with the Vice Admiral (Administration).

...

61. Relations with US Authorities: At the first I was somewhat doubtful about the reception that the BPF would get in the Pacific. It was thought that the insistence on strict British self-sufficiency was intended to act as much as an obstacle to exclude the BPF as to any factual necessity. Knowledge gained of the logistic set up in the Pacific has shown me that this latter [?] opinion was incorrect and that British self-sufficiency was essential if the American Fleet was not to be hampered in its operations.
62. When I saw Admiral Nimitz he was most cordial. In his mind there was clearly no political objection to the participation of the BPF in Pacific operations, and in fact he was delighted at the prospect of our co-operation. His only anxiety was that the BPF might find it necessary to make demands on American resources, and I am sure that his reaction was realistic and not political. Although his resources in the Pacific are vast they are not lavish ...
63. The Operational Commanders, of whom I met Admiral Spruance at Pearl Harbor, have been even more delighted at the addition to their forces provided by the BPF. ...
64. I have found that the American logistic authorities in the Pacific have interpreted self-sufficiency [liberally].
65. I have nothing but admiration for American command and staff work. The boldness of the plans conceived and the relentless efficiency with which they are carried out, the accuracy with which targets are adhered to and yet the readiness of all concerned to change their plans at the last moment, all must be the result of an admirable staff organisation.

Section IV – Effects

Suitability of BPF for Pacific Warfare

...

71. The entry of a British Fleet into the Pacific operations has been an exacting test which the Navy can reasonably congratulate itself on

having passed satisfactorily. … The fact that the BPF was able to take its place alongside the US Fleet and to enter at short notice into their highly specialised type of warfare demonstrates the two qualities of 'adaptability' and 'readiness' of which the British Navy is justly proud.

72. There can be little doubt that the Americans were much quicker than we were at learning the lessons of [the Pacific] war and of applying them to their ships and to their tactics. The vast shipbuilding resources enables them to build ships with such speed that they can embark on daring experiments even before these are shown to have a general application. Also the fact that their ships are always up-to-date enables them to engender an essentially modern and experimental habit of thought. As is often the case with experiments, these are not always successful, as has been shown in the vulnerability of their large carriers and in the somewhat doubtful handling of the Fleet in the face of Typhoon weather. We, on the other hand, are more cautious in our ship construction and in our tactics and unlike the Americans we would rather not change anything until the alternative has been thoroughly tested as an improvement. As a result the British Fleet is seldom spectacular, never really modern, but always sound.

73. The Endurance of our ships has proved adequate and has enabled the Fleet to keep at sea in the same manner as the Americans. In fact the distances are so vast that practically no operation can be contemplated without Fleet attendant tankers …

…

74. The armament of our ships has been designed primarily from an anti-ship point of view and generally speaking they are, as the Americans would say, 'Not able to look after themselves'. Suicide bombing has introduced new complications into the AA system, particularly as this type of attack has not proved vulnerable to anything smaller than the 40mm type of gun whereas our Fleet has been largely equipped with 20mm guns which had proved effective against the torpedo-bomber. This deficiency is being largely remedied locally by substituting a single Bofors for each twin Oerlikon. Sydney and other yards have in a short time installed a most impressive number of 40mm barrels …

76. The armoured decks of our Carriers have caused a great sensation among the Americans and have certainly proved their worth against suicide aircraft with their comparatively small penetrative power. The cost of the armoured deck in terms of aircraft carried and speed of operation, however, is enormous and it is questionable whether in future it would not be better to carry more aircraft in less safety, particularly as the confidence placed in the armoured decks may be quite misleading in the face of some future form of attack.

77. The aircraft which constitute the Fleet's main offensive weapon, leave much to be desired. In the first place the multiplicity of types is a grave hindrance in this type of warfare. It leads to tactical and logistic inflexibility and also is most uneconomical. Secondly the characteristics of the Seafire and the Barracuda make them very nearly incapable of reaching the enemy.[1] ...

... if we are to fight alongside the Americans again our aircraft should be interchangeable with the Americans.

...

83. XE Craft: Provided the *Bonaventure* is available to support them, the logistical cost of XE craft is practically nil, and the operational cost, in the form of towing submarines is light and acceptable. With so small an operational and logistic cost I have decided that it would be worthwhile to allow them to embark on two operations.

...

85. Submarine Operations: The work of the submarines has been hard but unspectacular due in the main to a lack of suitable targets. Working in the closest co-operation with US submarines they have however played an important part in cutting the enemy's sea communications. Their most spectacular success was the sinking by *Trenchant* in a most daring attack of the Japanese cruiser *Ashigara*, the only major enemy unit to be destroyed to date by the Fleet.

...

87. Second Task Group: At Pearl Harbor I promised Admiral Nimitz that I would operate a Second Task Group as soon as it became possible to support one, and even at that time he welcomed the idea.

88. However, my chief reasons for asking for the CVLs ... [were] firstly the strategic advantage of concentrating the maximum forces against the heart of the enemy, secondly the political value of having British forces engaged in the Pacific in the greatest possible strength and thirdly the importance of trying out this newest class of fighting ship in the most modern and advanced type of operations.

89. In this latter connection, as the British Navy of the future may have a high proportion of CVLs it seems to me to be of the utmost importance that their various disabilities should be overcome and the method

---

[1]Fairey Barracuda: 1940; 1 engine; 3 crew; 228mph; 2mg; 1620lbs bombs, depth charges or torpedo.

of operating [them] evolved which will allow them to play a major part as carriers rather than allowing them to be relegated entirely to a minor role which could be undertaken by CVEs.

90. ... American opinion ... regards them as too slow to be anything but an embarrassment to the rapid strategic moves of a fast carrier task force. These difficulties will I am sure be overcome. ...

Tactical Integration with the US Fleet.

...

92. In order to allow freedom of action it is clearly desirable that the British and American Fleets in the Pacific should be capable of operating either separately or together as the strategic situation demands. ...

93. ... it was clearly necessary for the BPF to adopt the American system of signals. I realised that this change was not liked by the Admiralty, but it was quite clear to me that we could not form part of the US Fleet until we spoke the same language. ... Events have justified the change-over ...

94. ... One of the stipulations of N-F 1, which is the outcome of the Pearl Harbour conference, is that to the maximum practicable extent the British ships will constitute a separate task force with no more direct tactical co-operation with US task forces than the situation requires.

95. I myself did not mean this to preclude the possibility of a British Task Group operating in the American Task Force, but C-in-C Pacific appears to have taken it to mean that, and during the July operations he co-ordinated Com3F's expressed intention to operate the British Task Group as part of the American FCTF.

96. It is an interesting sidelight on the American way of thought – in particular their rigid acceptance of the written word – that the C-in-C Pacific considers it necessary to enforce this small restriction. It is also interesting to note that Com3F, while accepting the restriction in its nominal sense, in fact disregards it completely and continues to operate the British Task Group as a group as part of his own Task Force. Provided he obeys the letter of the law, even if he completely disregards its spirit, every American is quite happy that the right and sensible action has been taken.

...

106. The Fleet Train: ... the ability of the BPF to operate at all in the Pacific has been entirely dependent on the success of an organisation quite new in the Royal Navy – the Fleet Train ...

107. At the start it was found that events in the Pacific had overtaken planning with regard to the composition of the Fleet Train ...

(a) The unexpectedly rapid advance into the Philippines had placed our advanced anchorage rather more than two times as far ahead of our shore bases as had been originally contemplated, and in the absence of shore facilities, this naturally had a direct effect on the number of ships required to keep the Fleet supplied at this Advanced Anchorage.

(b) The comparatively new American policy of replenishment had not been provided for. The chief effect of this was the modest number of Fleet attendant tankers allocated to deal with the older fashion harbour-based type of warfare were quite inadequate to deal with the style of warfare in which the Fleet, virtually based at sea off the enemy coast, is entirely dependent on its tankers.

108. The other most prominent deficiency was the absence of any means of transporting reserve aircraft from Australia to the Advanced Anchorage. ...

...

112. It was necessary to ask for a Fleet Train considerably greater than that which had been originally planned.

...

114. Logistic Support Groups: Hardly had this newly formed Fleet Train come into being than the new requirement for replenishing the Fleet at sea necessitated its giving birth to a still newer organisation – the LSF. ...

...

121. Operations: Palembang: The attack on the oil refineries at Palembang was the BPF's first operation, carried out on passage to the Pacific. At first the Admiralty were reluctant to sanction this attack. I believe this to have been mainly on account of an assurance given to the Australian Government that the BPF would reach the Pacific before the end of 1944 ... as it was ... thought that the heavy Japanese defences around the oilfields would make such an attack very costly to aircraft and air crews and would thus lower the Fleet's morale. It was also pointed out that experience in Europe had shown that prolonged mass attacks by vast fleets of heavy bombers were necessary before any vital damage could be inflicted.

122. In my estimation all these reasons were invalid. In the first place the carriers were not ready to reach the Pacific in December 1944. ...

123. In the second place I was rather sceptical of the heavy losses that were forecast. We seemed all along to have overestimated the Japanese strength in the East Indies ...

124. Thirdly I did not consider that the experience of 'Area bombing' by heavy bombers in Europe had any bearing on this case. ...

125. The result of the attack bore out this conclusion. Furthermore, this relation between target and weapon is now becoming of general interest in the Pacific since heavy bombers and carrier-borne aircraft frequently operate in the same area. ...

126. As a result of the Palembang operation, the Fleet arrived in the Pacific tested to some extent in the type of operation in which it was to be engaged. ...

127. ICEBERG: The Fleet's entry into its first operation in the Pacific was marked by a most unpleasant period of suspense. The assignment of the BPF to operation ICEBERG had been arranged in detail, but confirmation from COMINCH was needed before these plans could be put into effect. COMINCH was the deciding authority, and as long as he remained undecided the Fleet remained inactive. The precise cause of his indecision was unknown as I was not in a position to deal with him direct.

128. Eventually a decision was reached and COMINCH assigned the BPF to ICEBERG in time to arrive only two days late on schedule. A few days earlier a report which appeared in the press indicated the possibility the BPF might be relegated to a 'back area'. This report flared through the newspapers and simultaneously COMINCH made his decision. Apart from this coincidence I have no knowledge of any relevant factor that changed at that time.

129. This assignment to ICEBERG was made on condition that the BPF should be available for and redeployed at seven days' notice. After the operation had been in progress for a few weeks a re-deployment on those lines was in fact ordered by COMINCH and a proportion of the BPF was ordered to be assigned to the SWPA. Fortunately both Admiral Nimitz and General MacArthur were persuaded against this re-allocation and combined representation caused it to be annulled.

130. It is inconceivable, of course, that such a chaotic and nearly calamitous state of affairs could have arisen if there had been a Supreme Commander in the Pacific in whom all authority had been vested and on whom rested all responsibility. At the same time it is equally clear that the functions of a Supreme Commander cannot be exercised by an authority remote from the scene or close to and liable to become entangled in outside political considerations.

131. Between ICEBERG and OLYMPIC:[1] During this period ComB is, at the time of writing, carrying out a series of operations where both

---

[1] OLYMPIC: invasion of Kyushu.

strategy and tactics are designed on the most flexible plans. With easy grace he is striking here one day and there the next, replenishing at sea or returning to harbour as the situation demands.

132. With dogged persistence the BPF is keeping up and if anything is going to stretch its muscles these operations will. But it is tied by a string to Australia and much handicapped by its slow small tankers ...

SOURCES AND DOCUMENTS

Archives

UNITED KINGDOM

The National Archives, Kew, London

Cabinet Papers: CAB 86, 88, 99, 122
Admiralty Papers: Admiralty Secretariat, ADM 116
War Histories, 1939–1945, ADM 199
First Sea Lord's Papers, ADM 205

The National Maritime Museum, Greenwich, London

The Papers of Admiral the Fleet Lord Fraser of North Cape [Fraser]

Churchill Archives Centre, Churchill College, Cambridge

The Papers of Admiral Sir Bertram Ramsey [RMSY]

CANADA

These papers were furnished to me by Mr Michael Whitby, Senior Naval Historian,Department of Defence, Ottawa. [CAN]

UNITED STATES OF AMERICA

The National Archives, College Park, Maryland

Record Groups 13, 29, 38, 218 [RG ...]

Library of Congress (Madison Building), Washington, DC

The Papers of Fleet William D. Admiral Leahy [LC, Leahy]
The Papers of Fleet Admiral Ernest J. King [LC, King]
The Papers of Admiral William F. Halsey [LC, Halsey]

The Franklin D. Roosevelt Presidential Library, Hyde Park, New York

The President's Secretary's File [PSF 7]
The President's Map Room Files, boxes 17, 29, 33, 35, 39, 65, 88
[MRF ...]

Operational Archives, Navy Yard, Washington, DC

Office of Naval Operations, Strategic Plans Division, boxes 155, 156, 242, 243, 244, 250 [SPD...]
The Papers of Fleet Admiral Ernest J. King [Op Arch, King]
The Papers of Fleet Admiral Chester W. Nimitz [Op Arch, Nimitz]
The Papers of Admiral William V. Pratt [Op Arch, Pratt]
The Papers of Admiral Harold R. Stark [Op Arch, Stark]

The Naval War College, Newport, Rhode Island

The Papers of Fleet Admiral Ernest J. King [NWC, King]
The Papers of Admiral H. Kent Hewitt [NWC, Hewitt]

Numerical List of Documents

Part I: The High Command

1.	Chmn, Munitions Assessment Board: Memorandum	7 Oct 1943	CAB 88/19
2.	CCS, 122nd Meeting	8 Oct 1943	CAB 88/3
3.	CCS, 123rd Meeting	15 Oct 1943	CAB 88/3
4.	CCS, Memoranda	19 Oct 1943	CAB 88/14
5.	Capt Porter to Capt Douglas, US Navy	20 Oct 1943	SPD 243
6.	King to Secretary of Navy Knox	23 Oct 1943	Op Arch, King 4
7.	Stark to King	23 Oct 1943	Op Arch, Stark A2
8.	BAD Report, 1–31 Oct 1943	c. Nov 1943	ADM 199/1469
9.	JCS, 121st Meeting	2 Nov 1943	RG 218/196
10.	King to Stark	5 Nov 1943	Op Arch, King 4
11.	CCS, 126th Meeting	5 Nov 1943	CAB 88/3
12.	CCS 392: Memorandum by JCS	9 Nov 1943	CAB 88/19
13.	CCS 300/2: Memorandum by JCS	17 Nov 1943	CAB 88/14
14.	CCS 300/3: Memorandum by JCS	18 Nov 1943	CAB 88/14

15.	Admy Memorandum: Operational Functions & Design & Armament of Carriers & Aircraft	18 Nov 1943	ADM 205/33
16.	Leahy: Diary	24 Nov 1943	LC, Leahy
17.	CCS, 132nd Meeting	30 Nov 1943	CAB 88/3
18.	CCS, 133rd Meeting	3 Dec 1943	CAB 88/3
19.	CCS, 135th Meeting	5 Dec 1943	CAB 88/3
20.	CCS, 136th Meeting	5 Dec 1943	CAB 88/3
21.	CCS, 137th Meeting	6 Dec 1943	CAB 88/3
22.	A. V. Alexander to Stark	10 Dec 1943	Op Arch, King 4
23.	A. V. Alexander to Stark	12 Dec 1943	Op Arch, King 4
24.	Admiralty Memorandum	12 Dec 1943	Op Arch, Stark A2
25.	COS to JSM	23 Dec 1943	ADM 199/452
26.	Churchill to A. V. Alexander	10 Jan 1944	ADM 205/35
27.	A. V. Alexander to Churchill	21 Jan 1944	ADM 205/35
28.	Noble to Cunningham	25 Jan 1944	CAB 122/1140
29.	King to Adm Ingersoll, etc.	28 Jan 1944	Op Arch, King 4
30.	Cdre Rushbrooke to Stark	30 Jan 1944	Op Arch, Stark A2
31.	CCS, 149th Meeting	10 Mar 1944	CAB 88/4
32.	Blake to Cunningham	25 Mar 1944	ADM 205/38
33.	Cunningham to Blake	28 Mar 1944	ADM 205/38
34.	Blake to Cunningham	5 April 1944	ADM 205/38
35.	Notes on RN by Stark	c. 6 April 1944	Op Arch, King 4
36.	Post-War Research	12 April 1944	ADM 116/5395
37.	US Naval Attaché, Moscow, to King	8 June 1944	MRF 35
38.	CCS, 165th Meeting	14 June 1944	CAB 88/4
39.	Leahy: Diary	29 June 1944	LC, Leahy
40.	Blake to Cunningham	1 July 1944	ADM 205/48

41.	COS to JSM	12 July 1944	CAB 88/4
42.	King to Vice Adm Horne, US Navy	26 July 1944	NWC, King 7
43.	Naval Issues, W. Zones, Germany	3 Sept 1944	ADM 116/5359
44.	CCS, 174th Meeting	14 Sept 1944	CAB 88/4
45.	Meeting of King and Cunningham	15 Sept 1944	ADM 116/5359
46.	CCS, 176th Meeting	16 Sept 1944	ADM 116/5359
47.	US Aircraft to RN	28 Nov 1944	ADM 116/5347
48.	BAD to Admiralty	4 Jan 1945	ADM 116/5341
49.	First Sea Lord's Office: Memorandum	10 Jan 1945	ADM 205/49
50.	CCS, 182nd Meeting	30 Jan 1945	CAB 88/4
51.	CCS, 184th Meeting	1 Feb 1945	CAB 88/4
52.	Requirements from US	22 May 1945	ADM 116/5330
53.	Memorandum by First Lord	1 July 1945	ADM 205/54
54.	Memorandum by First Lord	7 July 1945	ADM 205/54
55.	Tripartite Committee: German Navy	1 Aug 1945	CAB 99/38
56.	Report of JSM	July, 1946	CAB 122/1579
57.	Memorandum by Rear Adm Dorling	July, 1946	ADM 199/1236
58.	Report by Rear Adm Waller	July, 1946	ADM 199/1236
59.	Report by Rear Adm Burt	July, 1946	ADM 199/1236
60.	Report by Capt Abel-Smith	July, 1946	ADM 199/1236
61.	Report by Capt Price	July, 1946	ADM 199/1236
62.	Report by Superintendent of Air Training	July, 1946	ADM 199/1236
63.	Report by Director of Armament Supplies	July, 1946	ADM 199/1236
64.	Report by Capt Roskill	July, 1946	ADM 199/1236

Part II: Anti-U-boat Warfare

65.	Admiralty to BAD	7 Oct 1943	CAB 122/1510
66.	Attack on U-boat	10 Oct 1943	ADM 199/1415
67.	Noble to King	16 Oct 1943	RG 38
68.	Rear Adm Low, US Navy, to King	16 Oct 1943	RG 38
69.	King to Noble	19 Oct 1943	Op Arch, King 4
70.	King to Noble	26 Oct 1943	Op Arch, King 4
71.	Anti-U-boat Warfare Committee	27 Oct 1943	CAB 86/2
72.	COS, 268th Meeting	3 Nov 1943	CAB 122/1510
73.	Capt Morey to Rear Adm Low, US Navy	5 Nov 1943	RG 38/32
74.	COS to JSM	7 Nov 1943	CAB 122/1510
75.	COS to JSM	7 Nov 1943	CAB 122/1510
76.	Memorandum from King to JCS	9 Nov 1943	CAB 122/1510
77.	King to Noble	10 Nov 1943	Op Arch, King 4
78.	Anti-U-boat Warfare Committee	11 Nov 1943	ADM 205/30
79.	Stark to Secretary of Navy Knox	15 Nov 1943	RG 13/24
80.	Syfret to Stark	28 Nov 1943	Op Arch, Stark A2
81.	A. V. Alexander to Churchill	1 Dec 1943	ADM 199/241
82.	Anti-U-boat Warfare Committee	1 Dec 1943	CAB 86/2
83.	Map Room Memorandum	4 Dec 1943	MRF 17
84.	King to Noble	13 Dec 1943	CAB 122/1510
85.	JSM, 47th Meeting	16 Dec 1943	CAB 122/1510
86.	Rear Adm Low, US Navy, to King	23 Dec 1943	SPD 243
87.	Stark to Rear Adm Wilson, US Navy	29 Dec 1943	SPD 243
88.	Air Marshal Slessor to Stark	n.d., Dec 1943	SPD 243

89.	Stark: Memorandum	11 Jan 1944	RG 38/24
90.	Vice Adm Ingram, US Navy to King	11 Jan 1944	Op Arch, King 4
91.	Sir R. Campbell to Foreign Office	3 Feb 1944	ADM 199/1887
92.	Horton to Secretary of Admiralty	5 Feb 1944	ADM 199/241
93.	Rear Adm Low, US Navy, to King	22 Feb 1944	RG 38/32
94.	Admiralty to King	29 Feb 1944	ADM 199/2403
95.	Anti-U-boat Warfare Committee	15 Mar 1944	CAB 86/6
96.	Attack on U-boat	2 May 1944	ADM 199/602
97.	Capt Isbell, US Navy, to FX-01	2 June 1944	RG 38/36
98.	Anti-U-boat Division, Admiralty	15 June 1944	ADM 199/1491
99.	RoP, HMCS *Statice*	5–6 July 1944	ADM 199/1460
100.	RoP, SO, Escort Group 11 [RCN]	14 July 1944	CAN 51/520-8440/EG11, Vol. 2
101.	Horton to Admiralty	14 Aug 1944	CAN 81/520–8440
102.	RoP, Escort Group 9	c.15 Sep 1944	ADM 199/1644
103.	Horton to Admiralty	26 Sep 1944	CAN 81/520–8440
104.	Stark: Memorandum for Capt Kline, US Navy	28 Sep 1944	RG 38/24
105.	Stark to Cunningham	29 Sep 1944	Op Arch, Stark A2
106.	Cunningham to Stark	2 Oct 1944	Op Arch, Stark A2
107.	Coastal Command: Anti-U-boat Campaign	2 Oct 1944	Op Arch, Stark A2

108.	Stark to King	22 Oct 1944	Op Arch, Stark A2
109.	Cunningham to Stark	2 Jan 1945	ADM 205/48
110.	Stark to King	3 Jan 1945	Op Arch, Stark A3
111.	Cdre Flanagan, US Navy, to Stark	5 Jan 1945	Op Arch, Stark A3
112.	Capt Ingram, US Navy, to Stark	11 Jan 1945	Op Arch, Stark A3
113.	Adm Ingram, US Navy, to King	15 Jan 1945	Op Arch, King 3
114.	Stark to Adm Edwards, US Navy	19 Jan 1945	Op Arch, Stark A3
115.	Stark to Cdre Flanigan, US Navy	22 Jan 1945	RG 38/32
116.	ACNS (UT) to Cunningham	24 Jan 1945	ADM 205/44
117.	Anti-U-boat Warfare Committee	26 Jan 1945	CAB 86/7
118.	CCS, Memorandum 774/3	2 Feb 1945	CAB 88/35
119.	Capt Miller, US Navy, to Stark	18 Feb 1945	Op Arch, Stark A3
120.	Stark to King	3 Mar 1945	RG 38/24
121.	HMCS *Guysborough* Survivors	Mar 1945	CAN DHH 81/520/8000
122.	Cunningham to Stark	6 April 1945	RG 38/24
123.	Cominch to Admiralty OIC	27 April 1945	ADM 199/2403
124.	A/Cdr J. B. McDiarmid, RCVNR	11 July 1945	Pte: M. Whitby

Part III: The Invasion of North West Europe

125.	R Adm Bieri, US Navy, to Asst CoS (Ops)	24 Oct 1943	SPD 243
126.	King to Stark	27 Oct 1943	SPD 243
127.	JCS, 121st Meeting	2 Nov 1943	RG 218/196
128.	R Adm Kirk, US Navy to Adm Cooke,	16 Nov 1943	SPD 243

US   Navy

129.	Roosevelt to Byrnes	23 Nov 1943	MRF 17
130.	Byrnes to Roosevelt	24 Nov 1943	MRF 17
131.	R Adm Kirk, US Navy to Adm Cooke, US Navy	28 Nov 1943	SPD 244
132.	Outline of Naval Forces	9 Dec 1943	ADM 199/628
133.	R Adm Kirk, US Navy to Capt Moon, US Navy	23 Dec 1943	SPD 243
134.	Noble to King	28 Dec 1943	SPD 244
135.	Notes on Comnaveu paper	4 Jan 1944	SPD 243
136.	COSSAC to Secretary of Admiralty	12 Jan 1944	ADM 199/1614
137.	R Adm Kirk, US Navy to V Adm Edwards, US Navy	13 Jan 1944	SPD 243
138.	King to Noble	15 Jan 1944	SPD 244
139.	Stark to King	26 Jan 1944	Stark A2
140.	JSM: Memorandum	10 Feb 1944	CAB 88/24
141.	Cdre Clarke to R Adm Cooke, US Navy	18 Feb 1944	SPD 243
142.	Capt Porter and Capt Osborn, US Navy	1 Mar 1944	SPD 244
143.	Marshall to Eisenhower	19 Mar 1944	SPD 243
144.	Stark to Secretary of Navy Knox	28 Mar 1944	Stark A2
145.	R Adm Hall, US Navy, to Stark	20 Mar 1944	Stark A2
146.	King to Noble	23 Mar 1944	SPD 242
147.	Stark to Cooke	25 Mar 1944	Stark A2
148.	Cunningham to King and Noble	30 Mar 1944	SPD 242
149.	Noble to King	1 April 1944	SPD 242
150.	Ramsay: Operation NEPTUNE	10 April 1944	ADM 199/1586
151.	Adm Little: Memorandum	11 April 1944	Stark A2

152.	King to Noble	11 April 1944	SPD 242
153.	Ramsay: Memorandum	13 April 1944	ADM 199/873
154.	Noble to King	13 April 1944	SPD 242
155.	Cunningham to King	27 April 1944	SPD 244
156.	CTF 125 to King, etc.	1 May 1944	SPD 244
157.	Kirk to Ramsay	4 May 1944	ADM 199/1556
158.	Force G: NEPTUNE Orders	20 May 1944	ADM 199/1558
159.	NEPTUNE: Operation	6 June 1944	SPD 250
160.	Admiralty Reports	7 June 1944	SPD 250
161.	RoP: Lieut Davis, RCVNR	9 June 1944	ADM 199/1659
162.	C-in-C Plymouth to Admiralty	18 July 1944	ADM 199/1644
163.	King to Stark	15 June 1944	NWC, King 8
164.	Cdr, CruDiv 7: Action Report	10 July 1944	ADM 199/1661
165.	Kirk to Stark	22 June 1944	Stark A2
166.	Cunningham to Churchill	22 June 1944	ADM 205/57
167.	Stark to King	23 June 1944	Stark A2
168.	King to Stark	23 June 1944	NWC, King 8
169.	Memorandum for F-1	24 June 1944	SPD 250
170.	Stark to Cunningham & reply	5 July 1944	Stark A2
171.	RoP, 9th Escort Group	8 Aug 1944	ADM 199/1644
172.	Little to Stark	11 Aug 1944	Stark A2
173.	Cdre Flanagan, US Navy, to Stark	15 Aug 1944	Stark A2
174.	NOIC, Arromanches, to FO, British Assault Area	19 Aug 1944	ADM 199/1614

175.	RoP, *Mauritius*	25 Aug 1944	ADM 199/1645
176.	Stark to King	13 Sept 1944	SPD 250
177.	Cdr Passmore to CO, US Advanced Bases	15 Oct 1944	ADM 199/1614
178.	Stark: Memorandum on Supplies	Autumn 1944	Stark A2
179.	Stark: Diary	3 Nov 1944	Stark A1
180.	Cunningham to A. V. Alexander	7 Jan 1945	ADM 205/43
181.	Operation NEPTUNE: Lessons	7 Mar 1945	ADM 199/1663
182.	Kirk to King	16 Mar 1945	Op Arch, King 5
183.	Cdr, US Bases, Plymouth	n.d., 1946	ADM 199/691
184.	Sir W. Monckton to COS	18 Jan 1946	ADM 199/1616
185.	Eisenhower: Dispatch on NW Europe	11 Feb 1946	ADM 199/1664

Part IV: The Mediterranean

186.	Eisenhower to the CCS and COS	10 Oct 1943	Map Rm 33
187.	King to Noble	16 Oct 1943	Op Arch, King 4
188.	King to Noble	25 Oct 1943	Op Arch, King 4
189.	Stark to King	3 Nov 1943	Stark A2
190.	Amended Cunningham-de Courten Agreement	17 Nov 1943	Map Rm 35
191.	Meeting: President, JCS, Hopkins, Adm Brown, US Navy	19 Nov 1943	Map Rm 29
192.	Meeting: President, JCS, Hopkins	28 Nov 1943	Map Rm 29
193.	Stark to R Adm Wilson, US Navy	23 Dec 1943	SPD 243
194.	Adm Leahy: Memorandum	28 Dec 1943	Map Rm 35
195.	Meeting: Adm Hewitt, US Navy, etc.	8 Jan 1944	SPD 244

196.	R Adm Moon to R Adm Bieri, US Navy	15 Feb 1944	SPD 244
197.	Meeting: President and JCS	21 Feb 1944	Map Rm 29
198.	R Adm Troubridge: SHINGLE Order	29 Dec. 1943	ADM 199/873
199.	R Adm Troubridge: RoP	24 Feb 1944	ADM 116/5459
200.	R Adm Troubridge to Adm Sir J. Cunningham	24 Feb 1944	ADM 199/873
201.	Adm Hewitt, US Navy to Cdre Ziroli, US Navy	13 Mar 1944	Map Rm 35
202.	King to Noble	23 Mar 1944	SPD 242
203.	R Adm Bieri, US Navy to V Adm Kirk, US Navy	24 Mar 1944	SPD 242
204.	Cunningham to King and Noble	30 Mar 1944	SPD 242
205.	Director of Plans: Memorandum	12 Apr 1944	ADM 205/37
206.	ANVIL: Naval Outline Plan	15 Apr 1944	SPD 250
207.	COSMED 156	24 July 1944	CAB 88/29
208.	Supreme Commander's Dispatch	16 April 1945	ADM 199/120
209.	Memorandum for F-1	24 June 1944	SPD 250
210.	Eisenhower to Marshall	29 June 1944	Map Rm 33
211.	Gen Wilson to COS	2 July 1944	Map Rm 33
212.	King to Hewitt	8 July 1944	SPD 244
213.	Noble to King	8 July 1944	SPD 244
214.	King to Noble	9 July 1944	SPD 244
215.	King to Noble	10 July 1944	SPD 244
216.	Noble to King	13 July 1944	SPD 244
217.	Outline of Operation DRAGOON	14 Aug 1944	ADM 205/57
218.	Invasion of Southern France	17 March 1945	ADM 199/120

219.	Adm Sir J. Cunningham to Admiralty	26 Sep 1944	ADM 199/864
220.	Report of Western Task Force	29 Nov 1944	ADM 199/865
221.	Adm Sir J. Cunningham to R Adm Morse	30 Nov 1944	ADM 199/864
222.	CCS to Eisenhower and Wilson	4 Dec 1944	Map Rm 35
223.	US LSTs to Greece	8 Dec 1944	Map Rm 88
224.	Lt Cdr Brine, USNR, to Hewitt	27 Feb 1945	NWC, Hewitt 1

Part V: The Far East

225.	Memorandum: C. T. Joy to ACOS (P)	20 Sep 1943	RG 38
226.	King to Noble	27 Oct 1943	Op Arch, King 4
227.	Adm Lockwood, US Navy, to Adm Nimitz	26 Nov 1943	Nimitz 1/121
228.	Cdr Hopkins to R Adm Pott	15 Dec 1943	ADM 199/117
229.	Cunningham to COS	22 Dec 1943	CAB 122/1140
230.	Mountbatten to Nimitz	24 Dec 1943	Nimitz 13/121
231.	Capt Porter to Capt Lambe	8 Jan 1944	CAB 122/1140
232.	JPS, Washington, to JPS, London	10 Jan 1944	CAB 122/1140
233.	Adm Cooke, US Navy: Memorandum	24 Jan 1944	RG 38
234.	King to Noble	25 Jan 1944	RG 38
235.	Noble to Cunningham	25 Jan 1944	CAB 122/1140
236.	Nimitz to King	31 Jan 1944	RG 38
237.	Nimitz to Mountbatten	26 Feb 1944	Nimitz 13/121
238.	Adm Cooke, US Navy: Memorandum	n.d., spring 1944	RG 38
239.	V Adm Boyd to Adm Kennedy-Purvis	2 May 1944	ADM 205/36
240.	King to MacArthur	21 July 1944	Op Arch, King 4
241.	Noble to King	22 July 1944	RG 38
242.	Memorandum: Cunningham	26 July 1944	CAB 122/1140

243.	Leahy: Diary	29 July 1944	LC, Leahy
244.	King to Stark and Hewitt	16 Aug 1944	SPD 244
245.	King to Marshall	17 Aug 1944	Op Arch, King 4
246.	Memorandum by Capt Dupre, Jr, US Navy	18 Aug 1944	RG 38
247.	JCS, 173rd Meeting	8 Sep 1944	RG 218/196
248.	JCS, 175th Meeting	13 Sep 1944	RG 218/196
249.	Memorandum by Capt Dupre, Jr, US Navy	18 Sep 1944	RG 38
250.	Movement of a British Fleet to the Pacific	24 Oct 1944	ADM 205/39
251.	Cunningham to Fraser	11 Nov 1944	NMM, Fraser 20
252.	King to Cunningham	12 Nov 1944	NMM, Fraser 20
253.	Capt Wheeler, US Navy, to Nimitz	13 Nov 1944	Nimitz 13/121
254.	Somerville to Cunningham	13 Nov 1944	NMM, Fraser 20
255.	Somerville to Cunningham	13 Nov 1944	NMM, Fraser 20
256.	Cunningham to Somerville	15 Nov 1944	NMM, Fraser 20
257.	Cunningham to King	15 Nov 1944	NMM, Fraser 20
258.	Cunningham to Fraser	n.d., c.15 Nov 1944	NMM, Fraser 20
259.	JCS to Roosevelt	18 Nov 1944	PSF 7
260.	Vice Adm Edwards, US Navy: Memorandum	23 Nov 1944	Op Arch, King 4
261.	Nimitz to Fraser	25 Nov 1944	RG 38
262.	Assignment of US aircraft to RN	28 Nov 1944	ADM 116/5347
263.	King to Nimitz	29 Nov 1944	Nimitz 13/117
264.	Admiralty to Fraser	6 Dec 1944	NMM, Fraser 20
265.	King to Nimitz	13 Dec 1944	NWC, King 7
266.	Nimitz to King	13 Dec 1944	Nimitz 13/117
267.	Brief for C-in-C, BPF	n.d., Dec 1944	NMM, Fraser 20
268.	Cunningham to Fraser	14 Dec 1944	NMM, Fraser 20
269.	Employment of BPF	20 Dec 1944	NMM, Fraser 21
270.	Mountbatten to Hewitt	23 Dec 1944	NWC, Hewitt 1

271.	Fraser to Admiralty	30 Dec 1944	NMM, Fraser 20
272.	Nimitz to Sir P. Mitchell	n.d., Dec 1944	Nimitz 13/121
273.	Leahy: Diary	1 Jan 1945	LC, Leahy
274.	BAD to Admiralty	4 Jan 1945	ADM 116/5341
275.	Stark to Adm Edwards, US Navy	11 Jan 1945	Stark A3
276.	Fraser to Nimitz	12 Jan 1945	Nimitz 13/117
277.	Fraser to Admiralty	17 Jan 1945	NMM, Fraser 21
278.	Fraser to Nimitz	22 Jan 1945	NMM, Fraser 23
279.	Fraser to King	27 Jan 1945	Nimitz 13/11
280.	CTF 77 to King	30 Jan 1945	Nimitz 13/117
281.	King to Nimitz	31 Jan 1945	Nimitz 13/117
282.	Kinkaid to MacArthur	8 Feb 1945	Nimitz 13/117
283.	MacArthur to Kinkaid	9 Feb 1945	Nimitz 13/117
284.	Cunningham to Fraser and Somerville	12 Feb 1945	ADM 205/58
285.	Fraser to Nimitz	15 Feb 1945	SPD 155
286.	Fraser to Nimitz	20 Feb 1945	Nimitz 13/117
287.	Fraser to Nimitz	20 Feb 1945	Nimitz 13/117
288.	King to Nimitz	21 Feb 1945	NWC, King 7
289.	Fraser to Nimitz	26 Feb 1945	Nimitz 13/117
290.	Fraser to Nimitz	7 Mar 1945	Nimitz 13/117
291.	Nimitz to King	9 Mar 1945	Nimitz 13/117
292.	V Adm Rawlings to Fraser	9 Mar 1945	NMM, Fraser 23
293.	V Adm Rawlings to Nimitz	15 Mar 1945	Nimitz 13/117
294.	R Adm Fisher to Fraser	18 Mar 1945	NMM, Fraser 23
295.	Fraser to Admiralty	21 Mar 1945	RG 38
296.	King to Kinkaid	21 Mar 1945	Nimitz 13/117
297.	King to Nimitz	22 Mar 1945	Nimitz 13/117
298.	R Adm Fisher to Fraser	27 Mar 1945	NMM, Fraser 23
299.	Fraser to Nimitz	30 Mar 1945	Nimitz 13/122
300.	Somerville to King	30 Mar 1945	RG 38
301.	Kinkaid to King	31 Mar 1945	Nimitz 13/117

302.	Overall Logistic Plan, US Navy	1 April 1945	Nimitz 13/122
303.	R Adm Vian to V Adm Rawlings	7 April 1945	ADM 199/595
304.	Nimitz to Fraser	9 April 1945	Nimitz 12/122
305.	British and US Action Reports	19 April 1945	ADM 199/591
306.	R Adm Fisher to Fraser	21 April 1945	NMM, Fraser 23
307.	R Adm Vian to Fraser	22 April 1945	NMM, Fraser 23
308.	Nimitz to King	26 April 1945	RG 38
309.	Nimitz to Fraser	27 April 1945	NMM, Fraser 23
310.	JSM: Naval Bases for BPF	28 April 1945	CAB 88/37
311.	V Adm Rawlings: RoP on ICEBERG	9 May 1945	ADM 199/555
312.	Nimitz to Fraser	22 May 1945	RG 38
313.	JSM: Base for BPF	25 May 1945	CAB 88/37
314.	Stark to King	28 May 1945	RG 38
315.	King to Nimitz	28 May 1945	RG 38
316.	Capt Dupre, Jr, US Navy: Memorandum for F-01	29 May 1945	RG 38
317.	Nimitz to King	30 May 1945	RG 38
318.	Fraser to Nimitz	4 June 1945	ADM 199/594
319.	Fraser to Nimitz	6 June 1945	RG 38
320.	V Adm Rawlings to Spruance	6 June 1945	ADM 199/1041
321.	King to Stark	9 June 1945	RG 38
322.	BPF: War Diary	9 June 1945	ADM 199/1457

323.	V Adm Vian to Fraser	12 June 1945	ADM 199/594
324.	Operation MERIDIAN [Sumatra]	13 June 1945	ADM 199/555
325.	Halsey to Fraser	15 June 1945	ADM 199/594
326.	JCS: Meeting	18 June 1945	RG 218/196
327.	Fraser to Nimitz	20 June 1945	ADM 199/594
328.	Adm Edwards: Memorandum	23 June 1945	RG 38
329.	Fraser to Nimitz	23 June 1945	RG 38
330.	Fraser to Admiralty	27 June 1945	ADM 199/594
331.	Fraser to Nimitz	4 July 1945	ADM 199/594
332.	King to Secretary of Navy Forrestal	23 July 1945	LC, King 11
333.	Capt Creighton, US Navy, to Nimitz	24 July 1945	Nimitz 13/122
334.	Leahy: Diary	8 Aug 1945	LC, Leahy
335.	Nimitz to ALPOA	10 Aug 1945	ADM 199/594
336.	V Adm Rawlings to Halsey	11 Aug 1945	ADM 199/594
337.	V Adm Rawlings to V Adm Vian	12 Aug 1945	ADM 199/594
338.	Attlee to Fraser	12 Aug 1945	NMM, Fraser 21
339.	Cunningham to Fraser	13 Aug 1945	NMM, Fraser 21
340.	Nimitz to Fraser et al.	12 Aug 1945	ADM 199/594
341.	Halsey to all Task Group Commanders	15 Aug 1945	ADM 199/594
342.	BPF: Task Organization	19 Aug 1945	ADM 199/593
343.	R Adm Portal: Report	Aug 1945	ADM 199/119
344.	BPF: Report	Aug 1945	ADM 199/1457
345.	Halsey to Nimitz	Sep 1945	Halsey 37

NAVY RECORDS SOCIETY – LIST OF VOLUMES
(as at 1 July 2020)

Members wishing to order any volumes should do so via the Society's website. All volumes are available on print-on-demand via scanned copies, apart from Volume 34 (for copyright reasons) and the two Occasional Publications (for reasons of size).

1. *State Papers relating to the Defeat of the Spanish Armada, 1588.* Vol. I. Ed. Professor J.K. Laughton.
2. *State Papers relating to the Defeat of the Spanish Armada, 1588.* Vol. II. Ed. Professor J.K. Laughton.
3. *Letters of Lord Hood, 1781–1783.* Ed. D. Hannay.
4. *Index to James's Naval History, 1886,* by C.G. Toogood. Ed. Hon. T.A. Brassey.
5. *Life of Captain Stephen Martin, 1666–1740.* Ed. Sir Clements R. Markham.
6. *Journal of Rear Admiral Bartholomew James, 1752–1828.* Eds. Professor J.K. Laughton & Cdr. J.Y.F. Sullivan.
7. *Hollond's Discourses of the Navy, 1638 and 1659 and Slyngesbie's Discourse on the Navy, 1660.* Ed. J.R. Tanner.
8. *Naval Accounts and Inventories of the Reign of Henry VII, 1485–1488 and 1495–1497.* Ed. M. Oppenheim.
9. *The Journal of Sir George Rooke, 1700–1702.* Ed. O. Browning.
10. *Letters and Papers relating to the War with France, 1512–1513.* Ed. A. Spont.
11. *Papers relating to the Navy during The Spanish War, 1585–1587.* Ed. J.S. Corbett.
12. *Letters and Papers of Admiral of the Fleet Sir Thomas Byam Martin, 1733–1854,* Vol. II (see Vol. 24). Ed. Admiral Sir Richard Vesey Hamilton.
13. *Letters and Papers relating to the First Dutch War, 1652–1654,* Vol. I. Ed. S.R. Gardiner.
14. *Dispatches and Letters relating to the Blockade of Brest, 1803–1805,* Vol. I. Ed. J. Leyland.

15. *History of the Russian Fleet during the reign of Peter The Great, by a Contemporary Englishman, 1724.* Ed. Vice-Admiral Sir Cyprian A.G. Bridge.

16. *Logs of the Great Sea Fights, 1794–1805,* Vol. I. Ed. Rear Admiral Sir T. Sturges Jackson.

17. *Letters and Papers relating to the First Dutch War, 1652–1654,* Vol. II. Ed. S.R. Gardiner.

18. *Logs of the Great Sea Fights, 1794–1805,* Vol. II. Ed. Rear Admiral Sir T. Sturges Jackson.

19. *Letters and Papers of Admiral of the Fleet Sir Thomas Byam Martin, 1773–1854,* Vol. III (see Vol. 24). Ed. Admiral Sir R. Vesey Hamilton.

20. *The Naval Miscellany,* Vol. I. Ed. Professor J.K. Laughton.

21. *Dispatches and Letters relating to the Blockade of Brest, 1803–1805.* Vol. II. Ed. J. Leyland.

22. *The Naval Tracts of Sir William Monson,* Vol. I. Ed. M. Oppenheim.

23. *The Naval Tracts of Sir William Monson,* Vol. II. Ed. M. Oppenheim.

24. *Letters and Papers of Admiral of the Fleet Sir Thomas Byam Martin, 1773–1854,* Vol. I. Ed. Admiral Sir R. Vesey Hamilton.

25. *Nelson and the Neapolitan Jacobins.* Ed. H.G. Gutteridge.

26. *A Descriptive Catalogue of the Naval Mss. in the Pepysian Library,* Vol. I. Ed. J.R. Tanner.

27. *A Descriptive Catalogue of the Naval Mss. in the Pepysian Library,* Vol. II. Ed. J.R. Tanner.

28. *The Correspondence of Admiral John Markham, 1801–1807.* Ed. Sir Clements R. Markham.

29. *Fighting Instructions, 1530–1816.* Ed. J.S. Corbett.

30. *Letters and Papers relating to the First Dutch War, 1652–1654,* Vol. III. Eds. S.R. Gardiner and C.T. Atkinson.

31. *The Recollections of James Anthony Gardner, 1775–1814.* Ed. Admiral Sir R. Vesey Hamilton and Professor J.K. Laughton.

32. *Letters and Papers of Charles, Lord Barham, 1758–1813,* Vol. I. Ed. Professor Sir J.K. Laughton.

33. *Naval Songs and Ballads.* Ed. Professor C.H. Firth.

34. *Views of the Battles of the Third Dutch War.* Ed. J.S. Corbett. (**Out of Print due to copyright**).

35. *Signals and Instructions, 1776–1794.* Ed. J.S. Corbett.

36. *A Descriptive Catalogue of the Naval Mss. in the Pepysian Library,* Vol. III. Ed. J.R. Tanner.

37. *Letters and Papers relating to the First Dutch War, 1652–1654,* Vol. IV. Ed. C.T. Atkinson.

38. *Letters and Papers of Charles, Lord Barham, 1758–1813,* Vol. II. Ed. Professor Sir J.K. Laughton.

39. *Letters and Papers of Charles, Lord Barham, 1758–1813*, Vol. III. Ed. Professor Sir J.K. Laughton.

40. *The Naval Miscellany*, Vol. II. Ed. Professor Sir J.K. Laughton.

41. *Letters and Papers relating to the First Dutch War, 1652–1654*. Vol. V. Ed. C.T. Atkinson.

42. *Papers relating to the Loss of Minorca, 1756*. Ed. Captain. H.W. Richmond.

43. *The Naval Tracts of Sir William Monson*, Vol. III. Ed. M. Oppenheim.

44. *The Old Scots Navy, 1689–1710*. Ed. J. Grant.

45. *The Naval Tracts of Sir William Monson*, Vol. IV. Ed. M. Oppenheim.

46. *Private Papers of George, 2nd Earl Spencer, 1794–1801*, Vol. I. Ed. J.S Corbett.

47. *The Naval Tracts of Sir William Monson*, Vol. V. Ed. M. Oppenheim.

48. *Private Papers of George, 2nd Earl Spencer, 1794–1801*, Vol. II. Ed. J.S. Corbett.

49. *Documents relating to the Law and Custom of the Sea*, Vol. I, *1205–1648*. Ed. R.G. Marsden.

50. *Documents relating to the Law and Custom of the Sea*, Vol. II, *1649–1767*. Ed. R.G. Marsden.

51. *The Autobiography of Phineas Pett*. Ed. W.G. Perrin.

52. *The Life of Admiral Sir John Leake*, Vol. I. Ed. G.A.R. Callender.

53. *The Life of Admiral Sir John Leake*, Vol. II. Ed. G.A.R. Callender.

54. *The Life and Works of Sir Henry Mainwaring*, Vol. I. Ed. G.E. Manwaring.

55. *The Letters of Lord St. Vincent, 1801–1804*, Vol. I. Ed. D. Bonner-Smith.

56. *The Life and Works of Sir Henry Mainwaring*, Vol. II. Eds. G.E. Manwaring and W.G. Perrin.

57. *A Descriptive Catalogue of the Naval Mss. in the Pepysian Library*, Vol. IV. Ed. J.R. Tanner.

58. *Private Papers of George, 2nd Earl Spencer, 1794–1801*, Vol. III. Ed. Rear Admiral H.W. Richmond.

59. *Private Papers of George, 2nd Earl Spencer, 1794–1801*, Vol. IV. Ed. Rear Admiral H.W. Richmond.

60. *Samuel Pepys's Naval Minutes*. Ed. Dr. J.R. Tanner.

61. *The Letters of Earl St. Vincent, 1801–1804*, Vol. II. Ed. D. Bonner-Smith.

62. *The Letters and Papers of Admiral Viscount Keith*, Vol. I. Ed. W.G. Perrin.

63. *The Naval Miscellany*, Vol. III. Ed. W.G. Perrin.

64. *The Journal of the 1st Earl of Sandwich, 1659–1665*. Ed. R.C. Anderson.

65. *Boteler's Dialogues*. Ed. W.G. Perrin.

66. *Letters and Papers relating to the First Dutch War, 1652–1654*, Vol. VI (& index). Ed. C.T. Atkinson.
67. *The Byng Papers*, Vol. I. Ed. W.C.B. Tunstall.
68. *The Byng Papers*, Vol. II. Ed. W.C.B. Tunstall.
69. *The Private Papers of John, Earl Sandwich, 1771–1782*. Vol. I, *1770–1778*. Eds. G.R. Barnes & J.H. Owen.
70. *The Byng Papers*, Vol. III. Ed. W.C.B. Tunstall.
71. *The Private Papers of John, Earl Sandwich, 1771–1782*, Vol. II, *1778–1779*. Eds. G.R. Barnes & J.H. Owen.
72. *Piracy in the Levant, 1827–1828*. Ed. Lt. Cdr. C.G. Pitcairn Jones R.N.
73. *The Tangier Papers of Samuel Pepys*. Ed. E. Chappell.
74. *The Tomlinson Papers*. Ed. J.G. Bullocke.
75. *The Private Papers of John, Earl Sandwich, 1771–1782*, Vol. III, 1779–1780. Eds. G.R.T. Barnes & Cdr. J.H. Owen.
76. *The Letters of Robert Blake*. Ed. Rev. J.R. Powell.
77. *Letters and Papers of Admiral the Hon. Samuel Barrington*, Vol. I. Ed. D. Bonner-Smith.
78. *Private Papers of John, Earl Sandwich*, Vol. IV. Eds. G.R.T. Barnes & Cdr. J.H. Owen.
79. *The Journals of Sir Thomas Allin, 1660–1678*, Vol. I, *1660–1666*. Ed. R.C. Anderson.
80. *The Journals of Sir Thomas Allin, 1660–1678*, Vol. II, *1667–1678*. Ed. R.C. Anderson
81. *Letters and Papers of Admiral the Hon. Samuel Barrington*, Vol. II. Ed. D. Bonner-Smith.
82. *Captain Boteler's Recollections, 1808–1830*. Ed. D. Bonner-Smith.
83. *The Russian War, 1854: Baltic and Black Sea*. Eds. D. Bonner-Smith & Capt. A.C. Dewar R.N.
84. *The Russian War, 1855: Baltic*. Ed. D. Bonner-Smith.
85. *The Russian War, 1855: Black Sea*. Ed. Capt. A.C. Dewar.
86. *Journals and Narratives of the Third Dutch War*. Ed. R.C. Anderson.
87. *The Naval Brigades of the Indian Mutiny, 1857–1858*. Ed. Cdr. W.B. Rowbotham.
88. *Patee Byng's Journal, 1718–1720*. Ed. J.L. Cranmer-Byng.
89. *The Sergison Papers, 1688–1702*. Ed. Cdr. R.D. Merriman.
90. *The Keith Papers*, Vol. II. Ed. C. Lloyd.
91. *Five Naval Journals, 1789–1817*. Ed. Rear Admiral H.G. Thursfield.
92. *The Naval Miscellany*, Vol. IV. Ed. C. Lloyd.
93. *Sir William Dillon's Narrative of Professional Adventures, 1790–1839*, Vol. I, *1790–1802*. Ed. Professor M. Lewis.

121. *The Keyes Papers*, Vol. II, *1919–1938*. Ed. Professor P.G. Halpern.
122. *The Keyes Papers*, Vol. III, *1939–1945*. Ed. Professor P.G. Halpern.
123. *The Navy of the Lancastrian Kings: Accounts and Inventories of William Soper, Keeper of the King's Ships, 1422–1427*. Ed. Dr. S. Rose.
124. *The Pollen Papers: The Privately Circulated Printed Works of Arthur Hungerford Pollen, 1901–1916*. Ed. Dr. J.T. Sumida.
125. *The Naval Miscellany*, Vol. V. Ed. N.A.M. Rodger.
126. *The Royal Navy in the Mediterranean, 1915–1918*. Ed. Professor P.G. Halpern.
127. *The Expedition of Sir John Norris and Sir Francis Drake to Spain and Portugal, 1589*. Ed. Professor R.B. Wernhan.
128. *The Beatty Papers*, Vol. I. *1902–1918*. Ed. Professor B.McL. Ranft.
129. *The Hawke Papers, A Selection: 1743–1771*. Ed. Dr. R.F. Mackay.
130. *Anglo-American Naval Relations, 1917–1919*. Ed. M. Simpson.
131. *British Naval Documents 1204–1960*. Eds. Professor J.B. Hattendorf, Dr. R.J.B. Knight, A.W.H. Pearsall, Dr. N.A.M. Rodger & Professor G. Till.
132. *The Beatty Papers*, Vol. II, *1916–1927*. Ed. Professor B.McL. Ranft.
133. *Samuel Pepys and the Second Dutch War*. Ed. R. Latham.
134. *The Somerville Papers*. Ed. M. Simpson with assistance from J. Somerville.
135. *The Royal Navy in the River Plate, 1806–1807*. Ed. J.D. Grainger.
136. *The Collective Naval Defence of the Empire, 1900–1940*. Ed. Professor N. Tracy.
137. *The Defeat of the Enemy Attack on Shipping, 1939–1945*. Ed. Dr. E.J. Grove.
138. *Shipboard Life and Organisation, 1731–1815*. Ed. B. Lavery.
139. *The Battle of the Atlantic and Signals Intelligence: U-boat Situations and Trends, 1941–1945*. Ed. Professor D. Syrett.
140. *The Cunningham Papers*, Vol. I: *The Mediterranean Fleet, 1939–1942*. Ed. M. Simpson.
141. *The Channel Fleet and the Blockade of Brest, 1793–1801*. Ed. Dr. R. Morriss.
142. *The Submarine Service, 1900–1918*. Ed. N.A. Lambert.
143. *Letters and Papers of Professor Sir John Knox Laughton, 1830–1915*. Ed. Professor A.D. Lambert.
144. *The Battle of the Atlantic and Signals Intelligence: U-boat Tracking Papers, 1941–1947*. Ed. Professor D. Syrett.
145. *The Maritime Blockade of Germany in the Great War: The Northern Patrol, 1914–1918*. Ed. J.D. Grainger.
146. *The Naval Miscellany*, Vol. VI. Ed. Dr. M. Duffy.

147. *The Milne Papers. Papers of Admiral of the Fleet Sir Alexander Milne 1806–1896*, Vol. I, *1820–1859*. Ed. Professor J. Beeler.
148. *The Rodney Papers*, Vol. I, *1742–1763*. Ed. Professor D. Syrett.
149. *Sea Power and the Control of Trade: Belligerent Rights from the Russian War to the Beira Patrol, 1854–1970*. Ed. N. Tracy.
150. *The Cunningham Papers*, Vol. II: *The Triumph of Allied Sea Power, 1942–1946*. Ed. M. Simpson.
151. *The Rodney Papers*, Vol. II, *1763–1780*. Ed. Professor D. Syrett.
152. *Naval Intelligence from Berlin: The Reports of the British Naval Attachés in Berlin, 1906–1914*, Ed. Dr. M.S. Seligmann.
153. *The Naval Miscellany*, Vol. VII. Ed. Dr. S. Rose.
154. *Chatham Dockyard, 1815–1865. The Industrial Transformation*. Ed. P. MacDougal.
155. *Naval Courts Martial, 1793–1815*. Ed. Dr. J. Byrn.
156. *Anglo-American Naval Relations, 1919–1939*. Ed. M. Simpson.
157. *The Navy of Edward VI and Mary*. Eds. Professor D.M Loades and Dr. C.S. Knighton.
158. *The Royal Navy and the Mediterranean, 1919–1929*. Ed. Professor P. Halpern.
159. *The Fleet Air Arm in the Second World War*, Vol. I, *1939–1941*. Ed. Dr. B. Jones.
160. *Elizabethan Naval Administration*. Eds. Professor D.M. Loades and Dr. C.S. Knighton.
161. *The Naval Route to the Abyss: The Anglo-German Naval Race, 1895–1914*. Eds. Dr M.S. Seligmann, Dr F. Nägler and Professor M. Epkenhans.
162. *The Milne Papers. Papers of Admiral of the Fleet Sir Alexander Milne 1806–1896*, Vol. II, *1860–1862*. Ed. Professor J. Beeler.
163. *The Mediterranean Fleet, 1930–1939*. Ed. Professor P. Halpern.
164. *The Naval Miscellany*, Vol. VIII. Ed. Mr B. Vale.
165. *The Fleet Air Arm in the Second World War*, Vol. II, *1942–1943*. Ed. Dr B. Jones.
166. *The Durham Papers*. Ed. Dr H.L. Rubinstein.
167. *Nelson's Letters to Lady Hamilton and Related Documents*. Ed. Dr M.R.E. Czisnik.

OCCASIONAL PUBLICATIONS

O.P. 1   *The Commissioned Sea Officers of the Royal Navy, 1660–1815*. Eds. Professor D. Syrett & Professor R.L. DiNardo.
O.P. 2   *The Anthony Roll of Henry VIII's Navy*. Eds. Dr. C.S. Knighton & Professor D.M. Loades.

INDEX

481

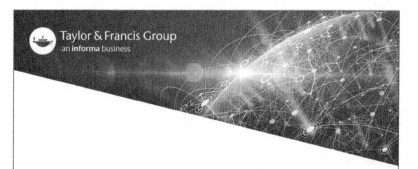